Kangzhan: Guide to Chinese Ground Forces, 1937–194
and-bolts handbook dedicated to coverage of the organ
National Revolutionary Army. It uses a mixture of
including document collections, along with primary sources held in the West, among them original Chinese documents from the files of the US China Theater, now in the US National Archives.

A brief description of the war in China is followed by detailed examinations of the national arsenals, and the NRA's tactical organization and weaponry, featuring illustrations and data never before seen in the West.

Leland Ness has been conducting and supervising defense analysis and writing military history for over 40 years. He served as director of special projects at DMS/Jane's, published a newsletter on ground ordnance for the defense industry, and has been an editor at Jane's for the last ten years (for *Jane's Ammunition Handbook* and *Jane's Infantry Weapons*). He is also the co-author of the classic *Red Army Handbook*, and the author of the HarperCollins *WWII Tanks and Combat Vehicles*, and the two-volume *Rikugun*, a study of the Japanese Army in World War II. He has been particularly interested in Asian military history since graduating with a degree in Oriental Studies and Language. During 28 years in the Army Reserve, he served with Headquarters, US Army Intelligence Agency, on active duty during Desert Storm.

Bin Shih was born in Tainan, Taiwan of first-generation mainlanders from the 1949 conflict. He graduated from Cheng Kung University with a degree in hydraulic engineering and later studied at Syracuse University. He was commissioned a second lieutenant in the infantry of the ROC Army and served as an S3 training officer. Always interested in Chinese history and small arms in general he started researching and collecting modern Chinese firearms in 1999 due to the absence of reliable information on the subject. He is also the author of *China's Small Arms of the Second Sino-Japanese War* (2005 in Taiwan; 2009 & 2014 in China; 2011 & 2014 in English).

KANGZHAN

GUIDE TO CHINESE GROUND FORCES
1937–1945

Leland Ness

with

Bin Shih

Helion & Company

Helion & Company Limited
26 Willow Road
Solihull
West Midlands
B91 1UE
England
Tel. 0121 705 3393
Fax 0121 711 4075
email: info@helion.co.uk
website: www.helion.co.uk
Twitter: @helionbooks
Visit our blog http://blog.helion.co.uk

Published by Helion & Company 2016
Designed and typeset by Donald Sommerville, Montacute, Somerset
Cover designed by Paul Hewitt, Battlefield Design (www.battlefield-design.co.uk)
Printed by Henry Ling Limited, Dorchester, Dorset

Text © Leland Ness 2016
Photographs © US National Archives unless otherwise noted
Front cover: The 74th Army was one of the few field armies to benefit from the arrival of new artillery in 1938–41. Here, one of its Soviet-made 76mm pack howitzers is in action in Hunan province in early May 1945. Within a few weeks these had been replaced by units with American 75mm pack howitzers. *Rear cover:* Light tank of the 1st Provisional Tank Group approaching Myitkyina in December 1944.

ISBN 978-1-910294-42-0

British Library Cataloguing-in-Publication Data
A catalogue record for this book is available from the British Library

For details of other military history titles published by Helion & Company Limited contact the above address, or visit our website: http://www.helion.co.uk

We always welcome receiving book proposals from prospective authors working in military history.

Contents

List of Illustrations

List of Maps and Tables

Maps

Tables

Abbreviations

AA	Anti-aircraft
AMMISCA	American Military Mission to China
AP	Armor-piercing
AT	anti-tank
Bde	Brigade
BN	Battalion
Cav	Cavalry
CCP	Chinese Communist Party
CD	Coast defense
CKS	Chiang Kai-shek (now usually Jiang Jieshi)
Enl	Enlisted
FA	Field Artillery
GD	Grenade discharger
GL	Grenade launcher
HE	High explosive
HQ	Headquarters
IGHQ	Imperial General Headquarters (Japanese)
IJA	Imperial Japanese Army
IJN	Imperial Japanese Navy
IMB	Independent Mixed Brigade (Japanese)
KMT	Kuomintang
LMG	Light machine gun
LPA	Loyal and Patriotic Army
MAC	Military Affairs Commission (also known as the National Military Council, or NMC)
MG	Machine gun
NCO	Non-commissioned officer
NRA	National Revolutionary Army (i.e. Chinese Nationalist Army)
Off	Officer
OSS	Office of Strategic Services
PLA	People's Liberation Army (Chinese communist)
Regt	Regiment
SACO	Sino-American Cooperative Organization
SGT	Sergeant
SMG	Submachine gun
TO&E	Table of organization & equipment
Y-FOS	Y Force Operational Staff

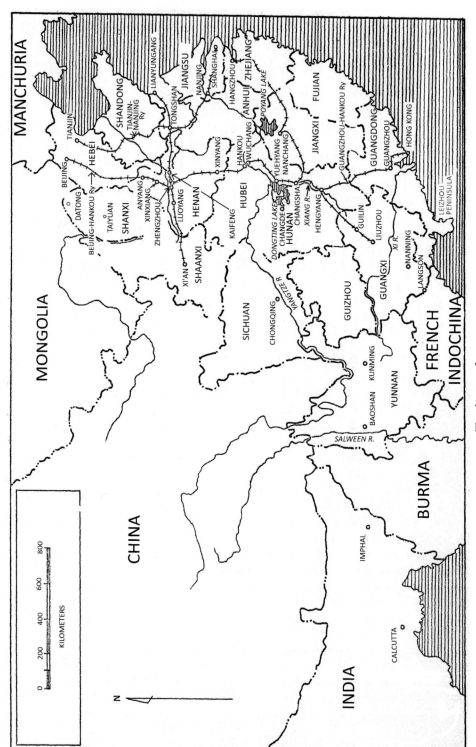

The theater of war.

Preface

The National Revolutionary Army (NRA) of China was one of the largest of World War II and its longevity in combat was equaled only by its foe, the Imperial Japanese Army (IJA). For over eight years bloody war raged over a land theater approached in size only by the more famous "Eastern Front" in Europe. Nevertheless, the activities and characteristics of the NRA during Kangzhan, the Second Sino-Japanese War of 1937–1945 have received scant attention from Western researchers and historians.

In part this is almost certainly due to the mistaken belief in the West that the Chinese military refused to engage the Japanese seriously, instead waiting for the USA and Britain to win the war for them. This is not new. Rather it was fed by a clique of malcontented American officers and politicians during the war and spread from there. It is certainly true that Chiang was content to define the minimum portion of his country that he needed for survival and then wait out and wear down the Japanese in much of the rest of it. But fighting was heavy for the first two years of the war, resulting in the loss of much equipment and casualties to elite formations. Thereafter the NRA moved to the defensive, but it was not a passive defense, as shown by the fierce counter-punching of Xue Yue in four battles around Changsha.

A second problem is the paucity of documentation. Although all are agreed that the war was a central, pivotal point in modern Chinese history there is no consensus on what actually happened. The two governments of China and Taiwan have long engaged in dueling histories of the war, each highlighting its own predecessors' contributions to the war against Japan while minimizing those of the other side. In an environment like that both parties, of course, will guard their archival resources jealously and only parcel out materials that clearly favor their own narrative, and even in those cases they tend to paraphrase or edit the texts.

Contributing to the relative lack of documentation is the fact that what is available is inaccessible to most Western historians due to the language barrier. Movement between English, German, French and Italian, for instance, is not terribly difficult. Using Russian is a bit more of a challenge, but alphabet-based languages lend themselves well to dictionaries. Chinese and Japanese, however, are an obstacle for most Westerners, and one that few take up.

For these reasons I decided to incorporate a chapter that provides a brief overview of the war in China. The definitive history of this conflict has yet to be written, and the brief chapter dedicated to the subject does not pretend to be that. Instead, it is intended merely as a very general guide to the ebb and flow of events in the China theater to complement the discussion of the evolution of the NRA.

Some aspects of the NRA have been left to others with more specialized knowledge of those areas. In particular, medical care, conscription practices, logistics, and the roles of personal loyalty and corruption are all ripe for in-depth examination.

*

This book has been about twenty years in the making for me. On the one hand that has proven invaluable, giving me time to delve into obscure corners for information and to rethink and refine my positions. The downside came in 2005 when I was hit with a catastrophic computer crash before I learned the true value of backing up. Almost all the source material could be found again or re-created; the tragedy was that the names and contact information of some of those who had been so helpful were wiped out. I did not fully realize that at the time and they are now lost in the mists of my memory. To those who expended time and effort on my behalf many years ago only to find themselves not mentioned here, my sincere apologies. Those who can be thanked here are Louis Capdeboscq and Nowfel Leulliot in France, Joan Hansen in Denmark, David Pazdera in the Czech Republic, Benny Tsang in Hong Kong, Stig Fransson in Sweden, Arthur Volz in Germany, and Akira Takizawa in Japan.

A final note: I have used the Hanyu Pinyin system of transliteration as that is the modern standard. For readers attempting to follow along with older maps or cross-reference with pre-1982 books, I apologise. Two exceptions have been made, where readers are likely to be far more familiar with the old Wade-Giles system, those being Chiang Kai-Shek (in Pinyin Jiang Jieshi) and the Kuomintang (KMT; or, in Pinyin, Guomindang/GMD). I have also supplied Wade-Giles names in parentheses in some cases where this may be helpful.

L. S. N.

1

The War in China

Following the death of Sun Yat-sen in 1925 Chiang Kai-shek emerged as the Kuomintang's new leader. In March 1926 he began his so-called Northern Expedition to consolidate his power and, at least nominally, unify China, aims which he had achieved to some extent by mid-1928. He had accomplished this with a relatively small "national" army that answered to his KMT government by entering into alliances with various provincial warlords that left each of them with varying levels of independence. Chiang may thus have been weak, but he was clearly working tirelessly to cement central power.

Each of the remaining semi-autonomous warlords had to be cajoled, bribed, and bullied into line, clearly a long-term effort, but this did not assuage Tokyo's alarm. A weak China was part of Japan's overall strategy in Asia. Zhang Zuolin, the warlord of Manchuria (to the Chinese the Three Eastern Provinces) had failed to stop Chiang's drive and he was assassinated by the Japanese Kwantung Army in June 1928, to be replaced by his son. In September 1931 the Kwantung Army staged an explosion that they blamed on the locals and used as a pretext for aggression. Within six months the Japanese had pushed Zhang's troops, who were under orders not to resist, out of their garrisons and finally south of the Great Wall. The Japanese then established the puppet state of Manchukuo in the region.

Escalating violence in Shanghai led to Japanese bombing on 28 January 1932 and 3,000 Japanese troops fanned out to take parts of the city. The 19th Route Army put up stout resistance. In mid-February the Japanese increased their strength to 90,000, while Chiang sent his German-trained 5th Army (87th and 88th Divisions) to Shanghai. In early March the 19th Route and 5th Armies pulled back, ending the fighting. The Japanese eventually largely withdrew, but insisted that Shanghai be demilitarized, including decommissioning of the arsenal facilities there.

In the meantime the Kwantung Army's leaders had come to believe that they needed both a buffer zone between China and their new Manchurian holdings and the mineral resources of North China. In February 1933 they invaded Jehol province and routed Zhang's troops there, with Chiang too concerned with the communists to send aid. In May the Kwantung Army pushed south on a broad front, forcing China to agree to a 13,000 square kilometer demilitarized zone that was, in fact, garrisoned by the Japanese. In mid-1935 bellicose posturing on the borders gave the Japanese the rest of Hebei province and forced the governor of Chahar, once again lacking support from Nanjing, to capitulate to the Kwantung Army.

In the meantime Chiang's full attention had been focused on his internal enemies, primarily the communists. When the latter set up a soviet in the province of Jiangsu he launched five successive campaigns against them. The First Campaign ran from the fall of 1930 to April 1931; the Second Campaign, from February to May 1931; the Third Campaign, from July to September 1931; the Fourth Campaign, from January to April 1933; and the Fifth Campaign, from October 1933 to October 1934. The first four, commanded by generals of indifferent talent and questionable loyalty, all failed. Chiang took command of the Fifth Campaign himself and, by improving the training of the army units involved and emphasizing civil affairs, won the day, at least temporarily. The communists fled the field on the "Long March."

If Chiang thought he would now have several years to finish off the communists, build up his army, and prepare for what most Chinese considered the inevitable Japanese aggression, he was mistaken. Public hostility to Japan had risen to new heights, spinning far our of his control. He was now a passenger rather than the pilot. In December 1936 he was kidnapped by senior generals and forced to form a coalition with the communists against the Japanese. The era of Chinese concessions to Japan had ended.

Ironically, this came about just as more moderate and realistic elements started to exert substantive influence over Japanese policy. Nevertheless, there were still hawks within the military, and they completely misread the new Chinese political environment. The opinion on the ground among Japanese forces in China was that they could continue to provoke minor clashes and use them as excuses to seize "bite-size" portions of China at a time or, failing that, they could launch a short, powerful, aggressive campaign that would thoroughly demoralize the Nanjing government.

Opening Drives South and West (July–December 1937)

One of the provocations used by the Japanese began with a clash near Beijing in July 1937. That the Japanese were prepared to act following this Marco Polo Bridge incident was

A soldier of the 29th Army shortly after the Marco Polo Bridge incident.

clear; their troops poured into Tianjin (Tientsin), where they had treaty rights, and then fanned out unopposed into the Beijing Plain. Defending Beijing was the 29th Army under the warlord Song Zheyuan with its headquarters at Nanyuan 16km south of the great city. Its 38th Division was near Tianjin, the 132nd just south of Nanyuan, and the bulk of the 143rd Division at Zhangjiakou (Kalgan), 190km away. On 25 July the Japanese 20th Division moved northwest along the Tianjin–Beijing railroad and encountered Chinese troops at Langfang and defeated them after a pitched battle the next day. Meanwhile, two Japanese brigades moved south from Rehe (Jehol) province (which had been annexed into Manchukuo in 1933) and occupied the area northeast of Beijing. On the 28th the Japanese attacked Nanyuan, catching the 29th Army and its 132nd Division by surprise, scattering the headquarters. On 29 July the Japanese 5th Division, still in Tianjin, attacked

Chinese soldiers on guard duty near Tianjin in July 1937.
Note the short swords carried on their backs.

and routed the 38th Division, driving it 80km south. At that same time Song took the remainder of his 29th Army on a retreat from Beijing, finally settling down at Baoding, about 110km south on the Beijing–Hankou railway and well out of harm's way for the time being. On 3 August Japanese troops marched into an undefended Beijing.

From Beijing the Japanese planned a drive west into Inner Mongolia, cutting about 130km northwest to Zhangjiakou via the southern Juyong pass, thence southwest to Datong in Yan Xishan's Shanxi province, defended by Yan's troops (nominally part of the National army) plus the communist 115th Division. Holding Juyong was the 13th Army, which inexplicably chose to mount its defense around the city itself rather than the narrow pass to the west, while the 17th Army was stationed to the north of the city. On 8 August advance elements of the Japanese 5th Division and 11th Independent Mixed Brigade (IMB) ran into the Juyong garrison, halted briefly before the main force arrived, but then took the city on 11 August. Three Chinese divisions were rushed up and fought at the Juyongguan pass, but abandoned it when the Japanese 5th Division entered the parallel Chenpien pass to the south, opening the way to Zhangjiakou from the east. That was not the only concern, for three Japanese IMBs were marching south on that city from southern Chahar, brushing aside the 143rd Division on 18 August. The 17th Army was rushed up to meet the threat, then retreated just as quickly. On 3 September the Japanese entered Zhangjiakou, turned somewhat southward and continued their advance towards Datong.

The Japanese drive to the southwest into Inner Mongolia actually had two "arms." The western arm, towards Datong, was formed from the force that had advanced from Chahar.

The eastern arm, based on the IJA 5th Division, marched parallel but about 50km to the east. Yan's 61st Army (one division and two brigades) from II War Zone conducted a widely spaced weak delaying action against the western arm, falling back about 30km at a time and on 13 September the Japanese occupied Datong. Chiang was bitterly disappointed, as this cut a main communication route with the Soviets, but there was little he could do. The eastern arm, headed by the 21st Brigade of the IJA 5th Division, moving down from Juyong Pass, was to meet an entirely different enemy.

At Pingxinguan Pass they met Yan's 73rd Division, later reinforced by the 71st, that stopped them in a see-saw battle for the heights. Needing resupply, the Japanese called on their supply train of 70 carts and 80 trucks to move up the sunken road with ammunition, food, and winter clothing.

The 115th Division of the Communist 8th Route Army had marched 500km from Shaanxi Province, arriving at Mount Wutai in front of the 21st Brigade on 20 September. For a day the commander, Lin Biao, made his preparations. Near the village of Pingxinguan the soldiers of the 115th Division moved in on the head and tail of the Japanese resupply column on the morning of 21 September. Chinese soldiers went the length of the column, throwing grenades down into the road while the Japanese, largely unarmed and unable to scale the 5–10 meter walls of the sunken road, flailed helplessly about. Longer sections of the road were raked from the ends by machine-gun fire. Central Army troops continued to attack the 21st Brigade, now running low on supplies, and losses were heavy on both sides. Relief forces finally reached the Japanese on 28 September and the Chinese withdrew. There are considerable discrepancies in the casualty reports,[*] but it is clear that the IJA should have learned not to take Chinese passivity for granted. Further, the battle was widely publicized and provided a much-needed morale boost to the Chinese forces and population.

The western arm of the Japanese advance, however, proceeded apace. Having taken Datong, the Japanese force of one division and nine Mongolian/Manchurian cavalry units turned west again, headed for Guisui, the Suiyuan capital. Chiang ordered the 35th Army and the 1st Cavalry Army south to avoid being cut off north of the Japanese drive, leaving four cavalry divisions and three brigades to hold back the Japanese advance. Their efforts were half-hearted at best and on 14 October the Japanese occupied Guisui unopposed.

With the exception of Pingxingguan and some of the smaller clashes with Yan's troops, the Japanese had outmaneuvered and outfought the Chinese decisively in every engagement. Wei Li-huang's 14th Army Group from the central government had performed fairly well, but with a few exceptions Yan's troops had given way quite easily. On the other hand the Japanese had failed to engage the Chinese decisively, resulting in the conquest of huge swatches of land that their numbers were insufficient to garrison.

The Japanese were not only interested in driving west from Beijing. The provinces of Shandong, Hebei and Anhui to the south were tempting targets that were both rich and blessed with good transportation routes that would ease any invasion. To guard against this, the Chinese had deployed the 1st Army Group on the Tianjin–Nanjing railway, with the 3rd Route Army in Shandong as a reserve. Further west, defending the Beijing–Hankou railway was I War Zone, commanded directly by Chiang.

---

[*] PLA histories claim that their forces annihilated the entire brigade of 4,000. A postwar history of the Japanese regiment involved, however, stated that the ambushed unit was only a 200-man transport column. Heavier losses definitely occurred with the main body of the 21st Brigade. In all likelihood the Japanese suffered about 3,000 casualties, and the Chinese 5–10 times that.

Bloodletting on the Central Coast

Meanwhile, far to the south and east, things were beginning to spiral out of control. The large foreign populations in their enclaves in Shanghai had not been known for their humility, usually treating the local Chinese as little more than a labor pool for servants. Even within this crowd, however, the Japanese stood out for their particular arrogance. The 5,000 Japanese troops stationed there under treaty rights had been a source of irritation for some time before 9 August, when a Japanese lieutenant, enraged that a Chinese sentry tried to stop him in his car, shot and killed the sentry before being killed himself by another sentry. It seems likely that the Japanese had not planned adventures in central China, at least not yet, but Chiang had decided this was the place to make his stand.

Chiang hoped to draw off Japanese troops from their depredations in north China that threatened supply routes from the USSR, but Shanghai was a strange place to chose for such an endeavor. True, it was the commercial center of China and putting on a good show there guaranteed favorable press coverage for China's plight around the world due to the large foreign population, but it had serious tactical drawbacks. The Japanese owned the seas, and the city's location on the sea at the mouth of a deep, navigable river gave the enemy flexibility and the availability of naval gunfire support over most of the front. The well developed port facilities allowed them to reinforce and supply almost at will. The level ground, combined with the ability to bring engineering equipment in, would allow the Japanese to create landing fields for their vastly superior air force. Nevertheless, Shanghai it would be.

On 11 August the 36th Division and two German-trained elite divisions, the 87th and 88th, closed around the Japanese positions north of the city, while the 55th, 56th, and 57th Divisions began moving north along the east bank of the river. On 13 August the Japanese landed two more divisions at Shanghai to bolster their forces. On that same day fighting broke out between the 87th Division and the Japanese in the Zhabei (Chapei) district;

Troops attacking near Shanghai, September 1937. The soldier on the left has just been shot.

after five days the Japanese had been forced back but their lines remained unbroken. Both sides then began to pour reinforcements into the area. On 22 August the Japanese landed elements of their 3rd and 11th Divisions upriver from the city, where they met the Chinese 15th Army Group, leading to a bitter two-week battle that ended in a stalemate.

Over a month of heavy fighting followed all along the front line, with the Japanese force, now known as the Shanghai Expeditionary Force, attempting to break out of the area around the city, and the Chinese III War Zone (commanded by Chiang personally) attempting to hold them in, and counterattacking on a regular basis. By late September the Chinese had thrown over 500,000 troops into the battle formed into Left Wing, Center, and Right Wing commands, and the Japanese over 200,000, including six divisions, four IMBs, the Formosa Brigade, and tank and artillery units.

That the Chinese managed to hold the line, and indeed counterattack successfully on occasion, was unexpected, not only to the Western observers in Shanghai, but also to the Japanese. The Rising Sun planes flew unaccosted above the battlefield, strafing and bombing at will. The old Wusong (Woosung) Fort had been captured early in the battle from the land side, its antique coastal guns no longer able to prevent Japanese warships from sailing up and down the river and pounding the Chinese lines with gunfire. Japanese tanks and artillery outnumbered their Chinese counterparts by a wide margin, both dealing death and destruction to Chiang's troops. By 20 October the Chinese had sustained over 120,000 casualties on the Shanghai front, and yet they hung on grimly, fighting, and dying in close combat for every meter they gave up. The next day the 21st Army Group of Guangxi troops, with a reputation as brave fighters, arrived and were thrown into battle.

Faced with such determined opposition and suffering horrendous losses themselves, the Japanese gave up on the idea of simply punching through Chinese lines. Instead, they landed their 10th Army of three divisions on the north shore of Hangzhou Bay, 50km south of Shanghai, on 5 November. This was something Chiang had not considered. The new army brushed aside light resistance and began marching north to Shanghai to attack the encircling Chinese from the outside. They quickly smashed through the Right Wing forces and joined up with the Shanghai Expeditionary Force. Emboldened, the Japanese in Shanghai began a massive assault along the whole line, heavily supported by air attacks and naval gunfire. This time, the Chinese line, already outflanked on the right, began to give. On 12 November the Japanese 16th Division made an amphibious landing about 70km upriver from Shanghai. This put them squarely behind the Chinese left flank, and the Chinese force began to crumble. Chiang issued an ambiguous order that could have been, and was, interpreted to mean retreat.

The Chinese troops had proven themselves brave, tough, and enduring soldiers. Western advisers, however, complained bitterly that staff work was abysmal, there was little coordination between adjacent units, the artillery fired most of its missions blind at maximum range, and that defensive positions usually consisted of a single trench line and gave way once that was breached.

If there was a retreat in the military sense, it lasted only one or two days. After three months of unremitting horror, pounded from the air and sea, of vicious hand-to-hand to fighting with no quarter given or asked, half-starved, lacking medical attention, their tactical leaders dead, the Chinese soldiers finally broke. And when they broke, it was total. Soldiers abandoned their weapons and the wounded, units mixed together in the flight to safety, and what had been a tenacious army a few days earlier turned into a panic-stricken

An 82mm mortar crew provides fire support outside Shanghai in early November 1937.

rabble fleeing west as fast as they could. Chiang had gambled most of his best units in Shanghai and he had lost. It cost him at least 187,000 of his finest troops killed or wounded, a loss that would extract its toll over the next eight years.

The Japanese troops, as eventual victors, had the opposite reaction. Having lost 11,000 killed and 31,000 wounded, and filled with rage at the humiliation of having been kept in check by an enemy they held in contempt, they now gave vent to an orgy of blood lust. They followed closely behind the Chinese, slaughtering the wounded, sick, and simply exhausted that Chiang's troops had left behind.

The Chinese attempted to make a stand at Suzhou, about 65km west of Shanghai, but were quickly outflanked and abandoned the city without a fight. Seeing the inevitable, the Chinese government was moved from Nanjing to Chongqing (Chungking) some 1,750km up the Yangtze on 20 November, although the Generalissimo moved to Hankou (Hankow), in between the two.

This was well timed, for now little stood between the rampaging Japanese Shanghai Expeditionary Force and Nanjing except disorganized, dispirited troops. The relatively intact 23rd Army Group moved up to stop them, but was hit from the flank and driven back. Chiang ordered Nanjing held "to the last man" and to that end two defense lines were formed in arcs in front of the city. The 36th and 88th Divisions, along with the Training Division were allocated to the outer line, 12–20km outside the walls of the city. They were shortly reinforced by the 74th Army and the 83rd Army, each of two divisions. The 41st, 48th, 87th, 103rd, 112th, 159th, and 160th Divisions manned the inner line, 2–5km outside the walls.* The Japanese Shanghai Expeditionary Force and the 10th Army arrived

---

* The 87th and 88th Divisions, formerly the central government's elite units, had been all but destroyed in the battles around Shanghai and rebuilt with untrained conscripts. They, along with the rest of the Nanjing defense forces, were essentially expendable.

in front of Nanjing on 6 December and immediately began their assaults, supported by artillery. On 8 December the outer line fell, followed by the inner line on 11 December. The next day the Japanese broke through the ancient city walls at the three main gates. Two days of heavy fighting was followed by a Chinese order to retreat. The only Chinese force to retain its coherence was the 66th Army (159th and 160th Divisions), which managed to fight its way out to the south and east. The rest of the soldiers trapped in Nanjing were hunted down and killed.

That, however, was the least of what would happen in Nanjing. For the next six weeks General Matsui's Japanese troops went on an orgy of murder, rape, pillage, and mayhem that has rarely been equaled.

Moving South from North China (August–November 1937)

The earlier northern campaign had left the Japanese in command of the three main rail hubs in northern China, Tianjin on the coast in the east, Beijing in the center, and Zhangjiakou in the west. From each of these hubs rail lines and roads ran south into the heart of China and these natural corridors served to channel the Japanese in their upcoming drive southwards. The Japanese had paused about a month after seizing the cities, regrouping and awaiting the expected Chinese negotiations that never came.

To block the Tianjin–Nanjing railway Chiang deployed the 1st Army Group of 27 divisions (including two cavalry) under General Song Zheyuan, an old warlord somewhat better at political intrigue than actual combat, about 65km south of the northern city.

Faced with an obvious threat down a narrow corridor, Song adopted the tactic common to the less competent Chinese generals, the "defense in depth." Unwilling to risk his force in a single battle, he placed defensive lines across the railway corridor all along its 250km length, one behind another, presenting his army to the Japanese for defeat in detail. Each of these defensive lines generally consisted of a field army of two or three divisions, with one division in the center to defend the railway and adjacent roads, the other(s) off to the side(s) to fall on the Japanese flanks after they had (inevitably) punched through the center division. In fact, the withdrawal of the center invariably precipitated the hasty departure of the flank divisions as well lest they be cut off.[*]

On 4 September the Japanese 2nd Army began its drive south from Tianjin. By 10 September it had travelled 60km and reached just north of Cangzhou, smashing the 29th Army with little difficulty en route. Uncharacteristically, Song decided to make at least a half-hearted stand at this city, collecting five divisions from different armies and rushing them to new positions just to the north. The appearance of this force stopped the Japanese temporarily while they brought up reinforcements, then they attacked on 21 September. Surprisingly, the Chinese forces held for two days under heavy air and artillery bombardment before breaking. The Japanese seized Cangzhou on 25 September, and Chiang responded by creating VI War Zone under Feng Yuxiang, the "Christian General," to take charge of operations along the Tianjin–Nanjing railway north of Shandong.

Feng's troops had performed fairly well during the Northern Expedition, but he was at heart another warlord and his days as a general had long since passed. He contributed

---

[*] Indicative of the confused chain of command common early in the war, Song commanded both the 1st Army Group and the 59th Army (the core of his earlier 29th Army) while Feng Chian commanded the intermediate 19th Army Group. Song was thus both Feng's superior and nominal subordinate at the same time.

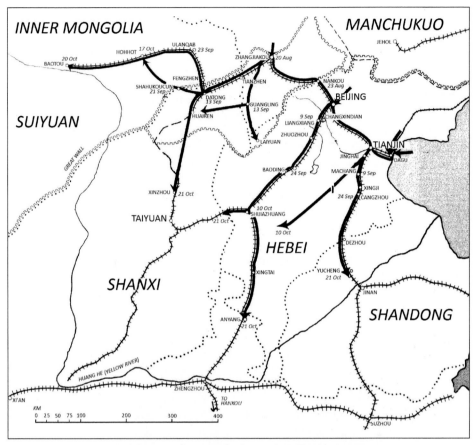

The Japanese drive south, September–October 1937.

nothing to the effort. The Japanese advance continued, delayed only a few days by a spirited counterattack by the 49th and 59th Armies under the war zone's deputy commander, Lu Zhonglin, and on 5 October Teh-Hsien fell, followed by Yuncheng on 15 October. The remaining Chinese units scrambled to safety behind the Yellow River. Thereafter Han Fuju, the governor of Shandong, kept his forces generally idle on the southeast bank of the river, giving lip service to the KMT government while carefully avoiding provoking the Japanese, until he could determine which way the wind was blowing.

Things went little better to the west. I War Zone, under the personal command of Chiang, was deployed "in depth" along the Beijing–Hankou railway corridor with three army group HQs and 22 divisions (including one cavalry). The forwardmost position was held by General Sun Lianzhong's 1st Army of four divisions at Liuliho, about 35km south of Beijing, with seven more divisions on the flank and in reserve. The Japanese 1st Army outflanked this position on 14 September, brushing aside the 53rd Army that was to have blocked them, and the entire Chinese force decamped 100km south to Baoding, excepting those who kept on going another 100km to Shijiazhuang. The familiar scene was repeated at Baoding, the capital of Hebei province, with a small Japanese frontal attack to fix the defenders, then a flanking movement from the east. Once again, the 53rd Army had been entrusted with security on this flank, but this time it did not even bother to pretend to fight and the line collapsed, with Baoding falling on 24 September. The atrocities of Nanjing were presaged here, on a smaller scale only because the city was significantly smaller, with the deaths of thousands of civilians and the destruction of much of the city.

The surviving Chinese forces joined those deployed in depth in defense of Shijiazhuang, 120km farther south. At this point morale in the area was so bad that even the 32nd Army, a usually reliable unit under General Shang Zhen, an able and intelligent officer, was unable to slow the Japanese drive significantly. And, once again, a Japanese force, here the 109th Division, was able to execute a wide enveloping move from the east against nominal opposition. On 10 October the three Japanese divisions entered Shijiazhuang with little fighting. The Japanese 14th Division continued south, scattering opposition, and finally halted on 19 October when it seized a bridgehead across the Zhang River just north of Anyang. The lack of a Chinese counterattack was fortunate for the Japanese, for the 14th Division was, in fact, all alone. Two Japanese divisions (6th and 16th) had been pulled out to reinforce the grim efforts in Shanghai, while two more (20th and 109th) were swung west out of Shijiazhuang to advance through an opening called "Ladies Pass" to attack Taiyuan from the east.

The main drive on Taiyuan was to come from the north, following the rail line down from Zhangjiakou. The heart of Shanxi province was a long and fertile valley running north–south, ringed on all sides by mountains. In the middle of this valley sat the ancient

Troops in fairly obvious defensive positions outside Tianjin in August 1937.

city of Taiyuan, the capital. Access from the north was via three easily defended passes, through one of which the Zhangjiakou–Taiyuan railway passed, near the city of Datong. Access from Hebei to the east was via Ladies Pass, through which ran the Shijiazhuang-Taiyan rail line.

Militarily, Shanxi was known as II War Zone under the command of General Yan Xishan, who had grown rich in his capacity of governor of Shanxi for the past 25 years. Yan's force totaled about 225,000 men in 4 army groups with 20 divisions and 13 brigades; 3 independent armies of 5 divisions and 2 brigades; 2 cavalry armies of 3 divisions; and the 18th Army Group, the former 8th Route Army, of communist forces under General Zhu De (Chu Teh).

Unfortunately, the Japanese had already crossed the northern passes and seized Datong in their opening advance, leaving the province vulnerable from that direction. Their Chahar Expeditionary Force began the drive south on 21 September and eight days later had breached the inner Great Wall about 130km north of Taiyuan. The Chinese set up their defenses about 80km north of Taiyuan in an arc and to reinforce the defenses Chiang, as noted earlier, ordered the 14th Army Group from their defense of Shijiazhuang through Ladies Pass into Shanxi. They arrived on 10 October, bringing the strength of this defensive arc up to 14 divisions and 9 brigades under the command of the 14th Army Group commander General Wei Lihuang.

On 13 October the (Japanese) Chahar Expeditionary Force (of three IMBs) and the 5th Division launched a furious attack on the Chinese positions. Infantry assaults, supported by artillery fire and air bombardment failed to dislodge the tenacious defenders. After three days of bitter combat the Japanese paused to reorganize and try again. On 21 October the Japanese unleashed a second assault, including the 20th Division hurriedly marched over from the east, and this time were successful. The Chinese pulled back in relatively good order to Blue Dragon Ridge, 35km north of the city. Once again the Japanese were stalled, this time for five days of bitter fighting, until Japanese engineers tunneled under a key redoubt and blew it up on 2 November. Having lost almost 30,000 men on the Blue Dragon Ridge, the Chinese withdrew again, this time to Taiyuan itself.

This, however, was not the only threat to Taiyuan and Shanxi. On 20 October the Japanese 20th and 109th Divisions had begun their move west from Shijiazhuang towards Ladies Pass. The Chinese 3rd Army was charged with defending this pass, but pulled back when the Japanese threatened to outflank the position via another pass to the south. The two Japanese divisions then marched unopposed from the east all the way to join with their brethren who were laying seige to Taiyuan from the north. A last-ditch stand in the city cost the Chinese about 20,000 men and 80 artillery pieces but lasted only a little more than a day. The Japanese then marched about 90km farther south to Pingyao, to establish their own defensive positions. This Japanese victory over a competent foe, in the back yard of the 8th Route Army, convinced the communist leader Mao Zedong (Mao Tse-tung) that the future for his forces lay in guerrilla warfare, rather than the conventional variety and henceforth they would concentrate their efforts on organization-building and sabotage.

All three Japanese drives to the south had achieved their objectives. Aside from some hard fighting north of Taiyuan, none had taxed their resources unduly. In all cases the Imperial forces were outnumbered and in a few cases they were significantly overextended, but the local Chinese commanders had been irresolute (except in a few instances of defense) and the invading forces had never been seriously threatened.

Connecting the Enclaves, early 1938

By December 1937 the Japanese had driven into China from two directions. The North China Front Army of 280,000 men held northernmost China, having advanced south from Tianjin to Jinan on the Yellow River, from Beijing to just north of Anyang, and from Zhangjiakou to Taiyuan. The Central China Area Army of 260,000 had driven west from Shanghai up the Yangtze to Nanjing.* The logical next move was to join the two forces by driving north from Nanjing and south from Jinan. At the same time the forces near Anyang would move south to the Yellow River to take the rest of the low ground in north–central China and cover the western flank of the main drive.

A drive south from Jinan would leave most of rich Shandong province cut off, a fact not overlooked by Shandong's old warlord chief, Han Fuju, concurrently commander of the 3rd Army Group of five divisions and a "pistol brigade," all provincial forces loyal to him. Han had spent the war so far sitting on the sidelines, pledging support to Chiang (without actually doing much), while putting out feelers to the Japanese. Also in Shandong was General Yu Xuezhong and his 51st Army of two divisions, a presence that restricted Han's freedom of action somewhat, much to his annoyance. In fact, the 51st Army had been ordered southward on 18 December, but Han blew the railway bridges, forcing the unit to march. Seeing the writing on the wall, and having received no response from his overtures to the Japanese, Han and his 3rd Army Group (and, of course, his bullion) began their departure from Shandong on 25 December. In early January he was arrested by KMT authorities, tried for treason and cowardice, and shot.

The Japanese North China Front Army drove east from Jinan in early January 1938, while a force of 1,500 Japanese sailors occupied Qingdao (Tsingtao) against no opposition on 10 January and on 17 January the Japanese 5th Division met up with the sailors just west of Qingdao. With the unopposed fall of most of Shandong province, the stage was set for the next great campaign, in which the Japanese would attempt to link their two forces in China. The North China Front Army would try to drive south, parallel to the Jinan–Xuzhou Railway, for which it had the 5th, 10th, 16th, 110th, and 114th Divisions, along with five brigades. The Central China Area Army was to drive north from the Nanjing area with the 9th and Konoye Divisions, plus six brigades. Standing in between them was the Chinese V War Zone under General Le Zongren. V War Zone consisted of 63 divisions plus the "pistol brigade," a cavalry brigade, the 1st Regiment of the 1st Artillery Brigade, and the 4th, 5th, 6th, and 7th Artillery Regiments.

On 25 January the Japanese driving northwest from Nanjing attacked the Chinese 11th and 21st Army Groups, driving them back and capturing Bengbu on the Huai River on 9 February.

Things went slower on the northern front. The Japanese 5th Division had moved south down the coast from Qingdao, but the division's brigade that attempted to move inland was repulsed at Linyi by the 40th Army with heavy losses on 14 March. The entire division was then brought up and resumed the assault on 24 March. By this time the 59th Army had reinforced the defenders and it took the Japanese four days of heavy fighting to occupy the town. Meanwhile the Japanese 10th Division, reinforced by tanks, was moving down

---

* The Central China Area Army had been formed on 7 November to handle the newly expanded war along the Yangtze River basin. In February 1938, after the fall of Nanjing, it was re-formed into the Central China Expeditionary Force.

the railway from Zoucheng. By 17 March they had captured Tengzhou, just 50km north of Xuzhou, a critical north–south and east–west rail junction.

Since strong Chinese forces still occupied the area east of the railway, the Japanese launched a double-pronged attack on the area, with the 10th Division attacking southeast from the rail line and the 5th Division southwest, converging on the area around Taierzhuang. The Japanese 10th Division was first off the mark, and ran into General Chi Fengcheng's 31st Division. There the Japanese experienced something new for them, a Chinese general who was not only a tough fighter, but a believer in aggressive maneuver as well. Between 23 and 26 March the two sides attacked and counterattacked in front of and in Taierzhuang in continual bloody fighting. As the Japanese brought up the full strength of their 10th Division, the Chinese reinforced also, with the 27th Division arriving on the 26th and the 30th Division on the 29th, the last accompanied by the first Chinese artillery, ten 75mm guns and two 150mm howitzers. On 31 March General Sun Lianzhong arrived to exercise field command over his 2nd Army Group. Heavy fighting continued within the walls of the old town, with grenades, bayonets, and shovels, over the next few days.

This was to be only the beginning of a period of trial for the Japanese, as on 26 March the 20th Army had launched a determined attack against the Japanese supply lines from east, and the 55th Army attacked from the south and west on 2 April. By 3 April the Japanese 10th Division was essentially cut off and isolated in Taierzhuang. The Japanese 5th Division broke through the Chinese lines south of Linyi and attempted a relief by marching southwest. Unfortunately for the Japanese, the 20th Army's General Tang Enbo was just as aggressive and tough as General Chi, and he simply wheeled a large part of his force around to face east and attacked, cutting off the advance guard of the 5th Division. The Japanese 10th Division and the bulk of one brigade of the 5th Division were now cut off, surrounded by the troops of two of Chiang's best generals, General Tang's 20th Army to the north and and General Sun's 2nd Army Group to the south.

Heavy fighting continued within the city through 5 April, but the Japanese were running out of food, water, and ammunition. Aerial resupply failed and the Japanese heavy weapons gradually fell silent. Sensing victory, the exhausted Chinese troops launched one bitter assault after another over the next two days. On 7 April the Japanese had had enough. The survivors fought through a narrow corridor to the north, leaving many of their dead comrades and all their heavy equipment behind.* But the Chinese had paid heavily too, a roll-call of the fierce 31st Division after the battle yielded only 2,000 of the original 9,000 men. The Chinese had won a great victory, but failed to follow up. Pursuit of the ragged Japanese survivors went no farther than about 25km and stopped. In particular, Li Zongren refused to launch a follow-on offensive with his Guangxi troops, demonstrating, if such was ever needed, the limits of using warlord armies.

The Japanese paused only briefly to lick their wounds. Although the 10th Division had been severely mauled, the 5th Division was quickly brought back up to strength and on 15 April began attacking again from Linyi. They drove due south, attempting to pass to the east of Taierzhuang. At the same time the 16th Division attempted once again to move down the rail line from Tsoushien. The 5th Division made some initial progress against ineffectual opposition, but on 27 April the 46th Army under the command of the

---

* The Chinese claimed they killed 16,000 Japanese and destroyed 40 tanks. Postwar Japanese accounts show actual losses to have been 2,000 dead (plus many more wounded, of course) for the 5th and 10th Divisions and a handful of tanks.

tough General Fan Congbu arrived on the scene after marching 400km from the west. In cooperation with the 59th Army it cut off the Japanese advance guard and destroyed it in hard fighting. The Japanese drive south along the rail line went only a little better. Four days of repeated assaults against the battle-worn but determined 20th Army yielded nothing until Japanese forces from the east threatened their right flank. They withdrew about 20km and made a stand again. Once again the Japanese pounded them with artillery and air strikes but furious assaults brought only more casualties. The Japanese responded by moving two further divisions, the 110th and 114th, down the railway to help out but this achieved little.

The Japanese Central China Expeditionary Force, now reinforced to four divisions (3rd, 11th, 13th, and Konoye) and attacking north from Nanjing, faced a different type of enemy. Their first opponent, the 24th Army Group, simply dissolved in front of them, while the 21st and 26th Army Groups put up only token fights before retreating to safety. The Japanese columns quickly reached about 100km beyond the Yangtze. V War Zone was now caught between two Japanese forces and in danger of becoming surrounded. The forces at the northern end continued to acquit themselves well, but were exhausted and short of ammunition. On 15 May Chiang finally ordered the V War Zone troops to break out to the southwest, although directing the useless 24th Army Group to remain behind and conduct guerrilla warfare. On 18 May the last Chinese troops skillfully withdrew from Xuzhou (Hsuchow/Tongshan), abandoning it to the Japanese, who entered it two days later. The Japanese hopes of trapping a major Chinese force had failed, but they had still inflicted heavy casualties.

In the meantime, things had been going even worse for the Chinese to the west. I War Zone was to defend the central railway corridor, from Beijing through Anyang and Zhengzhou, thence down to Wuhan, but had been weakened by the withdrawal of the excellent 20th Army and the 59th Army to reinforce the efforts around Jinan to the east. I War Zone under General Cheng Qian, had three army groups totaling 47 infantry and 2 cavalry divisions and 4 brigades, supported by the 6th Artillery Brigade, the 5th Regiment of the 1st Artillery Brigade, and the 7th, 9th, and 10th Artillery Regiments for a strength of about 290,000 men. The best of the commanders was the Eastern Henan Army's General Xue Yue, a tough fighter when he chose to be, but a man who picked his battles carefully. I War Zone's mission was to prevent the movement to the south of elements of the North China Front Army, mainly the 14th Division, with elements of the 11th and 108th Divisions, plus supporting artillery and armor for a total of about 45,000 men.

Cheng deployed his 1st Army Group "in depth," meaning one behind another over 80km of the railway north of Xinxiang. The Japanese simply marched parallel to the railway and threatened Xinxiang and, on 16 February, after putting up practically no resistance, the 1st Army Group fled to the west. The Japanese having seized the battlefield by default, the area became quiet for a while. In early May the Japanese 14th Division moved west and then south to cut the railway between Xuzhou and Kaifeng. Counterattacks by the Eastern Henan Army pushed them back off the railway, but only temporarily. On 31 May Chiang ordered the bulk of the I War Zone troops to pull back to west of the Beijing–Wuhan railway. The 20th Army Group fought a ferocious rearguard action for six days, but on 6 June the Japanese entered Kaifeng. Once again the IJA had been able to march almost anywhere it wanted, but the distances were so great, and the lines so porous, that even major Chinese units had little trouble slipping out of supposed encirclement.

Drastic action would be needed to stop the Japanese, and Chiang had just such a plan. He ordered the dikes of the Yellow River blown up at Huayuankou, east of Zhengzhou. The first dikes are traditionally believed to have been built some 4,000 years ago to hold in the frequently flooding river. Unable to dredge the river of its accumulating silt over the centuries, the Chinese had simply built the walls of the dikes ever higher. In some places the river bed was now as much as 10 meters higher than the surrounding countryside. The river waters now poured through the gaps in the dikes, flooding the countryside of Henan and Anhui, killing many civilians and leaving two million homeless and destitute. The Japanese were forced quickly to pull back east, but the people in the path of flood would never forgive Chiang.

The Fall of Wuhan

The advances of the Japanese forces in China through mid-1938 had been spectacular, although costly, but had brought them no closer to a final victory. The capture of Nanjing had not caused the government to surrender, nor had the Japanese been able to precipitate the kind of major encirclement battle that would destroy the Chinese Army. They now switched to a strategy of identifying significant points, the occupation of which would severely degrade the ability of the remnants of Chinese authority to threaten Japanese forces. With a failing economy and reduced legitimacy, Chiang and his government was to be defanged, a nuisance rather than a threat.

Strategically located upstream from Nanjing on the Yangtze River, where the Han River flows into it, are the three cities of Wuchang, Hanyang, and Hankou, the three so interconnected that they were usually referred to as one, Wuhan. Hankou was the largest, but Hanyang boasted a number of steel and iron mills and an important arsenal. Wuchang was the site of Chiang's new headquarters after having been driven out of Nanjing. Wuhan would be the next target.

In early June 1938 IJA forces moved west from Nanjing and cleared the area about 150km north of Wuhan of the 26th Army Group. The main thrust, however, was to move south from Nanjing in two columns. The 101st and 116th IJA Divisions would move upriver along the Yangtze, supported by Imperial Japanese Navy (IJN) warships, while the 6th IJA Division would move along the main road that paralleled the river about 40km west of it. The western arm, the 6th IJA Division, moved south down the roadway, brushing aside Chinese defenses until they reached Yuantanpu, about halfway between Nanjing and Wuhan. There, on 26 June, the Chinese 20th and 31st Armies with five divisions counterattacked straight into the Japanese forward units while the 26th Army of three divisions fell on the flanks. After three days of heavy fighting the Japanese were forced back, but as usual the Chinese took no advantage of this and instead simply returned to their defensive positions for another month.

In the meantime IJN vessels had moved upstream and they, and bombers, pounded Madang fortress while army units assaulted from the land side. The battle raged for three days, but finally the 53rd and 167th Divisions were driven out and the fort fell on 27 June. The supporting German-designed Hukuo fort fell without resistance on 4 July. The Japanese then moved upstream until they reached the entrance to Poyang Lake, where the Yangtze turned west to Wuhan. The Chinese arrayed themselves generally with the IX War Zone south of the river and the V War Zone west and south. On 23 July the Japanese launched their offensive to the west towards Wuhan and scored some initial successes. By then illness had hit both camps, malaria particularly affecting the Chinese and intestinal disorders the Japanese, and all significant operations in the area ground to halt for a month.

The Japanese restarted their offensive on 20 August, as their 11th Army attacked south of the river. The 1st Army Group stopped them in heavy fighting from 24 August to 1 September. Further attacks gained some ground, but at heavy cost. An attempt by the IJA 101st and 106th Divisions to outflank the operations to the south ran into the Chinese 2nd Army Group; the Japanese were badly mauled in heavy combat and had to halt operations on 10 October. In the meantime, the western prong of the Japanese offensive, advancing down the road parallel to the river, was having an equally tough time. The IJA 6th Division had to fight for ten days to seize the fortified town of Tianjiazhen (Tienchiachen) on the northern bank of the river, finally succeeding through the use of poison gas. Indicative of the heavy combat, the IJA 13th Infantry Regiment, the main assault force, suffered 1,000 casualties, about a third of its strength, including 80% of the platoon leaders and 65% of the company commanders.

What turned the tide was a wide outflanking maneuver in which the IJA 2nd Army, with about 80,000 men and supporting artillery, struck out due west from Nanjing, facing only the 51st and 77th Armies of Li Zhongren's V War Zone, totaling less than 25,000 exhausted men. This offensive had begun on 27 August and, meeting only sporadic resistance, reached the Pinghan railway that ran south from Beijing into Hankou on 10 October. In the meantime the IJA 11th Army to the south continued its assaults, battering the Chinese IX War Zone troops with artillery and air strikes. Finally, in mid-October the Chinese forces began to crumble and the Japanese were able to cut off Hankou from the south. Chinese resistance started to dissolve and then turned into a rout. On 26 October a Japanese flotilla advanced up the Yangtze, dropped anchor off the bund in Hankou and disgorged troops who quickly occupied the city with no opposition. Both sides had lost heavily in the four-month campaign, the Chinese more so, but Chiang and his entourage had fled Wuhan in September and the Japanese found themselves even deeper into China with no end in sight.

The Loss of the Coast

By mid-1938 the Japanese had managed largely to isolate China from the outside world by occupying the ports on the coast. There were two exceptions, Hong Kong and its upriver neighbor Guangzhou (Canton).[*] The former was inviolable (for the time being) as being British and occupation of the latter might provoke the British as well. Instead, reliance was placed on indirect means. While a naval blockade could prevent ships from sailing to Guangzhou there was no legal basis for stopping ships of neutral nations from sailing to Hong Kong, a neutral territory. There these ships would deposit their cargos of munitions for China, which would then be trans-shipped via the Hong Kong–Guangzhou Railway to Chinese authorities. The Japanese air forces began bombing this rail line and its yards almost immediately after the war began and these raids had become almost daily events, even if rather small by later standards, by October 1937. The Chinese had no shortage of

---

[*] It was also possible to land cargos at Haiphong in French Indochina and move them by rail into southern China, but Japanese diplomatic pressure had caused the French authorities to all but shut this route down for weapons in mid-1938.

labor to effect repairs, however, and significant quantities of weaponry continued to flow into China from overseas.

Clearly, more direct action was needed. On 12 October 1938 the Japanese 12th Army of three divisions landed at Bias Bay and marched westward in four columns towards Guangzhou. Defending the city was General Yu Hanmou and his 12th Army Group of seven divisions in three armies.* Leadership of the Chinese forces, including by General Yu, was both inept and timid and the force immediately dissolved into a routed mob that abandoned the city and left behind such heavy weapons as it had. The Japanese paraded into Guangzhou on 21 October unopposed.

The battle for Wuhan and the occupation of Guangzhou had tired out and dislocated both sides and for a few months relative peace prevailed. For the Japanese, however, it was merely a period to catch their breath and plan their next moves. At the beginning of 1939 the Japanese had a million soldiers in China, half of them in combat units, comprising 11 divisions, 4 IMBs, and a cavalry brigade in north China; 10 divisions and one cavalry brigade in central China; and two divisions in south China.

The Battle for Jiangxi and Hunan

The Japanese had come to the conclusion that in order to control the central Yangtze valley they would need to destroy IX War Zone south of Wuhan and west of Poyang Lake. To do that they would drive south on the west side of the lake to the city of Nanchang with their 11th Army, recent victors at Wuhan. The Japanese offensive kicked off on 17 March 1939 and met with only a few instances of hard fighting. On 27 March they launched their assault on Nanchang itself and conquered it that day.

On 19 April Chiang directed IX War Zone to counterattack and retake Nanchang with the 19th and 32nd Army Groups. This offensive was launched two days later and heavy fighting was rewarded with success. The Japanese were pushed back and from 30 April to 8 May savage close-quarters fighting raged in the city. On that latter date, however, the commanders of the 29th Army and the 26th Division, popular and fierce soldiers, were killed in action and all the fight seemed to go out of the Chinese. With success so close, they broke contact and withdrew.

The IJA 11th Army then used the break in the action to rebuild itself and prepare for the next offensive mission. The 11th Army, reinforced to four divisions and three brigades, was to move west from Nanchang and seize Changsha with three separate drives. The seizure of Changsha and the cities to the west would give the Japanese control of the Yangtze up to the Sichuan border and isolate the KMT base there from the rest of the war zones. The first element involved the IJA 101st and 106th Divisions attacking westward from Jingan on 13 September. Here the Chinese, particularly the 32nd, 60th, 72nd and 74th Armies, proved just as aggressive as the Japanese and after three weeks of bloody, confused fighting the Japanese were forced to withdraw to their starting point, arriving back at Jingan on 14 October.

The second element was a drive south by the IJA 3rd and 6th Divisions from about 100km north of Changsha. They launched their assault on 18 September, and on the night

---

* In March 1938 a British observer reported that Yu's chief of staff had told him that "approximately 10% of his officers were good, and the rest useless." *Report on Military Conditions in Guangzhou July 1937–March 1938*; PRO WO106/5303.

of 22 September one brigade of the 3rd Division used gunboats and commandeered junks to sail down Dongting Lake and land south of the Milou River. Outflanked, the Chinese resorted to a stratagem they had often trumpeted but never really implemented—they intentionally gave way and allowed the overconfident Japanese to advance into a large-scale ambush. When the two divisions got to within 30km of Changsha the 4th, 52nd, 70th, 73rd, and 87th Armies descended on them from all sides. Facing opposition and having reached the time limit for the operation, the Japanese withdrew, executing a fighting retreat back to their starting positions, arriving bloodied on 8 October.

The third part of the Changsha operation involved the IJA 33rd Division driving generally southwest on the city from Chongyang against the 27th Army Group. This was launched on 22 September and they moved about 100km into increasingly determined Chinese counterattacks. Attacked from the flanks and also having reached the time limit set for the operation, the Japanese here also executed a fighting retreat, arriving back at Tongshan on 14 October.

The battle for Changsha had proved a fruitless waste for the Japanese and a much-needed, if transitory, victory for China. IX War Zone commander Chen Cheng had given a textbook demonstration of how to use a force superior in numbers but inferior in equipment and training to win a victory via mobility and aggressive action.

Nevertheless, the Japanese 11th Army noted that Chinese tactical skill had declined since 1938, attributing this to poor leadership, reduced training, and shortages of weapons and ammunition, although the will to resist remained strong.

The "Winter Offensives"

In the fall of 1939 Chiang decided it was time to move over to a broad offensive against the Japanese. What prompted that is unclear, but his enemies had stopped for one of their periodic resupply and rebuilding pauses, and he may have interpreted that as weakness. In any event, in October the National Military Council issued instructions to each of the war zones directing them, in suitably aggressive yet ambiguous language, to undertake specific offensives. Of course, the war zone commanders used the directives more as a guide to writing their later reports than as a set of instructions.

I War Zone (Henan and northern Anhui) and VI War Zone (southern Hubei and western Hunan) contented themselves with raids that accomplished little. III War Zone did bloody the IJA 116th Division somewhat in mid-December, but achieved nothing that lasted more than a few days. Yan's II War Zone, his Shanxi warlord army that had been compressed down to Shaanxi and southern Shanxi, undertook some movements that alarmed the Japanese. On 3 December they attacked Yan's 4th, 5th, and 14th Army Groups precipitating a nine-day battle that exhausted both sides and left them pretty much where they started.

In IV War Zone the action was precipitated by a Japanese drive by their 104th Division north out of Guangzhou on 8 December to tie up Chinese troops and keep them from being moved elsewhere. In that, they were successful, for the Chinese counterattacked, forcing the Japanese to bring up elements of four other divisions for support. The Chinese 12th and 35th Army Groups launched a series of bloody attacks that forced the Japanese back to their starting point. As usual, however, there they stopped.

V War Zone launched two large-scale offensives. The Right Flank Army (based on the 29th Army Group plus the 55th, 59th, and 77th Armies) attacked across the Han River on 12 December and engaged in heavy, if sporadic, fighting against Japanese infantry and tanks until 20 January when things quieted down with little having been gained. The Southern Henan Army (built around the 2nd Army Group plus 92nd Army) launched its attack on the same day but accomplished little.

IX War Zone, previously engaged with the Changsha operations, was called upon to launch dispersed attacks against Japanese lines of communications. This it did with considerable gusto, ripping up railroad tracks, destroying bridges, burning buildings, and wiping out isolated Japanese patrols and detachments across a wide area. Japanese units up to the size of the 213th Infantry Regiment of the 33rd IJA Division were forced to retreat under pressure while smaller units were often butchered. The attacks petered out in mid-January 1940 with not much to show for the efforts except significant casualties on both sides.

Little had been expected of VIII War Zone but it remained active in this offensive longer than anyone else. In fact its 35th and 81st Armies and the 6th Cavalry Army launched significant attacks on Japanese forces and ambushes on relieving columns that bloodied the invaders, beginning in mid-December and continuing, on and off, into early April 1940 culminating in Japanese tactical withdrawals.

Overall, the Winter Offensives has discomforted the Japanese but had not altered the operational balance in the theater. They had inflicted casualties on both sides,[*] but neither side fundamentally changed its views or objectives.

The Invasion of Guangxi

Even though the coastal ports had been largely occupied or cut off, supplies were still reaching China through French Indochina and Burma. In fact, by the fall of 1939, Japanese intelligence was estimating that 30% of Chinese imports were coming in over the Guangxi Road. Diplomatic pressure on Britain to close Burma to Chinese arms imports had failed and had been only intermittently successful against France as regards Indochina. The military solution adopted by the Japanese Army's Imperial General Headquarters (IGHQ) was to seize Nanning and use it as a base to cut the southern supply routes.

The IJA 5th Army (5th Division and Formosa Brigade) was to land at Qinzhou Bay and drive northwest 90km to the city. The defenders counted one army of three divisions strung out along the coast and another near the mouth of the Xi River. Behind them were five army groups totaling 26 divisions (the largest being the 16th with 6 and the 38th with 13 divisions) under Bai Chongxi, Also available was the highly trained and well equipped 5th Army, comprised of the 1st Honor Division, the New 22nd Division, the 200th Motorized Division, the Tank Regiment, and a regiment of modern German 150mm howitzers.

The Japanese landed on 15 November 1939, surprising Chiang and the high command, and quickly formed into columns that cut off Nanning from the north and south with little fighting by 1 December, then moved north against moderate opposition to seize the pass at Kunlunkuan. On 18 December the Chinese 5th Army launched a counterattack that included significant numbers of tanks for the first time, along with accurate fire from the heavy howitzers. In heavy fighting they destroyed a reinforced infantry battalion occupying the Kunlunkuan area. Both sides rushed in reinforcements. Intense fighting see-sawed until

---

[*] Dorn estimated casualties (killed and wounded) in the Winter Offensives at 50,000 Japanese and 150,000 Chinese. Dorn, *The Sino-Japanese War 1937–41*, p. 320.

3 January, when both sides paused, exhausted, the Chinese in control of Kunlunkuan and Japanese in possession of the area to the south.

The fighting had been ferocious. Of the 55,000 men of the Chinese 5th Army who had entered the battle, 5,600 had died and over 10,000 were wounded. Japanese losses were over 4,000 dead and, tellingly, only 102 were reported by the Chinese as captured.

On 25 January 1940 the Japanese renewed their assaults and scattered heavy fighting ensued for three weeks before both sides paused again. The Chinese 46th and 64th Armies launched counterattacks on 12 March that lasted about two weeks and caused the Japanese to pull back somewhat.

An IJA regiment moved south to the French Indochina border in June, dispersing the Chinese 31st Army before it and then a relative calm settled down again. Pressure on the French Indochina government, which no longer had backing from Paris after Germany's victories in Europe, resulted in permission for Japanese troops to enter northern Vietnam, and in September 1940 the Japanese moved one of their 21st Army divisions by sea to occupy French Indochina. Nanning, which had been fought over so bitterly, was suddenly superfluous to Japanese plans. The IJA withdrew to the coast and on 17 November they abandoned Guangxi, having accomplished nothing except to bring misery to the population.

IJA 11th Army Back in Action

The area around Wuhan and Nanchang had been seized, but not pacified, by the brutal and hard-campaigning IJA 11th Army. The disastrous attempt to take Changsha had emboldened Chinese guerrilla and raiding forces and by the spring of 1940 the Japanese were clear that something would have to be done to quiet the area down. The method selected was to send flying columns out into the field in punitive raids. By this time the army consisted of the 3rd, 4th, 13th, and 30th Divisions, plus the bulk of the 6th and 40th Divisions. During the summer and fall the army was reinforced by the 39th Division and most of the 15th and 17th Divisions. This was an impressive show of strength by the Japanese Army since it was stretched somewhat thin on the ground on garrison duties and guarding Manchuria.

Hubei was to be defended by V War Zone under General Le Zongren. He commanded the 2nd, 11th, 22nd, 29th, 31st, and 33rd Army Groups, plus the army-group-size River Defense Force and separate units, for a total of 46 divisions, the 4th and 9th Cavalry Divisions, and 6 guerrilla divisions, all under 22 army HQs. These gave a total of about 380,000 men.

In late April 1940 the Japanese northern flank units, the 3rd, and 13th Divisions, moved north and west against ineffectual resistance, the Chinese units taking to their heels, until they reached the Han River on 10 May. By this time, however, the defenders had begun to gather themselves up and the 2nd and 31st Armies struck at the Japanese left flank, while the 29th and 33rd Armies smashed into their right, and one army plus the guerrilla divisions cut through the Japanese lines of communication. On 11 May the Japanese began a withdrawal, pursued with great vigor by the rejuvenated 31st and 33rd Armies. To speed the Japanese retreat the 33rd Army commander, the fierce General Zhang Zizhong, took his bodyguard battalion forward on 16 May and, waving his sword, personally led his army's charge into a mêlée of charging Chinese and retreating Japanese troops. There he was cut down by enemy machine-gun fire and the Chinese assaults ended almost immediately. The Japanese counter-counterattacked and drove back to the Han River with little difficulty.

In late May a second phase of the punishment columns stepped out, this time the IJA 3rd and 39th Divisions, which marched south through Nanchang aiming towards the river port of Yichang. The IJA 13th Division joined them by marching from the east and the three divisions moved to the city and launched an assault that captured it against only nominal opposition on 13 June. The Chinese 2nd and 31st Armies counterattacked on 18 June and scored some local successes, but finally pulled back to sit and watch.

For the next five months neither side launched major operations but on 25 November the Japanese 11th Army began a series of smaller punitive missions, usually battalion-size, that pillaged their way through the countryside with little opposition. The 11th Army launched a major punitive expedition on 20 January 1941 using the 3rd, 17th, and 40th Divisions and two tank regiments in southern Henan, against V War Zone. The Chinese troops retreated in the face of the attacks, usually before contact was made, and the Japanese contented themselves with working over the countryside through early February.

For its next offensive the 11th Army was directed to northwestern Jiangxi, about 80km west of Nanchang. Its IJA 33rd and 34th Divisions plus an IMB struck out in mid-March and ran through the area against only scattered opposition until 22 March when a three-day pitched battle broke out against the 49th Army. Having achieved its objective of punishment, primarily of local civilians, the 11th Army returned to the previous positions starting on the 26th.

The Hundred Regiments Offensive

Concern about flagging determination in Chongqing to continue the war effort caused the Chinese Communist Party to reconsider its reliance on low-level guerrilla warfare. Feeling they needed a dramatic gesture of their continued commitment, some members, including Peng De-huai, argued for a broad offensive by the 8th Route Army in northern China. Mao apparently opposed this, but was seemingly overruled. Chiang and his government were pointedly not told about the upcoming offensive.

The goal of the operation was to tie down large numbers of Japanese troops in north China by attacking their isolated garrisons and destroying rail and bridge lines of communications in Shanxi and Hebei provinces and to demoralize the Chinese puppet troops that the Japanese used for occupation duties. The operation was planned to consist of three phases, an initial campaign of sabotage against railways and bridges from 20 August to 10 September, a follow-on military offensive from 20 September to the end of October, and a defensive phase resisting the inevitable Japanese counterattacks from 6 October to 5 December. For this operation the 8th Route Army would have a strength of 47 regiments in the 129th Division, 22 regiments in the 120th Division, and 46 regiments in the 115th Division, although the actual forces committed were probably only about half of those.

After a careful reconnaissance effort lasting about a month by agents in civilian dress, simultaneous attacks on many Japanese garrisons between platoon and battalion size began on the evening of 20 September. The attacks continued, as planned, for a little over two months. They did considerable damage to rail lines, bridges, and mines, but were less successful in their efforts against Japanese bases. The communist forces had not yet seized significant numbers of heavy weapons and the attacks, although carried out bravely, turned into bloodlettings at the hands of Japanese machine guns, mortars, and artillery. Chinese casualties were reportedly around 22,000, while those of the Japanese were probably less than a quarter of that figure.

Communist forces continued to undertake sabotage missions and isolated Japanese and puppet patrols were never safe from ambush in north China, but this was to be last conventional offensive they undertook against the Japanese. It did spur the North China Area Army to engage in a more active form of defense, sending out punitive parties to raid, terrorize, and plunder through north China until the war's end.

The KMT forces in Shanxi, of course, appear to have done even less. Nevertheless, their very size was a source of concern to the Japanese so they reinforced their troops in the area and on 6 March 1941 launched an attack into the southern part of the province where the local and KMT troops had taken up residence. They quickly defeated the 15th Army and then moved west. The Chinese troops there retreated and by 14 May the Japanese were confident they had eliminated the Chinese threat. In the southeastern part of the province heavy losses were inflicted by three IJA divisions and the Shanxi operation was declared successfully completed by the Japanese on 15 June.

Changsha Again

What kept 1941 from being a fairly quiet year was Japanese determination to neuter the IX War Zone that had humiliated them in Changsha in 1939. Further, the War Zone's units were being retrained and re-equipped, becoming an obvious threat to the Japanese position in central China. In mid-March the Japanese advanced on the city of Shanggao along three axes but were defeated in detail and forced to retreat.

Six months later the IJA 3rd Army was again directed to seize the city of Changsha, which it had signally failed to do in September 1939. It would concentrate north of the Hsinchiang River, east of Dongting Lake and drive south in three columns using the 3rd, 4th, 6th, 13th, and 40th IJA Divisions. In doing so it would again be attempting to destroy the IX War Zone of the tenacious Xue Yue.

The Japanese troops crossed the Hsinchiang River on 17 September and on 20 September crossed the Milou River, about 35km to the south, against little opposition. On 26 September they had reached the outskirts of Changsha and here Xue Yue ordered the defenders to hold to the last man, and they did. The 10th, 26th, 37th, 72nd, 74th, 78th, and 79th Armies, totaling 20 divisions, entered into a savage mêlée with the Japanese soldiers. Simultaneously, two counter-strokes were launched. The 26th, 72nd, and 74th Armies moved in from the east and attacked the Japanese left flank, while the 4th, 20th, and 58th Armies, with 11 divisions, moved into the area between the Japanese front lines and base to the north and tore up the logistics net. The IJA 3rd Army was trapped.

On 30 September IJA 3rd Army launched an attack to the north to break out of the trap and retreat to its base. It succeeded but at heavy cost, having to fight through ambushes, road blocks, and surprise attacks all the way. On 8 October the Chinese pulled up to the south bank of the Hsinchiang River and halted. The Second Battle of Changsha had ended the same way as the first, with the Japanese beaten and the counter-puncher Xue Yue victorious.

Internecine Struggles

The formation of the united front against the Japanese reduced, but hardly eliminated, conflict between the Nationalist government and the Communist Party. Both sides jockeyed relentlessly to seize and hold favorable locations while forcing their opponents into unfavorable ones. This often involved low-level skirmishes and the deportation or execution of local officials answering to one side or the other.

The "December Incident" of late 1939 involved attempts by the KMT and Yan Xishan to wrest control of portions of Shanxi province from the communists and to bring the Shaanxi–Kansu Soviet under more stringent control. Local fighting continued into February 1940. Further fighting in the Shaanxi–Kansu area in May 1940 reportedly resulted in the deaths of 4,639 KMT supporters and an unknown number of communists, with the latter retaining their hold on the area.

Movement of the communist New 4th Army created further difficulties. In mid-1940 the 4th, 5th and 6th Detachments of that army began deploying eastward into western Jiangsu province. KMT and local forces pushed them back, but reinforcements from the 18th Group Army permitted the communists to seize northern Jiangsu. As the KMT began to marshal its forces for a counterattack the two sides appear to have reached an informal agreement that the communists would operate exclusively in north China, leaving the central portion to the KMT.

Nevertheless the communist side showed no urgency in complying. In December 1940 Chiang personally ordered all units of the nominally subordinate 18th Group Army north of the Yellow River by the end of the month, and units of the New 4th Army north of the Yangtze by the same date and north of the Yellow River by the end of January 1941.

On 4 January 1941 KMT forces of III War Zone moved to surround the HQ of the New 4th Army near Chinghsien in southern Anhui province (south of the Yangtze) and launched a series of hard-fought attacks over the next ten days, killing or capturing most of the 9,000 members. Included among the prisoners was Yeh Ting, the commander, while those killed included the vice-commander and the commissar.

The final clash came a few months later, when the 6th Detachment of the 4th New Army dallied in northern Henan until attacked by cavalry of the Guangxi Army (otherwise known as V War Zone), losing 4,000 men and 2,000 rifles.

Thereafter the two sides seemed content to limit their mutual antagonism to low-level skirmishes and running out or killing functionaries of the side in the contested regions between north and central China.

The Greater War Starts

By mid-October 1941 the Japanese had lost 132,000 killed in action, 48,000 dead of disease, and 36,000 permanently disabled in China. The initial hopes for a quick, cheap victory against China had clearly proven illusory. Nevertheless, Tokyo made the decision to expand the war by attacking the USA, Britain, and the Netherlands.

As part of the preparations for the war in the Pacific, Japanese IGHQ pulled the 5th, 18th, 21st, and 33rd Divisions out of China and reassigned them to the Southern Army in November 1941. In partial compensation the newly raised 51st IJA Division was sent to China. Further, the China Expeditionary Army was ordered to activate six divisions itself by expanding and reorganizing six of its independent mixed brigades, creating "security" or "occupation" divisions strong on infantry, but lacking artillery, and suitable mainly for garrison duties.

The most immediate ramification for China, of course, was the fate of British Hong Kong. The IJA 38th Division was moved from the Guangzhou area on 1 December and launched its attack on 8 December. Kowloon fell on the 12th and on the 18th the Japanese landed on Hon Kong Island; with the British surrender coming on Christmas Day, 1941.

The Third Battle of Changsha

At the outbreak of the Pacific War the commander of the IJA 11th Army suggested to his commander that he could contribute to the new operations by drawing Chinese troops away from the Burma border. This was approved and an IMB and an air brigade allocated to help him. His target, perhaps not surprisingly, was Changsha yet again, only a few months after his most recent humiliation.

For the Chinese the area between the Dongting Lake in the west and the Poyang Lake in the east was defended by the New 3rd, 20th, 58th, and 78th Armies, all facing north, with the 10th, 37th, and 99th Armies behind them, and the 10th Army in Changsha itself. Against this the IJA 3rd, 6th, and 40th Divisions, and the 9th IMB were arrayed on the west side of the front, to drive south on Changsha.

The Japanese assault began at dusk on 24 December 1941 and quickly broke through the 20th Army at the left end of the Chinese line. On the 26th the IJA 3rd Division continued south and routed the 99th Army with little trouble and pushed it to the west. As the Chinese retreated the IJA 3rd Division was ordered to pursue them and continue on to capture the city, while the 6th Division was to move to and secure the area to the east of it. On 1 January 1942 the IJA 3rd Division attempted a hasty assault of the city from the march but was repulsed by troops of the 10th Army in heavy fighting. The next day the IJA 6th Division was thrown into the fray and succeeded in penetrating into most parts of the city.

On 4 January the Japanese issued orders to begin a withdrawal back to the north, their mission of creating a distraction in central China apparently having been concluded. The return was to be harder than the advance. The 73rd and 99th Armies, having been bypassed to the west, attacked eastward and closed off the Japanese lines ahead of their retreat. Other Chinese forces moved in from all directions. The Japanese postwar military account stated:

> The withdrawal was carried out under considerable hardship. Not only did the Japanese forces have to fight off persistent assaults from large enemy forces—from the night of 4 January nine armies and more than twenty divisions had swarmed the battle areas and attacked the withdrawing troops—but they had also been compelled to escort a large number of casualties and rear service units.[*]

Fortunately for the Japanese the Chinese called off the pursuit on 12 January and a few days later were back in their starting position. The IJA 11th Army initiated a few subsidiary actions at the same time, including launching the 34th Division against the New 3rd Army,

---

[*] *Army Operations in China, December 1941–December 1943*, p. 71.

battering it about on 3 January, and making a few forays by the 18th IMB. For the Japanese the presence of the IJA 1st Air Brigade had proven invaluable in the battle, but even with that help the 11th Army had suffered 1,591 dead and 4,412 wounded.

After these engagements Japanese attention focused almost exclusively on the Pacific theater and as a result combat operations in China came to a halt for some time except for minor guerrilla attacks by the Chinese Nationalists and Communists.

Nevertheless, the overall situation for the Chongqing government continued to deteriorate. The loss of much of China's agricultural land and population centers to the Japanese invaders deprived the central government of much of its foundation. Taxes were switched from money to in-kind, which avoided problems with inflation, but made transfers across wide areas difficult. Further, reducing the supply route to the Burma Road made imports of all but the most essential of war materials impractical. Incremental movement towards a barter economy and widespread shortages due to lack of internal transport and a single congested import route led to a spiral of inflation that dramatically reduced wages of civil servants and soldiers. This, in turn, made military service less popular and desertion more common; in response forced conscription was introduced. Unable to feed, clothe, and equip the large army properly, Chiang was forced to trim its size. In November 1941 he directed the Military Affairs Commission (MAC) to come up with implementation plans. They suggested an army of 120 active divisions and 120 "citizen" divisions, including, among the former, 4 armies (12 divisions) of "offensive" divisions.* The General State Mobilization Law was passed on 29 March 1942 and the National Mobilization Committee formed in June to eliminate bureaucratic inefficiencies and infighting, but they were not enough.

In September 1942 troops in I, II, V, and VIII War Zones were directed to dedicate most of their energies to agriculture and other non-military efforts.

The Zhejiang–Jiangsu Operation

In the meantime, far across the Yellow Sea, on 18 April 1942 USAAF bombers under Colonel James Doolittle appeared in the sky over Tokyo. Physical damage was minimal but the psychological impact was great. Some of the planes landed in east China and IGHQ in Tokyo began to worry about American long-range bombers using bases in Zhejiang (Chekiang) and Jiangsu provinces as bases for operations against their homeland. They therefore directed the China Expeditionary Army to drop any other operations and concentrate on clearing the area south and west of Shanghai of any real or potential enemy air bases.

The Japanese 13th Army garrisoned the area around Shanghai and was arrayed along both sides of the Yangtze River all the way to Poyang Lake, a distance of a little over 600km, with five divisions and two IMBs. South of them, where the Japanese now wanted to go, was the Chinese III War Zone commanded by Gu Zhutong, a political general. This force was boxed in on the east by the East China Sea, and on the north and west by the IJA 13th Army but had been reinforced recently by 26th, 49th, and 74th Armies, all taken from the adjacent IX War Zone. The 23rd and 32nd Armies were deployed in a line facing the Japanese along the Yangtze River. The 10th Army faced the Japanese lines south of

---

* This was only partially implemented. Some of the "offensive" divisions were sent out of China and used in the 1942 Burma operations.

Despite Japanese operations in the area, these well-turned-out riflemen
belonged to a division in east China in mid-1945 that had not been worn
down by combat, but had largely been held back. (*J. Wisebram*)

Hangzhou Bay. To the extent there was a strategic reserve it was found in the 25th Army
gathered well to the south and the separate field army near the war zone HQ at Shangrao.

The IJA 13th Army launched probing attacks on 18 May in the area between Hangzhou
and the coast at the mouth of Hangzhou Bay with the ultimate objective of cutting off
and clearing the coastal area of Zhejiang. The main assault was launched on 25 April but
the 79th Division in Jinhua and the 63rd Division in Lanxi proved tough and it was not
until 28 April that the cities fell. At that the front settled down again while the Japanese
reorganized.

On 31 May the Japanese launched their second phase with the goal of clearing the
Zhejiang–Jiangsu Railroad. Attacks were to be made down both ends of the rail lines and
meet somewhere in the center in Chinese-held territory. The hard-charging IJA 11th Army
attacked eastward from below Poyang Lake and followed the rail line, scattering the 100th
Army with little trouble. The 79th Army of IX War Zone attempted to intervene from the
south but was destroyed during 6–8 June. The 100th Army re-formed along the railway and
was destroyed by the IJA 11th Army on 15–16 June. Meanwhile, the IJA 22nd Division of
the 13th Army moved westward down the rail line against the 26th and 86th Armies. The
two thrusts finally met at Hengfeng on the railway on 1 July.

Once the rail line had been seized, the IJA 3rd Division was ordered to clear out the
area to its south. The main objective was Linchuan/Fuzhou, where the Chinese 4th and

58th Armies had concentrated. On 25 June the IJA division attacked the city and three days later penetrated it, destroying the bulk of the 4th Army, while the 58th Army retreated south. The Japanese followed and on 3 July attacked the 58th Army, which fought hard but eventually succumbed on the 7th. The Japanese were able to destroy the airfields in the area, including those at Yushan, Zhaoxian, and Lishui. In mid-July the 3rd Division was ordered back north to rejoin its army, and on 28 July IGHQ directed that the offensive be terminated and units pulled back again, except for the retention of some key points around Jinhua. The general withdrawal began on 19 August 1942 and was completed by the end of the month without interference. The Zhejiang–Jiangxi operation had cost the IJA 11th Army 356 dead and 949 wounded, and the 13th Army 1,284 dead and 2,767 wounded.

With that operation completed the Japanese reverted to a period of relatively quiet garrison activity pending the next offensive. Plans were drawn up for a five-month campaign to seize Sichuan in the spring of 1943, but by late 1942 it had become clear that prosecuting the campaigns in the Pacific and Burma would require more troops than previously envisioned. Thus, in late 1942, IGHQ notified the China Expeditionary Force that large-scale offensives would not be supported for the next year and that the China theater would have to content itself with garrison duties with reduced forces.

The Lull of 1943

For the most part both sides were content to sit out much of 1943, engaging in only relatively minor operations through the year. The IJA 23rd IMB seized the Leizhou Peninsula in February against only nominal resistance, while the IJA 11th Army carried out some reconnaissance missions. In fact, outside the area of operations of 11th Army, the China theater remained quiet save for small-scale guerilla actions.

That exception was the area around Dongting Lake in northeastern Hunan province. The Japanese in the form of their 11th Army garrisoned both sides of the Yangtze River near the lake, but were concerned about Chinese forces concentrated north and south of the river near the lake. The Japanese units were initially directed to clear the area north of the lake, using forces that already had the area surrounded, albeit in a rather porous manner. The IJA 58th Division was to the north, west of Wuchang, the IJA 40th Division was to the south where the Yangtze entered the lake, and the IJA 13th Division was to the west, about 100km upriver from the lake. In mid-February they began their drive to converge in the center of that area.[*] The operation was successfully concluded in late March against only sporadic opposition, with Japanese casualties totaling 354 killed and 890 wounded. About 5,000 Chinese troops surrendered, but the majority simply melted away through Japanese lines, some to be re-formed as military units and some not. In contrast to earlier punitive operations here the Japanese stayed as occupiers, as it was agriculturally fertile land and provided a good base for the future in central China.

The next phase of the operation, more ambitious, was to clear the area south of the Yangtze and west of Dongting Lake. This was the home area of VI War Zone under General Chen Chung. Although he had a nominal 41 divisions under his command, combat support for the war zone was limited to the 4th Heavy Mortar Regiment under the River Defense Force and the 42nd (AA) Artillery Regiment. The Japanese forces would come, as before,

---

[*] As usual, each Japanese division had to leave substantial forces behind for garrison duty, so a division actually only fielded four or six infantry battalions and three artillery battalions for offensive operations.

from 11th Army, in the form of 3rd and 13th Divisions, 17th IMB, and two regimental combat teams.

The initial moves by the Japanese involved the 3rd Division driving south from just west of the lake to clear the area about 50km west of the lake and 60km south of the river, ending up on the western shore of the lake. That area was occupied by the Chinese 73rd Army, which was pushed back with little trouble, so that this operation, which began on 5 May was declared finished by the Japanese on 11 May.

The IJA 3rd Division was already in place well south of the river and would now drive west. The IJA 13th Division, on the north bank of the Yangtze about 150km west of the lake, would drive southeast and the two forces would assault the 87th and 94th Armies from two sides. This offensive was launched on 12 May and declared successfully terminated on 18 May. With that area cleared the two Japanese divisions now headed west, while the IJA 39th Division pushed south from its positions north of the Yangtze farther to the west. They completed the destruction of the 87th and 94th Armies and broke through the 10th Army. By 29th May the Japanese forces had breached many of the defenses west of Yichang.

The operation was declared completed on 31 May and orders for withdrawal issued. Chinese forces tried to block the withdrawal, but were defeated, the 79th Army by the 13th Division, and the 74th Army by the 17th IMB. By 10 June the Japanese were back in their original positions, having suffered 771 killed and 2,746 wounded.

The Battle of Changde

By mid-1943 the Japanese HQs at various levels noted that three Chinese armies had concentrated in Yunnan province with the apparent objective of attacking south into Burma. Not knowing that Chiang had no intention of launching them south until the Americans forced him to do so, their China Expeditionary Army proposed to IGHQ that they distract the Chongqing government. IGHQ approved this, but only as a temporary measure and one that had to be undertaken with existing forces, as no reinforcements could be spared.

The means chosen, almost inevitably, was unleashing the IJA 11th Army yet again on the populace of Hunan province and their ostensible guardians, VI War Zone, now under the somewhat erratic General Sun Lianzhong, on the west side of Dongting Lake. This would be accomplished by pushing south with the 3rd, 13th, 39th, and 116th IJA Divisions, which were strung out along the Yangtze west of the lake.

The four IJA divisions began their assault on 2 November. By 16 November they had thrust about 100km southwest, routing the 44th, 73rd, and 79th Armies. After a pause to resupply, the Japanese renewed their offensive on 19 November with the aim of driving south to encircle and capture the city of Changde. The IJA 13th Division on the right flank was stopped by heavy resistance from the rejuvenated 73rd Army, but the others continued their moves and by 23 November had encircled the city. Only one Chinese formation had been left in Changde, the 57th Division, but it fought ferociously. The 10th Army attempted to attack from the south to relieve the 57th Division, but was caught between the IJA 3rd and 68th Divisions and destroyed on 1 December. The city fell on 4 December and there then followed delicate negotiations within the Japanese command between the China Expeditionary Army and IGHQ. Tokyo wanted Changde held, but the theater commanders recognized they were stretched too thin for that. A slow and confusing withdrawal followed but by 24 December the IJA 11th Army was back to its original position. Fortunately for them, VI War Zone showed no inclination to take advantage of the Japanese moves back north. Nevertheless, the Changde operation had cost the 11th Army 1,274 dead and 2,977 wounded.

Overall, 1943 had passed relatively uneventfully for the vast majority of Chinese and Japanese troops in the theater, except for the periodic incursions of the 11th Army in Hunan. That was about to change.

Operation Ichi-Go

Through 1943 the Japanese had, for the most part, contented themselves with occupying the main lines of communication. They placed garrisons along the navigable portions of the major rivers, guarded railroad lines and bridges, and occupied the major cities and transport hubs in their areas of interest. Huge swaths of Chinese countryside, especially in the central and southern parts of the country, were left unoccupied, and indeed with a total force of only 24 divisions, 1 armored division, 11 IMBs, and 1 cavalry brigade in China at the start of 1944 the Japanese had few other options.

Both sides seem to have found this an acceptable, if far from optimal, arrangement. Chiang lacked the logistic support to launch broad offensives and could not mass large forces in any event. His troops still held most of China's territory and were being very slowly modernized with American Lend-Lease weaponry. The Japanese, for their part, were being ground down in the Pacific and Burma and were certainly not inclined to roil the waters in China any more than they felt they needed to.

The Japanese perspective changed in the fall of 1943. They had received word about improved American heavy bombers that could reach the Japanese homeland from airfields in east China and this was a major new source of concern. In addition, the US 14th Air Force was already savaging much of the Japanese lines of communications in China from their bases in Guangxi, generating a commonality of interest between the commanders in China and IGHQ. Further, US submarines were beginning to take a toll of Japanese shipping between the Home Islands and the resource-rich south and the possibility of establishing a land route between Malaya and northern China was becoming increasingly attractive.[*]

After some consultations IGHQ issued its orders for Operation Ichi-Go in January 1944, destined to be the largest IJA operation of the war. One goal was the destruction of Allied airfields in east China. Another was to seize several strategic rail lines running north–south through the country. The envisioned rail corridor would run from Beijing south to the Hankou industrial center, then south again and splitting at Hengyang with one branch going to the southeast to Guangzhou, and the other southwest to Nanning near the Indochina border.

Ichi-Go would be broken down into two component operations. The first, and preliminary, action was named Operation Kogo and involved the clearing of the Beijing–

---

[*] There is some uncertainty as to whether IGHQ envisioned a land route as a replacement for shipping from the southern part of the empire. It appears that this was considered in early planning, but once the operation was under way, in mid-1944, it was conceded that Japan did not have enough railway operating assets and instead the objective was simply to maintain land-based "liaison" with Southern Army in Indochina and Malaya.

Hankou railway, and was to take about six weeks starting in April 1944. Once Kogo had achieved its objectives Operation Togo would clear the area south of Hankou over a period of five months.

Unfortunately, many of Chiang's best troops had been pulled south for use in Burma. He had resisted this diversion of force for as long as he could, but Stilwell's complaints to Washington had yielded thinly veiled threats that if the partially US-equipped forces were not committed to the Burma enterprise American Lend-Lease deliveries would cease. In April 1944 Chiang bowed to the inevitable and gave the orders to prepare to move south across the Salween.* China would face the broad Japanese offensive with no operational reserve.

Operation Kogo

The Japanese North China Area Army already held the northern half of the Beijing–Hankou railway, down to where it crossed the Yellow River. At the river they concentrated the IJA 12th Army, reinforced to a powerful formation consisting of 37th, 62nd and 110th Divisions, the 3rd Armored Division (of two brigades), and the 4th Cavalry Brigade, a more mobile force than usually seen in China operations. The Japanese planners apparently envisioned little substantive opposition, for once the breakthrough over the river had taken place the army was to peel off elements to swing to the right and move west and northwest with the goal of destroying I War Zone near Luoyang. Only the 27th Division was allocated to move the full 120km down the railway and meet up with the 115th Brigade moving up from the south.

I War Zone was based in Henan province and was commanded by General Jiang Dingwen, noted more for his loyalty to Chiang Kai-shek than any military skills. Perhaps in recognition of this Jiang put most of the combat power of the area in a separate command group under his deputy commander, Tang Enbo, charged with guarding the rail line. The rest of the troops would be kept to the west, presumably to threaten the flank of any Japanese drive down the rail line. Tang had proven himself capable as commander of the 20th Army in 1937 and Colonel Frank Dorn, a US military observer at the time, referred to him as "courageous, intelligent and aggressive."† His performance here, however, was less stellar. Further, the population of Henan had been devastated by the flooding of the Yellow River in 1938, recent droughts, the apparent lack of concern for their predicament in Chongqing, and depradations from poorly disciplined and hungry soldiers. At the first opportunity many turned on KMT soldiers unwise enough to travel in small groups.

The IJA 37th Division began the operation with an assault against Chinese positions on the south side of the Yellow River on the night of 17 April 1944. The division, plus an IMB, smashed through Tang's forward positions and other divisions followed. The 28th and 31st Armies succeeded in slowing the Japanese advance only slightly and by 30 April

---

* Stilwell was convinced that Chiang was simply trying to conserve forces for use against the communists after the war, letting the Americans fight the war for him. More recent scholarship seems to show that Chiang was less concerned about the Burma Road than the Americans and more worried about rampaging Japanese forces in eastern and central China. In fact, overland deliveries did not start until January 1945 and even at the peak overall delivery month of July 1945 the airlift over the Hump provided a little over 70,000 tons, while the road provided only 21,000 tons and the pipeline about 10,000.

† Dorn, p. 106.

the Japanese were attacking Xuchang, which they seized the next day. That was the trigger for the Japanese advance to split, with the 27th Division continuing south down the rail line and the remaining elements of the 12th Army wheeling right for the drive northwest on Luoyang.

By 4 May the IJA 37th Division, 3rd Armored Division, and the cavalry brigade had arrived at Linru, about 50km west of the rail line, nearly cutting off the 85th Army, but it managed to break through an unguarded gap left by the slow-moving armored division. The 177th Division held up the IJA 9th Independent Infantry Brigade for several days of heavy fighting, but eventually succumbed. This was the exception, however, as the Japanese were able to push quickly south of Luoyang to the west, then turn around and come back to encircle it completely. They were helped by elements of the IJA 1st Army, which attacked south from its position across the Yellow River to the west. On 19th May the IJA 63rd Division, reinforced by part of the 3rd Armored Division, attacked Luoyang, which was garrisoned by the 15th Army. They were repulsed and a second assault was launched on 24 May, this time with the IJA 63rd Division attacking from the northeast, the 3rd Armored Division from the west, and the cavalry brigade poised to intercept fleeing Chinese. This attack succeeded and occupied the town the next day.

In the meantime, the 37th Division had continued south on the rail line, meeting up with Japanese forces driving north from Hankou on 11 May.

The Japanese had accomplished their missions in about a month. They had neutralized I War Zone and had cleared the northern portion of their planned rail corridor through China. The cost had been 869 killed and 2,280 wounded.

Fall of Changsha

With the preliminaries out of the way it was now time to initiate the second phase of Ichi-Go, Operation Togo. Once again the hard-charging IJA 11th Army would bear much of the burden, attacking once again into IX War Zone. The Japanese units were to drive south from the southern end of Dongting Lake following the railroad line and the Xiang River that runs parallel and to the west of it. About 80km south of the lake was their first objective, the city of Changsha, which the 11th Army had already seen in 1941. A farther 140km south was the second objective, Hengyang, where the rail line split, one branch going southeast to Guangzhou and the other south into Guangxi.

The Japanese launched their attack on 27 May 1944 with the 40th Division coming from the west side of the lake and the rest of the army from the east. The 20th Army put up substantial resistance to the IJA 68th Division for several days but was bypassed and did not threaten the Japanese advance. Similarly, the 99th Army stopped the IJA 34th Division in the hills, but after failing to dislodge their opponents the Japanese simply bypassed them as well.

Otherwise the Japanese were not slowed down and on 16 June the IJA 34th and 58th Divisions attacked Changsha, which was garrisoned by the 4th Army. The Chinese forces abandoned the city without much of a fight and it fell on 18 June. The 30th Army Group and the 44th Army had concentrated about 40km east of Changsha and these were defeated by the IJA 3rd and 13th Divisions with little difficulty on 18 June

Defense of Hengyang

With Changsha secured and the Chinese forces around it dispersed, the Japanese moved to the next phase, an advance farther south to the rail junction at Hengyang. Once again they would drive deep into Xue Yue's territory. Unlike in their earlier efforts in 1939–41 Changsha had fallen easily, but this time they were intent on driving farther and holding on to their gains.

On 22 June the IJA 40th Division moved south on the west side of the river and occupied Xiangxiang, brushing aside the 29th Army. On 26 June the IJA 68th Division captured Hengyang airfield and on the 27th it crossed the Xiang River south of Hengyang, surrounding the city. The IJA 116th and 68th Divisions launched their assault on the city on the 28th but were repeatedly repulsed in bloody fighting over the next three days that cost the Japanese heavy casualties, including the commander and chief of staff of the 68th Division. Li Yutang's group of the 24th Army formed the heart of the defense and they stood and fought for every block. On 2 July the Japanese suspended their attacks pending the arrival of additional artillery.

The Japanese reinforcements arrived on 10 July and the following day the offensive was resumed. Once again the attacks were rebuffed. The IJA 58th Division was brought forward to Hengyang, along with four 15cm howitzers and four 10cm field guns in preparation for a third round of assaults.

In the meantime, Xue had reverted to his old form of counterattacking at every opportunity. The 20th, 58th, and 72nd Armies were sent to attack the Japanese lines of communication, while the 37th, 62nd, and 79th Armies tried to break through to link up with the besieged forces in Hengyang. The relievers got to within 10km of the city but, exhausted and low on supplies, could finally push no farther against the newly arrived IJA 40th Division.

By early August the Japanese had completed their preparations for the final assault on Hengyang. The 58th, 116th, and 66th IJA Divisions were poised to the west of the city, from north to south; while the 13th IJA Division set up to the east across the Xiang River. On 4 August the 68th and 116th IJA Divisions launched their attacks but were stopped cold by a ferocious Chinese defense that simply refused to yield. Renewed efforts on the 5th and 6th accomplished little more. On 7 August the IJA 11th Army launched an all-out offensive against the whole perimeter of city. During the day it made no progress, but in the evening the 68th Division managed to break into a small section of the inner city and the Japanese renewed their efforts. Other units followed into the breach and attacked the defenders from the rear and finally, in the early morning of 8 August, General Fang Xianjue, commander of the 10th Army, and four of his division commanders surrendered what remained of their forces.

Battles between the tough Japanese 11th Army and the indomitable Xue Yue's IX War Zone were invariably bloody affairs. This one, however, was even worse than those that had preceded it. No final Japanese casualty figures are known, but by 20 July (before the final assaults on the city and much of action against the relieving columns) they had reached 3,860 killed and 8,327 wounded, along with 7,099 ill with disease. The Japanese estimated that about 10% of those casualties resulted from air raids by the US 14th Air Force, which conducted interdiction actions against their supply lines. As always, Chinese casualty figures were purely speculative, but must have been very high inside the city, while American observers with the attempted relief force noted heavy casualties there as well.*

The Fall of Guilin and Liuzhou

With the seizure of Hengyang the stage was set for the next phase of Operation Togo. The original plan to drive south on both branches of the railway had been deferred, and instead the Japanese generals decided to concentrate all efforts on the western rail line that ran from Hengyang southwest to Liuzhou (Liuchow) in Guangxi province. The main effort would come from the IJA 11th Army, victors of Hengyang, who would push down the rail line. A second effort would come from the IJA 23rd Army which would send two divisions west from Guangzhou up the Xi River basin and meet the 11th Army at Liuzhou.

The IJA 11th Army rested and resupplied after the heavy fighting of June and July and on 29 August began its attack down the rail line, aided by the presence of a regiment of new Japanese Army fighter aircraft that provided a good deal of protection to their supply lines from US aerial attacks. North of the rail line the IJA 37th and 116th Divisions pushed the Chinese 74th and 100th Armies westward with little trouble. The railway itself was defended by the 46th, 62nd, and 79th Armies and these were similarly dislodged by the IJA 40th and 58th Divisions. South of the line the IJA 3rd and 13th Divisions forced the 26th and 37th Armies to retreat. The Japanese offensive went smoothly and by 9 September they had reached the Guangxi border. They drove on a little farther and then

A mortar unit of the 2nd Division, 52nd Army, of Chiang's reserves, 1 August 1944.

paused to regroup and resupply. Afterwards 11th Army spent the rest of September and part of October clearing out the areas north and south of its positions without much difficulty.

---

* The Japanese estimated that 66,000 Chinese died, 27,500 were captured, and 132,500 became sick or were wounded, or a total of 226,000 casualties in the battle for Hunan. As is always the case estimates of enemy dead and sick/wounded were almost certainly considerably overstated, although the number of captured should have been roughly accurate. The Chinese Military Operations Office gave their casualties at 90,557 killed or wounded.

In the meantime the IJA 23rd Army began its drive to the west on 13 September and the advance moved smoothly until 24 October when the Chinese 46th and 64th Armies counterattacked at Guiping. That halted the Japanese until 29 October, when the Chinese forces began to withdraw. The advance then restarted, but by that time the IJA 11th Army was already on the move again.

Guilin (Kweilin) and Liuzhou were both important in their own right, the former as the site of a major American training base for the Chinese Army and the latter as a bomber base. The aggressive IJA 11th Army was determined to waste no more time. Its 37th, 40th, and 58th Divisions were ordered to invest Guilin and assault it by the end of October, and the 3rd and 13th Divisions to bypass that operation and speed on to the west to seize Liuzhou at almost the same time. The Americans had already evacuated both cities and on 9 November Guilin was attacked and fell with little resistance the next day. Simultaneously, on the 9th, elements of the IJA 104th Division occupied Liuzhou against token opposition.

A column of 75mm M1897 guns on the road from Liuzhou to Guiyang, October 1944.

Having the Chinese defenders on the run, 11th Army ordered its 13th Division to continue the pursuit from Liuzhou up the railway to the northwest. This they did to a distance of about 120km, scattering what Chinese forces remained. Similarly, the 3rd Division was directed to clear the area south of Liuzhou and the 22nd Division to pass through it even farther south and seize Nanning, which it did on 20 November.

Loss of the Guangzhou–Hankou Railway

The rail line between Guangzhou and Hengyang (en route to Hankou) passed through broken terrain that required the use of many bridges and tunnels. Since Japan lacked the resources at the time to rebuild these features, they would have to be seized intact. The IJA 40th Division formed four raiding detachments, each built around an infantry battalion, to occupy the vulnerable sites by coup de main. These groups moved out between 3 January and 12 January 1945 and executed their attacks during 19–22 January. The main force of the division, together with the 27th Division, occupied the whole of the rail line by the end of the month, and detachments from the divisions occupied airfields in the vicinity of the line.

Loss of the Northern Airfields, 1945

The operations of late 1944 had cleared out the Allied airfields in southern China at Liuzhou and Guilin, but had done nothing about the Laohekou or Zhijiang (Chihchiang) airbases in the central part of the country. As Japanese air strength in China diminished, the depredations of the US 14th Air Force continued and so Japanese commanders decided to minimize losses to air strikes the only way they could, by eliminating the enemy air bases. In late 1944 IGHQ ordered the China Expeditionary Army to destroy the air bases, and those orders were passed on to field units in January 1945.

The IJA 12th Army was made responsible for the seizure of Laohekou, in the area of I War Zone. The Japanese 110th and 115th Divisions launched their attacks westward on 22 March, bypassing the Chinese 143rd Division in Nanyang. They then fanned out, the 110th Division moving north of the airbase, while the 3rd Armored Division and 4th Cavalry Brigade rushed through the center of the hole. On 27 March the cavalry brigade captured the airfield but failed in a hurried attempt to take the city against the 125th Division defending it. On 28 March the IJA 39th Division moved up from the south to block Chinese reinforcements for the city and on 7 April the Japanese launched a more deliberate attack on the city with their 115th Division and occupied it the next day.

During this time the IJA 110th Division had been holding an area about 100km to the north around the town of Xixia in Henan. There it faced the Chinese 31st Army Group, which launched a counterattack on 5 April with its 68th, 85th, and 89th Armies. A small force of only six infantry battalions, the Japanese division quickly found itself in trouble and three battalions (two infantry and one artillery) of reinforcements were quickly sent. They proved insufficient and five more infantry battalions were dispatched. The situation then stabilized and on 29 April the Japanese division launched its own counterattack. According to a postwar Japanese military study, this proved an optimistic misjudgment and the Chinese "inflicted tremendous casualties on the Japanese and, on 10 May, the 110th Division suspended its attack in order to re-form its line. Taking advantage of this opportunity, the enemy attacked but this time the Japanese succeeded in pushing them back."[*]

Both sides having presumably made their points the front quieted down and stayed that way. The Chinese I War Zone reported its losses for the period 22 May to 23 June as 13,847 killed and wounded. There are no figures for Japanese losses.

The Test, April–June 1945

Through early 1945 the Japanese forces in China had not faced any Chinese divisions that had received American liaison teams and training. That would change in April with their

---

[*] Japanese monograph No. 72, p. 160.

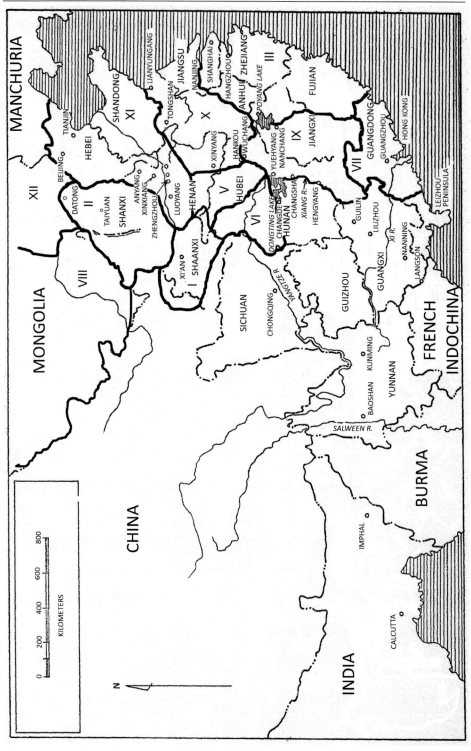

War zones, mid-1945.

decision to seize the airfield at Zhijiang. To get to the airfield the Japanese would have to go through mountainous western Hunan province, garrisoned by General Wang Yaowu's 24th Army.

The US Eastern Command had been set up in January 1945 to supervise the training and equipping of Wang's troops. By 1 April the command had a strength of 109 officers and 270 enlisted men with combat sections organized to advise the three US-sponsored armies: 18th, 73rd, and 74th. Training facilities were set up, starting in mid-April, and a first batch of small classes, officers and specialist enlisted, was brought in.

The force the Japanese entrusted to march 150km through the mountains and seize Zhijiang airfield was their 20th Army. To execute it the confident Japanese allocated the 116th Division, a garrison unit that had been roughly handled at Hengyang earlier, and one fresh, high-quality division, the 47th. Unfortunately, the movement of the 47th Division from Japan had been delayed by shipping shortages and only one regiment was available by the time the offensive was due to kick off.

The regiment from the IJA 47th Division moved out early, on 3 April, and traveled west parallel to the main road but about 50km north of it. On 28 April they were attacked by the Chinese 18th and 73rd Army and forced to dig in to await the rest of their division. Meanwhile, the 116th Division moved westward along the road in three columns until it encountered the 57th Division of the 74th Army on 8 April. The other two divisions of the army moved in to join the fray, with the 100th Army behind them. Then the 94th Army from Tang Enbo's 3rd Front Army also moved towards the battle from the south.

The 116th Division continued its attacks against increasingly unfavorable odds and on 4 May the IJA 20th Army commander ordered the division to cease its efforts. Withdrawals started the next day and were hotly followed by the troops of the 74th Army and parts of the 73rd Army. Pressure was maintained and isolated groups of Japanese wiped out. The 1st and 2nd Battalions of the 30th Field Artillery then joined the fray as part of the 74th Army and further increased the pressure on

Having been airlifted up from Burma four months earlier, troops of the CAI's New 6th Army at Zhanyi, China, 8 April 1945.

the Japanese. The combination of an aggressive Chinese spirit and US air support finally broke the IJA's 116th Division. It was forced to sacrifice its 109th Regiment, which lost 755 killed and most of the rest wounded, to cover its withdrawal. The remainder of the IJA 47th Division had arrived on 6 May but on 9 May, before it could be deployed, China Expeditionary Army terminated the operation as a lost cause and the Japanese retreated back to the east. On 26 May the Chinese called off their counterattacks, having driven the Japanese back to their start line. The Japanese had been soundly beaten and had lost 2,400 dead and over 25,000 wounded.

Clearly the Chinese Army that the Japanese ran into on this occasion was very different from many they had encountered before. Some little credit must be given to the American trainers and teams for improving staff work and liaison, but the bulk of praise must go to the Chinese units themselves.

Two divisions of each army were to be the Alpha-type divisions (see Chapter 10) with a field artillery battalion (11th and 18th Divisions of 18th Army; 15th and 77th of the 73rd Army; and 51st and 57th of the 74th Army), but in fact although all the artillery battalions existed, only one, that of the 15th Division, had actually joined its parent before the fighting ended. Although short of everything except ammunition, that unit fired for weeks and results were reportedly good, although no Americans were with it at the time. The artillery battalions of the 74th Army were originally part of the 30th FA Regiment and were very highly regarded, but did not join their divisions until just after the battle quieted down.

After-action summaries prepared by the Americans consistently praised the offensive spirit of the Chinese units with comments like "troops were anxious to close with the enemy," "Japs were made to engage in hand-to-hand combat in both offense and defense," "this army was completely offensive and in many instances wanted to continue attack but were unable to obtain authority from higher authority" and "good morale and discipline, soldiers were willing to fight. Soldiers fought bravely." Tactics on defense were usually good, although on offense there was still a reliance on costly frontal assaults. Use of machine guns was often inefficient, but the 60mm mortars received shortly before the action were popular and useful once the troops got used to them and were assured of ammunition resupply. Supply procedures were adequate, although just barely, but medical support was, as always, poor.

Chinese casualties are, as usual, unknown, but were undoubtedly quite high. The US liaison team with the 51st Division estimated it had taken 800 casualties (killed and wounded) during the operation, while the 94th Army, not fully engaged during the whole battle, reported the loss of 677 dead (including 390 in the 5th Division, 264 in the 121st Division, and 22 in the 43rd Division) and 651 wounded, a ratio that indicates either that only seriously wounded were reported or that poor medical care meant that a high percentage of the wounded died.

The Drive to the Coast

The US staff in China had long been frustrated by the pace of supply from India to China, either by airlift alone or supplemented by the Burma/Ledo Road. By early February 1945 General Albert Wedemeyer, Chiang's Chief of Staff, had begun sharing his thoughts with his staff that it might be possible to use the Alpha divisions in a drive to the coast to open up a port in July or August. The effort, the Beta Plan, as he envisioned it, called for an advance to the Liuzhou–Nanning area as Phase I, consolidating in that area as Phase II, and then preparing for an assault on Hong Kong and Fort Bayard (Guangzhou) as Phase III. Phase IV would then encompass the actual capture of those two cities. A variant included the development of port facilities on the Leizhou Peninsula during Phase II to support the final phase.

The Beta Plan was presented to the Generalissimo and the American staff held their breath. It would be the first major offensive effort conducted within China itself since Pearl Harbor and a major departure from Chiang's long-standing strategy of preserving his forces. On 14 February word arrived that he had approved the plan. Wedemeyer then flew to Washington to present it to the Joint Chiefs of Staff. The JCS agreed that operations in the western Pacific would stretch Japanese resources sufficiently to make Beta practical and, on 20 April, they also approved.

In the meantime, the Japanese had been conducting their own reassessments. As the Allies moved across the Pacific, the defense of south China began to look more like a matter of prestige rather than military necessity. The US landing on Okinawa on 1 April effectively cut off Japan from the south and speeded up the work on IGHQ's Plan Ketsu for the defense of Japan. The plan called for concentrating the troops in China around Hankou and Shanghai in the central part of the country and in a great swath of north China. South China, to include Changsha and Hengyang that had been bought at such great price in blood, was to be abandoned.

In May reports came in that the Japanese were prepared to abandon Nanning, having first destroyed the local utilities. On 26 May the Chinese attacked and drove out the small Japanese rearguard. The Japanese were clearly going to give up the objectives of Phase I of the offensive and a revised plan was drawn up in early June called Carbonado. The new plan differed little from the old except that Chinese forces were now to seize Fort Bayard, a small port on the South China Sea, as an interim supply base for the advance on Guangzhou/Hong Kong.[*]

The new effort was to come from IV War Zone under General Zhang Fakui, who commanded the remnants of six broken and dispirited armies that had been roughly handled in the Hengyang/Liuzhou battles: the 37th and 46th of the 16th Army Group, the 62nd and 64th of the 35th Army Group, and the 31st and 93rd. They had suffered heavy losses in the preceding battles, lost almost all their heavy weapons, the supply and medical systems had completely broken down, and their morale was almost nil. In addition, the area they were stationed in did not raise nearly enough food to feed them, and most were suffering from malnutrition as a result. Under American supervision a guerrilla battalion was activated in each of the two armies and provided with full equipment and better food to yield at least a small striking force.

Such a group would clearly be incapable of forcing the issue against any Japanese unit that wanted to hold on, so three Alpha Armies, the 8th, 54th, and New 1st, were moved to Zhang's control. In the meantime, his 46th and 64th Armies began shadowing the Japanese as they withdrew, the 64th occupying Nanning and the 46th stopping near Liuzhou as it ran out of supplies.

---

[*] Fort Bayard, at Guangzhou Bay, was a French concession that had been occupied by Japan in February 1943. US planners believed that the delivery of 25,000 tons per month at Fort Bayard would yield 15,000 tons per month to the forward area; whereas it took 60,000 tons at Calcutta to produce 15,000 tons in east China.

Troops of the 54th Army on the Red
River in Yunnan, 9 August 1945.

In fact, the 46th Army was something of a success story. Its morale had been dismal following the Liuzhou campaign, but on 1 July 1945 the inept General Li Xingshu was replaced in command by the capable General Han Liancheng and the situation quickly improved. Even though the army had only four 75mm howitzers as its artillery complement, with an 82mm mortar battalion providing the fire support for each division, and most weapons in poor shape due to lack of preservatives and cleaning gear, the 175th Division of the army had moved aggressively north, punched through some stiff Japanese resistance, and recapturing Liuzhou on 1 July. The entire army then moved south and the New 19th Division captured Limkong in a three-day battle, ending on 3 August 1945.[*] At that point the army ceased operations.

One area the Japanese were not prepared to give up was central China, particularly around the Laohekou airfield, which they had seized just a few months before. In mid-1945 I War Zone had 16 armies and 45 divisions, not counting the New 8th and 10th Armies that answered directly to Chiang Kai-shek. Also on the strength were the 1st, 3rd, 4th, 6th, 8th, 9th, 13th, and 23rd Guerrilla Columns with 41,000 troops, which operated sporadically behind Japanese lines. In addition, it held the 11th Artillery Regiment, 52nd AT regiment, 3rd Heavy Mortar Regiment, 2nd Armored Regiment, and signal and engineer elements, for a total of 358,704 officers and men. Japanese forces were formed into the 12th Army, which included the 3rd Armored Division and the 4th Cavalry Brigade. Both sides were still too tired after their recent battles to undertake any major actions, but the Chinese aggressively probed and skirmished through the end of July when they paused to resupply and reorganize. The 12th Army was ordered to "garrison" status with the pending departure of the 3rd Armored Division and thereafter fighting dropped off further.

Further north, Chinese efforts were mainly guerrilla raids, often small-scale operations

---

[*] The US liaison team noted that the division fought "magnificently" in this battle in spite of the inadequacies of supporting weapons and equipment. HQ, 46th Army Liaison Team, CCC, 6 Sept 1945, Secret Report on 46th Army.

by the communist forces. Thus, the IJA's 1st Army in Shanxi and Shaanxi in the north-west, and the 43rd to the northeast of that to the sea, including Beijing and the Shandong peninsula, were primarily garrison forces, although the latter had begun planning for the possibility of a US landing on the Shandong Peninsula in mid-1945.

At the end of the war the Chinese Army, spearheaded by about two dozen re-formed and trained divisions was advancing in the south, successfully engaging Japanese forces on offense and defense. In the central–eastern portion the provinces of Jiangxi, Fujian, and Zhejiang had never been strongly held by the Japanese and by mid-1945 they had essentially abandoned them, along with Guangxi and Hunan. In both these cases much of the motive for the Japanese pull-back was due to fears of a US invasion of the China coast. Nevertheless, the withdrawals and redeployments were accomplished against a much more aggressive and proficient foe than previously. The stage was set for a bloody civil war, one in which the shortcomings of cronyism and corruption, which had been papered over by hatred for the invaders, finally came to the fore.

2

Coalition Warfare—Burma

By 1940 the Burma Road into Yunnan province had become the only means of getting significant amounts of supplies from the outside world into China. As a result, the Chinese were almost as concerned with the security of Burma as the British. Immediately after Pearl Harbor the Chinese offered to send large numbers of troops into Burma to aid in its defense, but only on condition that they be deployed en masse and not committed piecemeal. The British were hesitant, in part because of problems in supplying them, and in part because of suspicions of unresolved Chinese border claims. In response to the Chinese offer of the 5th and 6th Armies, they originally agreed to accept only one division, then on 23 December two divisions of the 6th Army.

The First Burma Campaign

Japanese success in Malaya forced the British to rethink their position and in February 1942 they relented and requested full Chinese assistance. The Chinese Expeditionary Force in Burma consisted of two armies, later increased to three, under the command of American General Joseph Stilwell. The 6th Army was a mediocre unit, with one good division, the 49th, one average division, and the new and untrained Temporary 55th Division, all under the direction of a rather timid commander. The 5th Army, on the other hand, was one of Chiang's best. It included a tank regiment, a motorized reconnaissance battalion, and a troop-carrying motor transport regiment that was used to motorize the 200th Division. It also included an army artillery regiment of three 12-gun battalions of recently arrived 75mm US pack howitzers, a generous allocation by Chinese standards. One battalion of the efficient German 150mm howitzers was attached, but appears not to have ventured off the Burma Road in the north. The 66th Army included the crack 38th Division, formed from the Tax Police.

The 6th Army began to move into Burma in late January and by mid-March it was scattered about the Shan States area facing Thailand in regiment-sized packets. The 5th Army was stretched along the road and railway to the west, all the way from Toungoo in the south up into Yunnan, a distance of some 1,000km. The troop-carrying regiment had been attached to the 200th Division, enabling it to move all the way down to the southern end, where it took over from the 1st Burma Division. Once there, the Temporary 55th Division, a raw, untrained, and poorly led force, and the 5th Army Cavalry Regiment were subordinated to it. On 19 March the Japanese 55th Division launched its attack on the 200th Division at Toungoo, and on the 24th succeeded in outflanking it to the west and north, leaving only a single small supply route to the northeast. The Temporary 55th Division remained inert and ineffectual, while the 22nd Division ignored orders to move south in aid of the defenders of Toungoo. The 200th Division, fighting skillfully and ferociously, was on its own. Finally, on 30 March, after 11 days of heavy, close fighting, the division began its orderly withdrawal to the north. The Japanese regarded the stand of the

Chinese Expeditionary Force in Burma, 1942

HQ, Chinese Expeditionary Force in Burma

5th Army
>   96th Division (286th, 287th & 288 Regts, transport bn)
>   200th Division (598th, 599 & 600th Regts, transport bn)
>   New 22nd Division (64th, 65th & 66th Regts, transport bn)
>   Tank Regiment
>   Motorized (reconnaissance) Battalion
>   Artillery Regiment
>   1st Bn/10th Artillery Regiment (attached)
>   1st Bty/18th Artillery Regiment (attached)
>   Anti-Tank Battalion
>   Anti-Aircraft Battalion
>   Infantry Gun Battalion
>   Engineer Regiment
>   Motor Transport (troop-carrying) Regiment
>   Motor Transport (supply) Regiment
>   Special Service Battalion

6th Army
>   49th Division (145th, 146th & 147th Regts, mortar, engineer & transport bns)
>   93rd Division (278th & 279th Regts, mortar, engineer & transport bns)
>   Temporary 55th Division (1st, 2nd & 3rd Regts, mortar, engineer & transport bns)
>   Liu Guanlung Detachment (277th Regiment/93rd Div)
>   Special Service Battalion
>   Engineer Battalion
>   Transport Battalion
>   1st Bn/13th Artillery Regiment (attached)
>   3rd & 6th Btys/52nd AA Regiment (attached)

66th Army
>   New 28th Division (82nd, 83rd & 84th Regts, transport bn)
>   New 29th Division (85th, 86th & 87th Regts, transport bn)
>   38th Division (112th, 113th & 114th Regts, transport bn)
>   1st Bn/18th Artillery Regiment (attached)

CEF Troops
>   36th Division (106th, 107th & 108th Regts, transport bn)
>   one battalion/20th Gendarmerie Regiment

200th Division as the toughest fighting of the 1942 Burma campaign—the division had acquitted itself well.

Stilwell now intended to hold the line about 100km north at Allanmyo and Pyinmana, but ordered that line abandoned when the British pulled out on his right. In fact, the Burma Division probably would have been surrounded there at Yenangyaung but for a valiant attack by the 38th Division that forced the Japanese to redeploy. Stilwell then directed that the Japanese column advancing northward on Lashio be cut off by twin attacks meeting at Taunggyi, by the 200th Division from the west and the excellent and aggressive 49th Division from the east. The 200th Division captured Taunggyi on 25 March, but the 6th Army commander forbade the 49th Division from attacking, thus rendering the operation pointless. On 29 April the Japanese captured Lashio, the southern terminus of the Burma Road. That same day plans were made for a withdrawal from Burma.

The New 22nd and 38th Divisions withdrew westward into India, a grueling march involving firefights with pursuing Japanese and the near sacrifice of one regiment of the 38th Division as a rearguard. The US Army's official history noted:

> From the First Burma Campaign the 38th Division and its brilliant commander emerged with their reputations established. To the tactical feat of Yenangyaung, the gallant and capable Sun Li-jen [Sun Liren] added the unique achievement of bringing his division through the Chin Hills as an intact fighting unit with discipline and morale unimpaired.[*]

The 96th Division retreated to Fort Hertz in northern Burma, then across the largely unknown north Burma mountains into China, a feat of considerable endurance, although marred by some brutality against the native population. The gallant 200th Division moved north and then east, actually crossing behind advancing Japanese units, and into China, unfortunately losing its aggressive and skilled commander to Japanese fire in the process. Losses on the retreat had been very heavy, mostly due to starvation and disease.

Chinese Losses—First Burma Campaign (1942)			
	Original strength	Lost	%
5th Army	42,000	21,100	50.24%
6th Army	30,000	17,600	58.67%
66th Army	31,000	16,780	54.13%
Total	103,000	56,480	54.83%

The New 28th and New 29th Divisions attempted to halt the Japanese drive to the north at Wanting, but the latter was defeated there on 4 May and the retreat continued. To keep the Japanese on the west bank of the Salween, a major counterattack was launched on 9 May. The 71st Army (36th, 87th, and 88th Divisions, a few of the soldiers veterans of the 1937 Shanghai battles) opened a drive towards Lungling. The first attacks failed, but on 23 May the tide turned and the Chinese pushed the Japanese back in heavy fighting. Having given the Japanese a bloody nose, and convinced that this halted their plans to invade Yunnan across the Salween, the Chinese withdrew to the east side of that easily

---

[*] *Stilwell's Mission to China*, pp. 140–1.

defended river gorge. In fact, there was no Japanese plan to cross the Salween, and the front there remained static and relatively quiet for the next two years.

The Long Quick Pause

By early July 1942 Stilwell had come to the conclusion that the reopening of the land route through Burma would be critical to success in China. However, for a reconquest of northern Burma he could only count on the remnants of the 22nd and 38th Divisions that had retreated to India. On 1 August Chiang formally agreed to provide 20 divisions that could move south and west from Yunnan into Burma, although he only specifically identified 10 of them at the time. Stilwell took command of the Chinese Army in India (CAI),[*] set it up at the Ramgahr training center, and secured a promise from Chiang for an immediate influx of 23,000 soldiers, to be carried on the return flights over "The Hump" to fill out his two divisions.

Y-Force infantry overlooking the Salween River in June 1943.

Impatient as always, Stilwell wanted to begin operations as soon as possible. In meetings with the British he was given the northern part of Burma, the Hukawng valley, as his area of operations and began tentative planning for an offensive in early 1943. The timing was critical, because the monsoon season in Burma runs from May to September, inclusive, and military operations become extremely difficult, if not impossible during that

---

[*] American documents often refer to this as the Chih Hui Pu, but this generic term simply means command center and will not be used here.

time. He managed to get grudging acquiescence from Chiang for a move from Yunnan, but the British were clearly cool on the idea. Citing British reluctance, Chiang reversed himself in January 1943 and decreed that there would be no spring offensive.

In fact, the delay was almost certainly a blessing. Indeed, it was not until March 1943 that the War Ministry finally definitively (for the time being) nominated the 11 armies that would form the Yunnan Force (or Y-Force). At the Trident inter-Allied conference in May 1943 the British opposed an advance in Burma in the fall of 1943 and Roosevelt was luke-warm, so Anakim, as the overall Burma plan was now known, was reduced to operations in northern Burma, although only the CAI could be considered even partially ready.

Stilwell now turned his attentions to the training of Y-Force and set up an American liaison structure called Y-Force Operational Staff (or Y-FOS) to coordinate training and equipping in June 1943.

At the Quadrant Conference in August the British made it clear they had little enthusiasm for operations in Burma and demonstrated a decidedly lukewarm view of China's usefulness as an ally. They did agree to a February 1944 start for operations in northern Burma, but would commit little themselves. The goal of such an operation in northern Burma was twofold. First, the Japanese had to be dislodged from their airfields at Myitkyina, since their fighters there were forcing American transports to fly "The Hump" farther west, over the high Himalayas. The second was to open a route for the construction of a road from Ledo in Assam to connect up with the northern portion of the old Burma Road, thus opening a land route, albeit a tortuous one, to China.

Troops of the 64th Regiment, 22nd Division, under mortar
fire near Inkangahtawng, Burma, in May 1944.

By late 1943 the Japanese in Burma were either nearly surrounded, or operating on interior lines of communication, depending on your point of view, with the Japanese themselves clearly proponents of the latter and maintaining an offensive posture. The Japanese western front ran roughly along the Indo-Burmese border. At the southern end, in the Arakan area near the coast, was the IJA 55th Division facing the British XV Corps of three divisions. About 500km to the north the IJA 31st and 33rd Divisions faced the British IV Corps. At the northern portion of the Indo-Burmese border the IJA 18th Division was opposed by the CAI. From that point the border turned sharply south and southeast, following the Salween River, with Burma this time on the west

Troops of the 3rd Battalion, 226th Infantry Regiment, 76th Division, fire their 82mm mortar on Pingka Ridge on 1 June 1944.

and China on the east. Here Y-Force lined up against the IJA 56th Division. The Japanese reserve was their 54th Division.

The impatient Stilwell, in his capacity as commander of the CAI, had already launched his 38th Division into northern Burma as soon as the monsoons broke in October 1943. Expecting only token resistance, the division instead ran into the IJA 18th Division and quickly got bogged down in heavy fighting in the northern end of the Hukawng Valley, down which it hoped to advance. A slow advance by both Chinese divisions and elements of the Provisional Tank Group cleared the Japanese out of the Hukawng Valley by mid-March 1944 at a cost of about 2,700 Chinese casualties, dead and wounded.

In the meantime, however, the Japanese had launched their own offensive farther south. The IJA 55th Division was sacrificed against a newly competent Indian/British Army force in the Arakan in order to lure British reserves down into that area. On 8 March 1944 the IJA 15th, 31st, and 33rd Divisions were hurled against Imphal and Kohima in the central part of the front. The British proved masterful at maneuvering their forces and holding what needed to be held while Japanese supplies slowly disappeared with the arrival of the monsoon. By the time the Japanese finally called off their offensive in mid-July their force had been reduced to diseased, malnourished wretches pawing the jungle for food as they retreated. Out of 155,000 soldiers launched into the offensive, no fewer than 65,000 had died and the survivors were no longer an effective force.

The CAI moves into action

While Imphal and Kohima can be regarded as the turning point of the war in Burma, important actions were still taking place to the north. The US 5307th Regiment (Merrill's Marauders) had been brought in and helped clearing the Hukawng, and by April the CAI was poised at the top of the next valley, Mogaung, at the south end of which lay the Irrawaddy and Myitkyina. The Allied South-East Asia Command (SEAC), under Admiral

Mountbatten, could not figure out how to define the next objective in the face of conflicting requirements from Britain, the USA, and China, and in May 1944 US Army Chief of Staff General George Marshall broke the logjam by ordering Stilwell, in his capacity as commander of the US China–Burma–India Theater, to advance on and capture Myitkyina.

In fact, the Chinese forces moving out of India were growing stronger all the time. The New 30th Division was carried in to Hump airfields in early January 1944, followed by the 50th Division directly into the Hukawng Valley in mid-April and the 14th Division to Assam later that month. All of these arrived without heavy equipment, of course, but given the massive backup of supplies in India that did not present a problem.

In late April Stilwell ordered the excellent 22nd and 38th Divisions to move down the Mogaung to its southern end. They did, but with a slowness that agonized the Americans, who believed that Chiang had issued secret go-slow orders to the two divisions behind Stilwell's back. Apparently those orders were countermanded on 19 May because the next day the two divisions launched a fierce attack on the IJA 18th Division, including slipping a regiment in behind the Japanese on their supply route, that all but destroyed it.

On 28 April a force made up of the survivors of the 5307th Regiment and one regiment each from the 22nd and 38th Divisions made a difficult march over the mountains to the east of the Mogaung Valley, then south, and seized the Japanese airfields around Myitkina in a sudden and violent attack. Transport aircraft brought in reinforcements and the objective of the Myitkyina airbase had been attained.

Chinese and Japanese Losses—Second Burma Campaign (1944–5)			
Campaign	*Date*	*Japanese Losses*	*Chinese Losses*
Salween Crossing	1–21 May 1944	605	1,986
Tengchong	22 June–14 Sept. 1944	3,075	18,236
Songshan	24 June–7 Sept. 1944	1,280	7,600
Pingda	11 May 44–20 Jan. 45	523	802
Lungling	5 June 44–20 Jan. 45	10,620	28,384
Wanting	23 Nov. 44–20 Jan. 45	4,954	10,645
Total		21,057	67,403

However, that was not the same as seizing the town itself, and the Japanese poured reinforcements in through the jungle, bringing their peak strength up to about 3,500. The Sino-American forces loosely invested the town and, underestimating Japanese strength, launched a series of failed attacks starting on 21 May. Eventually the defenders started dying faster than replacements could be infiltrated through the jungle and the attacks became more successful. A final push at last cleared the town on 3 August, by which time the cost had risen to 972 Chinese and 272 Americans killed in action.

Crossing the Salween

The cumulative effect of several months of thinly veiled threats from the Americans to the effect that, if the Lend-Lease equipment were not used against the Japanese the flow would be cut off, finally came to a head. On 14 April 1944 General He Yingqin, as Minister of War, gave formal approval to a plan to cross the Salween, pass through the rugged mountains to the west into the smaller and parallel Shweli Valley and seize two key road junctions, Tengchong in the north and Lungling in the south, the latter on the old Burma Road. Although west of the Salween, both were in Chinese land that was occupied by the Japanese.

The front, 160km long in air distance, was exceptionally rugged and about 2,500 meters in altitude, but was defended only by a single division, the IJA 56th Division. Against this the Chinese would throw the Chinese Expeditionary Force (CEF). The old Burma Road would act as a central boundary, with the XI Army Group advancing along the road and to the south of it, crossing the river at two locations, while the XX Army Group was to cross the river at three places to the north.

The offensive kicked off on 11 May, just as the monsoon season began. All the river crossings were successful. After some firefights in the mountains the southern arm bypassed the Songshan mountain redoubt and reached Lungling on 8 June, but was pushed back by a counterattack. The XX Army Group in the north reached Tengchong in late June, but could not take it.

The advance over the mountains to the Shweli Valley had been grueling. The weather, unceasing rain and fog, made resupply flights unreliable and the absence of roads limited transport to coolies. Over 150 porters fell to their deaths from the slippery, winding mountain trails in the northern sector alone. The Chinese soldiers had shown themselves to be courageous and determined. Their leaders, however, ignored the advice that had

Bazooka teams from the CEF's 346th Regiment, 116th Division,
prepare for the final assault on Tengchong on 1 August 1944.

A 4.5-inch howitzer of Y-Force with its mule team en route to the front, 9 September 1944.

been pressed upon them for the previous six months and engaged in costly frontal attacks, exercised little initiative, and wasted huge amounts of precious ammunition through lack of fire discipline.

A second attack on Tengchong was launched on 2 July, surrounding it, and the assault on the city was opened on 26 July. The lessons of the previous month appear to have been learned and the XX Army Group assaults showed much improved tactical skills. Supported by P-40s and P-38s as weather permitted, the Chinese finally breached the city walls on 4 August after a month of ferocious fighting.

The decision to bypass the Japanese dug in on the Songshan mountain mass, overlooking the old Burma Road where it approached the Salween, appears to have been predicated on the expectation of a relatively quick campaign. With the failure of the Lungling attack the mountain would have to be taken quickly. The Japanese were well entrenched on the mountain and attacks begun in mid-June achieved little but Chinese casualties. In early July the 8th Army arrived and took over the assault and, after a few poor starts, launched a fierce attack with the 103rd Division on the 23rd. That unit brought its 75mm Lend-Lease pack howitzers right up to the front and used them in the direct fire role to knock out Japanese bunkers at close range, and coordinated its infantry and fire support well so that by early August the defenders had been reduced to a small perimeter. A brief siege followed, and final attacks on 20–2 August eliminated the last Japanese (by depositing huge amounts of dynamite under the Japanese main bunker and blowing it sky high). The battle for the Songshan had cost 1,200 Japanese and 7,675 Chinese dead.

The CAI Moves Out in Force

Active operations in Burma stopped for the heart of the summer monsoon, except for the central part of the front, where the energetic Slim directed the British forces to capitalize on their victory at Imphal. In the meantime the Northern Combat Area Command (NCAC) was reorganized and resupplied to consist of two Chinese armies with five divisions, the British 36th Division, and the US 5332nd Brigade (also known as Mars Task Force).

The British success at Imphal had made possible a realignment of objectives in Burma. NCAC, on the northern end of the Burma front, projecting to the west as a result of their offensive, was now to drive south in two phases. In the first phase to run from October to mid-December 1944, they were to move south about 120km to the east–west portion of the Irrawaddy River. In the second phase they were to drive about 110km farther south over rough terrain to the towns of Mongmit and Lashio.

CAI soldiers with a Thompson and a cut-down M1917 meet a CEF soldier with a CKS rifle in Burma.

The first phase kicked off on 15 October 1944 with a three-pronged effort, the British 36th Division (followed by the Chinese 50th Division) in the west, the Chinese 22nd Division in the center, and the Chinese New 1st Army (30th and 38th Divisions) in the east. The British moved quickly south, meeting opposition only at the town of Pinwe, and took the town of Katha on the Irrawaddy on 10 December. It was the same story in the center, where the 22nd Division simply marched down to their objective of Shwego on the south bank of the Irrawaddy on 7 November, and then continued to the southeast to cut off one of the roads leading to the Japanese stronghold of Bhamo on 14 November. The division, however, was called to China in response to Japanese activity there, and departed for the airfields on 12 December, leaving their front to an American regiment.

Things would not go as well on the eastern arm of the offensive. The objective there was Bhamo, the second largest town in northern Burma and the head of navigation on the Irrawaddy. A major river port before the war, it had been extensively fortified by the Japanese. With the 38th Division in the lead, Chinese forces moved south against little initial opposition, then skillfully outflanked the outer Japanese defenses, allowing the 30th Division actually to pass to the south of the city. While a regiment of the 38th Division worked its way into the city in ferocious fighting, half a Japanese division tried to muscle the 30th Division out of way. They failed, but on 15 December the garrison of Bhamo successfully disengaged and managed to break out to the south anyway. Of the 1,200 Japanese defenders of the city 950 made it to safety, but the city had fallen.

Opening the Route to China

With the fall of Bhamo the Japanese were left in control of only a relatively short portion of the road on the route between Ledo in Assam and Yunnan. The road that originated in Ledo extended southeast about 35km beyond Bhamo into the southern end of the Shweli Valley, where it turned northeast at the town of Namkham and proceeded up the valley another 50km until it joined the old Burma Road at Mong Yu. At Mong Yu they were about 100km south of Lungling, where the CEF had paused months earlier.

The area in the Shweli Valley north of Mong Yu was held by the dug-in IJA 56th Division, but the route to the west was only lightly held. Thus, the 30th Division of the CAI was able to drive down the Ledo Road to Namkham against little opposition and occupy the town on 16 January 1945.

In the meantime the CEF (Y-Force) was making a rather leisurely drive down from the northern part of the Shweli valley. The IJA 56th Division was having to look over its shoulder constantly, aware that the CAI was threatening to cut it off to the south. Thus, when the 200th Division outflanked the Japanese positions in Lungling, the IJA pulled out on 3 November. After an inexplicable pause the Chinese advance began again a week later, with the XI Army Group of four armies moving south down the old Burma Road through the valley. The IJA 56th Division contented itself with rearguard actions and Mang-shih

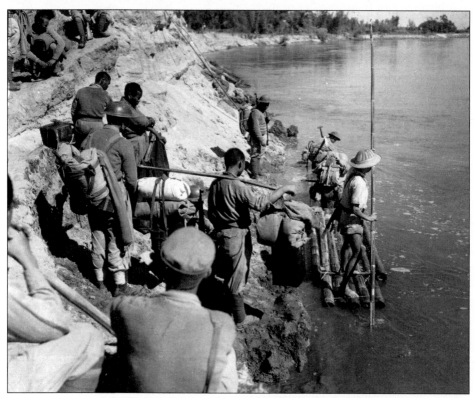

Troops of the 88th Regiment, New 30th Division, crossing the
Shweli River in Burma on bamboo rafts, January 1945.

fell to the Chinese on 20 November and Che-fang on 1 December, but there the CEF stopped again.

The CEF was certainly well under strength, its losses not having been made good by replacement personnel, but the Japanese were clearly worried and not inclined to fight to the last. Finally, a new attack was launched against the Japanese stronghold of Wanting at the new year and on 3 January the 9th Division broke into the town. The Japanese counterattacked and, following fierce close-quarters combat, forced the Chinese back out. Attempts to get around the flanks proved futile and finally the American liaison officers took an active part in the planning. For the first time the technical execution of the battle would match the courage and determination of the Chinese soldiers. On 19 January the XI Army Group launched a well-executed attack on the heights overlooking the town, and seized them, holding them against Japanese counterattacks. That night the Japanese withdrew and on the 20th elements of the CAI and the CEF met—the way to China was open. A formal ceremony was held on 27 January in Mongyu, which marked the opening of the Ledo Road to China. The Salween campaign of the CEF officially ended on 24 January as the CEF was ordered to concentrate for movement back to the eastern front in China.

3

Guerrilla Warfare

The communist forces, of course, were already experienced in guerrilla warfare by the time the Japanese invasion began. The formation of the united front following the Xi'an incident allowed them to come out of the small bases they had been forced into and spread out, this dispersal being a key feature of their subsequent success.

At the start of Japan's full-scale incursions into China in 1937 the communist regular forces numbered only 20,000 to 30,000, compared to about 1.7 million for the Nationalist government, giving them little initial leverage. The KMT issued guidance on 20 August that the communist 8th Route Army would be allowed to conduct independent guerrilla operations in the Japanese rear, but only in certain parts of Chahar and Hebei provinces in I War Zone.

Of course, this limitation was ignored, almost from the start. As the Japanese advance swept through much of China vast expanses of ungarrisoned territory were left in the rear. The communist forces moved into this vacuum. They did not move conventional forces in. Instead they covered areas of interest with small detachments of soldiers and party cadre to set up networks of village-based political cells and militia units. The militia units were

A guerrilla column in Hunan prepares to move out, 22 February 1945.

generally of two main types: the youth regiments of teenagers used for guard duty, and the local militia, made up of men between 18 and 45. They were poorly armed, especially early in the war and so concentrated on so-called sparrow warfare, involving snipers and improvised land mines.

The local militia also provided training and a "gateway" to the regular forces, ensuring a steady stream of new blood. This, together with low combat losses, enabled the 8th Route Army to expand to over 200,000 by the end of 1938. This 8th Route Army had been incorporated into the NRA as with the 115th, 120th and 129th Divisions, although clearly additional units were formed.

The Nationalists paid great lip service to guerrilla warfare, but do not seem to have understood its underpinnings very well. By the end of 1938 the KMT had between 600,000 and 700,000 of its troops behind enemy lines. For the most part these were conventional units that had been bypassed by the Japanese thrusts and told to switch to guerrilla warfare. They included 30 divisions moved to the mountains of Shanxi, the 3rd Army Group and 40th Army in southern Shandong, the 24th Army Group on the Tianjin–Pukou railroad, and the 48th and 89th Armies in Jiangsu. Many others followed as operations behind Japanese lines seemed to present easier rewards than facing them head-on. For the most part, however, they continued to think and operate like conventional units.

For one thing, they tended to stay concentrated. This placed a heavy burden on those unfortunate locales that were forced to host these large forces. Food, clothing, and other commodities were taken, often without compensation, from peasants already poor. This was in contrast to the communist forces that dispersed, spreading a much lighter load over a broader area. They also tended to attempt to defend their territory against the Japanese, usually with disastrous results, in contrast to the communists whose militia melted back into the villages while the main force retreated until out of reach.

The KMT left-behind forces did conduct some effective operations, for example in the winter offensives of 1939–40 and the second battle of Changsha in September 1941. For the most part, however, they lacked an understanding of guerrilla warfare, and what Mao would later term "mobile warfare." The battles that they fought usually ended in the destruction or neutralization of the KMT force. By the end of 1943 the KMT had lost most of its ability to conduct guerrilla operations.

The communist forces, on the other hand, continued to emphasize building up their infrastructure in the vast swaths of north China not occupied by the Japanese. In February 1940 the CCP determined to expand its force to 300,000 in the regular units and 3 million in the militia. Not only was this an expansion in size, but the New 4th Army was to increase its efforts in central China.

Nevertheless the expansion would come with a price. Guns and ammunition were in short supply, and redistribution yielded more, but less effective, units. Further, increasing the full-time force imposed additional burdens on the population. The solution to the last problem was to expand into new areas, resulting in the Battle of the Hundred Regiments, the largest communist operation of the war. Its failure led the communists to reaffirm their adherence to guerrilla warfare.

The KMT forces had already fought small scale battles (of one to two thousand men on each side) with the communist forces, with both sides guilty of initiating some of them, and the Chongqing government was understandably upset. The New 4th Army incident was the result.

The result of the failure of the Hundred Regiments Offensive and the battering of the New 4th Army was a decision by the CCP to bring the strength of its regular forces back down to 200,000 and to direct that non-productive personnel (party cadre, soldiers, administrators, and so on) in any base area should not exceed 3% of the population.

This dispersion reduced their ability to concentrate forces but they did conduct small-scale hit-and-run raids and sparrow attacks. In response, the Japanese dug kilometers of trenches and built hundreds of blockhouses, which served to disperse their strength as well. In addition, the Ichi-Go offensive of 1944 drew Japanese forces south, opening further possibilities in north China. As a result it proved possible to convert militia units to regular, so that by early 1945 the communists controlled 900,000 in their regular forces and perhaps 2–3 million in militia and local units. With this force, and the Japanese weakened near war's end, Mao began considering moving to "mobile operations" with conventional forces in late 1944. The transition to this phase, however, was not smooth and by the end of the war the communists were still adjusting their forces.

In the meantime the KMT had not been completely inactive. By early 1944 I War Zone had organized the guerrillas in the Hebei–Shanxi–Henan border area into nine "columns," each with a strength of 4,000 men. Although presumably slightly more agile than the old division structure, they were still quite large for true guerrilla operations.

Fine-tuning of the concepts continued. By the start of December 1944 the 24th Army Group had organized 11 "guerrilla groups" each with one or two companies. During the first half of December 1944 they claimed to have launched 71 raids that caused 729 enemy casualties and captured 51 POW and 84 rifles. For the second half of the month they carried out 17 raids and reported causing 307 enemy casualties and capturing 5 POW, 6 rifles, and 5 light MGs. The bulk of the raids appear to have consisted of ambushes of small Japanese supply columns. In January 1945 US Army/OSS teams were assigned to these groups, with unknown results.

A unique type of unit were the mine warfare groups formed to deny the enemy the use of the Yangtze River. In January 1940 the Chinese Navy designated the stretch of the Yangtze between Poyang Lake and Wuhu in Anhwei as the 1st Mine Laying Area and formed the Mine Laying Group of five companies. This launched drifting mines into the Yangtze River to the end of the war. The Japanese moved much of their small transport fleet farther up the river and in response the Navy formed the 2nd Mine Laying Area (four detachments) and the 3rd Mine Laying Area (two detachments). The detachments of the 3rd Mine Laying Area launched over 80 drifting mines and claimed more than 10 Japanese ships sunk.

4

Organization Overview

The warlord era ended in 1928, with the conclusion of the Northern Expedition. Chiang Kai-shek and his National Revolutionary Army had started small, but had accumulated followers as the campaign wore on, and, more importantly, Chiang had utilized alliances with some of the warlords in order to defeat the others. The successes had not been without a price to be paid in the future, however. Those warlords who had been co-opted, notably in Guangzhou, Yunnan, Shanxi, Xinjiang, and Guangxi, extracted concessions as the price of their cooperation. They remained semi-autonomous players who regarded the new central government in Nanjing more as a coordination center than one issuing orders that had to be obeyed.

Chiang had managed slowly to erode some of the independence of the remaining warlords. A significant piece of leverage was the requirement for an import permit for arms shipments, by which the Nanjing government could exercise some control over what weapons the warlords acquired. For example, the Guangxi government requested a quote for 36 mountain guns from Rheinmetall in 1935, but Nanjing informed the German Foreign Ministry that no import approval would be granted and the matter died there. Only the imminent outbreak of war finally forced the central government to permit a sale of similar Schneider guns in 1937.

Thus, by the mid-1930s only two of the warlords, those in Shanxi and the former Northeast Army, held GHQ artillery assets, and those resulted from indigenous production. As Japanese aggressive intentions became more clear, however, Chiang loosened the reins a little bit. Yunnan and Guangxi were able to purchase Schneider mountain guns and several warlords bought mortars and machine guns.

Restricting the armament acquisitions of the local powers worked to the advantage of the central government, but not so much as might be thought due to the shortage of foreign exchange available to the Nanjing regime and the limits that placed on its own armaments purchases. As a result, all of the militaries in China, provincial and national, were essentially infantry forces using machine guns and mortars as the sole heavy firepower to decide the battle. The national army had started to form GHQ pools of artillery and armor but they were far from complete and the sheer size of the country made concentration of force difficult.

Trying to figure out the strengths and allegiances of the various armed camps within China was an imprecise art even for the Chinese and that much more difficult for outsiders. Nevertheless, try they did. In 1935 the US Military Attaché spent considerable time and effort researching and working up a chart (*see overleaf*) dividing the military forces into those that were loyal, or semi-loyal, to Chiang, and those that were independent of him. The conclusion highlighted a "startling and extraordinary" expansion of the forces loyal to Chiang in the prior few years.[*] Nevertheless, the table was drawn up before the actual

---

[*] MA China Report No. 9093, 10 April 1935.

Military Affairs Commission (Chiang Kai-shek)

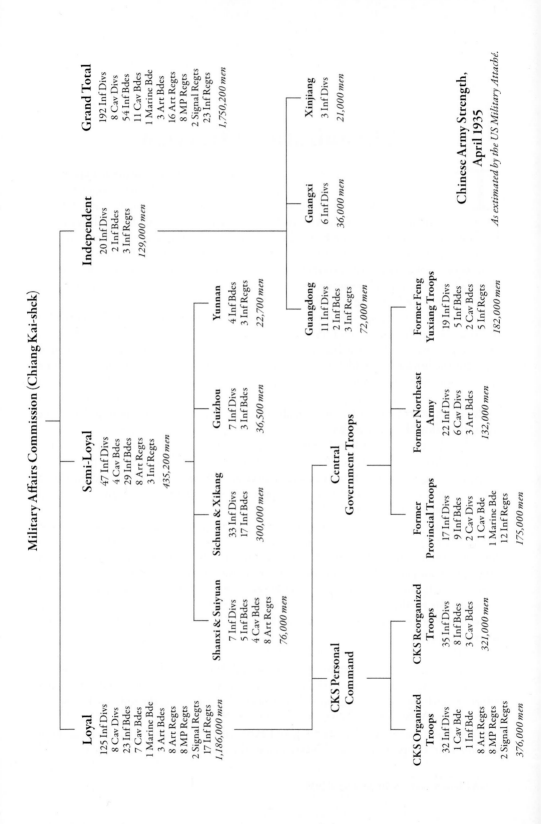

Grand Total
192 Inf Divs
8 Cav Divs
54 Inf Bdes
11 Cav Bdes
1 Marine Bde
3 Art Bdes
16 Art Regts
8 MP Regts
2 Signal Regts
23 Inf Regts
1,750,200 men

Independent
20 Inf Divs
2 Inf Bdes
3 Inf Regts
129,000 men

Xinjiang
3 Inf Divs
21,000 men

Guangxi
6 Inf Divs
36,000 men

Semi-Loyal
47 Inf Divs
4 Cav Bdes
29 Inf Bdes
8 Art Regts
3 Inf Regts
435,200 men

Yunnan
4 Inf Bdes
3 Inf Regts
22,700 men

Guangdong
11 Inf Divs
2 Inf Bdes
3 Inf Regts
72,000 men

**Former Feng
Yuxiang Troops**
19 Inf Divs
5 Inf Bdes
2 Cav Bdes
5 Inf Regts
182,000 men

Guizhou
7 Inf Divs
3 Inf Bdes
36,500 men

**Former Northeast
Army**
22 Inf Divs
6 Cav Divs
3 Art Bdes
132,000 men

**Central
Government Troops**

Sichuan & Xikang
33 Inf Divs
17 Inf Bdes
300,000 men

**Former
Provincial Troops**
17 Inf Divs
9 Inf Bdes
2 Cav Divs
1 Cav Bde
1 Marine Bde
12 Inf Regts
175,000 men

Shanxi & Suiyuan
7 Inf Divs
5 Inf Bdes
4 Cav Bdes
8 Art Regts
76,000 men

**CKS Reorganized
Troops**
35 Inf Divs
8 Inf Bdes
3 Cav Divs
321,000 men

**CKS Personal
Command**

Loyal
125 Inf Divs
8 Cav Divs
23 Inf Bdes
7 Cav Bdes
1 Marine Bde
3 Art Bdes
8 Art Regts
8 MP Regts
2 Signal Regts
17 Inf Regts
1,186,000 men

**CKS Organized
Troops**
32 Inf Divs
1 Cav Bde
1 Inf Bde
8 Art Regts
8 MP Regts
2 Signal Regts
376,000 men

**Chinese Army Strength,
April 1935**

As extimated by the US Military Attaché.

Japanese invasion of 1937, at which time the dynamics changed considerably, forcing some warlords farther into the central government orbit, while tempting others with the possible benefits of a separate peace. In any event these judgments proved more art than science, for the Shandong forces under Han Fuju were apparently included in the "former provincial troops" now loyal to the central government, but in fact Han sat on the fence early in the war and finally attempted to flee with his treasury after giving up the province to the Japanese.

Writing 43 years after the event a Soviet military adviser to the Nanjing government provided a darker appreciation, set at the start of the war:

> Out of a total of 169 infantry divisions, 47 separate brigades and 12 cavalry divisions, the Nanking [Nanjing] Government had only 71 infantry divisions, 10 separate brigades and one cavalry division. The rest belonged to the provincial governors, each of whom maintained an army according to his own establishment, and had his own system of armaments and his own ideas concerning the combat training of the troops and how they should be used in battle.[*]

Thus, Chiang's efforts towards military preparedness (as well as securing his personal power base) were two-fold. On the one hand he tried to restrict the power of the provincial warlords. Of course, for those satraps their armies were their power bases and they resisted the pull towards the central government. The second was to build up and modernize the forces that were directly loyal to him. To that end he brought in a German advisory mission (Deutsche Beraterschaft in China) that functioned under a succession of leaders. It provided logistical and administrative advice, helped draft the organizational templates for the army, and worked with the Handelsgesellshaft für industrielle Produkte (Hapro) to coordinate new military requirements with products available from the re-emerging German military industry.

Although the Germans added elements of modern military professionalism they also added yet another layer of complexity to the competing demands of organizational requirements. At various times they advocated a small, modernized army, and at others envisioned a war of attrition with Japan in which space would be traded for time and casualties, this latter implying a mass army. From Chiang's perspective not only could he not reduce the size of the remaining warlord armies; indeed, he needed to maintain forces in their areas to counterbalance those warlords lest they get grander ideas about their autonomy. Certainly the idea of a core of highly trained, well-equipped divisions, backed by modest artillery and armored forces appealed to him. But money and time were not working in his favor, nor was the fact that his primary benefactor, Nazi Germany, was laying claim to most of its arms output for its own rearmament and was moving towards friendship with Japan in any event.

In addition, of course, Chiang launched a series of campaigns against the communist forces that not only disrupted any grand reorganization plans, but also generated new organizational formats themselves.

The result was a confusing succession of organizational tables, none fully implemented and all of which supplemented, rather than replaced, earlier plans. By the outbreak of the war there was a bewildering array of organizational formats, not only among the various

---

[*] Kalyagin, A. Y., "Along Unfamiliar Roads, At the Bidding of the Heart"; in *Soviet Volunteers in China 1925–1945* (Progress Publishers, Moscow, 1980) p. 200.

warlords armies, each with their own organizational tables, but even within the troops answering to Nanjing.

The departure of the German advisers in mid-1938 left a void, but only a temporary one. The Americans, full of their own ideas, soon arrived. Faced with the irascible and highly opinionated "Vinegar Joe" Stilwell, the Chinese found themselves with no shortage of strongly worded advice. The unsuccessful foray into Burma in 1942 left Stilwell with a Chinese force in India, the CAI, that he could pretty much mold to his liking, and a complete set of TO&Es were drafted with little regard for the authorities in Chongqing.

As Lend-Lease materials started to flow across the Hump into Yunnan the Americans were able to influence the organization of the units of Yunnan Force (Y-Force) that received them. The finite aid that could be flown over the Himalayas both limited American leverage and also rendered impossible any thoughts of duplicating the divisions of the CAI.

In the meantime the bulk of the Chinese Army continued to fight on its own, although divided into multiple camps, not only by the influence of the conventional warlords but also by the failure of the Hundred Regiments Offensive in late 1940 and the subsequent abandonment of conventional warfare by the communist portion, followed by the assault on the New 4th Army HQ in January 1941.

A degree of standardization was finally achieved by the publication, and enforcement, of the 31st Year (1942) organization tables. These were the tables supposedly being followed by the bulk of the NRA in the fighting of the remainder of their war with Japan. Of the 281 divisions included in the NRA's order of battle at the end of the war, five were CAI divisions still on their original TO&Es, 34 were Alpha Plan divisions mostly reorganized and re-equipped into the American-sponsored organizational format, and about two dozen more had just started to receive some equipment as part of Z-Force. Of the balance about 50 were fairly independent forces under their warlords, about half of them under Yan of Shanxi.

In other words, progress had clearly been made, with well over half the NRA's divisions now on a single organizational format, but there were still outliers, both at the upper end of the spectrum as represented by the Alpha Plan, and at the lower end with the warlord forces. By that time the US had come to believe that the large-scale supply of arms and equipment necessary to bring more of the NRA up to Alpha standards would not be needed. Operations in China would have very little effect on the fall of Japan, even if the atomic bombs had not succeeded in convincing the Japanese to surrender. So the status in August 1945 was essentially that with which China would have continued the war, had it gone on.

With the small, simple divisions of the 31st Year organization the NRA appears to have arrived at close to the optimal balance. There had not been time, under the pressures of war, to train the many thousands of staff officers needed to handle the complex planning and logistics of hundreds of divisions and their constituent elements, so resort was made to the expedient of stripping divisions down to the bare minimum, essentially just triangular maneuver units. Not surprisingly, once the ensuing civil war had ended both sides opted to reorganize into more conventional divisional organizations, but as a wartime expedient the small, lean divisions of 1942–5 seem to have provided an eminently suitable response.

5

Central Government Divisions and Armies

The dramatic expansion of the National Revolutionary Army during the Northern Expedition eventually generated a need for a standardized organization. A divisional organization had been promulgated in 1924 and a year later the army was reorganized into three divisions and new tables of organization were issued, but it proved impossible to standardize even these three formations due to lack of manpower and equipment. As provincial armies flocked, if sometimes reluctantly, to the Kuomintang banner during the Northern Expedition, all attempts at standardization were temporarily abandoned.

With the expeditionary fighting nearing completion in January 1928 the Standing Committee of the Military Council issued new organization tables for the field army and its divisions, along with implementing orders. An army was now to consist of three divisions, a training regiment, an artillery regiment, a cavalry squadron, an engineer battalion, a signal detachment and smaller units for a total of 1,833 officers and 30,538 enlisted.

Fire support for the army was provided by an artillery regiment with three battalions each of three batteries. Each battery had four guns with caissons, 20 riding horses and 48 draft horses. The standard weapon was stated to be the Japanese 75mm Type 38 field gun as manufactured by the Hanyang Arsenal. In practice, a wide variety of weapons was used, and many armies had only battalions in lieu of regiments. In any case, the artillery was severely hampered by the lack of signal facilities of any kind.

The army also included what was termed an engineer battalion, although labor battalion might have been a better term. In addition to 54 rifles, each engineer company was meant to have 40 shovels, 10 picks, a small number of carpenter's tools, and explosives for demolition. Indicative of the light scale of equipment, no animals were provided and all equipment had to be hand-carried on the march.

The training regiment consisted of three infantry training battalions (each of four companies), a machine-gun company, an artillery battery, and a signal detachment. The artillery battery had three platoons, one with 82mm mortars, one with pack guns, and one with field guns. The mission of the regiment was to train enlisted men in the duties of NCOs, and trainees were selected by the division HQs and the other units under army command.

The heart of the army strength was found in its three divisions. There were two types of division: the Type A (four infantry regiments) and the Type B (three infantry regiments). In all other respects the two divisions were similar.

The basic unit was the section, which consisted of a sergeant section leader, two senior privates or corporals as assistant section leaders, and 13 privates. The standard personal weapon was to have been the 7.9mm Hanyang rifle, but a wide variety of rifle types was actually in use. Two of the men in each section were unarmed, serving as ammunition bearers, with one doubling as a cook. Three such sections, plus a lieutenant platoon leader and an orderly, made up the rifle platoon. The company headquarters consisted of the company commander (a captain), a special service officer, an administrative sergeant, a supply sergeant, two buglers, an orderly, and a cook.

Organization of the 1928 Field Army			
	Officers	*Enlisted*	*Notes*
Army Headquarters	89	120	
Signal Detachment			
Detachment HQ	6	9	
Radio Section	33	101	5 squads each 1 radio
Telegraph Section	5	52	4 x 11-man squads, total 2 field telegraph sets
Telephone Section	5	95	6 x 14-man squads, total 20 phones & 20km wire
Cavalry Squadron	9	168	4 platoons, each 2 x 20-man sections with carbines
Three Divisions, each			
Division HQ	61	148	
Political Department	13	5	
Signal Detachment	4	56	4 squads, total 10 phones & 15km wire
Three or four Infantry Regiments, each			
Regiment HQ	26	97	
Three Infantry Battalions, each			
Battalion HQ	3	16	
Four Rifle Companies, each	5	144	3 platoons, each 3 x 16-man squads with rifles
Machine-Gun Company	5	113	3 platoons, each 2 squads, each 1 Maxim & 3 rifles
Mortar Company	5	125	3 platoons, each 2 squads, each 1 x 82mm mortar & 4 rifles
Special Service Company	5	144	identical to rifle company
Transport Section*	5	306	12 squads, each 20 coolies
Medical Detachment*	10	116	

The battalion headquarters was a small affair, with only three officers—commander (a major), assistant commander (a captain), and an adjutant (a lieutenant)—and 16 enlisted. Communications for the battalion were limited to the bugle corporal and five messengers in the battalion HQ.

Fire support for the regiment was provided by a machine-gun company and a mortar company. A machine-gun squad consisted of a sergeant squad leader and 15 privates (one of whom was a cook) to man a 7.9mm water-cooled machine gun, usually a Maxim. With three platoons, the company had a total of six machine guns with 4,000 rounds of ammunition, and 20 rifles. A mortar squad consisted of two sergeants (squad leader and assistant squad leader), and 17 privates (including a cook) and carried an 82mm mortar and 30 rounds of ammunition.

The infantry regiment was commanded by a colonel, assisted by a lieutenant colonel and a major as deputies, six supply officers headed by a major, five medical officers, two adjutants, and four political officers. The regimental headquarters included a signal platoon with two 12-man wire squads, along with a 9-man messenger squad. Also included in the headquarters were 12 medics and 15 litter-bearers.

The division was commanded by a headquarters with limited staff capabilities. The "chief of staff office," which handled both operations and intelligence functions, had only

	Officers	Enlisted	Notes
Artillery Battalion			
Battalion HQ	5	22	
Three Batteries, each	5	147	2 platoons, each 2 x 75mm guns, total 20 rifles
Special Service Battalion	23	529	identical to infantry battalion
Engineer Battalion	26	455	
Transport Detachment*			
Detachment HQ	7	18	
Three/four Transport Sections, each	4	224	10 squads, each 20 coolies
Field Hospital*	17	100	capacity 400 patients
Stretcher-Bearer Detachment*	3	142	2 sections, each 5 squads each 30
stretchers			
Training Regiment	139	2,265	3 infantry bns, MG company, arty batty
Artillery Regiment			
Regiment HQ	21	120	
Three Artillery Battalions, each			
Battalion HQ	7	23	
Transport Detachment*	7	230	
Three Batteries, each	5	116	2 platoons, each 2 x 75mm guns, total 20 carbines
Engineer Battalion			
Battalion HQ		8	23
Three Engineer Companies, each	6	144	3 platoons, each 3 x 14-man squads, total 54 rifles
Military Police Company	5	88	3 platoons, each 2 squads, total 72 rifles

* wartime only

5 staff officers, 5 commissioned secretaries and clerks, and 5 messengers. The 72-man "adjutant section" had responsibilities for personnel duties, but most of its personnel were servants for the headquarters, including 11 stable personnel, 27 orderlies for officers, and 20 messengers. The quartermaster section, with 24 officers and 17 enlisted was responsible for supply and the maintenance of weapons within the division. The medical section provided 10 officers (of whom 7 were medical) and 58 enlisted, mostly stretcher-bearers and medics. The political department provided 13 political officers to monitor the division's political bearing.

The division's fire support was found in its artillery battalion of three batteries. Each four-gun battery had two platoons, each of two squads, each made up of two corporals and 30 privates (including two cooks) and provided with a 75mm pack gun. Officially, the gun was the Krupp pack gun made by the Shanghai Arsenal, but others were in use as well, such as the Japanese Type 41 and its copies. The weapons were most commonly pulled by draft horses rather than pack-carried. In any event, the divisional artillery battalion was absent in more divisions than not. Particularly notable in the organization of the artillery battalion was the complete lack of signal facilities. Each battery included two buglers, while the battalion headquarters had a four-man messenger section and a bugler corporal, but no telephones (much less radios) were provided, presumably limiting the artillery to direct fire or modified direct fire (spotting by the commander within visual signalling distance of the guns).

A divisional special service battalion, organizationally identical to an infantry battalion, provided local guards for the division HQ and supply areas, just as a special service company provided those duties for the infantry regiment. A cavalry squadron was designed to provide reconnaissance, but lacking any radios to convey information back it could not have contributed very much.

Logistics for the army were non-existent during peace and only mobilized for wartime operations. On mobilization, each infantry regiment would receive a transport section of 12 squads. Such a section would carry 92,000 rounds of small arms ammunition (50 rounds for each rifle and 3,000 for each MG) with 90 porters; 360 rounds of 82mm mortar ammunition with 60 porters each carrying 6 rounds; and one day's rations for the regiment (3,200 catties or 1,920kg) with 55 porters each carrying 58 catties (35kg). The divisional transport detachment was made up of four (A-type division) or three (B-type) transport sections, each of 10 squads. The divisional detachment generally carried one day's rations for the division, plus more small arms, mortar, and artillery ammunition. One company from the division's special service battalion could also be attached to the transport detachment, in which case it was called the escort section.

With the official conclusion of the Northern Expedition, signalled by the surrender of Zhang Xueliang on 29 December 1928, attention turned to reducing the size of the army. Preliminary plans were drawn up for a reduction of the army to 65 divisions with 16 artillery regiments, and in August 1929 a conference of the top army commanders was held to develop a new standard set of organization tables. The 1928 tables had only been implemented by the forces under Chiang's direct control, and then incompletely, so each of the four major army groups were organized differently (and even within them, consistency was not common). Not surprisingly, each of the army group commanders preferred an organization based on the one his forces were currently using.

The 4th Army Group of General Li Zongren, had 79 divisions built around the former Guangxi Army, a tough and well-regarded force that had performed ably during the Northern Expedition. They proposed that the standard division should have 3 brigades, each of 2 infantry regiments. Each regiment would have 3 battalions each of 4 companies; each company to consist of 3 platoons each of three 11-man sections. The regiment would also include a machine-gun company, a mortar company, a telephone squad, and a stretcher-bearer squad. Division support would be provided by an artillery battalion of three batteries and a telephone squad, a signal detachment, and a guard battalion.

The 3rd Army Group of 23 divisions and 9 brigades was under the command of General Yan Xishan, the boss of Shanxi province. They advocated their current organization, in which a division had 2 brigades of 3 regiments each. A regiment had 3 battalions of 3 companies and a heavy weapons company. A rifle company had 3 platoons of three 14-man sections. The heavy weapons company had 2 platoons each with two water-cooled MGs and one platoon with two 82mm mortars. The division does not appear to have included artillery.

The 2nd Army Group was under General Feng Yuxiang, and represented the leftish Guominjun (People's Army) and included 43 divisions, 5 mixed brigades, a cavalry brigade, and an armored command. They proposed a division built around two brigades, each of two infantry regiments. Each infantry regiment consisted of a mortar company, a transport platoon, a guard platoon, a stretcher-bearer platoon, a signal platoon, and three infantry battalions, each of the last consisting of 3 rifle companies and a machine-gun company. A division also included a cavalry squadron of 4 platoons, a 3-battery artillery battalion, a 3-company engineer battalion, a guard company, a signal company, and medical and repair units for a total strength of 15,396 men.

Organization of 18th & 19th Year Type A Divisions			
	Officers	*Enlisted*	*Notes*
Division Headquarters	79	147	
Two Brigades, each			
Brigade Headquarters	13	29	
Three Infantry Regiments, each			
Regiment HQ	22	68	
Signal Platoon	1	48	3 x 15-man squads, total 10 phones & 10km of wire
Three Infantry Battalions, each			
Battalion HQ	4	13	
Three Rifle Companies, each	5	104	3 platoons each 3 x 10-man squads with rifles
MG Company	5	121	3 platoons each 2 x 14-man squads each 1 Maxim & 4 rifles
Mortar Company	5	138	3 platoons each 2 squads each 1 x 82mm mortar & 4 rifles
Cavalry Squadron	6	169	4 platoons each 3 x 12-man squads with carbines
Artillery Battalion			
Battalion HQ	13	98	
Three Batteries, each	5	203	2 platoons each 2 x 75mm mountain gun
Engineer Battalion			
Battalion HQ	12	41	
Three Engineer Companies, each	6	180	3 platoons each 3 x 16-man squads
Signal Company	6	168	3 platoons each 3 squads, total 20 phones & 30km of wire
Special Service Company	5	104	
Transportation Battalion			
Battalion HQ	13	31	
Two Transport Companies, each	6	148	3 platoons each 3 squads each 12 coolies

The 1st Army Group came under the direct command of Chiang Kai-shek and contained 65 divisions and 5 mixed brigades. Not surprisingly, it was the 1st Army Group's proposals that formed the basis for the final draft of the Army Reorganization Committee. The new organizational scheme provided for three types of divisions. The Type A division had 2 brigades each of 3 regiments for a total strength of 805 officers and 11,720 enlisted. The Type B division had 3 brigades of 2 regiments for a strength of 818 officers and 11,749 enlisted. The Type C division had 2 brigades of 2 regiments for a strength of 586 officers and 8,357 enlisted.

The new 18th Year (1929) Division structure had several significant improvements over the old 1928-style division. Infantry firepower was significantly increased by raising the number of machine-gun companies from one per regiment to one per battalion. Equally significant, if not more so, was a dramatic increase in the signal facilities within the division. Not only was the divisional signal unit doubled in capability, with additional phones and wire, but similar sections were added to subordinate units. The infantry regiment gained a signal platoon with a 10-line switchboard, 10 field telephones and 10km of field wire, along with some steel wire and insulators. This permitted communications down to the battalion level and, in selected cases, individual companies. Unfortunately, the artillery was not similarly blessed. Although the artillery battalion HQ was enlarged significantly, it was mainly to accommodate 60 porters for ammunition and equipment. Lacking effective signal facilities, the artillery continued to rely on direct fire and modified direct fire for their support of the infantry.

The engineer companies continued to provide only manual labor, with each company being equipped with 72 rifles, 36 shovels, 18 picks, and some carpenter's tools. As before, no transport was provided. The transport battalion was made a permanent (peacetime) part of the division, aiding its mobility.

The organizational turmoil continued the next year, for in December 1930 a new TO&E was issued, this for the 19th Year Division, although this was merely the Type A Division of 1929 with a few small modifications.

The first of several significant turning points came with the arrival in 1932 of Georg Wetzell as the new German adviser. Although he had little influence on strategic thinking, he did propose an entirely new divisional structure known as the 21st Year Division. It was not intended that this would provide the basis for the entire army, but instead would

Some of the first products of German training: infantry at rifle
drill in February 1931. (*Bundesarchiv 102-11214*)

be applied to only a few "model divisions" that would inform the development of a small, hard-core for the NRA. The reorganization of two divisions, the 87th and 88th, was begun the following year with extensive German aid and advice.

21st Year Type Infantry Regiment			
	Officers	*Enlisted*	*Horses*	*Notes*
Regiment Headquarters	11	33	9	
Signal Company[a]				
Company HQ	2	13	1	
Two Signal Platoons, each	1	34	2	1 switchboard & 5 wire squads
Three Infantry Battalions, each				
Battalion HQ	5	17	2	
Three Rifle Companies, each				
Company HQ	2	14	0	
Three Rifle Platoons, each	1	51	0	2 automatic & 3 rifle squads, each 10 men
Machine Gun Company[b]				
Company HQ	2	28	5	
Signal Squad	0	12	4	
Three MG Platoons, each	1	26	11	2 squads each 1 medium MG
Infantry Gun Platoon	1	68	19	2 squads each 25 men with 1 x 2cm gun
Infantry Gun Company[c]				
Company HQ	2	21	4	
Signal Squad	0	12	5	
Two Gun Platoons, each	1	37	20	2 squads each 1 infantry howitzer
or **Mortar Company**[c]				
Company HQ	2	26	4	
Signal Squad	0	12	5	
Three Mortar Platoons, each	1	30	14	2 squads each 1 x 82mm mortar

a *In wartime supplemented by 2 more platoons plus 35 men with 70 pack horses.*
b *In wartime supplemented by 3 ammunition squads, each 8 men and 2 pack horses.*
c *In wartime supplemented by an ammunition platoon of 23 men and 18 pack horses.*

The most notable advance was the incorporation of light machine guns into the structure, on the basis of six per rifle company. At the lowest level of command the new table defined the rifle platoon as consisting of a platoon leader, platoon sergeant (an innovation in Chinese infantry organization), and 5 squads, each of a squad leader and 9 men. Three of the squads were armed solely with 10 rifles, while two of the squads were armed with a light machine gun (initially a KE-7 automatic rifle, later a ZB26) and 6 rifles. The rifle company HQ consisted of the company commander, a supply/armament officer, the first sergeant, 2 buglers, 2 orderlies, and 9 cooks. In action, one man was pulled from each squad (15 men total) and used as a messenger, 6 to the company HQ and 3 to each platoon.

The battalion machine-gun company was built around three platoons, each consisting of a platoon leader, platoon sergeant, a pack leader, and two mounted messengers, plus two squads each of a squad leader, 6 gun crew, and 4 drivers with pack horses for the gun and ammunition. In a significant break from tradition, the MG company was provided with its own signal squad with 2 sergeants, 8 privates, and 2 drivers with 4 pack horses for wire and phone equipment. In wartime an ammunition squad was added for each platoon, consisting of a squad leader, 2 drivers with pack horses, 4 reserve gunners/ammunition bearers, and a farrier. Some units enlarged their machine-gun companies to 9 or even 12 guns if weapons were available.

Also supporting the infantry battalion was an infantry gun platoon with two squads, each of a squad leader, 6 gun crew, and 18 drivers/ammunition bearers with 8 pack horses. Weapons were normally the 20mm Oerlikon Modell S, but in some cases the more cumbersome Solothurn S5-100 drawn by two horses was used. This was a strange choice for an infantry gun—the target set against which it was effective was quite small. True, it would have been useful against strafing biplanes and the thinly armored tanks of the time, but the HE charge was small and it was incapable of engaging targets in defilade. Even European armies eyeing mechanized potential foes chose mortars over an AA/AT weapon. Nevertheless, at least some of the Chinese units pronounced themselves pleased with the Oerlikon's performance in Shanghai in 1932.

The 21st Year regiment's fire support was found in either an infantry gun company or a mortar company. The infantry-gun company with German 75mm leIG howitzers was to have been standard, replacing the Dutch 47/75mm delivered earlier, each platoon having 16 pack horses. However, few such weapons were actually supplied. Instead, the common replacement was a mortar company with the Chinese 82mm mortar. In either case the company included a signal squad of 10 signalmen and 2 drivers, with 4 pack horses for wire and phones. A rapid-fire gun company with six 20mm Modell S guns was also incorporated into the regiments of selected divisions of the 19th Route and 5th Armies.

21st Year Type Division			
	Officers	Enlisted	Light Weapons
Division HQ 52		6275 pistols	
Special Service Company	6	218	15 pistols, 170 rifles, 8 LMG
Signal Battalion	43	422	106 pistols, 149 rifles
Two Brigades, each			
Brigade HQ	7	18	20 pistols
Two Infantry Regiments, each			Total 405 pistols, 79 carbines, 1,387 rifles, 56 LMG, 18 MG
Regiment HQ	11	33	
Signal Co	4	81	
Three Infantry Battalions, each			
Battalion HQ	5	17	
Three Rifle Companies, each	5	167	
Machine Gun Company	5	118	
Infantry Gun Platoon	1	68	
Mortar or Gun Battery	4	109	
Field Artillery Regiment			Total 549 pistols, 698 carbines, 42 rifles, 2 LMG
Regiment HQ	16	37	
Signal Company	7	228	
Three Artillery Battalions, each	34	459	
Engineer Battalion	25	589	99 pistols, 440 rifles
Transportation Battalion	17	288	69 pistols, 132 carbines
Medical Company	11	123	26 pistols

A special service (guard) platoon of the 32nd Army in 1935.

The regimental signal company had two platoons each of six 5-man squads, one to operate a switchboard and the other five for laying wire and operating the telephones. No transport was provided during peacetime, but in war 35 drivers with 70 pack horses were added, along with two more signal platoons.

For scouting the division could have a company-size cavalry squadron but this was not always part of the organization.

Another significant change was the nominal enlargement of the divisional artillery battalion to a full regiment of three battalions, to be equipped with either field or mountain guns. Communication was entirely by telephone, with each battery having a reel cart and an instrument cart to go forward to the front lines, and the regimental signal battery providing each battalion with four pack-carried signal platoons each of a 5-man switchboard squad and six 5-man phone squads; one for each battalion and one for the regiment HQ.

However, implementation of the artillery portion was not merely spotty, as it was with the infantry, but a complete non-starter. Some field and pack artillery guns were purchased in the 1930s, but on such a small scale due to cost that they were, without exception, diverted to GHQ artillery units rather than parceled out to divisions. Those divisions that originally held battalions of tired, old 75mm mountain guns kept theirs, but there would be no infusions of new weaponry for the divisional artillery.

As it happened, only the two German-sponsored divisions adopted the 21st Year Division organization. The rest muddled along with the variety of organization tables in force for their particular part of the army.

The disastrous outcome of the 4th Encirclement Campaign of early 1933 prompted yet another round of reorganization studies. The conclusion was that the brigade headquarters were superfluous, contributing only to the slowing of orders, and that lower-level units had to be brought up to strength.

As a result, a new organization table was issued in the spring of 1933 for the anti-communist division (officially the "anti-bandit division"). Such a division normally consisted of three regiments, but could have as many as five assigned, without intervening brigade headquarters. The other major change was an increase in squad size in the rifle and machine-gun units. Surprisingly, signal facilities were not improved, nor were light machine guns officially incorporated into the organization. The artillery battalion was retained, but few of the divisions actually took them into combat due to the rough terrain in the area of operations.

22nd Year Anti-Communist Division			
	Officers	Enlisted	Notes
Army Headquarters	89	120	
Division Headquarters	79	147	
Signal Company	6	168	3 platoons each 3 squads
Reconnaissance Company	5	144	
Three Infantry Regiments, each			
Regiment HQ	22	68	
Signal Platoon	1	48	3 x 15-man squads
Three Infantry Batallions, each			
Battalion HQ	4	13	
Three Rifle Companies, each	6	145	3 platoons each 3 x 14-man squads
Machine Gun Company	5	121	3 platoons each 2 x 16-man squads with Maxim MG
Mortar Company	6	138	3 platoons each 2 x 19-man squads with 82mm mortar
Special Service Company	6	145	Identical to rifle company
Transport Platoon	1	42	3 x 14-man squads
Stretcher-bearer Platoon	1	43	3 x 13-man squads
Artillery Battalion			
Battalion HQ	12	98	
Three Batteries, each	5	203	2 platoons each 2 75mm guns
Engineer Battalion			
Battalion HQ	11	41	
Three Engineer Companies, each	6	179	3 platoons each 3 x 17-man squads
Special Service Battalion	27	569	Identical to infantry battalion
Transport Battalion			
Battalion HQ	13	31	
Two Transport Companies, each	6	148	3 platoons each 3 x 14-man squads

The "anti-communist" organization was applied only to the divisions operating in Guangxi as part of the 5th Encirclement Campaign. They were apparently successful, at least in that the 5th Encirclement Campaign itself was successful, but no other units were reconfigured to this organization.

In the meantime, the German advisory mission had continued working in concert with the Chinese National Defense Planning Council on a new model reorganization scheme that would bring the Chinese army closer to the European standard. In December 1934 Chiang approved a massive reorganization of the NRA. The "National Army Reorganization Plan for 60 Divisions" was initially to be completed in three to four years, although this was soon extended to five.

Sixty divisions were to be raised almost de novo in in six-month batches. The enlisted troops were to be recruited from similarly numbered divisional districts to enhance unit cohesion and simplify communication. These "new divisions" (*xinbian shi*), however, would receive officers from around the country to eliminate regional allegiances.

In fact, the result, designated the 24th Year New Type Division, was simply a tweaking of the earlier 21st Year Division. The infantry battalion remained unchanged except for some minor personnel adjustments, and even retained the platoon organization of three rifle and two LMG squads. The only significant change to the infantry regiment was the introduction of a new unit that would be henceforth standard, the

24th Year New Type Division	Men	Horses
Division Headquarters	128	33
Cavalry Squadron	237	259
Signal Battalion		
Battalion HQ	36	129
Two Signal Companies, each	131	
Trains	74	
Two Infantry Brigades, each		
Brigade HQ	29	10
Two Infantry Regiments, each		
Regiment HQ	51	10
Signal Company	91	7
Three Infantry Battalions, each		
Battalion HQ	47	3
Three Rifle Companies, each	177	0
Machine Gun Company	126	43
Gun Platoon	71	20
Infantry Gun/Mortar Company	118	56
Special Duty Platoon	53	0
Special Duty Platoon	53	0
Field Artillery Regiment		
Regiment HQ	72	31
Signal Battery	237	106
Three Field Artillery Battalions, each		
Battalion HQ	66	348
Three Batteries, each	165	
Special Duty Platoon	53	0
or **Mountain Artillery Regiment**		
Regiment HQ	72	31
Signal Battery	237	106
Three Mountain Artillery Battalions, each		
Battalion HQ	66	342
Three Batteries, each	211	
Special Duty Platoon	53	0
Engineer Battalion		
Battalion HQ	33	89
Signal Platoon	37	
Three Engineer Companies, each	184	
Transport Battalion		
Battalion HQ	37	6
1st Transport Company	188	221
2nd Transport Company	107	105
Special Duty Company	234	0
Other	155	0

special duty element. In the case of the infantry regiment it was a platoon and adopted the organization of the rifle platoon to serve as a guard unit for the regiment HQ.

The cavalry squadron was enlarged and additional personnel added to the artillery regiment, although the latter never existed in practice so the change was academic. As before, the engineer battalion was equipped solely with hand tools and was closer to a labor unit than trained engineers.

Except for the absence of radios, the 24th Year model division was comparable on paper to Western divisions of the mid-1930s.

Planning for the implementation of the new division organization began in December 1934 and in late January 1935 a secret meeting of 83 of the highest-ranking officers was convened. The final plan called for the reorganization of 60 divisions onto the model division tables, in six-month "phases," 6–10 divisions in 1935, 16–20 in 1936, 20–30 in 1937, and any remaining balance in 1938, this schedule being slightly modified shortly thereafter. These would be the heart of the national army, answerable to Chiang and significantly better equipped (and trained) than those of the various semi-independent warlords.

These plans, however, were predicated on assurances from the German military mission that weapons and equipment for the divisions would be forthcoming. As Germany accelerated its own rearmament, however, delivery times lagged.

There were rifles aplenty for both the 21st Year and 24th Year New divisions, light machine-gun production was ramping up, and significant purchases from overseas filled most of the remaining shortages, and Maxim production was adequate. The 82mm Type 20 medium mortar was relatively easy to produce, and about a thousand had been turned out by the end of 1936, serving as effective surrogates for infantry guns. Those infantry guns, however, were destined never to show up. The 120 Oerlikon Modell S guns were enough for only 20 regiments (five divisions) and holdings of the regimental infantry guns were also very limited. Plans to provide each of the model divisions with a six-gun anti-tank company of German 37mm guns did not go much further. And, as mentioned, division artillery was never delivered.

In addition the plans were extravagant in light of China's resources, particularly in their intensive use of horses, which were not readily available and would have broken the logistical network that was already groaning under the strain of providing food for campaigning troops, much less fodder.

As a result, only 10 divisions were organized on the new-type configuration and equipped as best as could be done in 1935. A further 20 were nominally reorganized before the outbreak of the war in 1937, but without many of the arms that were to have made the divisions modern. The balance of the grand plan fell by the wayside.

The bulk of the NRA's divisions, those not destined for the "new division" program, were to be reorganized as "re-formed divisions" (zhengli shi). For them a new organization table was also prepared, the 24th Year Consolidation Type. This replaced the battalion machine-gun companies with a regimental company, specified a mortar company for regimental support, and made other reductions, including defining the artillery component as a battalion. As before, of course, the artillery component was rarely present.

Under the National Army Reorganization Plan the new divisions were to form the combat core of the NRA, while the re-formed divisions were to be used for security and bandit-suppression (often meaning anti-communist) duties, combat in lower threat environments, and as sources of replacement personnel for the new divisions.

This was followed by the 25th Year (1936) Adjusted Type, which combined elements of the 21st Year, New Type, and reformed divisions. In this, both the infantry battalion and regiment lost their gun units and the regiment gained a mortar company. The infantry regiment also included a special service platoon, stretcher-bearer platoon, signal platoon, and transport platoon. Divisional support was provided by an artillery battalion, engineer battalion, transport battalion, signal battalion, and special service company. Total division strength was about 11,000 men.

Since none of these organization tables had been adopted across the board the situation immediately before the war was little short of chaotic. Indeed, not only were there no fewer than six infantry division TO&Es in force simultaneously, but many of those were only incompletely implemented. In early 1937 the central committee decided to homogenize the divisions of the army along two lines.

> China currently has 182 Infantry Divisions, 46 Independent Infantry Brigades, 9 Cavalry Divisions and 6 Independent Cavalry Brigades, 4 Artillery Brigades, and 20 Independent Artillery Regiments. There are other special units and local units not included. The training and equipment varies a lot between units but unfortunately it is not up to our expectations in general. The combat strength also varies.
>
> There are many forms of TO&E currently in existence, besides those of the Sichuan, Yunan, Guangdong, Guangxi, Shenxi, Suiyuan, and the Northeastern Army types. There are also the 19th Year Division type, 21st Year Army Division type, 22nd Year Bandit Pacification type, 24th Year Model Division and Consolidation types, and 25th Year Adjusted type. In light of the modern combat requirement and equipment availability, the plan is to organize all troops into Type A and Type B:
>
> (A) Type is proposed to be based on the 25th Year Adjusted type. All the reorganized divisions will be organized according to this type. It is equivalent to the Regular Army Division of other modern nations.
>
> (B) Type is proposed to adopt the 24th Year Consolidation type. It is similar to the Reserve Division of other modern nations.[*]

The 1937 Division

These good intentions, however, lasted no longer than the earlier ones. War broke out mid-year and Chiang and many of his generals were immediately taken with the effectiveness of the Type 89 grenade discharger. They demanded that it be reverse-engineered and that, of course, mandated a new set of organization tables to incorporate the weapon into the force structure. The result was the 26th Year type infantry division, which differed a little from the immediately preceding 25th Year type.

A 45-man rifle platoon introduced the 14-man section, with two sections each consisting of an LMG squad and a rifle squad, and the third section with two rifle squads. Two Type 27 grenade dischargers were added to the platoon, although their nominal distribution is not clear. A rifle company would thus now have six LMGs and six grenade dischargers, and a battalion 18 of each, and a regiment 56 (including the two in the special service platoon).

Above that level through the brigade things were little changed, with a machine-gun company supporting the battalion and a mortar company the regiment. As before, the

---

[*] He Yingqin, February 1937, Report to 5th Conference of the 3rd Central Committee, the Nationalist Party.

26th Year Type Division	Officers	Enlisted
Division Headquarters	79	147
Special Service Company	5	144
Signal Battalion		
Battalion HQ	16	72
Two Wire Companies, each	11	100
Radio Company	36	121
Two Brigades, each		
Brigade HQ	13	29
Two Infantry Regiments, each		
Regiment HQ	22	69
Special Service Platoon	1	48
Signal Platoon	1	48
Three Infantry Battalions, each		
Battalion HQ	3	16
Three Rifle Companies, each	5	144
Machine Gun Company	5	113
Mortar Company	5	125
Transport Platoon	1	48
Stretcher-bearer Platoon	1	46
Artillery Battalion		
Battalion HQ	8	25
Three Artillery Batteries	5	159
Engineer Battalion		
Battalion HQ	8	18
Three Engineer Companies	6	144
Transport Battalion		
Battalion HQ	13	7
Two Transport Companies	6	148

brigade headquarters was not provided with a signal unit, rendering it primarily an administrative echelon. Similarly, the division tables continued to include an artillery battalion, although it seems likely that more divisions lacked this battalion than actually had them.

The one other significant change was the expansion of the previous signal company into a signal battalion. The unit now included a radio company that permitted radio communications upwards to the army HQ, but also down to the regiments, although it seems likely that the planned radios were actually in short supply.

The division was still a respectable size, if a little small, at 10,923 men in total. The practice of arming only the frontline combat personnel continued, as the division had a total of only 3,821 rifles and carbines.[*]

The 1938 Armies & Divisions

The success of the Japanese in the early phases of the war convinced the Chinese GHQ that their current array of organizations was obsolete and inefficient. A special committee was set up under Defense Minister He with remarkable alacrity to study the organizational structure of the army. They reported back in September 1937, proffering a standardized set of organization tables, an integrated numbering and designation system for all the regiments, divisions, and armies, financial and supply frameworks, and proposals to appoint loyal commanders.

The resulting organization tables were adopted as the 27th Year (1938) type organization. The most striking feature was the appointment of the field army as a fixed tactical unit. In keeping with that, the divisional artillery battalion was abolished, and the artillery moved up

---

[*] Chinese sources give a total for the division of 274 light and 54 heavy MGs, 243 grenade dischargers, 30 medium mortars, and 16 artillery pieces, although these numbers do not match the organizational structure.

to the army level, although division strength remained at about 11,000. In part, this was a recognition that the Chinese army was, indeed, the equivalent of the Japanese division in all but name. It was also, however, a result of massive losses of equipment in the first year of the war, such that even by consolidating assets, each army could only field a single artillery battalion, and even that was not always present. At the same time signal, transport, and engineer battalions were added to the army structure.

At the lower levels, the former regimental transport platoon was enlarged to an ammunition company to confer greater autonomy. Medical support within the division was strengthened slightly, but still remained abysmal, in large part for lack of qualified personnel.

27th Year Type Division		
	Officers	Enlisted
Division Headquarters	57	99
Special Service Company	5	167
Signal Battalion		
Battalion HQ	9	14
Two Wire Companies, each	6	115
Radio Platoon	27	49
Two Brigades, each		
Brigade HQ	8	15
Two Infantry Regiments, each		
Regiment HQ	15	27
Signal Company	4	81
Three Infantry Battalions, each		
Battalion HQ	5	16
Three Rifle Companies, each	5	147
Machine-Gun Company	5	134
Mortar Company	5	163
Ammunition Company	4	115
Medical Unit	2	29
Engineer Battalion		
Battalion HQ	13	55
Three Engineer Companies, each	5	183
Two Transport Companies, each	5	174
Two Medical Companies, each	12	189

The warlords, while accepting the uniform numbering and designation system, for the most part wanted nothing to do with the standardized organization tables, while the central government's divisions were often campaigning and unavailable for reorganization—thus the 1938 organization was implemented only very slowly and only a few divisions actually reorganized onto it, with many remaining on the 1929 or 1937 organizations.

Indeed, the orders to concentrate artillery at the army level were not actually issued until January 1941.

In any event, the brigade/regiment combination quickly proved too cumbersome for the mobile campaigning practiced by the Japanese and in March 1939 orders went out to "triangularize" the divisions by eliminating the two brigade HQs and one of the infantry regiments. This time around military common sense was reinforced by the heavy losses suffered, along with desire to inflate the number of units held by the various satraps, and even the warlords acquiesced. With only a few exceptions Chinese divisions henceforth consisted of a headquarters, three infantry regiments (initially the 1938 style) and small service elements.

A few reinforcing measures were undertaken outside of the formal table of organization process. In 1938–40, 16 divisions received an anti-tank company of six 47mm Bohler guns. In 1941 four anti-tank regiments were disbanded and their guns ordered to form additional AT companies (actually Western platoons, with only four guns) for the field army and divisions, bringing the total up to 161.* Twenty favored divisions also received four-gun light anti-aircraft "companies." Weapons known to have been used included the Solothurn 20mm S5-100 and the Hotchkiss 13.2mm single-mount.

Increasing production of the easy-to-make 82mm mortar made it possible to begin equipping divisions without artillery with a mortar battalion, although this was far from universal even by the end of the war.

At the lower levels it proved possible to equip the rifle platoons with grenade launchers, either the Type 27 hand-held version or the Type 28 rifle grenade launcher. By late 1944 about half the divisions had received these handy weapons, usually on a scale equal to the light machine guns.

The 27th Year Division TO&E and its improvements were applied first of all to loyal divisions directly under the MAC. Additional training was also mandated for these divisions, although it is not clear whether it proved possible to achieve a significant improvement. In October 1939 these divisions were sent out to reinforce the II, III, V, and IX War Zones.

The 1942 Division

In 1942 GHQ implemented the "picked troop policy," which was intended both to eliminate unused units and make existing units more compact and easier to control. The latter objective was to be attained by stripping the 1938-style division of all non-combat functions, which were to be assumed at field army level, and reconfiguring those divisions that had not already done so as triangular formations with three infantry regiments and no brigade headquarters. At that time the Chinese Army had 106 field army HQs and 299 infantry divisions.

Published in early 1942 the new TO&E was to be the definitive wartime baseline organization, applicable to all infantry divisions, and from which selected divisions would be upgraded later as equipment became available. The new division had a strength of only 366 officers and 6,428 enlisted, some 60% of the strength of the original 1938 division. The constituent combat units of the division were little changed, except for a reduction in the size of the battalion machine-gun company from three 2-gun platoons to only two.

The new rifle platoon consisted of a platoon leader and three sections, each of a sergeant, a corporal and 12 privates.

Strength of 1942 Type Division		
	Officers	Enlisted
Division Headquarters	30	41
Signal Company	32	191
Reconnaissance Company	8	181
Three Infantry Regiments, each		
Regiment HQ	17	27
Signal Platoon	2	74
Three Infantry Battalions, each		
Battalion HQ	5	15
Three Rifle Companies, each	5	150
Machine-Gun Company	4	83
Mortar Company	4	128
Engineer Company	5	167
Special Service Company	6	229

---

* In fact, it seems unlikely that more than about half of those AT companies were actually distributed to divisions and field armies, and of those about 50 were equipped with the near-useless Gruson/Rosenberg guns.

In the first and second sections of each platoon the sergeant commanded a light machine-gun squad (the corporal and 5 privates with a light machine gun) and a rifle squad (7 privates). The third section of each platoon lacked the light machine gun, but included a grenade launcher (Type 27 grenade launcher or Type 28 rifle grenade launcher) in each of its two rifle squads. The rifle company headquarters had the company commander (a captain), a warrant officer analogous to a first sergeant (who doubled as the HQ section leader), a supply sergeant, and a headquarters section. This last included 4 messengers, 2 buglers, 4 ammunition carriers, 2 stretcher-bearers, and 10 cooks.

Unit cooks had to carry their utensils and food. This cook was photographed in Burma with the 38th Division, but he could have been pictured in any army unit anywhere in China.

Such fire support as was available to the battalion commander was found in his machine-gun company. This unit was built around three platoons, each of two gun sections. A gun section was made up of a sergeant, a gunner, and 5 gun crew, who had to carry the machine gun, usually a heavy water-cooled Type 24 or Three-Tens. Each platoon also included an ammunition section of a corporal and 8 muleteers, each with a pack mule. The company also featured a signal section that included 2 telephone operators, 3 linemen, and 2 runners, although the telephone equipment, like the mules in the gun platoons, was absent more often than present in practice.

The battalion headquarters was an austere formation, consisting of a major (battalion commander), 2 captains (an assistant commander and a medical officer), 2 lieutenants, 2

Infantry Regiment, 1942 Type

	Officers	Warrant officers	Sergeants	Corporals	Privates	Pistols	Rifles	Grenade launchers	Light MGs	Medium MGs	82mm mortars	Horses	Mules
Regiment HQ	15	2	9	1	18	16	7	0	0	0	0	8	0
Special Service Platoon	1	0	7	5	56	6	56	0	0	0	0	0	0
Signal Platoon	1	1	9	6	62	46	8	0	0	0	0	0	7
Mortar Company													
Company HQ	1	1	9	0	18	15	46	0	0	0	0	2	0
Two Platoons, each	1	0	3	2	43			0	0	0	2	0	16
Three Infantry Battalions, each													
Battalion HQ	5	0	2	1	10	5	6	0	0	0	0	2	0
Three Rifle Companies, each													
Company HQ	1	1	3	1	21	15	82	0	0	0	0	0	0
Three Rifle Platoons, each	1	0	3	3	36			2	2	0	0	0	0
Machine Gun Company													
Company HQ	1	1	9	0	14	23	23	0	0	0	0	2	0
Signal Section	0	0	2	0	10			0	0	0	0	0	0
Three MG Platoons, each	1	0	2	1	22			0	0	2	0	0	8
Alternative organizations													
Battalion mortar platoon (in lieu of regimental mortar company)	1	0	49			4	19	0	0	0	2	0	16
Rifle Company													
Company HQ	1	1	3	1	21	15	82	0	0	0	0	2	0
Three Rifle Platoons, each	1	0	3	3	36			2	3	0	0	0	0

sergeants (a clerk and a supply sergeant), a bugler, a medical assistant, a 6-man messenger team, 2 cooks, and a stable orderly for the rarely present riding horses for the commander and assistant commander.

At the regimental level fire support was provided by a mortar company with two platoons each of two 82mm mortars. A mortar section consisted of a sergeant section leader, a corporal assistant leader, 6 gun crew, 3 ammunition bearers, and 3 muleteers with pack mules. A mortar platoon had two such sections, plus an ammunition section with 8 porters and 9 men with pack mules, and a headquarters with a messenger and a pack mule for instruments.

The regimental signal platoon held a switchboard squad of a sergeant and 6 privates, and five wire squads each of a sergeant, a corporal and 8 privates. The platoon HQ included 7 pack mules with handlers, one for each squad and one for the headquarters gear. The regimental special services platoon took the form of five sections, each of a sergeant, a corporal and 10 privates.

The regimental headquarters served the commander, a colonel, with a vice-commander (lieutenant colonel) an assistant commander (major), 2 adjutants, an ordnance officer with assistant, 3 supply officers with 3 assistants, a medical officer with assistant, a pharmacist, a veterinarian with assistant, a 12-man messenger section, and 3 cooks, along with other enlisted personnel.

A mortar company of a division in east China being inspected by a visiting US Army team in 1945. (*J. Wisebram*)

The only combat element of the division base was the reconnaissance company, which consisted of a 28-man headquarters (including 14 cooks), a 9-man signal section, a 38-man mounted platoon, and a 113-man dismounted platoon. The mounted platoon consisted of three sections, each of a sergeant, a corporal, and 10 privates. The dismounted platoon had 10 sections each of a sergeant, a corporal, and 9 privates. The divisional special service company was mainly a guard force, with four platoons. The first two platoons each had five sections, one with a light MG and 6 rifles, the others with 6 rifles. The third platoon was an "inspection" platoon and the fourth a scout platoon, similar to the first two platoons but without the light MGs.

Two variants to this organization were authorized when sufficient equipment was available. If enough mortars were issued the regimental mortar company could be replaced by a two-gun platoon in each battalion, thus increasing the number of weapons from four to six. The second served to increase the number of light machine guns in the rifle company from six to nine. This was accomplished by making all the sections in the rifle platoon identical (each with a light machine-gun squad and a rifle squad), and assigning the grenade launchers as needed, usually one each to two of the sections, to be manned by personnel there.

The utility of a division as thus organized was obviously extremely limited. It had no artillery, nor any anti-tank weapons. Of equal importance was that it had no organic transport or supply elements to move supplies. In static positions this could be worked around by pushing supplies forward from the rear, but once a battle became fluid it seems likely that such an arrangement would be found wanting. Communication up to the regimental HQ was by runner or, if enough wire was available, by telephone. The division signal company was supposed to provide radio teams to the regiments for division/regiment communications, but the equipment was in short supply and was broken at least as often as it worked.

The nominal 1942 TO&E proved to be exceptionally flexible. Minor changes were made by various commanders and the organization evolved over time. As a result, it is rare to find any two documents in agreement on the strength of the division or its constituent elements.

Although artillery was not authorized to non-US-sponsored divisions through to the end of the war, continued large-scale production of 82mm mortars did make it possible to increase their numbers. There were several ways of accomplishing this. One was to incorporate both the regimental mortar company (four 82mm) and battalion mortar platoons (each two 82mm), for a total of 10 mortars in the regiment, or 30 in the division. The same total could be achieved by adding a divisional mortar battalion of three companies, to yield a divisional total of six companies, half with four guns each and the other half with six each.

As an example of the evolution of the division is the organization table of the Temporary 20th Division as mandated on its formation in November 1944. The infantry regiments of this division were conventional, consisting of a headquarters, signal platoon, mortar company, and, new for a 1942-type division, transportation company; each of the three battalions had a HQ, three rifle companies, and a machine-gun company. Compared to the original 1942 standard, the division was strengthened by a mortar battalion, an anti-tank company, and a supply and transport battalion, while the engineer component was expanded to a battalion. Each of the regiments thus gained about 200 men, presumably

Organization Table for Temporary 20th Division, November 1944

	Officers	Warrant officers	Sergeants	Corporals	Privates	Total	Riding horses	Pack horses
Division HQ	46	12	14	3	53	128	24	0
Special Service Company	4	1	12	10	113	140	0	0
Signal Company	11	16	33	1	149	210	0	36
Three Infantry Regiments, each	89	17	215	126	1,720	2,167	22	143
Mortar Battalion	20	4	63	13	355	455	5	102
Anti-Tank Company	4	2	14	4	115	139	12	24
Engineer Battalion	18	3	50	19	344	434	2	54
Supply & Transport Battalion	25	4	62	1	944	1,036	48	288
Medical Unit	11	1	19	6	167	204	1	0
Field Hospital	10	1	15	6	104	136	1	0
Ordnance Repair Shop	0	2	3	3	14	22	0	0
Total	416	97	930	444	7,518	9,405	159	933
Attached Transport troops	4	1	2	9	119	135	0	0
Attached Chemical troops	10	6	43	21	79	159	0	0
Attached Political personnel	14	7	45	30	199	295	0	0
Attached other	112	55	0	0	0	0	0	0
Total, including attached	556	166	1,020	504	7,915	9,994	159	933

mostly in the transportation company, while the rest of the division gained about 2,000 men. The weapons strengths reported in January 1945 are consistent with those, with an additional six 60mm mortars per regiment, although this seems to reflect authorized strengths rather than actual.

The changes to the 1942 divisional organization were not applied in any regular pattern, except that field armies tended to be homogenous. Standardization above that level, however, was not guaranteed. For example, in late December 1944 the 31st Army Group had two field armies, the 78th and 85th, each with different variants of the 1942-type TO&Es for its constituent divisions. A division in the 78th Army had a strength of 7,314 men, while those of the 85th Army apparently resembled the Temporary 20th Division, being about 2,600 stronger on paper, with six-gun battalion MG companies (compared to four guns in those of the 78th Army), an anti-tank company, and additional mortars. In each case, a rifle platoon still had only two light machine guns, reflecting continuing shortages of those weapons, and two grenade launchers. All six divisions of the 31st Army Group were generally up to strength in weapons except that only one of the divisions actually had its anti-tank guns. The 78th Army was supposed to use Type 27 grenade launchers, while the 85th Army was supposed to use Type 28 rifle grenade launchers, but in fact the 78th Army used mostly Type 28s as well. For communications, each division was to have one 15-watt and four 5-watt radios, along with 42 telephones.

The smaller organization of the 78th Army was not unusual. The 4th Army Group with its 38th Army (17th and New 35th Divisions) and 96th Army (New 14th and 177th

Weapons & Ammunition Holdings of Temporary 20th–22nd Divisions, 8 Jan. 1945		
Weapons		
	T 20th Div	T 21st Div	T 22nd Div
Pistol, Mauser 7.63mm	93	94	94
Rifle, 7.92mm	2,100	2,100	2,100
Grenade Discharger	162	162	162
Light MG, 7.92mm	173	100	100
Light MG, 7.62mm	0	73	73
Medium MG, 7.92mm	36	36	36
Mortar, 60mm	18	18	18
Mortar, 81mm	27	25	25
Mortar, 82mm	0	5	5
Anti-Tank Gun, 20mm	4	4	4
Ammunition		
	Temp 20th Div	Temp 21st Div	Temp 22nd Div
Cartridge, Pistol 7.63mm	11,160	11,280	11,280
Cartridge, Rifle, 7.92mm	315,000	315,000	315,000
Cartridge, Light MG, 7.92mm	415,200	240,000	240,000
Cartridge, Medium MG, 7.92mm	162,000	162,000	162,000
Cartridge, Light MG, 7.62mm	0	175,200	175,200
Shell, 60mm mortar	2,160	2,160	2,160
Shell, 81mm mortar	3,240	3,000	3,000
Shell, 82mm mortar	0	600	600
Round, 20mm AT Gun	1,200	1,200	1,200
Grenade, Hand	9,000	9,000	9,000
Grenade, for discharger	4,860	4,860	4,860

Divisions) had similar authorized strengths in February 1945, except that the number of grenade launchers was doubled. On the other hand, the two divisions of the 17th Army (New 2nd and 84th) approximated the strength and equipment of the larger 85th Army in February 1945.

The NRA had been forced to undergo wrenching transformations with much of its homeland occupied and its forces under frequent attack by a brutal and competent foe. The first organizational challenge, and one that was never completely answered, was to integrate the various provincial forces into a common organizational framework. Some of the more independently minded provinces had been occupied, of course. Others had been slowly brought at least partially into the fold by the central government's near monopoly on arms and supplies. Nevertheless, some of the warlord forces remained on their own organizational patterns through to the end of the war, the most prominent being those in Shanxi and Yunnan.

The most glaring exception in all this, of course, were the communist forces, primarily operating in north China. Their force structure was fluid, being based on local conditions. In fact, the agreed-upon restrictions limiting the number of divisions to be supported by the communist party led to the term losing all military significance, with the Hundred Regiments Offensive being launched with no fewer than 46 regiments from the 115th Division, 22 regiments from the 120th Division and 47 regiments from the 129th Division.

A 76mm pack piece in full recoil, while serving as field army artillery in May 1945.

In fact, that operation in late 1940 was the last significant conventional operation of the communist forces.

The divisional structure the NRA established before 1937 proved almost completely inappropriate for the war that followed. The German-inspired model divisions of the 21st Year were completely beyond the capacity of China to form and maintain. The 25th and 26th Year division structures were more realistic, having abandoned the infantry-gun companies and reduced the artillery component, but remained clumsy square formations.

With the start of the war it became clear that it would be a long time before there was enough light artillery to fill out even the one battalion per division called for in the existing TO&E. As a consequence the artillery support for the forces in the field was now concentrated at field army level, at the necessarily modest nominal ratio of one battalion per field army.

These changes, however, still left the division a cumbersome square formation with two brigades each of two regiments. This had been favored in the First World War, featuring relatively static warfare and massive artillery support. Modern Western armies, however, abandoned the square division structure in the 1920s and 1930s as being inflexible. The NRA finally arrived at the same conclusion and, when it implemented the 1942 (31st Year) organization, the divisions were finally reconfigured into three directly reporting regiments. At the same time all the supporting services were abolished and consolidated at

A Maxim of the 57th Regiment of the 19th Division in action in Hebei province, May 1945.

the field army level. The division thus consisted of the three small infantry regiments and command elements. This was implemented fairly quickly, and from late 1942 onward this was the standard organizational format.

As 30-plus divisions were siphoned off for the Alpha Force program, with modest infusions of US equipment, it proved possible to improve some of the remaining divisions, primarily through the addition of some service support elements. By international standards they were still short of artillery firepower, signal facilities, and transport, but for their intended use in the environment in which they operated they were pretty well suited.

6

Cavalry

D ue to the limited availability of suitable horses and equipment, cavalry organization was even more diverse than infantry organization. The only large-scale use of cavalry was by the northeastern forces, where they were grouped into brigades, each of two cavalry regiments. The cavalry regiment consisted of four line squadrons, each of 175 men. Overhead, including administrative and trains personnel, was apparently significant because a squadron actually fielded only 90 effective combat personnel in four platoons. The northeastern cavalry was mounted on the sturdy Manchurian pony and was armed with rifles and light machine guns. Most of their experience was in fighting bandits, against whom they used the mounted frontal charge with the troopers firing their rifles from their hips over the heads of the ponies.

An attempt was made in early 1935 to standardize cavalry organization by setting up a "model" cavalry regiment at the Cavalry School at Nanjing, and a start was made in bringing field regiments to this configuration. By that time the central government had 8 divisions and 11 brigades of cavalry (including 7 divisions of the Northeastern Army).

Cavalry of the 29th Army prewar.

The model regiment had a strength of 65 officers and about 1,500 enlisted and was divided into four rifle squadrons, a machine-gun squadron, a gun squadron, and engineer, signal, and armored car platoons. A rifle squadron consisted of four 41-man platoons, each of three squads. Each 12-man squad was armed with 11 carbines and one ZB26 light machine gun, for which a pack horse was provided. The machine-gun squadron consisted of three platoons, each with four Maxim MGs carried on pack horses. The gun squadron had two platoons, one with two 37mm infantry guns, the other with two 75mm pack howitzers, each gun being pulled by two draft horses. The engineer platoon held a pioneer and demolition section and a bridging section, while the signal platoon had wire, visual, and radio sections, the last operating two radios. The armored car platoon, rarely present in practice, had two sidecar motorcycles with light MGs, and two armored cars, while the gun squadron was usually armed uniformly with 37mm infantry guns.

Reported Strengths of the Cavalry Armies, 15 December 1944

Cav Army	Divisions	Strength	Horses	Weapons
1st	1st Cav, 2nd Cav, 4th Cav	16,194	1,752	4,964 rifles, 603 LMG, 24 MG, 6 mortars
2nd	3rd Cav, Temp 14th	14,427	2,996	3,292 rifles, 256 LMG, 29 MG, 24 mortars, 5 mtn guns
3rd	New 7th Cav, 9th Cav	29,036[a]	4,095	3,421 rifles, 162 LMG, 22 MG, 2 mortars
4th	New 3rd Cav, New 4th Cav	8,582	5,096	3,083 rifles, 165 LMG, 28 MG, 15 mortars
5th	Temp 1st Cav, 5th Cav	9,733	7,059	3,258 rifles, 133 LMG, 8 MG

a   *This number appears erroneous, it probably should read 9,036.*

A small number of cavalry divisions was formed, each with three cavalry regiments, an artillery battalion, and supporting troops, and the prewar plan called for the inclusion of 10 cavalry divisions in the army force structure by 1938. The 1st Cavalry Army of Shanxi troops (1st, 2nd, 6th and 7th Cavalry Divisions, supported by four infantry brigades) participated in the campaign along the Beijing–Suiyan railway in August 1937, later joined by the 2nd Cavalry Army (3rd Cavalry Division); while the 3rd Cavalry Army (4th and 9th Cavalry Divisions) and the 4th Cavalry Army (10th Cavalry Division) participated in the Beijing–Hankou railway campaign of late 1937.

Following these disastrous initial campaigns the cavalry forces, mostly controlled by warlords in any event, were pulled back to their home bases and played little role in the subsequent war efforts. Such cavalry as was held by the central government remained on a close variant of the prewar organization table, but with the nominal addition of 82mm mortars and 37mm anti-tank guns. In fact, such weapons were rarely available. The newer divisions, however, used a much-reduced strength organization table. In fact, the new divisions were not only placed on a lower organizational strength, but fared no better in actual assignment of personnel and equipment. Indeed, an American observer noted in February 1945 that the Temporary 2nd Cavalry Division was "the most poorly equipped unit of any seen in [the 1st] War Area," noting that it had no artillery, mortars, or anti-tank weapons for its 313 officers and 2,967 enlisted men, and that its officers admitted the division had done no training.

Cavalry Strength Authorizations in Effect in February 1945			
	Officers	*Enlisted*	*Horses*
Corps Troops			
Corps HQ	89	162	214
Signal Squadron	25	159	202
Independent Cavalry Regiment	62	960	1,058
Special Service Battalion	22	378	412
Transport Squadron	7	237	298
Supply Section	12	25	0
Old-Type Cavalry Division			
Division HQ	85	108	183
Signal Squadron	27	215	262
3 Cavalry Regiments, each	83	1,445	1,552
Artillery Battalion	48	638	652
Transport Battalion	33	661	662
Special Service Squadron	7	194	212
Anti-Air Squadron	10	146	195
Engineer Squadron	11	237	315
Medical Battalion	10	172	93
Field Hospital	9	176	44
Saddle Shop	4	50	0
New-Type Cavalry Division			
Division HQ	58	97	152
Signal Squadron	12	110	143
Three Cavalry Regiments, each	62	949	1,058
Mortar Battery	7	140	185
Special Service Squadron	7	185	197
Transport Squadron	6	154	140
Medical Squadron	12	192	1

Nominally, there were five cavalry armies and a varying number of divisions in the Revolutionary Army, but many were under warlord control. A sizeable percentage formed the 1st Cavalry Army, but that was really an infantry force in all but name and was part of the Shanxi army of Yan Xishan. The 5th Cavalry Army and the separate 8th, 10th, and New 8th Cavalry Divisions were a mounted force, but were Muslim units raised in Qinghai and Ningxia provinces, under the control of the Ma clique, and fought only in 1940 in defense of their home area.* Four separate divisions (12th, New 1st, New 2nd, and Reserve 11th) were Xinjiang forces under Jin Shuren and remained in that distant province.

Two cavalry armies formed the core of the NRA's actual mounted force through most of the war. The 3rd Cavalry Army was formerly part of the Northeast Army and thus presumably still held on to a little bit of autonomy at least initially. The 2nd Cavalry Army and the separate 8th Cavalry Division spent most of their time in Anhui province, although the former held just a single cavalry division for much of its existence, being reinforced by an infantry division in 1944. The 4th Cavalry Army had been disbanded in September 1937

---

* The 8th Cavalry Division did move to Henan and serve under I War Zone in 1945.

Status of 3rd Cavalry Army, 26 February 1945						
	Army Troops		9th Cavalry Div.		New 7th Cavalry Div.	
	Auth	*Actual*	*Auth*	*Actual*	*Auth*	*Actual*
Officers	217	207	493	416	288	281
Enlisted	1,911	1,035	6,932	4,157	3,725	2,332
Horses	2,184	517	6,171	2,250	3,952	1,294
Mules	0	51	966	114	0	56
Pistols	168	0	185	123	205	13
Submachine Guns	0	29	0	2	0	9
Rifles	905	297	4,586	1,797	1,400	1,297
Light MGs	72	21	156	91	80	48
Medium MGs	4	2	18	16	12	4
Grenade Launchers	30	12	52	56	52	50
AA MGs	0	0	16	0	0	0
37mm infantry guns	0	0	12	0	0	0
37mm AT Guns	0	0	8	0	0	0
Mortars	0	0	6	2	4	0
Field Artillery	0	0	12	0	0	0

but was reactivated in 1944 for Suiyuan, where it joined one older and two new separate cavalry divisions, 7th, New 5th, and New 6th.

Thus, through most of the war, the only large mounted force available to Chongqing was the 3rd Cavalry Army. It appears to have taken little part in the fight against the Japanese after 1937 and its usefulness atrophied. An American observer who visited the corps in February 1945 noted that the equipment was in bad repair, the units untrained, and that the corps "would have little combat value."

7

Armored Units

The first armored unit formed by the Nationalist Army was based on 12 Carden-Loyd Mk VI machine-gun carriers delivered in 1930, which were formed into a single tank company of three armored platoons, a transportation platoon, and a workshop. This, and subsequent prewar units, were formed as part of the Transportation Corps.

With the acquisition of further British armored vehicles it proved possible to expand the force to a battalion in November 1934. By 1935 it consisted of three tank companies, each with three five-tank platoons and one HQ tank, the 1st Company (the so-called "Tiger Company") with Vickers 6-ton medium tanks, the 2nd Company ("Dragon Company") with Vickers amphibian tanks, and the 3rd Company with Carden-Loyd Mk VI machine-gun carriers. In addition, the battalion included security, reconnaissance, signal, and maintenance platoons. A mechanized branch was officially recognized in the army in July 1936. PzKw IA light tanks arrived from Germany in early 1937 and replaced the machine-gun carriers in the 3rd Company.

The German equipment made it possible to form a mechanized force of three battalions. The 1st battalion was the tank battalion. The 2nd battalion was a motorized reconnaissance unit, consisting of a headquarters, signal platoon, scout platoon, two motorcycle companies, and an armored car company (with German SdKfz 221/222 armored cars). The 3rd battalion was a motorized anti-tank unit with a headquarters, signal platoon, scout platoon, three 37mm Pak companies, and one 47mm Bohler company, with each company having six guns.

Also included in the mechanized branch (but not the mechanized force)

The Tiger Company pauses during a road march prewar.

The Dragon Company preparing for a demonstration in 1942.

was a training/reserve battalion with the old Carden-Loyds and some Renault FT-17s that had been inherited from warlord forces, and maintenance units.

The tank battalion never fought as a whole, and did not last long beyond the outbreak of the war. The 1st Company was decimated in the battle for Shanghai, attempting to support infantry in an urban environment, while the 3rd Company was lost outside Nanjing. The 2nd Company, with its little amphibians, was withdrawn to Sichuan province, where it was used mostly for the rare military parades as a symbol of central government power.

The only significant provincial armored force was that belonging to Guangdong province, with one company of Vickers amphibians and one of armored cars.

Second Generation Units

The Nationalists' wartime purchases all flowed into south China, first through Hong Kong, then through Rangoon and Haiphong. These included Soviet T-26s, Italian CV-35s, small numbers of Renault vehicles, and German light armored cars that had been ordered before the war but whose delivery had been delayed.

To accommodate the influx of these new vehicles a new 200th Division was raised as a mechanized division consisting of the 1149th and 1150th Tank Regiments, 1152nd Motorized Infantry Regiment, and reconnaissance, engineer, replacement, guard, signal, and transport battalions. The division at that time included no field artillery.

Each tank regiment consisted of two tank battalions, a (third) support battalion, a guard company, and a repair shop. A tank battalion had three tank companies, a mortar battery, a supply company, scout and guard platoons, and repair and medical sections. A tank company had two medium platoons (each three medium tanks), a light platoon (five

CV-35), and a headquarters (a medium tank and, in two of the companies, a CV-35). The medium tanks were almost entirely T-26s, although a few surviving Vickers 6-tons were also apparently present. A tank regiment's third battalion had four companies: one signal, one engineer, and two transport, along with a guard platoon and repair and medical sections. A regiment thus had a total of 42 medium tanks and 34 CV-35 tankettes.

The motorized infantry regiment had three infantry battalions (each three rifle companies and a machine-gun company) and a motor transport battalion to lift the infantry. Attached to the division was the 52nd Artillery Regiment, a GHQ anti-tank unit with 37mm Rheinmetall guns.

In the early summer of 1938 the division was directed to send a small task force built around two companies from the 1149th Tank Regiment to aid the Chinese forces attempting to hold Kaifeng and there lost three T-26s, three Vickers Es, and four L-3s to little effect, the city falling on 6 June.

The division had just barely been formed and equipped when another massive reorganization was ordered in October 1938. The new mechanized force was to be the 11th Army, consisting of the New 22nd Division, the 200th Division, the Honorable 1st Division, a single tank regiment, and support troops. The 200th Division was converted back to a regular infantry division and the tank and mechanized units pulled out and put under 11th Army command. In February 1939 the designation was changed to the 5th Army with a strength of 54,000 men.

In August 1940 the 5th Army's tank regiment was split into two, with the 1st and 2nd battalions forming the 1st Tank Regiment, still under 5th Army; while the 3rd and 4th battalions formed a new 2nd Tank Regiment in Shaanxi.

The 5th Army was ordered into Burma in early 1942 with the following organization:

- New 22nd Division (64th, 65th, and 66th Regiments)
- 96th Division (286th, 287th, and 288th Regiments)
- 200th Division (598th, 599th, and 600th Regiments)
- Training Depot (1st and 2nd Reserve Regiments)
- 5th Army Cavalry Regiment
- 5th Army Artillery Regiment
- 5th Army Engineer Regiment
- 1st Tank Regiment
- 5th Army Motor Regiment
- 5th Army Signal Battalion
- 5th Army Anti-Aircraft Battalion
- 5th Army Anti-Tank Battalion
- 5th Army Infantry Gun Battalion
- 5th Army Guard Battalion
- 1/10 and 1/18 Artillery Battalions (attached)
- The cavalry regiment was the former motorized reconnaissance battalion renamed (but not expanded).

The tank battalions were little changed from the earlier organization. A tank company had two medium platoons, with T-26s, and one light platoon with CV-35s, in each case with motorcycles with sidecars for scouting and liaison duties. The company also had a transport

5th Army Tank Regiment, 1941–2

	Officers	Enlisted	Pistols	Rifles	Light MGs	Armored cars	Renault UE	Light Tanks	T-26	Solo m/cycles	Sidecar m/cycles	Cars	Trucks
Regiment HQ	30	78	24	0	0	0	0	0	0	0		17	
Headquarters Company													
Company HQ	7	28	9	25	0	0	0	0	0	0	3	1	7
Scout Platoon	2	28	5	25	0	9	0	0	0	0	0	0	0
Tank Platoon	4	52	44	12	0	0	5	0	0	1	2	0	0
Rifle Platoon	2	46	8	40	3	0	0	0	0	0	0	0	0
Motorcycle Platoon	2	37	8	31	0	0	0	0	0	12	24	0	0
Signal Company													
Company HQ	6	47	4	0	0	0	0	0	0	0	3	1	5
Two Platoons, each	9	24	14	24	0	0	0	0	0	0	0	1	6
Two Platoons, each	7	54	10	24	0	0	0	0	0	0	0	1	6
Two Tank Battalions, each													
Battalion HQ	23	50	13	0	0	0	0	0	0	0	3	3	0
Headquarters Platoon	5	50	14	22	2	0	0	5	3	0	3	0	2
Scout Platoon	4	32	16	20	0	0	0	5	0	0	1	2	0
Three Tank Companies, each													
Company HQ	10	35	19	0	0	0	0	0	1	0	3	1	4
Light Tank Platoon	3	32	9	0	0	0	0	5	0	0	2	0	0
Two Medium Tank Platoons, each	3	32	9	0	0	0	0	0	3	0	4	0	0
Transport Platoon	2	34	14	10	0	0	0	0	0	0	2	0	26
Transport Company	13	144	43	0	0	0	0	0	0	0	4	0	68
Repair Group	6	103	0	0	0	0	0	0	0	0	0	20	

5th Army Tank Regiment, 1941–2 (continued)

	Officers	Enlisted	Pistols	Rifles	Light MGs	Armored cars	Renault UE	Light Tanks	T-26	Solo m/cycles	Sidecar m/cycles	Cars	Trucks
Engineer Company													
Company HQ	6	40	3	0	0	0	0	0	0	0	2	5	0
Camouflage & Demolition Platoon	2	69	8	0	0	0	0	0	0	0	2	8	
Bridging Platoon	3	66	18	0	0	0	0	0	0	0	2	10	
Road Building Platoon	3	49	7	0	0	0	0	0	0	0	2	5	
Supply Platoon	2	57	8	0	0	0	0	0	0	0	2	10	
Tank Transport Company	14	152	43	0	0	0	0	0	0	0	4	0	68
Two Supply Companies, each													
Company HQ	6	23	8	0	0	0	0	0	0	0	3	3	0
Fuel Platoon	2	48	6	13	0	0	0	0	0	0	2	0	13
Ammunition & Rice Platoon	3	29	5	8	0	0	0	0	0	0	2	0	8
Tank Supply Platoon	2	42	2	0	0	0	0	6	6	0	2	1	4
Repair Group	(454 civilians)		0	0					0		51		

platoon that presumably included trains personnel and trucks (including 16 defined as "Ford V-8 3.5-tons") to carry supplies and the excess personnel from the tank platoons.

The regiment was supported by two supply companies, each with a fuel platoon (four 2.5-ton and eight 4-ton trucks), an ammunition and rice platoon (four 4-ton and four field trucks) and a spare/replacement tank platoon. Also included was a tank transport company with four identical platoons with a total of 68 tank transporter trucks. The regimental signal company had an unusual organization of two small platoons each with a radio truck and four telephone trucks, and two large platoons each with a radio truck, a telephone truck, and four cargo trucks.

The regimental headquarters held a scout platoon (nominally with nine armored cars, although as of early December 1941 none were actually present), a tank platoon (with five light tanks, probably Renault AMR-ZBs, and five armed Renault UEs with trailers), a motorcycle platoon for scouting and liaison, and a rifle platoon for HQ defense.

The 5th Army (less 1st Tank Regiment) advanced into Burma in early 1942, but took few tanks with it. In order to conserve the operating lives of the tanks it was directed that all tanks would move into Burma on the backs of trucks. Unfortunately, there were few trucks that could carry the T-26s, and those that could would exceed the 10-ton weight limits of many of the bridges, so only the CV-35 tankettes and Renault tanks and UE tractors made the trip into Burma.

On 18 March 1942 the armored car company of the cavalry regiment briefly engaged Japanese forces, and later the CV-35s of the 5th, 6th, and 10th Tank Companies reportedly helped the 200th Division in its fierce defense of Toungoo, although Japanese accounts do

The pristine equipment and full uniform, seen here in March 1944
in Yunnan, mark the mechanized force as an elite unit.

not mention tanks. On 25 April the decision was made to pull the armored vehicles out of Burma. On return to China the 1st Tank Regiment was found have only 49 armored vehicles left, although this included all the precious T-26s.

On 1 January 1944 the armored elements of the 5th Army were reorganized into a new 48th Division. This consisted of the 142nd, 143rd, and 144th Regiments and a reconnaissance regiment, along with artillery, engineer, signal, and transport battalions, and a maintenance shop.

Only small elements of the division were committed to combat. In August 1944 the 142nd Regiment dispatched a reinforced platoon (six T-26) from its 3rd Battalion to support the 46th Army in Hunan. It was withdrawn again after losing two tanks on 7 August. Elements of the 2nd Battalion of the 142nd Regiment were sent to IV War Zone in November where at least one group of six T-26s engaged in brief combat.

In July 1945 the division was disbanded and the mechanized units subordinated directly to general headquarters as a reserve.

In the meantime the 2nd Armored Regiment had remained in northwestern China, where it was subordinated to I War Zone by 1945. In July of that year the war zone reported the regiment to have 29 3½-ton tanks, 6 6½-ton tanks, and 18 9½-ton tanks, supported by 59 trucks, probably representative of its strength since 1940.

US-Sponsored Armored Units

The initial order for armored vehicles placed in the US in May 1941, for Marmon-Herrington light tanks, was to have been shipped to China for use there. Even had the deal gone through to completion, however, they would have arrived too late to make it past India.

Stilwell began to plan for Chinese mechanized units to be raised in India in early 1943 and in March his staff arranged for the loan of one Sherman and three Lee tanks from the British for training. In May he directed the formation of two tank battalions at Ramgarh using the Universal carriers that would begin their journey from Australia that month. At the same time an initial allocation of 1,000 light tanks from American production was made.

Tentative tables of organization for a light tank battalion were drafted in March 1943. These provided for a 36-man HQ, three 101-man tank companies, a 105-man reconnaissance company, a 118-man support company, a 79-man service company, and 43 attached medical personnel. A tank company had three platoons, each with three light tanks, along with a mortar platoon with nine Universal-type mortar carriers and four 81mm mortars, and a company HQ with two more light tanks. The reconnaissance company had three scout sections, each with three jeeps, and three reconnaissance sections, each with three Universal carriers. The support company had four 75mm field howitzers towed by Universal carriers. Nevertheless, it was not until 8 August that creation of a tank force, consisting of a provisional tank group HQ and two light battalions, was approved and it was activated at Ramgarh on 1 October 1943.

In the meantime a new set of organization tables had been drafted and approved that covered the group headquarters, the light tank battalion, and the medium tank battalion, although no medium battalions were envisioned for the immediate future. Compared to the earlier proposals, the new light battalion lost the reconnaissance company and the

Tank Group, from August 1943

	Officers	Warrant officers	Sergeants	Corporals	Privates	Pistols	Submachine guns	Rifles	Machine guns	.50-cal. MGs	37mm AT guns	75mm howitzer	Universal carriers	Light tanks	Jeeps	2.5-ton trucks	Wrecker trucks
Group Headquarters																	
Command Section	5	0	0	0	5	5	5	0	0	0	0	0	0	0	3	0	0
Staff & Liaison Section	7	0	2	0	7	7	9	0	0	0	0	0	0	0	3	0	0
Headquarters Company																	
Signal Section	1	0	0	0	0	1	1	0	0	0	0	0	0	0	0	0	0
Maintenance Section	0	2	28	0	0	0	30	0	0	0	0	0	0	2	2	4	0
Supply Section	1	0	7	0	0	1	7	0	0	0	0	0	0	0	1	1	0
Mess Section	0	0	1	0	6	0	7	0	0	0	0	0	0	0	0	1	0
Attached Medical	0	3	0	0	0	0	3	0	0	0	0	0	0	0	1	0	0
Two Light Tank Battalions, each																	
Battalion HQ	15	1	30	0	18	24	22	18	0	0	0	0	5	3	6	1	0
Headquarters Company	13	1	80	19	71	13	100	71	0	5	15	0	27	0	6	9	0
Three Tank Companies, each	19	1	72	0	18	70	22	18	0	0	1	0	6	17	0	4	0
Assault Gun Battery	8	1	49	0	58	8	50	58	0	0	2	4	11	0	1	9	0
Service Company	12	8	55	22	165	12	85	165	3	0	12	0	19	0	5	62	5

Like other armies the Chinese sometimes removed the turrets from their M3 light tanks to make improvised scout and command vehicles, this one seen in Burma.

81mm mortars. It did retain the 75mm howitzers, apparently to supplement the rather poor HE firepower of the light tanks, in what was now rather optimistically termed an assault gun battery. The commander of the tank group and about half the officers and technical NCOs in the group HQ and HQ company were American, while the rest of the personnel were Chinese.

The Provisional Tank Group HQ and 1st Light Tank Battalion (less its assault gun battery) deployed to Ledo in Burma in early January 1944 and the battalion participated in five battles during March to May 1944, losing 18 light tanks in combat. The 2nd Light Tank Battalion (less assault gun battery) moved to Ledo in February but did not take part in combat. In April 12 M4A4 Sherman medium tanks arrived and these formed the "American Medium Tank Platoon" with US Army personnel. In early June, with the monsoon season arriving, the tank units stood down from combat.

In the meantime, expansion had continued at the Ramgarh Training Center. The 3rd Light Tank Battalion completed training in December 1943 and the 4th–7th Light Tank Battalions began forming in mid-1944. There were plenty of M3 light tanks available for these units, but the US had not provided support elements, such as trucks and maintenance sets, for any except the first two battalions. The 3rd Battalion was fitted out using a miscellany of equipment from China Defense Supplies, but the other four battalions were essentially only partially trained and completely immobile at the Ramgarh Training Center. To support the tank force two ordnance heavy maintenance companies were to be formed. Previously a

Tank Group, from July 1944

	Officers	Enlisted	Submachine guns	Rifles	Bren light MG	Water-cooled MGs	.50-cal. MGs	AT rocket launchers	37mm AT Guns	75mm howitzers	105mm howitzers	Light tanks	Medium tanks	Jeeps	¾-ton trucks	Semi-tractor trucks	2.5-ton trucks	Wreckers
Group Headquarters	16	68	59	0	0	0	0	0	0	0	0	2	0	9	0	0	6	0
Two Medium Tank Battalions, each																		
Battalion Headquarters	16	51	22	18	0	5	0	0	0	0	0	0	3	6	5	0	1	0
Headquarters Company	14	170	100	71	0	25	0	0	15	0	0	0	0	6	27	0	9	0
Three Tank Companies, each	20	107	22	18	0	6	0	0	1	0	0	0	17	0	6	0	4	0
Assault Gun Battery	9	115	56	66	0	11	0	0	0	0	4	0	0	1	11	0	9	0
Service Company	20	287	88	207	0	22	5	0	12	0	0	0	0	5	19	0	83	5
attached medical	3	40	0	0	0	0	0	0	0	0	0	0	0	1	1	0	4	0
Light Tank Battalion																		
Battalion Headquarters	16	48	22	18	0	5	0	0	0	0	0	3	0	6	5	0	1	0
Headquarters Company	14	170	100	71	0	25	0	0	15	0	0	0	0	6	27	0	9	0
Three Tank Companies, each	21	90	22	18	0	6	0	0	1	0	0	17	0	0	6	0	4	0
Assault Gun Battery	9	107	50	58	0	11	0	0	0	4	0	0	0	1	11	0	9	0
Service Company	21	277	85	165	0	22	5	0	12	0	0	0	0	5	19	0	62	5
attached medical	3	40	0	0	0	0	0	0	0	0	0	0	0	1	1	0	4	0
Ordnance Heavy Maintenance Company																		
Company Headquarters	1	31	0	26	1	0	0	1	0	0	0	0	0	1	0	0	1	0
Service & Supply Platoon	2	37	0	30	2	0	0	1	0	0	0	0	0	0	3	2	1	0
Armament Platoon	3	55	0	51	0	0	0	1	0	0	0	0	0	0	0	0	0	0
Tank Repair Platoon	3	78	0	69	2	0	0	3	0	0	0	0	0	1	0	0	1	1

provisional American unit had provided maintenance support, this found by scrounging personnel and equipment already in the theater. The 1st Ordnance Heavy Maintenance Company, for the tank group, was officially formed in July 1944, although it did not complete training until January 1945.

Training and reorganization of the tank group took place during July–October 1944. The opportunity was taken to issue a new series of organization tables for the armored force in India/Burma. The Universal carriers had arrived with no spare parts and had been kept running, in decreasing numbers, by cannibalization, and they were eliminated from the force structure.

Light tank of the 1st Provisional Tank Group approaching Myitkyina in December 1944.

The light tank company consisted, as before, of three platoons each with five M3A3 light tanks, each tank commanded by an officer. The company headquarters provided two more tanks for command purposes, a small dismounted scout section (presumably actually intended for headquarters security), and service units.

A light tank battalion had three such companies with fire support provided by an assault gun battery, plus service support elements. The assault gun battery was built around two platoons, each with two 75mm field howitzers drawn by 6 x 6 trucks. The battery held only four SCR-510 short-range FM radios for communications and was presumably used mostly in the direct or semi-direct fire mode. The service company had a recovery platoon with two 10-ton wheeled wreckers to bring back damaged tanks, a maintenance platoon, and a quartermaster (transportation) platoon. The battalion headquarters company included a light AA platoon with five .50-cal. machine guns, a pioneer platoon, and a dismounted reconnaissance platoon (with 37mm AT guns but no transport) that probably served at least as often as a guard platoon for the battalion headquarters.

In late 1944 the 1st and 2nd Battalions were ordered converted to medium tank battalions, while the 3rd Battalion joined the tank group as a light tank battalion. The organization table for a medium tank battalion was published at the same time as that for the light battalion and was almost identical except for the need for one additional crewman per tank. The major changes were the replacement of the 75mm howitzers in the assault gun battery with 105mm howitzers and the addition of cargo trucks to the service company for the additional fuel and larger ammunition to be carried.

In fact, the two battalions never received enough equipment for the conversion. Through most of 1945 the Provisional Tank Group had only 24 M4A4 Shermans, a dozen per battalion. The the rest of its strength comprised 145 M3A3 lights, along with a few dozen more M3A3 without turrets, and 18 half-track personnel carriers.

The commander of the Provisional Tank Group remained an American, as did many of the group staff officers. The American officers were of the opinion that the Chinese line officers were making progress in the combat leadership of armored units, but that the staff officers were "absolutely incapable of coping with supply and logistics" without American supervision and that "any Chinese armored units which are formed will have to be backed up by American supply agencies, and assisted by trained maintenance specialists for several years."[*]

Chinese Shermans, probably training at Ramgahr in 1944.

Back in April 1944 plans had been laid for expansion of the tank force in anticipation of the reopening of the Burma Road. These plans included entire, albeit small, armored divisions. Each of these was envisioned as consisting of about 800 officers and 8,000 enlisted, with a HQ battalion (signal and reconnaissance companies), service battalion, two medium tank battalions, two motorized infantry battalions, an armored artillery battalion,

---

[*] Letter, HQ, First Provisional Tank Group to Chief of Staff, Rear Echelon, Chinese Army in India (Chih Hui Pu), Subject: Requirements of the First Provisional Tank Group for 1945, dated 24 Nov. 1944.

a tank destroyer battalion, and a motorized engineer battalion. As it became apparent that the road would not be opened before the 1944 monsoon hit, however, the plans were quietly dropped.

In late November 1944, as the Tank Group prepared to depart for operations once again, the pendulum swung the other way as General Daniel Sultan, commander of US forces in India–Burma, made clear that he did not need more than three tank battalions, along with supporting troops, in the CAI. There simply was no opportunity in the close-in terrain of Burma for the employment of larger forces. This left the 4th–7th Light Tank Battalions, still with tanks but without trucks and maintenance equipment, and the 2nd Ordnance Heavy Maintenance Company, all still at Ramgarh, surplus to requirements.

On 1 December 1944 HQ US Forces India–Burma recommended that the excess tank units be disbanded. On 8 January 1945 the 4th–6th Light Tank Battalions and the 2nd Ordnance Heavy Maintenance Company began retraining and reorganization as motor transport units. The 7th Light Tank Battalion remained in being at Ramgarh as a training and replacement unit. In the late spring and summer the converted transport units began making their way to China over the Burma Road.

Thus, at the end of the war, the US-sponsored tank units, and the only effective tank units in the Chinese Army, comprised the 1st and 2nd Medium Tank Battalions (nominally with Shermans, actually mostly Stuarts), the 3rd Light Tank Battalion with Stuarts, the tank group headquarters, and the maintenance company, along with the 7th (Training) Tank Battalion.

8

Non-Divisional Artillery

The vast majority of modern artillery was held either as field army (= corps) assets or assigned to the GHQ pool. In general the old weapons held by the various warlord armies when they were incorporated in the KMT force structure were retained by those armies. Weapons acquired after 1932 by the central government were generally formed into separate regiments for the GHQ pool.

Heavy Mortar Units

The 15cm mortar had been popularized in China by the Northeastern Army, which included a four-gun company in each of its infantry brigades. The National Army, on the other hand, chose to concentrate its weapons into four heavy trench mortar regiments, each of two battalions, each with three batteries with four horse-drawn mortars. The strength of a regiment, under the 1942 organization tables, was 2,409.

A 15cm mortar of the 1st Battalion, 2nd Heavy Trench Mortar Regiment, supporting the 348th Infantry Regiment's attack on Tengchong in August 1944.

A mortar of 3rd Company, 1st Battalion, CAI Heavy Mortar Regiment,
being moved by cart near Wakaung, Burma, in April 1944.

The heavy trench mortar regiments appear to have seen little campaigning during the first three or four years of the war, but they were eyed for Y-Force use in late 1942. Three of the regiments, the 1st (24 guns) at Fengchieh in Sichuan, the 2nd (19 guns) at Changsha in Hunan, and the 4th (24 guns) at Shantuping, near Chongqing, were all to be allocated from the GHQ pool for operations across the Salween. In the event, the 4th Regiment was drawn off to the defense of western Hubei in April 1943, leaving only two regiments for the operation. The 2nd Regiment joined the fighting in July 1944, with its 1st Battalion supporting the drive on Tengchong and the 2nd Battalion at Tatung. The regiment was pulled out in October, and replaced by the 2nd Battalion of the 3rd Regiment, which operated around Lungling.

The four regiments served to the end of the war, with the 1st and 2nd Heavy Trench Mortar Regiments under direct command of the MAC, the 3rd under I War Zone and the 4th under VI War Zone for most of 1945. With the end of the war the regiments were redesignated the 15th, 35th, 45th, and 75th Mortar Artillery Regiments, of which only the 35th had a complement of horses to make it mobile.

There was no doubt among the American advisers to the Chinese Army in India that heavy mortars would also prove useful in the Burmese terrain. Nevertheless, a heavy mortar regiment (not to be confused with the heavy trench mortar regiments in China) was not formed as part of the first increment. Even after it was formed the 1st battalion did not move into Burma until the spring of 1944, followed by the 2nd battalion and the regiment HQ a few months later. It moved to China with the opening of the Burma Road and by May 1945 had concentrated in Zhanyi via Kunming. A second regiment was also formed, but was almost immediately converted to a separate infantry regiment to support the Mars task force.

Mortar Regiment Organization

	Officers	Sergeants	Other ranks	Submachine guns	Rifles	Bren guns	60mm mortars	4.2in. mortars	Jeeps	Light trucks	2.5-ton trucks	Hand carts
Heavy Mortar Regiment, CAI, from 21 October 1943												
Regiment HQ & Company	21	26	64	8	67	4	0	0	6	4	7	0
Attached Medical	15	18	60	0	0	0	0	0	6	25	0	0
Special Company												
Company HQ	3	6	18	3	10	0	0	0	1	0	2	0
Three Platoons, each	1	5	45	4	96	3	1	0	0	1	0	0
Three Battalions, each												
Battalion HQ & Company	19	32	98	24	92	8	0	0	7	6	18	0
Transport Company	14	22	211	16	38	8	0	0	4	6	8	0
Three Mortar Companies, each	11	24	164	20	120	6	0	8	2	4	2	27
Heavy Mortar Battalion, CAI, from 1 July 1944												
Battalion HQ & Company	19	32	98	24	92	8	1	0	7	6	18	0
Attached Medical	2	1	9	0	0	0	0	0	1	3	0	0
Transport Company	14	22	211	16	38	8	0	0	4	6	8	0
3 Mortar Companies, each	11	24	164	20	120	6	0	8	2	4	2	27
Heavy Mortar Regiment, from 5 July 1945												
Regiment HQ & Company	13	14	31	6	15	0	0	0	0	0	0	1
Three Battalions, each												
Battalion HQ & Company	15	17	52	19	37	4	0	0	0	0	0	3
Service Company	7	14	255	11	250	0	0	0	0	0	0	48
Three Mortar Companies, each	20	32	226	39	149	12	0	8	0	0	0	31

The regiment consisted of three battalions, each of three companies. Each battalion was provided with sufficient trucks to move the mortars on administrative journeys, but tactical movement was to be on foot, with a company being provided with 8 mortar carts, 16 ammunition carts, and 3 communications carts, all hand-drawn. The company was made up of two four-gun platoons, with 20 rounds per mortar carried in the carts, while the battalion transport company carried another 20 per mortar in trucks.

In practice the battalions often operated independently, and in July 1944 Stilwell recommended that the regimental headquarters and the "special company" (in essence a rifle company for close protection) be disbanded and to that end he had published an organization table for a separate heavy mortar battalion that differed little from the regimented battalion. This, however, was not accepted by the MAC.

Plans were also made for the incorporation of 4.2-inch mortar regiments into the American-sponsored forces in China. The initial 30-division plan included two such regiments, with two more being added when the plan expanded to 60 divisions. In December 1943 the allocation was officially set at two regiments per 30 divisions, paving the way for an eventual expansion to six regiments if and when the revised 90-division plan could be brought to fruition.

In the event, that proved slightly optimistic. Instead, attention was turned to expanding the force to four regiments for service in China on the CAI organization table. The 1st Heavy Mortar Regiment already existed, courtesy of the CAI, and the designation of 2nd Heavy Mortar Regiment was held open in the vain hope that the CAI's former 2nd Regiment might be converted back to mortars. In January 1945 the 1st Heavy Mortar Regiment (less 1st Battalion) was flown to China to form the basis for expansion of the force. The regiment's 1st Battalion remained with the CAI's New 1st Army as an organic element to the end of the war, usually with the simpler designation 1st Heavy Mortar Battalion, on the July 1944 TO&E. To complete the expansion a Heavy Mortar Training Center was set up at Na-chi in Sichuan and received its first students in April 1945.

Doctrine called for the mortars to operate in small packets. A platoon or company, depending on availability, would support an infantry regiment in the advance. Although the personnel were provided by the Chinese Army's chemical service and the regiments were regarded as chemical units, they would be trained primarily for infantry support using HE ammunition, with some training given in the use of smoke. No substantive training in chemical munitions was anticipated in the near term.

The 3rd Heavy Mortar Regiment was officially formed in mid-1945. Classroom and individual training proceeded apace, but unit training was delayed by shortages of equipment and was still ongoing when the war ended. The 4th Heavy Mortar Regiment was to have started unit training in September 1945, while no plans had been agreed to for the 5th Regiment (which would have completed the four-regiment structure, there being no 2nd Regiment). As a result, the only 4.2-inch mortar unit operational at the end of the war was still the capable 1st Heavy Mortar Regiment, veteran of the Burma fighting.

The Chinese high command wanted their 4.2-inch regiments to be semi-motorized formations, following the lines of the 1st Regiment formed by the CAI. This was vetoed by Wedemeyer, however, who insisted that all motor vehicles be used for logistics duties by the central supply service. After six months of wrangling, new organization tables for the heavy mortar regiments were issued in early July 1945. These abolished all motor vehicles from the regiment and instead each mortar company held 8 mortar carts, 16 ammunition carts, and

7 signal carts. These were supplemented by the battalion service company, which consisted of three 84-man platoons, each with 16 ammunition carts each drawn by four men. The regiment's "special company" had also been nominally abolished, but in fact each battalion HQ had been reinforced by a 24-man security platoon so the savings were less than might be supposed. Each company carried 80 rounds per mortar, while the battalion transport company carried a further 20 per mortar. No ammunition was carried at the regimental level. Most of the radios were also withdrawn from the organization table, leaving the unit reliant on field telephones.

Field Army Artillery

Given the paucity of artillery organic to the divisions, the mission of artillery support fell on the artillery battalions and regiments that were supposed to be organic to each army. The old warlord armies often had such an artillery battalion as the fire-support element of each field army. As these units were brought into the fold of the national army they generally retained their organization and equipment, but the national government was certainly not going to provide new artillery to forces with divided loyalties. Thus, such artillery as was available to the field armies was usually old and worn, the Krupp 75mm mountain gun and the Japanese Type 41 mountain gun (and Chinese copies of both) being by far the most common weapons. Although light and portable, both types of weapons had important limitations, the most important inherent one being the use of fixed ammunition. Even more significant was the fact that the warlords, and their KMT successors, seem never to have discarded artillery pieces. Tired weapons that would have been long consigned to the scrap heap in Western armies continued to be carried on the rolls. American observers reported that many of the guns were so worn that maximum range was in fact usually about 3km and that on the rare occasions when they were actually used, it was almost always in the direct fire mode.

A battery command post of the 32nd Army on maneuvers in 1935, showing that this army, at least, knew about indirect fire.

Each field army should have had a battalion of 12 guns organized into three

The 74th Army was one of the few field armies to benefit from the arrival of new artillery in 1938–41. Here, one of its Soviet-made 76mm pack howitzers is in action in Hunan province in early May 1945. Within a few weeks these had been replaced by units with American 75mm pack howitzers.

batteries, but it seems unlikely that more than half the armies were so provided at the outbreak of the war. Through most of the war there were six field armies with two-battalion artillery regiments (2nd, 5th, 16th, 59th, 90th, and 94th), 17 with three-battery battalions (1st, 8th, 22nd, 25th, 30th, 31st, 32nd, 46th, 52nd, 54th, 57th, 68th, 71st, 75th, 99th, New 2nd, and 1st Route), and thirteen with either one or two batteries (7th, 10th, 13th, 15th, 18th, 41st, 55th, 70th, 74th, 77th, 86th, 87th, and 2nd Cavalry).

An inspection of the 54th Army Artillery Battalion by US advisers in January 1943 highlighted such a unit. It was armed with 12 Japanese 75mm pack howitzers, all old and worn, with only one panoramic sight between them. The unit had 13 officers and 435 enlisted, along with 82 old and underfed horses and mules, and these were consolidated into a single battery as only four of the unit's pieces could be made serviceable. Signal equipment consisted of four telephones (with no batteries) a single switchboard and some unserviceable wire. Crew drills were demonstrated in a satisfactory manner, so presumably they could field a single battery for direct-fire missions, although it seems unlikely they would have been risked so close to the front.

A visit to the 52nd Army Artillery Battalion in March 1943 showed it to have 12 75mm Japanese-style mountain guns (four Japanese-made and the balance Chinese-made), all well-worn with excessive play in the traverse mechanism. Optical equipment was scanty and signal equipment consisted of 10 German telephones and about 7km of poor wire useless in rain. The strength of the unit was 34 officers and 390 enlisted, regarded as healthy and vigorous, with 48 horses and 70 mules in good condition. Gun drills were carried out efficiently, including packing and marching, but the conduct of fire by the officers was regarded as poor.

The arrival of artillery pieces in 1937–9 had allowed the formation of a few additional units, although most equipment went into the central GHQ reserve.

An example of a rare premier newly equipped unit was the 2nd Army's artillery regiment. In January 1943 a US inspection team visited the 2nd Army Artillery Regiment and found it to be composed of two battalions with a total of 22 Soviet 76mm pack howitzers and three old Krupp-style pack howitzers. The troops, totaling 170 officers and 2,560 enlisted, were found to be well trained and in good condition. Each howitzer was drawn by four mules hitched to a limber and enough men were available to porter the weapons short distances if required. The weapons were in excellent condition and optical equipment was relatively plentiful. The Achilles heel of the unit was communications, as it had no radios at all and only 73 field telephones (most lacking batteries) and 18km of poor quality wire. Nevertheless, overall it was rated "a mobile and effective artillery unit." Shortly thereafter, however, it was reduced to a battalion in strength and later re-equipped with US 75mm pack howitzers.

A similar field artillery unit was the 71st Army Artillery Battalion, which was given a cursory examination in February 1943. It had 11 75mm Mle. 1897 field guns drawn by horses and mules. Fire control equipment was mostly Soviet and the signal equipment was adequate for wire communications, although it had no radios.

The reluctance to employ artillery was to prove a source of continuing frustration for American advisers all the way through the end of the war. Following the disastrous losses of equipment in 1937 and 1938 and realizing the near impossibility of securing replacements, the Generalissimo issued an order threatening "dire consequences" for any general who lost artillery pieces to the enemy. Given the draconian punishments sometimes meted out it is not surprising that army and group army commanders thereafter tended to keep their artillery well to the rear, out of action and safe from loss. This did, it is true, reduce artillery losses to an almost negligible level after 1942, but it also removed artillery from the equation as far as Chinese capabilities were concerned.

While the enlisted men of these light artillery units were often competent at their crew drills in bringing the guns into and out of action, it proved difficult to retrain the leadership of artillery units that had only used direct fire in the past. When re-equipped from their old Krupp- and Japanese-type pack guns to the more modern US and Soviet weapons the American-led retraining proved inappropriate. The Field Artillery Training Center (FATC) taught use of fire direction centers (FDC) to mass battalion fires. But opportunities for such rarely showed up on the Salween front and battery commanders tended to sit idle awaiting FDC orders rather than exercise initiative and fire their batteries independently. Those who did fire their batteries proved less than efficient in their new role. Frank Dorn, Stilwell's artillery officer, wrote a scathing critique of Y-Force artillery in mid-1944:

Forward observation posts are seldom, if ever, used. Batteries are emplaced so far to the rear in combat that often they are firing at targets between the maximum effective range and the extreme range; resulting in inaccuracy and waste of ammunition.

Batteries have opened fire with no observation of any kind. One battery commander (a graduate of the FATC) when questioned as to his reasons for firing into a blue haze, answered that he was "directing the fire by the sound of the bursts."[*]

Subsequent training improved, and so did the light artillery's performance in 1945.

In addition, shortages of ammunition, both in the absolute sense and in terms of getting it where it was needed, reduced live-fire training of the older weapons to almost nil during the war. American observers visiting the 90th Army in January 1945 noted that the Army's artillery regiment held only 150 rounds for each of its 8 Krupp 75mm field guns and 75 rounds for each of its 12 French 75mm field guns and that "replenishment of this stock is doubtful so no practice with live ammunition is possible." Re-equipping the light artillery with US 75mm pack howitzers, for which ammunition was readily available, if not always where it was needed, helped ameliorate this problem and raised unit efficiency.

GHQ Artillery

Since one of Chiang's goals was to reduce the influence of the warlords in his army, it is not surprising that almost all the artillery procured by the Nationalist government was allocated to separate artillery regiments and brigades directly under GHQ control.

GHQ Light Field Artillery Regiment (Prewar)				
	Officers	*Enlisted*	*Animals*	*Guns*
Regiment HQ	16	37	26	0
Signal Battery				
Battery HQ	3	27	3	0
Regimental Platoon	1	19	23	0
Three Battalion Platoons, each	1	26	26	0
Three Battalions, each				
Battalion HQ	13	45	21	0
Three Batteries, each				
Battery HQ	3	14	9	0
Signal Section	0	14	10	0
Firing Battery	3	42	33	4
Ammunition Section	1	27	27	0
Trains	0	43	58	0

Two artillery brigades of the Fengtian Army were stationed around Beijing when the Japanese invaded Manchuria: the 7th and 8th Field Artillery Brigades, each with one regiment of 75mm Shenyang Type 13 field guns and one of Shenyang 77mm Type 14 field guns. After the fall of Manchuria they were reorganized to yield the 8th Brigade (77mm) and the 4th and 6th Field Artillery Regiments (75mm).

---

[*] Memo for Col Middleton & General Waters, from Brig Gen Dorn, Y-Force Operations Staff, 24 June 1944.

A Bofors 75mm mountain gun of the KMT in full recoil on manuevers about 1933.

The 6th Field Artillery Brigade was formed with two regiments of 75mm Krupp L/29 field guns turned out by the arsenals since the KMT take-over. The NRA also held five separate regiments. The 4th and 6th Regiments were equipped with Shenyang-made 75mm Type 38 field guns, the 8th and 17th Regiments with old 150mm Type 14 howitzers, and the 9th Regiment with one battalion each of 15cm mortars and Krupp field guns.

A light field artillery regiment equipped with 75mm or 77mm guns consisted of a headquarters, signal battery and three battalions, each with three 4-gun batteries. A battery consisted of a headquarters, signal section, firing battery, ammunition section, and trains elements. The heart of the organization was the firing battery, which was divided into two platoons, each of a platoon leader, 2 gun commanders, 10 gun crew, 6 drivers, and 3 mounted messengers. Three pairs of horses, each pair with a driver, pulled a limber/gun combination. The ammunition section was similarly divided into two groups, each with two 6-horse ammunition caissons. Three drivers and three ammunition bearers were assigned to each caisson. In wartime a second ammunition section was to be added to each battery. The trains held seven 3-horse carts for general supplies and 12 more for rations, forage, and kitchen. The battery signal section held a 6-horse wagon with reels for telephone wire and a 3-horse wagon for carrying instruments for use by the reconnaissance and observation party.

Communications, except between the batteries and their command/observation posts, was the responsibility of the regimental signal battery. This had four platoons, one to support the regimental HQ and one for each battalion HQ. The regimental platoon had a 5-man switchboard squad, four 5-man telephone squads, and five 2-man teams each with four pack horses for wire equipment. The battalion platoon was similar but had six telephone squads and a total of 21 pack horses.

The guns were usually pulled by three pairs of horses. In the case of a 77mm gun unit all the personnel rode, three on the gun limber and two stood on steps on the gun shield, and the others rode the caisson and limber. In 75mm units some of the personnel walked. The drivers and the gun commanders were the only members of the battery to carry personal weapons, Mauser-type carbines carried across the back.

In theory the light artillery regiments were capable of indirect fire, but little practice appears to have taken place and direct fire, sometimes with the battery CP/OP actually behind the guns, was the much more common method of engagement.

Even by the early 1930s it was becoming clear that this inventory was rapidly losing its usefulness. The Manchurian pieces were now cut off from their source of spare parts and ammunition, while the others were dated designs approaching obsolescence. Once the KMT had solidified its hold on the country they launched a search for a modern mountain piece that could be moved over China's poor road network while providing increased range and capabilities over the current GHQ artillery park.

Thus, the first purchase of foreign artillery by the KMT was of 72 modern Bofors 75mm L/20 mountain guns. These were formed into the 1st and 2nd Artillery Brigades, each of two regiments, each of two battalions, each of three 3-gun batteries. Although designed for pack use, they were normally pulled by draft horses.

The rising influence of the German military mission seems to have changed priorities. The emphasis would now be on fast-moving, road-bound modern medium artillery capable of delivering crushing firepower. The arrival of new artillery from Germany during 1935–7 permitted the creation of these new units. The 11th and 13th Regiments were each formed with two 12-gun battalions of 105mm leFH18 howitzers. The 10th and 14th Regiments were equipped with 150mm Rheinmetall howitzers (a mixture of L/30 and L/32 weapons), with the former having three battalions and the latter two. Unlike the other GHQ artillery units, these were fully motorized formations, using German trucks and cars.

A horsed field artillery unit on parade early in the war, with Japanese-type 75mm guns.

A massive reorganization of the GHQ artillery force was undertaken after the fall of Nanjing. The surviving Bofors mountain guns were concentrated in the 1st Brigade (with the 1st, 3rd, 5th, and 9th Regiments, all now under strength), while the 2nd Brigade HQ was disbanded. The 8th Brigade HQ was also disbanded and its two regiments, with weapons for which ammunition and parts were unavailable, were made independent units and essentially held back pending the arrival of replacement weapons. The 8th Regiment turned over its old howitzers to fortress troops and awaited the arrival of new weapons, while the 9th Regiment re-equipped with one battalion of Schneider 75mm mountain guns and two of old Krupp-type mountain guns. The 4th and 6th Regiments retained their organization and weapons.

By this time, however, an initially subtle shift in procurement had become pronounced. As Europe rearmed and Germany moved into alliance with Japan it became increasingly hard for China to find foreign suppliers of weapons with excess capacity for exports, particularly in the case of artillery which required specialized factories.

By 1938 China was no longer in the position of being able to choose its artillery suppliers, but instead was reduced to taking whatever anyone was willing to sell off. In practice that meant turning to the Soviet Union, which was disposing of older and non-standard weapons.

The arrival of the Soviet artillery shipments allowed some reconstitution of the artillery arm. The 2nd, 3rd, 7th, 15th, and 20th Regiments each had three battalions,

One of the surviving Bofors mountain guns in about 1942.

A pair of Russian-made 76mm M02/30 field guns in training at the FATC, May 1944.

each with three 4-gun batteries, one of 4.5-inch howitzers and two of 76mm M02/30 field guns. The 4th Artillery Regiment was re-equipped with Soviet 76mm M09 mountain howitzers. At the same time additional brigade headquarters were activated to control the artillery force.

The tremendous losses of equipment around Guangzhou and Wuhan in mid-1938 forced another major reorganization. The new organization was:

- 1st Brigade: 3 mountain regiments, each 2 battalions, each 3 batteries each 3 Bofors 75mm L/20 mountain guns.
- 2nd Brigade: 3 regiments, each 3 battalions mixed Soviet field guns and howitzers
- 3rd Brigade: as 2nd Brigade
- 4th Brigade: 3 regiments, each 3 battalions, each 3 companies of 82mm mortars
- 5th Brigade: 6th Regiment with 3 battalions, each 3 x 4-gun companies of 82mm mortars; 9th Regiment Schneider guns and mountain guns
- 6th Brigade: 12th Regiment of three 3-battery battalions, 17th Regiment of two 3-battery battalions, each battery 3 field howitzers
- 7th Brigade: 10th and 14th Regiments each of three 2-battery battalions, 11th Regiment of three 3-battery battalions, with German howitzers

In May 1940 the brigade headquarters were disbanded except for the 7th, which controlled the motorized heavy artillery force. In June the 7th Brigade HQ was disbanded and

Chinese New-Type Artillery as of 20 March 1942

	Artillery regiments																	Divs & armies	Schools	Total
	1	2	3	4	6	7	8	9	10	11	13	14	15	16	18	19	20			
Mountain gun, 75mm Bofors	19							19											12	50
Mountain gun, 75mm Schneider																		10	3	13
Mountain gun, 76mm Soviet				23														20	1	44
Field gun, 75mm French type					36		36	12						24	35	24		24	8	199
Field gun, 76mm Soviet		11	7			16							16				11	4	4	69
Field howitzer, 105mm German										19	12								2	33
Field howitzer, 4.5-inch (114mm) British		8	4			9							8				8		4	41
Medium howitzer, 150mm German									18		6	18							2	44

A mule-pulled 4.5-inch howitzer in Burma, September 1944.

used to form the new 1st and 2nd Brigade HQs to control the motorized artillery, which was configured into four regiments.

Later that year the Soviets provided 200 75mm French field guns, and these were used to form or re-equip seven artillery regiments. Shortly thereafter, faced with an almost complete cut-off of supplies of artillery weapons, Chiang issued a directive threatening severe consequences (implicitly including death) for any general who lost his artillery. As a result, the generals adopted the simple, if tactically unsatisfactory, response of not using any. Artillery was pulled well behind the lines and out of danger, rarely venturing forth to fire at the enemy, and then only in one- or two-gun detachments.

Not surprisingly, the strength of the GHQ artillery pool, which was mostly now in "new"-type weapons (at least in the sense they had been recently received) partially stabilized until the end of the war.

The influx of US 75mm pack howitzers in 1944–5 was used mainly to form artillery battalions for the sponsored armies and divisions, but a small number were allocated to the GHQ pool. In March 1944 the Ministry of War directed that two 2-battalion regiments, the 7th Artillery Regiment (Soviet equipment) and the 21st Artillery Regiment (old pack guns) would hand in their weapons, which would be sent to east China, and receive US 75mm pack howitzers in their place. This appears to have occurred in mid-year, with the battalions adopting the organization as used in the divisional and army pack howitzer battalions of Y-Force (see section on divisions and armies). These were followed by two more

A 15cm L/30 howitzer of the 10th Regiment
in action at Lungling, September 1944.

regiments, the 29th and 30th, formed by drawing off personnel from reserve artillery units (replacement units with personnel but little or no equipment). The 30th Regiment had two battalions, while the 29th had three, each battalion with the standard 12 75mm M1 pack howitzers. The 30th Regiment entered the FATC in August 1944 and completed its training in January, while the 29th Regiment was instead employed in the Hunan–Guangxi campaign, taking losses that necessitated reorganizing it into two battalions.

In February 1945 it was decided to break up the four US-equipped GHQ pack howitzer regiments, assigning one to each of four armies, with the regimental HQ serving as an army artillery headquarters, and the two battalions assigned to two of the divisions in each army. After the inevitable orders and counter-orders had been issued this was finally brought about in May.

The motorized German-equipped regiments, the 10th, 11th, 13th, and 14th, used this long respite to train. American observers and liaison personnel consistently praised these units for their training and skill. Some of these had been re-equipped to some extent early in the war. The Henschel tractors remained in service, but it proved necessary to add and replace some logistics vehicles. The 1st/10th Artillery (one of three identical battalions in the regiment) in January 1943, for instance, held six 150mm howitzers, 15 Henschel heavy tractors, 12 old-model GMC 2½-ton trucks (model 1937), 10 new versions (model 1941), and 4 Studebaker trucks. It also held 31 field phones, 2 switchboards, and a 15-watt radio. Another heavy howitzer unit, the 3rd/14th Artillery, consisting of a headquarters and three batteries, held 1 command car, 5 observation cars, 9 tractors, 3 caissons, and 15 trucks, all German, to support its nine 150mm howitzers in May 1945. A light howitzer unit, the 2nd/13th Artillery, held six 105mm leFH18 supported by seven Henschel tractors and six 1½-ton trucks, along with 26 field telephones and one 15-watt radio in January 1943.

To the south, for Chinese forces in India, the problem was not a lack of equipment. The original plans for the CAI included a motorized artillery brigade, consisting of a 56-man headquarters, two 1,486-man 105mm howitzer regiments, and a 1,580-man 155mm howitzer regiment. The 72 105mm and 36 155mm howitzers would need no fewer than 438 2½-ton trucks, 260 ½-ton light trucks, and 71 jeeps. The limiting factor, however, was not so much motor transport, of which there was at least a partial stock sitting in India, but manpower. There was also universal agreement that the heavy 155mm howitzers and their prime movers would prove of almost no use in Burma, and while the opinion regarding the 105s was more mixed, it was agreed that the artillery brigade would receive a low priority in calling on the air transports to bring troops in from China. Indeed, the main reason for forming the brigade in the first place appears to have been the simple one that the weapons were sitting there unused, which must have seemed a shame.

The troops of the 4th (Soviet pack howitzers), 5th (old pack howitzers) and 12th Artillery Regiments were flown to India in 1943, handing their equipment over to other units before departure. At the Ramgahr Training Center the first two converted to motorized 105mm regiments and the 12th to a motorized 155mm howitzer regiment.

105mm Howitzer Regiment (motorized), CAI, from 26 April 1943													
	Officers	*Sergeants*	*Other ranks*	*Pistols*	*Rifles*	*Submachine guns*	*Bren guns*	*105mm howitzers*	*Motorcycles*	*Jeeps*	*¾-ton trucks*	*2.5-ton trucks*	*Bicycles*
Regiment Headquarters	17	12	37	6	10	7	0	0	2	1	3	0	1
Three Battalions, each													
Battalion HQ	16	31	82	2	19	15	6	0	0	2	6	6	1
Three Batteries, each	11	23	90	1	15	23	6	4	0	1	3	10	1
Supply Battery	11	23	52	1	13	13	3	0	0	2	3	16	1
Special Service Battery	7	15	51	1	25	9	4	0	0	1	0	6	2

The definitive organization table for a 105mm howitzer regiment was published in April 1943 and called for three battalions each of three howitzer batteries and a supply battery. The battalion carried 2,154 rounds of ammunition for its howitzers in 2½-ton 6 x 6 trucks with 1-ton trailers, two in each battery and nine in the supply battery. The unit was well equipped with radios, with each howitzer battery holding three SCR-194 transceivers, and a battalion HQ three more plus two SCR-284s. Inexplicably, the regiment headquarters had no radios, serving as an administrative echelon.

A new organization table for the 105mm regiment was issued in July 1944 that made only detail changes. As before, the howitzer battery included a signal platoon with a 16-man wire squad and a 6-man radio squad, the latter with three SCR-194 transceivers. The battalion signal platoon was slightly larger, with a 17-man wire squad and a 12-man radio squad, this time with three SCR-194s and two SCR-284s. In this case the regiment was provided with a signal platoon, in the special service battery, with a 16-man wire section, and an 8-man radio section with four SCR-194s and one SCR-284.

The heart of the howitzer battery was its firing group, consisting of two platoons, each of two 9-man gun squads. All the vehicles of the battery, except the headquarters jeep, were held in the trains section for allotment as needed, the normal arrangement including one truck for each howitzer and two for ammunition.

105mm Howitzer Regiment (motorized), CAI, from 1 July 1944	Officers	Enlisted	Pistols	Submachine guns	Rifles	Bren guns	105mm howitzers	Jeeps	Light trucks	2.5-ton trucks
Regiment Headquarters	12	21	6	7	10	0	0	1	2	0
Attached Medical	5	28	0	0	0	0	0	0	2	0
Three Battalions, each										
Battalion HQ										
Command Group	5	6	0	5	2	0	0	2	0	0
Signal Platoon	2	29	0	3	0	0	0	0	0	0
Special Service Platoon	1	24	0	2	2	6	0	0	0	0
Survey Section	3	6	0	1	0	0	0	0	0	0
Liaison Section	1	5	0	1	2	0	0	0	0	0
Trains Section	4	43	0	3	13	0	0	0	12	0
Three Batteries, each										
Battery HQ	3	7	1	7	2	0	0	1	0	0
Signal Platoon	2	20	0	3	1	0	0	0	0	0
Machine Gun Squad	0	5	0	0	0	2	0	0	0	0
Firing Group	3	36	0	3	8	0	4	0	0	0
Ammunition Platoon	1	15	0	1	5	1	0	0	0	0
Trains Section	2	30	0	1	7	3	0	0	4	10
Supply Battery										
Battery HQ	3	11	1	3	4	0	0	2	0	0
Ammunition Platoon	4	18	0	4	0	0	0	0	0	0
Motor Transport Platoon	3	31	0	3	4	0	0	0	4	16
Machine Gun Squad	0	7	0	0	0	3	0	0	0	0
Special Service Section	1	8	0	5	0	0	0	0	0	0
Special Service Battery										
Battery HQ	3	10	1	2	5	0	0	1	0	0
Signal Platoon	2	23	0	3	2	0	0	0	0	0
Special Service Platoon	1	16	0	3	4	4	0	0	0	0
Motor Transport Squad	1	17	0	1	14	0	0	0	0	6

The 155mm regiment was slower in forming and its initial organization table was not finalized until October 1943. It was almost identical to the first 105mm TO&E except for a slight increase in strength to 1,997 of all ranks to man the heavier guns and a change in the mix of trucks to 110 2½-ton models and 45 4-ton models.

The revised and definitive TO&E was published on 1 July 1944. As before, it closely paralleled the organization for the 105mm regiment, the main differences being an enlargement of the gun squad to 11 men and the use of 4-ton 6 x 6 trucks to handle the heavier 155mm M1917A1s.

155mm Howitzer Regiment (motorized), CAI, from 1 July 1944

	Officers	Enlisted	Pistols	Submachine guns	Rifles	Bren guns	155mm howitzers	Jeeps	Light trucks	2.5-ton Trucks	4-ton trucks
Regiment Headquarters	17	49	6	2	10	0	0	1	2	0	0
Attached Medical	5	28	0	0	0	0	0	0	2	0	0
Three Battalions, each											
Battalion HQ											
Command Group	5	6	2	1	2	6	0	0	0	0	0
Signal Platoon	2	29	0	1	0	0	0	0	0	0	0
Special Service Platoon	1	24	0	1	2	6	0	0	0	0	0
Survey Section	3	6	0	1	0	0	0	0	0	0	0
Liaison Section	1	5	0	1	0	0	0	0	0	0	0
Trains Section	4	43	0	2	12	0	0	0	12	6	0
Three Batteries, each											
Battery HQ	3	7	1	7	2	0	0	1	0	0	0
Signal Platoon	2	19	0	5	1	0	0	0	0	0	0
Machine Gun Squad	0	5	0	0	0	2	0	0	0	0	0
Firing Group	3	44	0	7	8	0	4	0	0	0	0
Ammunition Platoon	1	15	0	1	5	1	0	0	0	0	0
Trains Section	2	30	0	2	7	3	0	0	4	5	5
Supply Battery											
Battery HQ	3	11	1	2	5	0	0	2	0	0	0
Ammunition Platoon	4	30	0	4	0	0	0	0	0	0	0
Motor Transport Platoon	3	31	0	1	10	0	0	0	4	13	0
Machine-Gun Squad	0	7	0	0	0	3	0	0	0	0	0
Special Service Section	1	8	0	3	2	0	0	0	0	0	0
Special Service Battery											
Battery HQ	3	10	1	1	5	0	0	1	0	0	0
Signal Platoon	2	24	0	1	2	0	0	0	0	0	0
Special Service Platoon	1	16	0	3	4	4	0	0	0	0	0
Motor Transport Squad	1	17	0	1	14	0	0	0	0	6	0

The skeptics were proven right about the utility of these units in the mountains and jungles of Burma. In the first place, it was clearly unlikely that entire regiments could be deployed and concentrated, so in July 1944 Stilwell recommended disbanding the regimental headquarters. This, of course, would have entailed eliminating a number of relatively high-level officer slots (including a brigadier general for each regiment) and this recommendation was disallowed. In the second place, the road-bound artillery could only be used in a few places. The fact that the 38th Division, alone among the Chinese divisions, already included a truck-drawn 105mm howitzer battalion, satisfied the need for such units for much of the early campaign. In fact, it was not until 17 July 1944 that the 5th Artillery Regiment (105mm) was alerted for possible movement, although it was told to remain for the time being at Ramgarh with the 4th and 12th Regiments.

In the event, it was the 5th Artillery Regiment that stayed at Ramgarh, while 1st Battalion of the 12th Regiment (155mm) and the 4th Regiment (105mm) began leaving for Ledo in late November, although it should be noted that when the towed howitzers were able to get to the battlefield they provided useful service. By January 1945, just before the opening of the Burma Road, the 5th Regiment and all but one battalion of the 12th Regiment were still at Ramgarh, with the 5th Regiment moving to the FATC in February and one battalion of the 12th Regiment shortly thereafter. By mid-1945 the 12th Regiment with its 155mm howitzers had moved to Panhsien.

The motorized artillery regiments were moved into Yunnan on the road fairly quickly, but the NMC had even greater hopes. At the end of January it requested equipment for 24 battalions (8 regiments) of 105mm howitzers and 6 battalions (2 regiments) of 155mm howitzers. It specified that the designations of the regiments were to be the 6th, 9th, 13th, 14th, 15th, 17th, 19th, 20th, 22nd, and 26th. The 105mm battalions were actually those intended for distribution at one per corps, mentioned earlier, but the 155mm units were to be new.

A 155mm howitzer section gets help from a bulldozer on
the Burma Road outside Lashio in 1945.

Once the allocations to the corps had been factored in, the Chinese were left with four regiments of US 105mm howitzers as GHQ troops: the 4th and 5th Regiments from the CAI, a new 10th Artillery Regiment (drawn from HQ and 1st Bn/10th and the 2nd/ and 3rd/14th Regiment), and the 13th Artillery Regiment. Of these, however, only the CAI units were fully operational by the end of the war. Each of the new regiments consisted of a headquarters and three battalions identical to those ordered for the Alpha program corps, described elsewhere.

The additional 155mm howitzers were a different story altogether. Excluding the weapons allocated for the CAI, only 24, instead of 36, M1917 howitzers were authorized under Lend-Lease and, although they were shipped to India in 1944, they were still there in depot storage when the war ended.

Little attention appears to have been paid to the GHQ artillery units that were not selected for re-equipping with US weapons. American aid to the artillery force was an "all-or-nothing" procedure—either a unit fully re-equipped and retrained, or it got nothing. Indeed, it seems likely that none of the legacy units had radios, and all relied on horse transport. The regiments equipped with French 75mm guns (6th, 8th, 16th, 18th, and 19th) appear to have seen little combat.

The Bofors units also saw little combat. Arsenals had the capacity to produce 5,000 rounds per month of ammunition for the weapon, provided raw materials were available, but do not seem to have reached this figure.

Of the provincial forces, only those of Yunnan had a separate artillery unit of note. That government had ordered three battery sets of Schneider SMP 75mm mountain guns in April 1936, these being delivered in mid-1938 to form the 1st Battalion of the Yunnan Provincial Artillery Regiment. Each of the batteries had 150 men, including 10 gun crew and 9 animal handlers in each of the four gun sections. The battery ammunition section had 20 animal handlers and 22 ammunition handlers. Two other battalions were formed using old Krupp 75mm mountain guns. Each battalion had three batteries each of four guns. Each battalion was provided with 12 field telephones and 10km of single-strand wire on reels, optical equipment, and sufficient pack animals, but no radios. Also included in the regiment was a mortar battery with four mule-drawn Brandt 120mm weapons. Although relatively well equipped they were not considered very well trained by American observers.

Anti-Tank Artillery

There were no dedicated anti-tank guns in the Chinese forces before the arrival of the German military mission. The initial purchases of Rheinmetall L/50 and Pak36 anti-tank guns in 1934–6 were used to form an infantry anti-tank training corps (three battalions, each four companies, each two 2-gun platoons), an anti-tank battalion of four companies, and a 6-gun divisional AT company for the 4th and 88th Divisions.

The use of tanks in the initial fighting persuaded the Chinese of the need for more such weapons, a need exacerbated by the loss of 46 of the Rheinmetall weapons in the early stages of the war. A large and diversified acquisition program launched in 1937 with deliveries in 1938 made it possible to raise new units, again, mostly for the GHQ reserve. The one exception was the 16 anti-tank companies raised with Bohler 47mm combination infantry/ AT guns (at six guns per company) for selected divisions.

The new units were generally homogenous as regards equipment in order to simplify training and logistics. Three regiments were formed with new equipment and one with the survivors of the German guns:

- 51st Artillery Regiment: five battalions, totaling 28 companies each with six 20mm Madsen AT guns.
- 52nd Artillery Regiment: eight companies each with four 37mm German AT guns, plus four companies awaiting delivery of Chinese 37mm Type 30 guns.
- 53rd Artillery Regiment: three battalions, each with four 6-gun companies of Soviet 37mm obr. 30 AT guns.
- 54th Artillery Regiment: three battalions, each with four 4-gun companies of Soviet 45mm AT guns.

This organization was rated as completed in September 1938, although Madsen deliveries would not be finished for another year. Two more regiments were formed in September 1939:

- 55th & 56th Artillery Regiments, each of six battalions each with four 6-gun companies of old 37mm Soviet Gruson and Rosenberg guns.

Shortly thereafter three more 24-gun battalions were added to each of the 55th and 56th Regiments, this time equipped with Soviet 37mm obr. 30 AT guns. Three more similar battalions were formed for school purposes.

In 1941 the forces were realigned to provide one regiment to each war zone, apparently by forming two new regiments out of existing assets. In 1942 the anti-tank force was again realigned. Four of the regiments were disbanded (including the 51st) and their companies assigned directly to armies and divisions, yielding a total of 161 companies distributed at that level. This left three regiments plus the three school battalions available at the GHQ level. Three further battalions were formed under the CAI and equipped with US 37mm guns for service in Burma.

Probably typical of the anti-tank distribution late in the war was the I War Zone in 1945, which reported a total of 89 AT guns, of which 8 were in Inner Mongolia (and thus unavailable for service), and 12 were old Russian Gruson/Rosenberg guns, worn out and with only 500 rounds of ammunition available between them.

The distribution of the weapons was:

- 52nd Anti-Tank Regiment
- 1st–6th, 10th & 11th Companies, each 4 x 37mm Pak 36
- 7th & 8th Companies, no AT weapons, serving as infantry
- 12th Company, 4 Chinese 37mm Type 30
- AT Company of the 1st Army: 4 Russian 37mm obr. 30
- 1st, 2nd, & 3rd AT companies of the 90th Army: each 4 Gruson/ Rosenberg 37mm
- AT companies of the 1st, 78th, & 167th Divisions: each 4 Bohler 47mm
- AT company of the Reserve 1st, 28th, 53rd, & 61st Divisions: each 4 Russian 37mm obr. 30

- AT company of the Temporary 59th Division: 5 unknown-type 47mm
- AT company of the New 43rd Division: 4 Chinese 37mm Type 30

Reshuffling of forces continued, so that in July 1945 the NRA held the 51st, 52nd, 54th, and 57th Anti-Tank Regiments, a line-up that remained past the end of the war.

Anti-Aircraft Artillery

The first GHQ anti-aircraft unit of the Nationalist Army was actually an outgrowth of the AA battalion of the "Bodyguard Brigade" of the Manchurian "Young Marshal." The regiment was formed in 1932–3 by concentrating almost all the AA machine guns in north China and had a strength of 1,250 men in a headquarters and three battalions. Each battalion had four batteries, each of a captain, two lieutenants, a first sergeant, and 100 enlisted, with four heavy AA machine guns. In two of the battalions the guns were twin-barrel Hotchkiss 13.2mm weapons, in the third battalion there were three batteries with Vickers .5-inch Type D machine guns and one battery with single-barrel 13.2mm Hotchkiss. Surprisingly, there were no enlisted men assigned to the battalion or regiment headquarters, which consisted of three and 16 officers respectively. In actual operations signal personnel were to be assigned from GHQ. The regiment was provided with 47 new 1½ ton Ford trucks, each to carry one gun and crew and ammunition.

A gun crewman drives the spades on a 75mm Bofors AA gun outside Nanjing.

The Solothurn S5-100, seen here with a German-equipped unit early in the war, remained the mainstay of Chinese low-level air defense for units in the field.

The Shanghai incident of 1932 brought home the need for high-altitude defense. A contract was quickly placed with Bofors for 75mm guns and ancillary equipment by the central government and these were used to form six 4-gun batteries, most of them deployed for the defense of Nanjing, under the command of the Anti-Aircraft School.

The Guangdong provincial government also purchased a battalion set of Vickers 75mm AA guns and formed these into a unit supported by searchlights and AA machine guns.

Low-level air defense of the field forces came back to the fore with input from the German military mission. The central government had earlier purchased 20mm Oerlikon Modell S guns, but these were more commonly used as infantry support weapons. In 1936 a major order was placed with Germany for 60 37mm Flak 18 guns and 120 Solothurn S5 guns.

With these, two light anti-aircraft regiments were formed in 1937. The 41st Artillery Regiment consisted of 18 batteries under 5 battalion HQs and manned the 60 37mm guns and an unspecified number of 20mm guns. The organization is not clear, but official histories refer to the 6th (37mm) and 15th (20mm) batteries participating in the defense of Nanchang in March 1938. Earlier the regiment had been involved in the defense of Shanghai, where it lost heavily. The 42nd Artillery Regiment had 16 batteries formed into 5 battalions and manned 108 Solothurn guns.

The heavy anti-aircraft forces received a boost with the arrival of the 20 76mm M1931 AA guns from the Soviet Union in 1938. These were formed into a battalion of five batteries, complete with all the equipment of a Soviet AA regiment (which had five batteries). The battalion was joined by the survivors of the Bofors 75mm guns to form the 45th Artillery Regiment of 10 batteries in three battalions. Two batteries of 76mm guns were lost in the defense of Guangzhou in 1938.

Anti-Aircraft Battalion, CAI, from October 1943										
	Officers	*Sergeants*	*Other ranks*	*Pistols*	*Submachine guns*	*Rifles*	*.50-cal. machine guns*	*Draft animals*	*Riding animals*	*Carts*	*Jeeps*
Battalion Headquarters	15	15	42	6	15	30	0	14	5	6	3
Three Companies, each	12	20	122	0	15	100	16	26	0	13	0

Under the tutelage of Soviet advisers a battery was deployed with a gun at each corner of a 70-meter square. In the center of each battery position was a 2-meter height finder operated by two men, a fire control computer with its crew of five, and a generator.

Following the Wuhan campaign the remaining Wuhan garrison AA troops were consolidated into an independent battalion with 14 light (20mm and 40mm) guns under the AA School.

In 1941 the AA units in Shanxi and the independent battalion were consolidated to form the 44th Artillery Regiment of 12 batteries in three battalions. The arrival of the .50-cal. AA machine guns from the USA in late 1941 allowed the formation of two more regiments, the 48th in Sichuan and Hubei, and the 49th along the Yunnan–Burma Road. Each of these consisted of three battalions each of three batteries. Each battalion had an authorized strength of 855, but they were usually under strength, the 3rd Battalion of the 49th Regiment reporting 38 officers and 420 enlisted in August 1944. The 49th was incorporated into Y-Force in 1943 and supported the Salween Offensive in 1944, albeit from Yunnan.

In 1942 20 light AA batteries with 13.2mm and 20mm weapons were removed from the AA command and assigned to selected field divisions.

Chiang had asked the Americans for substantial quantities of 40mm and 90mm AA guns and they reluctantly agreed. The reluctance flowed from the recognition that few 40mm and no 90mm guns would be useful in Burma, and that by the time they could be brought to China over the Burma Road Japanese air power would presumably have been much reduced. US misgivings notwithstanding, the Chinese pressed ahead and formed three anti-aircraft regiments to use these weapons, the 45th, 46th, and 47th. The weapons, however, remained in India until the end of the war, and although some members of the three regiments received training there, the units were never so equipped. At least some of these units manned extemporized weapons, as evidenced by a request from the 3rd Battery of the 46th Regiment in August 1944 for ammunition for their old British 3-inch naval AA guns manufactured in 1916 and 1919, these presumably having been removed from decommissioned Chinese naval vessels. A notation hand-written by a member of the US staff recommended, "suggest reply (in a few weeks) that this ammo is out of manufacture—as it undoubtedly is. The damned things only shoot 9,000' and belong properly in a museum." The Chinese were dutifully informed that a diligent search had turned up no ammunition.

The one American-trained and equipped anti-aircraft unit was the AA battalion of the Chinese Army in India. The battalion was built around three companies, each of four platoons, each of which, in turn, had two 12-man sections with two .50-cal. water-cooled machine guns. The initial organization table, issued in October 1943, provided carts to carry the machine guns and their ammunition. A later revision, of July 1944, eliminated the carts and substituted pack animals for draft animals one-for-one, without making any other substantive changes in the organization. The battalion moved into Burma in mid-1943, and spent the rest of the year and 1944 scattered along the Hukawng Valley protecting the supply route. When the Burma Road was reopened it moved into Yunnan.

9

Chinese Army in India

Chiang had given tentative approval to the training of Chinese troops in India to support operations in Burma in early April 1942. The defeat in Burma cast this into a wholly different light, however. Much of the 5th Army retreated into India and by mid-1942 the Chinese in India totaled about 5,000 from the 38th Division, 2,500 from the 22nd Division, and 12,000 from 5th Army HQ troops.

With Stilwell in command, the plan originally was to form these personnel into separate battalions of artillery and heavy weapons infantry. They would follow the British forces in their reconquest of Burma in the winter of 1942/3, then move into Yunnan to provide heavy weapons support for Y-Force. It quickly became clear, however, that the British were in no position to seize Burma by themselves, so the plan was recast as the creation of a full corps of two divisions plus supporting troops. To this end a training area at Ramgarh was acquired and rebuilding of the forces began. Fortunately, the cargo planes flying the Hump into China often returned empty, so it was possible to airlift Chinese troops (many of whom had never even seen an airplane before) into India, and the first batch of 4,000 arrived in October 1942. Shortly thereafter they were flying 400 troops a day into India.

A trainee learns the sights of the 75mm pack howitzer in India in late 1942.

Infantry Regiment, Chinese Army in India, from 16 March 1943

	Officers	Warrant officers	Enlisted	Pistols	Submachine guns	Rifles	Bren light MGs	Medium MGs	60mm mortars	81mm mortars	37mm AT guns	Riding animals	Pack animals	Draft animals	Carts	Jeeps	Trucks	Bicycles
Regiment Headquarters	7	1	18	7	3	13	0	0	0	0	0	3	0	0	0	2	0	3
Special Service Platoon	1	0	38	0	7	29	2	0	0	0	0	0	0	0	0	3	0	0
Signal Platoon	2	0	47	0	7	24	0	0	0	0	0	0	6	0	0	0	0	1
Three Infantry Battalions, each																		
Battalion HQ	4	0	11	4	0	10	0	0	0	0	0	1	0	0	0	2	1	1
Three Rifle Companies, each	4	1	171	0	17	134	9	0	6	0	0	0	0	0	0	0	0	1
Machine Gun Company	6	1	102	0	15	53	0	8	0	0	0	1	16	0	0	0	0	1
Mortar Company	8	1	169	1	20	75	0	0	0	12	0	5	0	24	12	0	0	1
Anti-Tank Company	6	1	127	0	37	59	0	0	0	0	8	0	0	0	0	18	8	0
Pack Transport Company	5	1	151	0	6	24	0	0	0	0	0	9	150	0	0	0	0	0
Porter Transport Company	6	2	135	0	19	69	0	0	0	0	0	0	0	0	0	0	0	0
Medical & Veterinary	9	1	79	0	0	0	0	0	0	0	0	1	0	4	2	0	0	0

The question of proper organization arose almost immediately. Initial planning worked on the assumption of 11,500 men for each of the two divisions, plus 9,500 men for GHQ troops. Draft guidance was provided by Stilwell's staff in October, specifying that each division should consist of three 2,600-man infantry regiments, three 600-man 75mm pack howitzer battalions, a 130-man reconnaissance company and service troops for a total of 11,500 men. An infantry regiment would have three infantry battalions, an anti-tank company, and a pack transport company, while an infantry battalion would have three rifle companies and a heavy weapons company. The GHQ troops were to consist of an artillery brigade of two motorized regiments of 105mm howitzers and one of 155mm howitzers, an MP battalion, two small engineer regiments, and service troops.

By December the two divisions were almost up to strength and final work on the applicable organization tables had begun. The official tables were published on 16 March 1943 and generally followed the outline set up the prior fall.

Two important characteristics that had to be considered were the terrain and availability of resources. Northern Burma, where this force would operate, had no good roads and few decent paths, so motor transport of heavy weapons was out of the question. As to resources, their constraints were the opposite of those applying to their colleagues in China: they had an almost limitless supply of weapons available as a result of delays in moving these from India into China, but few men.

The most striking feature of the new division was to be found in its lowest units, in particular the rifle platoon. The platoon consisted of three rifle sections, each of a sergeant, a corporal and 10 privates, and a mortar section of a sergeant and 10 privates. Each man in the rifle section was armed with an M1917 .30-cal. rifle except one who carried the .303-cal. Bren light machine gun. The mortar section had two 4-man teams, each with a 60mm mortar, along with a total of nine rifles. The provision of two light mortars (with a range of almost 1,800 meters) for a rifle platoon was a unique feature not duplicated in any other army of the time.

The platoon headquarters consisted of the platoon leader, platoon sergeant (a new feature to Chinese organization), and two messengers. The rifle platoon included three Thompson submachine guns, issued not to the rifle sections, but to the platoon sergeant and the two messengers. The rifle company had three such platoons, plus a headquarters with a captain, a lieutenant, a warrant officer (with the role the US Army assigned the first sergeant), and 21 enlisted. Those included a 10-man mess section, two medics, and four messengers. Once again, Thompson submachine guns were issued liberally to non-line personnel, eight weapons for the messengers, buglers, and so on.

The machine-gun company was built around four line platoons, each with two squads. A squad consisted of a sergeant, a corporal, and six privates, armed with five rifles and an M1917A1 water-cooled .30-cal. machine gun. The squad was provided with a mule for ammunition. The platoon HQ consisted simply of the platoon leader, platoon sergeant, and a messenger, the last armed with a Thompson. Also included in the company were an ammunition section of 10 men with eight pack mules, and a headquarters section.

The infantry regiment had two fire-support elements, a mortar company, and an anti-tank company. The mortar company had three platoons each of two sections. The section had a sergeant, two corporal squad leaders, six gun crew, six ammunition bearers, four drivers with two pack mules, and two 81mm mortars. In addition to two mortar sections, the mortar platoon had an eight-man ammunition section with four pack animals.

Infantry Division, Chinese Army in India, from 16 March 1943

	Officers	Warrant officers	Enlisted	Submachine guns	Rifles	Bren light MGs	Medium MGs	60mm mortars	81mm mortars	37mm AT guns	75mm pack how.	Riding animals	Pack animals	Draft animals	Carts	Jeeps	Trucks	Bicycles
Division Headquarters	58	13	137	8	78	0	0	0	0	0	0	8	22	14	7	9	16	7
Signal Battalion																		
Battalion HQ	8	1	29	5	10	0	0	0	0	0	0	2	0	4	2	1	3	0
Radio Company	22	5	104	10	44	0	0	0	0	0	0	3	0	6	0	3	0	6
Wire Company	22	5	153	0	63	0	0	0	0	0	0	3	0	6	0	0	0	9
Special Service Company	5	1	227	18	199	8	0	0	0	0	0	0	0	0	0	2	6	2
Reconnaissance Company	7	1	170	55	93	18	0	0	0	0	0	30	0	0	0	16	5	77
Three Infantry Regiments, each	110	19	2,642	297	1,688	83	24	54	12	8	0	24	204	28	14	29	11	21
Two Pack Artillery Battalions, each																		
Battalion HQ	17	1	89	8	35	4	0	0	0	0	0	8	4	8	4	0	0	2
Three Batteries, each	8	1	155	10	79	6	0	0	0	0	4	6	59	28	14	0	0	1
Service Battery	7	1	102	15	77	4	0	0	0	0	0	4	18	60	30	0	0	1
Engineer Battalion																		
Battalion HQ	8	1	39	4	33	0	0	0	0	0	0	0	0	0	0	0	1	1
Three Engineer Companies, each	3	3	147	10	123	8	0	0	0	0	0	0	0	0	0	1	1	1
Transportation Company	4	1	118	5	112	0	0	0	0	0	0	10	0	40	20	4	1	1

Infantry Division, Chinese Army in India, from 16 March 1943 (continued)

	Officers	Warrant officers	Enlisted	Submachine guns	Rifles	Bren Light MGs	Medium MGs	60mm mortars	81mm mortars	37mm AT guns	75mm pack how.	Riding animals	Pack animals	Draft animals	Carts	Jeeps	Trucks	Bicycles
Transport Battalion																		
Battalion HQ	8	0	36	2	9	0	0	0	0	0	0	5	0	0	0	0	0	2
Pack Company	6	2	137	19	69	0	0	0	0	0	0	9	150	0	0	0	0	2
Draft Company	6	1	65	13	34	0	0	0	0	0	0	6	0	52	26	0	0	2
Motor Company	3	1	71	28	34	2	0	0	0	0	0	0	0	0	0	2	29	0
Gas Platoon	2	4	38	6	30	0	0	0	0	0	0	0	0	0	0	0	3	2
Medical Platoon	10	1	126	3	3	0	0	0	0	0	0	2	0	12	6	0	0	1
Veterinary Platoon	2	1	24	0	9	0	0	0	0	0	0	1	0	2	1	0	0	1
Field Hospital	11	2	72	3	3	0	0	0	0	0	0	2	0	12	6	0	4	1

A member of the pack transport company of the 64th Infantry Regiment in May 1944.

The anti-tank company was, strangely, an entirely motorized formation. It consisted of four platoons, each of two sections, with each section provided with a 37mm M3A1 anti-tank gun and two ¼-ton jeeps. Once in the Burma jungles it proved difficult to keep the anti-tank guns apace with the infantry.

Resupply of the regiment was handled by two transport companies. One was a porter unit with four platoons, each of three sections, each with a corporal, six porters, and three cooks. The other was a pack transport company with 150 pack mules.

Radio signal assets for the regiment were held by the regimental signal platoon, which provided five SCR-284 portable transceivers for establishing the regiment/battalion net, eight SCR-195 backpack radios for distribution as needed by the tactical plan, and a single SCR-179 pack set. Headquarters guards were provided by the special service platoon.

The CAI infantry regiment was an unusual organization, largely due to its ability to throw HE firepower. The presence of no fewer than 54 60mm mortars, supplemented by 12 81mm mortars, was presumably a reaction to an anticipated inability of the artillery to keep up with infantry moving through the Burmese jungle-covered mountains. The presence of the anti-tank company is harder to explain, since it was an entirely motorized formation and even the redoubtable jeep would have had to await the construction of at least rough roads before the guns could be brought into action.

The division controlled three such infantry regiments, two pack artillery battalions and supporting troops. Each artillery battalion was equipped with 12 US 75mm pack howitzers carried on pack mules, with horse-drawn carts providing ammunition resupply.

A battalion had 14 SCR-194 backpack radios for communication between observers and gun positions, and an SCR-284 base radio at the battalion. In addition, the 38th Division was allotted a battalion of 105mm howitzers drawn by 2½ ton trucks, three batteries each of four guns, from July 1943.

The division reconnaissance company was built around two 33-man bicycle platoons, a 41-man jeep platoon, and a 30-man mounted platoon. Each of the bicycle platoons consisted of four 7-man squads (2 Thompsons and 5 rifles) plus a jeep with a Bren gun. The jeep platoon had three squads each with three jeeps and a motorcycle and armed with six rifles, three Thompsons, and four Bren guns. The mounted platoon had four squads each of seven men on riding horses, armed with six rifles and a Bren gun. It was provided with five SCR-203 radios that were designed to clamp onto a Phillips mule pack saddle but here also carried in jeeps, with a voice range of 8km and a CW range of 50km. The divisional transport battalion provided 150 pack mules, 26 carts, and 24 2½-ton trucks.

Although light in artillery support by world standards, the CAI division was designed specifically to operate in extremely rough terrain where mobility was difficult and long-range observation/target acquisition rare. Instead, reliance was placed primarily on 60mm mortars decentralized to the lowest possible level.

The pack transport company of the 22nd Division near Shadazup, Burma, in May 1944.

Army Troops, Chinese Army in India, from November 1943

	Officers	Warrant officers	Enlisted	Submachine guns	Rifles	Bren Light MGs	.50-cal. AA MGs	60mm mortars	155mm howitzers	Riding animals	Pack animals	Draft animals	Carts	Jeeps	Trucks	Bicycles
Army Headquarters	71	11	107	20	50	0	0	0	0	38	0	0	0	3	15	5
Signal Battalion																
Battalion HQ	11	1	32	5	30	0	0	0	0	6	0	4	2	1	3	?
Radio Company	24	2	123	5	75	0	0	0	0	6		8	4	2	3	?
Wire Company	9	5	120	5	75	0	0	0	0	7		8	4	2	3	?
Repair Section	4	0	10	0	0	0	0	0	0	0	0	0	0	1	0	0
Special Service Battalion																
Battalion HQ	8	1	19	5	7	0	0	0	0	4	0	0	0	0	4	2
Four Companies, each	5	1	154	18	93	9	0	6	0	0	0	0	0	0	0	2
Field Artillery Battalion	49	14	576	70	101	27	0	0	12	0	0	0	0	8	76	6
Anti-Aircraft Battalion																
Battalion HQ	14	1	57	15	30	0	0	0	0	5	0	12	6	3	0	0
Three Batteries, each	10	2	142	20	110	0	16	0	0	0	0	28	14	0	0	0
Military Police Battalion																
Battalion HQ	6	3	18	18	0	0	0	0	0	0	0	0	0	2	7	6
Attached signal section	5	0	8	8	0	0	0	0	0	0	0	0	0	0	0	0
Four Companies, each	5	1	120	22	98	4	0	0	0	0	0	0	0	1	1	4

Army Troops, Chinese Army in India, from November 1943 (continued)

	Officers	Warrant officers	Enlisted	Submachine guns	Rifles	Bren light MGs	.50-cal. AA MGs	60mm mortars	155mm howitzers	Riding animals	Pack animals	Draft animals	Carts	Jeeps	Trucks	Bicycles
Engineer Regiment																
Regiment HQ	24	2	30	6	0	0	0	0	0	0	0	0	0	3	2	0
Special Company	5	4	90	18	15	4	0	0	0	0	0	0	0	1	0	0
Transport Company	10	1	90	6	25	4	0	0	0	0	0	0	0	2	2	0
Railway Platoon	4	0	48	12	10	4	0	0	0	0	0	0	0	0	0	0
Two Battalions, each	25	13	379	21	250	18	0	0	0	0	0	0	0	6	4	0
Draft Transport Regiment																
Regiment HQ	15	0	59	5	1	0	0	0	0	8	0	4	2	0	0	0
Three Battalions, each																
Battalion HQ	7	0	17	6	1	0	0	0	0	7	0	4	2	0	0	0
Three Companies, each	5	1	94	13	44	0	0	0	0	6	0	76	38	0	0	0
Army HQ detail	0	0	10	0	0	0	0	0	0	12	8	0	0	0	0	0
Remount Company	6	0	162	0	0	0	0	0	0	0	0	4	2	0	0	0
Motor Transport Regt	122	13	1,029	269	328	88	0	0	0	0	0	0	0	17	383	10
Ordnance Battalion	42	25	594	2	33	14	0	0	0	0	0	0	0	9	44	5
Medical & Vet. Services	27	0	237	0	0	0	0	0	0	10	48	0	0	0	7	10

To coordinate the actions of the two divisions in the field the New 1st Army was formed, with a headquarters organization drawn up in July 1943. Unlike other Chinese armies, however, it had no fixed composition immediately. Initial planning assumed that the corps HQ and the CAI HQ would be the same unit, and so envisioned including an artillery brigade, an AA battalion, engineer battalion, two transport regiments, and a variety of other units. This, however, was not to be.

Some elements of the division organization were changed almost immediately. It was clear that the 37mm anti-tank guns would not be able to keep up with the line elements and in early July the 38th Division received an allocation of anti-tank rifles. Later that month the commander of the New 1st Army requested permission to organize an anti-tank platoon in each infantry battalion. Each 49-man platoon was to consist of four squads, each of a sergeant, a corporal, and eight privates, armed with three rifles, a Thompson (for the squad leader), and a Boys AT rifle. Permission was granted, but on the condition that the troops had to be found from within the current regimental strength. In October 12 bazookas were also authorized for each infantry regiment. Once again, no additional manpower would be provided and it was left to the regimental commanders to decide how to distribute these weapons. The 22nd Division formed a bazooka platoon for each battalion, similar to the anti-tank rifle platoon, but it is not clear if other divisions followed suit.

On 22 November a new organization table was issued for the divisional artillery battalion. A significant change was that it authorized so-called "Marine Hitches" that enabled the 75mm howitzers to be towed draft-style, rather than having to be pack carried, where terrain permitted. Another equipment change was that the SCR-195 backpack radios were replaced by SCR-194s, a nearly identical unit but operating in the artillery frequency band.

Divisional Pack Artillery Battalion, CAI, from 22 November 1943												
	Officers	Warrant officers	Enlisted	Submachine guns	Rifles	Bren light MGs	75mm pack howitzers	Riding animals	Pack animals	Draft animals	Carts	Jeeps
Battalion HQ	20	0	113	10	28	3	0	8	12	6	3	1
Three Batteries, each	8	1	163	12	50	6	4	6	65	20	10	0
Service Battery	6	2	124	17	34	4	0	4	18	60	30	0
Attached Medical & Veterinary	3	0	15	2	0	0	0	2	0	4	2	0

At the same time the organization of a field army was finally decided on. The fire-support element was much reduced compared to earlier thinking, consisting only of a single three-battery battalion of 155mm howitzers, moved by 4-ton 6 x 6 and 2½-ton 6 x 6 trucks. The battalion was well supplied with communications gear, having 14 SCR-610 vehicular radios and two SCR-694 base radios. Unfortunately, this meant that the forward observers needed their jeeps in order to call for fire unless they could borrow assets from the supported unit.

The other combat unit was a light anti-aircraft battalion with three batteries of water-cooled .50-cal. machine guns on high-angle mounts. The guns were carried on horse-drawn carts. The battalion had only a single SCR-583 radio for communications, so early warning would have been out of the question most of the time.

The army also had an engineer regiment, although the lack of transport to carry heavy equipment rendered it, in actuality, a labor unit. A military police battalion of four companies regulated traffic and provided some measure of rear area security.[*]

For transport the army had a motor transport regiment with 349 2½-ton LWB 6 x 6 cargo trucks to carry supplies forward to drop points, and a draft transport regiment with 342 carts to move it forward from there.

The CAI headquarters had proposed adding a reconnaissance battalion to the army troops, with two companies similar to those in the division, but that had not been acted on.

In the meantime, the flow of personnel from China via returning aircraft had continued and in July 1943 it had proven possible to raise the New 30th Division at Ramgarh, bringing the New 1st Army up to full three-division configuration, although the division did not rise to full strength until early 1944, and even then it was formed with only a single artillery battalion, a pack 75mm unit.

The organization of the New 1st Army actually proved somewhat flexible. Stilwell had opposed creation of the army, arguing that the CAI headquarters should function as the command element for the army in India, but Chinese authorities had insisted otherwise, leading to the situation where, for 1943, there were two headquarters elements to command two operational divisions plus a pool of smaller units. The CAI was the superior headquarters and controlled the New 1st Army HQ and all GHQ elements, and attached those units to the army headquarters as it saw fit. The result was that the dividing line between the GHQ troops of the CAI and the army troops of the New 1st Army was blurred and it was not always clear where a particular unit belonged in the chain of command.

As the airlift efforts picked up momentum it proved possible to move the troops of two more divisions to India, the 14th Division in April 1944 and the 50th Division the next month. These were flown in as complete units, personnel but no equipment, reorganized and re-equipped in India. They did not, however, pass through the Ramgarh Training Center the way the three earlier divisions had and were not provided with artillery battalions.

The two new divisions were equipped and ready for operations later in the year, but the crisis in China brought things full circle. On 30 November 1944 Wedemeyer and Chiang agreed that two of the CAI's divisions had to be hurried back to China by air. The New 6th Army HQ was formed and took over the veteran 22nd Division and the newly arrived 14th Division in December. The HQ (still incomplete) and two divisions were airlifted back over the Hump to China that month.

In the meantime proposals for changes in the TO&Es had been percolating through the chain of command. In January 1944 these were summarized as follows:

- The bicycles in the divisional reconnaissance company were universally regarded as useless in the jungle. The two divisions in combat wanted to see the two platoons re-equipped with light tanks or, failing that, Universal carriers. American staff simply wanted the bicycles removed so that one

---

[*] Through the end of 1943 the MP battalion adopted the personnel strength of the organization of a separate battalion in China, with four 133-man companies, here each armed with 9 Bren guns and 13 submachine guns.

platoon could function as a dismounted scout unit and the other as an intelligence unit.

- Both divisions wanted to add two privates to each rifle squad as ammunition carriers for the Bren gun and that two ammunition bearers be assigned to each 60mm mortar team.
- Both divisions wanted additional personnel to form a bazooka platoon for each infantry regiment, this to consist of a headquarters and four 12-man squads, with a total of 57 men, 6 Thompsons, 24 rifles, and 4 bazookas. They also wanted a bazooka squad added to the division reconnaissance company and the division special service company.
- A divisional jeep transport company was requested with 310 men and 200 jeeps.
- A reorganization of the infantry regimental signal platoon to provide a 17-man radio section (8 teams with backpack radios) and a 41-man wire section to run wire from the regiment HQ to the battalion HQ and operate the switchboard.

The recommendations were interesting, but ignored. They almost all involved additional manpower, which was more constrained out of the base in India than it would have been from a Chinese base.

Thus, the second official set of TO&Es for the CAI published in July 1944 differed only in small detail from the ones preceding them. The only change to the rifle company was that one rifle per rifle section was now defined as an M1903 Springfield. This was done because the M1917 usually issued was not able to mount the M1 or M2 grenade launcher, although only six grenade launchers were actually provided per company. Springfields with grenade launchers also replaced five M1917 rifles in the machine-gun company, three in the battalion headquarters, and three in the regiment headquarters. The only other change within the infantry battalion was that two Boys AT rifles were now authorized to be carried by each machine-gun company, although no dedicated crews were authorized—a codification of the prior ad hoc arrangement.

The only change at the regiment level was a reorganization of the anti-tank company, albeit without adding personnel. This company still consisted of a headquarters and four platoons, but the platoon structure was altered to accommodate light weapons for use where the 37mm guns could not go. A platoon now had a 7-man HQ and two 9-man sections. A section was armed with six rifles, a submachine gun, and a 37mm AT gun towed by a jeep. The platoon headquarters included two 2-man light AT teams, one with a Boys AT rifle and the other with a bazooka. The company HQ was divided into a 29-man command section and a 10-man ammunition section. The command section included two more 2-man bazooka teams but no signal means other than two messengers.

The only change to the divisional structure was the replacement of one of the 75mm pack artillery battalions by a 105mm truck-drawn battalion. This, however, was never actually implemented. Of the five CAI divisions, the 14th and 22nd remained on the earlier configuration of two 75mm pack battalions, while the New 30th and 50th only received one 75mm battalion as artillery. The 38th Division, on the other hand, had been re-formed with two 75mm pack battalions and one 105mm truck-drawn battalion in 1943 and it retained this organization.

A medium machine gun of the CAI in action at Bhamo in Burma, December 1944.

The other elements of the division base were unchanged. This included, surprisingly, the bicycles in the reconnaissance company, these having been disposed of by the divisions in Burma as totally unsuited to operations there.

The five CAI divisions retained their India-based organization through to the end of the war, this being noted by a message from the War Ministry to General Wedemeyer on 5 April 1945. The one component that was not standardized was the artillery allotment; for the operations in China up to the Japanese surrender the 38th Division had two 75mm battalions and one 105mm battalion, the 22nd Division two 75mm battalions, the New 30th and 50th Divisions one 75mm battalion each, and the 14th Division no artillery.

Tough, well trained, and battle-hardened, the divisions of the Chinese Army in India, particularly the original 22nd and 38th, provided a spearhead force that would have proven invaluable had the Japanese not surrendered when they did.

10

American-Sponsored Divisions

Proposals of March 1941 by Chiang Kai-shek's representative in the USA, T. V. Soong, for aid from peacetime America had implied a 30-division force and in November AMMISCA had been told of an existing plan to form 30 assault divisions (*kung chen tui*). It seems to have been assumed that the US would provide at least the heavy weapons and high technology items to outfit these divisions. Apparently those plans remained ephemeral, for a year was to pass from Soong's proposal before this was heard from again.

The loss of Burma in the spring of 1942 effectively cut China off from Western aid and thus one of General Stilwell's highest priorities became the re-opening of that route to ensure that China stayed in the war, tying down large numbers of Japanese troops. On 18 July 1942 he submitted a memorandum to Chiang that called for the Chinese to "offer to furnish an army of twenty picked divisions well backed up by artillery" should the US and Britain agree to cooperate in a joint venture to retake Burma.

Surprising Stilwell, on 1 August Chiang agreed, at least partially. He stated that he had in Yunnan ten divisions in the 6th Army (49th, 93rd, and New 28th Divisions), 32nd Army (82nd, 139th, and 141st Divisions), 71st Army (36th, 87th, and 88th Divisions), and the 2nd Reserve Division. To these he said he could later add six more divisions in the 2nd Army (9th, 76th, and New 33rd Divisions) and the 76th Army (24th, 196th, and Temporary 157th Divisions). On 3 November Chiang notified Stilwell that 15 divisions would be used to drive south and west into Burma. This force was henceforth known as Y-Force, or Yoke-Force, reflecting its base in Yunnan. No implementing orders to concentrate or prepare these forces were issued, however.

Thereafter the 30-division plan (and its various successors) and Y-Force ran in parallel and largely overlapping paths. Y-Force was a short-term fix intended quickly to field a Chinese force that could take part in the reconquest of Burma. The difficulties of flying materials over the Hump meant that for the most part only light equipment, much of which China already had, could be provided by the US. The US was able to send modest numbers of anti-tank rifles, Bren light machine guns, 60mm mortars, and, later, bazookas, but for the most part Y-Force would be equipped by the Chinese. The 30-division plan, on the other hand, was more of a long-term effort to create a modern core for the Chinese Army that could undertake effective offensive action against the Japanese in China.

Y-Force Organization

In March 1942 the MAC had proposed a new set of TO&Es for the 30 divisions to be supported by the Americans. This coincided with the plans for Y-Force and the Y-Force staff took over drafting their own necessarily more modest proposals along Stilwell's lines and by November a consensus of sorts had been reached on a new set of organization tables for application to Y-Force.

Infantry Regiment, 1942 Y-Force Type

	Officers	Warrant officers	Sergeants	Corporals	Privates	Pistols	Rifles	Submachine guns	Grenade launchers	Light MGs	Medium MGs	Boys AT rifles	60mm mortars	82mm mortars	Horses	Mules
Regiment HQ	15	2	9	1	18	16	7	0	0	0	0	0	0	0	8	0
Special Service Platoon	1	0	7	5	56	6	56	0	0	0	0	0	0	0	0	0
Signal Platoon	1	1	9	6	62	46	8	0	0	0	0	0	0	0	0	7
Mortar Company																
Company HQ	1	1	9	2	20	21	0	0	0	0	0	0	0	0	2	0
Three Platoons, each	1	0	3	2	44	0	66	0	0	0	0	0	0	2	0	16
Three Infantry Battalions, each																
Battalion HQ	5	0	2	1	10	0	0	0	0	0	0	0	0	0	2	0
HQ Platoon	6	0	5	2	16	0	0	0	0	0	0	0	0	0	0	0
Signal Section	0	0	2	0	11	8	0	0	0	0	0	0	0	0	0	0
Anti-Tank Squad	0	0	1	2	10	0	13	0	0	0	0	2	0	0	0	0
Supply Section	0	0	1	1	4	0	0	0	0	0	0	0	0	0	0	4
Three Rifle Companies, each																
Company HQ	2	1	3	1	21	20	0	0	0	0	0	0	0	0	0	0
Three Rifle Platoons, each	1	0	5	3	38	0	90	3	3	3	0	0	0	0	0	0
Mortar Section	1	0	1	4	30	0	0	0	0	0	0	0	3	0	0	0
Machine Gun Company																
Company HQ	2	1	9	1	17	21	0	0	0	0	0	0	0	0	2	0
Three MG Platoons, each	1	0	2	1	22	0	20	3	0	0	2	0	0	0	0	8
Bren Gun Company																
Company HQ	2	1	2	1	13	3	2	0	0	0	0	0	0	0	2	0
Three Bren Platoons, each	1	0	1	3	19	8	4	3	0	3	0	0	0	0	0	3
Pack Transport Company																
Company HQ	1	1	9	2	12	11	1	0	0	0	0	0	0	0	0	0
Four Pack Platoons, each	1	0	6	0	33	1	2	0	0	0	0	0	0	0	0	24

Although drawing on the experiences of the Chinese Army in India, Y-Force did not have the luxuries of that organization. It lacked the established training base at Ramgarh, and thus there was some reluctance to make drastic alterations in Chinese organization; furthermore, it could count on only the meager supplies that airlift was able to bring over the Hump. Thus, Y-Force organization tables drew heavily from the recently promulgated 31st Year (1942) standard tables for the NRA.

At the lowest level the strength of the rifle section was retained as a sergeant, a corporal (now defined as the assistant section leader), a five-man light MG squad, and a 7-man rifle squad. The difference was that the sections within the platoon were now identical, each containing a light machine gun, a grenade launcher and, new to the normal Chinese organization, a Thompson submachine gun. The rifle platoon headquarters was considerably strengthened to improve command and control, and now consisted of a platoon leader, a platoon sergeant, a sergeant "platoon guide," and two messengers.

For the first time the rifle company was given its own fire support element in the form of a mortar section, actually a platoon in strength. The mortar section consisted of a lieutenant section leader, a sergeant as assistant, three messengers, three mortar squads, and an ammunition squad. Each five-man mortar squad was provided with a 60mm mortar, either a Type 31 or an M2, while the ammunition squad provided a squad leader and nine ammunition bearers. The rifle company headquarters was unchanged except for the addition of an assistant company commander to aid control and supply of the unit.

The battalion machine-gun company was little changed from the 1942 standard tables, seeing only the addition of an assistant commander and the removal of its signal section to the battalion level.

A major change to the battalion came in the headquarters element. An operations officer, a captain, was added to facilitate planning, as was an intelligence/scout squad of a sergeant, a corporal, and six privates to locate the enemy. The signal section, formerly in the machine-gun company, was completely re-equipped. It now included eight radio operators, two telephone operators, and a lineman. This would permit the establishment of a battalion/company radio net using SCR-194 backpack transceivers, although these remained in very short supply through to 1945. Another new unit added was an anti-tank squad with two Boys .55-cal. anti-tank rifles.

Signal facilities at the regiment level were similarly improved. The overall strength of the regimental signal platoon was unchanged, but it now included a 6-man switchboard group, two 8-man radio groups, and three 8-man wire groups, along with the pack mule handlers, cooks, messengers, and other miscellaneous personnel. The radiomen would operate SCR-284 or the similar V-100 transceivers, large but still manportable units, using battery power for the receiver and a bicycle-type generator for transmitting.

Two new elements were added to the infantry regiment. The first was a Bren gun company. The water-cooled machine guns used by the battalions were useful for sustained fire, but were rather heavy for manporting over the rugged mountains of the Salween campaign area. The lighter Bren guns provided a highly mobile base of direct fire for the regimental commander and could aid in assaults. To enhance their utility the weapons would be provided with tripods for anti-aircraft use. They were separated from the rest of the regiment largely to simplify ammunition supply, as the Canadian-built Brens of the first contract were chambered for the .303-inch British cartridge rather than the standard Chinese 7.92mm. The company was a rather austere unit built around three platoons, each with three 6-man squads. Unlike the infantry in the battalions, the Bren company was provided with a mule for each weapon.

The second new unit was a pack transport company, intended to alleviate the problems of moving supplies forward into a foreign country and away from home bases. The company consisted of a headquarters and four identical platoons. Each platoon was divided into four sections, each of nine men (including two riflemen as guards) with six pack mules. Three of the platoons were dedicating to supplying the infantry battalions, with one section for each of the battalion's companies. In the fourth platoon, one section was dedicated to the Bren company, one to the mortar company, and the other two were available for duty as needed.

One further improvement to the regiment was to expand the mortar company from two 2-gun platoons to three. Observation was improved by providing each of the two observer sergeants in the company headquarters with two privates as assistants. The regimental HQ itself and the special service (guard) platoon were unchanged from the standard 1942 infantry organization.

The regiment emerged from the Y-Force reorganization a much more capable formation. Following the recognition that artillery would not always be available, mortar firepower had been increased dramatically. On paper, at least, signal communications were vastly improved, replacing wire and runners with radios down to the company level. In addition, the vexing problem of supply had been at least partially addressed. It was thus with not only surprise, but delight, that Stilwell received Chiang's approval of the new TO&Es in late 1942.

The divergence between Chinese demands and the American ability to supply was most apparent in discussions on the organization of the division. The MAC, with an eye to eventual organization of the 30 sponsored divisions, wanted one battalion each of pack artillery, anti-aircraft artillery, anti-tank artillery, engineers, signals, and pack transport added to the division structure. The Americans rejected all the artillery battalions immediately, although they did concede that a divisional mortar company with 12 82mm mortars might be practical. Eventually, the engineer battalion and signal battalions were dropped as well, these components remaining at company size.

For all the complex staff work and coordination needed to draft the new TO&Es, that was the easiest of the parts of the reorganization process. The MAC also needed to identify which units would be included in the American-sponsored reorganization, then bring them up to strength with personnel, and then the US needed to move the required equipment over the Hump into China.

The decentralization of command that characterized much of the Chinese military efforts came into play here as well. References were made to "Y-Force" and an American advisory staff, Y-Force Operational Staff (or Y-FOS) was formed, but in fact there was no such creature in the sense of units under a common command. Instead, the units that were referred to as Y-Force actually came under three entirely separate commands.

General Chen Cheng commanded the largest group, the Chinese Expeditionary Force (CEF), of five armies and 15 divisions which was to drive south and west into Burma. The movement of these troops, loyal to Chiang, into semi-autonomous Yunnan province would ruffle feathers, so a separate command called the Yunnan–Indochina Force was created and put under the command of the Yunnan warlord, Long Yun. This force guarded the border with Japanese-occupied Indochina with three armies and eight divisions, of which one army (60th, with the 182nd and 184th Divisions) was his own. Finally, there was to be

Y-Force Personnel Strenths as of 23 March 1943

		Prior TO strength	New TO strength	Actual strength	Replacements en route
Chinese Expeditionary Force					
XI Group Army	2nd Army				
	Army troops	14,500	11,700		
	9th Division	9,500	10,300	25,600	17,000
	76th Division	9,500	10,300		
	New 33rd Division	9,500	10,300		
	71st Army				
	Army troops	4,800	4,800		
	36th Division	7,800	10,300	18,750	9,500
	87th Division	7,800	10,300		
	88th Division	7,800	10,300*		
	93rd Army				
	Army troops	4,800	4,800		
	10th Division	7,800	10,300	8,200	17,000
	New 8th Division	7,800	10,300		
	Temp 2nd Division	7,800	10,300*		
	2nd Reserve Division	7,800	10,300	3,000	5,500
XX Group Army	6th Army				
	Army troops	4,800	4,800		
	93rd Division	7,800	10,300	14,700	10,500
	New 39th Division	7,800	10,300*		
	New 28th Division	7,800	10,300		
	53rd Army				
	Army troops	4,800	4,800		
	116th Division	7,800	10,300	15,900	4,500
	130th Division	7,800	10,300		
Yunnan–Indochina Force					
I Group Army	60th Army				
	Army troops	4,800	4,800		
	182nd Division	7,800	7,800	15,650	4,650
	184th Division	7,800	7,800		
IX Group Army	52nd Army				
	Army troops	4,800	4,800		
	2nd Division	7,800	10,300	20,450	7,544
	25th Division	7,800	10,300		
	195th Division	7,800	10,300*		
	54th Army				
	Army troops	4,800	4,800		
	14th Division	7,800	10,300	18,400	9,290
	50th Division	7,800	10,300		
	198th Division	7,800	10,300*		

		Prior TO strength	New TO strength	Actual strength	Replacements en route
	Y-Force Personnel Strenths as of 23 March 1943 (*continued*)				
Reserve					
V Group Army	5th Army				
	Army troops	25,500	21,850		
	49th Division	9,500	10,300	33,860	18,984
	96th Division	9,500	10,300		
	200th Division	9,500	10,300		
	8th Army				
	Army troops	4,800	4,800		
	Hon. 1st Division	7,800	10,300	21,050	7,300
	82nd Division	7,800	10,300		
	103rd Division	7,800	10,300*		
	74th Army				
	Army troops	14,500	11,870		
	51st Division	9,500	10,300	31,785	10,985
	57th Division	9,500	10,300		
	58th Division	9,500	10,300		

* Replacement division. New strength not finalized.

a reserve force of three armies and nine divisions that could be used to support either of the other two; this came under the Generalissimo's Chongqing HQ, nominally via Long Yun.

On 23 March 1943 the MAC announced its plans and, indeed, Y-Force would eventually form the core of the 30-division Alpha force. The Y-Force reorganization would be applied, in whole or in part, to 11 armies containing a total of 31 divisions. Six armies (6th, 8th, 52nd, 54th, 71st, and 93rd) each had three divisions, two of which were to be reorganized and re-equipped as "assault divisions," while the third division was reduced to a training and replacement pool for the other two, at full strength in terms of personnel but holding only a training scale of equipment. The 53rd Army had two divisions, both of which would be reorganized. The 2nd, 5th, and 74th Armies would see all three of their divisions reorganized. The 60th Army of two divisions (Yunnan provincial troops) would remain on the current 1942 organization. Y-Force would thus consist of 24 reorganized assault divisions, 2 standard divisions brought up to full strength, and 6 replacement divisions. Thus, the plans were still six divisions short of the goal, but since equipment was arriving only in small quantities that raised few eyebrows. No attempt was made to reorganize the army troops, which remained on their prior organization tables.

The fact that the MAC had nominated forces, however, did not mean that there was any actual commitment to moving them into harm's way. The deployment of forces to Yunnan was slow and half-hearted, so that by September 1943 the number of divisions allotted to Y-Force had fallen from 31 to 20.

In that month Stilwell proposed to Chiang that Y-Force be regarded as the heart of the 30-division plan and that a second batch of 30 divisions start training in the Guilin area. This may have been a subtle (for Stilwell) form of leverage to get Chiang to commit

Y-Force Organic Heavy Weapons, May 1943

	Mortars			Anti-Tank					Mountain					Field Guns			Howitzers	
	Obsolete	82mm	150mm	20mm Madsen	37mm old	37mm German	37mm Russian	47mm Bohler	75mm Krupp	75mm Japanese	75mm French	75mm US	76mm Russian	75mm Krupp	75mm French	76mm Russian	114mm Vickers	150mm German
Chinese Expeditionary Force																		
XI Army Group																		
2nd Army				4			8		9				22					
9th Division		30																
76th Division		30																
N 33rd Division		18																
71st Army					12		5	10							12			
87th Division		28																
88th Division		30																
N 28th Division		30																
93rd Army				6			4									8	4	
T 10th Division		29																
N 8th Division		24																
T 2nd Division		30																
R 2nd Division		30																
XX Army Group																		
53rd Army									8	4								
116th Division	15	7																
130th Division	15	6																
6th Army				3			4											
N 39th Division		30																
93rd Division		30																
CEF HQ units			26														8	12

Generalissimo HQ

V Army Group

5th Army			7						27			
49th Division	30											
96th Division	30							9				
200th Division	30										9	
8th Army				8		11						
H 1st Division	23											
82nd Division	29											
103rd Division	30	4										
74th Army		8		2	4		10			10		12
51st Division	30											
57th Division	30											
58th Division	30											

Yunnan–Indochina Force

IX Army Group

52nd Army		6			8		12					
25th Division	30											
H 2nd Division	30											
195th Division	30											
54th Army				8	6		11					
14th Division	30											
50th Division	30											
198th Division	30											

I Army Group

60th Army	12	5		4								
182nd Division	30											
184th Division	30											

more troops to Yoke, promising a second stage if only the first could be completed. If so, it worked for Chiang quickly issued orders adding three more armies to the force, directing the implementation of the reorganization of all three divisions of the New 1st Army (in India), and the two best divisions in each of the 2nd, 5th, 6th, 8th, 10th, 31st, 52nd, 53rd, 54th, 60th, 71st, 74th, and 93rd Armies, plus the 36th Division, a total of 30 divisions, of which 27 were in China.

The first practical problem to be encountered in the formation of Y-Force was that of finding troops. Units were under strength to start with, and moving them to an organization table with a higher strength level exacerbated the problem. Even the three relatively elite armies nominated for reorganization (2nd, 5th, and 74th) were well under strength.

The process of bringing them up to strength had begun with the dispatch of replacement and filler personnel in March 1943. Depending on how one counted authorized strengths (were the elite armies to be stripped of some of their army-level troops, did the replacement divisions really need to be up to full strength?) the initial tallies were somewhat confusing, but generally showed a shortage of about 185,000 men, against which the MAC had dispatched 122,750 replacements to be in place by 10 June. Promises of further reinforcements, however, disappeared in the face of a Japanese drive in central China, which drew off resources.

In terms of weapons the Chinese forces designated for Y-Force were pretty well set with rifles, machine guns, and 82mm mortars. Grenade launchers, a mix of Type 27 and Type 28, were issued on an irregular basis, with some divisions approaching full strength, and others having none.

There were no 60mm mortars available, Chinese production having not yet ramped up, so the Americans agreed to provide these weapons. According to the organization tables each division was to have no fewer than 81 of these weapons, yielding a requirement for 1,944 weapons even if the replacement divisions got none. This was clearly an impossible goal given the need to fly the mortars, and their ammunition, over the Hump into China. Nevertheless, a little under 720 were brought in from India in the fall of 1943 and distributed, and this provided at least a start.

Fine-tuning of the Y-Force organization continued as experience was gained with these units in training. As a result a final set of TO&Es was issued in November 1943 in anticipation of the imminent Salween offensive. The infantry regiment was very little changed from the initial tables. The ranks in the signal units were elevated to provide incentives for technically qualified personnel, although the total number of personnel assigned was not altered. At the battalion level, where the signal section's radio group had consisted of eight privates, it was now authorized a warrant officer, four sergeants, and four privates. A similar process took place within the regimental signal platoon.

The division was now also authorized 36 bazooka rocket launchers, although their distribution within the division was undefined. In any event, supplies of these weapons ran very late, and the first real deliveries did not take place until November 1943. A further 253 were issued in March 1944 which, added to the earlier deliveries, brought the strength up to within 30 of the target.[*] For these, however, only 1,700 rockets were available.

Supporting the three regiments in each division was a division base that included, at least nominally, signal, engineer, and transport battalions.

---

[*] The target was 27 per division for 15 divisions, in order to allow for the actual distribution of 36 per division for 10 divisions plus army units.

Division Base, Y-Force, from 1 November 1943

	Officers	Warrant officers	Sergeants	Corporals	Privates	Pistols	Rifles	Light MGs	Horses	Mules
Division Headquarters	52	12	14	3	53	36	13	0	24	0
Signal Battalion										
Battalion HQ	11	0	9	1	16	13	11	0	2	10
1st Company	5	3	16	1	91	47	28	0		24
2nd Company	4	2	15	1	101	50	18	0		24
Radio Platoon	9	17	11	0	57	45	16	0		10
Special Service Company										
Company HQ	1	1	2	0	23	54	149	0	0	0
Two Platoons, each	1	0	5	0	46			2	0	0
Two Platoons, each	1	0	5	0	46			0	0	0
Scout Company										
Company HQ	1	1	2	0	24	120	38	0	1	0
Signal Section	1	2	0	4	2			0	0	0
Cavalry Platoon	1	0	3	3	31			0	38	0
Infantry Platoon	2	0	10	10	92			0	0	0
Engineer Battalion										
Battalion HQ	10	1	15	1	74	22	48	0	0	42
Three Companies, each										
Company HQ	1	1	5	3	31	26	99	0	0	11
Three Platoons, each	1	0	3	3	37			3	0	0
Animal Transport Bn										
Battalion HQ	11	0	13	10	19	7	8	0	4	0
Two Companies, each	6	1	11	0	135	16	60	0	13	96
***or* Porter Transport Bn**										
Battalion HQ	7	0	4	1	10	5	6	0	0	0
Four Companies, each	6	1	18	0	281	23	68	0	0	0

The signal battalion had two wire companies with a total of 17 wire sections totaling 177 men and 48 mules. It also included a radio platoon with one 15-watt section of 18 men with 2 mules, and four 5-watt sections each of 16 men with 2 mules. In fact, however, most of the divisions only had signal companies due to the lack of equipment and technical personnel. Such a company would have one V-100 and one SCR-284 radio, along with three switchboards, 14 telephones, and 53km of wire.

The engineer battalion had a headquarters that included a 34-man wire signal platoon, and three engineer companies each of three platoons. The engineer platoons were organized similarly to rifle platoons with three sections, each of a section leader, assistant section leader, an 8-man rifle squad, and a 4-man light machine-gun squad. The similarity to infantry organization was apparently intended by the Americans to induce the Chinese to push their engineers forward instead of using them for construction labor. If that was the case, they were successful, for they were used essentially as infantry and took heavy losses. In fact, most divisions were only able to field a single engineer company due to the lack of trained personnel to start with and heavy losses.

Reconnaissance was the responsibility of the division scout company which was built around a mounted cavalry platoon with three 12-man sections, and a dismounted platoon with 10 11-man sections. The bulk of these troops were armed with pistols rather than rifles and may well have been intended to reconnoiter in civilian garb.

The divisional special service company had four platoons, each with five 10-man sections. The first and second platoons each consisted of two LMG and three rifle sections for guard duties, while the other two platoons had only rifles, the third as an inspection platoon and the 4th as a reconnaissance platoon. If a chemical disinfection platoon was ordered formed, 32 men from the special service company would be used to form it.

Finally, the division was to include a transport battalion, either with animals or porters. The animal battalion had two companies, each with four platoons each with 8 mule-drawn wagons, giving a capacity of 17½ tons of food and ammunition per company. Instead of an animal transport battalion, a division could include a porter battalion of four companies, each of four platoons, each platoon four sections, each with a sergeant and 16 porters. Each porter carried 66 pounds, or a total of 8 tons per company.

In December 1943 the Y-Force staff proposed adding a mortar battalion to each division, but in February 1944 the MAC, noting that they had already provided a mortar company, platoon, and section to each infantry regiment, battalion, and company respectively, stated that the current organization was "exceptionally strong" and needed no further mortars. Where they got the idea that battalion mortar platoons had been authorized is unknown.

With these components a Y-Force division at full strength had a strength of 503 officers and 10,287 enlisted, with 1,828 pistols, 4,174 rifles, 270 submachine guns, 270 light machine guns (including 27 Bren guns in .303 caliber), 54 medium machine guns, 27 AT rifles, 36 bazookas, 81 60mm mortars, and 30 82mm mortars. This was the organization they followed through the Salween campaign of 1944.

In addition, some divisions that had previously included other elements tended to keep them. For instance, a few divisions included an anti-tank company. These fielded a mixture of 20mm Madsens, old 37mm Gruson antiques, more modern German and Soviet 37mm guns, and 47mm Bohler guns.

In April 1944 the organization tables for the field army base elements of the China Expeditionary Force, a part of Y-Force, were published.

Army troops in Y-Force had an establishment strength of 555 officers and 7,849 enlisted, with 698 riding horses, 2,518 pack horses, and 259 pack mules. The largest component of the army base was the 3,796-man transport regiment that carried 128 tons by pack animal and 24 tons in the two 8-truck platoons of the motor transport company.

Fire support was to be provided by a field artillery battalion, using weapons of a type unspecified by the MAC. Each battery included a 29-man signal platoon (with three wire sections and a radio team), a five-man instrument section, a 16-man light MG section of two squads, four 22-man gun sections (each with 10 mules), and a 34-man ammunition section with 20 mules. The battalion signal section had a switchboard section, six light wire

Field Army Base Units, CEF, from April 1944

	Officers	Warrant officers	Sergeants	Corporals	Privates	Riding horses	Pack horses & mules
Army HQ	97	14	27	0	67	31	0
Signal Battalion							
Battalion HQ	11	0	9	1	16	2	10
1st Wire Company	4	6	16	0	90	0	24
2nd Wire Company	4	2	12	3	100	0	24
Radio Company	12	17	17	0	67	0	12
Reconnaissance Battalion							
Battalion HQ	12	2	7	0	18	4	0
Radio Platoon	5	0	2	0	9	0	0
Cavalry Company	5	1	17	13	160	189	12
Infantry Company	4	1	9	9	110	0	0
Special Service Battalion							
Battalion HQ	6	1	4	1	10	2	0
1st Company	4	1	11	9	129	0	0
2nd Company	4	2	24	1	113	0	20
Field Artillery Battalion							
HQ Battery	18	0	18	0	28	18	5
Signal Platoon	1	0	6	8	53	2	23
Three Batteries, each	7	2	25	9	172	31	77
Anti-Tank Battalion							
Battalion HQ	12	1	11	7	49	11	6
Three Companies, each	4	2	14	4	115	2	34
Engineer Battalion							
Battalion HQ	10	1	15	1	78	2	46
Three Companies, each	4	1	18	9	140	0	9
Artillery Ammo Train	4	1	1	12	197	0	0
Transport Company	6	1	6	16	365	0	0
Transport Regiment							
Regiment HQ	15	2	13	1	18	1	0
Signal Platoon	1	1	8	5	60	0	7
Motor Transport Company	5	1	28	4	58	0	0
Four Battalions, each							
Battalion HQ	13	0	14	10	23	8	0
Three Companies, each	6	1	19	1	251	24	194
Ordnance Company	3	4	45	0	7	0	0
Medical Units				*unknown*			

sections (including two to work with the battalion liaison section), and a radio section with an SCR-178 or SCR-179 and three SCR-609 or SCR-194 sets. The battalion HQ included a liaison section that formed two 3-man teams, and a 13-man observer section. Chinese armies had nominally included an artillery battalion for several years, so this itself was not a great change, although the provision of signal assets for indirect fire was, theoretically at least, a great step forward. The armies assembled for Y-Force in early 1943 generally had one battalion of artillery, although two (6th and 60th, the latter a Yunnan unit) had none, and three (2nd, 5th, and 74th) had three-battalion regiments.

The Americans had provided some 75mm pack howitzers prior to the formation of Y-Force, but these had simply been handed over to the Chinese who used them in their own fashion. The results, in the view of the Americans, was wasteful. A survey in early 1943 of the 5th Army Artillery Regiment, one of the better organic artillery units, found the training to be unsatisfactory and radios and transport assets completely lacking. Instead, the Americans now tried insisting that all Lend-Lease artillery be distributed in unit sets by the new Field Artillery Training Center (FATC) to units that had undergone training there.

Bren machine gunners of Y-Force train at the Infantry Training Center in April 1944.

The major factors in the improvement of the army artillery were the introduction of the new, modern 75mm pack howitzer, training in modern artillery methods, particularly indirect fire, and the provision of the equipment to carry that out. Thus, in addition to the 12 pack howitzers, each battalion also received 95 Phillips pack saddles, 4 BC (Battery Commander's) telescopes, 8 M2 aiming circles, 20 EE-8 field telephones, 4 switchboards, 9 SCR-194 and 1 SCR-179 radios, and plotting tables. In June 1944, in recognition of the continuing Chinese penchant for employing the batteries independently of the battalion headquarters, the signal allocation was changed to include three long-range radios instead of just one, these being defined as the V-100, SCR-583, SCR-284, or SCR-179, in decreasing order of preference. The rebuilt artillery units were the most capable in the Chinese Army. Unfortunately, the pace of training was necessarily slow due to the small size of the FATC.

The first unit to go through the FATC was the 71st Army artillery battalion. This had originally been equipped with 75mm French field guns, but these were unsuitable for use in Burma and were traded with another unit for US 75mm pack howitzers. The unit arrived for training at the end of March 1943 and left in September. The 2nd Battalion of the 2nd Army's regiment re-equipped from Soviet 76mm pack howitzers to US models and graduated in November, the same time as the new 6th Army battalion, formed from scratch, also finished. Thus, by the end of 1943 there were only three American-trained and American-equipped army artillery battalions. The 53rd and 54th Army artillery battalions graduated in April 1944, followed by the 3rd Battalion of the 5th Army regiment in May, the 8th Army battalion in July and the 1st Battalion of the 5th Army regiment in September, yielding five more for Y-Force in 1944.

The Y-Force field army was also provided with an anti-tank battalion with three companies, each built around two 34-man platoons (each with two guns and eight horses) and a 46-man ammunition platoon with 18 pack horses. The tank threat to Y-Force was low, and as a result so was the priority accorded their guns for delivery over the Himalayas. The 37mm guns finally started arriving in early 1944, but at a low rate. In May battalion-sets of weapons were issued to the 2nd, 53rd, 54th, and 71st Armies. In early June, however, a Hump crisis forced the freezing of deliveries of 37mm AT guns, along with Boys AT rifles, this lasting for a few months. For communications the battalion was to be allocated one V-100 radio for liaison with its higher HQ and four British No. 48 radios, along with 23 telephones and 30km of wire, for its internal net.

For scouting the army had one mounted and one dismounted company. The mounted cavalry company had four 38-man platoons, each with three sections. Each of the 12-man sections was provided with a light machine gun and a riding horse for each man. The dismounted (infantry) company had three 57-man platoons, each with three rifle and two light MG sections.

The special service battalion had two companies for its HQ guard duties. The first company was made up of three identical platoons, each of three sections, each in turn composed of a 7-man rifle squad and a 5-man LMG squad. The second company had a 12-man signal section, a 25-man medium MG platoon of two sections, and two 38-man reconnaissance platoons of three sections.

The main component of the army signal battalion was the telephone element. The 1st wire company had a 27-man switchboard platoon of two sections, and two wire platoons, each of 33 men and 8 pack horses divided into three sections. The 2nd wire company had three wire platoons identical to those in the 1st company. The radio company had two platoons, one with one 15-watt and two 5-watt sections, and the other with three 5-watt sections.

Overall, the delivery of signal equipment approximately kept pace with that of weapons, limited by capacity of airlift rather than tactical requirements. Through mid-1943 the only radios to be issued to Chinese troops by Y-Force were about 40 SCR-194s, which were to have been allocated at eight per infantry battalion. Small deliveries of various models took place through the rest of the year, with the only large issues being 270 V-100s in November and 50 SCR-284s in December. In early 1944, however, deliveries picked up considerably, especially in the smaller radios, so that by March 1944 a total of 346 of an authorized 443 SCR-284 and 516 of an authorized 702 US-built British No.48 radios had been issued to the nine armies (including 23 field artillery battalions). The picture was somewhat less rosy

Instruction in the British No. 48 radio for the 52nd Army in January 1945. It is not clear why these radios were chosen for issue to the army anti-tank battalions.

with regard to the longer-ranged sets, with only 75 of 132 V-100s and 60 of 207 SCR-194s released to the Chinese units.

Priority for equipment went to the units that would actually be doing the fighting, the CEF. Nevertheless, sufficient progress was made that by mid-1944 even Long's provincial 182nd and 184th Divisions of his 60th Army were feeling the results, those two divisions having received a total of 360 Thompson submachine guns, 36 Bren guns in .303cal, 36 Boys AT rifles, 62 60mm mortars, and 31 81mm mortars (to complement their 29 Chinese 82mm models).

The 30-Division Force

While Y-Force was preparing for its offensive into Burma using what was readily to hand, work continued in parallel on defining the ultimate US-equipped Chinese division. By August 1942 CBI estimated they would need 360 75mm pack howitzers and unspecified quantities of 37mm AT guns for the divisions and 105mm and 155mm howitzers for 10 army artillery regiments. That, however, was only a very small start in figuring out what would be required.

The Americans were to supply everything for these divisions except clothing. In order to requisition 30 divisions' worth of everything, from flashlight batteries to pup tents to howitzers detailed TO&Es for the division were clearly needed. The initial TO&E for sponsored divisions was issued in January 1943.* The new organization was radically different not only from the normal Chinese organization, but also from that adopted by Y-Force. It was predicated on the arrival and distribution of significant quantities of relatively heavy American equipment, such as 37mm anti-tank guns and 75mm pack howitzers, and massive quantities of other items, that could not become available in China until after the Burma Road was reopened. The tables thus represented a long-term goal and planning document rather than something to be implemented immediately.

The most striking feature was the incorporation of a mortar section with two 60mm mortars into each rifle platoon as in the CAI, for a total of six per company, or 54 per division. The division would include engineer, signal, and transport battalions, the last with two pack companies and a truck company. For fire support the division would have two artillery battalions, one of 75mm pack howitzers and the other of truck-drawn 105mm howitzers.

No sooner had these tables been officially issued than thought turned to expanding the program. In January 1943 Stilwell raised the issue of adding another 30 divisions to the program with T. V. Soong and reported to Washington that he and the Chinese leadership had agreed to complete the equipment of 30 divisions and begin procurement of a second set of 30 divisions' worth.

Stilwell's vision for what he called "the regular Chinese Army" involved three groups of 30 divisions each. The first "30-division" group was Y-Force which would campaign in Burma, get fully equipped there once the Burma Road reopened, and then be ready for further operations in China. That would be followed by the second 30-division batch that would begin training immediately so as to be ready when the Burma Road reopened to receive modern US equipment. Their training would complete while the first 30 divisions conducted operations against the Japanese. The final group would be garrison divisions used for static defense of important locales—these would not receive the full scale of equipment. Once sufficient progress had been made with the first two groups the remainder of the Chinese Army would be gradually inactivated, with the better personnel used to fill out the retained divisions or simply demobilized to save rations and expenses. Chiang was polite in his response, but nothing ever came of this plan.

In July 1943 the US War Department approved a Lend-Lease program for China that provided for equipping the first 30 divisions and providing 10% of the equipment needed for a second batch of 30 divisions in order to start training. The second batch, or Z-Force, was the subject of considerable disagreement between Stilwell and the MAC. Stilwell wanted to consolidate the existing forces in east China into 30 divisions, using the best personnel, getting rid of the rest, and then issuing new American equipment and training teams. The Chinese, on the other hand, viewed Lend-Lease simply as a spigot to be turned on to deliver additional equipment to be distributed as they saw fit to existing units. Stilwell asked the War Department for a commitment to equip Z-Force fully, but they declined in October, sticking by the 10% promise, giving him little local leverage.

Nevertheless, Stilwell continued to press for his vision of a modernized Chinese Army. In early November 1943 he drafted a memorandum for Chiang suggesting talking points for the upcoming Sextant Conference with Roosevelt and Churchill. Here he posited a force of no fewer than 90 re-formed and re-equipped divisions along with "1 or 2 armored

---

* The tables were republished in Washington, DC, in July 1943.

US-Sponsored Infantry Battalion, from November 1944

	Officers	Warrant officers	Sergeants	Corporals	Privates	Submachine guns	Rifles	Rifle grenade launchers	Light MGs	Medium MGs	60mm mortars	AT rifles	Riding animals	Pack animals	Motor vehcles
Battalion Headquarters															
HQ Detachment	2	0	1	0	3	0	4	1	0	0	0	0	2	0	0
Operations Team	2	0	1	0	0	0	1	1	0	0	0	0	0	0	0
Intelligence Team	1	0	1	0	0	0	1	1	0	0	0	0	0	0	0
Signal Section	1	0	2	3	3	0	0	0	0	0	0	0	0	0	0
Supply Detachment	1	0	1	4	2	0	4	0	0	0	0	0	0	6	0
Three Rifle Companies, each															
Company HQ	2	1	3	0	18	8	2	0	0	0	0	0	0	0	0
Three Rifle Platoons, each															
Platoon HQ	1	0	1	0	2	3	0	0	0	0	0	0	0	0	0
Three Rifle Sections, each	0	0	1	1	10	0	11	1	1	0	0	0	0	0	0
Mortar Section	0	0	1	0	10	0	9	0	0	0	2	0	0	0	0
Machine-Gun Company															
Company HQ	2	1	8	1	11	9	3	1	0	0	0	2	2	0	0
Ammunition Section	0	0	1	1	8	2	0	0	0	0	0	0	0	8	0
Four MG Platoons, each															
Platoon HQ	1	0	1	0	1	1	1	1	0	0	0	0	0	0	0
Two MG Squads, each	0	0	1	1	6	0	5	0	0	1	0	0	0	1	0

divisions." The divisions were to be re-formed in three groups of 30, with Y-Force plus the CAI as Group 1, Z-Force as Group 2 ready for the field in August 1944 (assuming the opening of the Burma Road), and a third group, yet to be defined, along with the armored divisions, in January 1945. In any event, shortly after Sextant, the USA and Britain cancelled plans for amphibious operations against the Burma coast, one of Chiang's prerequisites for an attack into Burma. With no immediate prospects for either employment of Y-Force or opening of the land route through Burma, the mass modernization plans for the Chinese Army slipped into irrelevance.

Further study apparently showed the divisional organization to be unworkable. There were too many trucks to be supported by available fuel, and mechanics were in short supply; further there were probably not enough technicians for a full signal battalion. A new organization table for the US-supported division and the army was issued in November 1944 by the (US) Chinese Combat Command and this was formally approved by US China Theater on 15 December.

The rifle section would consist of a sergeant, a corporal, and 10 privates, five forming a light MG team and five a rifle team. One of the privates was armed with a light machine gun (ZB26 or Bren), the corporal with a rifle with grenade launcher, and the rest with rifles. The rifle platoon's mortar section consisted of a sergeant and two 4-man teams, each with a 60mm mortar. The platoon HQ was made up of the platoon leader, platoon sergeant, and two messengers. The rifle platoon included three Thompson submachine guns, but they were issued not to the rifle sections, but to the platoon sergeant and two messengers.

The rifle company had three such platoons, plus a headquarters with a captain, a lieutenant, a warrant officer (with the role the US Army assigned the first sergeant), and 21 enlisted. Those included a 10-man mess section, two medics, and four messengers. Thompson submachine guns were issued liberally to non-line personnel, eight weapons for the messengers, buglers, and so on. The company HQ also included a single TP-3 telephone for communications with battalion HQ.

The main change to the battalion machine-gun company was the addition of a fourth 2-gun platoon. The platoons were reduced in size by eliminating the ammunition section and adding a muleteer with a pack mule to each section, thus saving six enlisted men per platoon, albeit at the expense of six pack mules for ammunition. The platoon headquarters consisted solely of the platoon leader (with a submachine gun), platoon sergeant (with a rifle grenade launcher), and a messenger. The company headquarters was similar to that of the rifle company except for the addition of eight muleteers with pack mules, and two Boys anti-tank rifles, which were carried for distribution within the company as needed.

The battalion HQ drew heavily on the Y-Force example except for the elimination of the anti-tank squad (whose weapons had been handed over to the MG company). The signal section had three corporals, each with an SCR-300 backpack radio for distribution to the companies, three linemen, two sergeants (a switchboard operator and a clerk), and a lieutenant. In addition to the three SCR-300s, the section held an SCR-694 radio for use as the base station, a switchboard, and three telephones.

The infantry battalion that emerged from this exercise was remarkable for the level of mortar firepower. The provision of two 60mm mortars for each rifle platoon, no less than six per rifle company, was without parallel in any other army. Since HE-throwing weapons were almost invariably used in the direct-fire role in the Chinese army, range was only rarely relevant and it made sense to move the weapons as far forward as possible in

US-Sponsored Division, from November 1944

	Officers	Warrant officers	Enlisted	Rifles	SMGs	Rifle grenade lanchers	Light MGs	Medium MGs	60mm mortars	82mm mortars	AT rifles	AT rocket launchers	37mm AT guns	75mm pack how	Riding animals	Pack animals	Motor vehicles
Division HQ & Company	41	4	84	42	8	0	0	0	0	0	0	0	0	0	0	0	3
Special Service Company	5	0	172	96	30	0	18	0	0	0	0	0	0	0	0	0	0
Signal Company	31	1	191	95	13	0	0	0	0	0	0	0	0	0	0	56	0
Reconnaissance Company	6	5	178	80	54	0	18	0	0	0	0	0	0	0	0	0	0
Three Infantry Regiments, each																	
Regiment HQ (incl att. medical)	16	4	109	15	7	0	0	0	0	0	0	0	0	0	4	6	1
Signal Platoon	2	0	37	28	5	0	0	0	0	0	0	0	0	0	0	4	1
Special Service Platoon	1	0	30	19	3	3	2	0	0	0	0	0	0	0	0	0	0
Three Infantry Battalions, each																	
Battalion HQ	7	0	21	10	0	0	0	0	0	0	0	0	0	0	2	6	0
Three Rifle Companies, each	5	1	171	128	17	9	9	0	6	0	0	0	0	0	0	0	0
Machine Gun Company	6	1	102	47	15	5	0	8	0	0	2	0	0	0	2	16	0
Mortar Company	8	1	170	75	20	0	0	0	0	12	0	0	0	0	5	24	0
Anti-Tank Company	6	1	132	59	26	0	0	0	0	0	4	6	8	0	2	40	0
Transport Company	6	2	135	12	9	0	0	0	0	0	0	0	0	0	0	0	0
Pack Artillery Battalion																	
Battalion HQ	18	2	130	44	11	0	6	0	0	0	0	0	0	0	5	28	0
Three Batteries, each	7	2	197	56	18	0	6	0	0	0	0	0	0	4	4	77	0

US-Sponsored Division, from November 1944 (continued)

	Officers	Warrant officers	Enlisted	Rifles	SMGs	Rifle grenade lanchers	Light MGs	Medium MGs	60mm mortars	82mm mortars	AT rifles	AT rocket launchers	37mm AT guns	75mm pack how	Riding animals	Pack animals	Motor vehicles
Engineer Battalion																	
Battalion HQ	7	1	31	20	4	0	0	0	0	0	0	0	0	0	1	4	0
Three Engineer Companies, each	5	1	147	102	10	0	8	0	0	0	0	0	0	0	1	8	0
Transport Company	8	1	55	10	5	0	0	0	0	0	0	0	0	0	0	144	0
Porter Transport Battalion																	
Battalion HQ	8	0	40	9	0	0	0	0	0	0	0	0	0	0	0	0	0
Four Transport Companies, each	6	2	135	12	9	0	0	0	0	0	0	0	0	0	0	0	0
Medical Battalion																	
Battalion HQ	3	1	6	0	0	0	0	0	0	0	0	0	0	0	0	0	0
Medical Company	8	0	165	0	0	0	0	0	0	0	0	0	0	0	0	0	0
Veterinary Platoon	2	1	24	0	0	0	0	0	0	0	0	0	0	0	0	0	0
Field Hospital	12	0	98	0	0	0	0	0	0	0	0	0	0	0	0	0	0

command terms. The organization appears to have been regarded as successful, for the battalion organization table remained unchanged through the end of the war, although the authorization for the Boys AT rifles was withdrawn in mid-1945 (without, however, deleting them from the organization tables).

The regimental structure looked nothing like the Y-Force predecessor. The Bren Gun company was deleted completely. It was replaced by an anti-tank company consisting of a headquarters and four platoons. Each platoon was made up of a 7-man HQ and two 9-man sections. A section was armed with six rifles, a submachine gun, and a 37mm AT gun with limber, and was provided two horses to tow the gun and two for pack loads of ammunition. The platoon headquarters included two 2-man light AT teams, one with a Boys AT rifle, the other with a bazooka. The company HQ was divided into a 29-man command section and a 10-man ammunition section, the latter with 8 pack animals. The command section included two more 2-man bazooka teams but no signal means other than two messengers.

The regimental mortar company was doubled in size in terms of firepower through the expedient of redefining the mortar section as a two-weapon unit instead of just one. The section now had a sergeant, two corporal squad leaders, six gun crew, six ammunition bearers, and four drivers with two pack mules. In addition to two mortar sections, the mortar platoon had an 8-man ammunition section with four pack animals. The company HQ was a large affair, mainly due to the incorporation of a 9-man mess section. It also included an observation sergeant and a signal sergeant, but no signal equipment.

Resupply of the regiment was the responsibility of the porter transport company, consisting of four platoons, each of three sections, each with a corporal, six porters, and three cooks. Three of the platoons were dedicated to support the three battalions, each carrying 5,000 rounds of 7.92mm, 1,800 rounds of .45cal, 84 rounds of 60mm mortar, and 90 AT grenades, along with 265 pounds (120kg) of rice. Defense of the regiment HQ was handled by the special service platoon, which was built around a 12-man light MG section of two 5-man teams, and a rifle section of 16 men with rifles (two with grenade launchers).

Communications within the regiment were handled by the signal platoon, which consisted of the platoon leader, a 6-man message center, a 15-man radio section, and a 17-man wire section. It was provided with four radios—two SCR-694, one SCR-583, and one SCR-300, a switchboard, a telegraph, and nine telephones.

A significant feature of the US-sponsored division organization was the reintroduction of divisional artillery. The modest artillery component was a pack howitzer battalion with a headquarters and three batteries equipped with US 75mm pack howitzers. Provision was made for indirect fire, with each battery being equipped with two SCR-619 radios, a switchboard, and seven telephones, enabling the battery observation group to operate on the front line and keep in contact with the firing battery to the rear. The battalion HQ included three SCR-619 radios (to provide one per battery) and two SCR-694 for the battalion command post, along with a switchboard and nine telephones.

Scouting for the division was carried out by the reconnaissance company, which consisted of three platoons, each of three sections. Each section was made up of a sergeant and two 8-man squads. A squad was armed with a light MG, two submachine guns, and four rifles. The company headquarters was authorized two fragile SCR-625 mine detectors, but no signal gear to transmit back any information they had gleaned from their efforts.

Alpha army base units, from November 1944

	Officers	Warrant officers	Enlisted	Rifles	SMGs	Light MGs	105mm howitzers	Riding animals	Pack animals	Jeeps	Light trucks	Trucks
Army HQ	100	16	94	50	20	0	0	38	0	5	12	9
Signal Battalion												
Battalion HQ	10	1	28	13	2	0	0	0	10	2	0	1
1st Wire Company	4	6	106	0	0	0	0	0	24	0	0	0
2nd Wire Company	4	2	118	0	0	0	0	0	24	0	1	1
Radio Company	12	17	85	0	0	0	0	0	12	0	1	0
Special Service Company	5	0	172	96	30	18	0	0	0	0	0	0
Field Artillery Battalion												
Battalion HQ	18	4	123	19	15	6	0	0	0	4	8	4
Three Batteries, each	8	3	127	23	10	6	4	0	0	2	5	8
Service Battery	9	3	98	13	8	3	0	0	0	0	5	17
Engineer Battalion												
Battalion HQ	9	1	39	20	4	0	0	1	4	0	0	0
Three Engineer Companies, each	5	1	147	102	10	8	0	1	8	0	0	0
Transport Company	8	1	55	10	5	0	0	0	144	0	0	0
Pack Transport Battalion												
Battalion HQ	9	0	44	9	0	0	0	5	0	0	0	0
Four Pack Companies, each	8	1	55	10	5	0	0	0	144	0	0	0
Porter Transport Regiment												
Regiment HQ	7	0	21	9	0	0	0	0	0	0	0	0
4 Battalions, each												
Battalion HQ	8	0	40	9	0	0	0	0	0	0	0	0
Four Porter Companies, each	6	2	135	12	9	0	0	0	0	0	0	0
Field Hospital	13	0	122	0	0	0	0	0	0	0	40	0
Veterinary Detachment	3	0	24	0	0	0	0	1	5	0	2	0
Weapons Maint. Co.	9	6	129	0	0	0	0	0	0	0	4	8

The divisional signal company consisted of a 27-man headquarters, a 109-man wire platoon, and an 87-man radio platoon. The wire platoon had a 10-man switchboard section and a 99-man installation section, the latter with no fewer than 46 pack animals and 26 telephones. The radio platoon included a 17-man section with two SCR-583 radios for the division HQ, and two 30-man field sections each with an SCR-694 for subordinate units.

34th Year Division, from February 1945

	Officers	Warrant officers	Enlisted	Rifles	SMGs	Rifle grenade launchers	Light MGs	Medium MGs	60mm mortars	82mm mortars	AT rifles	AT rocket lnchrs	37mm AT guns	75mm pack how	Riding animals	Pack animals	Motor vehicles
Division HQ & Company	45	4	84	42	8	0	0	0	0	0	0	0	0	0	4	6	6
Special Service Company	5	1	171	96	30	0	18	0	0	0	0	0	0	0	0	0	0
Signal Company	31	1	191	95	15	0	0	0	0	0	0	0	0	0	0	56	0
Reconnaissance Company	6	5	178	80	54	0	18	0	0	0	0	0	0	0	0	0	0
Three Infantry Regiments, each																	
Regiment HQ	12	4	30	16	7	0	0	0	0	0	0	1	0	0	2	6	4
Signal Platoon	2	0	40	28	5	0	0	0	0	0	0	0	0	0	0	2	0
Special Service Platoon	1	0	35	19	4	3	2	0	0	0	0	0	0	0	0	0	0
Three Infantry Battalions, each																	
Battalion HQ	4	0	16	10	0	3	0	0	0	0	0	0	0	0	0	0	0
Three Rifle Companies, each	4	1	171	126	17	6	9	0	6	0	0	0	0	0	0	0	0
Machine Gun Company	6	1	102	47	15	5	0	8	0	0	0	0	0	0	2	16	0
Mortar Company	8	1	170	75	20	0	0	0	0	12	0	0	0	0	5	24	0
Anti-Tank Company	6	1	132	59	27	0	0	0	0	0	4	6	8	0	2	24	0
Transport Company	6	2	135	12	9	0	0	0	0	0	0	0	0	0	0	0	0
Pack Artillery Battalion																	
Battalion HQ	20	2	130	41	11	0	6	0	0	0	0	0	0	0	5	28	0
Three Batteries, each	7	2	197	56	18	0	6	0	0	0	0	0	0	4	4	77	0

34th Year Division, from February 1945 (continued)

	Officers	Warrant officers	Enlisted	Rifles	SMGs	Rifle grenade launchers	Light MGs	Medium MGs	60mm mortars	82mm mortars	AT rifles	AT rocket lnchrs	37mm AT guns	75mm pack how	Riding animals	Pack animals	Motor vehicles
Engineer Battalion																	
Battalion HQ	12	1	41	20	4	0	0	0	0	0	0	0	0	0	1	4	0
Three Engineer Companies, each	5	1	149	102	10	0	8	0	0	0	0	0	0	0	1	8	0
Transport Company	8	1	72	10	5	0	0	0	0	0	0	0	0	0	0	144	0
Porter Transport Battalion																	
Battalion HQ	8	0	35	9	0	0	0	0	0	0	0	0	0	0	0	0	0
Four Transport Companies, each	6	2	135	12	9	0	0	0	0	0	0	0	0	0	0	0	0
Medical Battalion																	
Battalion HQ	incl in Med Co.			0	0	0	0	0	0	0	0	0	0	0	0	0	0
Medical Company	15	0	171	0	0	0	0	0	0	0	0	0	0	0	0	0	0
Veterinary Platoon	3	0	24	0	0	0	0	0	0	0	0	0	0	0	0	0	0
Field Hospital	12	0	98	0	0	0	0	0	0	0	0	0	0	0	0	0	0

The engineer battalion was built around three companies, each of three 33-man platoons. The company had little in the way of engineer equipment except for three SCR-625 mine detectors in each platoon. Indeed, the subordinate platoons were referred to as rifle platoons and the personnel as infantrymen. Interestingly, although the company was triangular, it was only provided with eight light MGs, which were held in company HQ to be distributed as needed. The transport company had four 12-man platoons each with 36 pack animals (including four as relief animals). In terms of specialized equipment the battalion was to be issued a total of four US platoon sets of carpentry equipment, five of demolition material, and three of pioneer equipment.

Security for the division HQ was the responsibility of the special service company, made up of three platoons, each of two 25-man sections of infantry. The division's supply was the responsibility of the porter transport battalion, with four companies identical to those in the infantry regiments. Three of those companies supported the infantry regiments, each carrying 9,000 rounds of 7.92mm, 7,200 rounds of .45cal., 400 rounds of 37mm for the AT guns, 168 rounds of 60mm mortar, and 52 rounds for 82mm mortars, along with 2,820 pounds (1,280kg) of rice. The fourth company supported the division base troops with 21,000 rounds of 7.92mm, 9,000 rounds of .45cal., and 3,360 pounds (1,524kg) of rice.

Established at the same time were organization tables for the next-higher echelon, the army, although the likelihood of organizing units to these standards was essentially nil for the foreseeable future. An army controlled three divisions, which it supported with a motorized field artillery battalion, an engineer battalion, and various service units.

The sole fire support element for the field army was to be a single battalion of 12 105mm M2 howitzers, the weapons to be drawn by 2½-ton 6 x 6 trucks. Although equipment had been authorized for eight battalions of 155mm howitzers as well, the utility of these weapons in the China theater was questioned, and no further units, other than those contributed by the CAI, were formed.

Each 105mm howitzer battery included a radio squad with three SCR-610 radios to provide communications between the observer party forward and the firing battery, along with a switchboard, 11 telephones, and 12 miles (19km) of wire. The weapon used was the 105mm M2 howitzer towed by a 2½-ton SWB truck. Two more trucks, with 1-ton trailers, were provided to the battery's ammunition section for the carriage of 271 rounds of ammunition. The battery also included a Bren gun section with 21 men with six weapons for local and AA defense. Trucks were provided to move the weapons and equipment, but the troops still had to walk.

The main elements of the artillery battalion headquarters battery were the operations platoon and the signal platoon. The operations platoon consisted of a 4-man fire direction center section and an 18-man survey and instrument section. The signal platoon was made up of a 28-man wire section and a 15-man radio section, the latter with three SCR-610s and SCR-194s.

The service battery held a 16-man battalion maintenance section and an ammunition platoon with nine 2½-ton trucks with trailers for 1,221 rounds.

The army signal battalion consisted of two wire companies and a radio company. The 1st wire company consisted of a 27-man switchboard platoon and two 33-man installation (wire-laying) platoons. The 2nd wire company had three 33-man installation platoons. The radio company had two platoons with a total of eight radios (1 SCR-177, 1 SCR-193, 3 SCR-583, and 3 SCR-694), all of them pack-horse carried.

Guard and other details for the army HQ were provided by the special service company, which was built around three 53-man platoons, each of which was made up of six 8-man squads, each with a Bren gun. The company had no organic signal or transport means.

The engineer battalion had three engineer companies each of three platoons. Each platoon had three 9-man squads, with each squad having a sergeant, a corporal, and seven riflemen privates, and being provided with three SCR-625 mine detectors. The company headquarters had eight 3-man Bren gun teams for distribution as needed. The battalion also included a transport company for engineer tools and equipment.

The field army had two transport units. One was a small pack transport battalion with four companies, each with 32 pack animals (plus four relief animals). Each company had a capacity of 1,742kg and the battalion a total of 6,970kg. This battalion usually carried 75mm howitzer ammunition, a total of 640 rounds. The porter transport regiment had four battalions each of four companies. A porter company had four platoons each of 27 porters, so that a company could carry 2,940kg and the regiment 47,030kg. One porter battalion carried ammunition for each division in the army (36,000 rounds of 7.92mm, 25,200 rounds of .45cal., and 528 rounds of 60mm mortar), while the fourth porter battalion carried rifle and submachine gun ammunition for the army troops.

Initial reorganization efforts utilized these TO&Es but in January and February 1945 the Chinese high command reworked them slightly and reissued them as the 34th Year Division and Army. The changes were very modest, the one significant change being that while the rifle company still had nine M1903 rifles for use with grenade launchers, only six launchers were actually provided. The distribution of these within the company is not clear. In the regimental signal platoon one of the SCR-694s was replaced by an SCR-583, heavier and with longer range.

New Life for the Sponsored Units

Through late 1943 and into 1944 Y-Force continued its build-up, albeit at a pace limited by small-scale deliveries over the Hump and a marked absence of urgency on the part of the Chinese in supplying formations and replacement manpower. In March 1944 the CAI had begun its campaign in Burma, but still Y-Force was not ready. Indeed, in April Chiang explicitly notified Roosevelt that he would not order Y-Force into Burma. A few days later Roosevelt bluntly responded that "it is inconceivable to me that your YOKE Forces, with their American equipment, would be unable to advance against the Japanese Fifty-Sixth Division in its present depleted strength." A comment that if Yoke was not committed the American supply and training efforts "have not been justified," seems a thinly veiled threat to halt the aid program. Shortly thereafter the Americans in Chongqing made that threat explicit and that had the desired effect. On 14 April 1944 General He, as Minister of War, gave his approval to a crossing of the Salween. With this delay, however, only about 40 days remained before the normal start of the monsoon season.

In the meantime visions of a reborn Chinese military were sliding backwards. With no land link to the outside world on the immediate horizon the equipping of Z-Force based around Guilin looked less likely. A Z-Force staff of Americans had been formed on 1 January 1944, but the Chinese made it clear that they would not actually assemble the second batch of 30 divisions until American hardware began flowing in. Since the US Lend-Lease budget still provided only 10% equipment authorization for these units, and even that was subject to delays crossing the Hump, there really was little the US could offer.[*]

Y-Force finally launched its offensive across the Salween on 11 May 1944. The participating portion was the CEF, which by this time consisted of the XI and XX Group Armies and a total of 5 armies and 12 divisions, with an additional army and 3 divisions added at the last minute. The Salween offensive began to wind down in December 1944 and officially ended in January 1945 and the CEF was ordered to return to China for duties there.

Artillery shortages had been a problem throughout the campaign. The pace of training at the FATC was agonizingly slow and only four army battalions had completed training by the end of 1943 (6th, 71st, 2nd/2nd and 1st/93rd). Two more completed in April and another two in July 1944. In fact, artillery equipment was being delivered more quickly than units could be trained, and in July the Americans released eight battalion sets of pack howitzers, for the 4th, 10th, 31st, 46th and 74th Armies in southern China around Guilin, and the 30th and 75th Armies east of Ichang, along with one set for the Guilin training center. Three more battalion sets were released later that year, to the 18th, 52nd, and 60th Armies, although no more army battalions graduated from the FATC until May 1945.

In the meantime, the Japanese had launched their Ichi-Go offensive in April 1944. By September the Chinese forces in east China had been roughly handled[†] and Stilwell urged Chiang to concentrate them near Kunming. Stilwell's replacement, Wedemeyer, continued pushing the plan with the codename Alpha. One portion of this complex plan called for the movement by air of two highly competent CAI divisions, 14th and 22nd, back to China to participate in the defense of Kunming, starting in December 1944.

Once the route through Burma was secure the CEF could be moved into position around Kunming and they would form the heart of the defense. After some shuffling and reshuffling of units the Alpha Plan forces would consist of the New 6th Army (the two divisions from the CAI plus one other division), seven armies from Yoke Force's CEF, many of them veterans of the Salween fighting (2nd, 5th, 8th, 53rd, 54th, 71st, and 74th Armies), and four armies already in the Kunming area (13th, 18th, 73rd, and 94th). The Alpha Plan now absorbed the 30-division plan, and expanded it to 34 divisions (not counting the two CAI divisions), earmarked for the defense of Kunming. In early 1945 the New 6th Army (14th and 22nd Divisions) was officially added to the program, bringing it up to 36 divisions. As the New 1st Army, the rest of the CAI, entered China it too was added to the Alpha program, increasing it to a 39-division effort in late May. Of these, the ex-CAI units remained the cream of the crop right to the end of the war, highly trained, battle hardened and fortified with the knowledge that they could, and had, beaten the Japanese.[‡] The former

---

[*] By September 1944 Z-Force had issued to Chinese units 6,000 Lee-Enfield rifles in .303-inch, 1,711 Thompson submachine guns (80 M1 and the balance M1928A1), 352 Bren guns in .303-inch, 60 M1917A1 machine guns, 14 M2 .50-cal. machine guns, 338 Boys AT rifles, 534 AT rocket launchers, 30 37mm AT guns, and 30 60mm mortars for distribution to the second 30 divisions.

[†] Indeed, of the six battalion sets of 75mm howitzers (72 weapons) sent to southeast China, over 60 were lost. The 30th and 75th Armies retained theirs and continued working with American training teams.

[‡] There was some dispute as to who was responsible for supplying the ex-CAI divisions. While they were in Burma the US had assumed responsibility for providing their ordnance, while the Indian Army provided everything else, including pay, rations, uniforms, medicine, etc. These scales were far above those of divisions in China, and when the first two of the CAI divisions were repatriated by air in December 1944 the question arose as to who would continue this level of support. Eventually, India agreed to support the five divisions of

Army	Strength	Combat efficiency	% equipped	Commander	Location
New 1st (N30, N38, 50 Divs)	43,231	Excellent	100	Sun Liren	Gaoling, Guangxi
2nd (R2, 9, 76 Divs)	23,545	Satisfactory	10	Wang Lingyun	Baoshan, Yunnan
5th (45, 96, 200 Divs)	35,528	Satisfactory	88	Qiu Qingquan	Kunming, Yunnan
New 6th (14, N22, 207 Divs)	43,519	Excellent	100	Liao Yaoxiang	Zhijiang, Hubei
8th (H1, 103, 163 Divs)	34,942	Satisfactory	93	Li Mi	Bose, Guangxi
13th (4, 54, 89 Divs)	30,677	Satisfactory	88	Shi Jue	Lipu, Guangxi
18th (11, 18 & 118 Divs)	30,106	Very satisfactory	100	Hu Lian	Yuanling, Hunan
53rd (H2, 116, 130 Divs)	34,465	Unknown	30	Zhou Fuzhen	Midu, Yunnan
54th (8, 36, 198 Divs)	31,285	Satisfactory	100	Que Hanqian	Wuming, Guangxi
71st (87, 88, 91 Divs)	30,547	Very satisfactory	96	Chen Mingren	Liuzhou, Guangxi
73rd (15, 77, 193 Divs)	28,963	Satisfactory	100	Han Jun	Xinhua, Hunan
74th (51, 57, 68 Divs)	32,166	Very satisfactory	100	Shi Zhongcheng	Shanshuwan, Sichuan
94th (5, 43, 121 Divs)	37,531	Very satisfactory	79	*unknown*	Guilin, Guangxi

Condition of US-Sponsored Armies at the End of WWII

Y-Force divisions had combat experience and some training, but had taken heavy losses in the Salween offensive, particularly in junior officers, the very folks who were expected to implement individual and small-unit training.

The whole 30/34/36/39-division program, now also referred to as the Alpha program, was, of course, a collaborative venture of sorts. The Americans provided the equipment and the Chinese the manpower. Both parties had strong views and each essentially held a veto power over the whole process. The Americans had drafted the November 1943 tables of equipment and then fleshed them out into organization tables later that year. These were then provided to the MAC as a basis for discussion.

General He had been pressing for an increase in the number of US-sponsored divisions from the then-figure of 36 to 45, but Wedemeyer had held firm. On 29 January He agreed that the forces allocated to the Alpha Plan would consist of 36 "offensive" or "attacking" divisions to be US-equipped and trained, and 9 "defensive" divisions. He also presented his version of the TO&E for a sponsored division.

The offensive division organization table was almost identical to the US tables of November 1944. In February the definitive tables were issued as 34th Year Division type, and they were almost reprints of the American November 1944 tables.[*] In order to bring these divisions up to strength six army HQs and 13 divisions were to be deactivated and their personnel sent to the offensive divisions. The defensive divisions under He's plan were to use the old Y-Force tables of organization.

With the opening of the Burma Road in early 1945 it finally proved possible to begin implementing the sponsored-unit program that had begun as the 30-division plan and was

the CAI until 90 days after they arrived in China, and in June 1945 they agreed to an additional 90 days for items that could not be procured by other means.

[*] Later the tables were again issued without change, dated 5 July 1945.

The 116th Division of the 53rd Army near Mangshi, Yunnan, in February 1945.

now known as the 39-division Alpha Program with the addition of the final three divisions from the CAI. In February the 5th Army was officially placed on the Alpha list, in March the 2nd, 8th, 13th, 18th, 53rd, 73rd, and 74th Armies joined it, and in April the 54th, 71st, and 94th Armies were added. In addition, the New 1st and New 6th Armies, formerly CAI, were included to complete the program.

Although the number of divisions to be modernized fluctuated somewhat over time, by early 1945 this force was clearly the heart of the American vision for China's military future. In March 1945 the major US leaders in China, Wedemeyer, Ambassador Hurley, SACO's Milton Miles, and others, were called to Washington for a top-level conference to decide American strategy for the China Theater. At this series of meetings the Joint Chiefs of Staff approved the Beta plan, the drive to the coast to seize Guangzhou and Hong Kong, and the nature of US support. For the long term they wanted to see a unified China with a core of competent forces.

They spoke against a background of China Theater's effort to create 36 US-sponsored Chinese divisions, well fed, well led, fully equipped, and trained, supported by an efficient service of supply and a revitalized air force, and thoroughly blooded by driving the Japanese out of south and central China. Their appraisals of China's future implicitly assumed the existence of such a force.[*]

Of course, the opening of the Burma Road was not a panacea for the supply problems. Priorities had to be established and Wedemeyer's plan was to equip 20 China-based divisions completely and the five CAI divisions first, and then worry about the others. His

---

[*] Romanus and Sunderland, *Time Runs Out in CBI*, US Army Center of Military History, 1959, p. 338.

more detailed plan called for a first group of six divisions (two each in the 13th and 8th Armies, one each in the 18th and 94th Armies), and a second group of eight more divisions (two each in the 5th, 54th, and 74th Armies and one each in the 18th and 94th Armies). The Chinese view was that it was preferable to equip two divisions in each army fully, and then go back and equip the third when possible.

In May the scheme was changed to divide the first batch of armies into two groups. The 13th, 54th, 71st, and 94th Armies were to be fully equipped by 1 August 1945, and the 5th, 8th, 18th, and 74th Armies two weeks later.

In some cases the reorganization proceeded fairly smoothly, for instance in the case of the 54th Army, a former CEF unit:

On the 25th of [February 1945] orders were received that the Army had been selected as one of the units to be equipped with American equipment and weapons. The order also stated that the three divisions of the Army would be the 8th, 36th, and 198th. In addition the Army was ordered to the vicinity of Hsing-Jen, Kweichow [Guizhou], China, for reorganization. The move to this area took place during the month of March.

During April, May, and June of 1945 the Army was reorganized according to the Table of Organizations set up for the Alpha Divisions. Recruits were received and new American weapons and equeipment issued. On or about the 1st of May 1945 an intensified training program, under American supervision and according to standards was started. This continued until the 1st week of July 1945 when orders were received on 2 July for the Army to move to the Nanning area in Kwangsi [Guangxi] province. The first units left their training area on 4 July and the last units closed in the Nanning area in the later part of August.. They were in this area when the Japanese Army surrendered.[*]

In some cases this involved some shifting of units, as in the 13th Army:

The XIII Army was brought down from the north in Nov–Dec 1944, to stop the Japanese drive on Kweiyang [Guiyang] in Kweichow province. On January 7, an American Combat Section joined them to conduct training and supervise the issue of US equipment. At that time, the Army comprised the 4th, 89th, and temporary 16th Divisions. On Feb. 15, the Army was reorganized. The T.16th Div. was broken up and used as fillers for the 4th and 89th, while the 54th Div. came in from the XCVII Army. The latter were inferior in physical condition, and were not initially scheduled to receive US arms.[†]

In this case training was halted in early July and the army committed to combat.

In the Eastern Command the 18th, 73rd, and 74th Army entered training in February, but had to be pulled back out in April to meet the Japanese attack on Baoching. They returned to training in late June, at which time the units were reorganized on to the Alpha

[*] *History of 54th Army and Subordinate Commands*; HQ, LIV Army, Chinese Combat Command (Prov), US Forces China Theater, 8 September 1945.

[†] *Historical Record*, HQ XIII Army Combat Section, Chinese Combat Command (Prov), US Forces China Theater, 1 September 1945

US-Sponsored Divisional Artillery Units, July 1945			
Unit	*Strength*	*Status of training*	*Original designation*
Divisional Artillery Battalions			
Hon 1st	758	Satisfactory	8th Army Artillery Battalion
Hon 2nd		Very satisfactory	1st Training Battalion, FATC
4th		Satisfactory	1/7 Artillery Regiment
5th*		*unknown*	1/21 Artillery Regiment
9th		Very satisfactory	2nd Army Artillery Battalion
11th*		*unknown*	2nd Training Battalion, FATC
14th	759	Very satisfactory	1st Battalion, 22nd Division Artillery
15th	511	*unknown*	1/29 Artillery Regiment
18th*		*unknown*	4th Training Battalion FATC
22nd	775	Very satisfactory	2nd Battalion, 22nd Division Artillery
N 30th		*unknown*	newly formed
36th	662	Satisfactory	54th Army Artillery Battalion
38th		*unknown*	newly formed
45th	740	Satisfactory	3/5 Army Artillery Regiment
50th	714	Excellent	newly formed
51st		Very satisfactory	1/30 Artillery Regiment
57th		Very satisfactory	2/30 Artillery Regiment
77th	627	*unknown*	2/29 Artillery Regiment
87th		Very satisfactory	71st Army Artillery Battalion
88th		Very satisfactory	71st Army Temp Artillery Battalion
89th		Satisfactory	2/7 Artillery Regiment
96th	770	Very satisfactory	1/5 Army Artillery Regiment
103rd	629	Satisfactory	3rd Training Battalion, FATC
116th	621	Very satisfactory	53rd Army Artillery Battalion
121st	1719	Excellent	2/21 Artillery Regiment
198th	700	Satisfactory	5th Training Battalion, FATC
200th	769	Excellent	2/5 Army Artillery Regiment
Res 2nd*		*unknown*	6th Army Artillery Battalion

* Units still at the FATC. All units were equipped with 12 US 75mm pack howitzers.

TO&Es. In that command, at least, the TO&E strength for an Alpha division had risen slightly to 680 officers and 10,329 enlisted (versus 673 and 10,317 in the November 1944 document), but the number of animals authorized had dropped from 997 to 871. Even by late July, however, those divisions were still about 20% under strength.

The most complex part of the implementation of the Alpha program was the redistribution of artillery units. The Y-Force elements, who formed the bulk of the Alpha units, had been operating with an allotment of no divisional artillery and one 75mm pack howitzer battalion per army. Under the initial concept of the sponsored (later Alpha) units, each division was to receive not only its own pack howitzer battalion, but also a motorized 105mm howitzer battalion. The latter, however, proved impractical and these

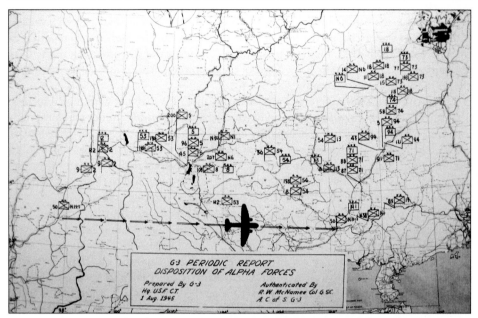

Disposition of Alpha forces at the end of the war.

were deleted in the November 1944 TO&Es. This reduction in requirements, however, did not eliminate the need for a complex and carefully choreographed realignment of artillery units, which was ordered, for the most part, by a series of telegrams sent out by the MAC on 20 February 1945.

The requirement for 75mm pack howitzers stood at 39, one battalion per division. They already had 10 army artillery battalions (including two in the 71st Army and three in the 5th Army), four two-battalion artillery regiments equipped with these weapons (7th, 21st, 29th, and 30th), and five training battalions at the FATC that could be released. A further four training battalions at the FATC were equipped except for animals. In addition, the CAI contributed six more battalions. There were also three battalions with non-sponsored units (52nd Army, 60th Army, and Yunnan–Guizhou Artillery Battalion).

In fact, as an interim measure it had been decided to afford priority to two of the divisions in each of the sponsored armies, as had been done earlier with Y-Force, and use the third division as a replacement pool for trained personnel until equipment could be found for it.

Thus, the immediate requirements were for only two battalions per army, a total of 26 battalions. This target could be, and was, met with little trouble, other than the usual reluctance of commanders to part with their units.

The Alpha program also envisioned 24 motorized battalions of 105mm howitzers. This would provide one battalion to each Alpha army as well as four regiments of GHQ troops. To that end the battalions of the 13th, 18th, 54th, 71st, and 94th Army were raised from cadres in India, that of the 53rd Army was converted from the CAI anti-aircraft MG battalion, while the 15th Artillery Regiment contributed the battalions for the New 6th and 8th Army, the 22nd Artillery Regiment for the 73rd and 74th Army, 2nd/6th Artillery Regiment became the 2nd Army battalion and 2nd/19th Artillery regiment was redesignated as the 5th Army battalion. The New 1st Army already had its own battalion from the CAI organization. The first of these battalions, for the 54th Army, reported to the FATC in March 1945, followed by six more (including one by conversion of the CAI anti-aircraft MG battalion) by June. None of these, however, had completed its training at the FATC by the end of the war.

The American effort to create a modern army in China had met with mixed success. That the Chinese soldier was tough and brave was beyond question. Junior and most mid-level officers were dedicated and similarly courageous. Unfortunately, they were almost completely untrained in the ways of modern war. Unlike the forces in India, which could almost be built from the ground up, here the Y-FOS advisers had to deal with existing units and leadership. Further, the small advisory teams that were attached to the divisions of the CEF had no command authority, but could only advise on training programs.

Initially training efforts centered on the field artillery branch, as that promised high payoff should the Chinese be broken of their habits of using direct fire almost exclusively and of parceling guns out individually. To that end the Field Artillery Training Center (FATC) was set up to train or retrain entire units from the ground up. That was a long process, however, and only two battalions were turned out in 1943 plus five more in 1944, all with 75mm howitzers. For the most part the artillery of the CEF fought the Salween offensive with little Western training beyond that which their advisers could impart.

An Infantry Training Center had been set up in 1943 in hopes of training mid-level infantry officers, but had closed less than a year later, its facilities taken over by a new general staff school, the need for which was apparently felt greater. It was reactivated in January 1945 to train both officers and enlisted.

Lower-level infantry training, at platoon, company, and battalion level, was carried out on site by the few advisers available to each division. The results were predictable. American observers reported that CEF troops often launched frontal attacks with little fire support and rarely used fire and movement. Loses were heavy as a result, including junior officers who often led from the front.

By the start of 1945 the CEF divisions had learned many lessons the hard way and, although still not as proficient as their CAI colleagues, were considerably improved over their state a year or two earlier. Further training and equipping during the year resulted in a force that was starting to show an aptitude for mobile warfare by the time the final battles were fought.

11

Provincial Units

The large number of units paid, administered, and directed by the provincial governors usually adopted local TO&Es. Because they are poorly documented only a few "snapshots" of these organizations can be provided.

Shanxi and Suiyuan

Governor Yan had built up a large and outwardly impressive force by 1937, well equipped with the products of his Taiyuan Arsenal. Controlled by him through a network of relatives, the forces nominally part of the National Army at the start of the war were the 19th Army (70th and 72nd Divisions), 33rd Army (66th and 69th Divisions), 34th Army (71st Division), 35th Army (73rd Division), 61st Army (68th and 101st Divisions), and the Cavalry Army (1st and 2nd Cavalry Divisions), along with the 1st Cavalry Brigade and 2nd, 3rd, and 7th Infantry Brigades. There were also three provincial formations, the 1st, 2nd, and 3rd Shanxi Brigades. All of the divisions were of the old six-regiment type with two or three brigade HQs, with a strength of about 7,000–9,000 men and 600–900 horses. The troops actually answerable to the central government consisted of the 21st Division in Shanxi and the 13th Army in Suiyuan.

The 1930 organization report showed the Shanxi forces organized their rifle companies as three platoons each of three 14-man sections, each with a light machine gun. A battalion had three rifle companies and a heavy weapons company, and the regiment three battalions. The heavy company had two machine-gun platoons, each with two 10-man squads, and a mortar platoon with two 11-man squads. The division had two brigades each of three regiments. Yan had a total of 107 such regiments, along with a machine-gun regiment, this having three battalions, each of four 6-gun companies. Yan's force also included 12 cavalry regiments each of four squadrons, each 120 men and 130 horses in four platoons. There were also one field and 12 mountain artillery regiments, each three battalions of three batteries. The field regiment had 27 pieces while the pack regiment had 36.

Even though reinforced by central units after the outbreak of the war, Yan's forces did not fight particularly well in 1937 and he was driven into the mountains in the south and west, taking most of his army with him. Content to wait the war out, he expanded his force into a fairly large one built around the 6th, 7th, 8th, and 13th Army Groups with eight army HQs and 25 infantry divisions (including three nominal cavalry divisions converted to infantry in 1939 for lack of suitable horses, and one division denominated a brigade for historical reasons). In fact, the army groups were not command headquarters, but merely served to provide high-rank billets for Yan's clique, and actual command ran straight to the army HQs.

By 1944 each of his divisions had an authorized strength of 702 officers and 7,502 enlisted, divided into a headquarters, a medical platoon, a "special mission" company, a scout unit, and three infantry regiments. An infantry regiment was made up of a headquarters, a machine-gun/mortar company, a signal platoon, a scout unit and a medical platoon, along with the three infantry battalions. The battalion had a headquarters and four rifle companies. Each of the rifle companies consisted of a headquarters, a small trains element, and three platoons, each of three sections, each of a sergeant, two corporals, 12 privates, a cook, and a laborer/porter. The sections were well armed, being divided into two squads, one provided with a Taiyuan-made Thompson submachine gun and the other a light machine gun, along with their rifles. Each platoon HQ included a Type 27 or Japanese grenade launcher.

Above the platoon level, however, armament was weak, probably reflecting the loss of heavy weapons during the retreat of 1937. There was no company- or battalion-level fire support and the regiment provided only a small machine-gun/mortar company. This unit consisted of two machine-gun platoons, each of two 13-man sections, and a mortar platoon of two 17-man sections, for a company total of four medium machine guns and two 82mm mortars. There was no divisional fire-support element. Thus, while the rifle platoons were well armed by Chinese standards, above the platoon level the only fire support in the whole division consisted of a dozen medium machine guns and six 82mm mortars.

The division special mission company had three identical platoons, each of three 12-man sections, although one was designated a signal platoon and the other two special mission platoons, presumably HQ guard units. Supplementing their communications efforts were four radio teams, one at the division level and one for each regiment. The medical unit at the division and regiment level consisted of four stretcher-bearer sections each of 12 men. The scout units were intelligence formations of 10 officers, who wore civilian clothes and gathered information in the countryside.

At the division and regiment levels there was also an "economic administrative unit," whose function was to supervise the farming the soldiers were required to perform in order to keep the units fed and to acquire food from the local communities. It also supervised the production of small items by the troops, such as gloves, shoes, and uniforms.

In any event, there was little likelihood that these units would see combat. That was probably fortunate, since a US Army team that observed the war zone for three months starting in early December 1944 reported most of the units to be untrained and not combat-worthy. The only exceptions noted were the three converted cavalry divisions, the 70th Division (selected for the final defense of the war zone HQ if needed), and the 66th Division, all of which were rated "satisfactory" by comparison with other Chinese units generally.

At the outbreak of the war the Cavalry Army was still a mounted formation, with the 1st and 2nd Cavalry Divisions. Each of these had three mounted regiments (3rd, 5th, and 6th in the 1st Division; and 4th, 7th, and 8th in the 2nd Division), giving a division a strength of 2,500 men with 1,750 horses. A 4th Cavalry Division was activated shortly thereafter, but after the fall of Taiyuan it proved almost impossible to secure replacements for old or sick horses and the three cavalry divisions were converted to infantry divisions, although keeping their cavalry designation.

There was one independent cavalry regiment that actually had some horses, the last remnant of Yan's former large cavalry force. This was built around four rifle squadrons, each of four rifle platoons, each of three sections, each section consisting of a sergeant, a corporal, and 12 privates. Each section was provided with a light machine gun, a Type 27 or Japanese grenade launcher, and rifles. The regiment also included a machine-gun squadron of two platoons, each of two 12-man sections and a scout platoon of three 11-man sections. The regiment thus had an authorized strength of 61 officers and 1,077 enlisted with 823 horses and 38 mules, armed with 33 pistols, 288 rifles, 8 submachine guns, 48 light and 4 medium machine guns, and 48 grenade launchers.

Yan's forces had lost much of their artillery in their retreat from Taiyuan in 1937 and the remaining pieces were concentrated in four line artillery regiments and a training regiment. The 23rd Regiment had eight batteries in three battalions, three batteries equipped with Type 13 mountain guns, three with Type 18 mountain guns, and two with Type 18 88mm field guns. The 24th Regiment also had eight batteries in three battalions, six armed with Type 13 mountain guns and the remaining two with Type 18 mountain guns. The 27th and 28th Regiments were identical, with eight batteries in three battalions, all equipped with Type 13 mountain guns. The Training Regiment had one 3-battery battalion for basic training and labor, with no guns, one 3-battery battalion with 105mm mountain howitzers, and one 2-battery battalion with 75mm mountain guns. In addition to the battalions, each regiment also had an observation/signal platoon of four sections, each of a sergeant, a corporal, and eight privates.

Yan also formed three "Guerilla Divisions." Each of these consisted of a special duty company and three guerilla regiments. The special duty company had a rifle platoon, a cavalry platoon, and a signal platoon. A guerilla regiment consisted of three battalions, a heavy weapons company, and a signal platoon. A battalion had three companies, each of three platoons, each of three 14-man sections. The guerilla regiment also included a "plain clothes detective" platoon of three 11-man sections to gather clandestine information. The guerilla divisions, however, received no special training and appear to have done little. American observers in early 1945 noted that the soldiers and lower-level officers were generally of good quality but not well trained, while the higher ranking officers were ineffectual.

The military police force consisted of three battalions, each of three companies, each of three platoons, each of these, in turn, made up of three sections each of a sergeant, a corporal, and eight privates. These were apparently well disciplined soldiers, but too few and too lightly armed to make a difference militarily.

The engineer group controlled three regiments, each consisting of three battalions with the same organization as an infantry battalion. No special equipment was provided.

Also present were nine garrison regiments, tasked to relieve the regular infantry troops of routine guard duties. The garrison regiments had no fixed strength and averaged 123 officers and 1,600 enlisted scattered in isolated posts ranging from platoon to battalion size. On average such a regiment had 21 pistols, 5 submachine guns, 475 rifles, and 26 LMGs.

The final force in II War Zone was Yan's militia. Theoretically this consisted of all able-bodied males in the area, these being given training. The strength of the militia was 6,394 officers and 47,157 enlisted and the rolls showed them as armed with 580 pistols, 68 submachine guns, 12,551 rifles, 599 light machine guns, and 64 grenade launchers. In fact, the weapons issued were aged and often non-functional. Their combat value was almost nil.

Yunnan

Lung Yun, governor of Yunnan, retained substantial autonomy throughout the war. During the early 1930s and even after the start of the war he equipped his own forces, mostly from the French, on a respectable scale, often adopting new types of weapons before the central government did.

Yunnan provincial troops with their French-style helmets,
Mauser rifles, and FN M1930 light machine guns.

In 1936 Lung reorganized his force to consist of six infantry brigades: 1st (1st and 2nd Regiments), 2nd (3rd and 4th Regiments), 3rd (5th and 6th Regiments), 5th (9th and 10th Regiments), 7th (13th and 14th Regiments), and 9th (17th and 18th Regiments). There were also two guard regiments and other smaller elements.

With the outbreak of the war a new force was formed for field service, the 60th Army, consisting of the 182nd, 183rd, and 184th Divisions. Once that was dispatched for combat service in the spring of 1938 a second force, the 58th Army, was formed for duty in Yunnan. When the 60th Army returned in 1939, the 58th Army was sent out to IX War Zone, where it partially lost its Yunnan affiliation over time.

There is evidence Lung had been considering expansion even before the war began, with large-scale orders placed in 1936–7 for machine guns, mortars, and even a few tanks.

Thus well-positioned in terms of supplies, he was able to expand his force quickly so that by late 1943 his command had been redesignated the 1st Army Group and consisted of the 60th Army (182nd and 184th Divisions) and the 2nd Route Army (18th, 20th, 21st, and 22nd Yunnan Divisions), along with the 23rd Yunnan Division and smaller units. During 1944 another army HQ was created, so that the 1st Army Group consisted of the 60th Army (182nd and 184th Divisions), 1st Route Army (18th and 20th Yunnan Divisions) and the 2nd Route Army (21st and 22nd Divisions). The 19th and 23rd Yunnan Divisions, along with the 2nd Independent Infantry Brigade (a division in all but name), the Yunnan Artillery Regiment, and an anti-aircraft battalion remained separate. At that time, the Yunnan Divisions were redesignated as "temporary" divisions with the same numbers.

In addition, the 58th Army (New 10th and New 11th Divisions) and the New 3rd Army (183rd and New 12th Divisions) served in Guangxi to the end of the war.

A late-war Yunnan rifle company consisted of three platoons each of three sections. Each section consisted of a section leader, a four-man light MG team with a Belgian-made BAR, and an eight-man rifle team. Three rifle companies plus a machine-gun company (including a 60mm mortar platoon) made up the infantry battalion. The regiment consisted of three battalions, a 300-man transport company, a mortar company (six 81mm or 82mm mule-packed weapons), a signal platoon, and a medical detachment.

Guangdong

The former Guangdong provincial units were concentrated in the 4th Route Army, along with the 11th and 67th Divisions of the central government. There were 10 such divisions, each of two brigades, each of three infantry regiments.

Most of these were formed into the 12th Group Army consisting of the 62nd Army (151st and 152nd Divisions), the 63rd Army (153rd and 154th Divisions), and the 65th Army (156th, 157th, and 158th Divisions). At the start of the war the 152nd Division (454th and 456th Brigades with six infantry regiments numbered 907–912) garrisoned Hainan Island, along with the 9th Independent Brigade (Infantry Regiments 625–627). The brigade returned to the mainland in September 1937 and between December 1937 and October 1938 the division essentially abandoned the island.

The Group Army commander was General Yu Hanmou, who apparently ran a headquarters good enough for peacetime, but which failed the test of war. In March 1938, before the Japanese attacked his

Guangdong Divisions, February 1937		
Division	*Brigades*	*Regiments*
151st	451st	901, 902, 903
	453rd	904, 905, 906
152nd	454th	907, 908, 909
	456th	910, 911, 912
153rd	457th	913, 914, 915
	469th	916, 917, 918
154th	460th	919, 920, 921
	462nd	922, 923, 924
155th	463rd	925, 926, 927
	465th	928, 929, 930
156th	466th	931, 932, 933
	468th	934, 935, 936
157th	469th	937, 938, 939
	471st	940, 941, 942
158th	472nd	943, 944, 945
	473rd	946, 947, 948
159th	475th	949, 950, 951
	477th	952, 953, 954
160th	478th	955, 956, 957
	480th	958, 959, 960

forces, a British military observer referred to Yu as honest and, although "not brilliant or smart," a thinker and of steady disposition. Further, he said that "his second in command is a good man, and his G.S.O.1 is brilliant." Following the debacle in Guangdong, a revised British report on a visit to the theater in May 1939 referred to "the inept Yu Han-

Mau and his still more incompetent chief of staff" as retaining their jobs despite their disastrous performances.[*]

The characterizations of the troops changed as well. The earlier report opined that "the Kwangtung [Guangdong] infantry are probably among the most effective in China" and that a good proportion were "seasoned and reliable fighters." By the time the second report was written they were noting that "the morale, discipline and training of the [12th Army Group] as a whole is low; the men have no confidence in their officers; whilst the latter are divided into internecine cliques whose only common concern is to indulge in as much squeeze and graft as possible."

If Yu's performance was disappointing, that did not appear to have reduced his power and indeed he was rewarded with command of VII War Zone in addition to his Group Army. By December 1941 Chinese staff in VII War Zone (Guangdong and southern Fukien) were telling the British in Hong Kong that their forces comprised over 251,000 troops and provided a detailed (although somewhat suspect) troop list as shown in Appendix V. In addition, the war zone received attachments from the general reserve, including two battalions of the 14th Artillery Regiment (12 x 150mm howitzers), the 2nd Heavy Mortar Regiment (19 x 150mm mortars), two battalions of the 1st Mountain Artillery Regiment (4 guns), seven companies of infantry guns (28 old Russian 37mm guns), and one AA company (4 x 37mm German guns).

By adroitly avoiding contact with the Japanese and remaining away from the coastline and the major cities Yu was able to keep his forces intact to the end of the war. Nevertheless, under pressure from the Japanese his 62nd Army (then consisting of the 151st, 157th and 158th Divisions) and 64th Army (then the 155th, 156th, and 159th Divisions) had pulled back into IV War Zone in Guangxi by mid-1944. Combat operations during the fall of 1944, however, reduced their fighting efficiency to almost nil by December.

By July 1945 the Guangdong troops, still formed into the 151st–154th and 156th–160th Divisions, were found in two areas, generally formed into armies with two Guangdong and one non-Guangdong divisions. The VII War Zone, and its nominally subordinate 12th Army Group, both concurrently commanded by Yu Hanmou, had the 63rd Army (152nd, 153rd, and 186th Divisions) and the 65th Army (154th, 160th, and 187th Divisions), along with the 158th Division and the 9th and 20th Brigades. The 2nd Area Army in Guangxi commanded the 62nd Army (95th, 151st, and 157th Divisions) and the 64th Army (131st, 156th, and 159th Divisions).

Guangdong was also the home of the only significant armored force outside central control. It had one company of Vickers amphibian very light tanks and one of Thornycroft-based armored cars prewar. These units moved to the town of Zengcheng, east of Guangzhou, on 18 October 1938, were attacked by Japanese naval aircraft, losing five armored cars, and then attacked by Japanese tanks. The Japanese infiltrated behind and cut the armored force off, occupying all the bridges. The remaining 70 armored vehicle crewmen destroyed their vehicles and escaped on foot shortly before the fall of Zengcheng on 22 October.

Also alone among the semi-independent provinces, Guangdong had a heavy anti-aircraft battalion. The Vickers 75mm guns were purchased by the provincial government

---

[*] The March 1938 report is entitled "Report on Military and General Conditions in Guangzhou, July 1937–March 1938, by Lieutenant H. F. G. Chauvin, RA." The later is entitled "Report on a Visit to the Headquarters of the IV War Zone at Shiukwan (North Kwangtung), by Captain C. R. Boxer and Captain H. Chauvin, April–May 1939." Both can be found at the UK National Archives in WO106/5303.

in 1933 for the defense of Guangzhou and were organized into an air defense unit of battalion size, consisting of three batteries, each of four guns. Each gun was provided with a light (3½-ton, 25hp) full-tracked Vickers tractor. The battery instruments, including the UB.2A height and range finder, fit into a trailer pulled by a medium (80hp) Vickers tractor. In addition, each battery had a 1½-ton truck for supplies. The battalion also included a searchlight section with three Barr & Stroud HCD 90cm lamps and sound locators.

The Vickers battalion was clearly purchased fully equipped and at the time was a capable collection of arms and equipment. By 1938, however, it was starting to show its age. The situation was exacerbated by the appointment of an idle and corrupt commander who was not relieved until after the start of hostilities. The bulk of the battalion and almost all its equipment was lost in the inept withdrawal from the Guangzhou area in 1938. The surviving personnel were withdrawn to Nam Po, where they briefly manned six naval-style Vickers 2pdr AA guns. Vulnerable points in Guangzhou, such as factories, bridges, power stations, and others, were defended by single-barrel Hotchkiss 13.2mm MGs, while the four railway bridges serving the Guangzhou–Hankou Railway around Sheklung were defended by single- and twin-barrel Hotchkiss.

Sichuan

Ringed by mountains, Sichuan remained relatively isolated through the mid-1930s. The province was politically fragmented with a number of minor warlords jockeying for position, but by 1932 the Chongqing-based Liu Hsiang had established himself as the preeminent power. Increasing communist presence in Sichuan led Liu to accept the presence of 20,000 Nationalist troops in 1934. In March 1936 the US military attaché reported that the central government had the 4th Army (45th and 90th Divisions), the 5th Army (23rd and 43rd Divisions), the 9th Army (47th and 54th Divisions), and the 36th Army (5th Division) in the province, each army having 18,000 men. In contrast, he reported the local Sichuan troops to consist of the 20th Army (133rd, 134th, and 135th Divisions), 21st Army (1st and 4th Division, and one undesignated division), 23rd Army (Training Division, 5th Division and 4th Brigade), 24th Army (136th, 137th, and 138th Divisions, and 1st Brigade), 41st Army (122nd, 123rd, and 124th Divisions), 44th Army (1st and 2nd Divisions, 1st Brigade), 45th Army (125th, 126th, 127th, 128th, and 131st Divisions), and three independent divisions: the 1st, 23rd, and 104th. The divisions had an average strength of 6,500 men and their idiosyncratic and sometimes duplicated numbering system was presumably a carry-over from the earlier multiple warlord armies.

In early 1937 Chiang moved further substantial forces into the province and Liu accepted the seemingly inevitable and handed over command of his troops to the central government, resulting in modest reorganization. The Japanese invasion of China, however, temporarily reversed the tide and Liu was placed back in charge of his troops. In October 1937 Liu's contribution to the Chinese Army consisted of the 122nd–128th, 134th–138th, 144th–150th, 161st–164th, 167th, and 168th Divisions, along with fourteen brigades (7th–20th). This proved to be short-lived, however, as Liu died of a stomach ailment in January 1938. The Sichuan troops were finally integrated into the national command structure shortly thereafter, and when the Nationalists moved their capital to Chongqing the absorption into the national fold was irrevocably completed.

The Ma Clique

The so-called "Ma clique" was a group of Muslim generals connected by family ties ("Ma" being a common Chinese rendering of "Muhammad") who served for three generations as leaders of the sparsely populated western provinces of Ningxia, Gansu, and Qinghai from the imperial regime through to the communist take-over. They tended to favor cavalry and the forces were relatively lightly armed.

Ma Hong-kui's 17th Army Group was based in Ningxia, where he was also provincial governor, and consisted of the 81st Army, 168th Division, 1st and 10th Cavalry Brigades, and two garrison brigades. In late 1944 the central government's 11th Army was moved in as well. Ma Hong-bin's 81st Army consisted of the 35th and Temporary 60th Divisions, plus a cavalry regiment. As the Japanese approached its home base the army moved east and engaged the enemy in the battle of west Suiyuan in 1940, performing well and stopping the Japanese advance before returning to its home base.

Qinghai recruits in 1942.

Ma Bu-fang was the provincial governor of Qinghai province, where he based his 40th Army Group consisting of the 82nd Army (which he also commanded directly) and the 5th Cavalry Army under Ma Bu-qing. The former was a large force, consisting of the 100th and Temporary 61st Divisions, plus the 8th and New 8th Cavalry Divisons, although the 8th Cavalry Division spent much of its time detached to serve as a mounted force for I War Zone in Henan province. The 5th Cavalry Army was based in Gansu, where Ma Bu-qing used it to rule the province, and consisted of the 5th, Temporary 1st, and Temporary 2nd Cavalry Divisions.

Reported Strengths of Ningxia, Qinghai & Gansu Forces, December 1944			
	Men	*Horses*	*Weapons*
42nd Army	16,394	2,337	5,115 rifles, 365 LMG, 110 MG, 52 mortars
Res. 7th Div.	6,718		
191st Div.	6,834		
81st Army	14,995	568	4,981 rifles, 183 LMG, 99 MG
(breakdown by divisions not available)			
82nd Army	18,518	4,099	11,069 rifles, 365 LMG, 26 MG, 33 mortars, 8 mtn guns
100th Div.	6,421		
Temp. 61st Div.	4,901		
New 8th Cav. Div.	2,798		
5th Cavalry Army	9,733	7,069	3,258 rifles, 133 LMG, 8 MG
(breakdown by divisions not available)			
8th Cav. Div. (det.)	2,877		
168th Div.	*Unknown*		

Xinjiang

Sheng Shi-cai took over as the final ethnic Chinese (Han) warlord of the remote majority-Turkic northwestern province of Xinjiang in 1933. He nominally inherited the 36th Division of Chinese Muslim ("Tungan") troops, primarily a mounted force, that had been formed a year earlier by General Ma Zhong-ying, who grew increasingly independent. The division put down several minor rebellions by local Turkic Muslim ethnic groups while Sheng moved into the Soviet orbit in return for badly needed financial and military aid. By 1935 the division, consisting of about 10,000 troops in two brigades, mostly mounted and well trained, had emerged as a Nationalist Chinese competitor to the Soviet-leaning Sheng. In 1937 the Soviets sent a 5,000-man force into the province and, with Sheng's assistance and the defection of the Tungan 2nd Brigade, destroyed the division.* This left the field to the ragtag forces of Sheng's assorted provincial allies which he gradually consolidated into the "Anti-Imperialist Army" independent of the central government. In May 1937, as Sheng consolidated his hold, the Soviets moved a task force (known officially as the Red Army 8th Regiment) to garrison the strategic oasis of Kumul without permission of either the Chinese or Sheng's government. After the outbreak of the war with Japan Xinjiang became the main supply route to China for Soviet materials and Moscow built further bases there.

The German attack on the Soviet Union (with Soviet suspension of aid to China) and the Japanese attack on the Western powers realigned Sheng's calculations considerably. He opened negotiations with Chongqing for reinstatement as a loyal provincial governor in early 1942. This was accomplished in October 1942, whereupon he demanded the withdrawal of all Soviet military from the province. The last of those left a year later.

---

* A new 36th Division was formed by the central government far to the east.

On the departure of the Soviet troops Sheng had about 20,000 men under his command, but probably only about 10% of them were formed into reliable, passably competent units. He expanded those forces, but Chiang moved quickly and inserted his own elements. His power-base gone, Sheng was called to Chongqing in September 1944 and the central government installed its own governor. Chiang moved his own 29th Army to the province, and shortly thereafter reorganized it from four small divisions into the New 2nd Army with the New 45th and New 46th Divisions. It was shortly bolstered by the 5th Cavalry and 42nd Armies of "Ma Clique" forces that were also brought into the province.

In the meantime the nomadic population of Xinjiang grew ever more restless. Already, by mid-1944 the provincial and central government forces in Xinjiang had their hands full dealing with local and Soviet-sponsored ethnic rebellions featuring repeated atrocities by all sides. In the end the Xinjiang forces never left the province and contributed nothing to the war against Japan.

12

Guerrilla Duties for Residual Forces

It was not uncommon in the opening phases of the war, when the Japanese were smashing their way through the countryside against ineffective opposition, for entire Nationalist divisions to scatter. When that happened commanders would sometimes assign a "guerrilla" mission to the division. That preserved the division, at least in name, pay continued, as did rations, and face was saved. Some of those divisions effectively ceased to operate, others split into small groups with varying objectives, and some formed the basis for more long-term forces.

In March 1945 the Ministry of War specified that it had 15 guerrilla or commando HQs controlling 65 "units" with a total strength of 14,429 officers and 209,987 enlisted, 31 "sub-units" totaling 2,635 officers and 34,994 enlisted, and 6 independent battalions with 158 officers and 4,501 enlisted. It is not known how accurate this count was, nor to what extent each of the varying elements actually answered to MAC's directives.

Some divisions formed guerrilla units of their own. Here guerrilla troops of the 58th Division are being trained in the M1 carbine and Thompson in January 1945.

Guerrillas as Elite Units

Plans had been laid out in mid-1941 at British urging for the creation of "elite" commando/guerrilla battalions for operations behind Japanese lines. Such a battalion would have a

headquarters and three companies. A company consisted of three platoons, each of three sections, for a total of 7 officers and 159 enlisted, armed with 6 light MGs and 107 rifles. Also proposed, although not definitively, was a mortar company with two sections of 82mm mortars and with, amazingly, the little 37mm French commando mortars. Ten of these battalions were actually formed and deployed in Zhejiang province by 32nd Army Group of III War Zone. In 1943 they were retitled as "surprise battalions" as "guerrilla" had taken on unpleasant connotations among the civilian populace.

Other units appear to have been formed on an irregular basis. One American unit reported that it trained "the Fourth Battalion of General Ho Yueh Ting," about a thousand men, in 1944. They were regarded as tough and experienced guerrilla fighters. Presumably other general officers formed guerrilla units as well.

Once in a while guerrillas were formed under American tutelage as elite units from existing units. An example was in IV War Zone where the Chinese forces were shattered following the fighting

A Chinese guerrilla stops to pose for a portrait west of the Salween in July 1944.

in the Liuzhou region in the spring of 1945. They were left poorly equipped, extremely malnourished, and their fighting spirit completely broken. As a stopgap measure the American Liaison HQ (Kwangsi [Guangxi] Command) supervised the creation of two guerrilla/commando battalions, one from the 16th Army and the other from the 35th Army. The personnel were given extra rations and some medical care to restore their strength, and new weapons. Each battalion consisted of two infantry companies (each with a demolition team) and a porter transport company for a total strength of 26 officers, 250 combat troops, and 150 porters. Training began in January 1945 and included ambushes, blowing of highways and bridges, scouting, and so on. The 1st (ex-35th) Battalion completed training in mid-March 1945 and the 2nd (ex-16th) Battalion in early April, but neither got a chance to enter combat.

Other divisions formed guerrilla units on their own, with varying degrees of success. These were used in central and eastern China and in the Salween offensive by the CEF.

Loyal & Patriotic Army

Among the power centers created by Dai Li, Chiang's head of intelligence, were the special operations brigades (*biedongdui*) formed from labor organizations and the criminal underground, primarily in Shanghai. Those who managed to escape from the cauldron of that city in 1937 regrouped at Liyang and re-formed into two "training units," each of about 2,000 men. A third was organized in 1938 and these were consolidated into the Loyal and Patriotic Army (LPA).

As the LPA expanded, eventually reaching about 100,000 strength, it was reorganized into brigades. The military nomenclature notwithstanding, these brigades were not tactical units but instead diffuse organizations, each responsible for a specific area, often one nominally under Japanese control. Although they conducted some effective, if small-scale, guerrilla operations in the fall of 1938 they were primarily concerned with the management of the huge and highly profitable network of smuggling routes, administration of order, and collection of intelligence.

Tactical drill for an LPA squad with M1 carbines and Thompsons.

In the meantime, the US Navy had taken an increased interest in China. Weather forecasting has always been important for fleets, but it assumed increased importance with the development of aircraft carriers, for whose pilots and planners visibility and winds were critical factors. Since weather tends to move from west to east, the US Navy in the Pacific eyed China as a huge platform for weather stations.

In May 1942 an American naval detachment arrived in China with a somewhat broader mandate that also included reconnoitering the coastline for potential landing sites, aiding downed airmen, and, in their spare time, harassing the Japanese occupiers. This relatively small contingent was designated the Sino-American Cooperation Organization (SACO).

In mid-1942 Dai Li raised the possibility of SACO training and equipping an LPA guerrilla force of 50,000. In response SACO set up a network of camps starting in April 1943 that eventually trained a total of 15,291 Chinese guerrillas, most of them from the LPA. The vast majority of those were trained at Camp 1 in Anhui province, Camp 2 in Hunan and Camp 3 in Henan.

These LPA guerrillas were formed into nine columns with strengths that varied from 550 to 1,500 men. In practice they operated in units up to platoon size, armed with Thompson submachine guns, M1 carbines, and demolition materials.

OSS Commandos

In early 1945 the Office of Strategic services (OSS) Operational Group in China was directed to form 20 company-size "commandos" for raiding duties. For the most part they were to be light infantry units, although plans were also laid for acquiring horses for use in mounted operations in north China. Troops were to be provided by the Chinese Ministry of Defense.

A commando had a strength of 22 officers (14 Chinese and 8 American) and 148 enlisted (137 Chinese and 11 American), plus 8 interpreters. It was divided into a headquarters and six "branches" that equated generally to platoons or sections. Three of the branches were rifle platoons, each of two rifle squads. A rifle squad consisted of one officer and 11 enlisted, all Chinese, armed with 10 M1903 Springfield rifles (one with a grenade launcher), 1 carbine, 1 BAR, and 2 M1911 pistols. The branch HQ consisted of one Chinese and one American officer, six Chinese and one American enlisted, and one interpreter, and was equipped with seven carbines, 2 submachine guns, and a bazooka. The fourth branch of the commando was a mortar platoon of three squads, each of five Chinese enlisted, armed with 3 rifles, a carbine, 2 pistols, and a 60mm mortar. The fifth branch was a light MG platoon of two squads, each of six Chinese enlisted, with 3 pistols, 3 rifles, 2 carbines, and a .30-cal. M1919A6 air-cooled machine gun. The sixth branch was a demolition section with two officers (one Chinese and one American), 17 enlisted (including one American), and an interpreter, armed with 8 pistols, 5 carbines, 3 submachine guns, and 12 rifles, plus C-2 demolition charges. In addition to the weapons, each commando was authorized two ¼-ton jeeps and two ¾-ton light trucks, and seven radios (two SCR 300 for the HQ and five SCR-536 for the branches).

The 1st Commando began training on 16 April 1945 and completed its eight-week course on 9 June. By that time it had been decided to deploy them via aircraft and they began jump training on 18 June. The 2nd–5th Commandos began training in late April, the 6th–17th in May, and the 18th in June. Only the 1st–6th Commandos completed their jump training before the end of the war and only the 1st and 2nd ever engaged in operations.

Operation "Apple" involved dropping the 1st Commando into the Lohting area on 12 July 1945 and in early August it attacked Japanese positions at the junction of the Namkong and West Rivers. The 2nd Commando parachuted into the Paoking–Hengyang–Changsha area on 27 July and launched an attack, together with an infantry regiment already in the

OSS guerrilla personnel in training in 1945.

area, on Taiyuantze on 5 August. The first mission was regarded as successful, the second less so due to poor cooperation with the conventional troops, and the 2nd Commando was broken up and its soldiers used as "agents."

A provisional battalion consisting of the 8th–10th Commandos was formed near the end of the war, but was never deployed operationally.

SOE Efforts

In March 1941 the British CinC Far East suggested to the War Office that the British and Indian Armies sponsor a "British led corps d'elite of Chinese guerillas." These would operate in five areas with a total of 15 companies, each company requiring 2 British officers and 15 British or Indian enlisted. The War Office made it clear that there was to be no provocation of Japan, including British troops in China or Chinese troops at training bases in Burma. In the absence of approval from the Chinese, who were suspicious of British motives and doubted the need for foreign leadership, the plan went nowhere. After the Japanese declaration of war against Britain, however, new life was breathed into the effort, but by that time Britain had neither the personnel nor equipment to help out. The MAC went ahead with the program on its own as "surprise battalions."

In December 1944 Force 136 (the British SOE contingent in southeast Asia) presented a plan to the US China Theater under which it would organize Chinese guerrillas around Guangzhou. For this they asked for the release of rifles, Bren guns, and miscellaneous equipment for 30,000 men. The Americans were adamantly opposed, giving as their reason a preference for arming regular troops first with the limited amount of arms that could be brought into China.

In its place the British Military Mission established a small commando training school in Fukien province in early 1945 but with the fall of the Ganzhou airfields in Jiangxi in February–March this had to be abandoned before much was accomplished. The Military Mission then proposed forming a regiment-size commando unit to be equipped with British equipment including, for unknown reasons, 42 vehicles and 24 x 2pdr AT guns. Once again, the Americans, controlling the supply lines, vetoed this.

13

Communist Forces

While the first four "extermination campaigns" conducted by the KMT against the communists had been dismal failures, the fifth, a much more methodical effort launched in October 1933, was more successful. Gradually the Red Army was forced to retreat and eventually undertake the Long March to remote western Sichuan. There the 4th Front Army remained temporarily, while the 1st Front Army moved north to Shaanxi, arriving in October 1935. The 4th Front Army joined them there a year later.

Chiang's plans for a sixth extermination campaign were resisted by the independent actors in the area, Shaanxi warlord Yang Hucheng and former Manchurian warlord Marshal Zhang Xueliang, both of whom were far more concerned about Japanese aggression than the small communist forces. To bring everybody into line Chiang called a conference of all the major players at the city of Xi'an in December 1936. There, however, he was kidnapped by the anti-Japanese faction and forced to agree to a national front effort against Japan.

That done, on 10 February 1937 the Chinese Communist Central Committee pledged that their army would be incorporated into the National Revolutionary Army of the KMT, and would serve under the direction of the Nanjing government. Chiang envisioned the assimilation of individuals and small units to facilitate control, but the communists wanted to retain their existing command structure. Negotiations proceeded in fits and starts until the Marco Polo Bridge incident provided the needed impetus. On 25 August 1937 the communist Central Military Commission ordered the reorganization of the bulk of their regular military forces (the 1st, 2nd, and 4th Front Armies) into the 8th Route Army of the National Revolutionary Army. The 8th Route Army, with Zhu De as commander, was to consist of three divisions: the 115th (under Lin Biao), 120th (He Long), and 129th (Liu Bocheng), and it was to have an authorized strength of 45,000 men, although the actual strength at the time was about 30,000. The army was soon redesignated the 18th Army Group, although this designation was not used by the communists, nor by many later commentators. In October the KMT directed that the communist guerrillas in eight southern provinces form into the New 4th Army.

Whereas the bulk of the National Revolutionary Army chose to posture as a conventional army the 8th Route Army and the New 4th Army never abandoned their more irregular roots. The collapse of Nanjing's forces in north China left a huge vacuum. The Japanese were far too few to occupy such a huge area, while most of the Nanjing government's agents and local authorities fled. Large areas of rural China were left to the mercies of marauding bands of bandits (sometimes calling themselves Nationalist guerrillas), Chinese puppet forces, Japanese troops on pillaging missions for food and supplies, and extemporized militias formed by frightened landlords.

The opportunity was simply too good to pass up. Already, in late 1937, Mao had issued a directive stating that in north China regular warfare, as conducted by the KMT, had been concluded, and that guerrilla warfare by the CCP was now the most important element of the struggle.* Into these huge swaths of China abandoned by governance flowed the agents of the CCP, both regular military formations and political cadres. In early 1940 the 115th Division moved into eastern Shandong, pushing the remaining KMT forces out, and in mid-year the 18th Group (ex 8th Route) Army moved into eastern Henan and northern Anhui, meeting elements of the New 4th Army that had discreetly moved northward.

The party established their own government offices through the *hsien* (county) and one step down to the *chü* (district) level. In addition to the regular forces of the 18th Army Group and New 4th Army, each district was to raise its own guerrilla force. These were then agglomerated at the *hsien* level to form independent battalions or regiments. The guerrilla units were full-time military formations, but were commanded by the local civilian party/ government leaders and were regional in nature, generally staying within the areas where they were recruited. In cases where coordination was vital the guerrilla units could be commanded by regular army officers. Another vital role performed by the guerrilla units was as a manpower pool from which the regular forces could draw new members.

In addition, each male between 15 and 55 was required to enroll in the self-defense force, or militia. These were part-time formations since agricultural production could not be disrupted without serious consequences. They were armed lightly, if at all, and were generally used for support tasks, such as digging trenches and carrying supplies.

The growth of the communist force in north China and parts of central China was phenomenal. The 8th Route Army started the war with a strength of 30,000, and in early 1938 another 12,000 were added in the form of the New 4th Army. By early 1939 the communist force had grown to 160,000 as a result both of co-opting existing armed bands into their fold and by raising new forces in villages they moved into. Although the 18th Army Group was limited to a strength of three subordinate divisions by the terms of the agreement with the Nanjing government, there was no restriction on the size of those divisions. Thus, for the Hundred Regiments Offensive of late 1940, the 115th Division fielded no fewer than 46 regiments, the 120th Division 22 regiments, and the 129th Division 47 regiments, for a total of 115 regiments.

The expansion surprised no one, especially not the KMT. As early as the December 1935 Wayaobu Resolution Mao had called for a million regulars in the Red Army, required both to vanquish the KMT and defend against the depredations of the Japanese. Once the opportunity to expand presented itself the communists proved both enthusiastic and prepared.

The regular and guerrilla units used the triangular unit structure. A rifle platoon had three squads, each of up to 16 men, while a rifle company consisted of three such platoons for a strength of about 130 men. Rifles were provided for only about nine men per squad. When available a light machine gun would be assigned to each squad, otherwise the allotment was one per platoon. A grenade discharger was also allotted to each platoon if available. An infantry battalion was made up of three such rifle companies plus, if available, a small machine-gun platoon with two medium machine guns.

Regiments came in a variety of configurations depending primarily on the availability of manpower and weapons. The taxonomy used by US intelligence at the time is probably as useful as any; this grouped them into three categories: Types A, B, and C. The Type A regiment was defined as a full-strength unit with three infantry battalions (each fully equipped with

---

* This decision, however, was not made without some opposition from military leaders such as Peng Dehuai and Zhu De, who argued unsuccessfully for a more conventional role for the 8th Route Army and New 4th Army.

light and medium MGs and grenade dischargers), a headquarters company with signal, mortar, supply, and medical platoons, and trains. The mortar platoon would be equipped with four 82mm mortars or 70mm or 75mm infantry guns. Such a regiment would have a nominal strength of 1,763 men. The Type B regiment was similar, but lacked one infantry battalion and the mortar platoon, for a nominal strength of 1,163. The Type C regiment consisted simply of a head-quarters company (signal, supply, medical, and service platoons) and four or five rifle companies, for a total of 866 men.

The regiments were grouped into brigades, and brigades into the existing divisions of the 18th Group Army and New 4th Army. In some cases

Ye Jianying, commander of the 359th Brigade, inspects one of many captured Japanese rifles used by his troops.

"columns" were inserted as intermediate HQs between the brigade and the division. There were no artillery or other heavy units in the communists' force structure, as they avoided direct conventional combat.

By mid-1940 the Japanese estimated communist forces in north China at 250,000 regulars and 150,000 guerrillas, while Peng Dehuai later stated the number of regulars to have been 220,000. As a result the CCP approached Chiang with the so-called "June Proposals," one of which called for the expansion of the 18th Group Army into nine divisions in three armies. At the same time the New 4th Army would be expanded into seven "detachments," roughly equaling large brigades. The KMT responded by authorizing expansion of the 18th Group Army to six divisions in three armies, plus five separate regiments, while the New 4th Army was to reorganize into two divisions. Instead, however, the 18th Group Army simply added a rather nebulous command, the Shanx–Chahar–Hebei (SCH) Military District, to control units on a territorial basis.

On 17 January 1941 the KMT directed the disbanding of the New 4th Army, following clashes south of the Yangtze. Ignoring that order the CCP reorganized the Army into seven divisions, sometimes also called "columns."

The strength of the communist forces was determined largely by the population under their control. In the early phases of the war the guidelines specified that the full-time personnel (military and party) should not exceed 3% of the population. Increasing Japanese pressure caused the party to rethink this ratio and in 1942 it was reduced to 1% of the population. To compensate the CCP increased its reliance on part-time fighters. They appear to have been aiming for a ratio of 1:1 of regulars to militia, although that varied according to locale, with more remote areas having more regulars and those closest to Japanese forces more part-time soldiers. Nevertheless, the communist forces were able slowly to expand their holdings, in particular as the Japanese drove KMT troops backwards, creating power vacuums. Further, the Japanese were withdrawing their best mobile troops from China for use in the Pacific, and by the summer of 1943 their North China Area Army had clearly begun withdrawing its more isolated garrisons, relying now on the "sweep and clear" punitive operations common to central and southern China rather than their earlier determination actually to hold large swaths of territory.

Nevertheless, the need to avoid draining the economy with a massive overhead of full-time (non-productive) military and party workers meant that most of the expansion thereafter came in the form of militia recruitment in areas from which the Japanese withdrew. In October 1944 the US estimated communist strength in China at 318,000 regulars (including 98,000 guerrillas) and 1,580,000 militia in the 18th Group Army area and 149,000 regulars (including 31,000 guerrillas) and 550,000 militia in the New 4th Army area. The regulars were estimated to be formed into 34 Type A, 74 Type B, and 91 Type C regiments in the 18th Group Army; and 25 Type A, 31 Type B, and 42 Type C regiments in the 4th New Army. By the end of the war the 18th Group Army was claiming 600,000 regulars, with the New 4th Army probably about half that. Of greater long-term importance was the network of administrative and party officials that had been established in north China and portions of central China during the war with Japan. In contrast to the fragmented, corrupt, and often non-functional administrators in the rest of China, who answered to a wide range of warlords, local power brokers, and landowners, these provided the mobilization base that would see the Communist Party through to success in 1949.

14

The Ordnance Industry during the War

What we are missing the most today isn't steel, isn't petroleum, isn't metal, isn't funding, isn't transport, isn't manpower, what we're missing is smart and efficient management.[*]

War is nothing new to China and since ancient times weapons have been produced on a large scale as well. As far back as the Northern Song dynasty (960–1127 AD) the central government was producing gunpowder and explosives, employing upwards of 40,000 workers.

By the mid-1800s, the Manchurian armies known as "Ba Qi" 八旗 that had brought the Qing dynasty to power had already faded away as a capable military organization. The "Lu Ying" 綠營 followed, but soon also decayed. The last resort was to raise troops on a provincial basis, called "Tuan Lian" 團練. These troops saved the Qing dynasty during the Taiping Rebellion and other various uprisings; however, this put military power into the hands of the various provincial authorities.

Inevitably, those same provincial governors soon began the quest to arm their forces with modern Western weapons. Arsenals sprang up in the various provinces, with no coordination between them in terms of production capability, model, and/or caliber. There were no production controls or standards, resulting in products that varied widely in quality.

The disadvantages of such a fragmented arms industry had not escaped the notice of the Qing government, which drew up plans to consolidate arms production into five big plants—North, South, West, East, and Central. These came to naught with the fall of the imperial regime. After the Republic of China was established in 1911, all arms production facilities came under the Military Arms Branch 軍械司 of the Army Department. However, China soon slipped into de facto civil war. Various warlords grabbed what they could and some even started their own arsenals—notably in Shanxi and Eastern Three Provinces. The Army Department's jurisdiction only reached a few arsenals such as Shanghai, Hanyang, Tehsien, and Gongxian. By about 1920 even these were only nominally under centralized control as the disintegration of China continued.

Prewar Arsenals
Gongxian 鞏縣 Arsenal

This had been established by the central republican government in 1915 in Henan province as a "model arsenal." Machinery and blueprints purchased from the US for Hanyang Arsenal were diverted to form the basis for the Gongxian Arsenal, and an artillery ammunition

---

[*] Zhou Zixin 周自新, Superintendent of the 22nd Arsenal, *The Factual Report of the 22nd Arsenal Relocation to Yunnan during the War, The Relocated Factories & Business to the Southwest during the War*

factory was also set up. Priority was given to heavy weapons, and production of shrapnel shells for 75mm guns, the first built in China, began in 1921, but it was not until 1922 that the rifle factory was actually established, the equipment having sat, deteriorating in storage, in Shanghai since 1920 due to shortage of funds to install it in Hanyang. A production report of October 1924 listed various shrapnel shells, fuzes, and 100 C96 pistols, along with the start of production of light aerial bombs, grenades, and 15cm shells. A copy of the Bergmann submachine gun entered production in the winter of 1926, this differing from other Chinese copies of this weapon by incorporating a selective fire switch.

In 1927 the arsenal began production of an 82mm mortar and its ammunition, along with wood-handled grenades. The following year it started turning out a 15cm mortar and its ammunition, and a copy of the Russian M1910 Maxim with Sokolov two-wheeled carriage.

Since it had been set up mainly as a heavy weapons factory, few shoulder-weapons had actually been produced on its deteriorated equipment. This changed with the construction of a new rifle factory in 1928, tooled to produce the Gong 98 (Type 4) rifle in 7.92mm round-nose.

By 1928 the arsenal employed 116 administrative staff and 2,224 workers. In June 1929 the Nanjing government took over the arsenal, lost it again in various warlord conflicts, then regained control in October 1930; production resumed two months later. By 1931 there were 2,400 employees producing 1,800 rifles, 12 Maxim machine guns, and 20,000 grenades monthly.

In August 1933 a new barrel configuration for the Type 4 rifle was developed that enabled it to fire the pointed type 7.92mm ammunition and the revised weapon went into production in 1934. The maximum production was reportedly 3,200 per month. In the meantime, however, the decision had been made by the Ordnance Office to standardize on the Model 1924 (Standard Modell) rifle. Drawings were acquired and the Finance Department ordered 10,000 of these weapons. Production was delayed by problems with the drawings, but low-rate production finally began in July 1935 as the Type 24 rifle, shortly thereafter being redesignated the Model Chiang Kai-shek (Jiang Jieshi) rifle.

On 11 November 1937, with Japanese troops advancing, the arsenal was ordered to evacuate to Hunan. The first train loaded with arsenal equipment left on 20 November. The relocated facility was renamed the 11th Arsenal in June 1938. The rifle factory was moved to Sichuan in 1940 and became part of the 1st Arsenal.

Jiangnan 江南 (Shanghai) Arsenal

The Jiangnan Arsenal was founded in 1865 through purchase of the American-owned Thos. Hunt & Co. Ironworks in Shanghai. There were several expansions to the arsenal in the following years to build a powder works, gun factory, cannon shell factory, sea mine factory, boiler factory, and cartridge factory. The arsenal produced many different rifles in short succession, starting with the Remington pattern rolling-block rifle in 1884, then the Kaili Rifle (a copy of the Mannlicher 1888 Rifle) in 1891, followed by the Hanyang/Commission rifle in 1899, and then the Type 1 (Yuan Nian) in 1908, and then its 7.9mm version, in 1915. In 1905 it became the first producer of modern artillery in China with the introduction of a license-built version of the Krupp 75mm mountain gun. By the time of the revolution it was the oldest and largest arsenal in the modern Chinese ordnance industry.

In 1915 it began production of an apparent variant of the Hotchkiss Mle. 1909 "portative" light machine gun as the Type 4, and a year later it placed the Browning 1900-pattern pistol in production in both 4-inch and 6-inch barrel versions. In 1917 the annual output was 37 Type 4 light machine guns, 400 Type 1 7.92mm rifles, and 285 Browning 6-inch pistols.

In October 1925 warlord Sun Chuan Fang captured Shanghai, including the arsenal. Monthly production under Sun reached 500 rifles, four 75mm mountain guns, eight mortars, and 2 million rounds of ammunition. In March 1927 the Northern Expedition led by the Guangzhou government recaptured Shanghai and its arsenal. Within a year production was in full swing again, with a monthly output that included eight 75mm mountain guns, 31 Type Three-Tens machine guns, 3 million cartridges, and 600 pounds of smokeless powder.

In 1931 the artillery factory moved to Gongxian arsenal, and then to Hanyang in 1934. Production in Shanghai in 1931 was thus focused on Type Three-Tens machine guns, Browning pistols, artillery shells, and bombs, built by 3,300 employees. In January 1932 the Japanese attacked Shanghai and the subsequent truce established Shanghai as a demilitarized area. This required the closing of the arsenal, and some of the machinery was shipped out to other arsenals, notably the Jin Ling arsenal, although much of the heavy machinery remained in place and unused until it was destroyed in 1937.

Hanyang 漢陽 Arsenal

Strategically located at the join of nine provinces, the tri-city region of Wuhan includes Wuchang, Hankou, and Hanyang. This industrial center would host one of the most important arsenals in modern Chinese history, consisting of the Gun Powder & Iron Works and the Rifle & Gun Works. The intention was to be self-sufficient in providing all ordnance needs.

Planning started in July 1888 when the Lowe Company of Germany was asked to provide machinery to make breech-loading repeating rifles and in 1891 the Commission Rifle of 1888 was selected as the model of choice. Trial production of the rifle at what was then known as the Hubei Rifle & Gun Factory began in August 1895, along with production of the round-nose 7.92mm cartridges it fired. Full production began the next year, yielding 1,300 rifles, and by the end of 1901 the arsenal had built 22,500 rifles, 316 carbines, 53 gingalls, and 14 million cartridges. Although large, the arsenal was inefficient and did not approach its full potential until after the collapse of the imperial regime in 1911.

A new superintendent improved efficiency under the republican regime, increasing rifle production to 70 per day and, in 1913, began production of the Krupp 75mm L/30 field gun (locally called the L/29). Starting in 1916 the arsenal formed much of the power-base of the warlord Wu Pei-fu and resources began to flow to modernize and expand the facilities. In 1917 the rifle production machinery of the Shanghai Arsenal was shipped to Hanyang and this increased rifle production to 100 per day. That same year Hanyang began producing the Krupp 75mm mountain gun, building 12 of them. A year later the arsenal started production of the Krupp 120mm L/14 howitzer, but only two were built before the project was canceled.

Engineering efforts increased even further and three new products, all copies of foreign models, were introduced in 1921. The first, and most significant, was the Browning

M1917 water-cooled machine gun, here in 7.92mm caliber. It was formally launched into production on 10 October, the 10th day of the 10th month of the 10th year of the republic, and was accordingly designated the "Three-Tens" model machine gun. Initial production was at 12 per month, later increased to 25 per month. The second was the Mauser C96 pistol, starting at 60 per month, increased later to 260 per month. The third was the Japanese 75mm Taisho Type 6 mountain gun, designated the Type 10 (= 1921) mountain gun. A total of 68 were built up to 1928 with production continuing at about one per month. Mortar production started in 1923, using the Japanese Type 11 as the model. After building 1,055 of these weapons in 75mm, production shifted to a more conventional 83mm in 1925 and 107 of these were built up to 1927.

On 1 September 1926 the Nationalist forces took Hanyang from Wu Pei-fu and in 1928 the arsenal was placed under the Ordnance Office of the Military Affairs Ministry. Production continued for the Nationalist government and in 1928 the arsenal began designing a 37mm infantry gun, this entering production the following year, although it proved unsuccessful.

Production of Type 88 Rifles by Hanyang Arsenal			
1895–1909	*1910–1932*	*1932–1938*	*Total*
130,036	463,180	283,100	876,316

Production data are fragmentary, but in 1932 Hanyang Arsenal produced 3,200 rifles, 30 Three-Tens machine guns, one Krupp field gun, and one Type 10 mountain gun. Rifle production increased slightly to 5,800 in 1933 and then dramatically in 1934, when the arsenal turned out 38,400 rifles, along with 240 Three-Tens machine guns and four 75mm field guns. By mid-1935 the arsenal was producing 150 rifles and 100,000 cartridges a day. The barrels for the artillery pieces were bought forged, but not bored, from Bohler and Krupp. A British steel salesman who visited the plant at the time reported that they were producing four 75mm guns per month and had 60 German- and Czech-made barrel forgings in stock.

In February 1938 the arsenal was renamed the 1st Arsenal and relocated to Chen Xi, Hunan, while the artillery factory was transferred to the Artillery Technology Office, where it later became the Zhong Shu branch of the 50th Arsenal, later relocating to Chongqing.

Shenyang 瀋陽 Arsenal

Around 1921, Manchurian warlord Zhang Zuolin set up a repair shop and cartridge factory within an old mint at the outskirts of the eastern gate of Shenyang (also known as Mukden), later renamed the Feng Tien Ordnance Factory 奉天機器局. The Feng Tien Ordnance Factory was itself renamed Eastern Three-Province Arsenal 東三省兵工廠 in 1922. The various designations were used essentially interchangeably by Westerners into the early 1930s.

The early influence was a mixture of European and Japanese, building Japanese-designed weapons on European machinery. In the mid-1920s Zhang sent a delegation, including a Japanese ordnance expert, on a tour of the defeated European powers, buying up arsenal equipment. A new rifle factory, an artillery ammunition factory, and a cannon factory were constructed under the supervision of the Danish company Nielson & Winther.

Between 1926 and 1928, the Eastern Three-Province Arsenal underwent a great expansion. A rifle factory and light machine gun plant were added, with over 8,000 machines. It became the largest and most advanced arsenal in China. In terms of infantry arms it started by producing its own Type 13 rifle and the Japanese Type 3 medium machine gun as its Type 13, both in 7.9mm caliber. It added a copy of the Japanese Type 11 light machine gun in 6.5mm in 1928 as the Type 17. Artillery production initially concentrated on Japanese models, 37mm infantry guns, 75mm field and mountain guns, 105mm guns, and 150mm howitzers. Zhang's purchasing delegation to Europe, however, returned with the components for 600 Austrian field pieces from Bohler, along with the machinery to finish them. These were completed as the Type 14 field gun and field howitzer. It also produced smokeless powder, explosives, and projectiles. It thus produced a large quantity of arms, all of high quality.

In 1929, Ordnance Office records referred it as the Liao Ning Arsenal 遼寧兵工廠, with daily output of 130 Type 13 Rifles and 410,000 cartridges, and annual output of 300 Type 17 light machine guns and 50 Type 13 heavy machine guns. There were 17,000 workers in the arsenal and it continued to expand until late 1931 when it was occupied by invading Japanese forces. Shenyang Arsenal weapons were brought south by the retreating Northeastern Army in 1932 and continued in service in China to the end of the war, albeit in decreasing quantities as spares and, in some cases, ammunition ran out.

The Shenyang Trench Mortar Factory was an entirely separate facility. Construction was begun in July 1926 and mostly German machines installed. It produced several different models of 82.5mm and 150mm mortars, along with ammunition. The steel tubes for the barrels were bought from several sources initially, before settling on Krupp. Steel was bought from Germany, and TNT and ballistite propellant from Norway. Phosphorus bought from France was successfully loaded into 3,000 rounds of 15cm ammunition, but they do not appear to have been used. It seems likely that the arsenal built over a thousand 8cm and about a hundred 15cm mortars before the Japanese invasion shut it down in 1932.

Shanxi 山西 Arsenal

This arsenal was established as the Shanxi Machinery Bureau by local governor Hu Penzhi in March 1898 to repair weapons used by the local garrison troops. Small quantities of weapons were built under the imperial regime, but the arsenal served mainly as a repair shop. After the republican revolution, Yan Xishan took power and, although he was not officially appointed governor by the Beijing government until 1917, he held power for the next 38 years. Although concerned about Marshal Zhang's Manchurian army directly to his north, he wisely avoided involvement in the internecine warlord feuds of the 1920s, and instead holed up in his mountain fastness in the relatively remote northwest.

That did not mean Yan remained idle, however. Indeed, he launched a massive expansion of the arsenal, renaming it the still innocuous-sounding "Shanxi Soldiers' Artisan Apprentice Factory" in 1920 to avoid attracting unwanted attention. The first phase of the expansion ran to about 1924 and involved hiring experienced managers and engineers away from the Shanghai and Hanyang Arsenals and buying materials and machinery from those and other sources, including Germany. By 1924 the factory was turning out copies of the Japanese Type 38 rifle in 6.5mm, Japanese Type 38 machine guns, and Type 13 mountain guns (copies of the Japanese Type 41), along with ammunition, gunpowder, bombs, and more. The arsenal had factories at three locations and employed almost 3,000 people.

The second phase of the expansion ran from about 1925 to 1930 and was built around purchases of machinery from Germany and the hiring of five German advisers. This led to production of the Type 16 105mm mountain howitzer and the Type 18 88mm field gun, Rheinmetall and Krupp designs respectively, that presumably involved the import of some components. There were even plans to build 150mm howitzers, probably of German design. The Mauser C 96 pistol in .45-cal. also began production. The only non-German weapons to be introduced into production during that period were the Thompson submachine gun in 1927 and an 82mm mortar.

The later portion of this phase was accomplished openly, as Yan had astutely waited until he was sure who would win in the Northern Expedition campaigns, and then allied himself with Chiang and the KMT. Thus, in 1927, the name was changed to the more accurate Taiyuan Arsenal.

The high-water mark of the arsenal came in 1930, when it was probably second only to Shenyang in capabilities. At that point it had 8,000 employees and turned out 500 pistols, 1,500 rifles, and 50 machine guns a month, presumably along with Thompson submachine guns. The mortar plant was turning out 300 medium mortars a month. The artillery plant had a rated capacity of 30 Type 13 mountain guns per month, although none were in production. Instead, efforts were concentrated on the 105mm Type 16, 88mm Type 18, and an unspecified "new model" 75mm mountain gun that had not yet entered production. In addition, material had been ordered from Germany for the 150mm howitzers, along with the facilities to build the tractors for them. Thus, by 1930, Yan had amassed 27 field artillery and 360 mountain artillery pieces, and 642 mortars.

In that year, however, Yan's political instincts failed him and he allied himself with the anti-Chiang forces in the Zhongyuan campaign. Having lost, he went into temporary exile and the Nanjing government placed severe restrictions on the arsenal, closing down the heavy weapons branches. Nevertheless, the small arms factories remained open and in 1931 the arsenal was producing 40 Type 38 Japanese rifles and 80,000 cartridges a day, plus 20 machine guns a month.

With the Japanese conquest of Manchuria, the Nationalists brought Yan back to power in 1931 as director of the Pacification Office, essentially once again running Shanxi. With the world economy in free-fall, however, he transformed much of the arsenal to civilian production, and abandoned many of the heavy weapons facilities. What military facilities remained in use were renamed the Taiyuan Arms Repair Depot, then becoming Renshen Manufacturing as a small-arms repair facility.

In 1936 he tried to sell the arsenal to the central government's Arsenal Administration Office. Yang Jiceng was sent by the office to inspect the facilities. He reported that there were 11 factories, the arms production was done by hand with a notable lack of precision, and much machinery had been left to rust. In addition, the steel used in production was substandard. The Arsenal Administration, not surprisingly, declined the offer.

Taiyuan was an early objective of the Japanese, and fell in 1937. Portions of the arsenal were evacuated ahead of the Japanese, one to Shaanxi and another to Sichuan. The former portion produced rifles, light and heavy machine guns, and Thompson submachine guns, mostly for the troops of Yan's II War Zone. However, the troops in this area saw little activity except the Winter Campaign between December 1938 and March 1939. Unfortunately, the machinery for producing 6.5mm ammunition was lost, so arms production switched to 7.9mm. The portion moved to Sichuan was eventually taken over by the Arsenal Office and became part of the 31st Arsenal, producing ZB26 light machine guns. The highest output of this facility was 800 rifles, 300 light MGs, a dozen pistols, and 10,000 grenades monthly.

The Jinling 金陵 (Nanjing) Arsenal

This arsenal was set up in 1865 at Nanjing after the Taiping Rebellion was put down, with Dr Halliday Macartney as the first superintendent. It was one of the earliest machine shops in China and went through several expansions over the years, producing fortress guns, Hale rockets, river mines, and other items.

A major event was the construction of the Black Powder Works in 1882. By 1885, during the Sino-Franco War, the arsenal provided 2pdr, 12pdr, and 24pdr guns, 10-barrel Gatling guns, 4-barrel Nordenfeldt guns, and muzzle loading gingalls. In 1889 the arsenal produced its first Maxim machine gun but only built about a dozen examples before production ceased and it went back to making Gatlings.

In 1898, the British Admiral Charles Beresford visited the arsenal. He mentioned that "the machineries are modern and first rate, but they use them to produce useless arms such as Gingals and a small gun firing one-pound projectiles." However, by 1905, the production had already switched to 37mm and 76mm breech-loading guns, as well as .43 Mauser black powder cartridges.

In 1908, the arsenal purchased 25 sets of cartridge manufacturing machines from Ludwig Loewe via Carlowitz & Co. and it became a major producer of rifle cartridges, manufacturing 6.5mm Japanese, 7.9mm Mauser, and 8mm Mannlicher.

In a report dated 1913 by the Beijing government, the arsenal was stated to have a monthly production of 60,000 7.9mm cartridges, 360,000 6.5mm cartridges and one 75mm gun. Production of 7.9mm Maxim machine guns, named Hwa-nin (China Peace) was restarted in February 1915, when the first six were turned out. At about the same time the arsenal began production of the 6-inch barrel Browning 1900 pistol—a copy of the .32 ACP M1900 Browning, and production of the 8-inch version started in 1919.

Two other weapons were also produced in smaller numbers during the 1920s. One was a copy of the Bergmann submachine gun in 7.65mm (.32 ACP). The second was the unfortunate Chauchat light machine gun, produced as the Nin 8mm automatic rifle. The latter proved no more popular in China than it had elsewhere and production was cut short. During that time the arsenal adopted the "reverse swastika" as its arsenal mark. It was a Buddhist symbol originally from India—meaning good fortune—and Jinling and the later 21st continued to use the symbol until the communists took over in 1949.

The Nationalist Northern Expedition forces reached Nanjing on 13 March 1927 and chased away the Beiyang troops. Nanjing became the capital of the Republic of China, thus bringing the arsenal firmly under the control of the central government.

The arsenal produced 170 Maxim machine guns under its new management in 1927 and the following year it became a branch of Shanghai Arsenal and added 82mm mortar shells and 30lb and 80lb aerial bombs to its product range. The monthly production rate was now 30 Maxims, 800,000 cartridges, 300lb of smokeless gunpowder, and 20lb of TNT.

In 1929 it was reassigned to report directly to the Ordnance Office and renamed Jinling Arsenal. By this time, however, the arsenal was showing its age and the lack of funds for modernization over the prior decades. A US Army officer visiting in May 1930 noted that the machinery was in poor condition and in need of constant repair, the buildings old and dark, morale among the workers poor, and the management "not so good." However, this was about to change dramatically. In July 1931, Lee Chunkan was appointed as the superintendent. He was a great manager and led the arsenal throughout the war. Under his leadership, it became the biggest arsenal in China by 1945 under its relocated designation as the 21st. Daily operation was about 14 hours and there were 1,100 workers.

Superintendent Lee accumulated 2 million yuan from his budget and obtained permission to renovate the arsenal. He acquired 223 Chinese acres of additional land, the cartridge factory was rebuilt and expanded, gun shop, wood works, warehouse, and other facilities. were also rebuilt. New machinery was also acquired, and production quality and capacity greatly enhanced.

Jinling Arsenal Production between 1927 and 1937

	Maxim MGs	7.65mm submachine guns	7.9mm round nose and pointed cartridges (1,000s)	82mm mortars	82mm shells	Gas masks
1927	170	385	544	·		
1928	228	280	1,656			
1929	324		1,092			
1930	348		2,100			
1931	372		2,004			
1932	280		1,728			
1933	336		1,896			
1934	280		1,932			
1935	330		2,808	180	113,160	
1936	610		3,600	480	204,000	34,000
1937	626		2,802	440	298,920	28,980

In 1935, the standard Maxim model was finalized with the designation Type 24 and blueprints of the MG 08/15 obtained from the German Army Ordnance Department. The arsenal switched from the commercial DWM MG 09 model that it had been building to the Type 24, using jigs and machinery purchased from Germany. In a major vote of confidence in the rebuilt Jinling Arsenal, that facility was also chosen as the major producer of the newly standardized 82mm mortar, and production of that weapon also started there in that year.

There were about 4,000 workers when the Sino-Japanese war broke out in 1937. The Japanese bombed Nanjing frequently in the early phases, inflicting some damage to the arsenal.

The cartridge factory was ordered to move to Chongqing in September and merged into the 1st Arsenal of Sichuan. The order came on 15 November to move everything else westward inland. In the next two weeks, almost 5,000 tons of machinery and materials were evacuated by trains, trucks, boats, and sampans to Hankou and then moved on to Chongqing. All personnel from superintendent down were also evacuated. The last boat left on 6 December. The Japanese troops occupied Nanjing on 13 December and started the infamous three-week massacre.

The arsenal finally arrived in Chongqing and started production on 1 March 1938. It was renamed as the 21st Arsenal and took over the Rifle Factory from the 1st Arsenal (originally Hanyang Arsenal) in July and resumed Han rifle (originally Hanyang rifle) production in January 1939.

Guangdong 廣東 Arsenal

The Guangdong Machinery Bureau was established in 1874 in Guangdong to produce arms and gunpowder, and in 1887 a cartridge factory was added to produce ammunition for Mauser, Martini, Snider, and Winchester rifles. A smokeless powder factory was added in 1897. In 1906 equipment was purchased from Carlowitz & Co. for the automated production of Mauser rifles and associated ammunition, along with machinery from Krupp for 300 pounds of smokeless powder per day. A year later lands were appropriated for expansion and all facilities of the renamed Guangdong Arsenal established there except the smokeless powder plant, the latter being completed in 1909.

Arsenal regulations of 1904 specified that the facility would concentrate on rifles and rifle cartridges. The Army Department had specified 6.8mm as the standard rifle caliber and the arsenal began building the Model 1904 Mauser rifle as the Guang Xu 33rd Year 6.8mm New Style 5-shot Smokeless Rifle, which laid the foundation for the Type Yuan Nian rifle later. On a 10-hour working day, the capacity of the newly acquired machinery was 25 rifles and 25,000 cartridges per day. In 1904 hand production began of the Madsen light machine gun, which yielded only 2–3 per month, and by 1908 an unspecified water-cooled machine gun was also in production. In 1909 the arsenal switched to the Mauser 1907 rifle in 6.8mm caliber, a weapon not in use by any other country.

In January 1913, the Republican Army Department issued a decree that made the contract Mauser 1907 pattern rifle the standard issue as the Type Yuan Nian (First Year). The caliber was changed to 7.9mm and Sichuan and Guangdong were ordered to start the re-tooling process; however this decision was contested, and no immediate action was taken.

In 1917 Superintendent Su Lun Yuan reported to the Army Department that the monthly production was 600 6.8mm rifles, 350,000 smokeless powder cartridges, 150,000 black powder cartridges, and 6 machine guns. Thus, the 6.8mm rifles were still in production in 1917!

In April 1925 rebellious troops from the Dian Army's Yang Ximin and the Gui Army Liu Zhenhuan seized Guangzhou, including the arsenal. On 12 June the Nationalist forces retook the arsenal, but the fleeing troops burned it down before leaving.

Rebuilding of the arsenal as the Guangdong Arms Manufacturing Factory was slow since it had to finance itself under the control of Provincial Governor Chen Ming Shu. Production quality was poor and sales to civilians without controls were the order of the day. Chen Jitang assumed control of Guangdong in 1930, and with it the arsenal.

The arsenal started producing a short rifle based on the Belgium FN 1930 pattern in 1932. It was called the Type 21 Mauser Rifle and featured several different kinds of markings on the receiver.

In 1935, the arsenal was renamed as the 1st Arms Manufacturing Factory and Chen appointed Huang Tao as the superintendent. As soon as he arrived, Huang started to change attitudes towards the inspection procedures—he asked that the standards be followed. It was said that only 10% of the cartridges produced could pass inspection in the beginning. During his one year in post at the arsenal, the quality of the products rose significantly. Guangdong Arsenal also started its ZB LMG production that year.

On 18 July, the Guangdong 1st Army led by Yu Hanmou defected on the drive to the north and Chen's rule in Guangdong collapsed. The arsenal was taken over by the Ordnance Office in November and renamed the 1st Arsenal of Guangdong. Zhong Dao Charn was sent to take over on 10 November. Jiang Biao was appointed as the superintendent of the 2nd (artillery) Guangdong Arsenal.

In 1937, a Carpentry Works was added. At that time, the arsenal had a rifle factory, machine gun factory for water-cooled MGs, smokeless cartridge factory, machine gun cartridge factory, smokeless powder plant, machinery plant (also producing light machine guns), bomb factory, power plant and carpentry works, a total of nine factories and about 2,300 workers. In June the rifle factory switched to Chiang Kai-shek (CKS) model production.

After the 7 July incident of 1937 the arsenal was ordered to relocate to Rong Xian, Guangxi Province. Starting on 22 December the machines were dismantled, and within the week they were all loaded on boats going west to establish the 41st Arsenal.

The 2nd Guangdong Arsenal

In July 1933, the governor of Guangdong, Chen Jitang, negotiated a deal with Hans Klein to purchase an artillery plant from Hapro via Siemssen & Co.* A location was selected at the mouth of Pa Jiang river, Hua County. It was to produce field artillery and its ammunition, gas, and gas masks. Chen was later defeated and escaped to Hong Kong and the arsenal was not completed. Some of the machinery was transferred to the 50th Arsenal and buildings were destroyed in a Japanese air raid.

Sichuan 四川 Arsenal

This was established in 1878 in Chengdu, although production was slow and of poor quality until new plant equipment from Germany was installed in 1910. By 1913, according to an Army Department report, the annual production was 15,000 6.8mm rifles, 7,500,000 cartridges, 45,000lb smokeless powder, and 21,000lb black powder. In March 1918, the warlord Xiong Kewu took over the arsenal and expanded production, adding Mauser pistols and Schwarzlose HMGs. In 1919, the caliber of the rifles changed to 7.9mm. Caught in internecine warfare, the arsenal shut down in 1925, reopened in 1926, then shut down again in 1932 when the Sichuan victor, Liu Xiang, relocated the machinery to Chongqing and it merged into Chongqing Repair Depot.

---

* Hapro—Handelsgesellschaft fur industrielle Produkte—was a trading company owned by Hans Klein. However, it was generally believed that it was a cover for the Reichswehr and German ordnance companies.

In November 1938, Zheng Daqiang was sent to Chengdu to clean up the remains of the arsenal. It was made into a Technical School of the 50th Arsenal and in 1941 it became a branch of the 50th Arsenal. There were about 800 employees and main products were 60mm mortar shells and primers. Production of 47mm mortar shells was reported to have been added in 1942, although it is not clear what weapon would have used these.

Dagu (Taku) Dockyard

The Beiyang Fleet Dagu Dockyard 北洋水師大沽船塢 was established in 1880 to support the coastal defense fleet being built up. Arms production started in 1891. It first produced 90 German pattern 1-pound artillery pieces. The following year, an artillery factory was added to the dockyard. In 1913, the dockyard was put under the Naval Department and started building naval and merchant ships.

The dockyard obtained a Maxim heavy machine gun in 1916 and successfully copied it in 1917. A special feature was that the Dagu Maxim had the rear sight calibrated for both pointed and round-nose cartridges.

The MP-28 II Bergmann submachine gun was successfully copied in 1926. The Dagu guns, in 7.63mm caliber, had the magazine turned downwards and enlarged to 50-round capacity. In addition, the ZB26 light machine gun was also successfully copied in 1927. In 1928 Dagu started production of Mauser pistols and carbines.

In December 1935, the Ordnance Office ordered the Dagu Dockyard to cease arms production. The quantity of small arms produced in Dagu was not very large but they were among the best in quality.

Other Arsenals
Chongqing Arms Depot 重慶武器修理所

This facility went under a variety of names over time, initially as the Hwa Xing Machine Factory set up in 1933 by two brothers, Hu Zhongshi and Hu Shuqian, to serve the requirements of Sichuan warlord Liu Xiang. In 1933 they bought much of the tooling of the China Iron Works in Shanghai and brought it to Chongqing with Liu's backing. They built 6,000 KE-7 light machine guns, apparently without benefit of license, during 1934–6. Production of a further batch of 1,900 was restarted on the outbreak of the war. It was taken over by the central government and made part of the 20th Arsenal, at which time it switched over to ZB26 production.

Jinan 濟南 Arsenal

Located in Shandong province, this facility apparently produced some weapons during the 1920s, but fell into partial disuse, retaining only ammunition production lines. By the mid-1930s its capacity was rated at 3 million rounds of 7.9mm ammunition and 60,000 handle-type hand grenades per month. On the outbreak of the war it relocated to Xi'an and then to Chongqing.

Establishment of the Ordnance Administration Office

The shortcomings of the semi-autonomous collection of arsenals were clearly apparent. Provincial arsenals were underfunded by contemporary international standards and never managed to adopt efficient mass-production techniques. Not only did this result in low volumes of production, but also in semi-handmade weapons, components of which were not interchangeable. This further reinforced the positions of the old-school foremen, who were highly experienced in craftsmanship but largely ignorant of, and resistant to, industrial method.

This decentralization also resulted in a wide array of similar weapons being under production simultaneously. Eventually this was remedied for the most part by the consolidation of power by the Nanjing government in the mid-1930s and by the movement and rationalization of arsenals in 1937–40, but it still left the army with stockpiles of various models of weapon for which replacement was slow even as the army was expanding.

After the Nationalist government established its capital in Nanjing, the Ministry of Military Affairs 軍政部 was inaugurated on 21 November 1928. Under the ministry, the Ordnance Administration Office 兵工署 was established. Its missions were to manage ordnance technology, ordnance production, and administrative matters related to arms.

There were several chiefs in rapid succession after the inception: Zhang Ch'un, Yang Weitseng, and Chen I. Finally, ballistics expert Dr Yu Dawei took office in 1933, and he proved to be the man they needed. He took a management system that had just finished transitioning from an early Confucian model to a political one and introduced modern, primarily German, production and management methods, most successfully at the Gongxian and Hanyang Arsenals. He also increased the variety of products such as optical instrument, gas masks, and so on, which proved fortuitous for the coming war. In 1934, he also established the Unified Ordnance Factory accounting system. Yu held the post the longest and made one of the greatest individual contributions to China's modern ordnance industry.

In a very significant move, Yu brought in Zhou Zixin, who had studied precision instruments and optics in Germany, to create the Baishuiqiao Precision Research Institute. It began work on gauges in 1934 and two years later it turned out the nation's first precision gauges, enabling standardization of tooling and parts in the manufacture of weapons. As a result, mass production finally began to supplant the older methods by the late 1930s.

In 1933, the Ordnance Administration Office was organized into Headquarters, Resource Branch, Executive Branch, and Technical Branch. In 1935, it was reorganized into Headquarters, Manufacturing Branch, Technical Branch, and Military Arms Branch. The charters of each branch were as follows.

The Manufacturing Branch was divided into four sections: General Affairs, Accounting, Inspection, and Material Acceptance, it managed:

- The organization of various arsenals, the materials warehouse, and depots.
- The personnel in various arsenals, the materials warehouse, and depots.
- Labor-related matters.
- Permits, transportation, and licenses for all ordnance matters for all units.
- Production fund distribution, budget drafting, and all accounting matters.
- Production planning, assignment, and cost validation.

- Real estate, machinery, and tool record keeping, acquisition, and validation.
- Unification of tolerances, engineering drawing, and other quality standards.
- Raw material distribution, accounting, validation, and storage procedure.
- Tools production, accounting, validation, and management.
- Waste and defect items validation and handling.
- New arsenal preparation, supervision, and guidelines.

The Technical Branch was divided into three offices and six sections. The three offices were Physics and Chemistry Research, Design, and Education. The six sections were Ballistics, Infantry Equipment, Artillery (Fortress) Equipment, Transportation Equipment, Communication Equipment, and Special Weaponry. Its responsibilites were:

- Standardization of arms.
- Military equipment design and improvement.
- Inspection, validation, and research of firearms, munitions, military equipment, and ordnance materials.
- Storage, safe keeping, translation, and compilation of instructions for arms and munitions.
- Ordnance training at home and abroad.
- Validation of invention, improvement of arms, munitions, and military equipment.

The Ordnance Branch was divided into Proofing, Safe Keeping, and General Accounting Sections. Its roles were:

- Armories organization.
- Personnel employment and promotion for the armories.
- Budget and accounting for the armories.
- Ordnance and munitions accounting, safe keeping, replenishment, repair, investigation, statistics, inspection, proofing, and transportation.
- Armories construction.
- Payment for ordnance, munitions, and military equipment, loss compensation, captured equipment recording, and damage reporting.
- Training of ordnance personnel.
- Disposal of obsolete arms, munitions, and military equipment.
- Arms control and civilian ownership.

According to the 6 April 1933 organization chart, each of the subordinate arsenals was managed by an accounting department, a benefit office, a general office, a technical department and an operation department.

The accounting department had four sections: general accounting, compensation, cost calculation, and book keeping. The benefit office had supply and education sections with attached school, farm, and hospital. The general office was in charge of employment, record keeping, general affairs, procurement, receivables and payables, meal preparation, transportation, products, and security. The technical department had a design office, a test lab, and an inspection and experiment lab.

The operation department was responsible for actual production. It handled production preparation, task distribution, and material warehousing, along with the distribution of the technical drawings, raw materials supply, task distribution, and employee training. It also owned the training facility to train qualified technicians.

Its subordinate factories, under the operation department, received the assigned tasks and organized resources to produce products. Based on the required components and skills, the department set up varying numbers of factories within the arsenals.

In June 1936, the Ordnance Office published "Temporary Outlines for Ordnance Products Acceptance Procedure" to unify ordnance products acceptance for all arsenals. The technical branch appointed inspectors to be stationed at the arsenals. The inspector was responsible for approval of the end products of each arsenal and without the acceptance approval, no product could leave the arsenal. The inspector applied the acceptance seal on the packing box or put a sealed slip over it. In the event of a failure to satisfy the inspection, the products would be returned to the factory to be refurbished or repaired. This practice is also the reason that there is no acceptance mark on Chinese-made weapons themselves, in contrast to the usual system in the US and Europe.

Wartime Production and Management

In 1939 an Ordnance Research Committee and a Procurement Committee were added to the Ordnance Administration Office. Even though it was under the civilian Executive Yuan all personnel held military commissions. The office was run like any military organization, the various points of daily life were announced by bugle calls, all staff members wore uniforms, and there was a duty officer in charge.

In May 1939 the office put out an order stating that: "A previous order stated that all workers during the War of Resistance are considered military personnel due to their critical role in ordnance production, this was done so the personnel can be put under Martial Law. However, these workers are skilled workers and should not be drafted into the Army, which would cause production interruption. All arsenals should put together a personnel list to be submitted to the Defense Department so they can be exempted from Conscription."

This view of arsenal workers as soldiers was reinforced in 1941 when the Chongqing Militia Corps put out a notice that all able males not in the services should participate in militia training. The Military Affairs Department decreed that "All workers in the arsenals are already enlisted and should be treated as current military personnel in the services." Even unskilled workers were compensated according to the military pay scale. To cope with wartime inflation arsenal workers also received allotments of subsistence items, such as rice, cooking oil, and salt.

Due to the tremendous demand for ordnance and munitions from the front line, the supply of raw materials and resources often became problems. Indeed, theoretical limitations of arsenal capacity were often irrelevant because of shortages of materials. Prior to the Japanese occupation of the southern coast, China was able to import both weapons and raw materials, largely through Hong Kong. When that route was shut the Indochina railway and the Burma Road were able to fill some of the gaps, particularly in finished weapons and ammunition. However, raw materials became increasingly scarce, and even more so after the Japanese occupation of French Indochina and then their conquest of Burma.

Perhaps the most critical requirement was for rifle and machine-gun ammunition, mostly in 7.92mm. Prewar capacity was 10.3 million rounds per month: 4.3 million at the Hanyang Arsenal and 3 million each at Jinan and Jinling. Actual production rose after the movement of the arsenals from 113.9 million in 1940 to 144 million in 1943. The latter worked out to an average of 12 million rounds per month which may sound like a lot, but the army at that point had 3 million men. In other words, they were producing 4 rounds per man per month for an army at war. Clearly, Chiang had to choose his battles (with their attendant ammunition expenditures) carefully. Production in September 1944 had risen to 14.6 million, representing about 70% of arsenal capacity had materials been available.[*]

The Wartime Production Bureau was established at the end of 1944 at the suggestion of American advisers. The bureau was to "achieve the maximum production capability for military and civilian alike." Its primary duties were to standardize military-related raw materials, and improve production efficiency, transportation, and distribution of raw materials. At the same time, the National Resources Commission under the Economy Department also set priorities to supply all arsenals with their production needs.

Overview of Wartime Production

The War of Resistance is a great dividing line to the Ordnance Industries. Most of the materials were imported before the war, most of the materials had to be domestically produced after the war broke out.[†]

Even before the war began the fourth meeting of the Fourth Nationalist Central Committee Conference passed the Tangible Nation Building Policy document on 20 January 1934. It decreed that:

The economy should not be threatened by foreign forces, it needs to be secured at the Defense Center ... all construction of major factories, railway and telephone lines should follow the guidelines of the Military and Civil Defense Planning, reviewed and approved by the government. Major enterprises, national- and civilian-owned alike, should avoid the coastline. Various cooperatives should be set up to stimulate farm production and economy. The taxation system needs to be modified to encourage commercial development and tax evasion needs to be curtailed. Highway construction should focus on the westward direction to obtain international access other than seaports.[‡]

It was thus explicitly proposed that economic development would focus on future national defense needs in an international war. The coastline was vulnerable and inland bases would be the key to the long-term struggle.

---

[*] Some relief was obtained via Lend-Lease. The US placed contracts for a total of 663.7 million rounds of 7.9mm ammunition for China between mid-1941 and mid-1944, with shipments out of the US completed in November 1944. Primarily used to supply Y-Force, some 138 million rounds had made it over the Hump into Yunnan by the end of 1943 and a further 18 million in January 1944. Further deliveries probably approximated to 20–25 million rounds per month.

[†] The Military Equipment Exhibition, *Da Kong News* 大公報, Chongqing, 18 March 1942.

[‡] "Guidelines for the ongoing Material Construction," 20 January 1934, Fourth Nationalist Central Committee Conference.

When the war broke out, "the strategy of the first stage wartime industry is to assist moving all factories and production facilities inland." Thus, on 10 August 1937, the 324th meeting of the Executive Yuan passed the decision to move the factories located in Shanghai.

The task of moving arsenals and supply factories was organized by the Department of Military Affairs. After October 1937, the Shanghai steel mill, the telegraph manufacturing and repair depot, the transportation machines factory, the artillery factory in Zhuzhou, the military uniforms factory, and the wool manufacturing factory were all moved to the west.

One of the critical tasks during the move was the preservation of the raw materials. Most of the critical materials at the time were imported. Without these materials, ordnance production could not continue. During the time in 1940–1 that Great Britain shut down the Burma Road, ordnance production dropped significantly. This problem was only resolved when domestic steel plants geared up to produce ordnance-grade materials. Strictly speaking, the prewar ordnance industries were only processing the imported raw materials into final products. Due to the lead time and high cost of the materials, they were expensive to produce and this, compounded with low production output, led to continuous procurement of arms in the international market. It should thus be noted that the claims by some experts that Chinese arms used dubious materials are completely untrue. These materials were the same as those used in the ordnance industries in Austria, Germany, and elsewhere.

All rifles and machine guns were required to pass high pressure rounds tests before they could be accepted. As a result the existing examples of CKS rifles today are as strong as their worldwide contemporaries.

German ordnance experts provided little help, being primarily interested in commerce. None of the factories they had proposed, such as an artillery factory, a shell factory, a big automotive factory, and a central steel mill, were completed before the war broke out and they had no significant impact on the war effort. Similarly, there were few or no German technicians involved in the existing Chinese arsenals. The German advisers, some 80 of them, were busy training the army.

For the arsenals, there were indeed various advisers but they were from all over the world. One example was that a naturalized Russian, Gregore Larikov, working in the Aero Weaponry Research Institute 航空兵器研究所. He later invented the Type 28 grenade launcher for the CKS Rifle. Even these foreign advisers were few in number. A review of the prewar production figures shows that although this had increased year by year, it was but an incremental gain. After the war started, the production skyrocketed without any additional foreign personnel.

In the early days of the war, the Ordnance Office implemented another important change. It started the effort of reorganizing arsenals by product categories. Each prewar arsenal had always tried to produce everything—from cartridges to cannon—and often found itself not very good at anything. This new structure would move cartridge production to a few arsenals and have them focus on it, small arms would be the primary products of others, and so on. This was an important step forward in the rationalization of production, allowing management to focus on a few things and be good at them. Some said later that it was a way for the central government to control the arsenals because arms and munitions were now separated. That may have been a side effect, but the motivation seems to have been that of production efficiency.

Thus, the Ordnance Office attempted to consolidate production facilities to increase efficiency. There were several types of arsenal:

- Artillery-centric: 51st,
- Ammunition-centric: 20th
- Arms-centric: 21st, 11th, 41st, 1st, etc.
- Steel & alloy: 24th, 28th, etc.

The machinery was moved accordingly among the arsenals and appropriate adjustments were made.

As soon as the war broke out, most of the arsenals were forced to move westward and inland. The primary location was in the Chongqing area in Sichuan. Some moved to Hunan but had to be moved again later due to the advance of the Japanese forces. The Guangdong Arsenal moved to Guangxi but had to move again later to Guizhou.

In February 1938 the Ordnance Office ordered a name change for all arsenals. Henceforth the arsenals were to be numbered, these numbers being assigned in blocks of ten to various provinces. The Hanyang Arsenal was the most famous, so it got the designation 1st. The other arsenals in Hubei province received 2–9. Hunan got the series 10–19; Gongxian was relocated to Hunan at the time so it got the 11th. Arsenals in Sichuan received 20–29; the Sichuan Arsenal was assigned the 20th; the Jinling Arsenal was relocated to Chongqing at the time and was designated the 21st. Shanxi was assigned 30–39 and Guangxi was assigned 40–49. The Guangdong Arsenal was in Guangxi at the time so it got the number after Guanxi Arsenal—41. From this point on, all arsenals in China used numeric designations only.

Once the arsenals had successfully moved and settled in, the primary limiting factor was the shortage of raw materials. China was cut off from its coastal trade first, and then the Burma Road was cut in early 1942. From then on, raw materials, often heavy, had to be flown in over the Hump, competing with other valuable cargoes. Initially this was the responsibility of the China National Aviation Corporation (CNAC). Stilwell's plan for his airlift as outlined in March 1943 called for 4,000 tons per month of cargo flying into China from India, of which 300 tons was to be raw materials for the arsenals.

In November General He Yingqin, chief of the general staff, notified Stilwell that "all the raw materials stored in China have been gradually used up" and that munitions production was in danger of ending, although this appears to have been a bit of an exaggeration. Part of the cause was that the CNAC aircraft had taken to flying at night to avoid Japanese fighters and this apparently reduced their payload by 40%, although it should be noted that CNAC was only carrying about a thousand tons a month both before and after the change. As a result, General He requested Stilwell, first, to honor the 300 tons per month allocation, and, second, to increase that to 1,268 tons per month, the largest components being materials for small arms ammunition (638 tons), materials for rifles and machine guns (200 tons), tin plates for moisture-proof boxes (200 tons), and materials for making steel (100 tons). The US Air Force managed to get its share up to the goal of 4,000 tons in mid-year and by the end of 1943 it was over 12,000 tons per month. The situation eased somewhat after that, but the arsenals rarely operated at capacity.

Wartime Arsenals Under Ordnance Office Management

A: Sichuan Province

> The construction of the buildings and machinery were under way in parallel, not wasting any time, the machinery was put back together as soon as it arrived, all people working days and nights to devote their efforts . . .[*]

20th Arsenal

The 20th Arsenal was the Munitions Plant of the Sichuan and Xikang Pacification Office 川康綏靖主任公署, located at the Tungyuan Chu, in southern Chongqing, controlled by Liu Xiang. The Ordnance Office took over the plant in August 1937 and renamed it the 1st Arsenal of Sichuan. It was renamed as the 20th Arsenal in March 1938.

The 20th was the primary munitions producer during the war. It produced cartridges for rifles, machine guns, and pistols. The 7.92mm pointed and round-nose cartridges were the primary products; annual output started as 7.9 million rounds. At the end of the war, the monthly output was 10.8 million rounds.

In 1938, the arsenal expanded and obtained another 1,849 acres of land for new facilities. The No.4 land mine was added to the production list, and by the end of the war it could produce 16,000 land mines monthly.

21st Arsenal

There were about 4,000 workers in the Jinling Arsenal when the Sino-Japanese War broke out in 1937. The Japanese bombed Nanjing frequently in the early phases and the arsenal suffered some damage. The cartridge factory was ordered to move to Chongqing in September and merged into the 1st Arsenal of Sichuan. A second order came on 15 November to move everything else westward.

The relocated Jinling Arsenal arrived in Chongqing and started production immediately on 1 March 1938 at Bojinshi and was soon redesignated as the 21st Arsenal. The first 20 Type 24 HMGs were produced out of the components brought from Nanjing.

In July, the relocated rifle factory from Hanyang Arsenal was transferred to the 21st; production resumed in January 1939. The marking was changed to a banner with Type Han 漢式 inside.

Also, on 14 January 1939, the 21st took over a light machine-gun factory from the 20th. In April it took over the Chongqing Arms Depot, originally set up for the local warlord. This factory had been producing KE-7 pattern and ZB26 pattern light machine guns. This marked the beginning of ZB26 production in the 21st Arsenal.

In March 1939 machinery for a new 82mm mortar factory arrived from Germany. A mortar factory was set up in Anning, Yunnan, as the Anning branch of the 21st Arsenal; production of mortar ammunition started in November 1940.

In August 1940, the 21st received an order to switch from the Hanyang rifle to the Chiang Kai-shek model. Neither the 1st nor the 41st had a full set of drawings so the 21st had to start from scratch. Over 8,000 drawings were made from studying German-

---

[*] Lee Chuan Kan, Superintendent of the 21st Arsenal, *Managing An Arsenal during the War.*

Type 24 machine guns at an arsenal, possibly the 21st, awaiting
shipment. Note the AA mounts at the far right.

and Chinese-made Mauser rifles. Production of Han rifles continued at the same time. The production line for the CKS rifle started working in October 1943, and Han rifle production finally ended in 1944. Barrels were made by the 24th Arsenal. In March 1941 the LMG factory, mortar factory, and the tool factory were all relocated to Tongluoyi, inside a cave to avoid Japanese air raids. A heavy mortar factory was set up in October 1943.

The 21st Arsenal was well-managed and relocated only once. It continued to expand during wartime with ever-increasing production capacity. It became the most important ordnance production facility during the war.

21st Arsenal Production, 1937–1945

	Type 24 Maxim	Czech Type ZB26 LMG	Hanyang rifle	Chiang Kai-Shek rifle
1937	626			
1938	1,060			
1939	1,971	892	41,500	
1940	2,468	900	53,813	
1941	1,860	150	31,500	
1942	1,980	930	46,600	
1943	2,680	2,041	33,400	
1944	2,986	2,020	350	24,500
1945	3,063	2,900		62,000

1st Arsenal

In February 1938 the Hanyang Arsenal was renamed the 1st Factory of the Ordnance Office. As the invading Japanese forces approached Wuhan, the 1st was relocated to Chenxi in Hunan. The cannon factory was transferred to the Artillery Technical Research Institute, where it later became the Zhong Shu branch of the 50th Arsenal.

In March 1939, the 1st Arsenal resumed production of cartridges in Chenxi. The machine-gun shop, welding shop, and machine shop followed in July. Shortly thereafter, however, the arsenal was ordered to move again to Chongqing. Er Gong Yan was the new location. Construction involved digging out a cave in a mountain to house the operation. This second move, however, did not go well. Due to the difficulties encountered in the process, the arsenal had to realign its operations with the 11th Arsenal, which was also experiencing problems. The 1st's cartridge factory, machine-gun factory, and the power plant were transferred to the 11th, while at the same time those parts of the 11th that were in Chongqing already, the rifle factory and cannon shell factory, were transferred to the 1st.[*] CKS rifle production resumed at the 1st Arsenal in July 1942 with monthly output rising to 4,000.

A worker in a wartime Chongqing arsenal. Note the belts driving
the machinery from an overhead rotating shaft.

The 1st Arsenal never really recovered from the chaotic disruption of the second move to Chongqing. As a result of this relocation, its importance as an ordnance facility declined after 1940. It was disbanded after the war.

---

[*] The swap later generated a great deal of confusion among the collectors of CKS rifles.

24th Arsenal

The 24th Arsenal was the former Chongqing Electric Steel Mill 重慶電力煉鋼廠, originally created in 1909. In 1929, Yang Jihui convinced Liu Xiang to consolidate the steel refinery capabilities of the province in order to boast local industrialization in Sichuan, as well as resolving a raw material supply problem for weapon making. Liu appointed Yang as the chairman to form a committee to consolidate the existing facility and buildings into a new one. At the start of 1937, the refinery was taken over by the Ordnance Office. On 8 January, it produced 4 tons of carbon tool steel.

It was renamed the 24th Arsenal on 1 January 1939, with Yang still in charge. The facility was also expanded significantly, adding a 1,000-ton water reservoir, a 2,000kw generator, a 3-ton Morgan furnace, a silicon iron furnace, a 2-ton steam operated hammer, a rolling mill, a steam operated cutter, a saw machine, and a 150-ton friction press.

The iron ore came from the local mines in Sichuan. However, some of the parts needed for steel production were no longer available from abroad. The arsenal devoted its resources to producing items such as electrodes and silicon shields. The 24th was one of the largest steel producers during the war, making 4,000 tons of steel and 3,900 tons of other steel materials such as nails and screws annually. The tungsten alloy barrels used by the 21st Arsenal CKS rifles were provided exclusively by the 24th Arsenal.

25th Arsenal

This was originally the Munitions Plant of the Artillery Technical Institute. It relocated to Chongqing in 1938 and became the 25th Arsenal in 1939. The main products were cartridges and hand grenades. With the 20th, it was one of the two main cartridge producers during the war. Its monthly output was 5.5 million cartridges and 60,000 hand grenades in 1945.

26th Arsenal

Once combat started there was a tremendous need for high explosives. To produce explosives with domestically available materials Ordnance Office Technical Manager Zhou Zhong Yang was assigned the task of developing a plan for indigenous production. The product chosen was a potassium chlorate-based explosive. All necessary materials were readily available.

The potassium chlorate was created by combining sodium chlorate (derived from salt by electrolysis) and tung oil. As directed by the Ordnance Office, the arsenal started working with the Sichuan Tung Oil Trading Co. to gather tung oil. The location of the facility was selected in 1939 and a preparatory office was moved to Zhang Shou in February 1940.

Facility construction began and production machinery was procured from the USA. Initial production started in January 1945, and was normally 20 tons per month; 30 tons was produced in March and May, but only 10 tons in July. The final test explosive was evaluated in June and was found satisfactory. The war ended, however, before mass production could take place.

30th Arsenal

This was the former Jinan Arsenal in Shandong. It relocated to Xi'an and changed its name to the 1st Arsenal of Shanxi 陝西第一兵工廠. It produced a variety of products but all in small quantity. It relocated to Chongqing in 1938 and was assigned the task of producing small munitions and launchers.

Most importantly, it was directed to develop and produce a grenade discharger based on the Japanese Type 10 in 1938. The final product was adopted as the Type 27 Grenade Discharger and was a simplified and improved version of the Japanese pattern. The discharger and its grenade became the primary product of the 30th Arsenal.

B: *Arsenals in Other Areas*

11th Arsenal

The Gongxian Arsenal was officially renamed the 11th Arsenal on 1 June 1938. In July it moved to Yanxi city in Hunan, a remote area where the arsenal was built among the hills and valleys. Much of the facility was set up inside specially dug caves and the entrances were all well covered. The more dangerous powder loading plant was set up in another location in Xu Pu county. The primary products were light machine guns, artillery shells, hand grenades, and CKS Rifles.

On 11 and 12 November 1939, just when the arsenal production capacity recovered from the move, it was hit by Japanese bombers. The location had somehow been discovered. More than 300 lives were lost in the bombing, the rifle factory suffered severe damage, and all office buildings were lost. Production ceased after the attack and workers were temporarily housed in the nearby villages. The arsenal had to move again.

It was first decided to move the arsenal to Chongqing and a liaison office was set up at Tong Guan Yi on 1 February 1940. However, the Japanese launched a major offense in the area in May 1940. The Yangtze River route to Chongqing was blocked at Yi Chang by Japanese forces after only a portion of the arsenal equipment had passed and the rest had to return to Hunan. Superintendent Li Dai Chen went to the western regions of Hunan and found a natural cave in Xiao Ping, Yuanling county. The cave was three stories high and several *li* (Chinese "miles" of variable length) long. It was a perfect air raid shelter and spacious enough for the arsenal operation.

By that time, the rifle factory had already successfully relocated to Tong Guan Yi and was absorbed into the 1st Arsenal, which restarted rifle production with the CKS model. The 11th started producing Three-Tens heavy machine guns. The other branches of the 1st Arsenal were still in Hunan—the ammunition plant, the machine-gun plant, and artillery shell plant—and they were transferred into the 11th Arsenal. Due to the merger, moves, and bombing losses, the importance of the 11th dwindled; records include comments about "falling apart in the moves."[*]

The 11th stayed in Hunan throughout the war.

Production of Three-Tens MG at 11th Arsenal					
1940	1941	1942	1943	1944	1945
514	520	480	0	0	0

---

[*] Yu Zhuo Zhi, "The Changes of the Jinglin Arsenal during the war," *Historical Records of Jiang Xu*, Issue 28.

40th Arsenal

Before the war the Kwei clique warlords owned seven facilities capable of producing rifles, machine guns, cartridges, mortars, and hand grenades in Guangxi. When the war broke out Li Zongren mobilized the province and to demonstrate willingness for unification, he handed over the arsenals to the central government. In September 1937, the Ordnance Office sent Jiang Shao to take over the arsenals. The several facilities were consolidated into the 1st Arsenal of Guangxi, employing about 2,000 workers, becoming the 40th Arsenal in late 1937. It was relocated to Qijiang, Sichuan, in 1944 due to the Japanese advances. There it was absorbed by the 21st Arsenal and became the Qijiang Branch of the 21st Arsenal.

41st Arsenal

The Guangdong Arsenal was relocated to Rong Xian, Guangxi, after the war broke out, and was renamed the 41st Arsenal in January, 1938.

On 24 December 1939 the 41st was ordered to move to Tongzi, Guizhou province, to avoid approaching Japanese forces. The cartridge factory was ordered to merge into the 40th Arsenal and the bomb factory merged with the Guilin Artillery Repair Works 桂林 修砲廠. The light machine gun factory of the 40th Arsenal was merged into the 41st. After the machinery was dismantled, it was shipped to Du Shan and then Tongzi by trucks. The secondary machinery was shipped by rail to Sichuan.

In September 1941 the arsenal reported that the principal products had been CKS pattern rifles and Czech pattern light machine guns. The total output had been 2,200 LMGs and 7,000 rifles since resumption of production in 1940. The monthly capacity was 260–300 LMGs and 1,100–1,300 rifles, barring any materials or personnel shortages.

At that time, there were eight production branches: the 1st produced rifles, the 2nd produced LMGs, the 3rd maintained machinery, the 4th milled the LMG chambers, barrels, and parts, and produced proof plates, the 5th was responsible for power generation and water supply, the 6th cast iron, the 7th mold and solder, and the 8th was the carpentry works.

In September 1944 the Ordnance Office reported the monthly production of the 41st was 1,000 rifles and 300 LMGs.

50th Arsenal

This was built around the Artillery Technology Office's factory, itself the former Hanyang Arsenal Artillery Factory. This became the Zhong Shu branch of the 50th Arsenal, later relocating to Chongqing. Facilities were supplemented by equipment that had arrived for the 2nd Guangdong Arsenal, but never been put to use, and by Sichuan Arsenal No. 1. Once set up the arsenal produced 37mm Type 30 anti-tank guns (at about two per month), 60mm mortars, 60mm mortar ammunition, 150mm mortar ammunition, and 75mm artillery ammunition; it also reworked 150mm mortars into the Type 29 configuration.

51st/53rd Arsenal

Before the war the Ordnance Office decided to adopt the Danish Madsen as the standard universal machine gun. In 1938 agreement was reached to produce the weapon under license in China, using German and American machines and Danish tools. A small Chinese engineering team was sent to Denmark and during 1939 engineers Yang Wen-hsi, Chou Tsu-peng, Chin Jen-fang, and Hu Yang-sen were trained there at the Madsen facility. On 1 April 1939 the 51st Arsenal Preparatory Office was established. The arsenal was to be

The 50th Arsenal rebuilding 15cm mortars in 1944.

located at Kunming with a production target of 500 Madsen light machine guns a month. By February 1940 about half of the machinery for the arsenal had arrived. However, the drawings and the tooling were lost in an air raid on the Burma Road in June 1940.

New orders went out that the arsenal would instead make the ZB26 machine gun, since this was already being produced in China. The first batch of 100 rolled off the production line in June 1941, and that September the 51st Arsenal was formally established.

In January 1942, the 51st (light machine gun) and the 22nd (optical equipment) Arsenals were ordered to merge to form the 53rd Arsenal. The 53rd continued to produce ZB26s and optical equipment as the main products.

The 53rd produced more ZB26s than any other arsenal; however, due to the remote location and lack of skilled workers, the products were the worst. The guns often could not fire in the full automatic mode and sometimes even discharged out of battery and damaged the receivers. By the end of the war the 53rd had produced 14,920 ZB26s, 11,480 Model CKS binoculars, 27,750 compasses, 297 rangefinders, and 2,608 mortar sights.

The Central Repair Depot—the 44th Arsenal

The 44th Arsenal started out as the Central Repair Depot 中央修械所 in Nanjing, in July 1936. It was evacuated in December 1937, before the fall of Nanjing, to Hunan, there it took over the old facility of the defunct Hunyang Ordnance Bureau 湖南軍械局 in Hunyang. It was relocated again in the winter of 1938 to Guizhou taking over the Guizhou Repair Depot facility 貴州修械所. It formed mobile repair units 遊動修理隊 that year and started sending them out to each war zone to perform repair duties.

It was expanded again in the spring of 1940, and the mobile units were further developed into smaller squads and teams and assigned to field troops as their main repair resources. A new location was found and a new facility built in the summer of 1940, at which time the Yuanlin Artillery Workshop 沅陵修炮廠 was merged into the Repair Depot.

Production of Smith & Wesson 32-40 revolvers and hand grenades started in the fall of 1942. The facility name was changed to 44th Arsenal in June 1943, although it continued to manage the mobile repair units in the field.

The 43rd Arsenal in Guilin was merged into the 44th in 1944. At that time, there were about 2,000 workers in the 44th Arsenal.

Other Arsenals

Zhejiang Iron Works 浙江鐵工廠

In December 1937 the Nationalist central government appointed Huang Shao Hong as chairman of the Zhejiang provincial government. To arm his Provincial Self Defense Forces and utilize the skilled workers and machinery evacuated from Hangzhou and Ningbo, Huang decided to set up his own ordnance production facility.

Production started in May 1939, initially of rifles only. The pattern used was the Belgian 1924/30 type, but with some small changes to simplify production. The daily output at first was four rifles. After a series of expansions, there were four factories: Factory 1, the largest, was at Xiao Siun, producing rifles and rifle grenade launchers; Factory 2 was at Shi Ton, producing modified ZB26 light machine guns; Factory 3 was at Yu Si, producing explosives and hand grenades; and Factory 4 was at Da Gon Tou and focused on producing machinery for the branch factories. There were about 2,000 workers altogether.

All arms produced in Zhejiang Iron Works were designated by Huang as Type 77 to commemorate the 7 July incident at the Marco Polo Bridge.

According to a report dated July 1939 by T. M. H. Pardoe of the British Embassy the monthly production capacity of the arsenal was:

- LMGs   75–100
- Rifles   360
- Cartridges   300,000
- Bombs & hand grenades   60,000
- Grenade launchers   unknown

By 1941 the arsenal employed about 4,000 workers, operating over 1,000 machine tools. It could produce over 1,000 rifles, 50 machine guns, and 50,000–60,000 grenades monthly. In March 1941, with the implementation of the central government policy of unified arsenal administration and armament standardization, the arsenal came under Ordnance Office control. In May 1942 the advance of the Japanese forces forced the move of the facilities to Nanping county in Fujian province. Later the factories were set up at Sha Men, Xi Qin, and Xia Yang, under the Special Administration, Southeastern Region, of the Ordnance Office.

According to a production record of the Nanping Factory, Southeastern Region, in a 1944 ordnance office report monthly production figures were 400 rifles, 10 x 82mm mortars, and 40,000 hand grenades. The production figures fell in 1945 to 10 x 82mm mortars, 25,000 hand grenades, and no more rifles.

Shanxi Arsenal

In 1937, the Japanese invasion forces quickly entered Shanxi and took Taiyuan. Some equipment was evacuated with Yan Xishan to the west. One batch moved to Shaanxi and another moved to Sichuan. The former continued to produce rifles, heavy machine guns, light machine guns, and Thompson pattern submachine guns. After the move the arsenals started out utilizing semi-finished parts they had brought with them to assemble arms. Later they had to use rail tracks as the raw materials, producing light machine guns at Cheng Gu, rifles at Xiang Ning, and pistols at Xiao Yi. The highest output was 800 rifles, 300 LMGs, a dozen pistols, and over 10,000 grenades per month. Due to the loss of the 6.5mm cartridge production facility, all arms were switched to the standard 7.9mm round.

The output was mostly supplied to Yan's relatively isolated forces in II War zone, except the element that had moved to Sichuan, which was eventually taken over by the Ordnance Office and became part of the 31st Arsenal, producing ZB26 pattern LMGs.

15

Submachine Guns

T he submachine gun was never very popular with the KMT central forces, but it was used by several of the warlord armies, particularly the forces of General Yan Xishan in Shanxi.

The Bergmann submachine gun had been developed in Germany during World War I as the MP 18/1 and small numbers were brought into China for the various warlords in the early 1920s. They proved popular and the Jinling and Shanghai Arsenals began building selective-fire models in 1926, in the end producing 1,000 and 5,000 respectively. Both arsenals also produced Browning pistols in 7.65 x 21mm caliber and their Bergmanns probably fired that round as well.

A Chinese soldier with a Bergmann in the 1920s.

In the meantime, the design had been further improved in Germany, to yield the MP-28 with selective fire and other design changes. This model was produced by the Dagu Dockyard and Hanyang Arsenal, in these cases in the 7.63 x 25mm caliber. In addition, the

This Shanxi-produced Thompson built in September 1927, above, was still in service in the Korean War. A standard American M1 model is below to highlight the difference in length.

Gongxian Arsenal built a Bergmann submachine gun in 7.63mm, although it is not clear what model it was derived from.

Bergmanns also arrived directly from Europe. Liu Xian's chief of staff recalled that Liu had ordered 1,200 Bergmanns and 6 million rounds of ammunition from Germany, and later 2,400 spare barrels from Belgium. In May 1931 the central government ordered 100 of the Swiss SIG version of the Bergmann in 7.63mm, along with spares and magazines, for SFr37,500.

All told, there were probably around 10,000–15,000 Bergmann submachine guns scattered throughout China in the early 1930s. By 1937, however, they appear to have lost much of their significance. Production of parts probably ceased around 1930 and the bulk of those still operational were probably lost in the first year of the war. They appear to have played only a small role thereafter.

Another European weapon was the Erma submachine gun, developed by Heinrich Vollmer and produced both by the Erferter Maschinenfabrik and, to avoid the restrictions of the Versailles Treaty, by the Swiss firm of Solothurn. A number of Solothurn-made weapons made their way to China before the war, but how many and for whom is unknown. The number was probably not large and their 9mm ammunition was not produced in China, so they played little role in the war.

Of more lasting significance than the European models was the Thompson submachine gun in .45-cal. Direct imports during the warlord era were small, but they did inspire local copies. The Taiyuan Arsenal began manufacturing a slightly shorter version of the M1921 Thompson in 1926 and production rose to 900 per month. That model was still in production in September 1927, but by August 1930 it had been replaced by a full-length version of the M1928, at which point a little over 30,000 Thompsons had been built. Surprisingly, given the temporary collapse of the warlord regime there, production continued at only slightly lower rates, so that Thompson serial number 37,216 came off the line in August 1931; manufacture ran until 1934 at a rate of about 250 per month.

Those figures are all the more remarkable for the fact that the initial batch of 15,000 Thompsons built in America by Colt did not sell out until 1937. By that time, in other words, the Shanxi Arsenal had built over twice as many Thompsons as were produced in the USA.

As a result of the Taiyuan Arsenal's efforts Yan's Shanxi troops were lavishly equipped with Thompsons through 1937 and only slightly less so during the war. Due to Yan's passivity, however, these weapons were probably only rarely fired at the Japanese.

Additional Thompsons were high on the list for initial aid to China and 11,000 of these weapons, in their M1928A1 configuration, arrived in Rangoon between 8 December 1941 and 16 March 1942, along with 4 million rounds of ammunition. The loss of the Burma Road in 1942 stranded most of those in India, but a portion were used to equip the CAI. Each division was authorized 1,212 Thompsons, and army troops a further 556. Not surprisingly the forces in India had little difficulty getting these weapons and by October 1943 the 22nd and 38th Divisions and the army troops were all fully equipped with them.

Getting the rest of the weapons the last leg to China proved more difficult, and only about 900 of them appear to have made it there by mid-1942. By September 1943 only 2,150 Thompsons and 4 million rounds had been delivered by air to Yunnan for Y-Force. The weapons issued to Y-Force were M1928A1 models, each with four 20-round magazines but no tools or accessories. Deliveries picked up starting in late 1943 and by the end of January 1945 some 12,688 Thompsons had been issued to units of the Chinese Army in China, with this number rising to 15,349 by the end of February and 29,014 by the end of May. By the end of the war, of 42,699 authorized for China, 30,858 were in service with the Chinese Army in China (mostly with the CEF), with the balance mostly being with the Chinese Army in India.

A cavalryman demonstrating a rather casual way of holding his M1928 Thompson in Chihkiang in May 1945.

The later deliveries were M1 and M1A1 models, which quickly became the standard submachine gun. In addition, SACO provided M1 Thompsons to the LPA, usually at the rate of four weapons per 12-man squad. The initial delivery, of 2,000 weapons and 4 million rounds, left the US in August 1942.

The other producer of the Thompson was the 21st Army Weapons Depot in Sichuan. It modified the weapon to fire 7.63 x 25mm ammunition and built it in two versions. One was a standard submachine model, the other was intended for use as a light machine gun, with longer barrel and bipod. The latter could not have been very effective, firing short-range pistol ammunition, and neither model appears to have played a significant role in the war.

A light machine gun version of the Thompson built by the 21st Army Weapons Depot. Note the long, thin barrel and bipod.

A total of about 4,700 (in both versions) were built.

A small number of M3 "Grease Gun" weapons were supplied with the tanks provided under Lend-Lease by the US. Although probably almost never used in combat, this weapon was apparently liked and was put in production in the late 1940s after the war ended.

The final submachine gun to see service in China was the United Defense M42. These had been developed in the US and significant numbers were bought by the OSS for equipping resistance units in occupied Europe. A smaller number were also purchased by SACO and provided to the LPA in China.

The MAC had not requested submachine guns in their 1941/42 Lend-Lease submissions, but when they presented their July 1943 request for Canadian assistance it included no fewer than 60,000 Sten submachine guns. When the Canadians informed the US aid offices the reactions were lukewarm. The Sten was recognized as "a nice light weapon" but there was concern about adding another type of ammunition to the China mix, the 9mm never having been used in significant numbers there. In fact, the US China Theater expressed its disapproval of Sten deliveries in April 1944, but by then it was too late.

A first batch of 7,000 weapons was shipped out of Canada in February 1944 and a second (and final, as it turned out) batch of 23,000 in June. Having arrived in India, however, they then needed the US China Theater to include them in the Hump airlift. No such provisions were forthcoming until the Burma Road was opened when permission was granted for the movement of 23,000 guns (and 25 million rounds of ammunition) to

Alpha force troops training on the M1 Thompson, January 1945.

China. Shortly after that the US authorities increased the allowed quantity to 37,000 guns. It is unknown, however, how many of the guns actually made it into the hands of troops before the end of the war. Certainly, US approval was based on equipping hypothetical light divisions to be used for mopping-up duties in the absence of any answer to repeated requests from the the US side as to how these weapons would be used. It seems unlikely that the Stens saw meaningful combat during the war in China.

Submachine Gun Specifications						
	Ammunition	*Operation*	*Weight*	*Length*	*Muzzle vel.*	*Rate of fire*
Chinese Bergmann	7.65 x 21mm	blowback	4.33kg	820mm	390m/s	550rds/min
M1928 Thompson	11.43 x 23mm	blowback	4.87kg	855mm	244m/s	650rds/min
M1 Thompson	11.43 x 23mm	blowback	4.4kg	808mm	244m/s	650rds/min
M42 United Defense	9 x 19mm	blowback	4.1kg	820mm	335m/s	700rds/min

Bergmann Submachine Guns

These were bought in the MP-18, MP-28 and SIG versions from Europe, and were built by the Jinglin and Shanghai Arsenals in 7.65 x 21mm caliber, and the Dagu Dockyard and Gongxian, Guangdong, and Hanyang Arsenals in the more powerful 7.63 x 25mm. All varied in some details, but retained the basic feature of simple blowback operation and firing from the open-bolt position. The weapon was reliable, if a bit underpowered.

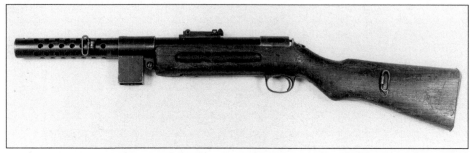

A Dagu-manufactured Bergmann submachine gun. Note the magazine well is turned 90° to point downward on the weapons from this plant.

Shanxi Thompson Submachine Gun

The Taiyuan Arsenal began making Thompsons in 1926, with a version of the M1921 model that was about 5cm shorter than the original. Around 1929 it switched to a full-length version of the M1928. There were no significant differences between the original M1928 and the Taiyuan copy except for the incorporation of sling points on the latter. The weapon was heavy but fired a powerful cartridge. Once the Taiyuan Arsenal fell to the Japanese, ammunition was no longer available to the isolated Shanxi forces so the weapons presumably would have seen little combat use.

A Taiyuan-made M1928 Thompson. Note the sling.

Thompson Submachine Gun

The initial version supplied was the M1928A1, a weapon with fearsome lethality but mediocre accuracy. The M1 was the M1928 but with a few changes to simplify production and lower costs. The finned barrel was replaced by a smooth one, the cocking handle moved from the top of the receiver to the side, the Cutts compensator was eliminated, and it used a 20- or 30-round box magazine. The weapon worked on a simple blowback operation, with the elimination of the Blish (friction) lock used on earlier versions. The weapon was heavy and difficult to control, but put out an impressive amount of lethal short-range firepower.

The M1928A1 Thompson submachine gun.

United Defense M42

This was developed as a cheaper and simpler replacement for the Thompson, a role it eventually lost to the even cheaper M3 submachine gun. The UD 42 was a straight blowback, selective-fire weapon in 9 x 19mm Parabellum caliber. It proved susceptible to blockage by mud and sand and the sheet metal magazines were prone to bend out of alignment. Nevertheless, it was widely distributed to guerrilla and resistance groups in Europe and Asia. In large part this was due to its use of ammunition that was common around the world except, ironically, in China.

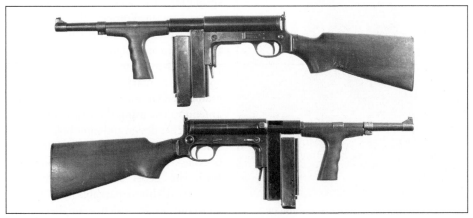

Side views of the United Defense M42.

16

Rifles

The Chinese invented both gunpowder and the associated weapons. Nevertheless, little development was undertaken and it was foreigners who made firearms practical and brought them back to China. The Chinese first encountered rifled shoulder arms in the 15th century, either via Arab traders overland from the west or from Portuguese and Dutch merchants on their ships. In either event, local copies soon appeared and this type of weapon was known as the "bird rifle" because of its supposed ability to hit small prey. Due to the lack of machinery and tools, however, it could take up to a month to produce a rifled barrel, so production was very limited and the vast majority of the Chinese troops remained equipped with smoothbore guns, swords, and spears.

This began to change in 1842 with the Chinese defeat at the hands of the British in the Opium War. The various provincial authorities were encouraged to establish machine shops to start the production of modern shoulder arms, although it would be another 50 years before repeating rifles would show up in significant numbers.

A sentry with the most common of the Chinese rifles, the Hanyang, with its long bayonet.

The first-generation repeating rifles, using black powder, were destined for quick obsolescence. The Hanyang Arsenal placed an order for the plans and tooling to build the 11mm Mauser M1871/84 in 1890, and the Sichuan Arsenal began building the 11mm Mauser Model 1871 in the mid-1890s, but only in small numbers.

In the meantime, however, a revolution in small-arms design was under way in Europe. The appearance of the Model 1886 Lebel rifle in France, the first to use high-energy "smokeless" powder, had completely changed the course of military rifle design. A hastily established German commission designed an equivalent using the magazine from a Mannlicher design and some bolt concepts from Mauser. The resultant M1888 model became known as the "Commission Rifle." Both the Lebel and the Commission rifles used this remarkable new type of ammunition in which a smaller bullet, with a full metal jacket, was propelled at higher velocities and to longer effective ranges than the earlier black-powder rounds. Other designers quickly followed suit in a small-arms arms race.

Two of the second-generation rifles were placed in production in China quite quickly. The Jiangnan Arsenal in Shanghai was first off the mark and began manufacture of its Kai Li rifle, based on the Steyr 1888 straight-pull model, in 1891. This, however, was to prove a dead-end. To the west a far more significant effort was under way. Viceroy Zhang Zhidong was building a new arsenal in Hanyang, Hubei, in 1891 when he heard about the new German Gewehr 1888 Commission Rifle. He immediately cabled the Chinese ambassador Xu Jing Cheng to change his contract from the M1871/84 to the new pattern. In 1894 the Hanyang Arsenal acquired templates for the Commission Rifle in 7.92mm, and began production of a trials batch in 1895.

The Kai Li and Hanyang rifles briefly competed but the Viceroy was by far a better promoter and in 1898 the Jiangnan Arsenal conceded the issue and bought machinery to build the Hanyang/Commission model as well, production beginning in 1899 and ceasing in 1908, with about 20,000–30,000 built. The Henan Ordnance Bureau at Kaifeng also began producing the Hanyang type rifle and reported an annual production of a very modest 300. By 1904 production at Hanyang had risen to 50 per day and in 1907 the Imperial Army Department directed all the provinces to buy their rifles from the Hanyang Arsenal in preference to importing foreign guns. The superiority of this first modern rifle

Chinese militia trainees practice rifle aiming. The first three trainees in front are equipped with three different types of Hanyang rifle— the regular long rifle, the short rifle, and the carbine pattern.

over the black-powder models used elsewhere was quickly apparent. The Hanyang Arsenal also built two variants of the design, a short rifle with cut-down barrel, stock and hand-guard; and a carbine version similar to the Gew. 91.

The Hanyang rifle was to become the most numerous rifle in China by the outbreak of the war, and retained that status through to the war's end. When the Hanyang Arsenal was forced to evacuate in 1938 the rifle factory, complete with the tooling to manufacture the Hanyang rifle, was transferred to the 21st Arsenal, which continued to build the Hanyang into 1944 before it was replaced on the production line by the Chiang Kai-shek model.

Meanwhile, back in Germany, Mauser continued its efforts on military rifles, aiming at replacing the 1888 Commission Rifle with a weapon purely their own. They did well enough to sell rifles overseas and then, in 1898, were selected to provide the new standard German Army rifle, the Gew. 98. This was followed by various commercial export models, one them developed specifically for China, the Model 1907 in the unique 6.8 x 57mm caliber. A contract was placed for delivery of a large number of these, but the Qing dynasty, lacking funds, defaulted and most of the weapons were converted to the standard 7.92 x 57mm caliber and issued to German troops during WWI.

The drawings and tools for the 6.8mm Model 1907 were delivered from the DWM company of Germany, however, and it was immediately placed in production at the Guangdong Arsenal as the Guang Xu Type 33. Thus, at the end of the Qing reign there were two modern rifles in production: the Hanyang, based on the Commission rifle, and the Mauser Model 1907 at Guangdong and elsewhere. With the establishment of the republic the Army Department declared that the Model 1907 was to be the standard rifle

Troops in a National Day parade in Chengdu, 10 October 1942,
with Type 4 pattern rifles. Note also the M35 helmets.

with the designation Type 1 Rifle, and directed all arsenals to switch to the manufacture of that weapon. With the exception of the Hanyang Arsenal, which claimed it lacked the funds to re-tool, the arsenals complied; with the Sichuan Arsenal, for instance, switching to the 6.8mm Mauser in 1912. Although the 6.8mm cartridge appears to have performed well enough, the fact was that no other country in the world used it, and maybe only one machine gun fired it (the Madsen LMG from Guangdong Arsenal). After much debate, the Army Department changed its mind and in 1915 switched back to the 7.92mm caliber. The Type 1 rifle in the new caliber was officially called the Type 4 Rifle, but was informally referred to as the 7.9mm Type 1 Rifle.

Estimated Production of Hanyang Rifles				
1895–1909	1910–1932	1932–1938	1939–1944	Total
130,036	463,180	283,100	207,164	1,083,480

The Guangdong Arsenal began building 7.92mm rifles in 1914, and thus produced rifles in both 7.92mm and 6.8mm during 1914–20. The Type 4 remained in production at the Guangdong Arsenal until 1932, with a probable total of about 55,000 during the period up to 1927, and another 20,000 after that under the central government Ordnance Office. The Jiangnan Arsenal began production of Type 1 rifles at about the same time, and then switched to 7.92mm, but in 1917 rifle production there was stopped after only a few thousand Type 1/Type 4 had been built. This permitted the machinery to be moved to the Hanyang Arsenal, but there put to the service of producing Hanyang (Commission) rifles, which allowed that facility to increase production to a hundred rifles a day. Finally, in 1919, the Sichuan Arsenal switched from 6.8mm to 7.92mm rifles.

The Gongxian Arsenal had been set up to produce heavy weapons, and did not start producing rifles until 1928. It chose the Type 4, but chambered for the round-nose 7.92mm Mauser also used by the Hanyang rifle. It produced them until 1935 at a rate eventually rising to about 20,000 per year, for a total of about 110,000. By the start of the war most of the Type 4 rifles had been displaced from front-line troops by Hanyang and CKS models, although they continued to serve with a few regular units and some second-line forces.

In Europe, the success of the Mauser pattern in World War I led to continued evolution of that design. These included the vz.24 from the Czech firm of ZB, the Model 1924/30 from FN, and the Standard Modell from Mauser. All three were purchased by China, and the second and third were placed in production there as well.

The FN 1924/30 replaced the Type 4 in production in 1932 at the Guangdong Arsenal. Known as the Type 21, it was produced for four years until the arsenal was taken over by the central government's Ordnance Office in 1936 following Chen Jitang's exile. Total production of the Type 21 was probably slightly in excess of 50,000.

Another source of FN-type rifles was somewhat more irregular. The governor of Zhejiang province, Huang Shaohong, had directed the creation of the Zhejiang Iron Works as an arsenal shortly after the war began in 1937. He ordered the production of rifles, but at the early stages this proved impossible. Instead, the workers took an FN M1930 rifle, ground off all the markings, and submitted that to Huang. Predictably, Huang was delighted and ordered the model into mass production. Needless to say, this caused great

A group of Chinese soldiers in Yunnan during the war, all armed with
FN 1930 pattern rifles. Note the facial expression of the man on the
left, seemingly trying to hold back an embarrassed grin.

consternation at the arsenal, but eventually they managed to reverse-engineer it and they not only armed the local troops, but some excess rifles were even sold to the regular army. As with all other weapons from the Zhejiang Iron Works, the rifles were designated the Type 77 to commemorate the 7 July incident at the Marco Polo Bridge. Total production of the Type 77 was around 32,000.

Mauser's inter-war efforts had yielded the Standard Modell in 1924. Samples were sent to China and, at the National Armament Standards Conference held in 1932 to determine suitable weaponry, the 7.92mm Mauser 1924 was chosen as the standard infantry rifle. Since the event was attended largely by ordnance experts and academics, most of the recommendations of the conference disappeared quietly without a trace (such as the US M1911 handgun), but in this case the decision was actually not only implemented, but quickly. In 1934 the Ministry of Revenue purchased 10,000 Standard Modell rifles from Mauser to arm the Tax Police and the Ordnance Office took the opportunity to request design prints, parts lists, and proof jigs from Mauser. These were turned over to the Gongxian Arsenal to produce templates and tools with the idea of starting production in 1934. Unfortunately, the jigs were found to be worn and the prints included errors, so the superintendent of the Gongxian Arsenal, Mao Yike, a graduate of the Technische Universität Berlin, was dispatched to Germany to get the correct parts and prints. The new materials arrived at the arsenal in early 1935.

The Gongxian Arsenal began low-rate production in July 1935 with the designation Type 24. During the trials process Chiang Kai-shek visited the arsenal with his wife. Chief Yu of the Ordnance Office requested and was granted permission to change the designation to the "Chiang Kai-shek Rifle Carbine" and full production officially started on 10 October 1935. In 1937 the Ordnance Office issued "the Material Standards Regulation for the Chiang Kai-shek Rifle," based on similar German regulations. It established a list of component parts, their names, and their chemical and mechanical specifications. It was the first attempt by the Ordnance Office to establish not only a standard rifle, but standardized specifications for its manufacture that all arsenals could implement.

The standardization, however, was more apparent on paper than in the field. In practice there were small variations between rifles from different arsenals and the parts were often not interchangeable as a result. The Gongxian Arsenal continued to manufacture the rifle under its new designation as the 11th Arsenal, although in decreasing numbers, until 1940. The Guangdong Arsenal switched from production of the Type 21 to the Chiang Kai-shek in June 1937 and production of that model continued after the arsenal evacuated and was redesignated as the 41st Arsenal. After giving up its rifle factory in 1938, the 1st (ex-Hanyang) Arsenal was given the rifle factory of the 11th in 1940, and continued producing the Chiang Kai-shek model using its blueprints and tools.

Wartime Production of Chiang Kai Shek Rifles										
	1937	*1938*	*1939*	*1940*	*1941*	*1942*	*1943*	*1944*	*1945*	*Total*
1st Arsenal	0	0	0	20,000	20,000	7,000	23,000	32,000	32,000	134,000
11th Arsenal	40,000	30,000	20,000	0	0	0	0	0	0	90,000
21st Arsenal	0	0	0	0	0	0	0	24,500	62,000	86,500
41st Arsenal	5,010	8,000	10,000	5,600	15,600	7,000	10,000	11,000	8,000	90,210

The strangest conversion was that of the 21st Arsenal, the former Jin Ling Arsenal, with Hanyang Arsenal rifle tooling, after its move from Nanjing. It received orders to switch production from the Hanyang rifle to the Chiang Kai-shek in 1940. Inexplicably, they began by examining blueprints of the Mauser Gew. 98 and used them as the basis for the new rifle. Of course, the Standard Modell differed from the Gew. 98, and as a result it took them three years to tool up and start production. In retrospect it is difficult to fathom why the 21st simply did not copy drawings used by the 1st and 41st Arsenals, both of which were producing the Chiang Kai-shek, unless the prints had been partially destroyed by air raids and those two arsenals were simply making them by jigs and templates. In any event, once production did start at the 21st, in October 1943, it ramped up very quickly and within a year the 21st was the largest producer of rifles in the country.

An exception to the dominance of the Mauser was the family of Japanese rifles. The imperial government purchased an initial batch of 14,000 Type 30 rifles in 1903. Through October 1917 Japan had exported to China no fewer than 97,996 Murata rifles, 126,867

A young Chinese with a CKS rifle poses for a photograph in front of some posters. The one on the left says "long live the Allies."

Type 30 rifles, and 10,000 of the newer Type 38 rifles. In the following year an additional 24,100 Type 30 rifles, 196,401 Type 38 rifles, and 2,033 Type 38 carbines were shipped, although only 125,000 Type 38 rifles went to the central government, the rest of the weapons being delivered to various favored warlords. Deliveries from Japan to assorted warlords continued in the 1920s, and in 1926, when the Huangpu (Whampoa) Military Academy was established, the Soviets sent 4,000 Type 38 rifles.

The Type 38 rifle was also produced at the Shanxi Arsenal in Taiyuan. It was built in the original 6.5mm caliber until 1937 at about 40–50 per day, when the arsenal facilities had to be evacuated. It had not proven possible to move the ammunition plant, so they switched over to 7.92mm caliber, as in the rest of China. The Type 38 rifle was the standard weapon of Shanxi troops, but according to Japanese intelligence was also widely used by the Northeastern Army, Northwestern Army, Guangdong, and Fujian troops. Such weapons as could be captured from the Japanese were also used, especially by the 8th Route Army. Indeed, some communist units were equipped almost entirely with Japanese rifles, captured from Japanese forces or captured or purchased from puppet troops. Relatively few Japanese units in China converted to the newer 7.7mm rifle, so most captured stocks were of the older Type 38.

> I captured a Type 38 rifle, it is black and shiny . . . load up a cartridge, put the hatred on the front sight, aiming at the invader, shoot that wolf-like animal. Bang!, went right through the heart . . .
> "I captured a Type 38 Rifle", movie theme song from *Two Young 8th Route Soldiers*.

One of the recipients of Japanese rifles had been Zhang Zuolin in Manchuria. In 1924, however, his Eastern Three-Province Arsenal (located in Shenyang) began production of a unique weapon, the Type 13. The origins of this weapon are unclear, but production started in 1924 at 400 per month and rose to 4,000 at the peak. Based on the known serial numbers, the total production was probably around 140,000. Chinese records indicate that the Japanese captured 72,679 Type 13 rifles in the take-over of Manchuria, the rest presumably being taken south with the retreating troops, where they were used by Northeastern Army troops during the war. Some were certainly lost in the anti-communist drives of the 1930s, so the number remaining in service in 1937 was probably not great.

In addition to local production, the warlord era also spurred purchases from abroad. The Western embargo on arms deliveries to China, agreed to by most nations in May 1919, proved quite porous with regard to rifles, which were much smaller and easier to conceal than aircraft, tanks, or artillery. The Czechs delivered 81,000 rifles and 40 million rounds of ammunition to the Fengtian army in 1925, and another 50,000 rifles in the fall of 1927 to Zhang Zongchang of Shandong.

The Italians were also active. In 1920 the Army Department agreed to purchase 40,000 rifles from an Italian company, although these may have been delivered to Cao Kun. Cao Kun bought another 14,000 in 1922, these being delivered in 1924. Wu Peifu also got 40,000 in 1924, and Zhang Qingyao 10,000 just before his ouster from Hunan. In 1924 the Army Department purchased all the cargo on board a cargo ship that included 40,000 M1891 Carcanos.

When the Huangpu Academy was first established, Russia sent 22,000 of its Mosin-Nagant M1891 rifles to support the Nationalists. The Northwest Army during the Northern Expedition and the troops in Xinjiang under Sheng Shicai were all equipped with large quantities of Mosin-Nagants due to their proximity to Russia. The Soviets delivered about 30,000 rifles, presumably Mosin-Nagants, to Feng Yuxiang in 1925–6.

France took an active interest in Yunnan province and during 1921–5 sold 3,000 Lebel Model Indochinois rifles plus 300 rounds per rifle for the railway guards. In June 1926 the French made a second sale, nominally to the Yunnan railway guards, of 5,000 refurbished Commission Model 1888 rifles and 5 million rounds of 7.92mm ammunition.

With the end of the Northern Expedition in 1928 rifle imports dropped and apparently stayed at a reduced level until the Japanese invasion of 1937.

One firm that did manage to find a niche market as supplier to Zhang Zuolin was ZB of Czechoslovakia. A Manchurian delegation arrived at the ZB facility in January 1927 and enquired about buying 130,000 rifles. Nothing came of this immediately, as the two sides could not agree on price, but in May a deal was struck for the sale of 40,000 rifles, including a mix of used and new weapons made with substandard parts, for the low price of $22.80 each.

Apparently both Chang and ZB felt comfortable with the deal, for they negotiated a series of contracts the next year for vz.24 rifles and vz.26 light machine guns, all new production. February 1928 saw a deal for 30,000 rifles, followed by 100,000 rifles in March, then 20,000 more late in the year. One other sale brought the delivery to Jehol of 10,000 rifles in mid-1930. This, however, marked the end of ZB rifle sales until the crisis of the Japanese invasion in 1937.

FN also made some significant sales during 1930–2 of its rifles and carbines, while Sichuan forces bought 3,000 Mauser rifles of unspecified model and 2 million rounds of ammunition from Arnhold & Co in 1930. An unusual series of transactions involved the Soley firm of Britain acting through Arnhold & Co to sell to the Guangdong provincial government. In 1932 Soley had sent 1,000 surplus Pattern 14 British rifles to Liége in Belgium where they were converted to 7.92mm caliber and the following year they were exported to Hong Kong, probably for sale to Guangdong. In January 1933 Soley applied for a British export license for 400 more converted Pattern 14 rifles to Hong Kong, and in mid-1934 applied for a third license for the export of 2,500 more to the Guangdong

Wartime Rifle Imports, through 1940					
		USSR	*Germany*	*Belgium*	*Czech.*
1937	Jul–Sep			2,500	
	Oct–Dec	none			
1938	Jan–Mar			12,000	
	Apr–Jun		5,000	34,540	27,000
	Jul–Sep		45,350	16,000	34,980
	Oct–Dec				
1939	Jan–Mar			18,000	18,000
	Apr–Jun		49,960	11,721	20,017
	Jul–Sep			11,000	
	Oct–Dec	50,000		1,700	
1940			*None*		

government. In addition, the government of British India sent 4,000 rifles and 4 million rounds of ammunition (presumably in the original .303 caliber) to Xinjiang warlord Jin Shuren in 1930.

An unusual purchase was the semi-automatic ZH.29 rifle from ZB. Zhang Zuolin contracted with the firm for 150 ZH.29 rifles in May 1929 and these were delivered in 1931. A second contract, for 100 of the improved ZH.32 model, was placed around 1932 and shipped in August 1933, the exact recipient within China being unknown. In addition, the Guangdong provincial government received 35 ZH.32 rifles in early 1933 in partial compensation for some seized machine guns. It is unlikely that any significant percentage of these small quantities remained in service against the Japanese.

The Shenyang Arsenal completed the trials of a semi-automatic rifle right before the Japanese took over in 1932, likely based on the ZH.29. The Japanese captured some ZH.29 rifles and this presumably influenced the design of a Tokyo Electric semi-automatic rifle that was entered into a Japanese Army competition in the 1930s.

The communist forces, denied supplies by the Nanjing government, relied for the most part on captured or purchased Japanese weapons. An exception was the Type 81 short rifle, which was placed in production at the Jin Ji Yu Operating Base Arsenal in September 1940. It was designed by Liu Guifu and took features from the Hanyang, vz.24, and Type 38 rifles. Prints and templates were made and distributed to other communist arsenals, but in the end only a reported 8,700 were built.

With the start of the Sino-Japanese war in 1937 the Nationalist government, as well as the provincial governments, scrambled to find suppliers for its rifle needs. ZB was approached for a second batch of their vz.24 Mauser derivatives and that firm produced 15,200 in 1937 and 73,000 in 1938 for China's account. These were delivered in 1938/39, along with about 12,000 used Mauser-type rifles.

Germany continued to supply China with rifles, but only via roundabout routes. Documents in the German Foreign Ministry archives seem to indicate that the Nazi government realized that it had at least to appear to stop sales to China in order to appease its new Japanese ally, and directives to that effect went out. However, the Chinese orders were a valuable source of revenue and materials for Germany and officialdom appears to

A Chinese airport sentry armed with a Mosin-Nagant watching a
bomber taking off. Note the spike bayonet mounted on the rifle.

have turned a blind eye to Mauser's efforts to keep the sales flowing. In addition, Germany
itself was rearming at the time, so China had to make do with what it could get, which
usually involved rifles assembled from a mixture of new and rejected parts.

> 5,000 Mauser rifles, disguised as Finnish procurement, loaded on SS *Hans Rickmer*,
> Hamburg on July 2 and designated for Hong Kong. It should arrive on 20 August.
> The manifest showed that the ship also contained 37,000,000 rounds of cartridges,
> vehicle parts, and sea mines from Hapro contracts. The payment must not be paid to
> the original manufacturers; it has to go through the company in Finland. This kind of
> transaction is strictly forbidden by the German Government and the manufacturers
> all stated that they did not engage in such transactions. We heard that this was secretly
> approved by Göring . . . it is going to be difficult going forward, if anything should
> happen to these cargos, there won't be any recourse because German Government has
> banned all armament shipment to China . . .*

Germany supplied slightly over 100,000 rifles, about evenly divided between those
delivered in 1938 via Hong Kong and those delivered in mid-1939 via Rangoon. The

---

* Commercial Counselor, Chinese Embassy, Tang Bo Yu 譚伯羽 to Minister of Finance, Kong Xiang Xi,
Berlin, 8 July 1938.

A soldier of the CAI's 22nd Division with his cut-down M1917 in Burma, May 1944.

latter shipment was listed on customs declarations as being "Mauser Model 1937 rifles," presumably a reference to Kar. 98k rifles with the 1937 crest. The earlier 50,000 rifles could have been used Mausers or Mauser crest Kar. 98k.

The FN firm of Belgium also got into the act, as the largest supplier of rifles during the early war period. Belgium had been a supplier of rifles before the war broke out, including almost 20,000 via Hong Kong alone between 1934 and the outbreak of the war, representing a mix of both new (Model 1924 and later 1930) and reconditioned Mauser-type rifles. The wartime records provide no clue as to what exact types were delivered except that one batch of 4,000 supplied in April 1938 were identified as being Model 30 weapons from FN. Presumably almost all of the other rifles delivered during the war were also new-build Model 30s.

The final supplier of rifles during the early war period was the Soviet Union. Under the arms sales agreements China purchased 50,000 Mosin-Nagant rifles and these were delivered via Rangoon in November 1939. Unlike all the other rifles discussed, however, they were chambered for the Russian 7.62 ammunition, so their usefulness would have been limited and it seems unlikely they ever saw significant combat use.

With the closing of the Burma Road the supply of foreign rifles ended until the US could begin re-arming the Chinese Army in India.

For the rebuilding of the CAI, the British provided the Lee-Enfield No. 4 Mk 1 and the US allocated M1917 rifles, which was the British Pattern 14 rifle of WWI adapted to fire the US .30-cal. cartridge. The M1917s had been in storage since the end of WWI, and some had been sold to Britain and others used for training in the US. An initial shipment of 20,000 of these rifles was made in 1942 and they were quickly issued to the 22nd and 38th Divisions and army troops. These were to be cut down in length to accommodate the shorter Chinese soldiers. This was accomplished in India, although some rifles were issued unmodified in late 1943 in order to fill out unit holdings. As the M1917 was not available in sufficient numbers, some of the Chinese were armed with the Lee-Enfield No. 4 Mk 1 at the time they entered Burma.

Since China produced rifles there was no initial need to provide them over the Hump to Y-Force. Thus, once the immediate requirements of Chinese forces in India had been met, no further deliveries were anticipated until the Burma Road could be reopened. The US recognized "requirements" for M1903 Springfield rifles in 1943, but did not supply any immediately. By late 1944, however, inspection teams began reporting on the worn condition of many of the NRA's rifles after seven years of war, and requirements for 200,000 M1903 and 90,000 M1917 rifles were approved, although significant shipments, in the form of 33,969 Springfields and 10,000 M1917s did not leave the US until the end of the year. The pace picked up during the first half of 1945, when a further 56,870 M1903s and 125,336 M1917s were shipped.

As with all other Lend-Lease items, getting them from India to China was at least as difficult as providing them in the first place. By the end of January 1945 the US had issued only 5,891 rifles to the Chinese Army in China, although a month later that had increased to 20,093. By the end of May 1945 the US had distributed 63,670 Springfields and 30,716 M1917s along with 6,324 British .303-inch rifles. At that time a further 9,200 Springfields, 42,199 M1917s, and 24,312 British rifles were in depots in China and India awaiting transport and distribution. By the end of the war a total of 183,246 M1903, M1917, and British rifles had been distributed to the Chinese Army, with a further 98,858 in depots in China.

An LPA squad in formation. The four on the left have
Thompson submachine guns, the rest M1 carbines.

Rifle Specifications

Chinese-Produced Rifles

	Ammunition	Operation	Length overall	Barrel length	Weight	Muzzle velocity	Feed
Japanese Type 38	6.5 x 50mm SR	manual turned bolt	1,280mm	797mm	3.97kg	762m/s	5-round internal magazine
Liao Type 13	7.92 x 57mm	manual turned bolt	1,250mm	740mm	4.27kg	859m/s	5-round internal magazine
Type 4	7.92 x 57mm	manual turned bolt	1,255mm	738mm	4.08kg	859m/s	5-round internal magazine
Hanyang rifle	7.92 x 57mm	manual turned bolt	1,250mm	740mm	4.06kg	600m/s	5-round protruding magazine
Zhejiang Type 77	7.92 x 57mm	manual turned bolt	1,110mm	600mm	4.08kg	853m/s	5-round internal magazine
Guang Dong Type 21	7.92 x 57mm	manual turned bolt	1,099mm	589mm	3.87kg	855m/s	5-round internal magazine
Chiang Kai-shek	7.92 x 57mm	manual turned bolt	1,110mm	600mm	4.0kg	810m/s	5-round internal magazine
Mauser M1896 carbine	7.63 x 25mm	recoil operated	895mm	254–406mm	1.3kg	490m/s	10–20 rd internal magazine

Imported Rifles

	Ammunition	Operation	Length overall	Barrel length	Weight	Muzzle velocity	Feed
Mauser M1898	7.92 x 57mm	manual turned bolt	1,255mm	646mm	4.08kg	859m/s	5-round internal magazine
Mauser Kar. 98k	7.92 x 57mm	manual turned bolt	1,110mm	600mm	3.9kg	845m/s	5-round internal magazine
Vz-98/22	7.92 x 57mm	manual turned bolt	1,244mm	724mm	3.85kg	870m/s	5-round internal magazine
Vz-24	7.92 x 57mm	manual turned bolt	1,110mm	590mm	4.08kg	810m/s	5-round internal magazine
Carcano 1891	6.5 x 52mm	manual turned bolt	1,285mm	780mm	3.8kg	700m/s	6-round protruding magazine
Mosin-Nagant 1891/30	7.62 x 54mm	manual turned bolt	1,235mm	800mm	4.1kg	731m/s	5-round protruding magazine
M1917	7.62 x 63mm	manual turned bolt	1,170mm	660mm	4.17kg	853m/s	5-round internal magazine
M1917 shortened	7.62 x 63mm	manual turned bolt	895mm	550mm	n/a	n/a	5-round internal magazine
M1903	7.62 x 63mm	manual turned bolt	1,098mm	610mm	3.94kg	853m/s	5-round internal magazine
Lee-Enfield No. 4 Mk I	7.7 x 56mm	manual turned bolt	1,129mm	651mm	4.1kg	744m/s	10-round box magazine
M1 carbine	7.62 x 33mm	gas short stroke	904mm	458mm	2.48kg	585m/s	15-round box magazine

A US weapon not provided by Lend-Lease was the .30-cal. M1 carbine. These were considered ideal by some for Chinese soldiers of short stature. Starting from 1943, SACO brought in M1 Carbines to arm the Loyal and Patriotic Army. With these weapons the LPA had considerable fire power and was feared by Japanese troops, who called LPA men "the Short Rifle Soldiers." The total number provided is not known, but was probably in the thousands.

(Japanese) Type 38 Rifle

The Japanese Army introduced the Meiji Type 38 rifle into service in 1905 and it remained in production into 1942 and in service with the IJA to the end of WWII. Large numbers were distributed to Chinese warlords and, later, puppet forces, and others captured on the battlefields. Copies were also produced by the Shanxi Arsenal and others.

The weapon used a proven design with a very strong action. The long barrel provided additional range in the north China plains and the dust cover protected the action on the battlefield. On the other hand, the small 6.5 x 50mm SR round had mediocre terminal performance and was not standard for Chinese troops.

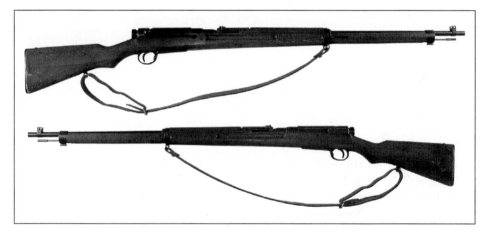

Type 38 rifle.

Liao Type 13 Rifles

Produced by the Eastern Three-Province (Shenyang) Arsenal in Manchuria prior to the Japanese take-over, the guns were of high quality, nicely milled, polished, and blued, and bore no visible tool marks. They used the proven Mauser action, but with some unique features, including a dust cover and two gas escape holes on the receiver. The bolt design did not have the bolt sleeve catch, so it could potentially rotate out of position and make the gun inoperable, and was not interchangeable with any other Mauser rifles. The bolt was similar to the Japanese Type 38 rifle, lacking the guide rib. The long barrel and powerful 7.92 x 57mm combination provided formidable firepower.

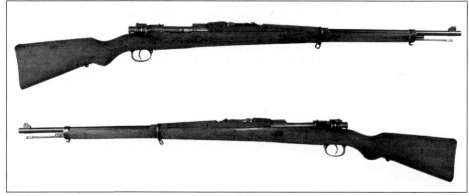

Type 13 rifle.

Type 1 and Type 4 Rifles

A small number of Mauser Model 1907s was imported before local production was undertaken as the Type 1 Rifle, still in the original 6.8mm caliber. By 1920 production had switched to 7.92mm caliber under the designation Type 4 Rifle. They were built by the Gongxian (where it was known as the Gong 98), Shanghai, Guangdong, and Guangxi Arsenals, with minor differences between the makers, including the rear sights. They used the proven Mauser action with a long barrel and powerful cartridge. Their bayonet lug was narrow and relatively weak.

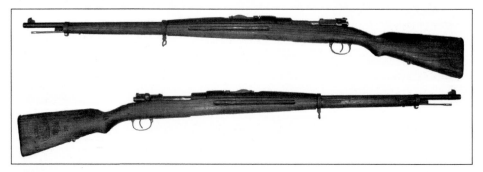

Type 4 rifle.

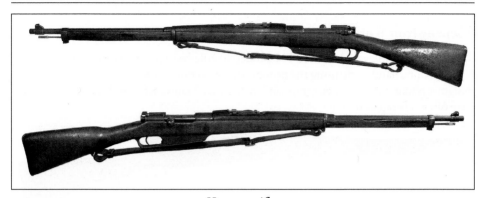

Hanyang rifle.

Hanyang Rifle

The Hanyang (Type 88) rifle was based on the German Commission Rifle of 1888. It had been in production since 1895 and it was proven, reliable, well understood, and trusted by Chinese soldiers. Unfortunately, it could feed only the round-nose version of the 7.92 x 57mm round and was not compatible with the newer "spitzer" pointed-tip version. It needed an en-bloc clip to charge. The bolt head was a two-piece design and easily lost; and the extractor was somewhat weak. The main producer of this rifle was Hanyang Arsenal, with production being transferred to the 21st Arsenal in 1939. Many other arsenals produced this rifle in various quantities, including Shanghai, Kaifeng, and Shanxi. There were several variations, including a short rifle (cut-down stock, hand-guard and barrel) and a carbine (similar to the Gew. 91), and one with built-in Mauser style magazine, sight, and pistol grip stock.

A Hanyang carbine.

Zhejiang Iron Works Type 77 Rifle

This was a wartime variant of the FN Model 30 rifle built by the Zhejiang Iron Works. It was a short, handy rifle using the proven Mauser action. Unfortunately, its unique bolt design, without a rib, was not compatible with other Mauser rifles and the materials used were often substandard.

Type 77 rifle.

Guangdong Arsenal Type 21/FN 30 Rifle

Large quantities of FN Model 30 rifles were imported before and during the war and copies were made by the Guangdong Arsenal as the Type 21. It was a short, handy rifle with the FN-type Mauser action, but featured significant muzzle blast and recoil.

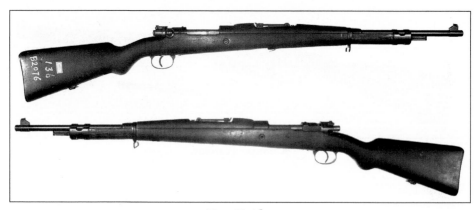

Type 21 rifle.

Chiang Kai-Shek Rifle

What was to become the standard Chinese wartime rifle was based on the Mauser Standard Modell and was built initially by the Gongxian Arsenal, with other arsenals being brought in over time. It was a short, handy, reliable rifle. As it was he standard issue rifle, official manuals and standardized training were available. As with the other shorter Mauser rifles it generated significant muzzle blast and recoil. About 400,000 of these weapons were made during the eight-year war in the four government arsenals. A small number were also built at smaller shops and entities.

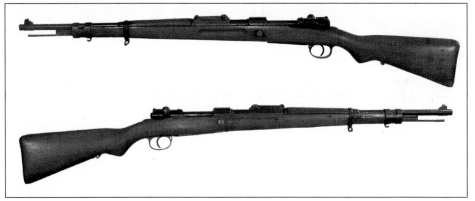

A Gongxian Arsenal Chiang Kai-shek rifle.

Mauser 1896 Carbine

This was a long-barrel version of the Mauser C96 pistol. It was a very light and handy carbine for cavalry troops or rear area use but fired a weak cartridge with limited stopping power and very short range. Some were imported and some manufactured domestically. Only small numbers were acquired and used.

A pair of Dagu-built M1896 carbines.

Type 81 Short Rifle

Little information is available on this weapon, which seems to have taken elements from various rifles built in China. It fired the 7.92mm ammunition and weighed 3.36kg. It was shorter than a rifle but longer than a carbine, and was fitted with an integral folding spike bayonet.

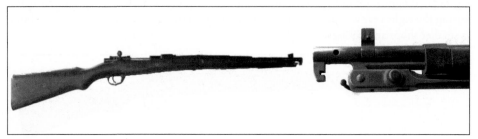

Type 81, with close-up of the bayonet mount.

Imported Rifles

German Mauser 1898 Rifle

This was Peter Mauser's ultimate battle rifle design and was made with superb material and workmanship. It was awkwardly long, especially for short Chinese soldiers, but reliable, accurate, and powerful. Most of the rifles were imported after WWI and had already seen varying degrees of use.

Mauser 1898.

German Mauser Karabiner 98k Rifle

The experiences of WWI showed that the Model 98 rifle was too long for trench warfare and too awkward for mobile operations. As a result the design was cut down after the war to yield the Kar. 98k (k = *kurz* = short) rifle. It retained all the advantages of the trusted Mauser design. All of these were imported after the Marco Polo Bridge Incident; some were made with rejected, but still serviceable, parts. They were marked with the Mauser banner on top of the receiver, and the Chinese 12-pointed star on the barrel, receiver and stock.

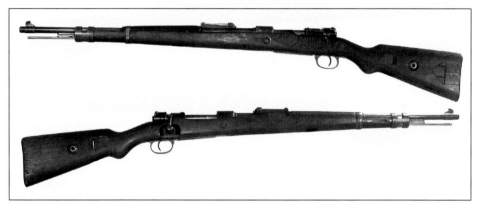

One of the Kar. 98k rifles sold to China in 1938–9.

Czechoslovakia vz.98/22 Rifle

A long rifle design based on the Mauser Model 98. It featured superb workmanship from the Brno factory, but the weapons sent to China were probably already used when imported in the late 1920s. The front sight was machined with the barrel and the upper hand guard covered the rear sight.

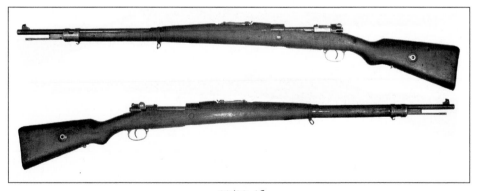

vz.98/22 rifle.

Czechoslovakia vz.24 Rifle

Built on the proven Mauser action with the best steel available in the world, this was arguably the best Mauser ever produced. It may have been a bit bit heavy for smaller soldiers. The sling swivels were configured for both side mount and bottom mount. The upper hand guard covered the full length of the stock from rear sight to the front band.

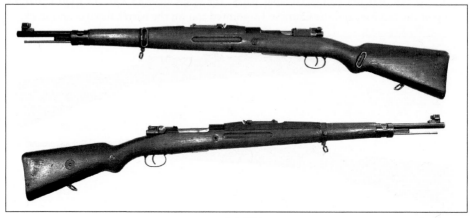

vz. 24 rifle.

Italian 1891 Carcano Rifle

An outdated design, most of these were probably well used when received in China. It needed an en-bloc to charge the protruding Mannlicher-type fixed magazine. It had a barleycorn front sight. The ammunition produced little recoil but had mediocre ballistics and was non-standard in China.

Carcano rifle.

Russian Mosin-Nagant 1891 & 1891/30 Series Rifles

A very simple and robust design. The /30 modification changed the bayonet socket, sights, and cartridge clips. By Chinese standards the weapon was long and unwieldy, produced severe recoil, and fired non-standard ammunition.

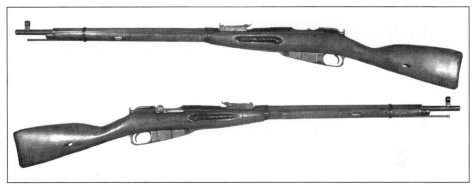

Mosin-Nagant M1891/30 rifle.

US M1917 Rifle

The M1917 was the British P14 rifle, a modified Mauser design, built in the US during WWI and chambered for the American .30-06 cartridge. To suit it better to Chinese soldiers most of the rifles were cut down in India, 110mm in the front and 30mm in the back, making it even shorter than the CKS. It was reliable and powerful, but fired non-standard ammunition. It could mount the M2 grenade launcher, enabling it to fire the M9 HEAT grenade, a very useful feature.

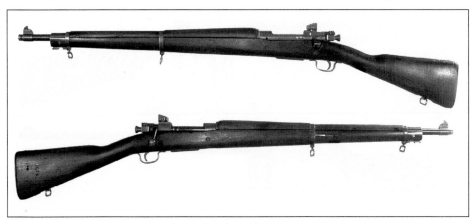

M1917 rifle.

US 1903A3 Rifle

This was a well-made weapon using a modified Mauser action. It was powerful and accurate but fired non-standard ammunition. It could mount the M1 grenade launcher, enabling it to fire the M9 HEAT grenade.

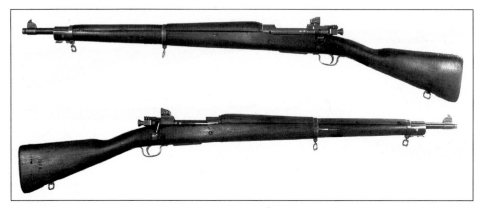

M1903A3 rifle.

US M1 Carbine

The M1 was developed as an intermediate weapon, between the rifle and the pistol. It was short and handy and its semi-automatic operation gave a good rate of fire. On the other hand, the small cartridges had limited stopping power and relatively short range, and were non-standard in China. The M1 carbine was not supplied by Lend-Lease, but was provided by SACO for guerrilla units.

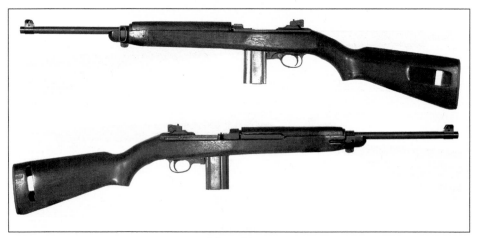

M1 carbine.

British Lee-Enfield No 4 Mk 1*

The standard British service rifle, it had a proven action and was very well made. The cock-on-close design permitted fast firing for a bolt-action weapon in experienced hands. Unfortunately, it fired non-standard ammunition and as a result was mostly used for training in India.

Lee-Enfield No. 4 rifle.

17

Grenade Launchers

A lthough made popular in the West by the First World War, grenade launchers appear not to have impressed the various Chinese warlords or the central government. There were small-scale purchases and production in the 1930s, but for the most part they remained curiosities rather than line infantry weapons.

All that would change with the Japanese invasion of 1937. The Chinese forces had had experience with the Japanese Type 10 grenade launcher during the earlier battles, but it took the full-scale campaigning of the first few months of war to bring home the need for an HE-throwing weapon for use at the lowest tactical level. Indeed, reports of the effectiveness of Japanese troops with their Type 10 and Type 89 grenade dischargers quickly reached the ears of Chiang Kai-shek himself. He noted their usefulness and demanded an equivalent be quickly put into production for his own forces.

> The agile movement of the troops, the good usage of the grenade discharger were all our enemy's strong points. We must learn their strong points then we don't have to be afraid of them. Once we learn those, we can use them against the enemy.[*]

The most immediate result was a simplified version of the Japanese Type 10 grenade discharger, known as the Type 27 grenade launcher. It worked, and was produced in large numbers and continually improved, but it meant one man per squad could not be armed with a rifle, the usual drawback for such a weapon. As an alternative, an effort was made to develop a rifle-launched grenade and this bore fruit the next year as the Type 28 grenade launcher.

 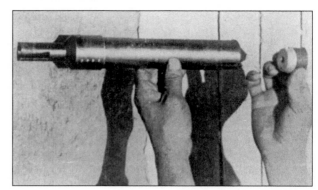

A Japanese soldier demonstrates a captured prewar warlord-type rifle grenade launcher in 1938. Nothing is known of it but the tiny size of the grenade must have limited its lethality.

---

[*] Chiang Kai Shek, 27 November 1938, speech to the 1st Nan Yue Military Conference

For the rest of the war the KMT forces produced and used both hand-held and rifle-mounted grenade launchers, in about equal numbers. Divisions tended to have either one type or the other, but there were instances of divisions with both. Armies often contained divisions with either or both types.

Rifle Grenade Launchers

The first documented acquisition of rifle grenade launchers came in May 1933 when the provincial government of Yunnan purchased 200 launcher attachments and 10,000 grenades from the Brandt firm, these being delivered in July and August. Presumably most of these were still available in 1937.

Photographic evidence confirms the existence of at least one prewar rifle grenade launcher that seemingly launched an exceptionally small munition. There may have been others, but any such would have been produced and used only in small numbers.

A wartime model was developed by the Zhejiang Iron Works and known as the Type 77, to be used with their Type 77 rifle. The weapon was supposedly designed by the warlord Huang Shaohong himself and production started in late 1938 and ended around 1943. It was probably only used by forces in Zhejiang Province.

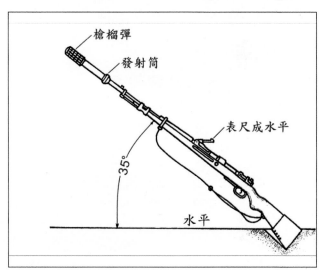

For firing the Type 28 a leather cup was placed over the buttstock to reduce cracking, a small pit dug in the ground, and the rifle sight used to establish a 35° elevation.

In February 1939 a Russian engineer Gregore Larikov began working on a rifle grenade launcher at the central government's Aerial Ordnance Research Institute. The design incorporated the Chinese preference for "potato masher" type grenades, although it used a special grenade for aerodynamic efficiency. The device was accepted for service as the Type 28 grenade launcher and entered production in June 1939. The grenades were produced at the Aerial Ordnance Research Institute (renamed the 27th Arsenal in 1943), while production of the launcher attachment was turned over to the 24th Arsenal, which built 39,000 during the war. They were widely used in all parts of China.

The launcher consisted of three parts: a tube to launch the grenade, a base by which the tube was attached to the rifle muzzle, and an interconnection section. In 1943 the 24th Arsenal recommended eliminating the interconnection section and forming the end of the tube into a cone for muzzle attachment. This simplified production but was not adopted until after the war ended.

A Type 27 grenade launcher behind a Lahti light machine gun
on the Yellow River in 1941. (*Rodger/Timepix*)

The grenades came in two varieties, the main one being an HE-fragmentation munition, supplemented by smaller numbers of a yellow phosphorus model for smoke and incendiary purposes. Both used a wooden handle that could either fit down the launcher tube or be thrown like a "potato masher" hand grenade. The launcher could be fitted directly to a CKS rifle or, by use of a copper shim, to the Hanyang rifle and later the US M1903 rifle.

For firing the rifle was set at a 35° angle of elevation, which was achieved by setting a range of 2,000 meters on the rear sight of a CKS rifle (or 1,800m on a Hanyang), which used a cam to raise the rear end of the sight. When the rifle was held such that the sight was horizontal the rifle was at the proper elevation.

For the Chinese Army in India the US provided M2 rifle grenade launchers for use on their M1917 rifles, and a smaller number of M1 rifle grenade launchers for use with M1903 rifles. An initial lot of 200 was allocated from US production in 1942, but not immediately delivered. No thought was given to shipping US grenade launchers over the

Hump, since Chinese forces already had such weapons, so the requirement was initially limited to the CAI. A further 3,723, including some spares, were produced for China during 1943, but only the 200 from 1942 plus 200 more were actually shipped to India. By that time it seems to have become apparent the anti-tank capability afforded by the US grenade launcher would be valuable in China itself, and stockpiling began, awaiting the opening of the Burma Road. Another 3,262 were built in 1944, and late that year deliveries finally

Soldiers pose with captured Japanese
Type 89 grenade dischargers.

started catching up with production, with 6,385 being shipped to India that year. Each of the five divisions in India was authorized 243 rifle grenade launchers and all were fully equipped, although it appears that this did not happen until late 1944. Through the end of 1944 the US had shipped to India for China 6,785 M2 rifle grenade launchers, along with 257,500 M9 shaped-charge anti-tank grenades, 5,000 M19 WP smoke grenades, and 1,660 M22 colored smoke grenades to go with them.

By the end of January 1945 the US listed 6,804 rifle grenade launchers as authorized under Lend-Lease for the Chinese Army in China, but only 33 had actually made the trip from the depots in India, where 3,933 were stored. The authorization was almost doubled to 11,016 in February, but while the holdings in India had increased to 5,966 no further launchers had actually made it to China. Things started to pick up in the spring and by the end of May 4,314 had made the trip over the Burma Road to China, of which 3,887 had been issued to Chinese units. By the end of the war in September 7,413 had been issued to Chinese Army units in China, a further 1,695 were in China awaiting distribution, and 2,971 were being staged through India. The M2s played a role in Burma and in China itself, but really only in the last year of the war.

Hand-Held Grenade Launchers

The Japanese were the world's foremost believers in the value of hand-held grenade launchers and used them extensively in China from the beginning. Since they were issued at the platoon level, significant numbers of both the Type 10 and the Type 89 were captured and used by the Chinese throughout the war.

Soon after the Marco Polo Bridge incident the Ordnance Bureau, impressed by the Japanese weapons, ordered the Hanyang Arsenal to manufacture something similar.

They reverse-engineered the Type 10, but it proved too complex to manufacture easily and the soldiers had difficulty using it. At the same time the arsenal was being moved, so responsibility for the new grenade launcher was switched to the 30th Arsenal. It simplified the design and this version passed Ordnance Bureau tests in 1938 and was standardized as the Type 27 Grenade Launcher. Production started in January 1939.

Production of Type 27 Grenade Launchers by 30th Arsenal						
1939	*1940*	*1941*	*1942*	*1943*	*1944*	*1945*
10,300	7,702	5,709	9,148	6,000	50	2,000

The Type 27 was slightly heavier than the Japanese Type 10 in spite of simplification in order to permit the use of lower-quality metal, but the production time was one-third that of the Japanese original. Detail improvements were made throughout the war and the weapon was liked by the troops. Ammunition was interchangeable with that of the Japanese Type 10, the Japanese Type 91 hand/launcher fragmentation grenade being especially popular, and both sides freely used weapons and ammunition from the other. The 30th Arsenal built 40,909 Type 27 grenade launchers and 1,551,313 grenades during the war.

Brandt Mle. 31 Rifle Grenade

The Mle. 31 rifle grenade and launcher were used by Yunnanese troops. It was unique for its time in using a "bullet trap" system featuring a central tube in the grenade. This tube absorbed the bullet, spreading the shock of impact over a period of time. Thus, unlike almost all other rifle grenades, it could be launched using ball (service) ammunition, rather than special blanks or wooden bullets. Brandt claimed a fair degree of accuracy with this weapon, dispersion being reported as 10 meters in range and 2.2 meters laterally at a range of 300 meters. No other major army adopted it, however.

Brandt Mle. 31, ready to fire.

Brandt Mle. 31 Specifications	
Grenade length	200mm
Grenade diameter	35mm
Grenade weight	450g
Weight of launcher	300g
Maximum range	325m

Zhejiang Type 77 Rifle Grenade Launcher

Little is known of this weapon other than a description provided by a British infantry officer who saw it being fired. He said that it was heavy, being made of iron rather than steel, and threw a grenade 2 inches (50mm) in diameter to a maximum range of 600 meters. For firing "it is attached to the muzzle end of the rifle, the range being adjusted by increasing or decreasing the aperture at the base of the discharger." He further commented that at maximum range it appeared "remarkably accurate." It was used only in Zhejiang and in relatively small numbers.

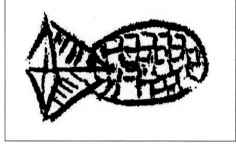

A sketch of a Type 77 rifle grenade drawn by the British observer.

Type 28 Rifle Grenade Launcher

The discharger was placed over the muzzle of the rifle and secured in place by a finger screw behind the front sight. A ballistite cartridge, similar to a blank round, was used to launch the grenade. There was no gas vent, the range being regulated by the extent to which the handle of the potato-masher type grenade was inserted in the tube, thus increasing or decreasing the gas pressure. The handle of the grenade was graduated up to a maximum range of 220m, and a felt washer was attached to the end of the grenade handle to prevent it from slipping farther into the tube than desired. The grenade had a time fuze with a nominal delay of 6.5 seconds, initiated after firing by the shock of the discharge and so, given luck and care, could achieve air bursts by varying the launch elevation. When used as a hand grenade, the same result was achieved by hitting the handle against some hard object. Two types of grenade were available, one with a yellow phosphorus payload, and the more common HE-fragmentation version with 55g of TNT for a burst radius of 10 meters.

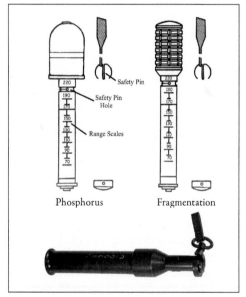

The Type 28 rifle grenade launcher and its two types of grenades.

Type 28 Specifications	
Tube caliber	25.8mm
Grenade weight	589g
Weight of launcher	750g
Length of launcher	250mm
Maximum range	220m

US Rifle Grenade Launcher

The US developed a pair of rifle grenade launchers in 1941 to launch the new M9 anti-tank grenade. These were the M1 for the M1903 Springfield rifle and the M2 for the M1917 rifle, identical except for small dimensional changes to accommodate the barrels. They formed a tubular extension to the rifle barrel with an outside diameter of 22mm, enabling the tail boom of projected grenades to slip snugly over the tube. The tube had a series of raised rings marked for range, the farther down the

M1/M9A1 Specifications	
Grenade weight	459g
Weight of explosive	113g
Weight of launcher	227g
Length of launcher	170mm
Maximum range	150m

tube the grenade was pushed, the longer the range achieved. Launching was accomplished by firing a special blank cartridge. An HE-fragmentation grenade was developed, but the munitions delivered to China were almost exclusively the M9 anti-tank model, which was also useful against bunkers.

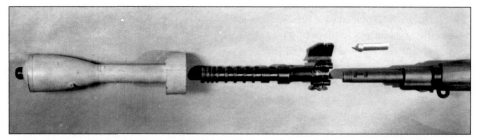

M1 grenade launcher (removed from rifle barrel) and M9A1 anti-tank grenade.

Japanese Grenade Launchers

The IJA introduced the small, hand-carried Type 10 grenade discharger in 1921 to fire the Type 10 HE hand grenade, along with pyrotechnics. This munition was replaced in 1931 by the Type 91 grenade. Both grenades had a cylindrical main body with a safety/fuze unit projecting from the top and a screw-in propellant unit at the bottom.

The Type 10 grenade discharger had a smooth bore and a moving firing pin. The grenade was dropped down the barrel and then a trigger was pulled, releasing the spring-loaded firing pin to move forward and strike the propellant unit at the bottom of the grenade. The weapon was

Type 10 (*left*) and Type 89 grenade launchers.

A Type 89 with its carrying case.

Type 10 and 89 Specifications

	Type 10	Type 89	
	Grenade	*Grenade*	*HE Shell*
Projectile weight	520g	520g	n/a
Range	230m	190m	650m
Weight	2.5kg	4.7kg	
Overall length	51cm	61cm	
Barrel length	24cm	25cm	

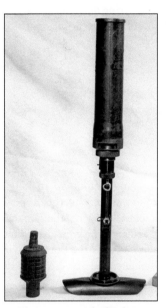

A Type 10 grenade discharger and Type 91 grenade.

normally fired from a 45° angle, with range being varied by rotating a knurled ring at the base of the barrel that allowed variable amounts of gas to escape. To the rear of the barrel was a tubular extension, at the end of which was a small curved baseplate.

The Type 10 proved exceptionally useful, but had one main drawback, that the fit between the grenade and the wall of the barrel was necessarily a poor one, allowing gases to escape and thus limiting range. The improved Type 89 had a rifled tube that permitted it to fire a special HE shell with a copper rotating band to greater distances. It could still fire the standard HE grenade if needed. The gas-bleed ring on the Type 10 was replaced by a knurled knob that moved a "stop" up and down within the barrel, varying the amount of empty chamber space.

Grenade Launcher, Type 27

The Type 27 was inspired by the Japanese Type 10, but had significant differences. The most obvious was the cruder finish, to speed production. The weapon was visibly distinctive in the use of a rectangular, L-shaped baseplate, rather than the curved baseplate of the original. A simple gas regulator valve governed the escape of propellant gases from a port in the base of the tube by covering or uncovering varying proportions of a gas-escape hole. A ball-and-spring device held the gas regulator in one of eight rotational positions calibrated

Type 27 Specifications	
Projectile weight	590g
Range	220m
Overall weight	2.6kg
Overall length	48cm

Side and front views of the Type 27 grenade launcher, showing the pull-type trigger and gas port.

for ranges from 50 to 220 meters. The round used was the Type 27 grenade, a close copy of the Japanese Type 91 fragmentation grenade, which could be used as a hand grenade or, with a propellant module screwed into the bottom, with a grenade discharger. The nominal kill zone was 20m in diameter and a well-trained team could put out 20 rounds per minute for short periods.

As the war progressed several improved versions of the weapon showed up, most of them retaining the Type 27 designation. In 1940 the base plate was made thicker and the 20cm-long aiming line on the barrel was narrowed. In 1941 the vent hole shape was changed from circular to wedge-shaped and later a push-type trigger mechanism replaced the pull-type to reduce tube movement during firing.

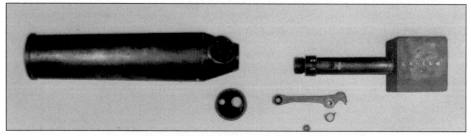

The Type 27 disassembled, less the firing pin and spring. The tube extension screws into an internally threaded blind hole in the barrel.

18

Light Machine Guns

Adoption of light machine guns trailed that of their heavier brethren in China as elsewhere. One of the earliest air-cooled portable machine guns was the Danish Madsen, some 84 of which had been purchased by the imperial regime via Bielefeld & Son, and a further 40 were bought in the early years of the republic. The Guangdong Arsenal began production for imperial forces in 1909 and the Kaifeng Arsenal reverse-engineered the weapon in the early 1920s, but the gun was complex and numbers produced appear to have been small. Although the Madsen was to make a return to China, these original batches played little role in the 1937 war.

In 1928 the Shenyang Arsenal began to build the Type 17 light machine gun for Manchurian forces, a copy of the Japanese Taisho Type 11. Production was cut short by the Japanese occupation after only about 400 had been built. Both the Japanese and Shenyang weapons remained in service to the early part of the war, but in limited quantities.

Another early purchaser of light machine guns was Marshal Liu of Sichuan. In 1929 he ordered 600 Lewis light machine guns from Soley Armament of the UK, who rebuilt the guns in their British facility, along with 6 million rounds of 7.7mm ammunition for them. The first batch of 348 guns arrived in March 1930 and the balance a few months later. A second contract, for a further 600 guns and 2 million rounds, was placed in March 1931. Their use seems to have been limited to Sichuan troops and that, combined with their non-standard ammunition, meant that they rarely fired against the Japanese.

In the meantime development in Europe was proceeding quickly on what would become the standard Chinese light machine gun. Engineer Václav Holek

A Madsen light MG being shown at the Kaifeng Arsenal in 1922.

279

A KE-7 of the 5th Army in 1932.

had been charged with developing a light machine gun for the Czech Army in 1923 and by 1926 his design had been adopted as the vz.26 and placed in production at the Brno factory of ZB. The firm immediately began looking for exports.

The initial customer in China was Zhang Zuolin, who had sent a delegation to ZB in Czechoslovakia in early 1927 looking for rifles. Apparently his locally produced Type 17 was not all that had been hoped for, for orders for the ZB26 light MG were placed concurrently with the rifle orders of 1928: for 500 in February, 1,500 in March, and 1,000 late in the year. A further 1,000 weapons were ordered in May 1929, then another 1,200 in early 1930. Most of these were delivered quickly, deliveries often starting a few months after the sale.

Those sales apparently filled the Manchurian requirements, but other warlords were not about to let Zhang leapfrog ahead of them. In December 1930 the German firm of Gollenhagen bought 200 of these light machine guns for resale in China, probably to the Guangdong provincial government. In April 1931 a further 300 weapons were shipped to southern China via Hamburg, although the recipient is unknown. At the same time the Guangdong provincial government placed a direct contract with ZB for 500 more ZB26s and these were shipped via the German Rickmers line, but the Nanjing government heard about it and persuaded Rickmers to divert the ship to Shanghai, where the weapons were confiscated. ZB shipped a batch of 1,500 light MGs to Nanjing in 1933, the first actual purchase of those weapons by the central government.

Exact details of all the sales are unknown, but the production records for ZB show output of 204 light machine guns in 1930 for China, followed by 1,200 in 1931, 1,050 in 1932 and 1,906 in 1933.

ZB was not alone in pursuing the China market. SIG of Switzerland had launched an aggressive marketing effort in China and was rewarded in November 1928 with an initial contract for 100 of their KE-7 guns at SFr1,800 each from the Nanjing regime, followed a month later by a second contract for 200 more at SFr1,640 each. As the orders increased in size the unit price dropped, so that the third contract, in June 1929 for 800 weapons, was priced at only SFr950 each, as was the fourth contract of September 1930 for another 125 weapons. A fifth contract, for 1,000 weapons, was placed in February 1931, bringing the prewar total to 2,225.

Apparently constrained by the arms embargo the third contender for supplier of light MGs to China fell somewhat behind the first two. Hotchkiss proposed their light machine gun firing 7.9mm ammunition from strips to the central government, and beat out the Vickers-Berthier, largely on cost. The first contract was awarded in early 1931 and covered 600 weapons, these being shipped in June/July. The second contract covered 500 more weapons with shipment in March 1932. A third contract covered 1,000 weapons for shipment in May/June 1932. Later orders provided for 120 more weapons with accessories for shipment in May 1932 and 200 for shipment in June. A final prewar order for 200 was placed in May 1933 and delivered in the second half of that year. In all cases the weapons were shipped with one spare barrel and 50 ammunition strips per weapon, and one machine for loading the ammunition into the strips for each ten weapons.

Not satisfied with three different models of light machine guns the Nanjing government went looking for yet another. The next model to be chosen was the M1930 version of the BAR, manufactured by FN in Belgium, in 7.9mm caliber. The initial contract, for 1,377 weapons, was placed in the first half of 1933. It was followed by five more contracts totaling 1,771 in 1934, and then two more contracts, for 500 each, in June and December 1935, for a total of 4,148, of which the 500 of the June 1935 contract were for the Opium Suppression Bureau in Guangzhou.

Troops practice with a Chinese-made ZB26 light MG. Note the sight to the side of the magazine and the magazine well cover flipped forward to allow insertion of the magazine.

Troops practice AA firing for the camera in Taiyuan in 1937. Note
the strip feed used in the Hotchkiss light machine gun.

Thus, by 1933 the BAR, KE-7, Hotchkiss, and ZB light machine guns were all in service, each very different in operation from the other. To simplify training and logistics a single weapon had to be chosen for this category and in late 1933 the ZB26 was selected. A contract was placed on 16 February 1934 for 5,000 weapons for CZK33 million. The delivery schedule insisted on by the Chinese side was far tighter than the firm could actually meet and as a result some 3,750 of the weapons delivered had to be diverted from orders placed earlier by the Czech Army. As a result of this expedient, the weapons were supplied in 1934, along with 820 from earlier orders. Another 400 were ordered and delivered in 1935.

With the selection of the ZB26, purchases of other machine guns ceased, except for the BARs, bought by Lung Yun for his Yunnanese forces.

The organizational changes in the army had a profound effect on the acquisition of light machine guns during the 1930s. The gradual shift towards providing a light machine gun for each rifle squad generated tremendous new requirements. One weapon per squad usually translated to about 81 per regiment, yielding a divisional requirement varying from about 320 for a four-regiment division to 480 for a six-regiment division. Within a few years the total requirement for light machine guns climbed from one or two thousand, for use by picked troops, to a figure of probably around 40,000.

The central government had no intention of purchasing such a large quantity of weapons from overseas. The Dagu Dockyard had already begun producing small quantities of ZB26s in 1927, but these were reverse-engineered weapons, largely hand-made, and parts could not be interchanged between weapons. With the decision to standardize on the ZB26 it was decided to launch large-scale indigenous production of the weapon. The Ordnance

Bureau attempted to get production drawings for the weapon along with the February 1934 order, but the Czechs turned them down, releasing only acceptance templates. Three Chinese technical experts were then sent to the Brno plant to observe production and secretly note the processes involved.

In the meantime more regional arsenals had got into the fray. In 1935 the Guangdong 1st Arsenal and the Northwest Casting factory in Shanxi both began low-rate production of the ZB26. A year later the Munitions Plant of the Sichuan & Xikang Pacification Bureau began production as well.

A soldier of the Honorable 1st Division fires a ZB26 from the hip in 1945.

In 1936 the three technical experts, now returned from Czechoslovakia, handed over their drawings and notes to the Gongxian Arsenal. Despite it being one of the better arsenals, the folks there never could get full production going and their capacity, even in wartime, never exceeded a few hundred a year.

In any event, these unofficial drawings were not perfect, and were subject to continuing modification as difficulties arose, and negotiations for a full official production license and technical data package continued. This seemed to bear fruit in the spring of 1937 when a Czech delegation arrived to finalize a license-production deal. The Marco Polo Bridge Incident, however, caused the delegation to hurriedly decamp for home without completing the deal, and the Chinese were left to continue the production efforts on their own.

With the outbreak of war some consolidation was mandated and many of the facilities moved inland. The Guangdong 1st Arsenal, moved and renamed as the 41st Arsenal, continued production to the end of the war at 260–300 weapons per month. The Sichuan and Xikang arsenal was renamed the 20th Arsenal in March 1938 and in 1939 its light machine gun factory was taken over by the 21st Arsenal (the former Jinling Arsenal, moved to Chongqing). Under the 21st Arsenal the factory continued to turn out ZB26s to the end of the war at about 2,000 per year. The 51st Arsenal began producing the ZB26 in June 1941 and had built 450 by the end of the year. It became a major producer, building 14,920 by the end of the war. Unfortunately, due to its remote location and shortage of skilled workers the quality of the ZB26s was poor.

The central government was not the only party interested in domestic production. The Hwa Xing Machine Factory in Chongqing had been set up as a private enterprise and began

The M1937 Madsens were supplied with their own complicated
tripod, seen here during training in June 1944.

production of the KE-7, apparently without a license, in 1934. Over the next two years
they built over 6,000 weapons for Liu's forces. Production was restarted at the outbreak of
the war and a further 1,900 were built in 1937–8. Once that batch had been completed,
the factory, by now taken over by the Nanjing government and made part of the 20th
Arsenal, switched to ZB26 production. The Hwa Xing-produced KE-7 was distinctive in
that the ventilation holes on the barrel's heat shield were round, in contrast to the original
elongated shape.

In addition, the Zhejiang Iron Works launched production of a modified ZB26 that
featured a side-mounted magazine and centered top-mounted front and rear sights, which
it designated the Type 77. Production began in 1938 and ran at about 60 per month.

Dreams of standardization fell by the wayside with the outbreak of the war, which
spurred frantic efforts to buy light machine guns from any source that would sell them.

Procurement of the Hotchkiss light MG had been halted after the standardization on
the ZB26, but the start of the war led to additional contracts being placed for Hotchkiss
weapons, 700 on 9 November 1937, 200 more the next day, and a final 500 in December.
With France rearming itself it is not clear how many of these later weapons were actually
delivered. Certainly, 200 passed through Hong Kong in July 1938 and 225 through
Rangoon in February–March 1939, but deliveries via Haiphong, if any, are unknown,
although a figure of 500 has been mentioned and seems likely. In addition to the wartime

orders by the central government, the Guangxi provincial government took delivery of 500 Hotchkiss light machine guns via Rangoon in late 1938.

At the same time the KMT renewed its contacts with FN, placing two orders totaling 8,000 BARs in early August 1937, and a third contract in December of that year for 1,500 more. These resulted in the delivery to Guangzhou via Hong Kong of 1,600 Model 1930s in January 1938, 462 in February, 100 each in April and May, then 1,500 in July, 500 in August and finally another 500 in September. Deliveries continued in 1939 via Burma, with 1,150 passing through in March and the final batch of 1,500 in May. These brought the total of M1930s to 11,560.

The central government also went back to Switzerland, contracting with SIG for 880 KE-7s in March 1938, these being delivered in July–September of that year via Germany and Hong Kong. This brought the acquisition of the KE-7 to slightly over 11,000 weapons, making it one of the more common of the Chinese light machine guns.

The failure to secure full production data and rights for the ZB26 was disappointing. Trials had already been conducted on a number of weapons and the Madsen, an earlier version of which had actually been produced locally by hand in small numbers, had proved satisfactory. Plans were made for both direct purchase and license production.

	prior	1937	1938	1939	1940	1941	1942	1943	1944	1945
Wartime Deliveries of Light Machine Guns										
Imports										
ZB26	13,236	1,243	7,629	8,141	0	0	0	0	0	0
Hotchkiss	2,620	0	700	225	0	0	0	0	0	0
KE-7	2,225	0	880	0	0	0	0	0	0	0
FN M1930	4,148	0	4,762	2,650	0	0	0	0	0	0
Lahti m/26	0	0	700	0	0	0	0	0	0	0
Madsen	0	0	500	2,000	600	200	0	0	0	0
Degtyarev	0	0	2,600	3,000	0	0	0	0	0	0
Maxim-Tokarev	0	0	1,000	400	0	0	0	0	0	0
Bren	0	0	0	0	0	0	925	1,500	1,000	9,400
Production										
KE-7	6,000	1,900		0	0	0	0	0	0	0
ZB26	?	?	?	?	1,324	2,440	6,000	9,391	13,574	13,863

Note: Bren figures are for issues to Chinese units.

An initial contract by the KMT for 1,500 weapons was signed in Bad Nauheim, Germany, on 21 October 1937 between Finance Minister Kung and Madsen president Henckel.[*] The initial batch, 35 guns, left the factory on 16 March 1938, arrived in Hong

---

[*] The Italian firm Simonetta had previously attempted to sell 200 Madsens to the Guangxi provincial government. For reasons that are unclear, it shipped them via Japan, arriving in Kobe in July 1932. The Japanese government impounded them and held them until February 1934, when they were returned to Italy. A second try was made when they were shipped again, this time to Hong Kong, arriving in June 1934. They were still there in 1936 and appear to have been returned to Europe once again.

Kong on 30 April and was trans-shipped to Guangzhou on 14 May. The next 500 guns were delivered via that route through 10 September, but a further 400 guns delivered to Hong Kong had to be re-shipped to Rangoon because the colony's inland links had been cut by the Japanese. The thousand guns remaining on the contract had been delivered to Rangoon by early May 1939 for movement onwards via the Burma Road.

A second contract for a further 1,800 Madsens was signed in June 1938 in Berlin, but was annulled by Kung because it was felt the price was too high. In mid-February 1939, however, Danish Colonel Halvor Jessen persuaded General Yu Dawei to appeal to Kung and on 25 February the contract was reinstated. The first batch of 100 weapons on this contract left the factory on 25 March and reached Rangoon in May. By the end of 1939 1,400 of the weapons on this contract had been built and 1,000 passed through Rangoon. Another large batch of 600 transited Rangoon in March 1940. The last weapons on the contract came out of the factory on 18 March, just three weeks before the German invasion of Denmark. The final 200 weapons were at sea on the Italian steamer *Calabria* when Italy entered the war and were seized by the British and stored at Calcutta until February 1941 when they were released and shipped to China via Rangoon.

China also negotiated for the purchase of license-production rights for the Madsen light MG. This would have involved machinery from Germany and the USA and gun-specific tools from Madsen. The first batch of tools left Copenhagen in June 1939 and the last on 4 April 1940. In anticipation of the arrival of the technical data package the 51st Arsenal was ordered to prepare for production of the weapon. It is not clear what happened next, Chinese sources merely noting that the tools and drawings were destroyed "on the Burma Road" by Japanese air attack. No production was therefore undertaken. Instead the 51st Arsenal was directed to produce ZB26 light machine guns.

Smaller sources were not overlooked, and in late 1937 a contract was signed for 1,000 Lahti m/26 machine guns from Finland. These weapons were not completely unknown to the Chinese, one such having been trialed in Guangzhou in December 1932, but no order followed at that time. The 1937 Lahtis, in 7.9mm, were delivered to Guangzhou in two batches, 200 in early July 1938, and 500 early the following month. The remaining 300 were apparently never delivered. Those that arrived remained in service to the end of the war, although probably in decreasing numbers for lack of spare parts.

Another source of light machine guns was the Soviet aid/sales package. Shipment 2 of the sale included 1,100 Degtyarev DP and 500 old Maxim-Tokarev light machine guns, these being delivered via Hong Kong in March 1938 and Haiphong a few months later. Shipment 4 provided a further 1,500 Degtyarevs and 500 Maxim-Tokarevs via Haiphong in August–September 1938. The final batch, of 3,000 DPs (with 14,000 drum magazines) and 400 Maxim-Tokarevs was delivered via Rangoon in October 1939. These were useful weapons but used non-standard ammunition and the operating system of the DP was unlike anything else in the Chinese armory.

The availability of Lend-Lease opened new possibilities. John Inglis of Canada was already manufacturing Bren guns for Britain under US Lend-Lease, and the Bren was a British adaptation of the Chinese-standard ZB26, albeit rechambered for the British .303-inch round. Little training would therefore be required to bring the Brens into Chinese service. Unfortunately, it would introduce a new family of ammunition, but converting the Bren back into the original 7.92mm caliber would have caused a significant break in production at Inglis, so this was dismissed immediately. In the summer of 1941 Lauchlin

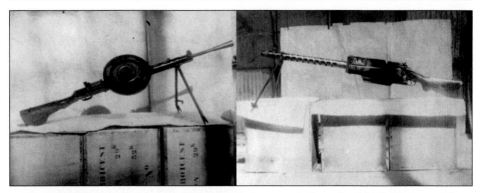

French officials in Haiphong examined and photographed much of the Soviet materiel passing through. Here a DP on the left and a Maxim-Tokarev on the right.

Currie, adviser to President Roosevelt, promised China Defense Supplies that the US would finance 1,750 Mk I Bren guns in .303-inch caliber from Canadian production, along with spares and ammunition, to be delivered by the end of the year. The bureaucracy moved slowly, however, and the Chinese went ahead and ordered 500 weapons from Inglis on their own. On 13 September Lend-Lease authorities allocated 1,750 Mk I Bren guns (including the 500 ordered by China), along with an equal number of spare barrels, 350 tripods, 38,500 magazines and 17.5 million rounds of .303-inch ammunition from Canadian production. The first 500 were shipped to New York and left that port in mid-September based on oral assurances from Currie that they would be paid for when negotiations with the Canadian authorities were completed.

No further orders were placed by the Lend-Lease Administration until mid-1942 but after that they flowed at a fairly steady rate, although the goal of 1,500 per month was not initially met. By the time the Canadians took over their aid to China in September 1943 a total of 18,135 of these weapons had been purchased and by November 1944 all had been produced and 14,563 exported.

Inevitably, the Brens piled up in depots in India. The CAI was

A Maxim-Tokarev in operation, probably on training maneuvers, in June 1939. (*CNA*)

completely equipped, using .303-inch Brens as the standard light machine gun, but this absorbed only about 350 per division. Y-Force allocated the Brens at only one company per regiment, so their requirements were fairly modest. An initial batch of 562 was flown into Yunnan in the spring of 1943 and these were issued during August–November, along with anti-aircraft mounts, an accessory not issued to the troops based out of India. Deliveries over the Hump were slow thereafter, so that by the start of 1945 only 1,117 had been issued to units in China, although 3,100 were sitting in depots in China. Once the Burma Road opened deliveries speeded up somewhat.

Lend-Lease Orders Placed for Brens for China	
Date	Quantity
1941	1,750
6 Jun 1942	1,500
28 Jul 1942	500
28 Aug 1942	1,237
28 Oct 1942	1,500
27 Nov 1942	1,500
26 Dec 1942	1,500
22 Jan 1943	1,650
25 Feb 1943	1,650
19 Mar 1943	1,350
22 Apr 1943	2,500
22 May 1943	1,498

The number of these weapons actually issued had climbed from 1,117 at the end of January 1945 to 2,324 at the end of February and then 6,993 at the end of May. By mid-1945 plans called for the equipping of 16 divisions and 6 corps troop sets of the Chinese Army in China with .303-inch Brens, along with 5 divisions and 1 corps troops set of the CAI, a total requirement of 7,846. At that point available stocks of the .303-inch Bren were 12,934.

A .303-inch Bren gun with the 22nd Division in the Mogaung Valley of Burma in May 1944.

Although useful as an interim measure, the supply of Bren guns in .303-inch caliber complicated logistics no end and, once Canadian production settled in, a Lend-Lease order was placed in early September 1943 for Mk II Brens in 7.92mm caliber, these to be produced starting in October. A few days after the order was placed, however, it was canceled as part of the Canadian assumption of military aid.

Canada duly assumed and reinstated the order and two shipments were made, a first one of 5,400 weapons and a second one of 13,500 more. They sat in India until the opening of the Burma Road, at which

Bren guns were issued with high-angle mounts. These were more common with Y-Force than the CAI, but the troops seen practicing here are in India in 1942.

point movement to China began. Of the 18,900 7.92mm Brens, 6,000 were allocated to the Chongqing Reserve and the balance was to be distributed to US-sponsored units of the Chinese Army in China. By mid-July 1945 a total of 13,806 had managed to make the trip to China, the balance still sitting in depots at Chabua in Assam.

Light Machine Gun Specifications					
	Ammunition	Weight	Length	Muzzle velocity	Cyclic rate of fire
Japanese Type 11	6.5 x 51mm	10.2kg	110.5cm	701m/s	500rds/min
Lewis	7.7 x 56R	11.4kg	128.6cm	747m/s	550rds/min
Bren	7.7 x 56R	10.1kg	115.1cm	732m/s	500rds/min
Degtyaryev DP	7.62 x 54R	9.3kg	129.0cm	841m/s	550rds/min
Maxim-Tokarev	7.62 x 54R	12.9kg	133.0cm	804m/s	550rds/min
Madsen M-1937	7.92 x 57mm	9.1kg	114.3cm	750m/s	450rds/min
SIG KE-7	7.92 x 57mm	7.3kg	119.1cm	800m/s	550rds/min
Hotchkiss Light	7.92 x 57mm	15.3kg	133.0cm	n/a	650rds/min
FN Model 1930	7.92 x 57mm	9.3kg	115.1cm	792m/s	500rds/min
Lahti-Saloranta m/26	7.92 x 57mm	9.3kg	118.0cm	n/a	500rds/min
ZB-26	7.92 x 57mm	9.7kg	116.3cm	792m/s	500rds/min

Japanese Taisho Type 11/Shenyang Type 17

This Japanese product used the Hotchkiss operating principle combined with a unique feed system designed by Colonel Nambu. The concept of the feed was ingenious, using a hopper that held six 5-round rifle clips. As the bolt opened, it pulled a round from the first clip, then drove it into the chamber on the return stroke. As the round was withdrawn from the clip, a spring-loaded arm in the hopper moved the next one into place. Once a clip was exhausted it was ejected and the next one slid into place. The hopper could be "topped off" by new clips any time there were fewer than six clips in place. Unfortunately, the conversion of the mechanism from the original French 8mm Lebel to Japanese 6.5mm was not successful. The 6.5mm cartridge case had much less taper than the 8mm Lebel and that, combined with the highly energetic propellant, resulted in some problems with ejection. The Shenyang Arsenal built this weapon as the Type 17.

A Shenyang Type 17, a copy of the Japanese Type 11 light machine gun.

Lewis

The famous and popular Lewis gun utilized a unique operating mechanism in which the underside of the gas piston included teeth that meshed with a gear wheel that wound a clock spring as the piston went to the rear. Once it reached full rear the spring pulled it forward again against the trigger sear. Once the trigger was pulled the piston was released to move forward and start the operation of the gun. The cooling mechanism consisted of a series of longitudinal aluminum fins that projected out from the barrel and were enclosed by a light metal casing open at both ends, giving it the appearance of a water-cooled weapon. The theory was that air would be drawn in the rear end of the casing and be pulled out the front by the action of the gases leaving the muzzle. British tests in the thirties found the casing made little difference, but in any event the guns did not overheat. Feed was from a 47-round pan magazine. The gun was moderately reliable, if somewhat susceptible to dirt fouling, but the 7.7mm British cartridge was non-standard in China and they do not appear to have been widely used in combat.

Lewis gun.

Degtarev DP

The standard Soviet light machine gun of the interwar years, the DP fired from an open-bolt position. The square bolt had a flap on each side, hinged at the front, that was forced outward by the forward movement of the firing pin, thus locking the bolt in place. After firing, cam surfaces in the piston forced the flaps back into the retracted position. The 49 rounds in the circular drum were horizontally set, pointed towards the center. The weapon was reliable and simple but, unfortunately, fired non-standard ammunition.

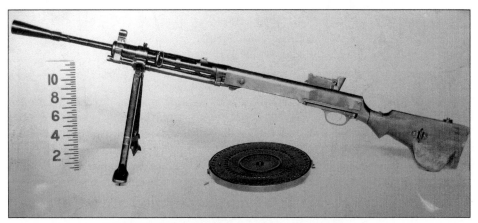

Degtyarev LMG with its 49-round magazine.

Madsen M-1937

The Madsen family of automatic weapons utilized a unique operating principle based on the dropping-block breech mechanism. This was accomplished by machining a pattern of curved grooves into the inner sides of the receiver such that the front of the breech pivoted upwards to permit extraction of the empty case to the bottom, and then downwards below the line of the chamber to allow feeding from the top. This yielded a complicated mechanism, but it proved fairly reliable in service. The distinctive features of the weapon were the curved 30-round magazine slightly offset to the left at the top (to give clear line of sight) and the rotating cocking handle on the right.

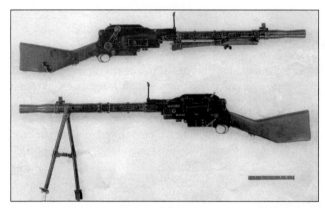

A Chinese M-1937 Madsen.

SIG KE-7

This weapon was recoil-operated, rare for a light machine gun, and fired from an open bolt. Ammunition was supplied via a 20-round box magazine that fitted below the receiver directly forward of the trigger guard. It had relatively few moving parts, which tended to keep costs down. It was also lightly built; in fact, it was one of the lightest light machine guns to enter service anywhere. While that made it handy, it probably also made it difficult to control in automatic fire and the light barrel was unlikely to take kindly to prolonged bursts.

A Swiss-made KE-7, minus magazine, captured in Korea in 1951.

Hotchkiss Light Machine Gun

This was a gas-operated weapon, selectable for fully automatic, semi-automatic or "safe." A gas regulator on some weapons permitted a choice of high (650) or low (350) cyclic rates of fire. The weapon was supplied from a 20-round metal strip, which was fed from the right by a pawl system, similar in principle to the Browning mechanism. The mainspring was housed in the stock, this collecting the energy from the recoiling bolt and then using it to return the weapon to battery. It had a smooth, reliable function except that the gas regulator had to be adjusted when the gun got hot.

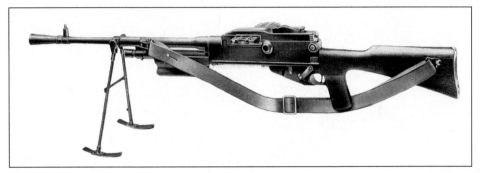

Hotchkiss LMG.

FN Model 1930

This was the Browning BAR license-produced by FN of Belgium with some minor modifications. The BAR was a gas-operated design introducing a bolt that tipped up at the rear, a concept later employed by several other popular automatic weapons. The most prominent changes to the original were the finned barrel to improve cooling and the addition of a pistol grip. FN also moved the bipod slightly to the rear and added their own gas regulator to the front end of the gas cylinder. The weapons were sturdy and reliable, but a bit complex to maintain. Their usefulness as machine guns

FN/Browning BAR.

was limited by the 20-round magazine. The early models sold to China had a fixed barrel, while the wartime batches had the removable barrel.

Lahti-Saloranta m/26

This barrel-recoil-operated weapon fired from a 20-round box magazine below the weapon (a 100-round drum magazine was apparently not purchased by China). It had a perforated barrel jacket and a light bipod at the front. The weapon could fire semi- and full-automatic and featured a barrel that could be replaced in 25–30 seconds. In Finnish service the Lahti-Saloranta's close tolerances led to a reputation for unreliability unless it was kept very clean.

A Lahti-Saloranta m/26. (*Sami H. E. Korhonen*)

ZB26

The standard light machine gun of the Chinese armed forces, the ZB26 was reliable and easy to maintain. It featured a gas-powered slide that tilted the rear of the bolt down from a recess in the top of the receiver to allow extraction and reloading as it moved rearward, then a spring moved the bolt forward again and up into the locked position for firing. The weapon fired from the open breech position. Feed was via a 20-round box magazine mounted over the receiver. Notable features of the time were the quick-change barrel and very good magazine speed loader.

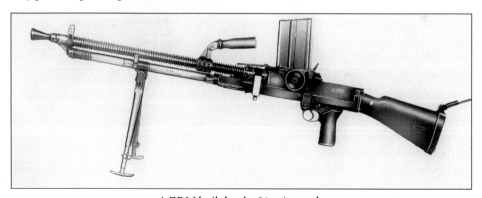

A ZB26 built by the 21st Arsenal.

Bren Gun

The Bren was a British modification of the original ZB26. Visually distinctive features of the Bren, compared to the ZB26, were the lack of fins on the barrel and the shorter gas cylinder. The 30-round overhead magazine was curved to accommodate the .303-inch rimmed British ammunition, but straight in the 7.92mm version. The Mk I had telescoping bipod legs and a rear pistol grip under the buttstock that were eliminated in the Mk II. The Mk II also replaced the dial type rear sight with a ladder type. China received mostly Mk II models, in both .303 (7.7 x 56R) and 7.92 Mauser calibers.

A Canadian-built Bren Mk II for China.

Maxim-Tokarev

This was a modification of the Russian version of the famous Maxim machine gun adapted as a light machine gun by removing the water cooling jacket and fitting a buttstock and rifle-type trigger. Soviet acceptance trials found it to be simple to operate and maintain, but a bit heavy and awkward to handle, and prone to jam. Remedies were unsuccessful and it was replaced in production in 1927 by the DP machine gun. By the mid-1930s these Maxim-Tokarevs were surplus to Soviet needs and were disposed of by sale overseas, including to China and Spain. From the Chinese perspective these weapons had the great advantage of commonality of operation with their standard medium machine gun, the Type 24, but used non-standard ammunition.

A Maxim-Tokarev Light MG. (*Maxim Popenker via Tony Williams*)

19

Medium Machine Guns

Machine guns were highly regarded during the warlord period, but lacking a central authority to enforce standardization a re-unified China found itself owning a disparate collection of such weapons.

By the 1880s the Jinling Arsenal had become famous for its 10-barrel Gatling and 4-barrel Nordenfeldt guns. As early as 1889 it produced its first copy of the Maxim machine gun. This latter weapon, however, proved a bit more complex than the arsenal was ready for, and they built only a few hand-made guns before production ceased.

There appears to have been little further effort under imperial rule, but with the slow disintegration of Republican China the warlords quickly realized that the machine gun would be the ideal weapon for use against potential competitors for power. There thus began a scramble to find suitable weapons and build them in their own arsenals. As centrifugal forces pulled the country apart a wide variety of weapons appeared, both imported and locally produced.

The early favorite of the warlords was the Maxim. The Sichuan Arsenal began Maxim production in 1912 but made only 20 due to difficulties encountered with parts, ammunition, and belts. The Dagu Navy Dockyard produced a DWM copy in 1916 and Jinling resumed production in 1923 based on the DWM 1909 model. The Gongxian, Fujian, Hunan, and Shangdong Arsenals joined the trend in the 1920s, all producing Maxims generally based on German models.

With the unification of the country following the Northern Expedition, the wide variety of Maxim guns, manufactured to different standards by the different arsenals, made logistical support difficult. In response, the Nationalist Ordnance Administration began a study on the advantages of standardization. The 1934 report by Yu Da Wei recommended adoption of the Browning M1917, but requests to the US and Belgium for drawings of this weapon met with silence. By this time, however, the Jinling Arsenal had acquired the design plans

A Chinese-made DWM Commercial Model 1909 Maxim on a rather questionable AA mount with the Northeastern Army in 1932.

of the MG08/15 from Germany and produced a set of standard drawings based on the already produced DWM 1909. The Nationalist Ordnance Administration reviewed the drawings and the product and decided that it was the best of the Maxim designs and officially standardized on it as the Type 24 Machine Gun in 1935.

Over the next few years Jinling continued to modify the design. In 1936 it changed the trigger to the pull-type to allow

Training on a Type 24 in April 1944.

A Shanghai Arsenal-made Type Three-Tens in action outside Shanghai in 1932.

A machine-gun unit of the 29th Route Army in Beijing in
July 1937 with their Type 38 machine guns.

Training on the M1917A1 machine gun at the
Infantry Training Center in July 1945.

single-hand operation. In 1941, as the 21st Arsenal, it launched another program to standardize the tolerances and dimensions of the components. On completion of that effort the internal parts were no longer serialized and were interchangeable among weapons. In the meantime, the displacement of the arsenals had essentially terminated production of Maxims other than the Type 24.

A notable exception to the dominance of German designs in the production of Maxims was found in the Gongxian Arsenal, which chose the Russian pattern M1910 in 7.62 x 54R cartridge, complete with wheeled mount. It appears to have begun building them in 1928, but by 1931 production was still only running at about 12 per month, and it ceased shortly thereafter.

It would have been naïve to believe that other machine-gun salesmen would not have noticed the power vacuum that followed the break up of Imperial China. In 1917 an American salesman approached the warlord Wu Peifu to sell him M1917 Browning (or the nearly identical Colt Model 1919) machine guns. The American soon found himself in prison for three months while Wu's Hanyang Arsenal reverse-engineered the weapon, after which he was released and the original gun returned to him. The Chinese copy was never quite right, but the arsenal went ahead and launched production on National Day, 10 October 1921. Since this was the tenth year of the republican calendar it was designated the Model Three-Tens (10th day of the 10th month of the 10th year).

Production began at 12 per month, with the rate doubling within a few years. Subsequently, the Shanghai and Hanyang arsenals began production of this weapon as well. In fact, by 1928 the Shanghai Arsenal was building 31 per month, although production there ceased in 1932. Production at Hanyang continued, even after it was relocated in 1938 and became the 1st Arsenal, although in steadily decreasing numbers as the war continued. Little effort appears to have been made to work out the bugs inherent in reverse-engineering, at least initially, for a report from 1928 stated that even in the best lot of Model Three-Tens tested from several arsenals only about a third could fire more than 200 rounds without some stoppage.

While the Type 24 and the Three-Tens were the dominant models of Chinese-made machine guns used during the war, other legacy weapons from the warlord period also saw service in smaller numbers.

A Hotchkiss used for high-angle firing in Shanghai, 1937.

Machine-gun practice by the 2nd Division at Lao Kai, Yunnan, in July 1944.
Note the Madsen on tripod in the foreground, with two Type 24s behind it.

While the Sichuan Arsenal had given up on the Maxim in 1913, it had not abandoned the machine gun as a useful product. In 1918 it began building the Schwarzlose machine gun, initially in 8mm caliber, switched to the standard 7.9mm the next year. Production, however, only ran at one or two per month and the total number produced was relatively small. The Guangdong Arsenal also produced small numbers of this weapon, probably in the early 1920s.

While most of the weapons built were water-cooled, Hotchkiss air-cooled designs also appeared, initially via the Japanese. They supplied machine guns to their favored warlords and local production of these was also undertaken. The first was their Meiji Type 38, a development of the original Hotchkiss Model 1900, and the Shanxi Arsenal placed it in production, joined later by the Guangdong Arsenal, both probably building it only in small numbers. The largest producer was the Shenyang Arsenal, which built about a thousand before it switching to a later model.

The replacement for the Type 38 in Japan was the Taisho Type 3, a similar Hotchkiss-type weapon improved by the redoubtable Colonel Nambu. The Shenyang Arsenal changed from the Meiji Type 38 to the Taisho Type 3, chambered for 7.9mm cartridges, in 1924, designating it the Type 13. Production did not actually start until around 1928, annual output was only 50 in 1929, and it ceased in 1931 when it fell to the Japanese, with total production only around a hundred or so. A more important source of Type 3 guns was battlefield capture, but these were chambered for the original Japanese 6.5mm round, making ammunition supply a bit less reliable.

Troops of the CAI firing an M1917A1 outside Bhamo, Burma, in December 1944.

A wide variety of machine guns were covertly exported by arms dealers to the various warlords in the 1920s, in contravention of the arms embargo, these including British Vickers guns in .303, the M1907 St Etienne in 8mm, and the Colt "potato digger" in Russian 7.62mm caliber. All of these, however, were acquired in small numbers only and few were left in service by 1937.

Given the desire to standardize on one type of medium gun, and even though that was already undercut by continued, albeit low-level, production of the Three-Tens, it is understandable that few foreign models were purchased during the 1930s. In fact, the only weapon purchased in other than trials quantities in the five years before the outbreak of the war was the Hotchkiss Mle. 14. In August 1930 Hotchkiss requested permission from the French Foreign Ministry to export 100 machine guns and mounts to the Northeast Army in Manchuria. This is the first noted sale of the Hotchkiss to China, although it is doubtful it went through before Japan seized the province. The first sale to the central government came in February 1932, and covered 100 machine guns in 7.9mm with mounts and accessories. Further orders were placed, comprising 200 in late 1932, 20 in March 1933, 200 in May 1933, 10 in September 1934, 10 more in December, and 20 in December 1936, with all being delivered within a few months of the order.

Of far more significance to Hotchkiss before the war were the purchases by the quasi-independent provinces. Yunnan purchased 30 in July 1935 and 102 more in January 1937, while Guangxi bought 120 in May 1935, and Guangdong was the largest purchaser with 110 in July–August 1935, 130 more in March–April 1936, and 200 more in May 1936, all of them in the standard 7.9mm caliber.

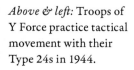

Above & left: Troops of Y Force practice tactical movement with their Type 24s in 1944.

The Communist forces were equipped in large part with captured Japanese weapons. Here a machine-gun unit of the 259th Brigade of the 8th Route Army shows off its 6.5mm Type 3 machine guns.

Once the Japanese onslaught began it was clear that, with the need to move the arsenals, it would take a while for indigenous production to catch up to requirements, and the central government went back to Hotchkiss, ordering 1,000 guns with 20 million rounds of 7.9mm ammunition in September 1937, and another 300 guns in December. A further quantity was ordered in mid- or late 1938 but the German invasion of France in May 1940 stopped deliveries after about 300 guns.

Another "emergency" weapon was the ZB37 from the Brno works in Czechoslovakia. Nanjing ordered 1,000 shortly after the Japanese invasion, but only 850 left the factory before the Germans clamped down, and those arrived in four batches in June and August 1938 via Hong Kong and January and June 1939 via Rangoon.

In July 1938 Vickers Armstrong was approached with a Chinese inquiry for 300 of their Class C water-cooled machine guns in 7.9mm caliber. The firm replied that they could deliver them within ten months of contract signing, but nothing ever came of this.

The final early war import was the M1910 Maxim from the Soviets. The second aid increment included 300 of these weapons. The sixth increment included a further 1,000 weapons. The former

Above: Two photos of a Hotchkiss-equipped machine-gun company in the early 1930s.

were delivered via Hong Kong and Haiphong in mid-1938, and the latter via Rangoon in October 1939. They stayed in service to the end of the war, their usefulness limited by the fact that they used non-standard ammunition not produced in China.

As noted in the chapter on light machine guns, it had been planned to standardize on the Madsen machine gun not only as the light machine gun, but also, by using a tripod, as the medium machine gun. Indeed, an unknown percentage of the Madsen machine guns supplied by Denmark were accompanied by tripods.

During the war the average monthly loss of medium machine guns was 119, while the actual production exceeded that, so provision of these weapons under Lend-Lease was not a high priority. The only units that immediately needed US medium MGs were those

Deliveries of Medium Machine Guns									
	1937	*1938*	*1939*	*1940*	*1941*	*1942*	*1943*	*1944*	*1945*
Imports									
ZB37	0	701	150	0	0	0	0	0	0
Hotchkiss	100[a]	203[b]	1,080	608	0	0	0	0	0
Maxim M1910	0	327	1,000	0	0	0	0	0	0
Browning M1917A1	0	0	0	0	0	0	144[c]	211[c]	2,160
Production									
Type 24	626	1,060	1,971	2,468	1,860	1,980	2,680	2,986	3,063
Three-Tens	n/a	n/a	n/a	514	520	310	260	n/a	n/a

a for Yunnan provincial government   b for Guangdong provincial government   c for Chinese Army in India

in the Chinese Army in India, and two division sets were provided in 1943, and another three division sets in 1944. These were the M1917A1, not much different from the Three-Ten models that many of the Chinese soldiers were already familiar with. The 30-Division Plan called for the distribution of 2,016 such weapons, raised to 2,448 in February 1945 to units in China.

As could be expected the need for these weapons was not pressing and it was not until February 1945 that the first batch of 144 (two division sets) were actually shipped over

A late-production Type Three-Tens, made by the 11th Arsenal in
December 1941, with Y-Force outside Tengchong in 1944.

Troops of the 50th Division practice firing the Type 24 from the
prone position at Mainkaung, Burma, in April 1944.

the Stilwell Road and issued to the regular Chinese Army. A further 716 were issued in
the next three months, and by the end of the war a total of 2,160 had been issued to units
in China, with another 821 in depots in China awaiting distribution and a further 1,228
in India pending delivery to China, even though the authorized quantity for the Lend-
Lease program remained at 2,448. Their delivery also complicated logistics, for they were

Medium Machine Gun Specifications

	Ammunition	Gun weight	Total weight	Muzzle velocity	Cyclic rate
Japanese Type 38	6.5 x 50SR	n/a	50kg	700m/s	450rds/min
Japanese Type 3	6.5 x 50SR	28kg	55kg	742m/s	450rds/min
Hotchkiss M 1914	7.92 x 57mm	n/a	55.7kg	737m/s	500rds/min
ZB-37	7.92 x 57mm	18.6kg	41.0kg	792m/s	700rds/min
Type 24	7.92 x 57mm	20.0kg	n/a	870m/s	600rds/min
Maxim M 1910	7.62 x 54R	23.8kg	59.8kg	804m/s	550rds/min
Type Three-Tens	7.92 x 57mm	15.5kg	39.1kg	824m/s	600rds/min
M1917A1	.30-06	14.8kg	38.9kg	853m/s	600rds/min

chambered for the standard US 30-06 round, thus necessitating additional deliveries of that ammunition, which was not produced in China.

The US also delivered 636 air-cooled M1919A4 machine guns to the CAI, but these were intended for armored vehicle use, not ground mount.

In addition, of course, the Chinese forces captured Japanese machine guns, the Type 3 in 6.5mm and the Type 92 in 7.7mm. Both were used, although ammunition supply may have presented problems at times.

Japanese Meiji Type 38 Machine Gun

This was the Hotchkiss machine gun of 1900 modified to suit Japanese manufacturing methods. The most notable differences from the standard Hotchkiss design were the seven cooling fins and the metal buttstock. It utilized the standard Hotchkiss gas-operated mechanism and fed from 30-round metal strips.

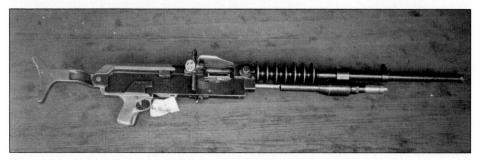

A Japanese Type 38 machine gun.

Japanese Taisho Type 3 Machine Gun

This was the replacement for the Type 38, using the same general operating principle but improved by the famous Colonel Nambu. It introduced the numerous small cooling fins characteristic of all successive Japanese machine guns. Another departure from Hotchkiss practice was the use of spade grips with two triggers, either of which could operate the weapon. It continued to use the somewhat underpowered 6.5mm Japanese cartridge, however.

A Japanese Type 3 machine gun, probably produced at the Shenyang Arsenal as a Type 13, of the Northeastern Army in 1931. Note the carrying handles inserted into sockets on the tripod, a characteristic of Japanese machine guns.

Hotchkiss Model 1914 machine gun

This was one of the most widely used machine guns of the interwar period, and gave good service to its owners, although it was a little heavy for an air-cooled weapon and the feed, via a 30-round strip, was often criticized. Since these weapons were purchased under Chinese contract in the 1930s, they were chambered for the standard 7.92mm Mauser cartridge.

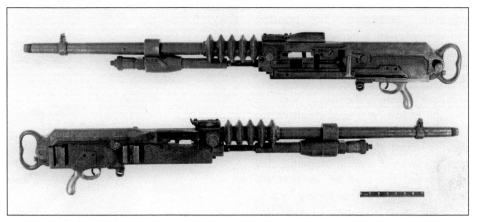

A rather worn Hotchkiss Model 1914 made for China and captured in Korea in 1951.

ZB37 machine gun

This was a gas-operated weapon that was unusual in having two rates of fire, 500 or 700 rounds per minute. Another distinctive feature, for a medium gun, was the quick-change barrel. It fired from 100- or 200-round metal link belts. It was reliable and accurate, and relatively light compared to other weapons in its category.

ZB37 machine gun on its tripod.

Fujian, Gongxian, Shangdong, Hunan, Dagu, Jinling Produced Maxim Medium Machine Gun & Type 24 Maxim Medium Machine Gun

The Maxim was the original modern machine gun. It did not have a traditional bolt; it used what is known as a lock instead to perform the firing, feeding, and ejection operations. The lock connected to a toggle-like mechanism. The principle was analogous to a human elbow, with strongest resistance when straight, the position while firing. It then bent when the barrel recoiled and allowed the lock to withdraw the empty shells.

The Maxim gun used recoil energy to operate the gun; the barrel and the slides recoiled together, rotating the handle clockwise before stopping. The lock opened the chamber to eject the empty shell and was then moved back by the main spring That spring was housed in a distinctive box on the left side of the receiver called the fusee box that clearly distinguished Maxim guns from other machine guns. A linear adjustment on the fusee box regulated the force exerted by the main spring. The different kinds of ammunition, environmental factors, wear, and assembly mandated changes to the spring force.

Side and rear views of the Type 24 (*above & top*).

Model 1910 Maxim

This was the Russian version of the Maxim, and was supplied complete with the Sokolov wheeled mount. The mount was heavy and clumsy, but this apparently did not bother the Soviets who valued its stability in firing. It featured a large turntable, two small wheels and a U-shaped trail. Although sturdy and reliable, the M1910's usefulness to the Chinese was limited due to the non-standard ammunition.

Model 1910 Maxim.

Type Three-Tens Machine Gun

This was the Browning M1917 machine gun built at various arsenals in China, the largest producer being Hanyang. It was recoil operated, with the barrel and barrel extension moving rearward, carrying the breechblock. An accelerator arm, activated by the barrel, pushed the breechblock even farther to the rear at high speed after the barrel had stopped moving, which moved the feed belt and cocked the firing pin. It fed from 250-round cloth belts from the left, unlike the Maxims, which fed from the right. The gun was robust, reliable and simple to manufacture.

Three-Tens machine gun.

M1917A1 Machine Gun

This was the M1917 to which a number of detail changes had been made, including a stronger belt feed mechanism to lift ammunition from boxes on the ground, an improved steam tube assembly, and a modified mount that permitted increased elevation up to 65°.

An M1917A1 medium machine gun.

Infantry Anti-Tank Weapons

The Chinese had not acquired manportable anti-tank weapons prior to the war, and the relative scarcity of Japanese tanks in the China theater meant that only modest priority was given to them once Lend-Lease began.

Two such weapons were available, the British Boys .55-cal. anti-tank rifle and the American M1A1 2.36-inch rocket launcher, the latter better known as the "bazooka." By 1942 the Boys AT rifle was nearing the end of its useful life in the European war, but the lighter Japanese tanks were often still vulnerable. The US contracted for 1,000 of these weapons from Canadian production in 1942 and they were delivered the same year and shipped to India. Further orders quickly followed so that a total of 6,129 had been programmed by the end of 1943; 500 shipped between July and the end of 1942 and another 3,600 the following year. This represented the full stated requirement for 60 divisions plus 865 spares and no further procurement was authorized. Nevertheless, another 900 were ordered directly from Canada in July 1943 and delivered in 1944.

The Chinese Army in India was quickly equipped with its scale of 36 per division and they took these into combat in Burma. Getting the weapons over the Hump and into the hands of the Y-Force units, however, proved somewhat more difficult. Nevertheless, a

Troops of the 2nd Division train on the Boys AT rifle at Lao Kai, Yunnan, in July 1944.

A Chinese bazooka team outside Tengchong in April 1944.

large initial shipment of 572 weapons was delivered to Kunming in July 1943, and 26 were immediately issued to the Infantry Training Center. The first major issue to field units came in August, with 342 weapons, followed by 82 in October, and 95 in November. Thereafter, issues of the Boys slowed with only 4 in December and 59 in all of 1944, but it still proved possible to provide eight weapons (a company's worth) to each of ten divisions of Z Force (41, 44, 59, 60, 90, 95, 151, 157, 175, and New 19) in May 1944, followed by 200 more to the 4th Army in IX War Zone in June. Shipments rebounded slightly with the opening of the Burma Road, the first half of 1945 seeing 185 more delivered.

An early adopter was the 31st Army Group, for which eight Boys teams were trained at Kunming in 1944 to form small anti-tank "companies" for the 78th and 85th Armies. Proof that these little weapons could still be effective against the elderly tanks Japan used in China came in early April 1945 when the 85th Army AT company chose a curve in a road in Zhong Yangdian in western Henan, and set out known-distance stakes to aid in range estimation. They ambushed an advancing Japanese tank force, knocking out at least two tanks and forcing the rest of the column to retreat.

In April 1945, however, Supreme HQ Chinese Armies requested that the Boys AT rifle be eliminated from the tables of equipment and replaced by bazookas. The reason they gave was that "the weight and recoil of the weapon is too great for the comparatively small and light Chinese soldier."* Further, its usefulness in attacking Japanese bunkers was limited in that its penetration into shingle-filled sandbags was rated at only 25cm under good circumstances. The end of the weapon was agreed to by the US China Theater and deliveries slowed to a trickle. Thus, of the over 6,000 produced for China less than a third actually made it into the hands of Chinese troops, while the bulk of them sat in India unused.

Perhaps indicative of the relative scarcity of Japanese tanks, only 47 rounds per Boys were issued during 1943, although a further 202 rounds per gun were kept in the Kunming depot.

Far more useful was the M1A1 rocket launcher, which proved valuable not only in destroying tanks, but also in the assault role to knock out bunkers. Unfortunately, these were new weapons and the US Army took priority on production to fill its own requirements. An initial allocation of 500 launchers had been given to China in 1942 from the November/December production, but none actually came off the production line that year. Another thousand were allocated in 1943 and the full 1,500 were produced, but only the 1942 allocation was shipped that year, followed by another 418 in 1944. The final allocation, 518 launchers, came in June 1944.

Naturally, deliveries began at a very slow pace. Even the Chinese Army in India received theirs late, with only 46 of the authorized 100 on hand in November 1943, although this may have been due to the lack of Japanese armor in their intended area of operations. For Y-Force, the first 40 launchers were delivered in July 1943, with six being immediately issued to the Infantry Training Center. Deliveries and issues proceeded at an agonizingly slow pace, with 14 weapons being handed out to field units in October, then 99 in November 1943. Even more troubling was the shortage of rockets, and by the end of 1943 only 1,070 had been issued for the 137 launchers on hand, with a further 600 rockets in depots in China. The situation with regard to both launchers and rockets improved considerably thereafter, with 1944 seeing the issue of 839 launchers to sponsored units in China, with another 78 in the first half of 1945. The first large units to see full-equipment issues were the 11th and 20th Army Groups, with six and five divisions respectively, each getting 27 launchers in April 1944.

The April 1945 decision to eliminate the Boys rifle increased the bazooka requirements from 27 per division to 36. Calculations made at that time showed that the initial 36-division increment now required 1,296 bazookas (at 36 per division), whereas actual holdings in China consisted of 1,124 launchers, of which 262 were in the hands of unsponsored units. At that date there were also 169 in depots in China and 194 in India. At the end of the war the Chinese Army stated it had 1,072 bazookas in its units.†

---

* Memo, Chinese Combat Command, 24 April 1945, "Substitute of Rocket Launchers for Boys AT Rifles," Decimal 471.94, CCC AG Decimal files.

† Another weapon used for assaulting fortifications was the flamethrower. There were no indigenous or foreign supplies of these weapons until late 1944. The US Lend-Lease program did not include any, but nonetheless an allotment of 120 M1A1 flamethrowers was agreed upon in April 1944 for the divisions and armies of Y-Force. It took a while for them to be delivered, however, and by May 1945 some 332 were in depots available for distribution.

Boys .55-inch Anti-Tank Rifle

This was an enlarged bolt-action rifle firing from a 5-round clip. It used a powerful 13.9 x 99mm cartridge with a steel-cored projectile reaching 990m/s and capable of penetrating 21mm of armor at 0° at 300 meters. That cartridge, however, also gave the gun a very nasty recoil and an unpleasant muzzle blast that, combined with the gun's 16.5-kg weight and awkward 1.6-m length, made it unpopular even with the larger British soldiers. The fact that it was essentially a single-purpose weapon reduced its attractiveness where the tank threat was minimal.

Boys anti-tank rifle.

2.36-inch M1A1 Anti-Tank Rocket Launcher

The famous "bazooka" was little more than a steel pipe open at both ends that directed a rocket carrying a shaped-charge warhead. With a weight of only 5.96kg it was significantly lighter than the Boys, although only slightly shorter. The rocket motor was initiated by means of a replaceable battery in the launcher giving a muzzle velocity of 83m/s. The 1.5-kg round was capable of penetrating 120mm of armor out to its maximum range of 700 meters, although the effective range was much less, about 150 meters. The fearsome backblast from firing restricted its tactical employment somewhat, but its light weight and great hitting power, against

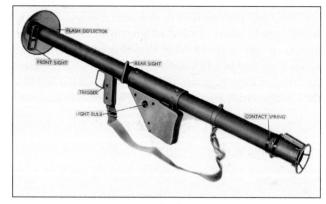

M1A1 rocket launcher.

bunkers and buildings as well as tanks, made it popular with every army that used it. The only targets it did not do well against were very thick concrete walls, and soft earth berms and walls, the latter often not activating the fuze.

21

Anti-Tank Guns

The few tanks held by the various feuding warlords in the 1920s could be dealt with by existing infantry weapons, in particular the popular 37mm infantry guns and later the 20mm Oerlikon weapons, so there was little early incentive for using scarce foreign exchange for the acquisition of anti-tank weapons. This would change.

The increasingly restive Japan never envisioned itself as a fielding a mechanized army, but it did starting designing and building its own new tanks, with some fanfare, in the early 1930s. Thus the German military advisory team quickly suggested the purchase of a small number of modern AT guns to the Chinese. Fortuitously, Rheinmetall had developed a new anti-tank gun as part of the covert rearmament of Germany. The initial effort had been a 37mm L/50 model, first shown in 1930. Subsequently a shorter, L/45, barrel was installed and this later version was adopted by the German Army as the Pak 36 and, surprisingly, by the Soviet Army, which purchased the license and made plans for local production.

In late 1934 a contract was placed for 20 of the 37mm L/50 models, probably trials and demonstration guns no longer needed by Rheinmetall. Unusually for China, these were to be motorized weapons. It was not immediately clear, however, what vehicles would be used

Troops of the 53rd Army practice with their Soviet-made 37mm AT guns, November 1944.

as prime movers. Against the advice of General Falkenhausen, the guns were accompanied by "Protzen" light trucks, which proved unjustifiably heavy and wide for Chinese conditions for such small weapons. Thus, a batch of 20 Kübelwagens was dispatched as replacements, again over Falkenhausen's objections. These too were found unsuitable as they had only rear-wheel drive and carried only four men. Nevertheless, at this point they had run out of options and the Kübelwagens remained in service, while the Protzen were handed over to the 105mm leFH unit being formed.

A contract for a further 124 37mm AT guns was signed in May 1936, but the L/50s were no longer produced so the weapons covered by this contract were standard German Pak 36 models, indistinguishable from the earlier guns except for the slightly shorter barrel. Twenty of these were to be the standard German Army model, while the other 104 included trail adaptors to permit animal draft. Bought at the same time were 20 Mercedes Typ 320WK medium cars to tow the motorized guns, along with 1,000 rounds per gun of ammunition. An initial batch of 40 (including the motor-drawn guns) was delivered almost immediately, but the final deliveries were not made until November 1937 (20 guns) and March 1938 (54 guns). It is possible that an additional 20 Typ 320WK were purchased for the original batch of guns bought in 1934. For the 1942 campaign in Burma, however, motor-drawn guns were towed by US-built 2½-ton trucks.

While Rheinmetall had been unable to build additional L/50 guns it did apparently have a stock of barrels. With this in mind China placed a supplementary order for components for 100 more L/50s, along with machinery to finish them and for ammunition production. The evacuation of the arsenals delayed the start of production and it was not until 1941 that the first weapon, now known as the Type 30 AT gun, came out of the 50th Arsenal, with the last of slightly less than 100 being delivered in 1945. These weapons were identical to the Rheinmetall original, except that they used Russian-style wooden-spoke wheels for horse-drawn traction.

The Soviets had acquired the plans for the 37mm L/45 from Germany and had begun production of a horse-drawn version as the 37mm obr. 30 anti-tank gun in 1930. They had only built a little over 500 of them by 1933, however, when production switched to the more powerful 45mm weapon. Using non-standard ammunition no longer in Soviet production, the 37mm weapons would be of limited utility in combat and all had been disposed of by 1941. The vast majority of them were sold to China.

The initial tranche of Soviet aid that arrived in Hong Kong in March 1938 included 80 of these obr. 30 anti-tank guns, along with 1,500 rounds for each gun. Another part of that package, arriving in Yunnan Province in February 1938, included 50 of the new 45mm obr. 37 AT guns with 7,000 rounds per gun, but these were the only examples of this model to be delivered and seemingly played little role in the war. The second tranche of Soviet equipment included a hundred more 37mm obr. 30 delivered to Yunnan in April 1939, followed by 200 more in November.

That second batch also included 200 elderly 37mm guns delivered in March. These were short-barrel L/21 weapons fitted on a small wheeled carriage with a shield but without any recoil mechanism. Unlike the 37mm infantry guns of the warlord era, these were used in the anti-tank role. The Russians held two models, the indigenous Rosenberg and captured German Grusons, and by 1936 they still had 153 of the latter and 170 of the former in stocks as surplus. The Chinese consistently referred to all these short-barrel weapons as "Gruson" guns, but they included Rosenbergs as well.

One of the diminutive Madsen 20mm AT guns being inspected by
troops of the 120th Division, 8th Route Army in 1938.

This second batch also included 66,800 rounds of 37mm AP and 222,919 rounds of 37mm HE, the latter mostly for the short-barrel weapons. Fortunately, the long-barrel versions, the obr. 30, fired the same ammunition as the German guns they were copied from, which was made locally after 1941, while the Rosenberg/Gruson models fired the ammunition of the 37mm infantry guns, also made in China. For that reason all the 37mm AT guns remained in service to the end of the war.

A happy result of this diverse mix was actually a remarkable degree of unintended standardization. The bulk of the anti-tank force was made up of four models of guns, all firing the same ammunition and visually identifiable only by the wheels used: the L/50 (Rheinmetall) and L/45 (Pak 36) with steel wheels and rubber tires, and the L/50 (Type 30) and L/45 (obr. 30) with wooden wheels.

By late 1937, however, it was becoming apparent that alternative sources would be needed. The Soviets had depleted their stocks of 37mm obr. 30 and world rearmament was picking up, with few countries having the capacity to supply exports as well as their own expanding forces. An exception was Denmark, whose Madsen firm was increasingly busy on the export market. It had developed a 20mm automatic cannon initially intended for the light AA role on its "universal" (later F7) mount. In the mid-1930s it also placed that weapon on a light wheeled mount for anti-tank use as the F5, also known as the "company mount" within Madsen. Two such weapons participated in the May 1937 Madsen demonstration in China and the exceptionally light weight of the piece and the limited armor protection of Japanese tanks made the F5 a suitable weapon. In addition to purchasing the two trials weapons the Nanjing government placed an order for a further 200 weapons, along with 3,000 rounds of AP per gun, in 1937. The first batch of 25 weapons (valued at DKK439,410)

37mm M3A1 guns of the 8th Division in August 1945.

left the factory on 22 December 1937, arrived in Hong Kong on 10 February 1938, and left there for Guangzhou on 17 February. Deliveries to Guangzhou via Hong Kong continued as five batches of 35 each, with the final batch leaving Hong Kong for Guangzhou on 5 August 1938, although only 40,000 rounds of ammunition was delivered by this route plus 71,000 more rounds from the UK, the latter not surprising since Madsen bought the bulk of its ammunition from ICI. In addition, the provincial government of Yunnan bought 15 F5 anti-tank guns and these were delivered via Rangoon between July and October 1939. Also delivered were 293,000 rounds moving between January 1939 and July 1940, destined for the central government and Yunnan.

The F5 gun remained in service to the end of the war. Thus, in April 1945 the 5th Division of the 94th Army included an anti-tank company with four Madson F5s, along with 30 magazines and 1,103 rounds of ammunition. Apparently the 20mm F5 was popular, for the 21st Arsenal reverse-engineered it and in March 1944 production was ordered. The first gun was completed in November but only five were built before production was halted.

The final anti-tank gun to be acquired was the US 37mm M3A1. The 1941 US Lend-Lease package did not include any anti-tank guns but 60, with a thousand rounds per gun, were quickly allocated shortly before the US entry into the war and these arrived in India in April 1942. It was clear that additional weapons would be forthcoming and the ammunition allocation was increased to no less than 135,000 rounds of M63 HE and 405,000 rounds of M51 AP shortly after Pearl Harbor.[*] There they were issued to the Chinese Army in India.

During 1942 a further 560 M3A1 guns were authorized and produced for Chinese Lend-Lease, along with 396 in 1943 and 653 in 1944. Shipments to India were 590 in 1943

---

[*] These numbers and ratios changed over time so that by October 1943 the quantity assigned and produced was 400,000 M63 HE; 582,000 M51 and M74 AP; and 160,000 M2 canister.

and 356 in 1944 (including 114 in December). As with other heavy weapons, getting the material to India was the easy part, and it was not until the Ledo/Burma Road had been opened that significant deliveries into China became possible. In fact, aside from an initial batch of 8 guns and 6,120 rounds of AP for the Infantry Training Center in the spring of 1943, there were no deliveries until early 1944. At that time the 2nd, 53rd, 54th, and 71st Armies were provided with 12 guns each.

As a result of difficulties in getting the weapons into China, by March 1945, of 864 guns authorized for the sponsored troops, only 220 were with sponsored units in China (along with 53 more in depots and 64 with unsponsored troops in China), while 664 were sitting in India. Also in China at that time were 169,000 rounds of ammunition. By the end of the war the situation had improved somewhat, with 542 guns having been issued to sponsored units and only 282 remaining in India.

The 37mm M3A1 proved effective in the China theater, but suffered one drawback. Having been designed for motor traction it proved awkward in mule draft. In early 1945 two proposals were put forward by the Chinese—one called for the fabrication in India of 600 locally designed limbers, and the second for the development and delivery of pack equipment suitable to adapt the M3A1 to pack transport on mules. Both were rejected by the US in July on the basis that there was already a shortage of mules for the mortars and pack howitzers provided. Instead, the weapons were to be transported on the backs of trucks for long moves and by manpower (pulling and carrying in pieces) for short moves.

Even before US entry into the war the Chinese had been eyeing the British 2pdr as a supplement to their anti-tank holdings. The day after Pearl Harbor Lauchlin Currie wrote to the general manager of War Supplies Ltd, noting that he understood that 25 2pdr guns were available for purchase in Canada and asking if they could be put aside on China's behalf pending a formal purchase order. Nothing appears to have come of this, but it was a harbinger of future interest.

The "wish-list" list provided by T. V. Soong to the British War Office in March 1942 included an unspecified quantity of 2pdr anti-tank guns to be diverted from US Lend-

Deliveries of Anti-Tank Guns									
	prior	1938	1939	1940	1941	1942	1943	1944	1945
Production									
37mm Type 30	0	0	0	0	0	24	28	33	9
Imports									
20mm Madsen	2	200	15	0	0	0	0	0	0
37mm Gruson/Rosenberg	0	200	0	0	0	0	0	0	0
37mm Rheinmetall L/50	20	0	0	0	0	0	0	0	0
37mm Pak 36	70	54	0	0	0	0	0	0	0
37mm obr. 30	0	80	300	0	0	0	0	0	0
37mm M3A1[a]	0	0	0	0	0	0	8	160	374
45mm obr. 37	0	50	0	0	0	0	0	0	0

a figures represent weapons issued to Chinese Army units in China

Anti-Tank Gun Specifications

	Barrel length (calibers)	Ammunition	Projectile weight	Muzzle velocity	Traverse	Elevation	Weight
Madsen F5	60	20 x 120mm	301g	730m/s	18°		173kg
37mm Rosenberg	23	37 x 94mm	680g	435m/s	0°	-5° to +15°	180kg
Rheinmetall L/50	50	37 x 250mm	n/a	n/a	60°	-8° to +25°	n/a
37mm Type 30	50	37 x 250mm	645g	825m/s	60°	-8° to +25°	343kg
37mm Pak 36	45	37 x 250mm	680g	762m/s	60°	-5° to +25°	330kg
37mm obr. 30	45	37 x 250mm	660g	820m/s	60°	-8° to +25°	313kg
37mm M3A1	53	37 x 223mm	730g	792m/s	60°	-10° to +15°	414kg
45mm obr. 32	46	45 x 130mm	1,430g	760m/s	60°	-8° to +25°	510kg

Lease allocations to China. The US was short of its own light AT gun at the time, and was funding Canadian production of the 2pdr for the British and, with British concurrence, an initial allocation covering 160 guns and 140,537 rounds of AP ammunition was agreed in early 1942. The first 124 weapons were taken from Canadian stock on hand, and replaced by new production, starting with 50 guns from the July 1942 output, followed by 16 more in August and 60 in September. The balance of the 160, however, was canceled. The first 28 guns left Canada in May 1942, followed by 48 each in June and July, together with 66,800 rounds of AP ammunition. They arrived in India starting in June but moved no farther. Little more was heard of the 2pdrs until March 1945 when General Chen, Minister of War, requested the US ship six regiments worth of 2pdr guns and two regiments worth of 6pdr AT guns to China immediately, with a further 22 regiment sets of 6pdrs to follow later, citing that all these guns were sitting in India unused. The guns were to be accompanied by 200 rounds per 6pdr and 500 rounds per 2pdr. The US China Theater, after some internal debate about the need for such equipment in the northeast of China, finally refused to readjust the transport schedule and they remained in India until the war ended. Indeed, in May 1945 the US India–Burma Theater, responsible for forwarding material to China, had declared as "excess to requirements" 332 2pdr guns and 368,000 rounds of ammunition, even though 275 of the guns and all the ammunition were actually Chinese property.

The request for 6pdr guns should not have been a surprise as Canada had agreed to supply 360 of those weapons, along with 240,000 rounds of AP ammunition, as part of its July 1943 mutual aid package. The first shipment, 108 guns and 253,000 rounds, left Canada in February 1944, followed by 180 guns and 20,000 rounds in June. The US had not approved transport of these weapons to China and would not relent, feeling that it added yet another ammunition type to the mix, the required motor transport was already in short supply, and the weapons were not justified in light of the limited Japanese armor threat. So in India they sat until the end of the war.

By 1943 the 37mm was obsolete as an anti-tank gun on all major battlefields of the war except the Chinese theater, where it continued to provide useful service. For the Japanese tank force China was a low priority and it continued to operate elderly vehicles there that were vulnerable to the high velocity 37mm Pak-family and M3 models and even, in some cases, to the Madsens and old Grusons. In addition, the light weight and small size of the 37mm weapons suited them well to the conditions in China. Furthermore, the Japanese tanks were not very numerous. By the end of the war the Japanese armored force in China consisted of the 3rd Armored Division (38 light and 126 medium tanks), the 3rd Tank Regiment (30 light and 60 medium tanks), and five tankette companies (total 60 tankettes). This was about half the strength they had mustered in mid-1944, but even then Japanese tanks had been a rare sight on the Chinese battlefield.

20mm Madsen F5 Anti-Tank Gun

To create this weapon Madsen took their 20mm automatic cannon, which they had been

selling as an anti-aircraft weapon, and placed it on a simple low-angle mount carried on bicycle-type wheels. Although it was obsolete as an anti-tank gun by European standards by 1941, against the Japanese armor faced in China it remained a fairly competent weapon to the end of the war. Its light weight and small size made it nearly ideal for Chinese conditions. It fired in the fully automatic mode from a 15-round magazine. Penetration at 0° was 42mm at 100 meters, 37mm at 300 meters and 32mm at 500 meters.

Two views of the 20mm F5 anti-tank gun being tested by Chinese troops at the 1937 trials. The bicycle-type wheels were replaced by small wooden wheels, albeit still with steel rims, on the production models.

37mm Gruson & Rosenberg Anti-Tank Guns

These two weapons, almost identical, were part of the rush to use the short 37mm cartridges popular in the 1890s. Grusonwerk in Germany and Rosenberg in Russia both developed small guns without recoil mechanisms for the infantry support role. In time, AP rounds were also developed for these weapons and the Chinese distributed these purchases from the Soviet Union exclusively to anti-tank units, for which role they were excruciatingly unsuited by low velocity, simple iron sights, and lack of traverse.

Russian soldiers with a 37mm Rosenberg.

37mm Rheinmetall Type

These were four nearly identical weapons, firing the same ammunition with similar ballistic results. They differed in the wheels and barrel lengths, and can be summarized as follows:

- Steel wheels & rubber tires with L/50 barrel: Rheinmetall commercial
- Steel wheels & rubber tires with L/45 barrel: German Pak 36
- Wood wheels & L/50 barrel: Chinese Type 30
- Wood wheels & L/45 barrel: Soviet obr. 32

A 37mm obr. 32 of the Chinese Army in 1938.

All used a semi-automatic horizontal sliding breechblock and hydrospring recoil system. The split-trail carriage was of tubular construction with coil springs for the wheels on the motorized versions. The most distinctive feature was the narrow, highly sloped shield that folded down at the top. All were powerful and effective weapons when introduced in the early 1930s. Although obsolete in Europe by 1942, they remained

A Type 30 AT gun leaving the 50th Arsenal.

effective against the second-line armor employed by Japan in China until the end of the war. Armor penetration at 500 meters range at 30° angle of impact was 36mm for the Pak 36 and 30mm for the obr. 30.

A Chinese 37mm Pak 36 with the shield folded down.

37mm M3A1 Anti-Tank Gun

This was a US development of the Rheinmetall carriage designs discussed above. Arc-shaped segments were fitted to the axle to swing down and raise the wheels off the ground for greater firing stability, and the traverse gear could be disengaged for free movement if needed. The vertically sliding breechblock was manually operated. The Chinese benefitted from the relatively late delivery of these weapons, as ammunition improvements during the war had raised the muzzle velocity from 790 to 878 meters per second, with

M3A1 37mm anti-tank gun.

concomitant increase in penetration. Penetration at 500 meters range at 0° angle was 36mm. In addition to AP, the US also provided HE and canister ammunition for these weapons.

45mm obr. 32 Anti-Tank Gun

This was a scaled-up version of the 37mm obr. 30, more powerful and with pneumatic tires for motor traction. The most powerful of the anti-tank guns available to China, the weapon could penetrate 38mm of armor at 1,000 meters range at 30°

A Chinese 45mm obr. 32 AT gun.

22

Infantry and Hybrid Guns

Infantry Guns

The unique conditions of warfare in 1916–18 gave rise to a new type of weapon, one that would fade from use quickly after the war but which briefly was almost universal in its adoption. This was the small-caliber infantry gun, which mated the widely used 37mm Hotchkiss pom-pom cartridge, or close variant, with a lightweight hand-loaded gun. The most popular of these was the French 37mm TR16. This short-barreled, low-velocity weapon was mounted on a tripod not much heavier than a machine gun-tripod and as a result it could be carried into action by infantry to engage machine gun-positions and hasty fortifications.

Troops in the standard Beiyang uniform, probably of the Northeastern Army, with a Shenyang 37mm Type 14 infantry gun in the 1920s.

By the late 1920s it had been recognized that newly improved medium (8cm) mortars with the same weight threw a much heavier shell, and could do so from a protected defilade position, but for a brief period the little TR16 reigned supreme for infantry support. Many nations built equivalent 37mm infantry guns, including Japan and Russia. The Japanese initially built a rather more substantial weapon called simply the Sogekiho (flat trajectory weapon) using a fairly powerful 37 x 133 round, but the resulting gun was rather heavy and bulky for infantry work. After only three years a replacement was standardized as the Taisho Type 11 Infantry Gun, this firing a less powerful 37 x 113 cartridge, but reaping the benefits of being lighter and more portable, and adding a semi-automatic breech function.

Perhaps the Japanese were unwilling to release the production rights for the Taisho Type 11, or maybe the Manchurian forces were simply impressed with the heavier round of the earlier weapon, but the Shenyang Arsenal acquired the production data for that weapon and began producing it in 1925 as the Type 14 Infantry Gun. They built 370 of these Sogekiho/Type 14 weapons and they were standard equipment in the Northeast Army. After the withdrawal to the south, following the Japanese occupation of Manchuria, they would have been cut off from all supplies of parts and, more importantly, the ammunition that was unique to that weapon. Their utility would thus have declined and presumably the Type 14s would have played little role after the initial phase of the 1937 invasion.

At about the same time the Hanyang Arsenal began working on its own light infantry gun. Their first effort was simply to take a 37mm barrel and place it in the carriage of their 75mm Type 10 mountain gun. The resultant weapon threw a 535g projectile containing 30g of picric acid at 420m/s to a range of 4,000 meters. Why in the world they did this is unknown, since it simply yielded an exceptionally heavy 37mm gun, and it is likely that few were built.

The second effort was a more conventional design fitted to a small wheeled mount. Once it was in its firing position the wheels and axle were removed and the weapon set up on its integral tripod. This reduced the weight of the gun from 193kg in traveling mode to 112kg in firing position. It used a screw-type breech system, highly unusual in such a small weapon. Little is known of the layout of this weapon except for notes made by a US military observer: "Appearance poor. Gun shield of very light material, easily penetrable. Wheels frail." Production probably began around 1929 and in May 1930 it was reported that 39 had been built and production was running about 8 per month. Deliveries probably slowed and then ceased around 1932–3.*

A larger weapon was developed by the Taiyuan Arsenal, which developed a very light 75mm gun, stripped of all but the most essential components in order to reduce weight to the absolute minimum. The plan was to create a weapon with a range of 5,000 meters that could be pulled by soldiers without the use of pack or draft horses. In fact, it was used as a mountain gun and is discussed in that section.

In addition, Japanese Taisho Type 11 infantry guns were captured and used by Chinese troops, presumably in small numbers.

In mid-1942 the Chinese Ordnance Office reported about 300 of these various 37mm weapons in service but neither the Japanese originals nor the Chinese copies appear to have been often used during the 1937–45 war.

---

* These short 37mm guns were designated as flat-trajectory guns (平射砲) to distinguish them from the curved-trajectory mortars. Here we will use the term infantry guns.

School troops demonstrate the 75mm leIG near Nanjing in October 1936.

The German influence was manifested in the purchase of 20 75mm leIG infantry guns in 1934. These few weapons, however, were lost early in the war, probably in the Shanghai fighting.

Japanese forces also captured at least one Soviet 76mm obr. 1927 regimental gun in China. It is not known how it got there, or how many others accompanied it, although any number would have been small.

Hybrid (Infantry/AT) Guns

In the late 1920s the development of infantry close-support artillery began to take two tracks. On the one hand there was a need for a counter to the increasingly common tank, and to this end developers worked on 25–40mm high-velocity guns that threw solid shot. On the other hand, there was also a requirement for high-explosive firepower and the period saw the development of small, ultra-light artillery of 60-80mm for this role.

Many armies, constrained by tight budgets, pronounced they could not afford both types of weapons and the armament firms responded with a variety of proposed hybrid weapons that could accomplish both tasks. The simplest approach was to design a weapon half-way in between the two categories. The main proponent of this concept was the Austrian firm of Böhler. In the early 1930s it built six trials guns of a medium-velocity 44mm L/39 design before switching to 47mm to create the widely sold 47mm M35 infantry/AT gun. The weapon was a commercial success and was most famous in its Italian license-built incarnation as the 47/32 gun. Tactically, however, the gun was simply not very good. In the nature of compromises, the velocity was too low for an effective anti-tank gun (at least after 1941), while its shell was too small to be very effective in the high-explosive role.

The Guangdong Opium Suppression Bureau purchased the six 44mm trials guns (two with and four without muzzle brakes) for HK$161,700 and 2,000 rounds of ammunition

Siderius infantry guns with the 5th Army in 1932, here with the 75mm barrels.

for HK$56,300, and these were delivered to Guangzhou in November 1935. These apparently proved fairly successful in the undemanding role of police artillery, and in 1937 an order was placed for 100 of the 47mm M35 version by the Army. No ammunition seems to have accompanied these weapons immediately, but shipments of 12,000 rounds in March 1938 and 18,000 rounds in September followed later. They were apparently organized into four-gun anti-tank "batteries," but the paucity of Japanese armor meant they were more commonly used in the infantry support role. Probably typical was a request from 3rd Army to IV War Zone in July 1945 for 600 rounds of HE ammunition and an equal quantity of AP ammunition for their Böhlers.

To avoid the inherent compromises of performance in having to chose a particular caliber, other manufacturers investigated the use of sets of barrels that could be swapped out in the field. In this case, the short, wide barrel of an infantry howitzer would be unscrewed from the breech ring assembly and a narrower anti-tank barrel screwed in. Since such weapons never attained widespread use it is impossible to tell whether the barrels and both sets of ammunition would be carried by the firing unit, or whether the "extra" barrel and its associated ammunition would be held in regimental or divisional trains. In any event it did reduce costs, but also added complexity, both in the gun itself and its accoutrements, and in a unique series of ammunition in which the two types of rounds of necessity shared a common cartridge case.

China purchased single examples of a number of these guns for trials, including the 25mm/70mm and 44mm/60mm from Vickers; the 37mm/62mm from Siderius, and the 37/70 from Skoda. Only two models were purchased for issue however, and those only in small numbers.

A Japanese Type 11 Infantry Gun.

A few (probably about a dozen) 47mm/75mm replaceable-barrel guns were purchased from the Dutch firm of Siderius around 1930 and these were used successfully in the 1932 Shanghai operation. They do not appear to have been significantly used post-1937, however, probably for lack of ammunition.

Another such weapon was produced in France by Schneider. These were known as the SEL (Schneider Extra-Leger) and featured 47mm and 75mm barrels. The initial order from China, the sole customer, was placed in 1932 and covered 24 carriages with 12 47mm and 12 75mm barrels (relegating each weapon to a single use). These were delivered in May 1933. In

A Chinese double-barrel Bofors 37mm/81mm piece.

July 1935 12 two-gun sections of 47/75 SEL (here each gun provided with one of each kind of barrel) were ordered and these were delivered half in June 1935 and the balance in March 1937. Another 14 sections (again, each gun with two different barrels) were ordered in April

Infantry Gun Specifications

	Bore	Barrel length (calibers)	Weight	Traverse	Elevation	Projectile weight	Muzzle velocity	Range
Japanese Type 11	37mm	28	91kg	30°	-5° to +14°	600g	450m/s	n/a
Hanyang	37mm	28	112kg	6°	6° to 16°	400g	434m/s	3,200m
Shenyang Type 14	37mm	28	110kg	20°	-3° to +15°	600g	450m/s	3,330m
Bohler	47mm	40	290kg	50°	-10° to +60°	1.5kg	650m/s	9,000m
leIG 18	75mm	12	400kg	12°	-10° to +75°	6kg	210m/s	3,375m
Siderius	47mm	30	367kg	50°	-10° to +43°	1.5kg	560m/s	6,000m
	75mm	13	345kg			4.5kg	233m/s	3,680m
Schneider SEL	47mm	n/a	n/a	8°	-10° to +60°	1.5kg	600m/s	n/a
	75mm	11	350kg			4.5kg	300m/s	6,000m
Bofors	37mm	45	450kg	50°	-8° to +80°	700g	800m/s	7,100m
	81mm	20				4.4kg	320m/s	6,000m

1936 and delivered in August 1937. The first order was accompanied by 4,000 rounds of 75mm HE and 2,000 rounds of 47mm HE; the second by 3,600 rounds each of 75mm HE and 47mm HE; and the third order by 14,000 rounds of 75mm HE, 9,800 rounds of 47mm HE, and (notably the first such order) 4,200 rounds of 47mm AP ammunition. Clearly, the anti-tank role was a secondary consideration for these weapons. No further ammunition for these guns was ordered, and subsequent ammunition shortages probably limited their usefulness after about 1938–9.

The final solution to the problem of providing two roles for one gun was championed by Bofors, and involved fitting two complete ordnance pieces in an over-under configuration on a single carriage. China acquired a single 47mm/75mm weapon from the firm, but settled on the lighter 37mm/81mm design. Twelve were purchased in 1933 and delivered in October 1934. Once again, limited quantities of the unique ammunition required seemly restricted their use once the war broke out and there is no record of their employment in combat.

37mm Infantry Guns

The Shenyang and Hanyang Arsenals both built 37mm infantry guns, but these do not appear to have served in large numbers or very long into the war. More common was the Japanese Type 11, captured during the war and some perhaps donated to select warlords in the 1920s. The breechblock was of the vertical sliding type and operated within a breech ring integral with the monobloc tube. The mount was a tripod of tubular metal, with a rather steeply sloped front leg and two long rear trails. In action it was usually carried by four men.

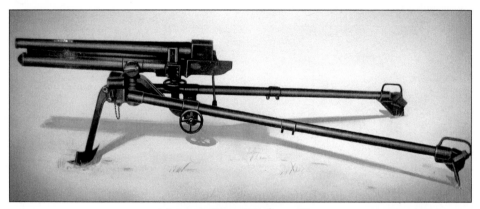

A Japanese Type 11 Infantry Gun.

75mm leIG 18

This was the standard German Army light infantry gun from 1927 to 1945. It had a box trail and used cross-axle traverse. It was effective as a direct-fire weapon and its high elevation enabled it to fire at targets in defilade, like a mortar. It fired semi-fixed ammunition with five charges, which gave good range coverage at various elevations. The most distinctive feature of the weapon was the break-open shotgun-type breech action, in which the rear end of the barrel was elevated to load the

A Chinese leIG 18 after capture by the Japanese.

ammunition, then dropped back down again to fit flush against the front face of the non-moving breech.

Böhler 47mm Infantry/AT Gun

The Böhler 47mm was an attempt to create a single gun that could undertake both infantry support missions with an HE round and anti-tank duties with an AP round. The projectile weight and muzzle velocity were the same for both rounds, resulting in only 44mm of armor penetration (at normal incidence) at 500m range—marginal by international standards but sufficient against the tanks the Japanese deployed to China. The weapon was fitted with a single axle with solid rubber tires on steel wheels, this assembly being removable for a lower profile in firing position. The weapon could be broken down into pack loads but was more commonly towed by a horse or the crew.

A Chinese Böhler in firing position, here a rare weapon of the first batch in 44mm caliber.

Siderius 47/75 Hybrid Gun

Developed in the mid-1920s this weapon featured a single breech mechanism into which could be screwed two barrels, one for a 47mm medium-velocity gun (for AP and HE ammo) and the other for a 75mm low-velocity infantry infantry gun (HE only). The gun could be broken down into ten loads for man transport or four loads for pack transport. It could also be towed behind a truck or, more commonly in China, by a horse team.

The Siderius 47/75, here with the 75mm barrel.

Schneider 47/75 SEL Hybrid Gun

As with the Siderius weapon, this featured a single breech mechanism and two inter-changeable barrels, one a 47mm for anti-tank use and the other a 75mm for infantry support. The gun could break down into four pack loads for mules or eleven loads for man-pack. It featured a box trail that could be folded for towing. The 47mm gun was capable of penetrating 30mm of armor at 1,000 meters range.

A 47/75 Schneider, here with the 75mm barrel.

Bofors 37mm/81mm Dual Mount Gun

This was a unique weapon with two complete guns on a coaxial mount: a 37mm high-velocity gun for anti-tank work on the top and an 81mm howitzer on the bottom for high-explosive fire power. The weapon could be broken down into six loads for pack horses or 12 loads that could, for short distances, be man-carried. The 37mm gun could penetrate 20mm of armor at 1,000 meters at 90° angle of impact.

The Chinese 37/81 guns in the Bofors factory awaiting shipment.

23

Light Mortars

The obvious utility of light mortars impressed various warlords who had lots of soldiers but little transport. Several types of light mortars were placed in production in local arsenals, but at this remove it is impossible to figure out who made what, in what quantities, or when. In any event, the numbers involved were small and they played little role in the Sino-Japanese War except in the very early phases.

The first appearance of what would become the standard Chinese light mortar came in late 1938 with a purchase of a hundred 60mm mortars and 40,000 rounds from Brandt by the Yunnan provincial government. These were to have been delivered in May 1939, but delays intervened and the mortars were actually supplied in two batches of 50 in October via Rangoon. Seemingly a separate contract for ammunition was agreed because a total of 138,000 rounds were delivered from Brandt in 1939. A second, similar, mortar order was planned but never placed. The weapons and ammunition were relatively light and manportable, and there was no Chinese analog. In fact, they were probably the ideal weapon for the transport-poor Chinese Army.

Chinese troops train on a 60mm mortar in April 1944.

Marshal Tang Enbo and Lieutenant General Shih Tsueh inspect
a US M2 mortar at Kweiyang, February 1945.

With France's entry into the European war supplies from that source ceased, but the US was making a copy of the 60mm Brandt for its own forces and a single example was purchased commercially and delivered in May 1940. Shortly thereafter, however, the US instituted controls on arms exports, and efforts to purchase this weapon also came to naught.

The weapons impressed the central government and it was decided to place them in production locally. On 18 May 1941 the 10th Arsenal was directed to produce the 60mm mortar. Apparently, this was not a straightforward task for them, for the first mortar was not turned out until 21 February 1943. The 50th Arsenal was also ordered to produce the mortar, in July 1941, and this seemingly went more smoothly, for their prototype mortar was delivered in September 1941, although full-scale production was still a long way off.

Both the 10th and 50th Arsenal mortars were given the same designation, 60mm Type 31 Mortar, although there were subtle differences between the two.* Production of ammunition was originally undertaken to support the Brandt mortars, but quickly expanded in light of Type 31 production and Lend-Lease imports. The Chengdu branch of the 50th Arsenal (originally the Sichuan Arsenal) was turned over almost exclusively to 60mm ammunition production. They ramped up quickly with 77,400 rounds produced in

---

* Production to a single set of specifications was finally achieved in 1947.

60mm Mortar Deliveries							
	1939	*1940*	*1941*	*1942*	*1943*	*1944*	*1945*
Imports							
Brandt	100	0	0	0	0	0	0
US M2[a]	0	1	0	0	798	1,000	150
Production							
Type 31 – 10th Arsenal	0	0	0	0	400	950	1,420
Type 31 – 50th Arsenal	0	0	0	200	800	900	1,500
HE rounds (thous)	0	0	8	92	203	*unknown*	860

a Not including deliveries to CAI

1942, although the haste showed when all of that year's production had to be discarded due to poor quality control. These problems were apparently overcome and the 1943 production of 172,000 rounds was accepted. Output peaked at 30,000 in a single month, although this was not maintained.

The Japanese attack on Pearl Harbor provided American impetus to review China's requests for mortars. On 27 February 1942 the War Department directed the diversion of 200 60mm M2 mortars and 200,000 rounds of HE ammunition from US production to the Chinese Lend-Lease account. This was only a start.

Within a few months the allocation had increased to 1,228 M2s and 350 had been shipped by mid-year. On their arrival in India, a portion was quickly used to equip the CAI, but the rest sat in depots awaiting transport to China. In the spring of 1943 it proved possible to move 270 to Kunming and Yunnan, along with 240,000 rounds of HE ammunition. A further 528 mortars and 35,550 rounds followed in August/September. Sixty weapons were quickly issued to the Infantry Training Center, but issues to field forces did not start until August when 131 were handed out, followed by 64 in September, 29 in October, and 523 in November.

Since the M2 was slightly lighter than the Type 31 and threw its shell to a longer range, distribution of the US-made weapon was often made to high priority units that already had Type 31s, with those weapons then being passed on to lower-priority units. For instance, in March 1944 the 53rd and 54th Armies in western Yunnan each had their full quota of 108 Type 31 mortars, but were placed on the list as the next to receive M2s by Wei Lihuang, commander of Chinese Expeditionary Forces.

Further deliveries brought the total up to 1,590 in field units and 295 awaiting distribution in depots in China at the end of January 1945. By the end of April US China Theater was noting that China had been authorized 5,832 M2 mortars but that only 2,209 were in China, with troops or in depots, and that only 36 remained in India with no immediate prospect for further deliveries. A week later, however, the picture brightened when they were informed that 200 mortars and 90,000 rounds would be made available due to the German surrender. These do not appear to have made it to China before the Japanese surrender, however.

In practice the 60mm mortars do not seem to have lived up to expectations. American observers and advisers with Yoke Force during the Salween campaign in the fall of 1944 were highly critical of Chinese mortar employment, and especially so with regard to 60mm weapons, held far to the rear under regimental command, contributing little. Even the well-trained CAI found less use for them than anticipated; the planning figures for combat in Burma were 7.5 rounds per day per 60mm mortar, and 8 rounds per day per 81mm mortar, but in the heavy fighting of November 1944 actual expenditure was only 3.9 for 60mm, compared to 9.6 for 81mm weapons.

An unusual weapon, outside the mainstream of light mortar procurement, was the little 37mm MAM (Matériel et Armement Moderne) developed by Ateliers et Chantiers de la Loire in France. Somehow the firm managed to convince the Chinese central government that this would be the ideal weapon for commando and guerilla units and in 1938 an order was placed for 200 mortars and 20,000 rounds, the latter apparently subcontracted to Brandt. They were shipped from France in September and October 1938 for Rangoon, and they left Burma for China in March 1939. Existing records only show the dispatch of 500 rounds of ammunition from France, however, and even this small number is not recorded as having transited Burma. The specialized ammunition required complex machining, which the Chinese arsenals were unable to provide, and it seems unlikely that any of these weapons ever saw combat. In February 1940 a request was made to France for an unspecified further quantity of these little weapons and ammunition, but nothing came of that.

Improvising aiming stakes for a 60mm mortar at Datun in May 1944.

Warlord Light Mortars

Little information is available on the light mortars manufactured for various warlords in the 1920s and 1930s.

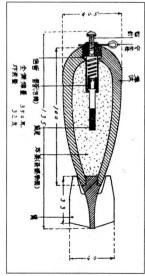

A 41mm mortar and its ammunition as illustrated by Japanese Army intelligence in 1938. No data were provided except that the mortar weighed 7.3kg and was said to have a range of 1,500–1,600 meters.

An unidentified 50mm mortar captured by Japanese forces early in the war.

This 45mm mortar was captured from Chinese forces by the US Army in 1951 in Korea. The barrel was 38 inches long and it weighed 5kg with the bipod. It carried the serial number 190.

A poor quality photo (*left*) of the short- and long-barrel versions of an unknown light mortar captured by Japanese forces early in the war. A Japanese display of captured equipment (*below*) in 1937 shows the same mortar, most in the short-barrel version. An example in the 202nd Arsenal Museum on Taiwan is mistakenly identified as a "55mm Type 37 grenade launcher," which may provide its caliber at least.

37mm MAM Guerilla Mortar

This little one-man mortar was developed in France in the late 1930s and featured a number of elements not seen before (or since, for that matter). First of all, the breech was set at a 90° angle to the barrel and had a separate opening mechanism. The propellant charge was separate from the projectile, contained in a rifle cartridge case, and was loaded into the breech. The projectile had a driving band, with three studs that matched three deep and wide rifling grooves in the barrel, and was muzzle loaded. Behind the barrel was a cylindrical "sprag" that enclosed a spring and hydraulic cylinder to reduce recoil and control return.

Apparently there were charges of three different strengths, the most powerful of which yielded a maximum range of 930 meters. The projectile weighed 500 grams, of which about 85 grams represented the explosive charge. The stated rate of fire was 10 rounds per minute. Since little ammunition was delivered, it seems unlikely these weapons saw much combat use.

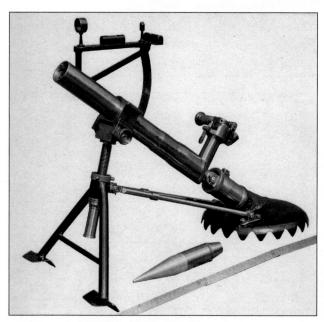

The unusual 37mm MAM mortar.

60mm Brandt Type Mortar

The Brandt original and the US copy, the M2, were almost identical, differing only to simplify production in the US. The Type 31 was also a copy of the Brandt mortar, but wartime China lacked the metallurgical facilities to reproduce it exactly, making it a little heavier and with a shorter range. It is unclear if US ammunition could be fired from the Type 31. The mortar was of conventional configuration with a tube (including base cap), a bipod mount, and a baseplate. The bipod included a cross-leveling device that attached to the left leg.

The Type 31 was produced at two arsenals, the 10th and the 50th. There were small dimensional differences that prevented the interchange of parts between the two versions. The data shown are for the version from the 10th Arsenal, which had a weight breakdown of 5kg each for the tube and baseplate, and 10kg for the bipod, plus 0.81kg for the sight.

The Chinese-made ammunition was exclusively of the HE type and used wrought iron bodies, which would have limited fragmentation effect. The propellant was in five charges which

60mm Mortar Specifications		
	M2	Type 31
Weight, complete	19kg	20kg
Elevation	40°–85°	45°–77°
Traverse each side	4°	3.5°
Projectile weight	1.38kg	1.36kg
Max. muzzle velocity	158m/s	133m/s
Max. range	1,815m	1,450m

A 60mm Type 31 mortar. This particular weapon was captured by US forces during the Korean War and may incorporate some post-1945 features.

provided muzzle velocities of 50, 75, 95, 114, and 133m/s. The fuze employed was of the point-detonating type, originally not very effective, but replaced by an improved version in December 1943.

24

Medium Mortars

Although developed for the trench warfare of the Western Front in Europe during World War I, the medium (70–90mm) mortar proved ideal in the almost opposite conditions of China in the 1920s to 1940s. Indeed, almost every facet of the mortar recommended itself to the Chinese authorities:

- It was light and small, easily carried by soldiers and thus largely independent of China's poor road system and limited stock of pack animals.
- It was simple to manufacture and maintain, having no moving parts except basic elevation and traverse screws, and required little in the way of raw materials.
- The low muzzle velocity resulted in low acceleration loads on the projectiles, which meant they demanded few specialty metals; in fact some projectile bodies were made of cast iron.
- Because of the low acceleration loads shell bodies could be made much thinner than artillery projectiles, and as a result an 81mm mortar round usually packed the explosive power of a 105mm howitzer round.
- Little training was needed for operation in the direct fire mode. Operation in defilade, using a simple alidade with the squad leader correcting the fire from near the weapon, demanded only a little more training, for the squad leader and gunner.

In fact, the one disadvantage of the mortar, its short range as compared to artillery, was largely negated by the paucity of signal equipment in the Chinese armies and the shortage of trained observers and fire-direction technicians such that long-range fire was impractical in any event.

The advantages were quickly recognized and in 1922 the Shenyang Arsenal began building an 80mm mortar designated the Type 11. This was apparently promising enough that in 1925 a special trench mortar arsenal was established at Shenyang to manufacture these weapons for the Northeast Army, yielding the 83mm Type 13 and the improved Type 15.

Other arsenals quickly joined in. In 1923 the Hanyang Arsenal began building 75mm mortars, configured like the Japanese 70mm Type 11, with a weight of 62kg and a range of 1,500 meters, and by 1928 had built no fewer than 1,055 of them. It simultaneously produced an 83mm mortar with a range of 1,600 meters starting in 1925 and produced 107 of them the following year. Neither of these appear to have survived in use past the early phases of the war.

In 1925 the Shandong Arsenal developed an 84mm mortar and began producing it at a rate of 12 per month. The Shanghai Arsenal began producing medium mortars in 1924 and in 1927 introduced a Stokes-type mortar with a nominal bore of 82mm (actually 79mm) and built 780 of them between 1927 and 1929. The Shanxi Arsenal began building 75mm

An early-type Chinese 82mm mortar being used by the
19th Route Army in the fighting near Shanghai, 1932.

mortars in 1927. In March 1928 the Chongqing Arsenal introduced an 82.5mm mortar and by July 1938 they had built 750. By 1930 the Taiyuan Arsenal was reportedly producing 300 82mm mortars per month, although production probably ceased around 1933. In addition, the Jiangnan Arsenal also began producing an 82mm mortar in September 1928 at about 8 per month.

A major revolution in mortar design came in the mid-1920s, when Frenchman Edgar Brandt devised a modified bipod. Previously the elevating mechanism, the telescoping tube between the bipod legs, was fixed in relation to those legs. That meant that if the ground was not completely level the elevating mechanism would be off kilter, left or right, and elevating the mortar also traversed it, and vice-versa. Brandt's design had the elevating mechanism pivot at the top of the bipod and incorporated a cross-leveling adjusting link at the bottom so that the mechanism could always be aligned vertically. This was incorporated into the famous Brandt 81mm Mle. 27 mortar, later modified slightly into the Mle. 27–31.

This did not go unnoticed by the Jinling Arsenal which, in 1931, took the Shanghai 82mm mortar and a French Brandt 81mm mortar and combined their features, along with high-quality Austrian steel for the barrel, to yield the 82mm Type 20, which became the standard Chinese medium mortar. In 1932 the Jinling Arsenal established a separate mortar factory in its facility to make the Type 20. Production got off to a slow start, however, and by 1934 only 16 had been produced, reaching a peak of only 5 per month against a capacity of only 20 per month. Demands for this new, improved weapon spurred significant expansion and during 1935–7 the arsenal produced no fewer than 1,100. In addition, the Northwest Casting Factory of the Shanxi Arsenal began production in 1934, with a capacity of 150 per month. The Type 20 proved an excellent weapon, if still a bit heavy, and it served through the war, again through the Korean War, and some even turned up in Vietnam in the 1960s.

The loss of the Shenyang, Jiangnan, and Taiyuan Arsenals in 1931–2 severely reduced production, leaving only the Jinling (Nanjing) Arsenal in low-rate production. Orders were issued to move the work to the Hanyang Arsenal and it began turning out Type 20s in 1935, later moving to the 21st Arsenal, which continued to produce them through the war, with 2,000 being built as late as 1947.

The only ammunition mass-produced for the 82mm Type 20 was high explosive. The projectile weighed 3.56kg (excluding fuze and propellant cartridge), of which 255g was the explosive filler, a coarse granular mixture of 60% TNT and 40% potassium perchlorate. This compared to 540g of TNT in a Japanese 81mm mortar projectile, the Chinese projectile having thicker walls and base. The propellant system consisted of a metal propellant cartridge (many of which were imported from the UK) and three silk bags each weighing 4.5g. There were two fuzes available for these rounds, super-quick and a combination SQ/delay. The former was very simple, a weighted plunger that moved forward against a spring on impact, hitting the primer. The only safety was a pin that was removed prior to firing. The dual-mode fuze was more complicated, including a setback safety armed by firing and a rotating cylinder that either allowed the initiating flash to travel directly through a hole, or interposed a pyrotechnic delay element. A screwdriver or other flat blade turned the cylinder to select the operating mode.

A white phosphorus round weighing 4.05kg was also produced, but apparently only in small numbers.

Production of 82mm ammunition was a source of concern throughout the war. The goal was 1.68 million rounds per year, with production of shell bodies and fuzes split evenly between arsenals (40th and the Anning branch of the 21st) and commercial firms. Filling was done by arsenal personnel. The limiting item in production was the fuze, which consistently lagged behind potential shell body production by about half. In late 1944 it was proposed that the 21st Arsenal and US ordnance personnel examine the possibility of using the US M52B1 fuze in the 82mm bodies. It was found that the nose of the body had to be shaved somewhat and the fuze well modified, but firing tests showed that once that was done the combination worked from a ballistics point of view. The US allocated 4,608 M52B1 fuzes in 1945 as an initial increment but it seems unlikely they made it to China in time for wartime use.

The loss of production capacity in the early 1930s and the improvements offered by the Brandt design also caused the army to look to foreign suppliers for temporary help. The obvious source was the Brandt firm of France, foremost designer and producer of mortars during the interwar years. An initial trials batch of two 81mm Mle. 27 mortars and 400 rounds was ordered in 1930 and shipped later that year. It was probably these that provided the basis for the Jinling Arsenal mortar program. A slightly more substantial order came in mid-1932 and covered 20 mortars and 550 rounds (500 HE and 50 heavy HE).

The first major order, for 260 of the 81mm Mle. 27–31 mortars with 39,000 HE rounds, 3,900 heavy HE rounds, and 1,300 smoke rounds, was placed in February 1933 and delivered in May–August of that year. Further small orders followed, including 41

CAI troops train on an 81mm M1 mortar at the Ramgarh Training Center in November 1943.

for the Yunnan government and 20 for the Guangxi government in 1934, with the next large order (150 for the Guangzhou government) coming in March 1936 with deliveries five months later. That year also saw 52 more ordered by the Guangxi government and 40 by the Yunnan government. Thereafter, all purchases appear to have been for the central government. Major orders were placed in August 1937 (150 weapons and 128,000 rounds, delivered in December), and April 1938 (250 weapons and 200,000 rounds, the mortars being delivered in September 1938 to Guangzhou and the ammunition in early 1939 via Rangoon). The last deliveries of Brandt 81mm mortars, 20 weapons and 10,500 rounds, came through Burma in March 1940.

The only other source of mortar equipment during the 1930s was a single purchase of 100 of the Austrian copy of the Mle. 27 and 22,000 rounds from Austria (actually finally delivered by Germany) and some 81mm ammunition from Finland delivered via Rangoon. The imports were significant in bridging the gap in supply in the early and mid-1930s, but were quickly overshadowed by the Type 20 once production got into full swing in 1939. Nevertheless, manufacture of 81mm ammunition for those weapons was undertaken at the 21st Arsenal in the early war years to make up for by then unavailable European suppliers.

As part of its Lend-Lease program the US supplied China with its version of the Brandt mortar, the 81mm M1. Because China was largely self-sufficient in mortar production (assuming raw materials were delivered) provision of medium mortars was accorded a lower priority than many other items. As a result production for China totaled only 18 in 1942, 334 in 1943, and 496 in 1944, all using the M1 mount. Small additional quantities were probably diverted to China from the US supply stream. A further 312 using the M4 mount were produced in the spring of 1945, but it seems unlikely they reached Chinese troops before VJ-Day.

The modest requirements of the Chinese Army in India were met with little trouble. Since the Chinese built an equivalent weapon themselves, priority for the 81mm over the Hump was low. In fact, the first significant deliveries did not take place until after the opening of the Stilwell Road. An initial goal of 1,008 M1 mortars for the Chinese forces in China was raised to 1,224 in February 1945, but only 36 had actually been issued by that time. That number increased to 144 by the end of February and 500 by 31 May 1945. By the end of the war 864 had been issued, with another 321 awaiting issue in Chinese depots and 284 still in depots in India. Initially the US had intended to provide pack hangers for the 81mm mortars, to permit the use of pack horses, but in January 1945 these were eliminated from the Lend-Lease list as there were too few horses and mules available in China to take advantage of them.

The availability of US ammunition inevitably led to the question of whether it could be fired from Chinese 82mm mortars. The need was particularly critical in the case of smoke rounds, which could be produced only with great difficulty in China. In response the Chief Ordnance Officer at the Ramgarh Training Center in India set up an 81mm M1 and an 82mm Type 20 side-by-side with identical settings and fired five rounds of US 81mm smoke ammunition from each. The results are summarized in the table. They disclosed a loss of range and a significant increase in range error. The expected increase in lateral error, due to the shell bouncing around inside the larger tube (balloting) did not occur, however. No denting of the fins was found from balloting

Test Results of 81mm Smoke Ammunition		
	81mm M1	82mm Type 20
Range obtained	1,182m	921m
Depth of pattern	38m	97m
Width of pattern	15.5m	14.5m

inside the barrel, nor were there any misfires due to off-center impact on the fixed firing pin at the bottom of the barrel. As a result Y-Force requested 1,365 rounds of 81mm smoke in August 1943 for use with their Type 20 mortars. Although 171,718 rounds of 81mm WP smoke were shipped for China, few such rounds appear to have been delivered past India and Burma.

In addition to smoke rounds, of course, the US provided HE ammunition in far greater quantities. Lend-Lease shipments comprised 1,130,300 rounds of the M43A1 light HE shell and 705,829 rounds of the M56 heavy HE shell. These were more effective than the Chinese rounds as they featured bodies made of steel, which created lethal fragments,

Mortar Deliveries

	1932	1933	1934	1935	1936	1937	1938	1939	1940	1941	1942	1943	1944	1945
Mortars														
81mm Brandt Mle. 1927	0	260	61	12	202	170	230	52	0	0	0	0	0	0
81mm Austrian	0	0	0	0	0	0	100	0	0	0	0	0	0	0
81mm US M1	0	0	0	0	0	0	0	0	0	0	0	72	108	1,080
82mm Type 20 (Hanyang/21st)	0	0	0	180	480	440	110	1,136	900	500	760	1,381	1,140	1,084
82mm Type 20 (other arsenals)	50	30	200	0	85	n/a	n/a	n/a	0	0	0	0	n/a	1,316
Ammunition (thousand of rounds)														
81mm from France	0	55	7	40	60	148	13	165	0	0	0	0	0	0
81mm from Austria	0	0	0	0	0	0	7	15	0	0	0	0	0	0
81mm from Finland	0	0	0	0	0	0	0	45	0	0	0	0	0	0
81mm from USA	0	0	0	0	0	0	0	0	0	0	0	2,008		0
81mm Chinese	0	0	0	0	0	1	0	68	82	51	18	0	0	0
82mm Chinese (Hanyang/21st)	0	0	0	113	204	299	481	568	509	323	319	380	424	208
82mm Chinese (other arsenals)	66	159	155	33	44	n/a	n/a	n/a	33	91	226	336	n/a	1,932

Note: 943 and 1944 deliveries of US mortars were to CAI, 1945 figure is for deliveries into China.

Chinese Mortar Specifications					
	Weight complete	Traverse	Elevation	Range	Projectile weight
75mm Stokes type	221kg	20°	45°–75°	2,100m	3.35kg
82mm Type 20	69kg	8°	45°–85°	2,850m	3.8kg
83.5mm Shenyang	191kg	7°	46°–65°	3,031m	4.0kg

as opposed to the Chinese mortar ammunition of cast iron, which tended to shatter so that a portion of the body was simply turned into small particles and even dust. Nevertheless, the 81mm US rounds worked only inefficiently in the 82mm Type 20 mortar and not many were delivered into China before mid-1945.

Medium Warlord Mortars

Several arsenals copied the British Stokes mortar in the early and mid-1920s in calibers ranging from 75mm to 82mm. Little information is available on any of them and most would have been replaced by Type 20s by the outbreak of the war.

The Hanyang Arsenal 75mm was a completely different design and was designated the Type 15. The weapon was complex, including a recoil cylinder on each side that supported the recoiling barrel, making the weapon heavy and difficult to disassemble. As a result, it was carried in tactical movement by four men using handles that projected out from the large baseplate, a difficult and awkward task. The 75mm mortar appears to have seen little use after about 1938, presumably for lack of ammunition.

An unknown Stokes-type 75mm mortar, possibly from the Shanxi Arsenal.

75mm Type 15 mortar.

81mm Brandt Mle. 1927–31 and copies

The predecessor of almost all modern medium mortars, the French Brandt 81mm was widely copied before and during World War II. The seamless drawn-steel tube featured a cap with fixed firing pin at its rear; a spherical protrusion on the cap fitted into a socket in the rectangular baseplate. The bipod was formed by two legs attached to a center trunnion by a compass joint. The left leg carried a cross-leveling mechanism operating a sliding bracket. The mortar broke down into three main parts, barrel (20.7kg), baseplate (20.5kg), and bipod (18.5kg), for man transport. The Austrian mortar was essentially a direct copy of the Brandt model.

The American version of the 81mm Brandt, known as the M1, differed from the original only in detail mainly related to US manufacturing methods. As with the original, the mortar was carried in three components, the barrel (20.2kg), baseplate (20.5kg), and bipod (21.1kg). The most significant difference between the two was in the ammunition, with the American mortar benefiting from developments in propellant that yielded longer ranges.

The Americans retained the concept of two types of HE round, one light (M43A1) and one heavy (M36), but the latter was significantly lighter than the French original. On the other hand, the M57 smoke projectile was heavier than its French equivalent.

81mm Mortar Specifications		
	Brandt	**M1**
Weight complete	59.7kg	61.8kg
Traverse	7°	7°
Elevation	45° – 80°	40° – 85°
Range, light HE	1,900m	2,990m
Range, heavy HE	1,000m	2,325m
Range, smoke	1,900m	2,245m
Weight, light HE	3.25kg	3.12kg
Weight, heavy HE	6.90kg	4.83kg
Weight, smoke	3.25kg	4.89kg

A Brandt 81mm mortar.

82mm Type 20

This modern design was of conventional construction, although the use of lesser-quality metals apparently added to the weight. The distinctive feature inherited from the Shenyang design was the bipod, with each leg being made of two struts, joined at the top and bottom, and by a center bar. Several designs of bipod were used, with circular or flat struts. The cross-levelling knob was held between the struts of the left leg. A single folding bar attached to the front strut connected the two legs about half-way down. The sight provided was simpler than Western designs, using simple metal leaves in lieu of optical lenses.

Top right: Troops practice with a Type 20 mortar at the Infantry Training Center in 1944. This weapon uses the flat-sided struts for the bipod legs.

Right: A Type 20, showing the bipod design.

83.5mm Shenyang Mortar

The Type 13 was made from steel tubes provided by Shanghai Mills and Bofors, while the later Type 15 used tubes from Krupp. The original model had a long barrel, some 132cm (L/16), but the Type 15 had a 109cm (L/13) barrel, while at the same time switching from steel to nickel-chrome steel to reduce the wall thickness slightly. About 300 Type 13s and 1,200 Type 15s were built. The Type 15 was a well-made weapon with good finish and an excellent range of 3,000 meters, with 5,000 meters reportedly being achieved on a trials basis with supercharge. The weapon was set on a single-axle mount in which the wheels could slide and lock 15cm in or out to adjust for different track widths on trails. In action the mortar was usually detached from the axle, a simple and quick operation, and fired from its bipod and baseplate. Nevertheless, the weapon was rather heavy for its type: 101kg for the mortar and mount, and 90kg for the wheels.

Three views of a Shenyang 83mm mortar with Fengtian troops in 1932. *From top*, in traveling position on its wheels; ready for firing from its wheels (note the plumb bob arrangement); in firing position off its wheels.

Although some features were modern, others were archaic, in particular, the lack of a sight. Aiming was accomplished by looking down a rod stuck in the barrel before firing and elevation was determined by a plumb bob at the end of the rod.

Useful weapons, a number were brought into China proper with the fall of Manchuria and they served, albeit in decreasing numbers, into the early phases of the 1937–45 war until replaced by the Type 20.

25

Heavy Mortars

An outstanding design from the Shenyang (Mukden) Trench Mortar Arsenal was their 150mm heavy mortar. They built an initial batch of 35 with steel barrels, followed by the main production run using nickel-steel barrels, of which about 50 had been made by 1928. The weapon used an ingenious carriage in which the barrel was mounted in a rotatable cradle set on the 2-wheel axle. Boxes on each side of the barrel carried sights and other equipment. To bring the piece into action the baseplate was placed on the ground and the mortar tube and cradle rotated to set the rear of the tube into the plate. The mortar could be fired from its wheeled carriage, although it was more commonly rested on a conventional bipod. The tubes were initially purchased from Shanghai Mills, Britain, or Bofors, but by the late 1920s all came from Krupp.

The weapon proved almost ideal for Chinese conditions, being light enough to transport virtually anywhere, throwing a powerful shell, and being simple to operate and maintain. Indeed, it was so successful that other arsenals began to build similar weapons. By 1931 the Gongxian Arsenal had a rated capacity of 22 per month and the Hwayang

A captured 15cm Shenyang mortar in traveling position. (*Osamu Shimoharaguchi*)

A 15cm mortar crew training during the war.

Arsenal 10 per month. These were built to a slightly modified design that simplified the carriage, dispensing with some of the fancier features, such as the equipment boxes and attachment points for the baseplate. Thus, even though the Shenyang Trench Mortar Arsenal fell under Japanese control, by the mid-1930s the KMT army fielded four heavy trench mortar regiments, each with 24 of these mortars.

With the outbreak of war the wheeled mount was discontinued as unduly complex and expensive, and the mortar was now simply loaded into a cart for transport. The new design was standardized as the Type 29 in 1940 and the 50th Arsenal ordered to build 360 of them, with the order actually being placed in 1939. This was accomplished in large part by the rebuilding and conversion of existing mortars and the type quickly became the standard heavy mortar during 1942–5. Ammunition was produced through the war by various government arsenals, after 1938 mainly at the 50th Arsenal.

The 15cm mortar proved effective, its light weight and heavy firepower compared to the bulkier artillery being especially appreciated in south China and Burma in 1944. Nevertheless, by the late 1930s it was starting to show its age, as it was heavier than contemporary heavy mortars being developed elsewhere and, even after rebuilding, did not incorporate the Brandt leveling-type bipod.

50th Arsenal 15cm Mortar Production							
	1939	*1940*	*1941*	*1942*	*1943*	*1944*	*1945*
15cm mortar rebuilds	86	0	47	1	33	40	69
15cm mortar ammunition	0	2,000	2,500	9,000	16,827	18,623	25,650

In June 1936 the Yunnan provincial government became the first customer for the French 120mm Brandt mortar, purchasing four mortars with their transport rigs, caissons, and 400 rounds of HE ammunition. Delivery seems to have occurred in 1938 and they were formed into a separate battery of the Yunnan Provincial Artillery Regiment where they remained in service to the end of the war.

In 1938 the central government purchased a pair of 120mm mortars from Brandt for trials, along with 275 rounds of HE ammunition. These were delivered in late March 1939 via Rangoon. The mobilization, and subsequent fall, of France made further purchases impossible, but the weapons were turned over to the 21st Arsenal as part of an effort to build a local equivalent. A competition between the 21st and 50th Arsenals led to the former's design being chosen, amid allegations by the 50th Arsenal that their competitor had intercepted components built in the US intended for their work. The resulting design borrowed heavily from the Brandt original, particularly in the design of the bipod, although the barrel was somewhat shorter to reduce weight. The 21st Arsenal placed the 120mm mortar in production in 1945, with 49 mortars and 3,288 rounds of ammunition being turned out that year. Although not confirmed, it seems unlikely that they saw combat before the Japanese surrender. Development continued even during production, so that the original batch, probably few in number, became designated the Type 33 Model 1 mortar, while the more common postwar weapons were known as the Type 33 Model 2.

The heavy mortar for the Chinese Army in India was, of necessity, the US 4.2-inch chemical mortar. The initial requirement for 72 weapons was filled in 1943 and weapons served in Burma during 1944. A further requirement that arose in 1943 was for two 4.2-inch mortar regiments for each of the 30 American-sponsored divisions in China. No weapons, however, were flown in, so that although the requirement stood at 288 (four regiments) in February 1945, only 48 had been issued to Chinese units, and only 87 more had made it to China over the Burma Road. These weapons were turned over to the Heavy Mortar Training Center for use in activating further regiments, but this

A 4.2-inch mortar in action in the Mogaung valley of Burma in April 1944.

took longer than anticipated, so that at the end of the war only 168 of these weapons had been issued to units in China, with a further 158 sitting in depots there.

107mm (4.2-inch) M2 Mortar

This weapon had originally been developed to throw chemical (gas and smoke) shells, but served in WWII mostly as a conventional HE-throwing weapon. It was unusual in that it featured a monopod, known as the "standard," that sat on its own small baseplate at the front. A pair of rods connected the main baseplate to the standard to keep recoil from driving them apart. Another unusual feature was that the tube was rifled and the ammunition spin-stabilized. The range with the original HE shell was 2,910 meters, but an improved propellant became available in 1944 that increased that figure to 4,020 meters.

4.2-inch M2 Mortar Specifications	
Weight	150kg
Traverse	40°
Elevation	45° – 60°
Muzzle velocity	255m/s
Range	4,020m
Projectile weight	11.4kg

4.2-inch M2 mortar on a concrete slab.

120mm Brandt Mortar

This served as the prototype from which the later Type 33 was developed. It was a modern design, well in advance of its time and featured a long barrel for long range and modern ammunition. An axle attached to the bipod, which swiveled back for transport, making the weapon easy to move and quick into and out of action.

A Brandt 120mm on trials in France in 1936.

120mm Type 33-1

This was the Brandt 120 as modified by the 21st Arsenal to suit local conditions and manufacturing methods. The barrel was made shorter, the traverse reduced, and the high-speed wheels on the original were replaced by wooden wheels for animal draft. The weapon was towed by a hook that attached to the muzzle. Despite the shorter tube, the weapon retained a long range and was, in fact, an excellent weapon. Unfortunately, they were produced too late to see much service against the Japanese.

Type 33-1 Mortar Specifications	
Bore	120mm
Barrel length	1,500mm
Elevation	+25° – 85°
Weight complete	212.7kg
Projectile weight	10.5kg
Muzzle velocity	256m/s
Range (charge 6)	4,925 m

A Type 33-1 mortar on its wheels with the towing hook fitted.

150mm Shenyang Mortar

This mortar featured an unusual mount, incorporating an integral cart. The tube was on a cradle which rotated the tube onto the base plate when placing it in action. Aiming instruments and accessories were carried in boxes on either side of the cart. The barrels of the first models were made from steel tubes from Shanghai, Britain, and Sweden, but this was later changed to nickel-chrome steel tubes from Krupp. It was usually accompanied by a one-mule caisson carrying 10 rounds of ammunition. Maximum range was about 2,700 meters.

A 15cm mortar of the Northeastern Army parading in Shenyang in 1930.

150mm Gongxian/Hwayang Type Mortars

These similar designs drew on the Shenyang 15cm mortar but reduced the weight and simplified production. Like the Shenyang model, they could be fired from their cart/mount, but were also provided with a bipod. That, however, necessitated removing the mortar from the cart. Maximum range was about 3,000 meters.

15cm mortars with the 19th Route Army in 1932: on the left with a bipod; on the right firing from the wheeled mount.

150mm Type 29 Mortar

This design dispensed with the wheeled mount completely in favor of the conventional bipod arrangement. Shock absorbers were added to mitigate the loading on the bipod mount and the tube was apparently strengthened to permit firing with more propellant. In fact, the Type 29 was manufactured with barrels of three different lengths.

An American technician examines a disassembled Type 29 mortar and its accessories in August 1944.

Type 29 Mortar Specifications

Bore	153mm	153mm	153mm
Barrel length	190cm	160cm	145cm
Barrel weight	178kg	156kg	148kg
Total weight	310kg	288kg	230kg
Muzzle vel.	196m/s	182m/s	177m/s
Range	3,143m	2,807m	2,680m
Projectile	22kg		
Elevation	45° – 75°		

26

Pack Artillery

In a country where narrow paths were far more common than roads and bridges were fragile, it is not surprising that the lightest members of the artillery family would prove the most popular. That mountain, or pack artillery could be broken down into separate loads for transport appears to have been less important than overall weight, as draft transport was still the preferred means. This was particularly true in the south, which tended to have smaller horses and mules.

The first large-scale procurement of such weapons resulted in the delivery of 257 Schnellfeuer-Gebirgskanone 7.5cm L/14 mit Rorhrücklauf by Krupp between 1904 and 1912. These were part of the family of Krupp mountain guns generally designated the M03, despite a range of detail changes made to suit the numerous customers. The weapons were light and threw a useful shell for the time, and quickly became the standard light artillery piece of the Imperial Chinese Army. Almost all of the subsequent Chinese pack artillery through 1942 was derived, directly or indirectly, from the pioneering work done by the Krupp concern at the turn of the century.

Pleased with the weapons, the Jiangnan Arsenal in Shanghai started building them for the imperial government in 1905. With the collapse of the imperial regime and then the republican government the Krupp mountain guns were dispersed widely amongst the warlords. Nevertheless, the Jiangnan Arsenal continued building them and by 1928 a total

A 75mm Krupp-type mountain gun in 1937.

A 75mm Meiji Type 41 or Chinese variant with the 32nd Army in 1935.
Note that the horses have pack gear as well as draft harnesses.

of 494 had been made. By early 1931 production had reached six per month, although it ceased shortly thereafter. No distinction seems to have been made between the Chinese-built guns and the Krupp originals, both being referred to as Type Ke mountain guns.

There were probably about 250–300 of these guns still in service in 1937, and about 190 in 1942. By the latter date, however, the weapons, although well cared for, were aged and very worn. Effective range had dropped to about 3,000 meters due to the worn barrels and they were rated as effective only as direct-fire weapons. Nevertheless, they remained in service as divisional and army artillery, serving mostly as infantry guns, to the end of the war, albeit in decreasing numbers.

Krupp had also sold its mountain gun to the Japanese, who modified it extensively to yield their Meiji Type 41 mountain gun. The Japanese lengthened the barrel, replaced the sliding breech with an interrupted-screw type, and changed the box trail for a unique Y-shaped pole unit. The Japanese had distributed numbers of these to friendly warlords after the First World War and in 1918 modified the recoil system, probably to ease manufacture, and offered it as an export weapon to China with the designation Taisho Type 6. The Hanyang Arsenal began production of the Type 6 in 1921 as the Type 10, but apparently manufacture got off to a slow start because a total of only 68 had been built by 1928, although they were still building them at two per month in early 1931. Production probably ceased shortly thereafter.

Other warlords got into this new arms race and in 1921 the Shanxi Arsenal launched an effort to build mountain guns, buying machinery and materials from Germany. In 1923 it began production of an unknown model of 75mm ultra-light gun, with a very short

76mm obr. 09 mountain guns with caissons, probably from Feng's original purchase, now belonging to Yang Hucheng's 17th Route Army in the mid-1930s.

barrel,[*] a screw-type breech, and a reported range of 5,000 meters, as its Type 12 infantry gun, designed to be pulled by manpower without the need for pack or draft horses. In 1924 it produced 30 pieces. In the event, they proved impractical and were used in the role of mountain guns. In that year, however, the arsenal also launched production of a copy of the Hanyang Type 10 (itself a Taiho 6) as its Type 13. In 1928 it introduced the Type 17 mountain gun, based on the Type 13, but featuring an increase in range to 7,000 meters. The arsenal had a production capacity of 40 of these weapons per month, although it is not clear if this was actually achieved. By 1929 it had built 700 75mm mountain guns of the various types. In April 1931 the arsenal reported producing 75mm mountain guns at 30 per month. Production of these weapons probably ended in 1932 but as war loomed the old Type 12 was placed back in production and 200 more were built in 1936–7 before the Japanese forced the evacuation of the arsenal.

The Shenyang Arsenal designed a version of the Japanese gun, either the Meiji 41 or the Taisho 6, with a shorter barrel, as the Type 14 but only built 72 of them between 1925 and 1931 using materials bought from Japan and Austria, pack guns being considerably less useful in Manchuria than elsewhere in China.

These warlord weapons were widely used as divisional and army artillery although losses were very heavy early in the war, so that there were only 270 of them still in service in the spring of 1942. As with the Krupp weapons, ammunition was locally made, subject to the availability of raw materials.

---

[*] Modern Chinese sources give a barrel length of 600mm (L/8) although it is not clear what definition of barrel length they are using.

Ammunition production for the 75mm mountain guns ran at 40,400 in 1932, rising to 86,300 the following year and totaled 335,162 for the period 1932–6. Despite the evacuation of the arsenals, production was maintained during the war, with no fewer than 267,280 rounds being produced during 1940–3. Given the extreme reluctance of Chinese commanders to commit their artillery, this was probably sufficient for their needs.

The one type of early mountain gun that did not owe anything to the Krupp design was the Russian 76mm obr. 09, which was the Schneider-Danglis mountain gun bored out from 75mm for Russian ammunition. It would seem that 42 of these weapons, along with limbers and 84 caissons, plus 22,692 rounds of ammunition (equally divided between HE and shrapnel) had been delivered to Feng Yuxiang by the Soviet Union in 1926 and at least some of these remained in service with the Northwest Army into the mid-1930s and probably saw some use in the opening phases of the war.

By the time Chiang's Nanjing government got around to buying mountain artillery for its own general artillery reserve much had changed in the capabilities of the weapons being offered. In particular, manufacturers had begun offering weapons with higher elevation limits and semi-fixed ammunition with variable charges. This made indirect fire a practical option, in contrast to the Krupp- and Schneider-type weapons from the turn of the century which were really only useful for direct fire except in rare circumstances.

With the completion of the Northern Expedition and the end of the arms embargo in 1929 the central government was able to go overseas for the latest in mountain artillery for its own GHQ artillery reserve. They held trials in 1931 and finally two models were chosen. From Bofors it picked the 75mm L/20, and an initial batch of 12 was delivered in February 1933. These proved satisfactory and three more batches of 20 each were delivered in January, March, and April 1934, bringing the total to 72. These weapons proved effective and popular, providing much of the firepower in the defense of Shanghai in 1937. By early 1942 only 50 remained, but with locally made ammunition available they soldiered on to the end of the war.

The other weapon was the Schneider 75mm M1928, sold commercially under the designation SMP. A few earlier M1919 (commercial SM) models had apparently been sold in China, but not in great quantity. An order for four SMP guns was placed in 1932 and these were delivered in March 1933. A second order, this time for three 4-gun batteries, was placed in July 1935 and delivered a year later. A third order covered three more batteries, and these were delivered in July 1937. In addition, the Yunnan provincial government placed an order for three batteries worth in April 1936 (delivered between August 1937 and June 1938).

Schneider backed into one other sale. In late 1935 the Guangxi

A Bofors 75mm mountain gun firing.

A 76mm obr. 09 mountain gun without its shield being fired in 1944.

provincial government had requested a quote from Rheinmetall (via Siemssen & Co) for 36 of its commercially marketed 75mm L/20 mountain guns but the Nanjing government refused an arms import permit for them and in March 1936 the German foreign ministry reluctantly told Rheinmetall not to proceed. Frustrated, the Guangxi government ordered three batteries of Schneider SMP guns in May 1937 and, with war appearing imminent, the central government this time approved and these were delivered in July–December 1938.

By early 1942 the central government was reporting that it only had 13 Schneider pack guns left in service. This does not seem to have included the provincial troops, as the 1st Battalion, Yunnan Provincial Artillery, still had its full complement of 12 weapons, along with pack animals and wire signal gear, in January 1943. Ammunition was in short supply, since the central government had ordered only 290 rounds per gun, and Guangxi only 300 rounds per gun. Yunnan, on the other hand, ordered a thousand rounds per gun and so was well provided for. There was no local production of ammunition for the SMPs.

Another weapon that found its way into the central government arsenal was the Russian 76.2mm obr. 09 mountain gun. Fifty guns, similar to those delivered to Feng in the 1920s, were delivered via Rangoon in October 1939. By the spring of 1942, 44 were listed as still in service with central government forces, with 2,000 rounds per gun. These guns were apparently late-production pieces, for they were reported to be in excellent condition by US observers, and proved useful when they were heavily used in the Salween campaigns of 1943–5. No ammunition was produced in China, but some was extemporized by converting the ammunition for the Soviet field guns, which were less used due to their flat trajectory.

All of these weapons required ammunition and the US shipped over propellants both to support production and to renew aging stocks. Apparently, however, this was a low priority. The depot in Assam reported in March 1945 that it was holding 136,000kg of propellant for the Bofors guns, 66,000kg for the Japanese-type guns, 20,000kg for the old Krupp guns, and 400kg for the Schneider guns, which had been sitting there for two years. Deterioration, although not yet severe, was beginning to take a toll and they urged the material be taken to China quickly.

What would become the standard artillery piece for the Chinese Army did not start showing up until 1942. The May 1941 Lend-Lease Ordnance Program envisioned the delivery of 600 75mm pack howitzers worth $9.2 million beginning in mid-1942. As expected, deliveries had to await the ramp-up in US production. By mid-May 1942 32 pack howitzers and 89 of the less common field howitzer versions (along with 6,500 rounds) had arrived in Burma and India, but none had made it to China.

The 75mm M1A1 at the FATC. *Top*, gun crew drill; *above*, practicing cart transport that was more common in China than pack transport and needed because there was no draft harness available for the weapon.

The most common model was the M1A1 cannon (barrel & breech) on the M1 carriage, which was the standard break-apart pack version. To equip airborne troops the US had developed the M8 carriage, which simply replaced the wooden wheels with steel ones with pneumatic tires, this being suitable for towing behind jeeps for short and medium distances. For some reason 12 of these were sent to India, where they equipped one battalion of the 30th Division of the CAI for its battles in Burma.

By the end of 1942 some 250 pack howitzers on the M1 carriage (along with the 12 on the M8 carriage) had been shipped out of the US for India. Of those 20 were sent to Rangoon and appear to have made it to China for the 5th Army, but the majority were diverted to India, where they equipped the CAI or sat in depots.

Mountain Artillery Specifications

	Barrel length (calibers)	Weight (firing position)	Traverse	Elevation	Projectile weight	Muzzle velocity	Range
75mm Krupp	14	421kg	4°	-10° to +25°	5.3kg	300m/s	4,800m
75mm Shanghai	14	386kg	4°	-8° to +23°	5.3kg	280m/s	4,300m
75mm Mle. 1928	18.6	680kg	10°	-10° to +40°	6.33kg	440m/s	9,600m
75mm Bofors L/20	20	800kg	6°	-10° to +50°	6.5kg	405m/s	9,200m
75mm M1A1	15.9	577kg	6°	-5° to +45°	6.3kg	381m/s	8,930m
75mm Type 41	19.2	525kg	6°	-8° to +25°	6.4kg	360m/s	6,270m
75mm Hanyang & Shanxi	19.5	610kg	5°	-8° to +25°	6.4kg	342m/s	6,000m
75mm Shenyang	17.3	512kg	6°	-8° to +25°	6.5kg	335m/s	6,000m
76mm obr. 09	16.5	670kg	2.5°	-6° to +28°	6.2kg	381m/s	7,100m
105mm Shanxi	12	853kg	7°	-15° to +40°	12kg	300m/s	5,964m

An initial increment of pack howitzers was flown over the the Hump in the summer of 1943, resulting in Y-Force issuing 18 more weapons in September 1943, 17 in October, and 24 in November, so that by the end of October there were already five army artillery battalions in Y-Force equipped with these weapons. The November shipment equipped one more battalion at the FATC as a demonstration unit. Thereafter most deliveries of these weapons were made through the center, which both equipped and trained units to guarantee maximum return on the investment.

By the end of 1943 the Y-Force requirement stood at 277 howitzers and 230,000 rounds of ammunition, of which only 97 howitzers and 91,900 rounds had been delivered. Things picked up a bit early the next year and by April 1944 Y-Force had been fully equipped to its authorized scale of 17 battalions (204 howitzers). In the spring and summer of 1944, however, an emergency issue of 96 pack howitzers had to be made to unsponsored units in east China to meet the Japanese offensive, and most of these were lost shortly thereafter.

By the end of January 1945 the requirement, for all Chinese troops, had increased to 28 battalions, and then the next month to the final figure of 34 battalions (408 howitzers). Actual issues, however, had been reduced to a trickle, due this time not to the difficulties of delivery from India but to an actual shortage of the weapons. Thus, early in 1945, 284 weapons had been issued to Chinese units in China (plus 115 to CAI units), but with only a further 22 in depots in China and 29 in India. No further issues to Chinese units were made until mid-year, although in the last three months of the war a further 105 weapons were issued.

Little use appears to have been made of heavier mountain artillery, though given the mountainous nature of much of Shanxi province, it is not surprising that Yan's forces experimented with larger mountain guns. The Taiyuan Arsenal bought the plans and equipment for the old 105mm Krupp L/12 pack howitzer from Rheinmetall (via Solothurn) in the 1920s and began producing a slightly modified version in 1927 as the Type 16 mountain howitzer. Only 16 were built, however, during 1927–30, and by late 1944 only six remained on the strength of II War Zone.

The central government also ordered a single example of the Schneider 105mm SMP mountain howitzer for trials in July 1936, but it does not appear to have been delivered until 1939 and then saw no service use.

75mm Krupp Mountain Gun

One of the most common of the divisional support weapons, this was used both in the original Krupp-built model and a slightly modified version built by the Shanghai Arsenal. The gun broke down into four pieces, the heaviest of which weighed 120kg, for pack transport, although draft transport was more commonly used in China. The weapon used a horizontal sliding breechblock and a shield was provided, but was not always fitted. It fired fixed ammunition (no variable charges) and this, together with the limited elevation afforded by the box trail, must have reduced its flexibility in other than direct fire. By the late 1930s all of these weapons, but particularly the Krupp originals, were badly worn. Range, already short, was further reduced by worn barrels, while the elevating and traverse gears usually no longer held true aim, and the wheels were loose on the axles. Nevertheless, these guns soldiered on to the end of the war, useful for their light weight and portability.

The Krupp (*above left*) and Shanghai (*above right*) 75mm mountain guns.

Two more views of a Shanghai 75mm mountain gun, *above left*
in traveling position with the rarely used shield.

75mm Schneider Mle. 1928 Mountain Gun

Schneider developed a range of 75mm mountain guns between the wars. The original model, the Mle. 1919, sold commercially as the Model SM (Schneider Montagne) initially featured a complex angular shield, but this was later replaced by a curved design. The next offering was the Mle. 1928, marketed as the SMP (Schneider Montagne Poussant) and was generally similar to the earlier model but featured an improved recoil system to handle slightly more powerful ammunition. The ammunition was of the separately loaded variety with four charges. Initially, the Mle. 1928 continued to use the curved shield, and this was offered as an option throughout the production run, although the guns purchased by the French Army used a simpler angular shield.

The most distinctive feature of the Schneider mountain guns was the use of a cranked axle arrangement. This permitted the height of the trunions to be raised for high-angle firing, increasing the elevation from 22° to 40°. The gun broke down into seven pieces for pack transport, the heaviest being 120kg, but in Chinese service draft transport was more common. The Mle. 1928 was a modern design, featuring a lower weight and longer range than the Bofors L/20 weapon used concurrently.

Two views of a Chinese 75mm Mle. 1928. *Above left*, the axles are in the normal traveling position, while *above right* the gun has been raised to permit high-angle fire.

75mm Bofors L/20 Mountain Gun

A popular and efficient weapon, the Bofors 75mm mountain gun remained in front-line service to the end of the war. Although heavy, it had a good range and was of generally modern construction. It broke down into eight loads for pack or cart transport. It fired separately loaded ammunition with three charges.

A Bofors factory crew test-fires an L/20 mountain gun before delivery.

75mm M1A1 Pack Howitzer

The M1A1 howitzer on various carriages was the standard US pack howitzer, used mostly by airborne troops. Although a late arrival, by the end of the war the M1A1 on the M1 carriage with wood-spoke wheels equipped the bulk of the effective Chinese artillery units. The weapon had a distinctive feature, the use of a heavy "upper sleigh" that surrounded the barrel on the top and sides, giving the weapon its unique "hump-back" appearance. The weapon broke down into six loads for pack or cart transport. A smaller number of field howitzers on the M3 carriage, with split trails and pneumatic tires, were also supplied. The M8 carriage was similar but featured pneumatic tires on steel wheels. It fired semi-fixed ammunition with four charges.

A Chinese crew train on an M1A1 howitzer at the ATC, clearly showing the cross-axle traverse, here all the way to the right.

75mm Type 41 Mountain Gun

The Japanese extensively modified the Krupp mountain gun and placed it in production as the Type 41. The main changes were a longer barrel, the replacement of the sliding breechblock with an interrupted-screw mechanism, and the use of a Y-shaped pole trail that provided a simple identification feature. For horse draft the single-pole extension was removed and replaced by two extensions for the main trail elements. It fired fixed ammunition with no charge

A Japanese Type 41 regimental gun showing the distinctive trail arrangement.

variations. These weapons were purchased by various warloads before and shortly after WWI. The Taisho Type 6 was a Japanese export model with a modified recoil system. The Hanyang Type 10 and Shanxi Type 13 were local copies of the Taisho 6, while the Shenyang Type 14 used a shorter barrel. The Taiyuan Arsenal modified the weapon to give a range of 7,000 meters with the designation Type 17. For the most part the Chinese-built guns dispensed with the gun shield. A small number of Japanese Type 41 regimental guns, with the small shields, were captured and used during the war.

A Shanxi Type 13 mountain gun. (*Osamu Shimoharaguchi*)

76mm Soviet M09 Mountain Gun

An efficient weapon, the M09 remained in production in the Soviet Union until 1939. Like

the Schneider weapon, it had cranked axle shafts that allowed the gun crew to raise the height of the trunnions, and hence improve the elevation from 22° to 28° in the firing position. The weapon was heavy compared to the Krupp guns (although 62kg of that weight was the shield) but it outranged them considerably. It broke down into seven sections (the heaviest 119kg) for pack transport. The sound design was betrayed by the fixed ammunition it fired.

An M09 76mm mountain gun with its distinctive S-shaped shield, with Y-Force in December 1943.

105mm Shanxi Type 16 Mountain Howitzer

This was the Krupp pre-WWI commercial 105mm L/12 mountain howitzer as produced

by the Shanxi Arsenal. It broke down into nine pieces weighing 90–110kg each for pack carriage. The ammunition was provided with six propellant charges that varied the muzzle velocity from 165 to 300m/s. Like most mountain guns of the period it utilized cross-axle traverse.

Shanxi Type 16 in the Beijing Military Museum.
(*Photo Lam Chun Wing*)

27

Light Artillery

Field artillery was never as popular in China as pack pieces due to the poor road network. The Imperial government purchased about 500 non-recoil 75–87mm field guns from Krupp in the late 19th century but even by the turn of the century these had been rendered obsolete by the new generation of rapid-fire guns. For their replacement they chose the widely sold Krupp L/30 model (known as L/29 models in China), which they purchased in two batches: one of 68 guns delivered in 1904–6, and the second of 132 guns delivered in 1910–12. The non-recoil guns appear to have been little used after the fall of the warlords in 1928, but the L/29s were to see considerable use. In fact, the Hanyang Arsenal was preparing to produce the Krupp L/29 when the imperial regime collapsed. Production there finally got under way in 1913 and continued for about the next 20 years. The Krupp originals and Hanyang copies continued to serve through 1945, although in declining numbers and with reduced effectiveness as they wore out.

The fall of the dynasty caused a scramble among the warlords for artillery. Under a contract signed just before the arms embargo the Zhili (Chihli) forces took delivery of six 4-gun batteries of 75mm M1911 field guns and 24,000 rounds of ammunition from Italy in November 1921. A second delivery in 1924 added 27 more guns and 50,400 rounds. These weapons were eventually incorporated into the national army and were still in service in 1937, some being captured in the initial Japanese offensives although the remainder saw little service after that, probably for wear and lack of ammunition.

Arrival of Italian 75mm guns for Zhili forces, October 1924.

A 75mm Type 38 field gun with the 29th Route Army outside Beijing in 1937.

The Guominjun (or Northwest Army) acquired almost all of its artillery from the Soviet Union. These included 66 field guns in 1925, probably 76mm Model 1902 guns. There were also two purchases in 1927, with the first covering 18 field guns with limbers, 36 caissons, and 35,308 rounds of ammunition (evenly split between HE and shrapnel). The second was for 42 76mm weapons with limbers, caissons, and 11,346 rounds of ammunition, but this later one appears to have been for mountain guns.

Other weapons acquired in small numbers by the various warlords included British 18pdr guns in Mk IV and Mk V configurations, Krupp 77mm M1916 guns, and French 75mm M1897s. None of these appear to have played a significant role in the events after 1937.

In Manchuria, Zhang Zhoulin purchased from Japan both Type 38 and Improved Type 38 75mm field guns. The former design was placed in production at the Shenyang Arsenal as the 75mm Type 13 field gun and 108 were built before the Japanese occupation in 1932. All three types continued in Chinese Army service through the war, with the original Type 38 and Type 13 predominating.

The largest, if short-lived, contribution to the Chinese armory resulted from Zhang Zhoulin's dispatch of agents to the Bohler works in 1922. There they found components and machinery for building the new Austro-Hungarian 76.5mm M18 field gun and tubes for the 100mm M14 field howitzer. These were purchased, shipped back to Shenyang and the machinery installed at the arsenal. From the components the arsenal was able to complete and assemble 300 field guns and 300 field howitzers, the latter created by mating the M14 barrel with the carriage of the M18 field gun. Some were lost to the Japanese in the occupation of 1932 but others withdrew south of the border and were incorporated into the national army. Ammunition production capacity had been lost, as had that for spare parts, so their usefulness declined quickly. The 8th Brigade was equipped with the

77mm guns before the war, but this was soon reduced to a single (16th) regiment, which in turn was re-equipped with French 75s in 1941. By 1942 the only remaining Shenyang/Bohler weapons appear to have been about a dozen of the howitzers with very little ammunition.

The Type 14 howitzer was apparently a useful weapon, for the Japanese converted about 60 of them to fire Japanese ammunition by enlarging the chamber in 1938–9 and issued them to troops in China and Korea.

A similar acquisition strategy paid off for the Taiyuan Arsenal, also immediately after WWI. It bought components and machinery for the production of the 88mm field gun from Krupp, a weapon that had just missed

Two photos of Chinese troops with the 76mm M1902/30 field gun at the FATC.

entering service with the German Army. The arsenal was able to assemble and complete 150 of these weapons as the 88mm Type 18 Field Gun between 1929 and 1932. When the arsenal was all but shut down in 1932, however, production of ammunition and spares halted. It seems that little ammunition had been made up to that point; these fairly modern weapons had all but disappeared from the Chinese inventory by 1937 and none were in service by 1942.

The KMT central government took a little longer to join this arms race, but among the purchases in the May 1936 contracts signed with Germany were 60 105mm leFH18 field howitzers, along with a thousand rounds of ammunition apiece and Henschel 6x4 Model 33 trucks as prime movers. Deliveries were exasperatingly slow, however. In fact, only four weapons had been delivered and another 36 were in transit when Germany cancelled further shipments in mid-1938. Losses in the early campaigns reduced the number to 33 by March 1942 and thereafter the very limited ammunition stocks restricted their use, resulting in few subsequent losses.

With the prewar field artillery crippled by lack of spares and ammunition, the burden of fire support would fall for the most part on the wartime acquisitions. The major contributor early in the war was the Soviet Union. The second shipment of Soviet arms included 160

Chinese troops of Y-Force load a projectile into their 4.5-inch howitzer at the northern end of the Burma Road in September 1944. Note the open-box trail.

M1902/30 76mm field guns and these were delivered via Hong Kong to Guangzhou in April 1938. That shipment also included 80 ex-British 115mm (4.5-inch) howitzers, delivered via the same route in April–May 1938. The howitzers were used by Y-Force in Burma in 1944/45. The field guns, however, were not as useful. They were concentrated in Yunnan Province, and most combat envisioned was in Burma. The rugged terrain in Burma did not lend itself to employment of flat-trajectory field guns and the M1902/30s appear to have been little used. In fact, some of the ammunition provided with the guns was converted for use with M1909 mountain guns, which were much more versatile.

The 1940 batch of artillery from the Soviet Union was to have included an additional 200 76mm guns according to the Sino-Soviet agreement, but in fact the Soviets provided ex-Polish 75mm M1897 guns instead. They were sent in mid-to-late 1941. Having come overland, the weapons were delivered into Sinkiang Province, and the process of moving them closer to the action took quite some time. As a result, they played little role in the fighting.[*]

The final batch of light artillery came from the United States. The initial Lend-Lease package provided for 89 75mm howitzers on the M3A1 field carriage, this being the ordnance of the M1A1 pack howitzer with a field howitzer carriage. Twenty-four were landed at Rangoon after Pearl Harbor and quickly moved up to China while the balance were diverted to India. Eight were used to form a two-battery battalion for the CAI while the rest sat in depots. Eventually the number delivered to India rose to 118 in spite of the fact that there were no trucks available in China to tow them, so in India they sat. In mid-1945 30 were converted to pack howitzers with the arrival of that number of empty carriages from the US.

The 1942 request for Lend-Lease by China included 360 105mm field howitzers, on the premise of one battalion for each of the 30 planned modernized divisions. This was

---

[*] In addition, in February 1940 the Chinese government requested the sale of 240 75mm guns and 600,000 rounds from France in exchange for tungsten, the same sort of arrangement that had worked with Germany. All that could be spared, however, were 32 75mm guns and 44 antique deBange 90mm guns, and even these were never delivered.

Chinese troops manhandle a
105mm leFH18 howitzer.

An apparently pristine 75mm M1897
field gun complete with limber takes
part in the Communist victory
parade in Guangzhou in 1948.

approved and 218 M2A1s were shipped out for Indian ports during the second half of
1942. A further 258 were approved and shipped in 1943. A portion of these benefited the
Chinese Army in India, permitting the raising of two regiments, but getting the bulk of

A 105mm M2A1 howitzer of the Chinese Army in India
fires on Pinwe, Burma, November 1944.

them to China was another matter completely. The howitzers were of little use without their prime movers, and that would have put too much strain on an already overburdened Hump fleet, so in India they stayed.

The opening of the Ledo/Burma Road to convoys in February 1945 finally permitted the delivery of 105mm howitzers. US advisers made certain that these weapons were delivered to the FATC where they could be incorporated into trained units, rather than simply handed out in the field. As it turned out, the first new 105mm howitzer battalion to be formed by the FATC was still in training there when the war ended.

Along with the 105mm howitzers, the 1942 Chinese Lend-Lease mission also requested 360 25pdr gun-howitzers from Canadian production. These were disallowed by the US Lend-Lease office on the basis that their introduction would add another non-standard ammunition family into an already complicated mix and that they required motor traction that China simply did not have. Nevertheless, 36 of these weapons managed to make it to Chinese depots in India in 1942, followed by 24 more in 1943, possibly from British stocks in-country.

Not easily discouraged, the Chinese went directly to Canada in 1943, requesting this time no fewer than 720 of these artillery pieces. The Canadians agreed, but when the American authorities discovered this they informed their northern neighbors that they would refuse to ship them to India and, if they made it to India, would refuse to ship them thence to China. At that the Canadians quietly informed Chongqing that it was not possible to supply the 25pdrs after all. None had made it to China before the end of the war.

Light Artillery Specifications							
	Barrel length (calibers)	Weight (firing position)	Traverse	Elevation	Projectile weight	Muzzle velocity	Range
75mm Hanyang L/29	30	1,243kg	7°	-8° to +16°	6.0kg	510m/s	6,000m
75mm Mle. 1897	36	1,140kg	6°	-11° to +19°	6.2kg	575m/s	11,100m
75mm M1911	27	1,076kg	52°	-15° to +65°	6.3kg	502m/s	10,240m
75mm Type 38	31	950kg	7°	-8 to +17°	6.4kg	506m/s	8,180m
75mm Type 38 Improved	31	1,136kg	7°	-8° to +43°	6.4kg	506m/s	9,455m
75mm Type 13 Shenyang	31	874kg	6°	-8° to +16°	6.5kg	500m/s	8,250m
76mm M1902/30	40	1,320kg	5°	-5° to +37°	6.4kg	635m/s	12,400m
77mm Type 14	30	1,350kg	7°	-8° to +45°	8.0kg	529m/s	11,000m
88mm Type 18	31	1,360kg	6°	-5° to +45°	9.0kg	525m/s	10,500m
105mm Type 14	19	1,350kg	6°	-6° to +43°	13.5kg	360m/s	7,700m
105mm leFH18	28	1,985kg	56°	-6° to +40°	14.8kg	470m/s	10,675m
105mm M2A1	23	1,936kg	46°	-5° to +65°	15.0kg	470m/s	11,360m
114mm 4.5	13	1,370kg	6°	-5° to +45°	16.0kg	306m/s	6,360m

75mm Krupp L/30 and Hanyang L/29 Field Gun

One of the earlier of the modern field guns, this design was clearly dated by the mid-1930s. It utilized a closed box trail that limited the elevation (and hence range), although additional elevation could be obtained by digging in the spade. The cradle had a vertical trunnion that sat in the transverse saddle, which itself was pivoted on the horizontal grunions in the trail brackets. The rear portion of the saddle formed the traversing bed, against which the elevating screw operated. As with similar field guns, the L/29 fired fixed ammunition, and the lack of a means to alter the muzzle velocity, along with

A Krupp L/30 field gun still in service at the FATC in 1943.

the small elevation range, reduced its utility in rough terrain. The weapon was also placed in production at the Hanyang Arsenal as the 29-caliber field gun, to which the data here refer.

75mm French Mle. 1897 Field Gun

The most widely used light field in the world in 1939, this was a relative late-comer to the Chinese theater. The gun used a built-up barrel and a Nordenfelt eccentric screw breech. An unusual feature of the weapon was the provision of a reinforcing band with two rollers beneath it at the muzzle end of the barrel. This was necessitated by the long recoil, the rollers engaging the cradle slides in the latter part of the recoil movement. The weapon had a pole trail, limiting elevation, and a 7-piece shield. Ammunition was of the fixed type. The gun was sturdy and reliable, but apparently saw little action in China, at least until after 1945.

Modèle 1897 75mm gun.

75mm Italian M1911 Field Gun

This was a license-built version of the French Deport M11 field gun and was better known by its Italian Army designation of 75/27 M1911. The split trails and spade plates were innovative when the gun was introduced, these permitting an exceptional elevation that gave it a long range for its time. An unusual feature was that the recoil mechanism remained fixed in a horizontal orientation even when the barrel was elevated.

An Italian 75/27 M1911 showing off its maximum elevation. The recoil mechanism projects horizontally forward to the left of the wheels.

76mm Soviet M1902/30 Field Gun

In 1930 the Soviets launched a modernization of their old M1902 Putilov field guns to yield the M1902/30. The modernization included lengthening the barrel and opening a hole in the trail for increased elevation. The weapon had a shield and a distinctive curved open-box trail. As modified they were sturdy and powerful weapons, but their flat trajectory limited their usefulness.

An M1902/30 field gun at the FATC in December 1943.

75mm Japanese Type 38/Improved Type 38 & Shenyang Type 13 Field Gun

Adopted by the Japanese Army in 1905 the Type 38 was a derivation of the Krupp design of the same period. It utilized a sliding-wedge breechblock and a hydrospring recoil mechanism. The cradle was trunnioned to the upper carriage at the point of balance, eliminating the need for an equilibrator. It had a closed-box trail that limited maximum elevation and had steel-rimmed wooden wheels.

A modernization program was undertaken by the Japanese starting in 1915. The main objective was to increase elevation (and hence range). This was done by adopting an open-box trail, through which the breech could recoil, and moving the trunnions

A row of Japanese Type 38 improved field guns. Note the open-box trails.

closer to the breech, with the concomitant addition of two spring-and-cable equilibrators. At the same time the hydrospring recoil mechanism was modified from a constant to a variable type, increasing the rate of fire slightly.

The Shenyang Arsenal placed the basic Type 38 field gun into production as the Type 13 75mm gun.

A Type 38 field gun in firing position.

77mm Type 14 Field Gun

This was the Bohler 76.5mm M18 field gun, introduced into the Austro-Hungarian Army near the end of WWI. Machine tools and components were purchased from Bohler in 1922 by the Shenyang Arsenal, which placed it in production as the Type 14. For unknown reasons the gun was bored out to 77.7mm by the Shenyang engineers. The gun had a horizontally sliding breechblock and the carriage an open-box trail that gave full elevation, yielding good range. The weapon featured cross-axle traverse, hydrospring recoil, and spring equilibrators.

Right: Two views of the 77mm Type 14 field gun.

Type 14 field guns with limbers on parade in Manchuria.

88mm Type 18 Field Gun

This was the 8.8cm type Z.A. field gun that Krupp had developed at the end of World War I but had been unable to place in production in time. The production machinery

and some components were purchased by the Taiyuan Arsenal and it was made there as the Type 18 (1929) field gun. It used a horizontally sliding breechblock and an open-box trail that gave good range but limited the traverse somewhat. A solid, modern design for the 1930s, it appears that little ammunition was built and it played little if any role in the fighting.

The Krupp 8.8cm Z.A. field gun.

105mm Type 14 Field Howitzer

This hybrid weapon consisted of the carriage of the Bohler M18 (Shenyang Type 14) 77mm gun and the ordnance of the 100mm Skoda M14 howitzer, bored out to 105mm caliber.

The production machinery and components had been obtained by the Shenyang Arsenal in 1922. This weapon never entered service in Austria-Hungary and the Type 14 was rarely used, so little information is available on the weapon. It had an open-box trail that permitted good elevation but the axle-traverse mechanism meant it had limited traverse. It utilized hydro-spring recoil and spring equilibrators. It was a fairly light weapon for its type, which undoubtedly recommended it for Chinese use.

A Type 14 howitzer in Japanese service after capture.

105mm German leFH18 Field Howitzer

This Rheinmetall design was the first modern light artillery piece to be received by China. It was of conventional construction, with split trails with folding spades, allowing good traverse and elevation ranges. The recoil system placed the buffer in the cradle and the hydropneumatic recuperator above the

German 105mm leFH18.

barrel. A single hydropneumatic equilibrator was fitted. The ammunition fired was of the separate-loading type, with six charges in the cartridge case. The weapon was a sound, rugged design and was highly regarded in Chinese service, but required motor draft.

105mm US M2A1 Field Howitzer

The M2A1 was the standard light artillery piece in the US Army and was provided to China under Lend-Lease. It was one of the few artillery pieces in Chinese service optimized for motor transport. It fired semi-fixed ammunition, with both HE and smoke being provided

An M2A1 howitzer of the New 6th Army in Hunan in June 1945.

to China. The weapon used a constant-length hydropneumatic recoil system, and a single-unit spring-type equilibrator compensated for mounting the trunnions well to the rear. The split-trail design gave good traverse and it was designed with exceptionally high elevation to yield useful plunging fire. The elevating mechanism could be operated from either side of the carriage. It was a modern and useful design, although its distribution was limited by the need for trucks and the fact that all ammunition had to come through Yunnan province.

4.5-inch (114mm) British Field Howitzer

This elderly piece, placed in production in 1908, was supplied by the Soviets, who had acquired them from a variety of sources after the First World War. The ammunition was separately loaded, with five charges contained in a brass case. The weapon had a horizontal sliding breechblock, a variable hydrospring recoil system, a shield, and an open-box trail to permit high elevation. Although fairly light by the standards of field howitzers, it was still a little too heavy for the limited resources and poor roads of China and its tactical utility was limited by its short range.

A Chinese 4.5-inch howitzer.

28

Medium Artillery

The poor road system in most of China limited the utility of weapons heavier than light field guns. The imperial government appears to have purchased none and its successor warlords, with but few exceptions, showed no more interest

Initially the most common of the weapons were the various Chinese copies of the Japanese 15cm Type 38 howitzer, an elderly weapon with short range. The Shenyang Arsenal built 21 of these (designated the Type 14) between 1925 and 1931. The Taiyuan Arsenal also built some during the 1920s, probably about the same number. Shenyang also put the Japanese 105mm Type 38 gun into brief production that ceased after only 12 had been built. In all cases the loss of the armories (Shenyang to the Japanese, Taiyuan to neglect) also spelt the end of ammunition production and as a result the weapons appear to have fallen out of use by about 1940. Fourteen of the 15cm Type 14s were still on strength with I War Zone in 1945, but these were held at schools and little ammunition seems to have been available.

Of more lasting import was the influence of the German advisory team. They persuaded the KMT that a small number of powerful, motorized heavy field howitzers would serve as an exemplary reserve of firepower for the central government. In mid-1934 a competition was held between three models of 15cm howitzer, one each from Skoda, Krupp, and Rheinmetall. The Skoda was quickly eliminated leaving the two weapons that

A Chinese 15cm howitzer, probably a Type 14, in defense of Nanjing early in the war.

One of the Henschel tractors used by the Chinese to tow the 15cm German howitzers.

were also competing back home for the German Army requirement, an L/30 weapon from Krupp and a very similar, but longer-barreled L/32 from Rheinmetall.

The two firms were competing solely on price in China, and in early September Krupp proposed a deal to their competitor: they would abandon the heavy field howitzer competition, if they were allowed to supply light field howitzers and cross-country light trucks without competition, and provide logistical support for 75mm mountain guns and AA guns. It is not clear if this proposal was accepted, but a contract was placed with Rheinmetall for 24 weapons, ammunition, and prime movers. The question of the prime movers was a troublesome one. Büssing tractors were tried, but proved under-powered for the task and too complicated. In the end the 6x4 Henschel Model 33 tractor was selected, for lack of an alterative, although it was regarded as too heavy for local conditions. Nevertheless, the Henschels and other German vehicles supporting them served through to the end of the war. In April 1935 a delegation from the Ordnance Office arrived in Germany with Chinese seals and plates and accepted and marked the howitzers the following month. On arrival they were used to form the 10th Artillery Regiment.

A second order was placed in 1936, but the Rheinmetall models were no longer offered, having lost the German Army competition to Krupp, so the Chinese accepted the Krupp L/30, now standardized as the sFH18 in Germany and manufactured by both firms. The total number appears to have been 48, including 16 delivered in 1937 and the final 8 in March 1938. These were formed into the 13th and 14th Artillery Regiments. The two orders were accompanied by a large shipment of ammunition, at least 37,000 rounds of which passed through Hong Kong during 1937–8.

Following heavy losses in the 1937 campaigns, the 150mm German howitzers appear to have been carefully husbanded, for by early 1942 there were still 44 available, although by May 1945 the number had dropped to 15 Rheinmetall L/32 and 18 Krupp L/30 models.

An officer familiarization course on the 15cm L/32 howitzer.

The ammunition supply was adequate at about 1,000 rounds per gun, but only because they were not often used. The US did provide propellant formulated for the German 15cm weapons starting in 1943, but that may well have been aimed simply at keeping the stockpile fresh. In late 1944 the Chinese government requested the supply of 15cm German ammunition captured by the Allies in Europe and Middle East and 4,400 HE and 1,778 anti-concrete projectiles with 11,000 propellant charges were shipped to India in early 1945, but made it no further due to the limited transport capacity thence into China.

Medium Artillery Specifications								
	Barrel length (calibers)	Weight (firing position)	Traverse	Elevation	Projectile weight	Muzzle velocity	Range
105mm Type 14 Gun	32	2,594kg	8°	-2° to +15°	18kg	540m/s	11,000m
150mm Type 38 Howitzer	12	2,091kg	4°	0° to +43°	36kg	276m/s	5,915m
150mm Shenyang Type 14 Howitzer	12	1,852kg	3°	0° to +43°	36kg	275m/s	5,900m
150mm sFH18 Howitzer	30	5,512kg	64°	-3° to +45°	43kg	495m/s	13,250m
150mm Rheinmetall L/32 Howitzer	32	5,650kg	64°	0° to +45°	43kg	598m/s	15,300m
155mm M1918 Howitzer	15	3,720kg	6°	0° to +42°	43kg	447m/s	11,270m

A 15cm L/30 howitzer firing in practice at the Artillery Training Center.

As early as January 1942 Stilwell had asked for 36 old-style (horse-drawn) 155mm howitzers with 1,500 rounds each for China from the US. Later that year 36 motor-drawn 155mm M1918 howitzers on M1917A4 carriages were shipped to Ramgahr, along with 44 heavy trucks for draft and 48,000 rounds of HE ammunition, and formed an artillery regiment for the support of the CAI. By the end of 1944 the ammunition figures had increased to 60,614 rounds of HE and 1,808 of smoke. These weapons supported the CAI in its drive across Burma in 1944–5, but played no role in the battles in China itself. At various times proposals were floated to provide up to 100 more of these heavy weapons, and about two dozen actually made it to India outside of Lend-Lease channels, but none went farther due to their limited mobility in Burma and China.

105mm Type 14 Gun

This was the Japanese 105mm Type 38 gun built by the Shenyang Arsenal. The single box trail restricted elevation, which in turn severely limited range. It utilized a combined hydrospring recoil system and a spring recuperator. The relatively short barrel and rear placement of the trunions meant that no equilibrator was needed. It fired fixed ammunition, probably limited to HE.

A Shenyang Type 14 105mm gun in firing position.

150mm Japanese Type 38 / Shenyang Type 14 / Taiyuan 15cm Howitzer

The original Japanese Meiji Type 38 was derived from the Krupp 15cm L/12 howitzer, which was then copied by the Shenyang and Taiyuan Arsenals. The Shenyang version was lighter by about 200kg than the Japanese original. This utilized an interrupted-screw breech and an open-box trail, along with a combined hydrospring recoil system with tapered grooves, and a spring recuperator. There were no equilibrators. The ammunition was separate loading, with three propellant charges available. The weapon was normally drawn by eight horses. With their short range, these were obsolete by the mid-1930s. The data shown are for the Shenyang Type 14.

A Japanese Type 38 15cm howitzer. (*Volz*)

150mm sFH18 Howitzer

This modern piece was the standard heavy field howitzer of the German Army during WWII. In Chinese service it was commonly known as the L/30 to distinguish it from the similar L/32 versions also in use. It used a horizontal-sliding breechblock and fired separate-loading ammunition. Eight charges were nominally available, but the top two (which would extend the range to 13,250 meters) were not normally fired by the German Army and may not have been provided to China. The weapon was motor-drawn on a single axle with pressed-steel wheels and solid rubber tires, with a limber carrying the trails.

The German sFH18 heavy howitzer.

150mm Rheinmetall L/32 Howitzer

This was generally similar to the competitor Krupp sFH18 and fired the same projectiles, but featured a slightly longer barrel. The two can be easily distinguished by the longer (taller) equilibrators on the longer-barrel Rheinmetall.

A Chinese 15cm L/32 howitzer with tractor.

155mm M1918 Howitzer

The US supplied the M1918 howitzer (the American version of the Schnieder C17) on the M1917A3 carriage, which had been adapted for high-speed towing without a limber. It fired separately loaded ammunition with seven charge ranges. This gave quite a bit of flexibility in firing, but was partly negated by the old-style box trail that limited traverse significantly. Nevertheless, although not as modern as the German 15cm howitzers, it was lighter and threw a heavy shell to a useful range.

A Chinese 155mm M1918 preparing for action in Lashio, Burma, in 1945.

29

Light Anti-Aircraft Weapons

As elsewhere, little attention was paid to low-level air defense in China in the 1920s. Airpower played only a very minor role in the campaigns of the Northern Expedition and until 1932 there was no serious air threat. To the extent units in the field needed protection against low-flying aircraft the requirement could reasonably be filled with the standard Maxim machine gun. To this end several arsenals built anti-aircraft adapters for the field machine-gun mount that added a long pedestal enabling high-angle fire. In this configuration the weapon used a cylindrical magazine on the side with an enclosed spool around which the belt was wrapped, necessary since the feed mechanism could not pull the heavy belts all the way up from the ground.

By the mid-1920s several European firms were finally offering dedicated light anti-aircraft guns for sale and China was one of the first purchasers. The Swiss firm of SEMAG was the pioneer and had had some small success in selling a few of its 20mm automatic cannon to at least one of the warlords in the early 1920s.

When Oerlikon took over the SEMAG product line it refined the designs and in 1927 introduced the new "Modell S" firing the more powerful 20 x 110RB round still in use today. The weapon was a multi-purpose gun designed to be used both for infantry support and anti-aircraft. With AP ammunition it could also be used against the tanks of the period, although it is not clear if such ammunition was purchased by China. In fact, these guns were distributed as infantry guns in infantry regiments of the 19th Route Army and the 5th Army, although these do not show up in any official TO&E. In the ground role it could be fired from its wheeled mount. For anti-aircraft use the wheels were removed and a tubular-frame rectangular mount was set on the ground and extended upwards to give high elevation. The weapon fired from a 15-round box magazine and the time from wheels to AA mount for a trained

A Type 24 machine gun on AA mount on prewar exercises in Suiyuan province, 1937.

crew was less than one minute. The usefulness of such a weapon for infantry support was limited, with its light projectile and flat trajectory; the anti-aircraft mount does not appear to have been very stable, particularly when firing to the side.

A 20mm Modell S of the 19th Route Army in the infantry
support mode outside Shanghai in 1932.

Nevertheless, Oerlikon concluded a sale of an initial batch of 10 of these Modell S guns to China in December 1928. They were apparently well-liked for a second order was placed in June 1929 for a further 90, and a few months later for 104 simple Zeiss M/4a anti-aircraft sights. A final order for 20 guns was placed in 1930. All the weapons came with the infantry mount with the high-angle AA adaptor and five extra magazines per gun. The weapons were supplied with at least 54,000 rounds of HE, HE-I, HE-T, and training ammunition, and there may have been other types. They were used extensively in the 1932 fighting in Shanghai. German advisers had thought the guns too complex for the troops, but the Chinese commanders reported no stoppages except to enemy action and they were quite popular. A further 52,000 rounds of ammunition to replace combat expenditure were purchased in April 1933. Combat losses and wear seem to have reduced the numbers available to about 50 by 1942 and they do not appear to have played much of a role after that time.

The emergence of Japan as a likely enemy, rather than ill-equipped warlords, spurred the development of an air defense force for the protection of cities, airfields, and vital points such as bridges. A competition was held for the role of low-level air-defense gun in mid-1932.

Two competitors for this role quickly emerged. Vickers had reworked its .5-inch heavy machine gun design in the mid-1920s to accept the more powerful 12.7 x 120SR cartridge, in lieu of the underpowered standard 12.7 x 81mm round. This ammunition featured two types of steel-jacketed ball ammunition, one with a lead filler in the back half and a light alloy in the nose (like the .303 Mk VII ball) and another with a mild steel core with a lead tip filler. Known as the .5-inch Class D machine gun, this heavy, water-cooled design was a commercial failure, slightly fewer than 100 being built, of which China purchased 20 in November 1932, along with 34,000 rounds of ammunition (subcontracted to ICI). A further 44,000 rounds (in 10:1 ball/tracer mix) was ordered three years later. This was China's only purchase, however; an effort to sell an additional 24 guns in early 1936 was frustrated by the lower prices and longer payment periods offered by the competing Hotchkiss design.

The more successful competitor to the .5-inch Class D was the Hotchkiss 13.2mm, which underwent its trials with the French Army in 1927 and was accepted for service there in 1930. The Chinese apparently began purchases shortly thereafter.

By mid-1933 a diminutive light AA regiment had been formed at Beijing with 12 Vickers Class D and 4 single-barrel Hotchkiss 13.2mm in one battalion, and a total of 32 twin-barrel Hotchkiss weapons in two other battalions. A further 100 single-barrel Hotchkiss weapons were held in storage for use by the field army, although the army purchased 20mm weapons for its use and the single-mount 13.2mm weapons remained with the air-defense forces.

The twin-mount guns were actually too heavy for the firepower they put out given the poor roads in China, so procurement shifted to the single-mount version. Two batches totaling 30 weapons were purchased and delivered in 1932, followed by no fewer than 267 in 1933, 44 in 1935, and then 8 in 1936 and early 1937. The final purchases came in August 1937 for 2 more guns, then, at the end of November 1937, 20 guns, these being delivered in January 1938. These brought total procurement to no fewer than 478, all of them for the central government except six purchased by the Guangdong provincial government in 1936.

Officers of the Light AA Regiment at Beijing inspect a
twin-mount 13.2mm Hotchkiss in 1932.

Prewar purchases of 13.2mm ammunition were mostly from Hotchkiss, 1.7 million rounds before the outbreak of the war, along with a small batch of 20,000 rounds from Italy. A further 2,240,000 were ordered from France and Belgium in late 1937 and early 1938. After the start of the war China had to scramble for ammunition suppliers and between December 1937 and October 1938 took delivery of 1.6 million rounds of 13.2mm from the UK and 636,000 from

Troops of the AA Company, 2nd Division, practice bringing their S5-100 into action in July 1944.

Belgium. A further 181,000 from Britain and 192,000 from Belgium arrived via Rangoon in 1939. The ammunition supplied included normal ball, AP, and tracer in varying mixes. In addition, China purchased 10,000kg of propellant for 13.2mm ammunition from France in 1933, but it is not clear how much ammunition was actually locally produced. In early 1938 China approached Hotchkiss for the sale of a further 300–500 of the 13.2mm weapons in single and double mounts and in March the firm requested export permission from the French government. Preliminary approval was granted in July, but by that time France was rearming and final approval was denied.

The Air Defense Force may have been happy with the 13.2mm weapon but the field army was sticking with the 20mm. If the Modell S had proven its value as an infantry gun in the 1932 fighting in Shanghai, it was clearly far from ideal as an anti-aircraft weapon. The heavy recoil and highly leveraged mount in the AA mode caused accuracy to suffer. This failing had not escaped the notice of the European designers, and both Solothurn and Oerlikon responded with new, more stable, mounts. By the early 1930s Oerlikon had realized that the firing height of the weapon had to be lowered

A Chinese 20mm Breda in action.

A 37mm Flak 18 in Chinese service.

significantly to achieve stability and that geared traverse and elevation were necessary for accuracy of aiming. These resulted in the mating of the Type S gun with a new mount, the JLa, to yield the JLaS anti-aircraft gun. Oerlikon was not to be alone, for Rheinmetall's Swiss subsidiary Solothurn had come to the same conclusion. Its solution was similar (indeed, the Oerlikon and Solothurn mounts were almost identical), and was titled the Type S5-100. The main difference was in the ammunition, with Oerlikon continuing to use the 20 x 110RB of the Modell S, while Solothurn opted for the more powerful 20 x 138B.

Solothurn was first into this new market, aided by the German advisory mission. An initial order for about 70 appears to have been placed in the winter of 1932/33, with deliveries starting about 1933.* An immediate follow-on order for 60 more S5-100s was placed in 1933, but this was annulled as a result, according to the Germans, of intervention by the Italian politician Count Ciano then visiting China, and was replaced by a similar size order for Breda 20mm M.33 L/65 guns. These weapons remained in service (some of them mounted on railroad cars) through the war, and in 1942 the Army Ordnance Office reported holdings of 111 Solothurn and 35 "other" 20mm AA guns, but by then the Bredas' ammunition supply must have been running low, although they shared the same ammunition as the Solothurns. For example the 1st Army had only 200 rounds for each of the eight Breda guns held by its AA battalion in early 1945, or less than one minute's worth of firing.

---

* The contract was for 130 weapons and 200,000 rounds, but about half were actually destined for the secret rearming of Germany.

Solothurn S5-100 guns, like this camouflaged piece, provided
the bulk of the low-level air defense through the war.

Ordered at the same time as the Solothurn 20mm was the Hotchkiss 25mm, albeit in modest numbers. A single gun was purchased in February 1933 for trials and delivered immediately. These were apparently successful for a second order, for four guns and 40,000 rounds (along with 6,000kg of propellant for local ammunition manufacture), was placed in May of that year and delivered in October. A third order for four more guns and 24,000 rounds was placed in March 1936, this time by the Guangdong provincial government, and these were delivered in June 1937. In August a further eight guns were ordered, along with 26,000 rounds of ammunition, and these were delivered in early 1938. The central government requested quotes for eight twin-mount 25mm AA guns and an unspecified number of single-barrel 25mm guns in mid-1938, and Hotchkiss secured French government permission for export in August, although the deal does not appear to have been consummated. The final delivery of 3,400 rounds of 25mm ammunition occurred in July 1938. Shortages of ammunition restricted their use and they appear to have been withdrawn from service by early 1942.

The largest contract for light anti-aircraft material, placed in March 1936, came via Hapro, the German arms agency for China, and Rheinmetall. This covered 120 S5-100 and 3,000 rounds per gun and 60 37mm Flak 18 also with 3,000 rounds per gun. The first batch of each type of gun rolled out of the factories in September 1936 and production was completed in February 1937. Deliveries of the Solothurn were all but finished before the outbreak of China's war, although many of the 37mm appear to have been on the high seas when the war broke out and were not delivered until March 1938 via Hong Kong.

The S5-100s provided the backbone of the Chinese field army's low-level air defense through the war, with 111 weapons still in service in March 1942. By August 1942 50 of the Flak 18s remained in service, but with only 6,000 rounds of ammunition available their usefulness was limited.

Oerlikon, without a German sponsor, fared less well than their fellow Swiss competitor. On 9 September 1937 the Hunan provincial government placed an order for 20 JLaS AA guns and 40,000 rounds of 20mm ammunition. Each gun would be accompanied by a spare barrel, five 15-round magazines, a sight and a tool box. These guns were delivered to Hong Kong aboard the SS *Sophie Rickmers* on 18 November 1937 and departed via the Kowloon–Guangzhou Railway by the end of the year.

There were two further deliveries of this Oerlikon model, each of four guns and 8,000 rounds, this time for the 5th Route Army in Guangxi. The first arrived and departed Hong Kong in January 1938 and the second in March 1938. Oerlikons remained in service, although once again ammunition shortages probably severely reduced their usefulness.

A captured Chinese Oerlikon in traveling mode. (*Osamu Shimoharaguchi*)

In 1937 Madsen demonstrated two of its heavier weapons, the 20mm automatic cannon on the "Universal" (AA) mount and on the F5 (ground) mount. Both were selected for use, with the F5s to be purchased directly and the Universal mount and gun to be built at the new 51st Arsenal. An initial batch of 18 AA guns was funded and these were produced in January 1938 and delivered to Guangzhou in April. Production tools were delivered

The Madsen 20mm on Universal mount at its China trials in 1937. Just visible behind the row of soldiers is the 20mm F5 AT gun which was purchased directly from Madsen.

via the Burma Road, but were destroyed by Japanese bombing after crossing the Chinese border in June 1940. The 51st Arsenal gave up the attempt to build the Madsen 20mm, but the 21st Arsenal took up the challenge. The first gun was turned out in November 1944, but only three more were completed before the war ended production.

Once the war broke out China, in desperation, turned to the UK, hardly a world leader in low- and medium-level air defense at the time. All that could be purchased were six 40mm 2pdr guns and 18,000 rounds of ammunition for £42,685 in late 1937. These were naval equipment, on pedestals fitted for bolting to ships' decks. The one-man sighting and aiming system was designed to take input from the ship's director of target speed, course, and altitude, but this was not available here, rendering them, according to a visiting British artillery officer, "practically useless." They were delivered in June 1938 and set up at Nampo, on the Guangdong–Guangxi border, in early 1939 where they were manned by the battalion that formerly held the Vickers 75mm AA guns, but no more was heard of them after that.

Two photos of GIs training Chinese soldiers on the M2 water-cooled machine gun on M2A2 mount, astride the Burma Road in August 1944.

Light AA Gun Specifications

	Ammunition	Weight	Barrel length	Cyclic rate of fire	Practical rate of fire
.50-cal. M2 machine gun	12.7 x 99mm	215kg	1.14m	600rpm	n/a
.5-inch Vickers D	12.7 x 120SR	n/a	1.14m	450rpm	n/a
13.2mm Hotchkiss single	13.2 x 99mm	n/a	1.65m	450rpm	n/a
Oerlikon Modell S	20 x 110mm	197kg	1.4m	300rpm	100rpm
Oerlikon JlaS	20 x 110mm	185kg	1.4m	300rpm	100rpm
Madsen on F7	20 x 120mm	248kg	1.2m	400rpm	175rpm
Solothurn S5-100	20 x 138mm	260kg	1.3m	300rpm	200rpm
Breda Model 33	20 x 138mm	308kg	1.3m	220rpm	n/a
25mm Hotchkiss	25 x 163mm	850kg	1.5m	350rpm	n/a
37mm Flak 18	37 x 263mm	1,748kg	2.1m	160rpm	80rpm
Bofors L/60	40 x 311mm	1,920kg	2.25m	120rpm	90rpm
40mm M1	40 x 311mm	2,522kg	2.25m	120rpm	n/a

The Soviets were responsible for introducing yet another type of ammunition for the light anti-aircraft park. The final, overland, shipment of arms from the USSR in early 1941 was planned to include 30 37mm AA guns, but such weapons do not show up in any Chinese inventory from 1942. It seems almost certain that the Soviets substituted 40mm Bofors guns captured in Poland. The Chinese Ordnance Department did report the presence of 34 Bofors 40mm in the spring of 1940, but with only 1,600 rounds of ammunition.

The German invasion in 1941 stopped all further shipments from the Soviets. China had been made eligible for American Lend-Lease but the US had little to offer except the venerable water-cooled .50-cal. M2 machine gun. Among the pre-Pearl Harbor items on the Lend-Lease list were 285 of these weapons (although with only 249 AA tripod mounts), along with 1.7 million rounds of ammunition, these being intended for the air defense of the Burma Road. These arrived in Rangoon in early 1942, where 40 were turned over to the British for the defense of Burma. The remainder, along with about 950,000 rounds of ammunition, had arrived in China by June 1942. These were used to form two light AA regiments and portions moved back into northern Burma.

The .50-cal. machine gun was a reliable and versatile weapon, but both the gun and ammunition were heavy compared to rifle-caliber weapons, and, as the Japanese drew off air strength for the Pacific Theater, the need for anti-aircraft machine guns declined. In fact, the division TO&Es for both the army in India and Y-Force did not include any .50-cal. machine guns. The only such weapons authorized were the 48 water-cooled guns in the CAI's anti-aircraft battalion. There were some intra-theater transfers in Yunnan from US units sent there for air defense, but even that yielded only 58 weapons, 6 each in the 116th and 130th Divisions of the 53rd Army, 12 in the 2nd Army, and 34 as training weapons with the 5th Army.

Although no .50-cals were authorized for the Chinese Army in China, Lend-Lease requirements were inexplicably calculated on the basis of 12 water-cooled .50-cal. machine guns per division. An allocation of 100 weapons from the January 1943 production, when combined with the 285 shipped earlier, more than met the requirements for the first 30 divisions. A further 352 were allocated from production in February–July of that year to complete the requirements for the second batch of 30 divisions with some to spare. All had been exported by early 1944. The fact that these weapons were not actually authorized for forces in China, combined with the difficulty of transporting them over the Hump, meant that they never made it. Thus, no fewer than 534 air-cooled and 402 water-cooled weapons had accumulated in depots in India by the end of January 1945 when they were finally released for other uses, none having been distributed to Chinese forces.

Chiang had insisted on including 300 40mm Bofors guns in the Lend-Lease aid package, against the objections of the US War Department. The first 180 of these were to be supplied by the US as the 40mm M1. With their directors they were too heavy and bulky for practical employment in the mountainous jungles of Burma and there was no hope that they could compete with other Chinese needs for tonnage on the Hump, but to placate the Generalissimo the 180 weapons were allocated from US production in early 1943. These finally arrived in late 1944. The other 120 were allocated from Canadian production and an initial batch of 48 had been delivered by July 1944. At that point the US China Theater command sent a message telling Washington not to send any more and noting that 80 of the guns already present in India had been transferred to US units. By mid-April 1945 only 49 guns, with directors, generators, and remote-control systems, had been shipped from India to China. All of them, except one gun sent to the AA School at Kweiyang, had been distributed (with American advisers) in twelve 4-gun batteries for the defense of seven airfields in the south and east.

.50-caliber M2 Machine Gun

Still in widespread first-line service 80 years after its introduction, the .50-cal. M2 machine gun has proven to be reliable and hard-hitting. The Chinese received theirs in the original water-cooled configuration with high-angle tripod mounts for anti-aircraft fire. The weapon was recoil-operated and fired from 110-round fabric or disintegrating-link belts. Cooling was by means of a water jacket with a capacity of 9.5 liters connected to a condensing can. Sights were conventional, a covered blade in the front and a folding-leaf rear sight with adjustments for windage and elevation, although a speed-ring sight could also be fitted.

GIs with a water-cooled M2 with speed-ring sight in Assam.

.5-inch Vickers Class D Machine Gun

This utilized the standard Vickers water-cooled short-recoil operating principles, but scaled up to take advantage of a new, more powerful cartridge. Most Vickers heavy-caliber machine guns, the Class B weapons, used the low-powered 12.7 x 81mm round, but the firm saw the need for a more powerful weapon in the late 1920s and developed a new 12.7 x 120SR round that was actually more powerful than the round used in the Browning M2. The maximum vertical range claimed was 4,750 meters, but the effective AA range would probably have been around 1,000m. In any event, few were

A Chinese Vickers Class D in August 1937.

bought and ammunition would have been prohibitively difficult and expensive to acquire after the mid-1930s.

13.2mm Hotchkiss Machine Gun

The 13.2mm was the big brother of the generally successful Hotchkiss range of rifle-caliber machine guns. It was a gas-operated design fed from a 30-round overhead magazine. With its two-man crew and more complex sighting the weapon was more accurate than the .50-cal. M2, although it is open to question whether much benefit was actually gained with such a light weapon. It's usefulness was also somewhat limited by its small magazine and air-cooled barrel.

The 13.2mm Hotchkiss on the single-gun R1 mount.

20mm Solothurn S5-100

The competitor to its fellow Swiss JLaS, the S5-100 was similar in concept with a low-mounted gun, two-man crew with geared controls and wide-spread legs. The gun was developed by Ehrhardt and passed via Rheinmetall to Solothurn, and retained the recoiling barrel and rigidly locked breech of the original design. Compared to the Oerlikon, it fired a slightly heavier projectile at a slightly higher velocity due to the larger cartridge case. Ammunition feed was from a 20-round magazine on the left. The mounting was almost identical to the JLaS, providing 360° of traverse and 85° of elevation when fully set up. The weapon could be broken down into four loads for pack transport.

The S5-100 in traveling position (*above right*) and firing position (*right*).

20mm Oerlikon Modell S

The Modell S was the first of the famous range of Oerlikon 20mm products and was derived directly from the SEMAG gun, to which Oerlikon acquired the rights. The gun itself was an exceptionally sound design that remained in production even through the end of WWII. The mount, however, left quite a bit to be desired. It was adequate in the ground-fire role as an infantry-support weapon, which was the primary role of the Chinese weapons, but when extended to its rickety high-angle mode it provided little stability, to the detriment of accuracy. It used the API blowback system common to Oerlikon products. The top-mounted 15-round magazine distinguished Oerlikons from the Solothurn products. The weapon could break down into nine loads, the heaviest of which weighed 60kg.

A Modell S of the 19th Route Army in hasty anti-aircraft mode in 1932.

20mm Oerlikon JLaS

The inability of the Modell S to fire in the AA mode with accuracy was recognized and the same 20mm gun was mounted on a new carriage as the JLaS (Jnfanterie Lafette S) starting around 1930. The gun was mounted closer to the ground, the legs extended out, and geared traverse and elevation for two men were added. Stub axles on two wheels were fitted to the mount for towing, although it could also be dis-assembled into six loads for pack transport.

A JLaS demonstrated at the factory.

20mm Breda Model 33

Predecessor of the well-known Model 35 adopted by the Italian Army, the commercial Model 33 differed from the later version mainly in the use of wooden-spoke wheels. The gun crew (not counting loaders) consisted of three: the gunner in the seat (traverse and elevation), one to set the lead (on the left) and one to set off the data on the sight (on the right). The gun was fed by 12-round strips. It was designed to be pulled by a single animal, but could also be drawn by hand or carried by four pack animals.

Breda Model 33.

20mm Madsen gun on F7 "Universal" Mount

This was actually the standard Madsen machine gun scaled up to 20mm. It was thus a short-recoil weapon, and fired from 10- or 15-round magazines. The ammunition used was unique to Madsen weapons, although produced in Britain, and would presumably have been in short supply after 1942.

A Madsen 20mm on F7 mount in traveling position in China for a demonstration.

25mm Hotchkiss

Developed as a result of the firm's belief that the 20mm caliber was too small to be effective, the 25mm used a scaled-up version of the gas-operated system employed by the 13.2mm heavy machine gun. The ammunition was fed from 15-round box magazines and the 9-man crew could bring it into action in 3 minutes from the traveling position. Ironically, the weapon saw most of its use in the Japanese-built version, several thousand being built there during the war.

Hotchkiss 25mm AA gun in the firing position.

37mm Flak 18

Although not as capable as its contemporary, the famous Bofors 40mm L/60, the Rheinmetall 37mm Flak 18 was a competent and reliable weapon. Nevertheless, the Germans found it heavy and cumbersome for its firepower, and it had been replaced in German Army production by a lighter model after only a small number had been built in 1935–6. The gun used a rotary-locked short-recoil operating system in which the cocking handle on the bolt traveled in a slot in the receiver that curved as it neared battery, twisting the bolt and locking it to the barrel. It fired its ammunition from an eight-round clip. The mounting was a cruciform platform that for transport was carried on a pair of two-wheeled limbers.

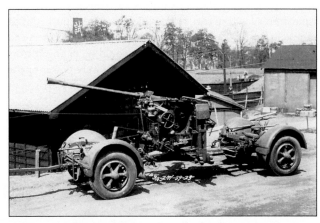

A Chinese Flak 18 on its wheels after capture by Japanese forces in December 1937.

Bofors 40mm L/60

The famous Bofors 40mm was the best-known and most widely used light/medium AA gun of the war. The gun was mounted low on the carriage with trunnions well to the rear, using twin equilibrators to balance the load. The gun was fired from a cross-shaped mount (although firing from the wheels was possible in an emergency). Two gunners (one for elevation, one for traverse) aimed the weapon via two-handed handles. Ammunition was fed into the autoloader in four-round clips from the top. The Polish-made guns received by China lacked the facility for central fire control found on Swedish models.

A Bofors 40mm at the factory in Sweden.

40mm M1 Anti-Aircraft Gun

This was the US-built version of the famous Bofors 40mm L/60 gun, one of the outstanding weapons of its type. The gun was recoil-operated with a vertical-sliding breechblock. The automatic loading mechanism took cartridges from 4-round clips and fed them, one at a time, into a loading tray, from which they were pushed into the chamber by a mechanical rammer. The M2 carriage provided front and rear girders and two hinged outriggers carried on two 2-wheel axle trees. The gun could be changed from the traveling position to the firing position in 25 seconds. The US guns were power-operated and remotely controlled by an M5 director, the US adaptation of the British Kerrison predictor.

The 40mm M1 gun on its carriage but ready for fire.

30

Heavy Anti-Aircraft Guns

The paucity of combat aircraft in China made heavy AA guns relative latecomers. The Zhili forces purchased a small number of truck-mounted Italian 76/40 AA guns (copies of the British 12pdr) in the early 1920s, but these appear to have been reduced to static mounts by the mid-1930s and saw little if any combat use. The Shenyang Arsenal placed a 75mm AA gun in production as the Type 16, but sources disagree on what it was. It was probably the Japanese Type 11 AA gun. It could, however, have been the barrel of the Type 38 field gun, which they already had in production, placed on a Japanese-type high-angle pedestal mount. The exact model is largely irrelevant, however, for only four were produced and it seems unlikely they survived the Japanese take-over in 1931.

The fighting in Shanghai in 1932 brought home the need for protection against enemy aircraft. Late that year an order was placed with the German firm of Carlowitz & Co. of Hamburg and Nanjing for five modern AA batteries. The guns chosen were the Bofors 75mm L/50 and 20 were delivered in batches of four between May and December 1933. These were accompanied by Bofors HE ammunition with Krupp clockwork time fuzes, Hungarian Gamma fire control systems (one per battery), and German rangefinders. German searchlights and sound locators followed shortly thereafter. Originally the ammunition came from Sweden, but there appears to have been local license production as well. This local production could not keep up with wartime demands and in 1938 the government contracted with Hungary (which built an 80mm version of the gun and its ammunition under license) and 16,000 rounds were delivered from that source to Yunnan in April–May 1939. The Bofors guns were apparently withdrawn in time during each retreat, for in March 1942 the

An Italian 76/40 AA gun of the Zhili forces in 1924.

Chinese Ordnance Bureau reported on hand 21 (!) guns and 24,000 rounds of ammunition.[*]

The combination of the Bofors guns and the old Gamma fire control system was showing its age by 1940. The same pairing was used by the Hungarians (albeit with their 80mm guns) and they reported that the combination was obsolete by 1942, unable to engage aircraft traveling faster than 360km/hr at 8,000 meters altitude.

A further eight guns were ordered in 1937, this time with German fire control and Zeiss optical rangefinders, but were never delivered, being taken over by the Swedish military in 1939.

Almost simultaneously, an order was placed with Vickers for 12 of their 75mm AA guns in February 1933, along with

A Bofors 75mm in service near Chongqing in March 1943.

three battery sets of equipment, each including a U.B.2 Barr & Stroud height finder and a Mk V Vickers predictor. Each gun was provided with a Vickers Carden-Loyd light tracked tractor and the fire control equipment with a VCL medium tractor. In addition, three searchlights and sound locators were provided, along with 12,000 rounds of ammunition. The last of the guns was shipped in December 1933. The guns were formed into a battalion for the defense of Guangzhou, where a visiting British artillery officer commented that sandbags had to be placed over the outriggers to keep the guns steady in action and that parts broke in the course of normal firing. They were lost there in the fall of the city in 1938. A few damaged guns were subsequently recovered and apparently put back into service but appear to have played no further role.

In October 1937 the Chinese ambassador to London had met with Lord Cadogan of the British Foreign Office and pressed for permission to place an order for twenty more Vickers 75mm AA guns with 2,000 rounds per gun to aid in the defense of Guangzhou. The War Office vetoed this, although it did permit accelerated production of an order for

---

[*] At least one Bofors 75mm was captured by the Japanese and reverse-engineered as their Type 4 AA gun.

a further 12,000 rounds placed in early 1938. It seems unlikely that they were delivered, however.

Possessing only two battalion-sets of heavy AA guns up to that point, the Chinese included such weapons in their request to the Soviets. The Soviets not only had their 76mm AA guns in large-scale production, but were about to convert to 85mm, and so could spare weapons. The initial Soviet aid package included five AA batteries, consisting of 20 7.62cm obr. 1931 guns with PUAZO-1 fire control stations, 4 searchlights, 2 sound locators, 30 Komintern tractors, and 40,000 rounds of ammunition, delivered to Guangzhou in February 1938. A further batch, of 20 obr. 1938 model guns with battery equipment, was delivered overland in late 1940. Two batteries of the earlier guns were lost in the defense of Guangzhou in October 1938, The bulk of the surviving guns, some 20, formed the backbone of the defense of Chongqing. A total of 32 guns were reported in service in March 1942.

Nevertheless, by 1938 almost all nations had concluded that the day of the 75mm/76mm anti-aircraft gun had passed. The ballistic coefficient of

Chinese soldiers man the UB2 optical rangefinder.

Vickers 75mm AA guns set up for airfield defense at Guangzhou in August 1937.

Chinese and US troops inspect a 76mm M1931 AA gun.

Komintern tractors, used to tow the 76mm Soviet AA
guns, at Liuzhou Station in September 1944.

the shells meant that they lost velocity quickly, which increased their time-to-altitude, thus rendering fire control very difficult in the case of modern fast-flying aircraft. In response, those nations turned to 85–94mm guns, which not only suffered less velocity decay, but also featured a larger lethal burst radius. China, however, was in no position to take advantage of this. Most of these guns were just entering production at the time and no one had guns to spare for sale.

The German coast-defense sale of 1934 included 10 8.8cm SKC 30 naval-type dual-purpose guns, followed by 10 more shortly thereafter. They were not modern long-barrel guns and had

Chinese troops with a German sound locator.

Heavy AA Gun Specifications

	Barrel length (calibers)	Weight (firing position)	Max. elevation	Projectile weight	Muzzle velocity	Max. altitude
75mm Vickers	40	2,464kg	90°	6.5kg	750m/s	9,235m
75mm Bofors	53	3,400kg	85°	6.5kg	840m/s	10,200m
76mm obr. 1931/38	52	3,750kg	82°	6.6kg	813m/s	9,000m
88mm SKC/30	45	5,760kg	80°	9.0kg	790m/s	9,700m

limited utility. These were emplaced primarily to support and defend the 15cm guns delivered at the same time, 8 in Jiang En Fortress, 8 in Jiang Nin (both by the Yangtze near Nanjing) and 4 in Baiwushan Fortress outside Wuhan. Being in static emplacements, all were quickly lost in the opening phases of the war and played no role in the conflict.

Chinese troops with a German AA searchlight.

Finally, the US shipped 24 90mm M1 AA guns (out of 28 originally allocated) to India en route to China in 1943 as part of Lend-Lease. Their subsequent fate is unknown, although they almost certainly did not make it to China before the end of the war.

A sound locator and searchlight position in 1942.

75mm Vickers AA Gun

China purchased the L/40 version of the Vickers 75mm (an L/46 was later offered). An unusual feature of the weapon was that the trunions were set well to the rear of the breech, allowing a low firing height. The gun was mounted on four tubular steel jackarms and featured a horizontal-sliding breech block and a replaceable barrel liner. The gunners aimed the weapon using a follow-the-pointer system of data from the Vickers predictors. Most users of the L/46 version were happy with their guns, but a British officer inspecting the Chinese weapons in early 1938 found them "much too lightly made." In any event, their Chinese service was sufficiently short that it probably made little difference.

The Vickers 75mm L/40 gun in firing position.

75mm Bofors L/50 AA Gun

With its longer barrel, this weapon gave slightly better performance than the Vickers model. An excellent weapon for its time, by 1939 the design was nonetheless beginning to lose its effectiveness against high-speed bombers. The tube recoiled in a sleeve-type cradle, on which were set the recuperator above the barrel and the recoil cylinder below it. The recoil length was adjusted automatically as the gun elevated by a cam and lever that regulated the throttling of the liquid inside the cylinder. The semi-automatic breechblock was of the horizontal-sliding type. The equilibrator device was a chain that was attached to the elevating arc, leading down into the pedestal where it was connected to a spring. The fuze-setter, pointer dials, elevating and traversing handwheels, and two seats for the gunners were mounted on the upper (rotating) carriage.

A Bofors 75mm in firing position. (*Yang Yeh*)

76.2mm obr. 1931 & obr. 1938 AA Guns

These weapons featured a semi-automatic sliding breechblock, variable hydraulic recoil mechanism below the barrel, and hydro-pneumatic recuperator above it. The equilibrator was a twin spring arrangement passing almost vertically through the yoke to the bottom of the rotating mount. A platform folded down over the four outriggers for the crew to walk on while servicing the gun. The obr. 1931 used a two-wheel carriage which proved top heavy in transit and slow to bring

Soviet 76mm M1938 AA guns in the 1941 May Day parade in Moscow. They are being towed by Komintern tractors, also delivered to China with the AA guns.

into action, resulting in the adoption of a four-wheel carriage for the obr. 1938. Otherwise the weapons were identical except for a change to the barrel liner.

88mm SKC 30 Dual-Purpose Guns

Not to be confused with the more powerful 88mm Flak family developed for the German land forces, these were shorter-barrel naval guns designed for dual-purpose use. The MPLC 30 mounting was set in concrete for land use in China and featured a 10–15mm shield and a fuze-setter machine. Traverse and elevation were by hand. The gun had a barrel with a half-length loose liner and a vertical-sliding breechblock. Nose-fuzed HE shells with and without tracer were the most common rounds, but AP ammunition was also available and was probably supplied to China for coastal defense. Although mediocre performers, captured guns were moved by the Japanese to their fortifications and further examples were produced as the 8cm Type 99.

A Chinese 8.8cm SKC 30.

31

Coastal Artillery

During the later 1800s the imperial government spent large sums to build up Chinese coastal defenses in a vain attempt to slow the incursions of the Western powers, the two principal beneficiaries being Krupp and Armstrong. During the period 1880–1900 deliveries to China from Krupp totaled 38 x 12cm, 62 x 15cm, 12 x 17cm, 65 x 21cm, 51 x 24cm and 6 x 28cm coastal guns, plus 6 x 28cm coastal howitzers. Deliveries from Armstrong, although not known in detail, were probably on a similar scale, favoring 12cm (4.7-inch) and 15cm (5.9-inch) guns. Such purchases tailed off after 1900, with an emphasis on local production of those same guns.

During the descent into the warlord era little attention was paid to coastal defenses, with the various factions more concerned with each other than external threats. Thus, by the time the KMT unified the country, the coastal forts had largely fallen into disrepair and the weapons were obsolete. The largest forts were those guarding Shanghai, in particular

Typical of the antiques still in service was this Armstrong-type 12-inch muzzle-loaded rifle from the 1880s at Wusong Fort in 1932.

A row of Vickers-Armstrong guns, probably 15cm, at Wusong fort in 1932.

the large fort at Wusong. The capture of those forts in landward assaults by the Japanese in 1932 demonstrated the limited utility of coastal forts without a field army to defend them from the rear.

Most of these guns were on open barbette mounts, the smaller ones (up to 8-inch) with shields. A small percentage were in concrete emplacements with overhead cover.

A German delegation photographed these former German 15cm guns at Fort Huitschumhuk in Qingdao in 1933. Although looking good from the outside they were almost certainly non-operational. (*Bundesarchiv 137-035454*)

A modest attempt to rebuild the coastal and river defenses, particularly those guarding Nanjing, was made in the mid-1930s under German supervision. Sales in 1935–6 provided 20 8.8cm SKC 30 dual-purpose coastal/AA guns and at least eight 15cm SKC 28 coastal guns. Of the 88mm guns, 16 were installed along the Yangtze near Nanjing (8 at the Jiang En fortress and 8 at Jiang Nin fortress), and the remaining 4 at Wunan. In addition a single battery (4 x 15cm guns) was placed at Jiang En. The Nanjing forts fell to land assault from the Japanese Army in 1938 without having engaged any enemy ships. The other coastal forts fared little better, and by the end of 1938 the Chinese coast artillery had essentially ceased to exist.

Armstrong Guns

The most common guns remaining in the Chinese inventory after 1932 were the Armstrong 12cm (4.7-inch) in L/40 and L/45 models, the 15cm (6-inch) L/40 and, in smaller numbers, the 20cm (8-inch) Model 1890. All were obsolescent weapons with limited elevation (and hence range).

Right: The breech of an Armstrong 20cm gun.

An Armstrong-type 15cm gun at Wusong fort, 1932.

Armstrong Guns Specifications				
	12cm L/40	**12cm L/45**	**15cm**	**20cm**
Barrel length (calibers)	40	45	42	46
Weight	1,230kg	n/a	7,000kg	20,455kg
Elevation	-5° to +15°	-7° to +20°	-6° to +15°	-5° to +15°
Traverse	360°	360°	360°	360°
Projectile weight	20kg	20kg	45kg	100kg
Muzzle velocity	634m/s	n/a	666m/s	792m/s
Range	7,200m	8,000m	8,400m	15,000m

15cm Krupp SKC 28

The only modern coast-defense piece in the Chinese inventory, the SKC 28, was widely used on German warships. Elevation and traverse were manual, and it featured a vertical-sliding breechblock. The ammunition was separately loaded, with projectiles including APC and HE types. The range figure given in the table is from Japanese tests of Chinese weapons, although the Germans quoted a figure of 23,000 meters, perhaps reflecting different ammunition models.

15cm Krupp SKC 28 Specifications	
Barrel length (calibers)	55
Weight	n/a
Elevation	-10° to +35°
Traverse	360°
Projectile weight	41kg
Muzzle velocity	875m/s
Range	20,000m

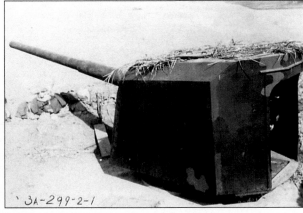

Two views of the Krupp SKC 28 coast gun.

32

Armor

A rmored vehicles did not play a large role in Chinese military operations through the mid-1930s. To be sure, a few warlords bought small numbers of vehicles and often showed them in parades, but the paucity of good roads and the absence of supporting infrastructure severely limited their usefulness.

Tanks

Tracked vehicles are thirsty for fuel, and thus require a substantial supply train; and are prone to mechanical failure, so must be accompanied by trained mechanics with spare parts. These factors limited the appeal of tanks to the various Chinese factions.

The first Chinese tanks were ex-French Renault FTs acquired by Zhang Zuolin from the French when their forces withdrew from Vladivostok in 1920. Fourteen more FTs were purchased by the Marshal in 1924–5, armed by the Japanese, and these were used against Wu Pei-fu's army in 1926. In 1929 they were attached to the 1st Cavalry Brigade of the National Revolutionary Army as part of the integration of Manchurian forces into the KMT army. Their fate in 1931 is unknown, but most were probably captured by the Japanese and then scrapped a few years later. Two made the trip south and were given to

Manchurian FT tanks fitted with Japanese armament parade in Shenyang in October 1930.

the Central Military Academy as training vehicles. Other warlords may have bought small quantities of FTs, but used them little. Any FTs acquired by the national army appear to have been discarded by the start of the war.

In this environment Vickers saw a market for their little Vickers-Carden-Loyd Mark VI machine-gun carrier. A Vickers representative showed up in December 1929 with a single vehicle and gave a demonstration. This was apparently successful, for T. V. Soong awarded a contract to the firm for the trials vehicle plus 11 more new vehicles with trailers for £16,270. These were delivered in April 1930. At about the same time a second order was placed, this time for 12 more Mk VI MG carriers plus six trailers for £15,770.

A Chinese Mk VI Vickers Carden-Loyd machine-gun carrier and trailer, probably about 1934. (*Karl Martin collection via Gunter Hartnagel*)

This was the start of a significant relationship with that firm. The Vickers amphibian light tank found its sole customer in China. The Guangdong provincial government ordered 12 of these vehicles in January 1933 for £37,380 and later that year the central government ordered a single example for trials. These were apparently successful, for in early 1934 the central government ordered a further 12 amphibians, followed by four more a few months later, with the last being delivered in May 1935.

The heavier tanks were to be the Vickers 6-ton Type E tanks. In March 1934 the central government ordered 12 single-turret models, without radios, and 3,200 rounds of 47mm ammunition for them. A second order followed in May of that year for four more tanks and 6,000 rounds of ammunition. A further 4,000 rounds of AP ammunition were purchased in the late summer of 1934. The final purchase came in September 1935, four tanks and 2,400 rounds of practice ammunition. Of these 20 tanks, all were the single-turret model with the Vickers-Armstrong 3pdr (47mm) gun, and only the final batch were fitted with radios. The final deliveries of the Vickers Type Es came in October 1936.

Only one purchase of conventional Vickers light tanks was concluded, as part of the September 1935 contract, for four tanks. The last was delivered in October 1936.

Many of the 6-ton tanks were destroyed in the Shanghai fighting in 1937, and the Guangdong government's amphibians around Guangzhou in 1938. The central government's amphibians were evacuated to Sichuan and appear to have played no role in the war.

In late 1935 the Henry Disston company of the US received an order from China for four of its light tanks with 37mm guns. These were crude vehicles featuring a thinly armored shell that the firm dropped onto a Caterpillar bulldozer body. They were apparently built, but in April 1937 the Nanjing government informed the US State Department that the tanks were no longer needed and should not be shipped. No further information is available, although this

Japanese troops face a Chinese Vickers 6-ton tank in Shanghai, 1937.

has the hallmarks of a provincial order that was finally blocked by the central government.

By 1934 the German advisers were suggesting that China increase its armored vehicle holdings with armored cars and light tanks. Both were useful, given the long distances involved and weak bridges, and coincidentally that was all Germany had to offer at the time. Near the end of that year China ordered 36 armored cars from Germany, although the designs had not yet been completed. These appear to have been the Krupp Radpanzer models.

A second order was placed in May 1936 for 15 PzKw IA light tanks and 15 more armored cars. The tanks arrived in early 1937, but were not unpacked at Nanjing by the Chinese ordnance department until mid-June, by which time they had suffered water damage to their electrical components. The tanks turned out to be unsuited

Chiang Kai-shek (*center*) inspects an L3/35 tankette.

A T-26 tank captured by the Japanese and dug in as a bunker at
Tengchong, then recaptured by the Chinese in September 1944.

to Chinese conditions, overheating and proving very susceptible to thrown tracks in the
soft ground, far more so than the Vickers vehicles with their twin roadwheels and center
guides. These tanks were lost outside Nanjing in December 1937.

The next source of supply was France. Zhang Xueliang had asked for demonstrations
of the UE infantry tractor and the VL armored car back in 1933, but nothing came of it
immediately. Finally, the national army placed an order in March 1936 for 10 Renault UE
Chenillettes fitted with small armored superstructures with machine guns, and trailers. At
the same time they ordered 12 Renault AMR-ZB light tanks, half armed with the short
37mm gun and the other half with 13.2mm machine guns. A few months later the Yunnan
provincial government ordered four more ZBs, half with 37mm and half with 13.2mm.
Export documentation for the UE tractors, with an assessed valuation of FFr1,600,000,
was issued in France in March 1937 and the vehicles probably delivered that summer. Of the
tanks, the Yunnanese vehicles were delivered first, in October 1938, overland via Haiphong.
The Central Army's ZBs appear to have been held up in Indochina, but were at least partially
delivered in February (two vehicles) and June (eight vehicles) 1940 via Rangoon.

Another source of armored vehicles was Italy, and from this country the Chinese
purchased 101 L-3/35 tankettes on 8 August 1937.[*] These vehicles were delivered in
January–February 1938 via Hong Kong and based initially at Changsha. An initial batch of

---

[*] Records of the Groupe Chine, as reported to the French government, show only 94 tanks as being sold on
that date, but British customs records for Hong Kong are explicit that 101 arrived, 61 on the SS *Ischia* in
January 1938 with Czech-made machine guns, and 40 on the SS *Franken* in February with Belgian-made
machine guns. The additional seven tanks may have been a later sale.

CAI troops training on Universal carriers at Ramgarh, November 1943.

20 was based at Nanchang and saw little action; the remainder were used in the formation of the 5th Army Tank Regiment, and would see heavy, if intermittent, combat through 1942.

Yet another early war supplier was the Soviet Union. The military assistance protocols provided for the delivery of 82 T-26 tanks, and the first 50 arrived at Guangzhou in March 1938, and the remaining 32 in Yunnan via Haiphong a month later. These were formed into the 5th Army Tank Regiment. They remained in service through the war and would have been a match for any tanks the Japanese deployed to China, but appear to have seen little combat. Contemporary eyewitness reports speak of large numbers of Soviet armored cars arriving overland via Mongolia, but these do not show up in the protocols and were probably merely escort vehicles for truck convoys.

Supplies from all these sources dried up in 1940. US Lend-Lease approval for China in January 1941 actually provided few immediate benefits, since the US tank industry was still in the midst of expansion and US and British requirements had priority. All the Chinese had to show for it was an initial shipment of 36 M3A1 White scout cars delivered in October to Yunnan via Rangoon.

One firm that remained outside the US tank production plan was Marmon-Herrington, which preferred to market its own designs, primarily to overseas customers. Its tanks were obsolete and sub-standard, but during the crucial years of 1940–1 they were the only source for countries that did not have their own tank industry. In May 1941 China placed a contract with the firm for 240 of its little CTLS light tanks. These were strange vehicles with an archaic configuration of two turrets each with a light machine gun. The Chinese specified that the vehicles must be capable of mounting either a .50-cal. machine gun or a 20mm automatic cannon, but this was either not conveyed to the firm or it chose to ignore it, and when the tanks started coming off the production line in March 1942 they were still fitted only for .30-cal. machine guns. The Chinese refused to accept them, and they were eventually taken over by a reluctant US Army and used for training.

In compensation for the failed CTLS deal the US offered 1,200 Universal carriers. The contracts were placed through the Eastern Supply Group with Australia and the actual number supplied was 1,100 machine-gun carrier versions and 400 3-inch mortar carrier versions. These vehicles were delivered to the Chinese training base at Ramgarh in India from June 1943, but apparently saw no combat.

It was not until June 1943 that the US assigned tank production against Chinese requests, in the form of 1,000 M3A3 light tanks. In fact, only 536 were actually shipped from the US, and of those only 100 actually made it to Chinese forces in Burma before the end of the war. In their place the British provided 116 Shermans from their stocks in India in late 1944. The US-built tanks served in Burma but do not appear to have engaged in combat in China prior to the end of the war.

The mixture of US, British, German, French, Italian, and Soviet tanks made maintenance difficult, especially given the lack of spare parts deliveries after 1939 for all but the US-made tanks, and those only operated in Burma prior to 1945. In any case, with endemic fuel shortages, the tanks could not be extensively used, and played little role in the fighting.

Armored Cars

The various warlords had bought small quantities of armored cars before the conclusion of the Northern Expedition, and those who retained some degree of independence continued to do so afterwards. Liu Hsiang of Sichuan bought three armored cars from Arnhold & Co. in 1931. These used armored bodies provided by the Eagle & Globe Steel Co. of Britain, identical to those sold to the Japanese Special Naval Landing Forces on Crossley chassis, but here mounted on GMC chassis. Another similar vehicle was sold to the Chengdu authorities at the same time. Photographic evidence suggests that the Nationalist Army may have bought a small number as well, but this is unconfirmed.

The view into the turret of a Chinese SdKfz 222 armored car. For unknown reasons the 2cm gun and MG are reversed from the normal German arrangement.

The Guangdong provincial government bought nine armored cars in 1931, all based on Thornycroft chassis. Three were heavy vehicles and were armored by the Hong Kong & Whampoa Shipyard with the same body as used by the Hong Kong Volunteer Defence Corps on its armored cars. Each of these had two turrets arranged en echelon, the rear one with a short 37mm cannon and the front one with a machine gun. The other six vehicles were lighter vehicles, about which nothing is known.

Although armored cars of the period tended to be road-bound, a considerable disadvantage in much of China, they were faster, less thirsty, and had lower maintenance requirements than tanks and one of the first suggestions made by the German advisory mission was the purchase of small numbers, presumably for use in urban areas. German records show the purchase of 36 Strassen-Panzerwagen, or armored road vehicles, in late 1934. Photographic evidence suggests that these were Krupp Radpanzer models, but this is not certain.

Within a few years Germany had begun to field slightly more modern armored cars, including those with 4x4 drive and moderate cross-country performance. In April 1936 the Chinese ordnance office requested a quote from Germany for 13 armored cars armed with 20mm guns and got a price of RM 62,000 each. The actual order, when it was placed in May, was for 15 vehicles. The distribution of vehicles is not clear. It

Two views of a Chinese SdKfz 260 armored radio vehicle, with bed-frame antenna up and down.

appears that the majority were the 20mm-armed SdKfz 222 models and two were MG-armed SdKfz 221. At least one SdKfz 260 radio version was also supplied. These vehicles arrived in Guangzhou via Hong Kong in December 1937. The armored cars served briefly

A camouflaged Chinese M3A1 scout car near Lungling in September 1944.

in the 1942 Burma campaign, then retreated to Yunnan where they remained for the rest of the war.

An early request for Lend-Lease aid resulted in the delivery of 36 M3A1 Scout Cars to Yunnan in October 1941 via Rangoon. Shortly thereafter, however, that route was closed and all attention turned to the upcoming fighting in the jungles and mountains of Burma, where armored cars would be of little use. As a result, no further scout cars or armored cars were delivered by the US, nor were any half-tracks provided. The scout cars that did arrive served mostly in Yunnan through the war, including a few that moved west to support the drive to Lungling.

Warlord Armored Cars

During the late 1920s and early 1930s various warlords purchased a wide range of armored cars and even fabricated some themselves. They were invariably large vehicles, with thin armor and limited cross-country mobility. Ideal to intimidate the populace and would-be domestic rivals, they were of little use against a modern army.

Above: Two views of an unknown model of armored car destroyed by Japanese forces in 1937.

A heavy armored car of the Guangdong forces based on the Thornycroft A3 chassis. Note the rear-right turret has been refitted with a hand-held light machine gun in lieu of its cannon.

Two of the GMC-based armored cars of the Sichuan provincial forces. They used the same Eagle & Globe armored bodies as the Japanese Vickers-Crossley armored cars, fitted to the American chassis in Shanghai around 1930. There are reports that they were also armed with a short-barrel 37mm infantry gun pointed forward next to the driver.

Armored Vehicle Specifications

	Weight (tons)	Length	Width	Height	Front armor	Side armor	Engine	Road speed
Wheeled								
M3A1 Scout Car	5.6	5.6m	2.0m	2.0m	12mm	8mm	87hp	84km/hr
SdKfz 222	4.8	4.8m	1.9m	2.0m	8mm	8mm	75hp	85km/hr
Tracked								
Universal carrier	3.6	3.8m	2.1m	1.6m	12mm	9mm	85hp	53km/hr
VCL Mk VI MG Carrier	1.2	2.5m	1.8m	1.2m	9mm	9mm	40hp	40km/hr
CV-35 (L-3/35)	3.2	3.2m	1.4m	1.3m	13mm	9mm	43hp	42km/hr
Vickers Amphibian	2.2	4.1m	2.1m	1.9m	9mm	7mm	90hp	44km/hr
PzKw IA	5.4	4.0m	2.1m	1.7m	13mm	13mm	57hp	37km/hr
Vickers 6-ton	7.0	4.5 m	2.2m	2.4m	17mm	n/a	80hp	37km/hr
T-26B	9.4	4.6m	2.4m	2.2m	15mm	15mm	90hp	35km/hr
M3A3 Light Tank	14.4	5.0m	2.5m	2.3m	37mm	25mm	250hp	60km/hr
M4A4 Medium Tank	29.7	6.1m	2.6m	2.7m	75mm	50mm	425hp	40km/hr

Scout Car, M3A1 White

This was an open-topped armored body placed on a commercial 4 x 4 truck chassis. Seats for the driver and commander were provided at the front, and for up to six troops in the rear. Normal armament in Chinese service was a .50-cal. M2 water-cooled machine gun and a .30-cal. M1919 machine gun on a skate rail that encircled the open top. An armored shield hinged at the top could be dropped to cover the windshield, while armored louvers, controlled by the driver, protected the radiator. An armored truck, the M3A1 was too large and poorly protected and lacked the cross-country mobility

A US Army M3A1 Scout Car.

required for its original role of scouting, but it proved a useful jack-of-all-trades vehicle for communications, liaison, repairs, and so on. In Chinese service it appears to have been used primarily as a command vehicle.

Armored Car, SdKfz 221/222

These were the first purpose-built German armored cars, based on the Horch 801 chassis with 4 x 4 drive. The two vehicles were almost identical except for the turret. The SdKfz 221 was armed with a single 7.92mm machine gun in a one-man turret, while the SdKfz 222 had a larger two-man turret with a 20mm autocannon and a coaxial light MG. The vehicle was lightly built and thinly armored, and the shortage of motor roads in China limited its usefulness. They served mostly Yunnan and appear to have seen no combat.

An SdKfz 222 (*center*) and two SdKfz 221s in a parade in Yunnan, 1944.

Universal Carrier

These were full-tracked open-topped vehicles developed by the British to transport machine guns and mortars near the front lines. There was space for the two-man basic crew in the front, the driver on the right and the gunner on the left, the latter usually manning a Bren LMG, although a water-cooled Vickers could be fitted instead. Two more men could be accommodated in the rear

A Universal carrier at Ramgahr in 1943.

compartment. The vehicles used by China were built in Australia to local specifications, which differed only in detail from the original. Although delivered in substantial numbers and used in training at the Ramgarh center, they were not suitable for use in Burma and do not appear to have been issued to units at the front or to have seen any combat.

Vickers Carden-Loyd Mark VI Machine-gun Carrier

In these tiny vehicles the crew sat side-by-side with the engine between them, the driver on the left and the gunner

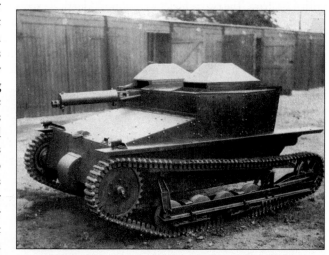

on the right. Armament was a single .303-inch water-cooled Vickers machine gun, with a very limited traverse facing forward. The crew were provided with head covers in the form of truncated pyramids, and the vehicles had tracked trailers to facilitate their use as forward area resupply tractors. Their armor was proof only against ball ammunition from rifle-caliber weapons and their suspension was a bit

A factory photo of a Mk VI machine-gun carrier.

weak. They would still have been around in 1937, but there is no record of them engaging in combat.

CV-35 (L-3/35)

This little vehicle was a derivative of the Carden-Loyd, above. As with the original, the crew could hear nothing but the engine behind them, and see little outside the vehicle.

The armament in this case consisted of two air-cooled machine guns, ZB models in half the vehicles, Belgian in the other half. The mounting could traverse 40° total and elevate from −20° to +20°. The armor was slightly thicker at the front than in the Carden-Loyds, but the Chinese found them deathtraps, easily knocked out, with little chance of crew survival. Nevertheless, they served through the war, mainly for lack of alternatives.

A Chinese L-3/35.

Vickers Amphibian Light Tank

Two slightly different models were in service in China, 12 vehicles bought in 1933 by the Guangdong provincial government, and 16 vehicles bought in 1934 by the central government. The differences between the two were largely cosmetic, the most noticeable being a smaller turret hatch on the earlier models. The tanks had a crew of two, a driver in the hull and a gunner/commander in the turret, and were armed with a single rifle-caliber water-cooled machine gun. The armor was thin and the vehicles lacked radios, so their usefulness was quite limited.

Amphibian tanks of the Dragon Company.

PzKw IA

This vehicle was slightly better than the Carden-Loyds and CV-35s in that the armament was turret-mounted, but it otherwise proved unsuited to use in China. The lack of ventilation turned them into ovens in the summer around Nanjing and they frequently threw their tracks on Chinese terrain due to the short height of the guide teeth. In German service they were found to be under-powered and prone to engine overheating. Armament was two air-cooled 7.9mm MG13 machine guns in the manually operated turret, and the crew was two, a driver in the hull and a gunner/commander in the turret.

A Chinese PzKw IA after capture by Japanese troops.

Renault ZB Light Tank

This vehicle mated the body and turret of the AMR-35 reconnaissance tank with the suspension of the R-35 infantry tank. Little information is available on these vehicles, which were built in very small numbers and only for China, except that the turret could be fitted with either a short 37mm gun or a 13.2mm heavy machine gun. Assuming the original AMR specifications were not greatly changed it would have had a two-man crew and turret frontal armor 13mm thick. Their sole combat use appears to have been in Burma.

A ZB light tank with 13.2mm armament in Burma, 1942. (*George Rodger/Timpix*)

Vickers 6-ton Type E Medium

The only modern tanks in the Chinese arsenal in 1937, these vehicles featured a medium-velocity 47mm (3pdr) gun and a water-cooled rifle-caliber Vickers Type C machine gun in the turret. Power came from a horizontal, air-cooled 4-cylinder Armstrong Siddeley engine. The suspension used two clusters of two 2-wheel bogies, an adequate design although it limited cross-country speed. Only four of the tanks were fitted with radios, Marconi G2A models.

A factory photo of a Vickers 6-ton.

T-26B Tank

This was the significantly improved Soviet version of the Medium E, immediately above. It featured a new turret with a more powerful 45mm Model 1932 20K main gun with coaxial Model DT machine gun, and had a radio. The crew was three: a driver in the hull and two men in the turret: the gunner sitting on the left with the gun controls in front of him, and the commander on the right, doubling as the loader.

A T-26 at a parade in Yunnan in 1942.

M3A3 Light Tank

This was a hybrid light tank, utilizing an all-welded modified version of the hull of the M5 light tank with the M3A1's radial gasoline engine and a new turret with a bustle for a radio.

The armament consisted of a 37mm M6 gun and a coaxial .30-cal. machine gun in the turret, a .30-cal. machine gun in a ball mount in the hull front, and a third .30-cal. on an AA mount. The 37mm and the coax were carried in an M44 mount, a new design that reduced dispersion compared to earlier versions of the M3 light. The tank had a crew of four, a driver and assistant driver in the hull front, and a gunner and commander in the turret.

A pair of Chinese M3A3 light tanks on the Stilwell Road in February 1945.

M4A4 Sherman Medium Tank

This was the Sherman variant with the welded hull powered by the liquid-cooled 30-cylinder Chrysler A57 multibank engine, most of which were turned over to the British as Lend-Lease. Power was transmitted to the front sprocket by a 5F1R transmission. The armament consisted of a 75mm M3 gun and coaxial .30-cal. M1919A4 machine gun in a hydraulic power turret, along with a second M1919A4 on a ball mount in the hull front and a .50-cal. HB M2 machine gun on an AA mount. The tank carried 97 rounds of 75mm and 4,750 rounds of .30-cal. ammunition. There was a crew of five: driver and assistant driver in the hull, and loader, gunner and commander in the turret.

A Chinese Sherman near Lashio in February 1945.

Appendix I

National Revolutionary Army Orders of Battle

A: Defense of Beijing (July 1937)

29th Army   37th, 38th, 132nd, 143rd Divisions

B: Defense of Shanxi (August 1937)

Taiyuan Pacification HQ

    Tang Enbo's Command

        13th Army   4th, 86th Divisions

        17th Army   21st, 84th Divisions

    7th Army Group

        72nd, 143rd Divisions; 7th, 27th, 200th, 211th Brigades

    Direct Command

        1st Cavalry Army   1st, 2nd, 6th, 7th Cavalry Divisions; New 2nd Cavalry Brigade, New 3rd, New 5th, New 6th, 218th Infantry Brigades

I War Zone

    14th Army Group (part)

        14th Army   10th, 83rd Divisions
                85th Division

C: Battle of Shanghai (October 1937)

Right Wing Forces

8th Army Group

28th Army	62nd, 63rd Divisions
	55th Division, 45th Brigade
	2nd Artillery Regiment

10th Army Group

11th Reserve, 45th, 52nd Divisions; 11th Temporary, 12th Temporary, 37th Brigades

Central Forces

9th Army Group

8th Army	61st, Salt Tax Divisions
71st Army	87th Division
72nd Army	88th Division
78th Army	36th Division
	18th Division
	I/3 Artillery Regiment

21st Army Group

1st Army	1st, 32nd, 78th Divisions
48th Army	173rd, 174th, 176th Divisions
	16th, 19th, 171st Divisions

Left Wing Forces

19th Army Group

2nd Army	9th Division
20th Army	133rd, 134th Divisions
25th Army	13th Division
59th Army	57th Division
66th Army	160th, 195th Divisions
75th Army	6th Division

15th Army Group

4th Army	90th Division
15th Army	23rd, 53rd, 102nd, 103rd Divisions
18th Army	11th, 60th, 67th Divisions
39th Army	56th Division, 34th Brigade
54th Army	14th, 94th Divisions
57th Army	111th, 112th Divisions
73rd Army	15th Division
74th Army	51st, 58th Divisions
	44th Division

River Defense Forces

11th Army	33rd, 40th Divisions
12th Army	76th Division
43rd Army	26th Division
	I/8, I/3, 4th Artillery Regiments, I/10 Heavy Artillery Regiment

D: Northern Sector of the Tianjin–Nanjing Railway (early September 1937)

VI War Zone

12th Army	20th, 81st Divisions
67th Army	107th, 108th Divisions
3rd Cavalry Army	4th, 9th Cavalry Divisions

1st Army Group

3rd Army Group

40th Army	39th Division
49th Army	105th, 109th Divisions

19th Army Group

59th Army	38th, 180th Divisions
77th Army	37th, 132nd, 179th Divisions

E: Northern Sector of the Beijing–Hankou Railway (August–Sept. 1937)

I War Zone

2nd Army Group

1st Army	27th, 30th, 31st Divisions; 44th Independent Brigade
3rd Army	7th, 12th Divisions
14th Army	42nd, 169th Divisions
52nd Army	2nd, 25th Divisions
4th Cavalry Army	10th Cavalry Division
Direct Command	17th, 47th, 177th Divisions; 5th, 46th Independent Brigades; 14th Cavalry Brigade

14th Army Group (part)

14th Army	10th, 83rd Divisions

20th Army Group (part)

32nd Army	139th, 141st, 142nd Divisions

Direct Command

53rd Army	91st, 116th, 130th Divisions

F: Battle of Taiyuan (early September 1937)

II War Zone

6th Army Group

33rd Army	73rd Division; 3rd, 8th Independent Brigades
34th Army	71st Division; 196th, 203rd Independent Brigades
	New 2nd Division

7th Army Group

17th Army	21st, 84th Divisions
35th Army	205th, 211th, 218th Independent Brigades
61st Army	101st Division; 7th, 200th Independent Brigades
6th Cavalry Army	7th, 1st Temporary Cavalry Divisions
	New 2nd, New 6th Brigades, New 2nd Cavalry Brigade

14th Army Group

9th Army	47th, 54th Divisions
14th Army	10th, 83rd Divisions
	85th Division, 5th Independent Brigade

Deputy Commander Group

1st Army	27th, 30th, 31st Divisions; 44th Independent Brigade
3rd Army	7th, 12th Divisions
14th Army	42nd, 169th Divisions
	17th, 94th Divisions

Direct Command

13th Corps	4th, 89th Divisions

G: Battle of Xuzhou (December 1937)

V War Zone

    2nd Army Group

30th Army	30th, 31st Divisions
42nd Army	27th, 44th Divisions

    3rd Army Group

12th Army	20th, 81st Divisions
55th Army	29th, 74th Divisions
56th Army	22nd Division, Pistol Brigade

    11th Army Group

31st Army	131st, 135th, 138th Divisions

    21st Army Group

7th Army	170th, 171st, 172nd Divisions
48th Army	174th, 176th Divisions

    22nd Army Group

41st Army	122nd, 124th Divisions
45th Army	125th, 127th Divisions

    24th Army Group

57th Army	111th, 112th Divisions
89th Army	33rd, 117th Divisions

    26th Army Group

10th Army	41st, 48th Divisions
	199th Division

    27th Army Group

20th Army	133rd, 134th Divisions

    3rd Army

40th Army	39th Division

    19th Army

77th Army	37th, 132nd, 179th Divisions

    20th Army

52nd Army	2nd, 25th Divisions
85th Army	4th, 89th Divisions

    27th Army

59th Army	9th, 38th, 180th Divisions; 13th Cavalry Brigade

    Direct Command

2nd Army	3rd, 9th Divisions
22nd Army	50th Division
46th Army	28th, 49th, 92nd Divisions
51st Army	113th, 114th Divisions
60th Army	182nd, 183rd, 184th Divisions
68th Army	119th, 143rd Divisions
69th Army	181st, New 6th Divisions
75th Army	6th, 93rd Divisions
	95th, 104th Divisions
	4th, 5th, 6th and 7th Artillery Regiments, 1st Regiment/1st Artillery Brigade

H: Northern and Eastern Henan (February 1938)

I War Zone

Eastern Henan Army

8th Army	40th, 102nd Divisions
64th Army	155th, 187th Divisions
74th Army	51st, 58th Divisions

1st Army Group

53rd Army	116th, 130th Divisions
69th Army	181st, New 9th Divisions
77th Army	37th, 132nd, 179th Divisions

3rd Army Group

12th Army	20th, 22nd, 81st Divisions
55th Army	29th, 74th Divisions

20th Army Group

32nd Army	23rd, 139th, 141st and 142nd Divisions, Salt Tax Brigade

Direct Command

39th Army	34th, 56th Divisions
71st Army	87th, 88th Divisions
90th Army	195th, 196th Divisions
91st Army	45th, 166th Divisions
3rd Cavalry Army	4th, 9th Cavalry Divisions
	24th, 61st, 91st, 94th, 95th, 106th, 109th, New 8th, New 35th, Reserve 8th and Reserve 9th Divisions
	2nd, 28th Brigades; 13th, 14th Cavalry Brigades
	6th Artillery Brigade, 5th Regiment/1st Artillery Brigade; 7th, 9th, 10 Artillery Regiments

I: Battle of Wuhan (July 1938)

IX War Zone

1st Group Army

20th Army Group		
	18th Army	11th, 16th, 60th Divisions
	32nd Army	139th, 141st and 142nd Divisions; Salt Tax Brigade
9th Army Group		
	4th Army	59th, 90th Divisions
	8th Army	3rd, 15th Divisions
	25th Army	52nd, 109th Divisions
	64th Army	155th, 187th, 9th Reserve Divisions
	66th Army	159th, 160th Divisions
	70th Army	19th Division
Direct Command		
	29th Army	40th, 79th Divisions
	74th Army	51st, 58th Divisions
	167th Division	

2nd Group Army

3rd Army Group		
	12th Army	20th, 22nd, 81st Divisions
30th Army Group		
	72nd Army	New 13th, New 14th Divisions
	78th Army	New 15th, New 16th Divisions
31st Army Group		
	13th Army	23rd, 35th, 89th Divisions
	98th Army	82nd, 193rd, 195th Divisions
32nd Army Group		
	52nd Army	2nd, 25th Divisions
	92nd Army	21st, 95th Divisions
Tienpei Fortress		
	2nd Army	9th, 57th Divisions
Tiennan Fortress		
	54th Army	14th, 18th Divisions

Wuhan Garrison

Yangtze North		
	6th Army	93rd Division
	16th Army	28th Division
Yangtze South		
	75th Army	6th, 13th Divisions
Wuhan Garrison		
	94th Army	55th, 185th Divisions
Direct Command		
	37th Army	92nd Division

Direct Command

	53rd Army	116th, 130th Divisions
	60th Army	49th, 102nd, 184th Divisions

V War Zone

3rd Group Army

    2nd Army Group

	30th Army	30th, 31st Divisions
	42nd Army	27th Division;
		44th Independent Brigade

    Direct Command

	26th Army	32nd, 44th Divisions
	55th Army	29th, 74th Divisions
	87th Army	198th Division

4th Group Army

    11th Army Group

	48th Army	173rd, 174th, 176th Divisions
	84th Army	188th, 189th Divisions

    29th Army Group

	44th Army	149th, 162nd Divisions
	67th Army	150th, 161st Divisions

    Direct Command

	68th Army	119th, 143rd Divisions
	86th Army	103rd, 121st Divisions

Direct Command

    19th Army Group

	77th Army	37th, 132nd Divisions

    21st Army Group

	7th Army	171st, 172nd Divisions
	31st Army	131st, 135th, 138th Divisions

    24th Army Group

	57th Army	111th, 112th Divisions
	89th Army	33rd, 117th Divisions

    26th Army Group

	10th Army	41st, 48th Divisions
		199th Division

    27th Army Group

	59th Army	38th, 180th Divisions;
		13th Cavalry Brigade

    Direct Command

	1st Army	1st, 78th Divisions
	20th Army	133rd, 134th Divisions
	45th Army	125th, 127th Divisions
	51st Army	113th, 114th Divisions
	71st Army	36th, 61st, 88th Divisions

J: Battle of Nanchang (February 1939)

IX War Zone

1st Army Group

3rd Army	184th, New 12th Divisions
58th Army	183rd, New 10th Divisions
60th Army	182nd, New 11th Divisions

19th Army Group

32nd Army	139th, 141st, 142nd Divisions
49th Army	105th, 9th Reserve Divisions
70th Army	19th, 107th Divisions
79th Army	76th, 98th, 118th Divisions
Direct Command	
	5th Reserve Divisiion

30th Army Group

72nd Army	New 14th, New 15th Divisions
78th Army	New 13th Division

Hunan–Hubei–Jiangxi Border Area Guerrillas

8th Army	3rd, 197th Divisions
73rd Army	15th, 77th Divisions
	128th Division

Direct Command

74th Army	51st, 58th, 60th Division

K:　First Battle of Changsha (September 1939)

IX War Zone

1st Army Group
58th Army	New 10th, New 11th Divisions
60th Army	183rd, 184th Divisions

15th Army Group
37th Army	60th, 95th Divisions
52nd Army	2nd, 25th, 195th Divisions
79th Army	82nd, 98th, 140th Divisions

20th Army Group
53rd Army	116th, 130th Divisions
54th Army	14th, 23rd, 50th Divisions
87th Army	43rd, 198th Divisions

27th Army Group
20th Army	133rd, 134th Divisions

30th Army Group
8th Army	3rd, 197th Divisions
72nd Army	New 14th, New 15th Divisions
78th Army	New 13th, New 16th Divisions
	1st, 3rd Advance Columns (= divisions)

Direct Command
4th Army	59th, 90th, 102nd Divisions
5th Army	1st Honor, 200th, New 12th Divisions
New 6th Army	5th, 6th Temporary Divisions
70th Army	19th, 107th Divisions
73rd Army	15th, 77th Divisions
74th Army	51st, 57th, 58th Divisions
99th Army	76th, 92nd Divisions
	11th Division

L: Southern Guangxi (December 1939)

Generalissimo's Guilin HQ

16th Army Group

	31st Army	131st, 135th, 188th Divisions
	46th Army	170th, 175th, New 19th Divisions

26th Army Group

four infantry regiments

35th Army Group

	64th Army	155th, 156th Divisions

37th Army Group

	66th Army	159th, 160th Divisions

38th Army Group

	2nd Army	9th, 76th Divisions
	5th Army	1st Honor, 200th, New 22nd Divisions
	9th Army	49th, 93rd, 2nd Reserve Divisions
	36th Army	5th, 96th Divisions
	99th Army	92nd, 99th, 118th Divisions

Direct Command

43rd, New 33rd Divisions

M: V War Zone (April 1940)

V War Zone

2nd Army Group
30th Army	27th, 30th, 31st Divisions
68th Army	119th, 143rd Divisions; 27th Independent Brigade

11th Army Group
84th Army	178th, 188th Divisions
92nd Army	21st, 47th Division

22nd Army Group
41st Army	122nd, 124th Divisions
45th Army	125th, 127th Divisions

29th Army Group
44th Army	149th, 150th Divisions
67th Army	161st, 162nd Divisions

31st Army Group
13th Army	89th, 110th, New 1st Divisions
85th Army	4th, 32nd Divisions; 11th Independent Brigade

33rd Army Group
55th Army	29th, 74th Divisions
59th Army	38th, 180th Divisions; 9th Cavalry Division
77th Army	37th, 132nd, 179th Divisions

River Defense Force
26th Army	23rd, 41st, 44th Divisions
94th Army	12th, 55th, 185th Divisions

Eastern Hubei Guerrilla Force
7th Army	3rd, 4th Guerrilla Divisions
	16th, 19th Guerrilla Divisions

Direct Command
2nd Army	33rd, 76th Divisions
New 12th Army	1st Honor, 5th Divisions
18th Army	18th, 77th, 199th Divisions
39th Army	56th Division
75th Army	6th, 13th Divisions; 4th Cavalry Division

N: Second Battle of Changsha (August 1941)

IX War Zone

19th Army Group

New 3rd Army	12th, 183rd Divisions
	195th, 5th Reserve Divisions; 2nd Advance Column

30th Army Group

78th Army	13th Division
Southern Hubei	4th, 5th, 8th Advance Columns

Direct Command

2nd Temporary Army	7th, 8th Temporary Divisions
4th Army	59th, 60th, 90th, 102nd Divisions; 7th Advance Column
10th Army	10th Reserve, 3rd, 19th Divisions
20th Army	54th Temporary, 133rd, 134th Divisions
26th Army	22nd, 41st, 44th Divisions
37th Army	95th, 104th Divisions
58th Army	New 10th, New 11th Divisions; 6th Advance Column
72nd Army	New 14th, New 15th, New 16th Divisions
74th Army	51st, 57th, 58th Divisions
79th Army	6th Temporary, 82nd, 98th Divisions
99th Army	92nd, 99th, 197th Divisions

O: Third Battle of Changsha (December 1941)

IX War Zone

19th Army Group

New 3rd Army	12th, 183rd Divisions
	5th Reserve Division, 2nd Advance Column

Luo Zhuoying Group

26th Army	32nd, 41st, 44th Divisions
69th Army	6th Temporary, 98th, 194th Divisions

Wang Lingji Group

78th Army	New 13th, New 16th Divisions
	New 15th Division

Yang Sen Group

20th Army	5th Provisional, 133rd, 134th Divisions
58th Army	New 10th, New 11th Divisions

Direct Command

4th Army	59th, 90th, 102nd Divisions
10th Army	3rd, 10th Reserve, 190th Divisions
37th Army	60th, 95th, 140th Divisions
72nd Army	34th Division
73rd Army	5th Provisional, 15th, 77th Divisions
74th Army	51st, 57th, 58th Divisions
99th Army	92nd, 99th, 197th Divisions
	New 20th Division

P: Western Hubei (April 1943)

VI War Zone

River Defense Force

18th Army	11th, 18th, 34th Divisions
32nd Army	5th, 139th, 141st Divisions
86th Army	13th, 78th Divisions
	4th Heavy Mortar Regiment,
	II/42nd Artillery Regiment

10th Army Group

87th Army	23rd, 43rd, 118th Divisions
94th Army	35th Provisional, 55th, 121st Divisions

26th Army Group

66th Army	185th, 199th Divisions, 1st Marine Brigade
75th Army	4th Reserve, 6th, 16th Divisions

29th Army Group

44th Army	149th, 150th, 161st, 162nd Divisions
73rd Army	5th Provisional, 15th, 77th Divisions

33rd Army Group

30th Army	27th, 30th, 31st Divisions
59th Army	38th, 53rd Provisional, 180th Divisions
74th Army	51st, 57th, 58th Divisions
77th Army	37th, 132nd, 179th Divisions
79th Army	6th Provisional, 98th, 194th Divisions

Direct Command

42nd Artillery Regiment

Q: Battle of Changde (late October 1943)

VI War Zone

10th Army Group

66th Army	185th, 199th Divisions
79th Army	6th Provisional, 98th, 194th Divisions

26th Army Group

32nd Army	139th, 141st Divisions
75th Army	4th Reserve, 6th, 16th Divisions

29th Army Group

44th Army	105th, 161st, 162nd Divisions
73rd Army	5th Provisional, 15th, 77th Divisions

33rd Army Group

59th Army	34th Provisional, 38th, 180th Divisions
79th Army	30th, 132nd, 179th Divisions

River Defense Force

18th Army	18th, 55th, 118th Divisions
86th Army	13th Division

Wang Yaowu's Force

74th Army	51st, 57th, 58th Divisions
100th Army	19th, 63rd Divisions

IX War Zone

Li Yutang's Group

10th Army	3rd, 10th Reserve, 190th Divisions
99th Army	54th Provisional, 92nd, 197th Divisions

Ou Zhen's Group

58th Army	New 10th, New 11th Divisions
72nd Army	New 13th, New 15th Divisions
	7th Provisional Division

R: Central Henan (April 1944)

I War Zone

Tang Enbo's Command

15th Army Group		
	2nd Cavalry Army	3rd Cavalry Division, 14th Provisional Division
	8th Cavalry Division	
	2nd, 3rd Provisional Brigades	
19th Army Group		
	9th Provisional Army	30th Provisional, 111th, 112th Divisions
28th Army Group		
	15th Provisional Army	27th Provisional, 29th Provisional Divisions
	85th Army	11th Reserve, 23rd, 110th Divisions
	89th Army	New 1st, 20th Divisions
31st Army Group		
	12th Army	22nd, 29th, 55th Divisions
	13th Army	4th, 81st, 117th Divisions
	29th Army	16th Provisional, 91st, 193rd Divisions
Direct Command		
	78th Army	New 42nd, New 43rd, New 44th Divisions

Direct Command

4th Army Group		
	38th Army	17th, New 35th Divisions
	96th Army	New 14th, 17th Divisions
14th Army Group		
	15th Army	64th, 65th Divisions
36th Army Group		
	47th Army	
39th Army Group		
	New 8th Army	New 6th, 29th Provisional Divisions
Direct Command		
	14th Army	83rd, 85th, 94th Divisions

VIII War Zone

Direct Command

1st Army	167th Division
16th Army	3rd Reserve, 109th Divisions
27th Army	128th Division
40th Army	New 4th, 39th, 106th Divisions
57th Army	8th, 97th Divisions

S: Battle of Changsha/Hengyang (May 1944)

IX War Zone

24th Army Group

    Li Yutang's Command

	10th Army	3rd, 10th Reserve, 54th Provisional, 190th Divisions
	46th Army	New 19th, 175th Divisions
	62nd Army	151st, 157th Divisions

    Direct Command

	73rd Army	15th, 77th Divisions
	74th Army	51st, 57th, 58th Divisions
	79th Army	6th Provisional, 98th, 194th Divisions
	100th Army	19th, 63rd Divisions

27th Army Group

    Ou Zhen's Command

	2nd Provisional Army	7th Provisional, 8th Provisional Divisions
	26th Army	32nd, 41st, 44th Divisions
	37th Army	60th, 195th, 140th Divisions

    Direct Command

	20th Army	New 20th, 133rd, 134th Divisions
	44th Army	150th, 161st, 162nd Divisions

30th Army Group

	58th Army	New 10th, New 11th, 183rd Divisions
	72nd Army	New 13th, New 15th, New 16th, 34th Divisions 1st, 2nd, 3rd, 4th Advance Columns

Direct Command

	4th Army	59th, 90th, 102nd Divisions
	99th Army	New 23rd, 92nd, 99th, 179th Divisions 160th Division

T: Battle of Guilin/Liuzhou (August 1944)

IV War Zone

16th Army Group

31st Army	131st, 135th, 188th Divisions
46th Army	New 19th, 170th, 175th Divisions
93rd Army	8th, 10th Divisions

27th Army Group

20th Army	133rd, 134th Divisions
26th Army	41st, 44th Divisions
37th Army	9th Division

35th Army Group

62nd Army	151st, 157th, 158th Divisions
64th Army	155th, 156th, 159th Divisions

Li Yutang's Group

79th Army	98th, 194th Divisions

Tang Enbo's Command

9th Army	New 24th, 54th Divisions
13th Army	4th, 16th Provisional, 89th Divisions
29th Army	11th Reserve, 91st, 193rd Divisions
57th Army	8th, New 34th Divisions
87th Army	New 23rd, 43rd, 118th Divisions
94th Army	5th, 35th Provisional, 121st Divisions
98th Army	42nd, 169th Divisions

U: Western Henan/Northern Hubei (March 1945)

I War Zone

4th Army Group

38th Army	17th, New 35th Divisions
40th Army	39th, New 40th, 106th Division
90th Army	7th, 61st Divisions
96th Army	New 35th, 177th Divisions

31st Army Group

27th Army	4th Provisional, 28th, 47th and 64th Divisions
78th Army	New 42nd, New 43rd, New 44th Divisions
85th Army	23rd, 55th Provisional, 110th Divisions
89th Army	New 1st, 62nd Provisional Divisions

Western Henan Garrison

15th Army	55th Provisional, 64th, 65th Divisions

Hebe–Chahar War Zone

New 8th Army	New 6th, 29th Provisional Divisions

V War Zone

2nd Army Group

55th Army	29th, 74th, 81st Divisions
68th Army	36th Provisional, 119th, 143rd Divisions

22nd Army Group

1st Provisional Army	
41st Army	122nd, 124th Divisions
45th Army	125th, 127th Divisions
47th Army	104th, 178th Divisions

33rd Army Group

59th Army	38th, 53rd Provisional, 180th Divisions
69th Army	28th Provisional, 181st Divisions
77th Army	132nd, 179th Divisions

Direct Command

	16th Artillery Regiment

X War Zone

8th Provisional Army	3rd, 27th Provisional, 173rd Divisions; 4th, 13th, 20th Replacement Divisions

[total 148,000 men]

V: Battle of Western Henan (April 1945)

HQ, Chinese Army Forces

10th Army Group

39th Army	51st Division
92nd Army	21st, 142nd Divisions

3rd Front Army (part)

27th Army Group

New 6th Army	14th, New 22nd Divisions
26th Army	44th Division
94th Army	5th, 43rd, 121st Divisions

4th Front Army

18th Army	11th, 18th, 118th Divisions
73rd Army	15th, 77th, 193rd Divisions
74th Army	51st, 57th, 58th Divisions
100th Army	19th, 63rd Divisions
Direct Command	6th Provisional, 13th Divisions

Distribution of Troops, Early 1937
According to US Military Attaché[*]

Hebei – Feng Chian, provincial chairman

	commander	location	strength
Central Government Troops			
32nd Army – Shang Chen			
139th Division	Huang Kuang-hua	Hantan	7,000
141st Division	Sung Kan-tang	Shunteh	7,000
142nd Division	Lu Chi	Shaho	7,000
4th Cavalry Division	Wang Chi-feng	Taming	2,000
Ind Cavalry Regiment		Shunteh	1,000
Ind Artillery Regiment		Shunteh	1,000

Nominal Central Govt. Troops, actually controlled by Hebei–Chahar Political Council

	commander	location	strength
29th Army[*] – Sung Che-yuan			
37th Division	Feng Chih-an	Baoding	12,000
38th Division	Chang Tze-chung	Tianjin	9,000
132nd Division	Chao Teng-yu	Beiping	8,000
13th Ind. Brigade	Liu Chen-shan	Kaopaitien	3,000
26th Ind. Brigade	Li Chih-ta	Tsangchow	3,000
1st Cavalry Brigade	Chang Jen-chih	Chochow	2,000
Special Service Regt.		Beiping	1,600
Training Corps		Beiping	1,200

Nominal Central Government Troops, former Northeastern Army

	commander	location	strength
53rd Army[†] – Wan Fu-lin			
116th Division	Liu Yuan-hsun	Tingchow	6,000
119th Division	Tsung Chao-lin	Shihkiachwang	5,000
130th Division	Chu Hung-hsun	Baoding	5,000
91st Division[‡]	Fen Chan-hai	Kaoyi	10,000

Provincial Troops

	commander	location	strength
1st Ind. Brigade	Tai Shou-yi	Hokien	3,000
2nd Ind. Brigade	Kao Shu-hsun	Shunteh	3,000
North Hebei Peace Preservation Corps			
1st Brigade	Chang Hsi-hsien	Beiping	3,000
2nd Brigade	Feng Shou-peng	Beiping	3,000

[*] *Former Guominchun forces.* [†] *Former Northeastern Army forces.* [‡] *Personal troops of Chiang Kai-shek.*

---

[*] Colonel Stilwell. English spellings in the original of this document do not allow the normal conversion to the Pinyin forms to be made with certainty. Original spellings have therefore been retained in many cases.

	commander	location	strength

East Hebei Autonomous Government of Yin Ju-keng (not controlled by Nanjing)

	commander	location	strength
1st Corps	Chang Ching-yu	Tongzhou	4,000
2nd Corps	Chang Yan-tien	Tsunhwa	4,000
3rd Corps	Li Yun-sheng	Iwanchow	4,000
4th Corps	Han Tze-hsi	Tangshan	4,000
Training Corps	Yin Ju-keng	Tongzhou	2,000

Chahar – Liu Jun-ming, provincial chairman

Nominal Central Govt Troops, actually controlled by Hebei–Chahar Political Council

29th Army* – Sung Che-yuan

	commander	location	strength
143rd Division	Liu Jun-ming	Zhangjiakou	8,000
3rd Ind. Brigade	Ku Tze-wen	Zhangjiakou	3,000
3rd Cavalry Brigade	Tao Ching-chuan	Hwailai	2,000
8th Cavalry Brigade	Hsia Tze-ming	Kangchwang	2,000
39th Cavalry Brigade	Juan Hsuan-wu	Xuanhwa	2,000

Shanxi – Chao Tai-wen, provincial chairman

Central Government Troops

	commander	location	strength
21st Division†	Li Hsien-chow	Fenchow	9,000
94th Divisonc	Chu Huai-pin	Fyuncheng	8,000

Nominal Central Govt Troops, actually controlled by Yen Hsi-shan

33rd Army – Sun Chu

	commander	location	strength
66th Division	Feng Peng-chu	Pingyao	8,000
69th Division	Yang Chen-yuan	Fenchow	8,000

34th Army – Yang Hsia-ou

	commander	location	strength
71st Division	Kuo Tsung-chun	Pingyang	8,000

61st Army – Li Fu-ying

	commander	location	strength
68th Division	Li Fu-ying	Yangkao	9,000
101st Division	Li Chun-kung	Tatung	8,000
Temporary 2nd Division	Chin Hsien-chang	Kiehsiu	2,800

Provincial Troops

	commander	location	strength
1st Ind. Brigade	Tu Chun-yi	Taiyuan	3,000
2nd Ind. Brigade	Chou Yuan-chien	Yuanping	3,000
3rd Ind. Brigade	Feng Yu-hsi	Yangchwan	3,000

* *Former Guominchun forces.*   † *Former Northeastern Army forces.*   ‡ *Personal troops of Chiang Kai-shek.*

Shandong – Han Fu-chu, provincial chairman

	commander	*location*	*strength*
Nominal Central Government Troops, actually controlled by Han Fu-chu			
3rd Route Army* – Han Fu-chu			
20th Division	Sun Tung-hsuan	Yanchow	12,000
22nd Division	Ku Liang-min	Chowtsun	9,000
29th Division	Tsao Fu-lin	Jinan	10,000
74th Division	Li Han-chang	Jinan	8,000
81st Division	Chan Shu-tang	Kiaochow	8,000
Ind. Cavalry Brigade		Jinan	1,500
Pistol Brigade	Wu Huan-wen	Jinan	3,000
1st Artillery Regiment		Jinan	1,000
2nd Artillery Regiment		Jinan	1,000

Provincial Troops
Militia Troops

	commander	*location*	*strength*
1st Corps	Chao Ming-yuan	Lintsing	2,000
2nd Corps	Chao Jen-chuan	Lintsing	2,000
3rd Corps	Ku Liang-yu	Kufow	2,000
4th Corps	Hsueh Shu-hsien	Chaoyuan	2,000
5th Corps	Chang Hsieh	Tsining	2,000

Suiyuan – Fu Tso-yi, provincial chairman

Central Government Troops

	commander	*location*	*strength*
13th Army† – Tang Enbo			
4th Division	Wang Wan-ling	Hsingho	8,000
89th Division	Wang Chung-lien	Tsining	8,000
7th Cavalry Division*	Weng Ping-yueh	Chotzeshn	4,500
Nominal Central Government Troops, actually controlled by Yen Hsi-shan			
19th Army – Wang Ching-kuo			
70th Division	Wang Ching-kuo	Paotow	8,000
72nd Division	Chen Chang-chieh	Fengchan	8,000
35th Army – Fu Tso-yi			
73rd Division	Fu Tso-yi	Wuchwan	8,000
7th Ind. Brigade	Ma Yen-shou	Wuchwan	2,500
1st Cavalry Brigade	Shih Yu-Shan	Hsingho	1,200
Cavalry Army – Chao Chen-shou			
1st Cavalry Division	Peng Yu-pin	Wuchwan	1,500
2nd Cavalry Division	Sun Chang-sheng	Taolin	1,500

* *Former Guominchun forces.*   † *Former Northeastern Army forces.*   ‡ *Personal troops of Chiang Kai-shek.*

Shaanxi – Sun Yu-ju, provincial chairman

	commander	location	strength
Central Government Troops			
5th Army[†] – Yueh Sen			
23rd Division	Li Pi-fan	Wainan	8,000
43rd Division	Tai Yueh	Paoki	8,000
17th Army[‡] – Hsing Chen-nan			
2nd Division	Cheng Tung-kuo	Tungkuo	12,000
25th Army[‡] – Wan Yueh-huang			
140th Division	Wang Wen-yen	Fengsiang	6,000
46th Army[‡] – Fan Sung-pu			
79th Division	Chen An-pao	Fuping	8,000
28th Division[‡]	Tung Chao	Sanyuan	7,000
36th Division[‡]	Sung Hsi-lien	Sian	8,000
53rd Division[‡]	Li Pao-ping	Hanchung	8,000
61st Division	Yang Pu-fei	Pucheng	7,000
84th Division	Kao Kuei-tze	Suiteh	8,000
86th Division	Kao Shuang-cheng	Yulin	9,000
95th Division[‡]	Li Tieh-chun	Shanghsien	8,000
27th Route Army under Feng Chin-tsai			
7th Army – Feng Chin-tsai			
42nd Division	Liu Yen-piao	Tali	8,000
169th Division	Wu Shih-min	Tali	7,000
Nominal Central Government Troops, actually controlled by Yang Hu-cheng			
17th Route Army – Yang Hu-cheng			
38th Army – Sun Wei-ju			
17th Division	Chao Shou-shan	Sanyuan	8,000
177th Division	Li Hsing-chung	Tsingyang	7,000
1st Ind. Brigade	Tang Tse-feng	Sanyuan	3,000
2nd Ind. Brigade	Kung Tsung-chow	Fuping	3,000
3rd Ind. Brigade	Wang Chen-hua	Hsingshih	3,000
Nominal Central Government Troops, former Northeastern Army			
1st Cavalry Army[†] – Ho Chu-kuo			
3rd Cavalry Division	Kuo Hsi-peng	Singping	1,500
6th Cavalry Division	Pai Feng-hsiang	Sienyang	1,500
Provincial Troops			
E. Shanxi Garrison Bde	Wang Kuang-tsung	Shanghsien	4,000
Ankang Garrison Bde	Chang Hung-yuan	Ankang	4,000

* *Former Guominchun forces.*   † *Former Northeastern Army forces.*   ‡ *Personal troops of Chiang Kai-shek.*

Gansu – Ho Yueh-tsu, acting provincial governor

	commander	location	strength
Central Government Troops			
25th Army – Wan Yueh-Huang			
49th Division[†]	Li Chi-lan	Tienshui	8,000
51st Division[†]	Wang Yueh-wu	Lanzhou	8,000
37th Army[†] – Mao Ping-wen			
8th Division	Chen Shih-tao	Tungwei	10,000
24th Division	Li Ying	Lungsi	8,000
Temporary 1st Army – Ten Pao-shan			
165th Division	Lu Ta-chang	Minhsien	7,000
10th Ind. Brigade	Tu Chieh	Lanzhou	3,000
11th Ind. Brigade	Liu Pao-tang	Lanzhou	3,000
18th Division[†]	Chu Yueh-hua	Pingliang	8,000
25th Division[†]	Kuan Lin-cheng	Pingliang	10,000
97th Division[†]	Kung Ling-hsun	Lanzhou	8,000

Ningxia – Ma Hung-kuei, provincial chairman

	commander	location	strength
Central Government Troops			
15th Route Army[•]			
35th Division	Ma Hung-pin	Ningxia	10,000
1st Mixed Brigade	Lu Chung-liang	Yuwang	4,000
2nd Mixed Brigade	Ma Chuan-liang	Ningxia	4,000
3rd Mixed Brigade	Ma Ying-tsi	Kinki	4,000
1st Cavalry Brigade	Ma Hung-kuei	Chungwei	2,500
2nd Cavalry Brigade	Ma Chung-ching		2,500

Qinghai – Ma Lin, provincial chairman

	commander	location	strength
Central Government Troops			
Temporary 2nd Army – Ma Pu-fang			
100th Division	Ma Pu-fang	Sining	8,000
5th Cavalry Division	Ma Pu-ching	Sining	4,000
Provincial Troops			
1st Garrison Brigade	Ma Yuan-hai	Lotu	3,000
2nd Garrison Brigade	Ma Piao	Tatung	3,000
Lapuleng Garrison	Huang Chen-ching		5,000

[•] *Former Guominchun forces.*   [†] *Former Northeastern Army forces.*   [‡] *Personal troops of Chiang Kai-shek.*

Xinjiang – Li Yung, provincial chairman

	commander	location	strength
Provincial Troops			
Border Defense Army – Shang Shih-tsai			
5th Division		Tihwa	4,000
6th Ind. Brigade		Ili	3,000
15th Ind. Brigade		Tacheng	3,000
20th Ind. Brigade		Tihwa	4,000
1st Ind. Brigade		Tihwa	3,000
4th Ind. Brigade		Ili	3,000
Bodyguard Brigade		Tihwa	2,000
Cavalry Brigade		Hami	1,000
1st Artillery Regiment		Tihwa	600
White Russian troops		Tihwa	1,200

Zhejiang – Chu Chia-hua, provincial chairman

Central Government Troops

	commander	location	strength
Temporary 20th Division	Kao Tze-chu	Kashing	8,000
19th Division[†]	Li Chueh	Tsingtien	8,000
34th Division	Ku Chia-chi	Chuchow	8,000
55th Division[‡]	Li Sung-shan	Kashing	8,000
63rd Division[†]	Chung Kuang-jan	Kiangshan	9,000
3rd Ind. Brigade	Chiang Tso-chun	Shaohing	3,000
35th Ind. Brigade	Li Yi	Hangchow	4,000
38th Ind. Brigade	Pan Shan-chai	Hangchow	4,000

Provincial Troops

six peace preservation regiments			8,800

Jiangsi – Hsiung Shih-hui, provincial chairman

Central Government Troops

	commander	location	strength
20th Route Army – Chang Fang			
75th Division	Sung Tien-tsai	Kwangtseh	8,000
76th Division	Li Mo-lin	Linchwang	8,000
27th Army[‡] – Liu Hsing			
92nd Division	Liang Hua-sheng	Pingsiang	8,000
[separate units]			
50th Division[†]	Cheng Kuang-yueh	Wantsai	8,000
67th Division[†]	Hwang Wei	Kanchow	8,000
117th Ind. Brigade	Lu Feng-nien	Nanchang	4,000
7th Artillery Brigade[†]	Chia Fang	Nanchang	2,000
1st MP Brigade	Lin Ping-chou	Kiukiang	3,000

● *Former Guominchun forces.*　† *Former Northeastern Army forces.*　‡ *Personal troops of Chiang Kai-shek.*

Henan – Shang Chen, provincial chairman

	commander	location	strength
Central Government Troops			
3rd Army[‡] – Tseng Wan-chung			
7th Division	Tseng Wan-chung	Chengchow	10,000
12th Division	Tang Huai-yuan	Kaifeng	10,000
40th Army[•] – Pang Ping-hsun			
39th Division	Li Yun-yung	Sinsiang	12,000
13th Division[‡]	Hsia Chu-chung	Loyang	10,000
58th Division[‡]	Yu Chi-shih	Loyang	8,000
106th Division	Shen Ka	Junan	1,000
167th Division	Yang Chu-tung	Yencheng	7,000
10th Cavalry Division	Tan Tze-hsin	Hsuchang	2,000
118th Ind. Brigade	Liu Yueh-ting	Sincheng	3,000
24th Cavalry Brigade	Ho Cho-lien	Kioshan	1,500
6th Artillery Brigade[†]	Wang Ho-hua		1,800
26th Route Army[•] – Sun Lianzhong			
42nd Army – Sun Lianzhong			
27th Division	Feng An-pang	Mienchih	8,000
31st Division	Chih Feng-cheng	Shanchow	8,000
Nominal Central Government Troops, former Northeastern Army			
49th Army[†] – Liu To-chuan			
105th Division	Liu To-chuan	Nanyang	12,000
112th Division	Huo Shou-yi	Chenping	6,000
129th Division	Chu Fu-cheng	Tengchow	5,000
57th Army[†] – Miao Cheng-liu			
109th Division	Ho Kuei	Hwaiyang	6,000
111th Division	Chang En-to	Sihwa	5,000
115th Division	Liu Chi-wan	Chowkiakow	5,000
120th Division	Chao Yi	Luyi	6,000

[•] *Former Guominchun forces.*   [†] *Former Northeastern Army forces.*   [‡] *Personal troops of Chiang Kai-shek.*

Anhui – Liu Shang-ching, provincial chairmain

	commander	location	strength
Central Government Troops			
14th Army – Wei Li-huang			
10th Division	Li Mo-an	Liwan	8,000
83rd Division	Liu Kan	Hwoshan	8,000
85th Division[†]	Chan Tieh	Pengpu	7,000
40th Ind. Brigade	Sung Shih-ka	Chengyangkwang	3,000
44th Ind. Brigade	Ho Chi-hsiung	Yingshan	2,000
46th Ind. Brigade	Pao Kang	Guizhou	4,000
11th Cavalry Brigade	Tan Fu-lieh	Mengcheng	2,000
15th Cavalry Brigade	Chang Hung-chun	Hwoshan	2,000
11th Route Army[•] **– Liu Mao-en**			
15th Army – Liu Mao-en			
64th Division	Wu Ting-lin	Anking	8,000
65th Division	Liu Mao-en	Tungcheng	8,000
Nominal Central Government Troops, former Northeastern Army			
67th Army – Wu Ke-jen			
107th Division	Chin Kuei-pi	Pochow	4,000
108th Division	Chang Wen-ching	Fuyang	6,000
110th Division	Chang Li-heng	Kuoyang	5,000
117th Division	Wu Ka-jen	Taiho	5,000
Provincial Troops			
Garrison Brigade	Juan Chin-Ching	Anking	3,000

[•] *Former Guominchun forces.*   [†] *Former Northeastern Army forces.*   [‡] *Personal troops of Chiang Kai-shek.*

Hubei – Huang Shao-hsiung, provincial chairman

	commander	location	strength
Central Government Troops			
26th Army[‡] – Hsiao Chih-chu			
44th Division	Hsiao Chih-chu	Sianyang	10,000
30th Division[•]	Peng Chen-shan	Tungshan	7,000
33rd Division[•]	Feng Hsing-hsien	Chungyang	8,000
34th Division[†]	Chang Nai-wei	Shasi	7,000
40th Division[†]	Liu Pei-hsu	Hankow	7,000
47th Division[‡]	Pei Chang-huei	Siangyang	8,000
102nd Division	Ho Chih-chung	Sungfow	5,000
103rd Division	Po Hui-chang	Macheng	6,000
121st Division	Wu Chian-ping	Kichow	6,000
Temporary 8th Division	Chiang Pei-hsu	Yangsin	5,000
43rd Ind. Brigade	Liu Tseng-ching	Chienli	3,000
Provincial Troops			
Garrison	Shen Chen	Wuchang	4,000
1st Ind. Brigade	Wu Chen-ping	Wuchang	3,000
2nd Ind. Brigade	Li Ting-wu	Kwangki	3,000

[•] *Former Guominchun forces.*   [†] *Former Northeastern Army forces.*   [‡] *Personal troops of Chiang Kai-shek.*

Jiangsu – Chen Kuo-fu, provincial chairman

	commander	location	strength
Central Government Troops			
1st Army[†] – Hu Tsung-nan			
1st Division	Li Tieh-chun	Xuzhou	14,000
78th Division	Ting Teh-lung	Xuzhou	8,000
87th Division[‡]	Wang Ching-chiu	Changshu	8,000
88th Division[‡]	Sun Yuan-liang	Nanjing	9,000
Tax Police Division[‡]	Huang Chieh	Haichow	10,000
Training Division	Kuei Yun-ching	Nanjing	8,000
4th Ind. Brigade[‡]	Li Tseng-kai	Nanjing	3,000
1st Artillery Brigade[‡]		Nanjing	3,000
2nd Artillery Brigade[‡]		Nanjing	3,000
8th Artillery Brigade[‡]	Huang-Yun-an	Xuzhou	2,000
10 MP Regiments		Nanjing	12,000
3 Signal Regiments		Nanjing	3,800
2 Engineer Regiments		Nanjing	1,000
1 Transport Regiment		Nanjing	800
1 Railway Corps		Nanjing	800
3 Armored Train Corps		Nanjing	1,500
22nd Route Army – Chiang Ting-wen			
2nd Army – Chiang Ting-wen			
9th Division	Li Yen-nien	Chinkiang	9,000
Nominal Central Government Troops, former Northeastern Army			
51st Army[†] – Yu Hsueh-chung			
113th Division	Li Chen-tang	Sutsen	6,000
114th Division	Mo Chung-hang	Hwaian	6,000
118th Division	Chow Kuang-lieh	Shuyang	7,000
Artillery Regiment	Chang Wei-pin	Hwaian	1,500

• *Former Guominchun forces.*   † *Former Northeastern Army forces.*   ‡ *Personal troops of Chiang Kai-shek.*

Hunan – Ho Chien, provincial chairman

	commander	location	strength
Central Government Troops			
28th Army[†] – Tao Kuang			
15th Division	Wang Tung-yuan	Changteh	7,000
16th Division	Chang Liang-chi	Hengchow	7,000
62nd Division	Tao Liu	Changsha	7,000
18th Army[†] [part] – Li Shu-sen			
14th Division	Ho Kuei-chang	Yochow	10,000
43rd Army[†] – Kuo Ju-tung			
26th Division	Liu Yu-ching	Shenchow	8,000
59th Division[†]	Han Han-ying	Yochow	10,000
60th Division[†]	Chen Pei	Laiyang	8,000
96th Division[†]	Chao Hsi-kuang	Chenchow	8,000
32nd Ind. Brigade[†]	Hu Ta	Paoking	3,000

• *Former Guominchun forces.*   [†] *Former Northeastern Army forces.*   [‡] *Personal troops of Chiang Kai-shek.*

Sichuan – Liu Hsiang, provincial chairman

	commander	location	strength
Central Government Troops			
10th Army – Jsu Yuan-chuan			
41st Division	Hwang Hsin	Wanhsien	8,000
48th Division	Hsu Chi-wu	Chongqing	10,000
36th Army[†] – Chow Yun-yuan			
5th Division	Hsueh Pu-fu	Chengdu	8,000

Nominal Central Government Troops, actually controlled by Liu Hsiang

	commander	location	strength
6th Route Army – Liu Hsiang			
21st Army – Liu Hsiang			
145th Division	Jao Kuo-hua	Kiating	6,000
146th Division	Fan Shao-tseng	Suining	6,000
Temporary 2nd Division	Peng Cheng-fu	Nanchwan	3,600
23rd Army – Pan Wen-hua			
147th Division	Yang Kuo-chan	Tzechung	4,000
148th Division	Chan Wan-jen	Tungchwan	4,000
Temporary 9th Division	Pan Tso	Jungchang	2,000
Temporary 10th Division	Mu Shao-ching	Neikiang	1,800
41st Army – Sun Chen			
122nd Division	Wang Ming-chang	Kwanhsien	5,000
123rd Division	Tseng Hsien-tang	Sinfan	5,000
124th Division	Sun Chen	Mienchu	5,000
44th Army – Wang Tsan-pin			
149th Division	Kuo Chang-ming	Neikang	5,000
150th Division	Liao Chen	Tzeliutsing	4,000
Temporary 9th Brigade	Chen Lan-ting	Tzechung	3,400
45th Army – Teng Hsi-hou			
125th Division	Chen Ting-hsun	Tehyang	4,000
126th Division	Huang Ying	Chengdu	4,000
127th Division	Ma Yu-chih	Tzetung	4,000
128th Division	Yang Hsui-chun	Hwangyuan	5,000
131st Division	Chen Li	Chaohwa	5,000
104th Division	Li Chai-yu	Anhsien	5,000
144th Division	Kuo Hsun	Chengdu	6,000
161st Division	Hau Shao-tseng	Tungliang	7,000
Temporary 23rd Division	Lo Tze-chou	Lifan	5,000
Temporary 1st Brigade	Chang Pang-pen	Sufu	1,800
Temporary 2nd Brigade	Tang Kuo-chang	Kusung	1,800
Temporary 3rd Brigade	Chang Chieh-chang	Penshui	1,800
Temporary 4th Brigade	Shih Hsi-yi	Yungchwan	1,800
Temporary 6th Brigade	Fan Nan-hsuan	Tsangki	2,000
Temporary 7th Brigade	Tien Chung-yi	Chengdu	1,800
Temporary 8th Brigade	Hsiung Yu-chang	Kintang	1,800

• *Former Guominchun forces.*   † *Former Northeastern Army forces.*   ‡ *Personal troops of Chiang Kai-shek.*

Sikang – Liu Wen-hui, provincial chairman

	commander	location	strength

Nominal Central Government Troops, actually controlled by Liu Wen-hui

24th Army – Liu Wen-hui

	commander	location	strength
136th Division	Chen Kuang-tsao	Kangting	5,000
137th Division	Liu Yuan-tang	Luting	5,000
138th Division	Tang Ying	Yakiang	4,000
1st Ind. Brigade	Yu Sung-lin	Kangting	2,000

Guizhou – Hsueh Yueh, provincial chairman

Central Government Troops –Wu Chi-wei

4th Army† – Wu Chi-wei

	commander	location	strength
46th Division	Liu Tze-hsia		8,000
90th Division	Ou Chen	Hweiyang	8,000

9th Army† – Hao Meng-ling

	commander	location	strength
54th Division	Hao Meng-ling	Tsungyi	9,000
99th Division†	Kuo Sxe-yen	Hweiting	8,000
34th Ind. Brigade†	Lo Chi-kiang	Chinyuan	3,000

Fujian – Chen Yi, provincial chairman

Central Government Troops

39th Army – Liu To-ting

	commander	location	strength
56th Division	Liu Shang-chih	Pucheng	9,000
45th Ind. Brigade	Chang Luan-chi	Kienyang	3,000
3rd Division†	Li Yu-tang	Yenping	10,000
45th Division†	Tai Min-chuan	Foochow	7,000
52nd Division	Lu Hsing-jung	Yungan	8,000
80th Division	Chan Chi	Chwanchow	8,000
Temporary 10th Division	Chen Ta-chun	Fuan	6,000
6th Ind. Brigade	Chow Chih-chun	Chengho	3,000
37th Ind. Brigade†	Chen Teh-fa	Shahsien	3,000
2nd MP Brigade	Lin Tung	Mamoi	3,000

Nominal Central Government Troops, actually controlled by Yu Han-mou

4th Route Army [part] – Yu Han-mou

	commander	location	strength
156th Division	Teng Lung-kuang	Lungyan	6,000
157th Division	Huang Tao	Changchow	6,000

• *Former Guominchun forces.*   † *Former Northeastern Army forces.*   ‡ *Personal troops of Chiang Kai-shek.*

Guangdong – Wu Tieh-cheng, provincial chairman

	commander	location	strength
Central Government Troops			
18th Army[‡] [part] – Li Shu-sen			
11th Division	Chou Tze-shou	Canton	10,000
6th Division[†]	Chow Yen	Samshui	9,000
82nd Division[†]	Jung Ching-fang	Shiuchow	8,000
93rd Division[†]	Chen Lieh	Yingtak	8,000
98th Division[†]	Hsia Chu-chung	Fachow	8,000
9th Ind. Brigade[†]	Wang Ting-hua	Kiungtung	3,000
Nominal Central Government Troops, actually controlled by Yu Hanmou			
4th Route Army [part] – Mo Hsi-teh			
151st Division	Mo Hsi-teh	Shiuhing	6,000
152nd Division	Chang Chang	Kiungshan	6,000
153rd Division	Chang Jui-kuei	Chungfa	6,000
154th Division	Wu Chien-hsiung	Yeungkong	6,000
155th Division	Li Han-yun	Chaoan	6,000
158th Division	Tseng Yu-jen	Tsiuleng	6,000
159th Division	Tan Sui	Muiluk	6,000
160th Division	Yen Chao	Tsengcheng	6,000
Training Brigade	Lo Tze-hsia	Shiuchow	3,000

Guangxi – Huang Hsu-chu, provincial chairman

	commander	location	strength
Nominal Central Govt Troops, actually controlled by Li Tsung-jen & Pai Chung-hsi			
7th Army – Liao Yen			
19th Division	Hsi Chi-ming	Kweilin	8,000
21st Division	Yang Chun-chang	Liuchow	8,000
24th Division	Chang Shu-fan	Chwanchow	8,000
48th Army – Ho Wei-chen			
43rd Division	Ho Wei-chen	Kweilin	8,000
44th Division	Wang Tsan-pin	Wuchow	8,000
45th Division	Mo Shu-chieh	Jungyun	8,000
Temporary 1st Division	Shou Nian	Kweilin	6,000

* *Former Guominchun forces.*   † *Former Northeastern Army forces.*   ‡ *Personal troops of Chiang Kai-shek.*

Yunnan – Lung Yun, provincial chairman

	commander	location	strength

Nominal Central Government Troops, actually controlled by Lung Yun

10th Route Army – Lung Yun

	commander	location	strength
3rd Ind. Brigade	Lung Yu-tsang	Yunnan	6,400
5th Ind. Brigade	Lu Tao-yuan	Chiupei	4,400
7th Ind. Brigade	Kung Shun-pi	Chaotung	4,000
9th Ind. Brigade	Chang Chung	Yunnan	2,500
Guard Regiment	Chang Yi	Yunnan	2,000
Mixed Regiment	Wu Chung	Yunnan	1,000
Ind. Regiment	Tuan Tsan-kuai	Yunnan	1,600

• *Former Guominchun forces.*   † *Former Northeastern Army forces.*   ‡ *Personal troops of Chiang Kai-shek.*

Appendix III

Army Order of Battle
As ordered on 17 January 1938

I War Zone

1st Army Group
>> 53rd 68th, 77th, & 92nd Armies; 3rd Cavalry Army
>> 17th, 106th, 118th, New 8th, New 35th, & 4th Cavalry Divisions

20th Army Group
>> 32nd Army
>> 14th Cavalry Brigade

[total 25 infantry & 2 cavalry divisions, 2 infantry & 1 cavalry brigades]

II War Zone

South Route Commander
>> 3rd, 9th, 14th, 15th, 17th, 19th, 47th, 61st, & 93rd Armies

North Route Commander
>> 18th Army Group HQ
>> 33rd, 34th, & 35th Armies, 1st & 2nd Cavalry Armies
>> 66th, 71st, New 2nd Divisions

[total 27 infantry & 3 cavalry divisions, 3 infantry brigades]

III War Zone

10th Army Group
>> 28th, 70th Armies
>> 19th, 79th Divisions
>> 12th, 13th Provisional Brigades

19th Army Group
>> 4th, 18th, 25th, 73rd, & 79th Armies

23rd Army Group
>> 21st Army

28th Army Group
>> 23rd Army

New 4th Army

6th Independent Brigade

[total 24 infantry divisions, 6 infantry brigades]

IV War Zone

12th Army Group
>> 8th, 62nd, 63rd, 64th, & 65th Armies
>> 9th & 20th Independent Brigades

[total 9 infantry divisions, 2 infantry brigades]

V War Zone

3rd Army Group
  12th, 51st, 55th & 56th Armies

11th Army Group
  31st Army
  4th Column of New 4th Army

21st Army Group
  7th & 48th Armies

22nd Army Group
  41st & 45th Armies

24th Army Group
  57th Army

27th Army Group
  20th Army

3rd & 59th Divisions

[total 27 infantry divisions, 3 infantry brigades]

VIII War Zone

17th Army Group
  81st Army
  168th Division
  1st & 10th Cavalry Brigades
  Ningxia 1st & 2nd Garrison Brigades

80th & 82nd Armies, 5th Cavalry Army

191st Division

[total 5 infantry divisions, 5 cavalry divisions, 4 infantry & 4 cavalry brigades]

Wuhan Garrison HQ

2nd, 49th, 54th, 60th and 75th Armies

13th, 77th & 185th Divisions

River Defense HQ (57th Division)

[total 14 infantry divisions, 1 infantry brigade]

Xian HQ of the Generalissimo

11th Army Group
  37th & 43rd Armies

17th Army Group
  1st & 8th Armies

21st Army Group
  New 1st Army
  86th & 165th Divisions

38th & 46th Armies

1st Temporary Cavalry Division

[total 12 infantry & 3 cavalry divisions, 4 infantry brigades]

Fujian Pacification HQ

75th & 80th Divisions

Fujian 1st, 2nd, & 3rd Peace Preservation Brigades

2nd Marine Brigade

[total 2 infantry divisions, 4 infantry brigades]

MAC Direct Subordinate Units

2nd Army Group
>   30th & 42nd Armies

8th Army Group
>   36th, 50th, 92nd, 93rd, & 167th Divisions

20th Army Group
>   13th, 52nd, & 85th Armies

26th Army Group
>   10th & 87th Armies

[total 17 infantry divisions]

Units undergoing training & reorganization

Total 26 infantry divisions under reorganization & training; and 14 infantry divisions and 7 infantry brigades in rear

Appendix IV

Order of Battle
June 1940

I War Zone (Henan & northern Anhui provinces)

2nd Army Group
>> 30th, 42nd, & 58th Armies

3rd Army Group
>> 12th Army

40th & 76th Armies

[total 12 infantry & 1 cavalry divisions, 1 infantry & 1 cavalry brigades]

II War Zone (Shanxi & part of Shaanxi provinces)

4th Army Group
>> 38th, 47th, & 96th Armies

5th Army Group
>> 3rd, 15th, & 17th Armies

6th Army Group
>> 19th & 61st Armies, 1st Cavalry Army

7th Army Group
>> New 1st, 22nd, & 35th Armies

14th Army Group
>> 14th, 93rd, & 98th Armies

18th Army Group (ex 8th Route Army)

9th Army

Temporary 1st, Temporary 2nd, 66th, & 71st Divisions

[total 32 infantry & 5 cavalry divisions, 14 infantry & 3 cavalry brigades]

III War Zone (southern Jiangsu & Anwhei, Zhejiang, & Fujian provinces)

10th Army Group
>> 28th & 91st Armies

23rd Army Group
>> 21st & 50th Armies

25th Army Group
>> 100th Army
>> New 28th Division

32nd Army Group
>> 25th & 29th Armies
>> 67th Division

New 4th Army

[total 22 infantry divisions, 2 infantry brigades]

IV War Zone (Guangdong & Guangxi provinces)

9th Army Group
    4th & 65th Armies

12th Army Group
    62nd, 63rd, 66th, & 83rd Armies

16th Army Group
    46th & 64th Armies

[total 18 infantry divisions & 2 separate brigades]

V War Zone (western Anhui, northern Hubei, & southern Henan provinces)

11th Army Group
    39th & 84th Armies

22nd Army Group
    41st & 45th Armies

29th Army Group
    44th Army

33rd Army Group
    55th, 59th, & 77th Armies

Guerrilla Force
    7th & 48th Armies

[total 26 infantry & 1 cavalry divisions, 1 cavalry brigade]

VIII War Zone (Gansu, Ningxia, Qinghai, & Suiyuan provinces)

17th Army Group
    81st & 168th Divisions

New 2nd, 80th, & 82nd Armies

2nd, 5th, & 6th Cavalry Armies

191st Division

[total 6 infantry divisions, 9 infantry & 4 cavalry brigades]

IX War Zone (northwest Jiangxi, southern Hubei, & Hunan provinces)

1st Army Group
    New 3rd, 58th, & 60th Armies

19th Army Group
    32nd, 49th, 70th, 78th, & 79th Armies

20th Army Group
    53rd, 54th, & 87th Armies

27th Army Group
    20th Army

30th Army Group
    72nd Army

31st Army Group
    13th, 18th, 37th, 52nd, & 92nd Armies

Border Area Guerrilla Command
    8th & 73rd Armies

[total 52 infantry divisions]

X War Zone (Shaanxi province)

34th Army Group
27th & 90th Armies

16th Army

[total 9 infantry & 1 cavalry divisions, 1 infantry & 1 cavalry brigades]

Shandong–Jiangsu War Zone (northern Jiangsu & Shandong provinces)

51st, 57th, & 89th Armies

[total 7 infantry divisions]

Hebei–Chahar War Zone

New 5th, 69th, & 99th Armies

[total 5 infantry & 1 cavalry divisions]

IV and VII War Zones
Strengths, December 1941

The following tables were provided to the British Military Mission in Chongqing by the Chinese government, presumably as part of joint Sino-British assessments for the defense of Hong Kong.

In addition to the organic units listed below and on the following pages, attached artillery units from the GHQ pool were noted as opposite:

				Personnel	Horses	
IV War Zone						
16th Army Group	31st Army		131st Division	9,117	387	
			135th Division	11,455	534	
			188th Division	9,417	480	
			Army Troops	3,933	79	
	46th Army		New 19th Division	11,530	184	
			170th Division	11,632	162	
			175th Division	11,632	220	
			Army Troops	4,904	280	
	74th Army		51st Division	8,815	272	
			57th Division	8,707	150	
			58th Division	7,688	484	
			Army Troops	9,510	1,039	
	2nd Ind. Engineer Regt.			2,323	0	
	2nd Signal Regt.			2,578	0	
	Army Group Troops			1,346	152	

For IV War Zone:

- 5 AA artillery companies (total 4 Soviet 76mm guns, 8 x 37mm and 15 x 20mm German guns)

For VII War Zone:

- 2 battalions of the 14th (Medium) Artillery Regiment (total 12 German 150mm howitzers)
- 2nd Heavy Mortar Regiment (19 x 150mm mortars)
- 2 battalions of the 1st (Mountain) Artillery Regiment (total only 8 Bofors 75mm guns)
- 7 companies of infantry guns (total 28 Russian 37mm guns)
- 1 company AA artillery (4 German 37mm AA guns)

Although the data were provided by official sources the British Military Liaison office noted that the figures indicating strength and equipment must be accepted with considerable reserve.

Source: PRO WO208/230

Pistols	Rifles	Grenade throwers	Light MGs	Medium MGs	Mortars	37mm guns	AT guns	Mountain guns	Field guns	Anti-Aircraft guns
449	2,923	96	175	71	28	0	4	0	0	0
436	2,609	68	215	61	13	0	40	0	0	0
511	425?	62	168	54	30	0	4	0	0	0
246	1,269	0	35	5	0	0	0	0	0	0
672	2,475	0	204	53	30	0	4	0	0	0
466	3,084	0	222	53	27	0	4	0	0	0
640	2,487	0	207	47	24	0	4	0	0	0
274	425	0	34	1	2	4	0	10	0	0
0	2,020	0	774	50	31	0	0	0	0	0
0	1,656	0	141	50	25	0	0	0	0	0
0	1,472	0	67	36	21	0	0	0	0	0
0	1,204	0	30	4	0	0	16	16	18	6
96	1,112	0	30	0	0	0	0	0	0	0
96	1,112	0	20	0	0	0	0	0	0	0
0	0	0	0	0	0	0	0	0	0	0

			Personnel	Horses
VII War Zone				
12th Army Group	62nd Army	151st Division	9,089	50
		154th Division	10,539	70
		157th Division	8,880	65
		Army Troops	1,916	35
	63rd Army	152nd Division	11,068	601
		153rd Division	11,700	89
		186th Division	11,590	38
		Army Troops	2,932	21
	65th Army	158th Division	9,998	44
		160th Division	7,776	63
		187th Division	9,681	81
		Army Troops	2,931	28
	9th Ind. Brigade		6,441	12
	Army Group Troops		25,221	172
35th Army Group	4th Army	59th Division	12,134	118
		90th Division	9,111	115
		102nd Division	7,136	168
		Army Troops	4,790	40
	64th Army	155th Division	8,521	84
		156th Division	10,170	120
		159th Division	10,771	687
		Army Troops	3,076	469
	79th Army	Temp. 6th Division	7,375	91
		98th Division	8,674	197
		Army Troops	4,387	46
	Temp. 2nd Army	Temp. 7th Division	8,377	21
		Temp. 8th Division	8,099	36
		Army Troops	3,583	17
	25th Ind. Engineer Bn.		381	3
	26th Ind. Engineer Bn.		351	2
	27th Ind. Engineer Bn.		348	1
	Army Group Troops		897	22
Guangdong–Fujian–Jiangxi Border Command				
		6th Reserve Division	7,328	31
		20th Ind Brigade	5,184	55
		HQ Troops	1,003	2

Note: The mountain guns in the 12th Army Group were new-type Schneider 75mm weapons.

Pistols	Rifles	Grenade throwers	Light MGs	Medium MGs	Mortars	37mm guns	AT guns	Mountain guns	Field guns	Anti-Aircraft guns
255	1,711	162	282	47	13	0	4	0	0	0
0	2,665	89	246	47	12	0	6	0	0	0
353	2,504	90	206	51	14	0	4	0	0	0
43	231	0	14	0	0	0	0	6	0	0
628	2,614	89	211	48	14	0	4	0	0	0
373	3,398	89	233	43	13	5	2	0	0	0
514	2,820	0	248	43	14	0	4	0	0	0
48	529	0	31	0	6	0	0	6	0	0
47	2,798	153	186	52	18	0	0	0	0	0
90	1,911	185	214	59	14	0	4	0	0	0
224	2,024	160	207	32	17	0	4	0	0	0
17	322	0	14	0	0	0	5	0	0	0
201	1,857	38	159	24	3	0	0	0	0	0
553	7,698	23	446	54	11	12	0	0	0	
97	1,629	81	105	44	24	0	0	0		
152	2,155	73	144	46	31	0	2	0	0	0
264	1,788	157	154	50	23	0	4	0	0	0
0	413	0	0	20	7	8	0	0	0	0
346	2,544	0	127	52	0	0	0	0	0	0
165	2,480	175	196	39	29	0	8	0	0	0
21	2,659	0	143	59	28	0	4	0	0	0
65	150	0	22	0	0	12	0	0	0	0
22	1,857	153	175	7	30	0	0	0	0	0
192	2,269	160	194	61	30	0	6	0	0	0
78	842	16	34	19	0	12	0	0	0	0
262	2,892	51	141	48	14	0	0	0	0	0
461	2,784	46	187	58	8	0	0	3	0	0
168	970	4	15	9	0	0	0	0	0	0
9	200	0	6	0	0	0	0	0	0	0
9	199	0	6	0	0	0	0	0	0	0
9	200	0	6	0	0	0	0	0	0	0
10	248	0	12	4	0	0	0	0	0	0
74	1,749	50	390	0	6	0	0	0	0	0
306	2,307	41	170	35	9	0	0	4	0	0
15	186	0	13	0	0	0	0	0	0	0

Appendix VI

Army Order of Battle and Strength, October 1944

			Personnel	Animals	
15th Army Group					
	HQ Troops		3,270	174	
	2nd Cavalry Army	HQ troops	2,577	714	
		3rd Cavalry Division	4,708	1,870	
		Temp 14th Division	7,812	1,211	
	8th Cavalry Division		2,877	1,131	
	Temp 1st Division		1,826	59	
19th Army Group					
	Temp 1st Army	HQ troops	1,770	339	
		33rd Division	7,946	284	
		117th Division	13,671	892	
	Temp 9th Army	HQ troops	3,591	346	
		New 29th Division	4,401	76	
		119th Division	9,166	266	
28th Army Group					
	HQ Troops		895	100	
	13th Army	HQ troops	6,595	311	
		4th Division	6,660	393	
		89th Division	6,612	269	
		Temp 16th Division	6,022	105	
	78th Army	HQ troops	4,063	58	
		New 42nd Division	4,267	36	
		New 43rd Division	4,662	70	
		New 44th Division	5,814	31	

I War Zone

Notes to Appendix VI Tables

1: The data shown were supplied by the Military Affairs Committee to the US in September 1945, but dated from October 1944.
2: Only divisions and organic army units are shown. Independent GHQ units, such as the artillery pool, are not included.
3: Communist forces are not included.
4: No data are available for submachine guns or hand-held grenade dischargers.

Rifles & carbines	Rifle gren. lars	Light MGs	Medium MGs	Mortars	Infantry guns	Anti-tank rifles	Anti-tank guns	Flamethrowers	AA MGs	AA guns	Mountain guns	Field artillery
948	?	21	8	11	0	0	0	0	0	0	0	0
1,052	?	60	9	5	0	0	0	0	0	0	0	0
1,599	?	122	7	7	0	0	0	0	0	0	8	0
1,100	?	117	24	9	0	0	0	0	0	0	0	0
1,506	?	95	19	0	0	0	0	0	0	0	0	0
456	?	6	4	0	0	0	0	0	0	0	0	0
1,797	?	121	2	5	0	0	0	0	0	0	1	0
1,827	?	137	21	7	0	0	0	0	0	0	0	0
5,470	?	384	44	19	0	0	0	0	0	0	1	0
1,622	?	121	2	5	0	0	0	0	0	0	0	0
2,378	?	55	12	2	0	0	0	0	0	0	0	0
2,443	?	184	64	26	0	4	0	0	0	0	0	0
98	?	6	2	0	0	0	0	0	0	0	0	0
830	?	40	2	0	0	0	0	0	0	0	6	0
1,679	?	231	53	21	0	0	3	0	0	0	0	0
1,685	?	111	38	24	0	0	4	0	0	0	0	0
1,539	?	135	48	8	0	0	0	0	0	0	0	0
3,041	?	181	60	19	0	0	0	0	0	0	0	0
987	?	56	24	3	0	0	0	0	0	0	0	0
576	?	57	17	3	0	0	0	0	0	0	0	0
496	?	79	43	4	0	0	0	0	0	0	0	0

I War Zone (*continued*)

			Personnel	Animals
31st Army Group				
	HQ Troops		924	154
	85th Army	HQ troops	6,826	575
		23rd Division	7,127	175
		110th Division	8,164	336
		Temp 55th Division	8,031	94
	89th Army	HQ troops	3,328	204
		New 20th Division	4,100	129
		New 1st Division	5,193	114
		Temp 62nd Division	2,583	11
4th Army Group				
	38th Army	HQ troops	2,985	142
		17th Division	6,271	271
		New 35th Division	4,782	142
	96th Army	HQ troops	3,381	287
		177th Division	6,541	172
		New 14th Division	5,569	235
36th Army Group				
	HQ Troops		1,053	80
	27th Army	HQ troops	3,155	134
		45th Division	?	?
		46th Division	5,782	93
	Temp 4th Army	HQ troops	2,327	66
		47th Division	6,177	177
		Temp 4th Division	4,734	177
	15th Army	HQ troops	2,923	13
		64th Division	5,807	10
		65th Division	5,073	22
	Direct Command	New 36th Division	6,507	1,753
		Temp 12th Division	8,518	2,102

Rifles & carbines	Rifle gren. lnrs	Light MGs	Medium MGs	Mortars	Infantry guns	Anti-tank rifles	Anti-tank guns	Flamethrowers	AA MGs	AA guns	Mountain guns	Field artillery
?	?	0	0	0	0	0	0	0	0	0	0	0
4,161	?	15	0	0	0	0	0	0	0	0	0	0
1,734	?	153	59	26	0	0	0	0	0	0	0	0
1,703	?	136	36	34	0	0	0	0	0	0	0	0
1,215	?	33	25	11	0	0	0	0	0	0	0	0
1,699	?	126	38	21	0	0	0	0	0	0	3	0
949	?	75	27	8	0	0	0	0	0	0	0	0
1,140	?	80	25	15	0	0	3	0	0	0	0	0
1,021	?	81	24	15	0	0	3	0	0	0	0	0
397	?	24	6	0	0	0	0	0	0	0	0	0
945	?	136	36	8	0	0	0	0	0	0	0	0
919	?	130	31	4	0	0	0	0	0	0	0	0
3,565	?	193	42	23	0	0	0	0	0	0	0	0
1,528	?	87	25	11	0	0	0	0	0	0	0	0
1,436	?	90	27	12	0	0	0	0	0	0	0	0
1,719	?	0	0	0	0	0	0	0	0	0	0	0
1,719	?	32	42	14	0	0	0	0	0	0	0	0
1,638	?	95	36	24	0	0	0	0	0	0	0	0
1,578	?	149	36	12	4	0	0	0	0	0	0	0
186	?	12	0	0	0	0	0	0	0	0	0	0
1,560	?	140	33	10	0	0	0	0	0	0	0	0
1,520	?	101	32	9	0	0	0	0	0	0	0	0
309	?	25	5	0	0	0	0	0	0	0	4	0
818	?	65	22	10	0	0	0	0	0	0	0	0
836	?	62	22	10	0	0	0	0	0	0	0	0
4,556	?	108	2	6	0	0	0	0	0	0	0	0
5,150	?	70	4	27	0	0	0	0	0	0	0	0

				Personnel	Animals	
34th Army Group						
		HQ Troops		3,321	134	
		1st Army	HQ troops	7,548	955	
			1st Division	11,486	778	
			78th Division	11,428	960	
			167th Division	11,972	960	
		16th Army	HQ troops	4,269	940	
			109th Division	8,322	552	
			Reserve 1st Division	7,479	523	
			Reserve 3rd Division	8,271	715	
		90th Army	HQ troops	4,607	1,233	
			28th Division	8,572	485	
			53rd Division	8,640	661	
			61st Division	8,971	597	
37th Army Group						
		HQ Troops		1,023	83	
		36th Army	HQ troops	3,857	570	
			Temp 52nd Division	5,274	188	
			Temp 15th Division	5,766	245	
			Temp 59th Division	5,329	463	
		80th Army	HQ troops	3,903	463	
			165th Division	7,276	466	
			New 27th Division	6,408	347	
			New 37th Division	6,063	554	
		New 7th Army	HQ troops	2,536	370	
			Temp 24th Division	4,430	129	
			Temp 25th Division	5,480	168	
			Temp 26th Division	4,662	132	
	3rd Army		HQ troops	2,543	238	
			7th Division	6,890	416	
			12th Division	7,726	37	
			New 3rd Division	3,839	no data	
	57th Army		HQ troops	3,199	357	
			8th Division	8,163	494	
			New 34th Division	6,054	307	

I War Zone (continued)

Rifles & carbines	Rifle gren. lsrs	Light MGs	Medium MGs	Mortars	Infantry guns	Anti-tank rifles	Anti-tank guns	Flamethrowers	AA MGs	AA guns	Mountain guns	Field artillery
815	?	81	13	0	0	0	0	0	0	0	0	0
1,926	?	24	4	0	12	0	0	0	0	0	0	0
2,872	?	237	67	30	0	0	0	0	0	0	0	0
2,537	?	274	16	30	0	0	12	0	0	0	12	0
2,381	?	180		29	0	0	0	0	0	0	0	0
832	?	35	2	0	0	0	0	0	0	0	21	0
2,155	?	163	52	30	0	0	0	0	0	0	0	0
2,391	?	171	54	30	0	0	4	0	0	0	0	0
2,395	?	171	54	30	0	0	9	0	0	0	0	0
8,575	?	548	166	131	27	0	10	0	0	0	21	0
2,437	?	164	54	30	2	0	3	0	0	0	0	0
2,510	?	175	54	18	4	0	3	0	0	0	0	0
2,300	?	164	54	29	4	0	4	0	0	0	0	0
200	?	12	6	0	0	0	0	0	0	0	0	0
726	?	18	2	0	0	0	0	0	0	0	0	0
2,351	?	171	54	12	0	0	0	0	0	0	0	0
2,371	?	171	54	12	0	0	0	0	0	0	0	0
2,392	?	177	53	18	0	0	5	0	0	0	0	0
548	?	16	2	0	0	0	0	0	0	0	0	0
2,350	?	171	54	18	0	0	0	0	0	0	0	0
2,220	?	119	52	9	0	0	0	0	0	0	0	0
1,648	?	156	43	18	0	0	0	0	0	0	0	0
257	?	6	0	0	0	0	0	0	0	0	0	0
1,966	?	101	27	12	0	0	0	0	0	0	0	0
1,560	?	171	36	12	0	0	0	0	0	0	0	0
2,011	?	104	28	12	0	0	0	0	0	0	0	0
3,596	?	19	2	0	0	0	0	0	0	0	0	0
1,751	?	163	44	8	0	0	0	0	0	0	0	0
1,473	?	189	44	12	0	0	0	0	0	0	0	0
663	?	22	6	0	0	0	0	0	0	0	12	0
2,732	?	175	46	31	0	0	0	0	0	0	0	0
1,942	?	120	54	12	0	0	0	0	0	0	0	0

			Personnel	Animals
I War Zone (continued)	**3rd Cavalry Army**		HQ troops	1,272	594
			9th Cavalry Division	3,115	2,478
			New 7th Cav. Div.	2,713	1,142
	17th Army		HQ troops	4,687	87
			84th Division	6,740	215
			New 2nd Division	6,765	286
	40th Army		HQ troops	2,248	54
			39th Division	7,347	131
			106th Division	5,802	157
			New 40th Division	2,848	93
			Temp 2nd Cav Division	3,280	1,254
	Temp 15th Army		HQ troops	3,787	68
			New 29th Division	9,820	37
			Temp 27th Division	7,582	79
	12th Army		HQ troops	10,593	359
			111th Division	8,439	169
			112th Division	9,379	214
	I War Zone Totals			527,329	39,278

				Personnel	Animals
II War Zone	**HQ Troops**			952	135
	6th Army Group				
		HQ Troops		*no data*	
		19th Army	HQ troops	1,294	137
			68th Division	6,850	236
			Temp 37th Division	6,414	212
			Temp 42nd Division	6,382	252
		23rd Army	HQ troops	1,349	124
			Temp 40th Division	6,362	284
			Temp 46th Division	6,172	255
			Temp 47th Division	6,562	221

Rifles & carbines	Rifle gren. lrs	Light MGs	Medium MGs	Mortars	Infantry guns	Anti-tank rifles	Anti-tank guns	Flamethrowers	AA MGs	AA guns	Mountain guns	Field artillery
376	?	22	2	0	0	0	0	0	0	0	0	0
1,797	?	91	16	2	0	0	0	0	0	0	0	0
1,329	?	48	4	0	0	0	0	0	0	0	0	0
771	?	64	2	6	0	0	0	0	0	0	0	0
1,760	?	117	34	9	0	0	0	0	0	0	0	0
1,536	?	102	36	9	0	0	0	0	0	0	0	0
325	?	11	2	0	0	0	0	0	0	0	0	0
1,382	?	162	39	16	0	0	0	0	0	0	0	0
103	?	162	39	12	0	0	0	0	0	0	0	0
923	?	55	13	8	0	0	0	0	0	0	0	0
1,470	?	41	6	0	0	0	0	0	0	0	0	0
125	?	6	2	0	0	0	0	0	0	0	0	0
2,578	?	45	12	2	0	0	0	0	0	0	0	0
1,756	?	5	2	6	0	0	0	0	0	0	0	0
1,672	?	112	2	5	0	0	0	0	0	0	1	0
1,794	?	131	21	4	1	0	0	0	0	0	0	0
1,846	?	122	21	7	1	0	0	0	0	0	0	0
155,462	?	10,157	2,670	1,118	1	0	58	0	0	0	68	0
26	?	15	6	0	0	0	0	0	0	0	0	0
no data												
272	?	26	0	0	0	0	0	0	0	0	0	0
1,756	?	341	18	6	0	0	0	0	0	0	0	0
1,893	?	332	17	6	0	0	0	0	0	0	0	0
1,500	?	197	17	6	0	0	0	0	0	0	0	0
235	?	35	0	0	0	0	0	0	0	0	0	0
1,612	?	247	9	6	0	0	0	0	0	0	0	0
1,654	?	209	2	6	0	0	0	0	0	0	0	0
1,385	?	49	1	2	0	0	0	0	0	0	0	0

			Personnel	Animals	
7th Army Group					
	HQ Troops		956	119	
	33rd Army	HQ troops	1,347	135	
		71st Division	6,414	263	
		Temp 38th Division	6,375	206	
		Temp 41st Division	6,385	191	
	34th Army	HQ troops	6,476	240	
		73rd Division	6,404	240	
		Temp 44th Division	6,413	190	
		Temp 45th Division	6,411	148	
8th Army Group					
	HQ Troops		954	120	
	43rd Army	HQ troops	1,302	56	
		70th Division	6,419	87	
		Temp 39th Division	6,173	271	
		Temp 43rd Division	6,413	181	
	61st Army	HQ troops	501	96	
		72nd Division	7,868	160	
		69th Division	237	944	
		Temp 48th Division	8,172	300	
13th Army Group					
	HQ Troops		957	132	
	83rd Army	HQ troops	1,341	135	
		66th Division	6,172	219	
		Temp 49th Division	6,412	233	
		Temp 50th Division	6,173	235	
	1st Cavalry Army	HQ troops	1,347	136	
		1st Cavalry Division	6,173	1,166	
		2nd Cavalry Division	6,486	182	
		4th Cavalry Division	6,171	187	
	196th Brigade		6,477	246	
II War Zone Totals			183,287	7,967	

II War Zone (continued)

Rifles & carbines	Rifle gren. bars	Light MGs	Medium MGs	Mortars	Infantry guns	Anti-tank rifles	Anti-tank guns	Flamethrowers	AA MGs	AA guns	Mountain guns	Field artillery
121	?	11	0	0	0	0	0	0	0	0	0	0
290	?	25	0	0	0	0	0	0	0	0	0	0
1,388	?	216	16	6	0	0	0	0	0	0	0	0
1,860	?	16	9	4	0	0	0	0	0	0	0	0
1,634	?	226	6	6	0	0	0	0	0	0	0	0
1,255	?	249	6	6	0	0	0	0	0	0	0	0
1,369	?	256	4	6	0	0	0	0	0	0	0	0
1,338	?	272	7	5	0	0	0	0	0	0	0	0
1,041	?	173	3	5	0	0	0	0	0	0	0	0
101	?	14	0	0	0	0	0	0	0	0	0	0
191	?	27										
883	?	210	2	10	0	0	0	0	0	0	0	0
1,300	?	238	4	6	0	0	0	0	0	0	0	0
795	?	237	1	2	0	0	0	0	0	0	0	0
944	?	151	7	6	0	0	0	0	0	0	0	0
883	?	210	2	10	0	0	0	0	0	0	0	0
	?	151	7	6	0	0	0	0	0	0	0	0
898	?	82	14	6	0	0	0	0	0	0	0	0
144	?	15	0	0	0	0	0	0	0	0	0	0
330	?	34	0	0	0	0	0	0	0	0	0	0
1,530	?	110	14	0	0	0	0	0	0	0	0	0
1,500	?	140	18	6	0	0	0	0	0	0	0	0
1,559	?	320	6	13	0	0	0	0	0	0	0	0
249	?	27	0	0	0	0	0	0	0	0	0	0
1,873	?	310	12	6	0	0	0	0	0	0	0	0
1,687	?	235	11	6	0	0	0	0	0	0	0	0
1,404	?	227	8	0	0	0	0	0	0	0	0	0
1,211	?	244	1	6	0	0	0	0	0	0	0	0
38,085	?	5,876	228	153	0	0	0	0	0	0	0	0

			Personnel	Animals
32nd Army Group				
	HQ Troops		991	28
	88th Army	HQ troops	3,382	5
		79th Division	1,379	11
		New 21st Division	6,478	14
		Temp 33rd Division	4,373	16
	Temp 11th Brigade		2,365	15
25th Army Group				
	HQ Troops		899	15
	49th Army	HQ troops	3,079	24
		26th Division	10,820	66
		105th Division	2,198	10
		Reserve 5th Division	6,286	26
23rd Army Group				
	HQ Troops		902	20
	28th Army	HQ troops	6,416	26
		62nd Division	8,187	2
		52nd Division	4,108	37
		192nd Division	6,427	72
		28A total	25,138	137
	50th Army	HQ troops	5,548	24
		144th Division	4,308	57
		148th Division	7,481	167
		New 7th Division	9,862	45
	21st Army	HQ troops	5,194	19
		145th Division	6,784	22
		146th Division	8,375	40
		147th Division	4,333	20
25th Army		HQ troops	3,134	49
		40th Division	8,161	64
		108th Division	8,900	62
		Temp 13th Division	6,360	21
70th Army		HQ troops	2,472	24
		80th Division	7,573	139
		107th Division	7,197	24
		Reserve 9th Division	5,849	25
		33rd Brigade	5,150	48
III War Zone Totals			174,565	1,237

III War Zone

Rifles & carbines	Rifle gren. bars	Light MGs	Medium MGs	Mortars	Infantry guns	Anti-tank rifles	Anti-tank guns	Flamethrowers	AA MGs	AA guns	Mountain guns	Field artillery
180	?	12	6	0	0	0	0	0	0	0	0	0
5,257	?	489	144	46	0	0	0	0	0	0	0	0
1,913	?	168	45	28	0	0	2	0	0	0	0	0
942	?	187	33	12	0	0	0	0	0	0	0	0
1,270	?	104	35	8	0	0	0	0	0	0	0	0
925	?	40	3	0	0	0	0	0	0	0	0	0
5,972	?	448	148	69	0	0	8	0	0	0	0	0
900	?	27	12	0	0	0	0	0	0	0	0	0
2,008	?	185	50	30	0	0	4	0	0	0	0	0
2,106	?	185	60	31	11	0	4	0	0	0	0	0
1,953	?	36	12	7	0	0	0	0	0	0	0	0
783	?	38	0	0	0	0	0	0	0	0	0	0
852	?	?	?	?	0	0	0	0	0	0	0	0
?	?	?	?	?	0	0	0	0	0	0	0	0
?	?	?	?	?	0	0	0	0	0	0	0	0
?	?	?	?	?	0	0	0	0	0	0	0	0
5,257	?	489	114	56	0	0	0	0	0	0	0	0
266	?	19	10	0	0	0	0	0	0	0	0	0
929	?	19	10	0	0	0	0	0	0	0	0	0
1,624	?	150	32	11	0	0	0	0	0	0	0	0
2,259	?	179	55	11	0	0	0	0	0	0	0	0
5,596	?	401	159	196	0	0	0	0	0	0	0	0
1,800	?	162	54	21	0	0	0	0	0	0	0	0
1,800	?	162	54	21	0	0	0	0	0	0	0	0
1,213	?	60	29	9	0	0	0	0	0	0	0	0
758	?	39	2	0	0	0	0	0	0	0	12	0
2,037	?	211	53	22	0	0	3	0	0	0	0	0
2,039	?	211	57	20	0	0	4	0	0	0	0	0
1,266	?	131	24	8	0	0	0	0	0	0	0	0
367	?	14	0	0	0	0	0	0	0	0	2	0
2,391	?	247	66	30	0	0	4	0	0	0	0	0
2,316	?	208	63	30	0	0	4	0	0	0	0	0
1,381	?	118	26	10	0	0	0	0	0	0	0	0
?	?	?	?	0	0	0	0	0	0	0	0	0
57,407	?	4,739	1,325	662	11	0	33	0	0	0	14	0

			Personnel	Animals
16th Army Group				
	HQ Troops		1,031	24
	31st Army	HQ troops	6,014	477
		131st Division	8,908	325
		135th Division	5,995	595
		188th Division	8,537	404
	79th Army	HQ troops	4,565	64
		98th Division	6,669	143
		194th Division	6,554	69
		Temp 6th Division	5,967	60
		79A total (undist)	19,755	336
	46th Army	HQ troops	6,836	309
		170th Division	6,949	51
		135th Division	8,888	228
		New 19th Division	8,521	238
	93rd Army	10th, Temp 2nd, New 8th Divs	7,055	?
	20th Army	133rd, 134th, New 20th Divs	21,922	122
27th Army Group				
	26th Army	32nd, 41st, 44th Divs	19,246	158
	37th Army	60th, 95th, 140th Divs	20,467	281
	44th Army	149th, 150th, 161st, 162nd Divs	31,468	237
	62nd Army	151st, 157th, 158th Divs	20,987	137
	64th Army	HQ troops	3,071	42
		155th Division	7,388	41
		145th Division	6,074	7
		159th Division	7,294	76
IV War Zone Totals			227,605	4,084

IV War Zone

Rifles & carbines	Rifle gren. lnrs	Light MGs	Medium MGs	Mortars	Infantry guns	Anti-tank rifles	Anti-tank guns	Flamethrowers	AA MGs	AA guns	Mountain guns	Field artillery
231	?	12	4	0	0	0	0	0	0	0	0	0
1,551	?	115	3	0	0	0	0	0	0	0	11	0
2,504	?	252	63	36	0	0	4	0	0	0	0	0
1,443	?	146	66	36	0	0	4	0	0	0	0	0
2,654	?	225	66	36	0	0	4	0	0	0	0	0
?	?	?	?	?	0	0	?	0	0	0	0	0
?	?	?	?	?	0	0	?	0	0	0	0	0
?	?	?	?	?	0	0	?	0	0	0	0	0
?	?	?	?	?	0	0	?	0	0	0	0	0
4,236	?	540	114	100	0	0	12	0	0	0	0	0
519	?	35	5	0	0	0	0	0	0	0	11	0
2,436	?	150	63	31	0	0	4	0	0	0	0	0
2,525	?	225	66	36	0	0	4	0	0	0	0	0
2,516	?	224	64	36	0	0	4	0	0	0	0	0
1,951	?	271	73	23	0	0	0	0	0	0	0	0
1,077	?	211	66	26	0	0	0	0	0	0	0	0
3,446	?	303	108	33	0	0	9	0	0	0	15	0
5,753	?	574	147	62	10	0	0	0	0	0	0	0
815	?	101	70	133	0	0	0	0	0	0	0	0
1,864	?	207	59	11	0	0	0	0	0	0	3	0
358	?	33	2	0	8	0	0	0	0	0	0	0
950	?	5	21	20	2	0	0	0	0	0	0	0
804	?	150	30	13	0	0	0	0	0	0	0	0
1,100	?	134	39	20	4	0	0	0	0	0	0	0
38,733	?	3,913	1,129	652	24	0	45	0	0	0	40	0

			Personnel	Animals
2nd Army Group				
	HQ Troops		961	144
	55th Army	HQ troops	5,476	462
		22nd Division	no data	
		29th Division	4,768	372
		74th Division	6,851	372
		81st Division	no data	
		55th Army total	17,095	1,206
	68th Army	HQ troops	7,557	629
		119th Division	8,944	266
		143rd Division	8,577	242
		Temp 36th Division	6,910	38
21st Army Group				
	HQ Troops		1,018	151
	7th Army	HQ troops	5,321	935
		171st Division	7,792	180
		172nd Division	8,536	110
		173rd Division	8,085	95
	48th Army	HQ troops	5,305	193
		138th Division	7,992	90
		176th Division	8,756	458
	84th Army	HQ troops	3,805	566
		174th Division	7,130	100
		189th Division	9,138	101
22nd Army Group				
	HQ Troops		1,006	22
	45th Army	125th, 127th Divs	19,306	506
	47th Army	104th, 178th Divs	18,210	134
	69th Army	181st, Temp 28th Divs	14,949	138
41st Army		HQ Troops	5,568	281
		122nd Division	9,222	164
		123rd Division	5,734	74
		124th Division	9,948	150
51st Army		HQ Troops	8,564	103
		113th Division	7,466	68
		114th Division	7,234	22
V War Zone Totals			232,524	8,282

V War Zone

Rifles & carbines	Rifle gren. lnrs	Light MGs	Medium MGs	Mortars	Infantry guns	Anti-tank rifles	Anti-tank guns	Flamethrowers	AA MGs	AA guns	Mountain guns	Field artillery
286	?	17	6	0	0	0	0	0	0	0	0	0
888	?	32	12	11	0	0	0	0	0	0	5	0
no data												
1,880	?	144	54	22	0	0	0	0	0	0	0	0
1,862	?	141	50	1	0	0	0	0	0	0	0	0
no data												
34,630	?	317	116	34	0	0	0	0	0	0	0	0
475	?	21	4	0	0	0	0	0	0	6	12	0
2,443	?	185	64	26	0	0	4	0	0	0	0	0
2,480	?	214	68	27	0	0	4	0	0	0	0	0
1,102	?	60	10	8	0	0	0	0	0	0	0	0
286	?	17	6	0	0	0	0	0	0	0	0	0
3,692	?	63	25	3	0	0	0	0	0	0	8	0
2,585	?	205	56	20	0	0	4	0	0	0	0	0
2,297	?	205	53	20	0	0	4	0	0	0	0	0
1,319	?	133	36	18	0	0	0	0	0	0	0	0
1,411	?	15	13	18	0	0	4	0	0	0	0	0
2,189	?	151	51	14	0	0	0	0	0	0	0	0
3,308	?	16	54	19	0	0	0	0	0	0	0	0
1,423	?	15	18	16	0	0	4	0	0	0	0	0
1,890	?	151	48	10	0	0	0	0	0	0	0	0
1,887	?	150	39	10	0	0	0	0	0	0	0	0
2,101	?	13	4	0	0	0	0	0	0	0	0	0
3,169	?	279	87	19	0	0	0	0	0	0	0	0
2,871	?	307	52	37	0	0	0	0	0	0	0	0
4,397	?	226	94	24	0	0	0	0	0	0	0	0
868	?	74	27	7	0	0	0	0	0	0	0	8
2,010	?	187	49	30	0	0	0	0	0	0	0	0
1,071	?	117	25	15	0	0	0	0	0	0	0	0
2,335	?	209	53	30	0	0	0	0	0	0	0	0
1,902	?	107	7	4	4	0	0	0	0	0	0	3
751	?	93	15	3	0	0	0	0	0	0	0	0
765	?	62	14	3	0	0	0	0	0	0	0	0
89,057		3,771	1,181	443	4		24	0	0	6	25	0

			Personnel	Animals	
Upper Yangtze River Garrison Force					
	HQ Troops		3,765	11	
	94th Army	HQ troops	9,603	448	
		5th Division	7,980	70	
		121st Division	9,645	137	
		Temp 35th Division	6,803	15	
	30th Army	HQ troops	8,524	272	
		27th Division	9,503	302	
		30th Division	9,190	392	
		31st Division	9,204	741	
10th Army Group					
	HQ Troops		868	10	
	18th Army	HQ troops	6,081	219	
		11th Division	8,622	93	
		18th Division	8,683	107	
		55th Division	9,026	66	
	87th Army	HQ troops	2,757	120	
		43rd Division	7,616	69	
		118th Division	7,173	49	
		New 23rd Division	4,626	66	
	66th Army	HQ troops	2,357	18	
		185th Division	7,993	43	
		199th Division	8,210	45	
	92nd Army	HQ troops	6,240	303	
		21st Division	6,569	379	
		142nd Division	6,291	140	
		Temp 56th Division	3,045	102	
26th Army Group					
	HQ Troops		869	33	
	75th Army	HQ troops	3,124	289	
		6th Division	8,289	43	
		16th Division	7,627	35	
		Reserve 4th Division	9,115	57	
	32nd Army	HQ troops	3,195	242	
		Temp 34th Division	3,691	17	
		139th Division	8,964	72	
		141st Division	9,863	56	

VI War Zone

Rifles & carbines	Rifle gren. lnrs	Light MGs	Medium MGs	Mortars	Infantry guns	Anti-tank rifles	Anti-tank guns	Flamethrowers	AA MGs	AA guns	Mountain guns	Field artillery
394	?	11	21	5	0	0	0	0	0	0	0	0
1,077	?	14	10	0	0	0	0	0	0	0	22	0
1,625	?	135	57	36	0	0	4	0	0	0	0	0
1,837	?	149	64	35	0	0	4	0	0	0	0	0
1,806	?	136	29	12	0	0	0	0	0	0	0	0
1,281	?	43	8	0	0	0	0	0	0	0	12	0
1,898	?	145	55	23	0	0	0	0	0	0	0	0
1,464	?	145	54	26	0	0	0	0	0	0	0	0
1,973	?	145	53	26	0	0	0	0	0	0	0	0
120	?	6	4	0	0	0	0	0	0	0	0	0
7,022	?	41	26	11	0	0	4	0	0	0	5	0
1,997	?	174	62	32	12	0	4	0	0	0	0	0
2,102	?	164	45	30	0	0	4	0	0	0	0	0
2,475	?	157	32	14	0	0	4	0	0	0	0	0
958	?	25	6	0	0	0	0	0	0	0	7	0
1,581	?	159	54	27	0	0	4	0	0	0	0	0
1,768	?	173	54	25	0	0	4	0	0	0	0	0
1,467	?	83	30	12	0	0	4	0	0	0	0	0
522	?	90	16	6	0	0	0	0	0	0	0	0
1,860	?	171	54	23	0	0	2	0	0	0	0	0
2,088	?	171	54	30	0	0	4	0	0	0	0	0
772	?	39	19	12	0	0	0	0	0	0	0	0
1,508	?	167	633	28	0	0	0	0	0	0	0	0
1,582	?	169	62	25	0	0	0	0	0	0	0	0
920	?	80	25	9	0	0	0	0	0	0	0	0
159	?	6	6	0	0	0	0	0	0	0	12	0
715	?	28	4	0	0	0	0	0	0	0	0	0
2,043	?	194	60	33	0	0	4	0	0	0	0	0
2,135	?	138	52	24	0	0	0	0	0	0	0	0
1,989	?	212	62	33	0	0	4	0	0	0	0	0
429	?	28	6	0	0	0	0	0	0	0	12	0
1,085	?	32	9	6	0	0	0	0	0	0	0	0
1,894	?	178	49	28	2	0	4	0	0	0	0	0
1,950	?	199	51	25	0	0	0	0	0	0	0	0

			Personnel	Animals
24th Army Group				
	HQ Troops		938	50
	73rd Army	HQ troops	6,131	108
		15th Division	9,239	15
		77th Division	8,905	0
		Temp 5th Division	2,197	15
	74th Army	HQ troops	9,644	626
		51st Division	10,132	146
		57th Division	8,941	91
		58th Division	9,655	188
	100th Army	HQ troops	1,789	37
		19th Division	7,034	50
		63rd Division	6,152	56
		75th Division	16,211	8
33rd Army Group				
	HQ Troops		1,394	158
	59th Army	HQ troops	3,472	627
		38th Division	8,852	317
		108th Division	7,832	380
		Temp 53rd Division	5,737	229
	77th Army	HQ troops	3,195	310
		37th Division	7,582	442
		132nd Division	7,606	417
		179th Division	8,658	340
86th Army		HQ troops	2,573	49
		13th Division	7,892	36
		67th Division	7,415	22
		Temp 32nd Division	1,490	15
VI War Zone Totals			395,777	9,793

VI War Zone (continued)

Rifles & carbines	Rifle gren. lnrs	Light MGs	Medium MGs	Mortars	Infantry guns	Anti-tank rifles	Anti-tank guns	Flamethrowers	AA MGs	AA guns	Mountain guns	Field artillery
200	?	12	6	0	0	0	0	0	0	0	0	0
1,965	?	210	53	27	0	0	0	0	0	0	0	0
1,554	?	118	38	17	0	0	2	0	0	0	0	0
1,314	?	144	32	9	0	0	0	0	0	0	0	0
402	?	36	8	6	0	0	0	0	0	0	0	0
1,478	?	40	14	0	0	0	11	0	0	6	7	0
2,370	?	187	53	32	0	0	0	0	0	0	0	0
2,039	?	152	37	19	0	0	14	0	0	0	0	0
2,122	?	151	47	28	0	0	0	0	0	0	0	0
502	?	41	9	7	0	0	0	0	0	0	0	0
1,678	?	138	48	10	0	0	0	0	0	0	0	0
1,295	?	150	37	13	0	0	0	0	0	0	0	0
196	?	16	0	4	0	0	0	0	0	0	0	0
226	?	39	14	0	0	0	0	0	0	0	0	0
9,211	?	46	4	0	0	0	4	0	0	4	19	0
2,393	?	168	60	28	0	0	21	0	0	0	0	0
2,489	?	186	57	30	0	0	0	0	0	0	0	0
2,156	?	152	54	18	0	0	0	0	0	0	0	0
392	?	25	2	4	0	0	0	0	0	0	5	0
2,058	?	164	43	18	0	0	24	0	0	0	0	0
2,038	?	148	47	18	0	0	0	0	0	0	0	0
3,017	?	159	54	17	0	0	0	0	0	0	0	0
645	?	25	1	0	0	0	0	0	0	0	4	0
1,695	?	154	54	27	0	0	2	0	0	0	0	0
1,571	?	156	42	25	0	0	1	0	0	0	0	0
701	?	58	17	0	0	0	0	0	0	0	0	0
100,203		6,682	2,657	953	14	0	133	0	0	10	105	0

				Personnel	Animals
VII War Zone	**12th Army Group**				
		HQ Troops		12,015	179
		63rd Army	HQ troops	2,992	22
			152nd Division	7,683	28
			153rd Division	7,426	25
			186th Division	6,986	34
		65th Army	154th, 160th, 187th Divs	28,675	144
		9th Ind Bde		7,970	18
		20th Ind Bde		6,685	46
	VII War Zone Totals			51,757	497
VIII War Zone	**Shanxi, Shaanxi & Suiyuan border forces**				
		22nd Army	HQ troops	5,424	317
			86th Division	6,416	146
			6th Cavalry Division	3,480	2,366
		New 26th Div.		*no data*	191
		7th Cav. Div.		*no data*	2,685
	Northeast Shock Troops		HQ troops	1,148	193
			New 5th Cavalry Division	3,537	808
			New 6th Cavalry Division	2,013	446
	35th Army		HQ troops	2,265	454
			101st Division	6,600	440
			New 31st Division	6,329	383
			New 32nd Division	6,410	3,773
	Temporary 3rd Army		T 10th, T 11th, T 17th Divs	17,281	1,971
	4th Cavalry Army		HQ troops	1,344	799
			New 3rd Cavalry Division	1,795	1,824
			New 4th Cavalry Division	2,104	2,179
			1st Division	2,565	247

Rifles & carbines	Rifle gren. lnrs	Light MGs	Medium MGs	Mortars	Infantry guns	Anti-tank rifles	Anti-tank guns	Flamethrowers	AA MGs	AA guns	Mountain guns	Field artillery
6,261	?	332	35	5	0	0	0	0	0	0	4	0
776	?	24	4	0	0	0	8	0	0	0	0	0
2,535	?	170	47	12	0	0	4	0	0	0	0	0
2,317	?	170	47	12	0	0	4	0	0	0	0	0
1,272	?	171	43	14	0	0	4	0	0	0	0	0
7,865	?	682	53	45	0	0	12	0	0	0	3	0
1,251	?	137	24	7	0	0	0	0	0	0	0	0
1,685	?	164	34	11	0	0	0	0	0	0	0	0
23,922	?	1,846	289	105	0	0	32	0	0	0	7	0
2,860	?	66	36	57	0	0	0	0	0	0	12	0
3,533	?	90	36	18	0	0	0	0	0	0	8	0
2,271	?	67	12	6	0	0	0	0	0	0	0	0
1,643	?	30	4	3	0	0	0	0	0	0	0	0
2,360	?	143	12	6	0	0	10	0	0	0	0	0
174	?	20	0	2	0	0	0	0	0	0	0	0
890	?	23	9	1	0	0	0	0	0	0	0	0
1,278	?	20	7	0	0	0	0	0	0	0	0	0
861	?	26	36	18	0	0	0	0	0	0	0	0
1,526	?	0	30	9	0	0	4	0	0	0	0	0
1,526	?	148	31	0	0	0	0	0	0	0	0	0
1,512	?	142	30	9	0	0	4	0	0	0	0	0
3,142	?	140	48	7	0	0	0	0	0	0	0	0
476	?	8	4	3	0	0	0	0	0	0	0	0
720	?	21	4	2	0	0	0	0	0	0	0	0
432	?	56	12	6	0	0	0	0	0	0	0	0
1,460	?	80	80	4	0	0	0	0	0	0	0	0

			Personnel	Animals
17th Army Group				
	HQ Troops		4,000	899
	11th Army	HQ troops	1,379	256
		168th Division	9,847	332
		Temp 9th Division	7,841	273
		Temp 31st Division	7,847	227
		1st Cavalry Brigade	7,787	1,211
		2nd Cavalry Brigade	*no data*	1,141
	81st Army	35th, Temp 60th Divs, Cav Regt	14,995	568
3rd Army Group				
	HQ Troops		870	5
	91st Army	T 58th, New 4th Divs, 10th Cav Div	20,326	3,627
29th Army Group				
	HQ Troops		918	91
	42nd Army	191st, Reserve 7th Divs	18,014	803
	New 2nd Army	New 45th, New 46th Divs	16,420	1,271
40th Army Group				
	HQ Troops		894	7,069
	8th Cav Army	5th, T 1st Cav Divs	*no data*	
	82nd Army	100th, T 61st Divs, New 8th Cav Div	17,526	4,101
128th Division			5,474	1,249
Temp 3rd Div			4,524	856
11th Cav. Div.			1,803	1,592
12th Cav Div			2,027	1,827
New 1st Cav Div			2,065	1,935
VIII War Zone Totals			213,268	48,555

VIII War Zone (continued)

Rifles & carbines	Rifle gren. lnrs	Light MGs	Medium MGs	Mortars	Infantry guns	Anti-tank rifles	Anti-tank guns	Flamethrowers	AA MGs	AA guns	Mountain guns	Field artillery
1,587	?	19	3	0	0	0	0	0	0	0	0	0
204	?	4	0	0	0	0	0	0	0	0	0	0
2,143	?	171	89	14	0	0	0	0	0	0	0	0
1,014	?	90	71	10	0	0	0	0	0	0	0	0
1,233	?	81	15	7	0	0	0	0	0	0	0	0
71	?	10	0	0	0	0	0	0	0	0	0	0
43	?	14	0	0	0	0	0	0	0	0	0	0
4,981	?	183	99	0	0	0	0	0	0	0	0	0
200	?	12	6	0	0	0	0	0	0	0	0	0
6,566	?	4100	128	44	0	0	0	0	0	0	0	0
320	?	12	6	0	0	0	0	0	0	0	0	0
4,799	?	367	110	52	0	0	0	0	0	0	0	0
5,517	?	371	116	38	0	0	8	0	0	0	12	0
468	?	150	6	0	0	0	0	0	0	0	0	0
3,285	?	133	8	0	0	0	0	0	0	0	0	0
365	?	26	33	0	0	8	8	0	0	0	0	0
4,072	?	59	36	12	0	0	0	0	0	0	0	0
3,885	?	58	34	12	0	0	0	0	0	0	0	0
1,794	?	34	20	0	0	0	0	0	0	0	0	0
1,677	?	37	23	0	0	0	0	0	0	0	0	0
1,727	?	26	13	0	0	0	0	0	0	0	0	0
72,615		7,037	1,207	340	0	8	34	0	0	0	32	0

				Personnel	Animals
IX War Zone	HQ Troops				*no data*
	1st Army Group				
		HQ Troops		3,726	146
		58th Army	New 10th, New 11th Divisions	10,674	222
		New 3rd Army	183rd, New 12th Divisions	18,986	383
	30th Army Group				
		HQ Troops		974	122
		72nd Army	34th, New 13th, New 15th, New 16th Divs	29,816	332
		4th Army	59th, 102nd Divisions	13,632	168
		99th Army	HQ Troops	3,430	138
			92nd Division	6,661	80
			99th Division	3,512	64
			197th Division	885	10
	IX War Zone Totals			92,296	1,665
Hebei–Chahar War Zone	HQ Troops			1,010	221
	New 8th Army		HQ troops	1,800	101
			New 6th Division	4,040	90
			Temp 29th Division	3,815	115
	Hebei–Chahar War Zone Totals			10,465	527

Rifles & carbines	Rifle gren. lnrs	Light MGs	Medium MGs	Mortars	Infantry guns	Anti-tank rifles	Anti-tank guns	Flamethrowers	AA MGs	AA guns	Mountain guns	Field artillery
no data												
168	?	12	4	0	0	0	0	0	0	0	0	0
4,704	?	324	128	40	0	0	8	0	0	0	0	0
996	?	52	4	0	0	0	8	0	0	0	0	0
996	?	52	4	0	0	0	0	0	0	0	0	0
6,589	?	768	215	98	0	0	4	0	0	0	0	0
4,544	?	296	96	30	0	0	0	0	0	0	0	0
1,635	?	509	164	70	0	0	12	0	0	11	0	0
1,081	?	96	19	14	0	0	18	0	0	0	0	0
963	?	102	29	14	0	0	14	0	0	0	0	0
217	?	21	2	1	0	0	1	0	0	0	0	0
21,893		2,232	665	267	0	0	65	0	0	11	0	0
0	?	0	0	0	0	0	0	0	0	0	0	0
237	?	0	0	0	0	0	0	0	0	0	0	0
1,172	?	100	18	10	0	0	0	0	0	0	0	0
2,714	?	94	15	9	0	0	0	0	0	0	0	0
4,123	?	208	33	19	0	0	0	0	0	0	0	0

			Personnel	Animals
MAC direct	9th Army	54th, New 24th Divs	20,177	778
	10th Army	3rd, Res 10th Divs	4,714	*no data*
	29th Army	91st, 193rd, Reserve 11th Divs	21,681	786
	39th Army	56th, Temp 51st Divs	21,442	715
	76th Army	24th, New 5th, Temp 57th Divs	30,920	828
	97th Army	166th, 196th Divisions	14,114	0
	98th Army	42nd, 169th Divisions	12,023	234
	Temp 2nd Army	Res 6th, Temp 7th, Temp 8th Divs	23,279	106
	MAC Totals		148,350	3,447
Generalissimo Temporary HQ Kunming	**1st Army Group**			
		HQ Troops	1,428	81
	1st Route Army	HQ troops	23,960	0
		182nd Div.	*no data*	*no data*
		184th Div.	*no data*	*no data*
		total	24,963	81
	2nd Route Army (Temp 20th, Temp 21st, Temp 22nd Divs) tot	HQ troops	964	155
		Temp 20th Div.	10,053	266
		Temp 21st Div.	9,391	290
		Temp 22nd Div.	9,600	275
	Temp 18th Division		10,197	295
	5th Army Group			
		HQ Troops	889	36
	5th Army	HQ troops	11,295	1,125
		49th Div.	6,062	129
		96th Div.	8,325	92
	Temp 19th Division		9,837	339
	Hon 2nd Division		8,281	57
	9th Army Group			
		HQ Troops	988	40
	52nd Army	HQ troops	7,396	526
		2nd Div.	8,697	646
		25th Div.	8,369	625
		195th Div.	7,606	592
	Temp 23rd Division		9,351	213
	Generalissimo HQ Totals		143,629	3,787

Rifles & carbines	Rifle gren. lnrs	Light MGs	Medium MGs	Mortars	Infantry guns	Anti-tank rifles	Anti-tank guns	Flamethrowers	AA MGs	AA guns	Mountain guns	Field artillery
2,655	?	225	53	18	0	0	0	0	0	0	8	0
2,725	?	253	70	23	0	0	0	0	0	0	0	0
1,222	?	126	34	10	0	0	0	0	0	0	0	0
8,505	?	694	200	154	0	0	8	0	0	0	0	0
5,738	?	377	110	60	0	0	8	0	0	0	0	0
2,520	?	248	72	24	0	0	0	0	0	0	0	0
8,226	?	434	154	36	0	0	0	0	0	0	0	0
31,591		2357	693	325	0	0	16	0	0	0	8	0
275	?	26	10	6	0	0	0	0	0	0	0	0
817	?	47	2	0	0	0	0	0	0	0	12	0
2,396	127	166	38	51	0	18	5	0	0	0	0	0
1,919	84	163	55	62	0	18	4	0	0	0	0	0
5,132	?	376	95	133	0	36	9	0	0	0	12	0
126	?	3	2	0	0	0	0	0	0	0	0	0
1,700	?	173	36	29	0	0	4	0	0	0	0	0
2,100	?	173	36	33	0	0	4	0	0	0	0	0
2,100	?	173	36	33	0	0	4	0	0	0	0	0
2,100	?	191	36	79	0	0	3	0	0	0	0	0
no data												
1,438	?	277	6	9	0	0	6	0	0	0	24	0
2,400	?	380	48	54	0	0	0	0	0	0	0	0
2,040	?	380	53	53	0	0	0	0	0	0	10	0
2,100	?	173	36	31	0	0	4	0	0	0	0	0
2,748	?	175	54	30	0	0	0	0	0	0	0	0
450	?	25	6	2	0	0	0	0	0	0	0	0
756	?	33	15	2	0	0	0	0	0	0	13	0
2,292	?	245	63	86	0	0	4	0	0	4	0	0
1,785	?	193	55	81	0	0	4	0	0	7	0	0
2,043	?	239	76	81	0	0	3	0	0	6	0	0
2,100	?	173	36	30	0	0	4	0	0	0	0	0
30,597		2,934	564	607	0	72	49	0	0	0	71	0

			Personnel	Animals
11th Army Group				
	HQ Troops		1,091	158
	2nd Army	HQ troops	7,430	572
		9th Division	9,062	179
		76th Division	4,495	195
		New 33rd Division	6,544	251
	6th Army	HQ troops	5,090	594
		Reserve 2nd Division	5,072	1,242
		New 39th Division	4,491	150
	71st Army	HQ troops	7,625	1,290
		87th Division	5,295	506
		88th Division	4,024	404
		New 28th Division	3,592	241
2th Army Group				
	HQ Troops		1,944	51
	53rd Army	HQ troops	5,042	1,124
		116th Division	6,125	115
		130th Division	5,590	105
	54th Army	HQ troops	5,248	980
		36th Division	4,394	517
		198th Division	5,054	329
8th Army		HQ Troops	6,430	607
		82nd Division	5,634	?
		103rd Division	6,265	?
		Hon 1st Division	7,851	?
CEF Direct		93rd Division	6,437	214
		200th Division	8,859	?
Chinese Expeditionary Force Totals			138,684	9,824

(Side heading: Chinese Expeditionary Forces)

Rifles & carbines	Rifle gren. lnrs	Light MGs	Medium MGs	Mortars	Infantry guns	Anti-tank rifles	Anti-tank guns	Flamethrowers	AA MGs	AA guns	Mountain guns	Field artillery
156	0	16	0	0	0	0	0	0	0	0	0	0
1,404	0	51	17	0	2	0	22	0	0	0	18	0
2,273	168	699	42	82	0	18	0	27	0	0	0	0
1,446	88	177	44	79	0	17	22	27	0	0	0	0
2,513	53	107	54	83	0	18	0	27	0	0	0	0
5,864	0	246	65	18	0	0	8	0	0	0	0	0
78	48	27	58	15	0	15	0	23	0	0	0	0
1,986	0	118	29	53	0	0	0	0	0	0	0	0
1,339	?	61	5	16	1	0	16	0	0	0	12	1
2,466	?	187	76	79	0	0	0	0	0	0	0	0
2,166	?	189	54	80	0	0	0	0	0	0	0	0
2,027	?	199	60	89	0	0	0	0	0	0	0	0
722	2	33	12	0	0	0	0	0	0	0	0	0
?	?	?	?	?	?	?	?	0	0	0	?	0
?	?	?	?	?	?	?	?	?	0	0	?	0
?	?	?	?	?	?	?	?	?	0	0	?	0
592	18	49	2	0	18	0	12	0	0	0	12	0
1,554	76	174	27	74	101	18	0	24	0	0	0	0
982	28	169	31	71	65	16	0	19	0	0	0	0
952	60	19	2	0	0	12	0	0	0	0	12	0
1,562	22	149	43	73	0	0	0	26	0	0	0	0
1,834	87	183	36	81	0	18	0	27	0	0	0	0
2,043	154	153	54	77	0	18	0	2	7	0	0	0
1,831	?	227	59	94	0	5	0	0	0	0	0	0
2,508	?	229	59	65	0	0	0	0	0	0	9	0
38,298	804	3,462	829	1,129	184	155	80	202	0	0	63	1

			Personnel	Animals
Chinese Army in India				
New 1st Army		(New 30th, New 38th Divs)	21,769	2,535
New 6th Army		HQ Troops	1,642	914
		14th Division	9,807	491
		50th Division	10,051	498
		New 22nd Division	12,423	1,745
Chinese Army in India Totals			55,692	6,183
Rear Pacification Units				
Chongqing Garrison				
	14th Army	HQ troops	2,499	208
		83rd Division	5,708	297
		85th Division	4,488	197
		94th Division	1,494	13
	New 25th Div.		4,673	?
Sichuan–Zikang Border Defense Command				
	HQ troops		1,798	247
	95th Army	126th, New 9th Divs; Ind Bde	27,322	789
		New 13th Division	?	?
		New 18th Division	7,391	410
		136th Division	6,916	394
		137th Division	6,916	396
		New 1st Brigade	6,066	?
		Ind Brigade	4,214	240
		Ind Regiment	1,986	111
		6th Cavalry Regt	370	388
Sichuan–Shanxi–Hebei Pacification Forces				
		HQ troops	2,319	604
		163rd Division	6,945	393
		164th Division	6,945	393
		Ind Brigade	4,199	240
Rear Pacification Units Totals			98,050	4,687

Rifles & carbines	Rifle gren. lnrs	Light MGs	Medium MGs	Mortars	Infantry guns	Anti-tank rifles	Anti-tank guns	Flamethrowers	AA MGs	AA guns	Mountain guns	Field artillery
11,625	269	748	144	395	0	68	48	60	0	0	60	0
2,651	0	67	21	71	0	10	44	0	0	0	0	0
2,863	263	162	53	125	18	12	0	25	0	0	0	0
2,205	162	349	66	154	0	26	0	38	0	0	0	0
6,137	394	362	71	197	0	36	24	32	0	0	24	0
25,481	1,088	1,688	355	942	18	152	116	155	0	0	84	0
591	?	56	20	10	0	0	1	0	0	0	0	0
1,601	?	146	29	15	0	0	3	0	0	0	0	0
1,051	?	75	22	12	0	0	2	0	0	0	0	0
124	?	12	6	2	0	0	0	0	0	0	0	0
2,496	?	104	0	72	0	0	0	0	0	0	0	0
150	0	0	0	0	0	0	0	0	0	0	0	0
9,306	?	486	175	24	0	0	0	0	0	0	0	0
2,579	?	420	0	88	0	0	0	0	0	0	0	0
1,860	?	333	8	120	0	0	0	0	0	0	0	0
2,987	?	27	36	12	0	0	0	0	0	0	0	0
2,990	?	27	36	12	0	0	0	0	0	0	0	0
1,530	?	162	16	60	0	0	0	0	0	0	0	0
1,886	?	18	24	8	0	0	0	0	0	0	0	0
940	?	9	12	4	0	0	0	0	0	0	0	0
320	?	0	0	0	0	0	0	0	0	0	0	0
305	?	19	0	0	0	0	0	0	0	0	0	0
2,622	?	162	36	66	0	0	0	0	0	0	0	0
2,622	?	162	36	66	0	0	0	0	0	0	0	0
1,748	?	106	24	46	0	0	0	0	0	0	0	0
33,338		2,218	420	505	0	0	6	0	0	0	0	0

Army Strength, July 1945

	Supreme HQ Chinese Army		
	HQ & direct control	1st Front Army	2nd Front Army
Army Group HQs	0	0	0
Army HQs	3	3	3
Divisions	6	9	9
Brigades	1	0	0
Officers	7,624	8,559	6,637
Enlisted	107,396	103,476	75,186
Horses & mules	7,644	8,924	1,717
Rifles & carbines	29,167	18,781	15,264
Submachine guns	7,734	1,597	384
Rifle grenade launchers	1,114	966	757
Grenade dischargers	0	646	25
Pistols	0	1,972	2,763
Light machine guns	2,628	1,819	1,924
Medium machine guns	571	427	425
Mortars	931	613	317
Anti-tank rifles	65	144	72
Bazookas	194	50	51
Anti-tank guns	194	87	30
Flat-trajectory infantry guns	48	0	0
Anti-aircraft machine guns	5	3	0
Anti-aircraft guns	0	0	0
Pack artillery	85	25	0
Field artillery	12	0	0
Signal pistols	188	502	58
Flamethrowers	0	0	0
Fortress artillery	0	0	0
Howitzers	0	0	0
Medium & heavy artillery guns	0	0	0

Note: Figures do not include Communist or local-defense units.

3rd Front Army	4th Front Army	Kunming Defense Forces	Kunming Defense HQ	HQ & direct command
1	0	0	0	1
5	4	2	2	2
14	11	7	7	6
0	0	0		0
10,837	9,856	8,157	6,262	4,815
115,352	107,299	89,386	64,699	33,763
5,581	2,937	4,708	4,117	1,045
34,523	32,197	28,519	19,663	7,381
2,827	4,469	4,672	1,922	0
1,726	614	1,093	1,285	406
1,164	223	1,302	247	162
1,471	656	208	383	142
2,078	2,810	1,815	1,579	757
586	569	357	297	207
519	540	639	629	123
51	52	138	147	6
175	165	105	70	1
99	46	72	27	2
0	0	0	0	0
0	0	4	6	5
0	0	0	0	0
108	60	60	36	3
0	0	0	0	0
212	157	139	133	6
36	36	0	0	0
0	0	0	0	0
0	0	0	0	0
0	0	0	0	0

	Generalissimo's Field HQ in Hanchang			
	I War Zone	*V War Zone*	*X War Zone*	*XI War Zone*
Army Group HQs	5	2	3	0
Army HQs	11	4	5	2
Divisions	29	10	13	6
Brigades	0			
Officers	20,673	8,358	10,340	5,063
Enlisted	217,659	85,663	121,375	50,923
Horses & mules	17,207	4,879	4,346	1,054
Rifles & carbines	47,171	16,173	33,368	16,103
Submachine guns	0	0	0	0
Rifle grenade launchers	1,632	233	360	283
Grenade dischargers	1,402	705	1,758	198
Pistols	1,311	1,126	3,121	469
Light machine guns	3,654	1,354	1,788	510
Medium machine guns	1,096	394	453	92
Mortars	643	221	125	59
Anti-tank rifles	163	36	0	0
Bazookas	42	0	0	0
Anti-tank guns	38	19	10	0
Flat-trajectory infantry guns	16	0	16	0
Anti-aircraft machine guns	16	3	6	0
Anti-aircraft guns	0	0	0	0
Pack artillery	21	0	20	0
Field artillery	43	0	0	4
Signal pistols	65	59	83	0
Flame throwers	0	0	0	0
Fortress artillery	0	0	0	0
Howitzers	8	0	0	0
Medium & heavy artillery guns	0	0	0	0

Note: Figures do not include Communist or local-defense units.

G'mo's Field HQ in Southeast

III War Zone	VII War Zone	IX War Zone	G'mo's HQ in Chongqing	II War Zone	VI War Zone	VIII War Zone
3	1	2	0	5	3	4
7	2	7	0	7	8	6
21	7	21	1	24	19	15
2	2		1	1		
18,110	8,375	14,958	1,027	18,701	14,891	10,064
21,865	84,043	156,819	17,297	146,719	210,011	115,648
1,969	647	2383	471	?	6,222	15,401
43,097	15,196	25,810	0	?	50,437	37,985
276	14	12	0	?	1,584	210
365	693	240	0	?	2,933	2,622
1,550	5	978	0	?	1,349	519
647	233	856	0	?	1,988	2,374
4,100	1,689	2,281	0	?	4,418	1,565
1,080	308	581	0	?	1,086	454
754	105	220	0	?	943	152
0	0	84	0	?	104	0
0	0	2	0	?	69	0
37	32	48	0	?	55	16
0	0	0	0	?	0	0
6	0	6	0	?	10	12
7	0	0	0	?	20	8
12	10	3	0	?	77	26
0	0	0	0	?	33	27
46	0	12	0	?	74	5
0	0	0	0	?	0	0
0	0	0	0	?	86	0
0	0	0	0	?	0	0
0	0	0	0	0	0	0

	XII War Zone	Inspectorate General of Org & Training	Chinese Army in India	Chongqing garrison	Pacification Troops	
Army Group HQs		0	0	0	0	
Army HQs	4	0	0	1	3	
Divisions	9	8	0	4	8	
Brigades	1	0	0	0	4	
Regiments		1	2		4	
Battalions			3			
Companies						
Officers	4,698	7,214	740	3,807	5,393	
Enlisted	57,268	68,300	7,819	38,237	68,006	
Horses & mules	5,534	1,881	?	1,217	4,435	
Rifles & carbines	17,480	14,841	?	13,372	21,082	
Submachine guns	178	2,351	?	169	572	
Rifle grenade launchers	592	992	?	808	0	
Grenade dischargers	77	0	?	0	0	
Pistols	492	41	?	1,023	1,084	
Light machine guns	754	1,502	?	924	1173	
Medium machine guns	241	368	?	227	212	
Mortars	129	568	?	347	538	
Anti-tank rifles	0	135	?	0	0	
Bazookas	0	0	?	0	0	
Anti-tank guns	11	0	?	65	8	
Flat-trajectory infantry guns	0					
Anti-aircraft machine guns	0	0	?	0	0	
Anti-aircraft guns	0	0	?	0	0	
Pack artillery	10	0	?	17	12	
Field artillery	0	0	?	0	0	
Signal pistols	4	66	?	20	0	
Flame throwers	0	0	?	0	0	
Fortress artillery	0	0	?	0	0	
Howitzers	0	0	?	0	0	
Medium & heavy artillery guns	0	0	0	0	0	

Note: Figures do not include Communist or local-defense units.

Under direct command	Cavalry	Artillery	Engineer	Motor Transport	Mechanized	Signal	Gendarmerie	Irregular forces
0	0	0						
1	5	0						
4	22	0						
1	3							
2	1	23	25	20	2	7	28	
		2		9	6	10	5	
			2		1	1		
3,210	8,716	3,816	5,603	4,333	2,740	6,885	3,896	21,977
33,931	85,777	41,399	48,294	32,192	16,078	32,813	29,555	214,442
642	42,882	5,393	1,037	0	0	91	33	?
10,278	42,152		0	0	3,599	0	21,462	
263	385		0	0	1,352	0	144	
505	256		0	0	0	0	0	
99	296		0	0	0	0	0	
327	2,353		0	0	341	0	6,135	
896	1,965		0	0	134	0	297	
225	333		0	0	281	0	43	
126	72	149	0	0	11	0	1	
0	0		0	0	0	0	0	
0	0		0	0	0	0	0	
7	0	98	0	0	95	0	0	*unknown*
			0	0	40	0	0	
0	0		0	0	17	0	0	
0	0		0	0	0	0	0	
11	0	94	0	0	0	0	0	
0	0	60	0	0	0	0	0	
3	97		0	0	27	0	29	
0	0		0	0	0	0	0	
0	0		0	0	0	0	0	
0	0		0	0	12	0	0	
0	0	190	0	0	0	0	0	

Army Strength, September 1945

Formations and Personnel

		Army Group HQs	Army HQs	
GHQ Chinese Army	HQ & Direct Units	0	3	
	1st Front Army	0	3	
	2nd Front Army	0	3	
	3rd Front Army	1	5	
	4th Front Army HQ	0	3	
	Kunming Garrison	0	2	
	Burma Road	0	2	
Generalissimo's SE HQ	III War Zone	3	7	
	VII War Zone	1	2	
	IX War Zone	2	5	
Generalissimo's Kunming HQ		0	0	
I War Zone		5	10	
II War Zone		4	7	
V War Zone		2	4	
VI War Zone		2	6	
VIII War Zone		4	6	
X War Zone		2	4	
XI War Zone		1	7	
XII War Zone		0	4	
Youth Army		0	3	
Chongqing Garrison		0	1	
Pacification Troops		0	3	
AMC Direct Command		1	2	
Cavalry Branch		0	3	
Artillery Branch		0	0	
Engineer Branch		0	0	
Quartermaster Branch		0	0	
Signal Branch		0	0	
Mechanized Branch		0	0	
Military Police		0	0	
Shock Troops		0	0	
Grand totals		28	97	

Note: Figures do not include Communist or local-defense units.

Divisions	Brigades	Regiments	Battalions	Companies	Officers	Enlisted	Animals
9	0	0	0	0	9,154	109,156	9,119
11	0	0	0	0	8,243	116,415	7,031
9	0	0	0	0	6,547	76,405	1,846
14	0	0	0	0	9,832	122,353	4,505
8	0	0	0	0	8,373	77,569	2,364
7	1	0	0	0	6,597	8,4431	4,750
6	0	0	0	0	5,569	58,954	4,529
19	0	0	0	0	15,074	185,857	2,127
6	0	0	0	0	6,554	6,4157	600
15	0	0	0	0	11,898	129,275	2,255
0	1	0	0	0	454	8,248	0
26	0	0	0	0	19,919	213,712	14,996
21	0	0	0	0	19,599	160,578	?
10	0	0	0	0	8,454	103,647	4,366
15	0	0	0	0	12,223	164,666	4,205
15	0	0	0	0	11,186	123,770	15,564
9	0	0	0	0	7,318	76,500	3,969
19	0	0	0	0	14,161	183,776	5,037
8	0	0	0	0	5,150	42,381	4,874
8	0	0	0	0	8,223	85,090	2,495
4	0	0	0	0	6,571	57,136	1,420
6	0	2	0	0	5,385	68,774	4,505
6	2	0	0	0	5,621	56,132	937
19	3	0	0	0	7,308	78,119	40,784
0	0	31	2	0	5,198	55,466	3,740
0	0	26	0	0	5,455	49,269	1,055
0	0	20	10	0	4,522	32,686	0
0	0	7	10	0	5,805	30,779	74
0	0	2	7	1	2,356	15,137	0
0	0	2	5	0	3,903	29,754	41
0	0	27	0	0	21,747	210,668	0
270	7	115	34	1	268,399	2,870,860	147,188

Infantry Weapons

		Pistols	Submachine guns	Rifles & carbines
GHQ Chinese Army	HQ & Direct Units	0	11,076	46,232
	1st Front Army	1,043	1,597	20,185
	2nd Front Army	2,375	379	14,903
	3rd Front Army	1,471	2,827	34,523
	4th Front Army HQ	656	4,469	32,197
	Kunming Garrison	208	4,672	28,519
	Burma Road	362	1,922	19,663
Generalissimo's SE HQ	III War Zone	469	189	44,928
	VII War Zone	333	1	15,909
	IX War Zone	756	13	24,344
G'mo's Kunming HQ		?	?	?
I War Zone		1,346	3	51,521
II War Zone		?	?	?
V War Zone		1,845	0	8,830
VI War Zone		873	3,359	44,607
VIII War Zone		1,770	3,190	36,472
X War Zone		4,136	70	26,672
XI War Zone		1,286	566	32,291
XII War Zone		1,510	259	13,510
Youth Army		31	1,229	13,713
Chongqing Garrison		3,418	1,105	21,316
Pacification Troops		923	408	20,312
AMC Direct Command		287	561	40,390
Cavalry Branch		3,048	545	38,330
Artillery Branch		0	0	0
Engineer Branch		0	0	0
Quartermaster Branch		0	0	0
Signal Branch		0	0	0
Mechanized Branch		477	1,352	4,026
Military Police		5,674	17,236	4,930
Shock Troops		?	?	?
Grand totals		34,296	57,029	638,323

Note: Figures do not include Communist or local-defense units.

Rifle grenade launchers	Grenade dischargers	Light machine guns	Medium machine guns	Trench mortars	Flame-throwers	Anti-tank rifles	Anti-tank rocket launchers
0	0	3,617	668	1,170	60	155	263
966	658	1,346	457	742	0	180	74
855	1	1,644	403	291	0	71	51
1,726	1,164	2,078	586	519	36	51	175
614	223	2,810	569	540	36	52	165
0	1,302	1,805	372	643	0	138	105
1,285	383	1,408	266	327	0	129	76
1,091	1,341	3,985	1,008	1,150	0	2	0
546	0	1,512	325	94	0	0	0
152	1,322	1,927	510	231	0	88	3
?	?	?	?	?	?	?	?
1,178	1,687	3,219	850	996	0	548	36
?	?	?	?	?	?	?	?
364	436	977	384	127	0	21	0
2,256	1,182	3,854	814	987	0	149	84
811	233	1,578	1,007	172	0	0	0
144	625	1,895	478	190	0	38	0
409	1,113	2,575	402	317	0	26	35
531	48	503	107	74	0	1	0
979	6	2,609	354	548	0	135	0
850	0	1,497	240	411	0	0	0
0	0	1,112	220	480	0	0	0
566	97	1,335	315	217	0	33	0
180	297	2,013	257	60	0	0	0
0	0	0	0	165	0	0	0
0	0	0	0	0	0	0	0
0	0	0	0	0	0	0	0
0	0	0	0	0	0	0	0
0	1	238	289	11	0	0	5
0	0	11	305	0	0	0	0
?	?	?	?	?	0	0	0
15,503	12,119	45,548	11,186	10,662	132	1,817	1,072

Support Weapons

		Anti-tank guns	Infantry guns
GHQ Chinese Army	HQ & Direct Units	133	48
	1st Front Army	83	0
	2nd Front Army	19	0
	3rd Front Army	99	0
	4th Front Army HQ	46	0
	Kunming Garrison	72	0
	Burma Road	0	0
Generalissimo's SE HQ	III War Zone	35	12
	VII War Zone	22	6
	IX War Zone	29	0
G'mo's Kunming HQ		?	?
I War Zone		109	0
II War Zone		?	?
V War Zone		4	0
VI War Zone		63	2
VIII War Zone		16	0
X War Zone		38	0
XI War Zone		6	0
XII War Zone		0	0
Youth Army		0	0
Chongqing Garrison		16	7
Pacification Troops		0	8
AMC Direct Command		7	62
Cavalry Branch		0	0
Artillery Branch		340	0
Engineer Branch		0	0
Quartermaster Branch		0	0
Signal Branch		0	0
Mechanized Branch		95	80
Military Police		0	0
Shock Troops		0	0
Grand totals		1,232	225

Note: Figures do not include Communist or local-defense units.

Anti-aircraft machine guns	Anti-aircraft guns	Mountain artillery	Field artillery	Howitzers	Fortress artillery	Heavy artillery
8	1	100	0	0	0	12
0	0	25	0	0	0	0
0	0	8	0	0	0	0
0	0	108	0	0	0	0
0	0	60	0	0	0	0
4	0	60	0	0	0	0
6	0	36	12	0	0	0
21	0	6	0	0	0	0
0	0	47	0	0	0	0
6	0	0	0	0	0	0
?	?	?	?	?	0	0
12	30	0	30	0	0	0
?	?	?	?	?	0	0
3	6	0	3	0	0	0
57	2	90	18	0	58	0
0	0	0	27	0	0	0
6	18	24	17	0	0	0
0	0	14	0	0	0	0
0	0	12	0	0	0	0
0	0	0	0	0	0	0
0	26	27	0	0	0	0
0	0	12	0	0	0	0
0	0	11	0	0	0	0
0	0	0	0	0	0	0
0	0	99	52	0	0	20
0	0	0	0	0	0	0
0	0	0	0	0	0	0
0	0	0	0	0	0	0
57	0	0	0	18	0	0
0	0	0	0	0	0	0
0	0	0	0	0	0	0
180	83	639	156	18	58	220

Chinese Army in India Strengths

As of 30 April 1944

	TO strength	Chinese reported strength	Y-FOS estimate of strength
Chinese Expeditionary Force			
CEF HQ	n/a	?	?
54th Army			
Army HQ & Troops	8,404	?	728
54th Army Artillery Battalion	777	?	800
36th Division	11,460	9,016	7,000
198th Division	11,460	?	7,200
93rd Division	11,460	?	?
Special Service Regiment	3,260	1,649	?
3rd Bn/49th AA Regiment	855	660	?
1st Engineer Regiment (Fort)	871	798	?
2nd Engineer Regiment (Independent)	3,288	2,052	?
24th Engineer Battalion (Independent)	705	544	?
HQ 6th Signal Regiment	19	18	?
3rd Bn/3rd Signal Regiment	1,165	756	?
CEF Artillery HQ			
Artillery HQ	n/a	?	?
7th Artillery Regiment	2,003	1,628	?
10th Artillery Regiment (less 3rd Battalion)	2,086	1,346	?
13th Artillery Regiment (less 3rd Battalion)	n/a	?	?
21st Artillery Regiment	2,871	1,522	?
2nd Heavy Mortar Regiment (less 3rd Battalion)	2,509	1,334	?
1st Army Group			
Army Group HQ	n/a	?	?
60th Army			
Army HQ & Troops	8,404	?	5,000
182nd Division	11,460	?	6,500
184th Division	11,460	?	6,500
2nd Route Army			
18th Yunnan Division	n/a	?	6,500
19th Yunnan Division	n/a	?	4,000
20th Yunnan Division	n/a	?	4,000
21st Yunnan Division	n/a	?	4,000
22nd Yunnan Division	n/a	?	4,000
23rd Division	n/a	?	4,000

	TO strength	Chinese reported strength	Y-FOS estimate of strength
5th Army Group			
Army Group HQ	n/a	?	?
5th Army			
Army HQ & Troops	8,404	?	5,500
5th Army Artillery Battalion	777	?	887
49th Division	11,460	6,027	5,314
96th Division	11,460	8,100	6,840
200th Division	11,460	7,000	5,250
9th Army Group			
Army Group HQ	n/a	?	?
1st Bn/1st Heavy Mortar Regiment	n/a	?	?
8th Army			
Army HQ & Troops	8,404	?	?
Hon 1st Division	11,460	?	7,500
82nd Division	11,460	?	6,500
103rd Division	11,460	?	7,500
52nd Army			
Army HQ & Troops	8,404	?	2,382
2nd Division	11,460	?	7,300
25th Division	11,460	?	7,502
195th Division	11,460	?	6,500
11th Army Group			
Army Group HQ	1,514	1,498	?
6th Army	?	?	?
Army HQ & Troops	?	?	?
6th Army Artillery Battalion	777	?	700
2nd Reserve Division	11,460	7,600	6,500
New 39th Division	11,460	?	6,000
71st Army			
Army HQ & Troops	9,909	?	?
71st Army Artillery Battalion	777	?	800
New 28th Division	11,460	6,800	4,000
87th Division	11,460	7,000	5,500
88th Division	11,460	?	5,000
20th Army Group			
Army Group HQ	2,265	2,018	?
2nd Army			
Army HQ & Troops	6,989	?	?
2nd Army Artillery Battalion	777	?	850
9th Division	11,460	?	4,000
New 33rd Division	11,460	?	4,350
76th Division	11,460	?	4,000
53rd Army			
Army HQ & Troops	6,439	?	?
53rd Army Artillery Battalion	777	?	819
116th Division	11,460	?	7,180
130th Division	11,460	?	5,785

As of 31 July 1944

	TO strength	Chinese reported strength	Y-FOS estimate of strength
Chinese Expeditionary Force			
CEF HQ	3,260	429	?
8th Army			
Army HQ & Troops	8,404	4,260	?
Hon 1st Division	11,460	6,500	2,454*
82nd Division	11,460	6,100	?
103rd Division	11,460	5,960	?
93rd Division	11,460	8,049	8,049
Special Service Regiment	3,260	1,598	?
3rd Bn/49th AA Regiment	855	458	?
1st Engineer Regiment (Fort)	871	450	?
2nd Engineer Regiment (Independent)	3,288	1,195	?
24th Engineer Bn (Independent)	705	1,085	?
HQ 6th Signal Regiment	19	352	?
3rd Bn/3rd Signal Regiment	1,165	605	?
CEF Artillery HQ			
Artillery HQ	n/a	132	?
7th Artillery Regiment	2,003	1,300	?
10th Artillery Regiment	2,086	1,210	?
1st Bn/5th Army Artillery Regiment	777	842	842
2nd Bn/5th Army Artillery Regiment	777	540	540
21st Artillery Regiment	2,871	1,140	1,140
1st Heavy Artillery Regiment	n/a	1,200	?
2nd Heavy Mortar Regiment	2,509	385	?
1st Army Group			
Army Group HQ	n/a	?	5,000
60th Army			
Army HQ & Troops	8,404	?	5,000
18th Division (Yunnan)	n/a	?	10,000
182nd Division	11,460	?	10,000
184th Division	11,460		10,000
5th Army Group			
Army Group HQ	n/a	?	?
5th Army			
Army HQ & Troops	n/a	8,404	?
49th Division	11,460	6,027	5,317
96th Division	11,460	8,100	6,840
200th Division	11,460	7,000	5,220
9th Army Group			
Army Group HQ	n/a	?	?
52nd Army			
Army HQ & Troops	8,404	?	6,522
2nd Division	11,460	?	9,753
25th Division	11,460	?	9,797
195th Division	11,460	?	9,821

	TO strength	Chinese reported strength	Y-FOS estimate of strength
11th Army Group			
Army Group HQ	1,514	1,440	?
2nd Army			
Army HQ & Troops	7,406	6,740	?
2nd Army Artillery Battalion	777	557	?
9th Division	11,460	6,500	1,000*
New 33rd Division	11,460	5,500	1,500*
76th Division	11,460	5,900	2,832*
6th Army			
Army HQ & Troops	7,253	3,480	?
6th Army Artillery Battalion	777	407	?
New 39th Division	11,460	3,980	?
71st Army			
Army HQ & Troops	6,615	5,800	2,000
71st Army Artillery Battalion	777	368	?
3rd Battalion/5th Army Artillery Regiment	777	457	?
Provisional Artillery Battalion	777	437	?
New 28th Division	11,460	4,400	1,721*
87th Division	11,460	4,600	2,423*
88th Division	11,460	4,920	2,514*
20th Army Group			
Army Group HQ	2,265	2,960	?
53rd Army			
Army HQ & Troops	8,404	3,530	?
53rd Army Artillery Battalion	777	507	?
116th Division	11,460	5,500	1,250*
130th Division	11,460	5,500	1,250*
54th Army			
Army HQ & Troops	8,404	150	?
2nd Reserve Division	11,460	4,762	2,048*
36th Division	11,460	5,175	2,484*
198th Division	11,460	3,700	2,200*

* Indicates that American estimates cover only line troops, not other divisional elements.

As of 31 October 1944

	TO strength	Chinese reported strength	Y-FOS estimate of strength
Chinese Expeditionary Force			
CEF HQ	3,260	429	?
8th Army			
Army HQ & Troops	8,404	4,260	580
82nd Division	11,460	?	3,679
103rd Division	11,460	?	2,914
93rd Division	11,460	8,049	5,000
Special Service Regiment	3,260	1,598	?
3rd Battalion/49th AA Regiment	855	458	?
1st Engineer Regiment (Fort)	871	450	?
2nd Engineer Regiment (Independent)	3,283	1,195	?
24th Engineer Battalion (Independent)	705	1,085	?
HQ 6th Signal Regiment	19	352	?
3rd Battalion/3rd Signal Regiment	1,165	605	?
CEF Artillery HQ			
Artillery HQ	n/a	132	?
7th Artillery Regiment	2,003	1,300	435
10th Artillery Regiment	2,086	1,210	666
1st Battalion/5th Army Artillery Regiment	777	842	400
2nd Battalion/5th Army Artillery Regiment	777	540	500
21st Artillery Regiment	2,871	1,140	1,100
2nd Battalion/3rd Heavy Mortar Regiment	777	?	?
1st Battalion/30th Artillery Regiment	777	500	606
2nd Battalion/30th Artillery Regiment	777	667	536
1st Army Group			
Army Group HQ	n/a	?	?
60th Army (Yunnan)			
Army HQ & Troops	8,404	?	5,000
60th Army Artillery Battalion	777	?	507
18th Division (Yunnan)	n/a	?	10,000
182nd Division	11,460	?	10,000
184th Division	11,460	?	10,000
5th Army Group			
Army Group HQ	n/a	?	?
5th Army			
Army HQ & Troops	8,404	?	5,500
49th Division	11,460	6,027	4,000
96th Division	11,460	8,100	5,500
48th Division	11,460	14,000	6,000
2nd Hon Division	11,460	7,000	5,500

	TO strength	Chinese reported strength	Y-FOS estimate of strength
9th Army Group			
Army Group HQ	n/a	?	?
52nd Army			
Army HQ & Troops	8,404	?	6,500
52nd Army Artillery Battalion	777	?	507
2nd Division	11,460	?	7,500
25th Division	11,460	?	7,500
195th Division	11,460	?	7,500
11th Army Group			
Army Group HQ	1,514	1,440	562
Hon 1st Division	11,460	?	4,267
36th Division	11,460	?	4,174
200th Division	11,460	?	8,222
2nd Army			
Army HQ & Troops	7,406	2,901	2,630
2nd Army Artillery Battalion	777	557	?
9th Division	11,460	5,066	4,175
New 33rd Division	11,460	5,500	4,100
76th Division	11,460	3,965	3,865
6th Army			
Army HQ & Troops	7,253	3,480	?
6th Army Artillery Battalion	777	274	345
New 39th Division	11,460	?	1,592
71st Army			
Army HQ & Troops	6,615	3,184	4,714
New 28th Division	11,460	4,420	2,569
87th Division	11,460	4,847	3,627
88th Division	11,460	4,338	3,733
1st Battalion/71st Army Artillery Regiment	777	368	?
2nd Battalion/71st Army Artillery Bn	777	437	?
3rd Battalion/5th Army Artillery Regiment	777	457	?
20th Army Group			
Army Group HQ	2,265	2,960	824
53rd Army			
Army HQ & Troops	8,404	3,530	4,700
53rd Army Artillery Battalion	777	500	?
116th Division	11,460	5,097	4,127
130th Division	11,460	5,827	4,614
54th Army			
Army HQ & Troops	8,404	?	5,279
54th Army Artillery Battalion	777	507	507
2nd Reserve Division	11,460	4,632	4,726
198th Division	11,460	5,558	3,628

Appendix X

Chinese Army in India Equipment Holdings

These tables provide the status of the Chinese Army in India on three representative dates as reflected in official strength returns.

CAI Troops in Burma, 15 October 1943

	Army troops	22nd Division	38th Division
Officers	384	782	878
Enlisted	2,817	6,912	10,125
Horses	310	1,316	1,446
Mules	27	0	496
Carts	118	0	195
Pack saddles	3	0	1,183
Pistol, .45-cal.	2	0	9
Submachine guns, .45-cal.	608	1,210	1,212
Rifles, .30-cal. M1917 (mod)	1,475	3,370	4,494
Machine guns, .30-cal.	0	72	72
Machine guns, .303-cal.Bren	177	353	355
Machine guns, .50-cal. HB	0	0	0
Machine guns, .50-cal. WC	48	0	0
AT rifles, .55-cal. Boys	0	30	30
Rocket launchers, AT	0	0	26
Mortars, 60mm M2	0	162	150
Mortars, 81mm M1	0	36	36
AT guns, 37mm	0	24	24
Pack howitzers, 75mm M1	0	24	24
Motorcycles	9		30
Station wagons	0		1
Truck, ¼-ton	14		95
Truck, ½- or ¾-ton	14	unknown	96
Lorry, ¾-ton	0		19
Truck, 2½-ton	225		32
Ambulances	0		5
Radios, SCR-177B	0	0	1
Radios, SCR-179	1	1	6
Radios, SCR-194	1	28	28
Radios, SCR-195	0	22	24
Radios, SCR-288 & V-100	0	21	21
Telephones, EE-8A	29	152	104

Note: Main army troops were 6th Motor Trans Regt, AA Bn, 12th Engineer Regt, and Special Service Bn.

Chinese Army in India, 30 November 1944						
	CAI troops	14th Division	22nd Division	30th Division	38th Division	50th Division
Officers	2,618	745	872	903	945	618
Enlisted	22,809	11,362	12,883	10,992	13,501	10,170
Animals			*unknown*			
Submachine guns, .45-cal. M1928A1	3,220	1,844	1,315	1,098	1,245	1,044
Submachine guns, .45-cal. M1	0	0	0	34	0	0
Rifles, .30-cal. M1917	3,657	0	6,554	6,990	6,004	219
Rifles, .30-cal. M1903 & A3	3,619	4,005	243	0	0	4,271
Rifles, .303-cal. Lee-Enfield	126	0	0	0	0	0
Grenade launchers, M1 or M2	0	243	243	243	223	276
Machine gun, .30-cal. M1919A4	721	0	0	0	0	0
Machine guns, .30-cal. M1917A1	0	74	73	72	72	77
Machine guns, .303-cal. Bren	525	301	351	322	351	301
Machine guns, .50-cal. HB	41	0	0	0	0	0
Machine guns, .50-cal. WC	59	0	0	0	0	0
Mortars, 60mm M2	3	162	162	150	162	162
Mortars, 81mm M1	0	32	36	35	36	36
Mortars, 4.2-inch chemical	72	0	0	0	0	0
Anti-tank rifles, .55-cal. Boys	0	24	36	30	36	30
Anti-tank rocket launchers	0	36	36	36	36	39
Anti-tank guns, 37mm	64	24	24	24	24	24
Pack howitzesr, 75mm	0	0	24	12	24	0
Pack howitzers, 75mm M8	0	0	0	12	0	0
Field howitzers, 75mm	8	0	0	0	0	0
Field howitzers, 105mm	48	0	0	0	0	0
Field howitzers, 155mm	4	0	0	0	0	0
Motorcycles	28	0	3	22	25	0
Trucks, ¼-ton	263	51	131	194	130	58
Trucks, ½-ton	11	21	0	0	0	34
Trucks, ¾-ton	442	29	85	99	52	28
Trucks, 2½-ton	971	13	32	27	33	7
Trucks, 2½-ton shop	23	0	0	0	0	0
Trucks, 4 ton	5	0	0	0	0	0
Trucks, wrecker	14	0	0	0	0	0
Trucks, 750-gal tanker	2	0	0	0	0	0
Lorries, British 15cwt (¾-ton)	1	0	0	0	0	0

Chinese Army in India, 30 November 1944 (*continued*)

	CAI troops	*14th Division*	*22nd Division*	*30th Division*	*38th Division*	*50th Division*
Personnel carriers, half-track	28	0	0	0	0	0
Light tanks, M3A3	145	0	0	0	0	0
Medium tanks, M4A4	45	0	0	0	0	0
Radios, British No. 48	50	27	4	46	5	27
Radios, SCR-177B	4	1	1	1	1	1
Radios, SCR-179B	1	0	0	2	0	0
Radios, SCR-193	5	0	1	1	1	0
Radios, SCR-194	60	0	28	14	28	0
Radios, SCR-195	0	0	24	0	26	0
Radios, SCR-284	37	18	2	22	2	6
Radios, SCR-299	2	0	0	0	0	0
Radios, SCR-610	6	0	0	0	6	0
Radios, V-100	6	2	22	1	21	16
Telephones, EE-8A	453	102	175	195	160	100

Chinese Army in India, 31 January 1945

	Army troops	14th Division	22nd Division	30th Division	38th Division	50th Division
Officers	2,376	17	57	929	1,068	727
Enlisted	20,889	649	1,465	10,961	13,378	11,695
Submachine guns, .45-cal. M1928A1	3,040			1,140	1,236	1,224
Submachine guns, .45-cal. M1	0			22	0	0
Rifles, .30-cal. M1917	3,894	*no data given*		7,000	6,004	243
Rifles, .30-cal. M1903A3	3,497			0	0	4,271
Rifles, .303-cal. Lee-Enfield	0			0	0	0
Grenade launchers, M1 or M2	0			243	223	230
Machine guns, .30-cal. M1919A4	795			0	0	0
Machine guns, .30-cal. M1917A1	0			72	56	83
Machine guns, .303-cal. Bren	497			338	341	325
Machine guns, .50-cal. HB	60			0	0	0
Machine guns, .50-cal. WC	59			0	0	0
Mortars, 60mm M2	19			162	162	198
Mortars, 81mm M1	0			36	36	46
Mortars, 4.2-inch chemical	24	*no data given*		0	0	0
Anti-tank rifles, .55-cal. Boys	0			30	36	30
Anti-tank rocket launchers, M1A1	0			36	36	38
Anti-tank guns, 37mm M3	62			24	24	24
Pack howitzers, 75mm M1	0			12	24	0
Pack howitzers, 75mm M8	0			12	0	0
Field howitzers, 105mm	48			0	0	0
Field howitzers, 155mm	12			0	0	0
Motorcycles	30			27	25	0
Trucks, ¼-ton	228			201	139	57
Trucks, ½-ton	11			8	30	1
Trucks, ¾-ton	388			120	52	28
Trucks, 2½-ton	879			26	33	7
Trucks, 2½-ton shop	24	*no data given*		0	0	0
Trucks, 4-ton	15			0	0	0
Trucks, wrecker	19			0	0	0
Trucks, 2½-ton tanker	2			0	0	0
Lorries, British 15cwt (¾-ton)	0			0	0	0
Personnel carriers, half-track	27			0	0	0
Light tanks, M3A3	157	*no data given*		0	0	0
Medium tanks, M4A4	54			0	0	0

Chinese Army in India, 31 January 1945 (*continued*)

	Army troops	14th Division	22nd Division	30th Division	38th Division	50th Division
Radios, British No. 48	50	35	4	46	5	27
Radios, SCR-177B	4	11	1	1	1	1
Radios, SCR-179B	1	0	0	2	0	0
Radios, SCR-193	5	0	1	1	1	0
Radios, SCR-194	62	0	30	14	33	0
Radios, SCR-195	0	0	24	0	24	0
Radios, SCR-284	37	27	2	22	3	11
Radios, SCR-299	2	0	0	0	0	0
Radios, SCR-610	6	0	0	0	6	0
Radios, V-100	6	2	22	1	22	16
Telephones, EE-8A	453	100	175	195	160	100

Note: The bulk of 14th & 22nd Divisions had been airlifted to China.

Appendix XI

Strength & Weapons Reports

US Liaison Officers began filing strength reports on the units to which they were attached or observing in 1944. Although fragmentary, they provide the best view of the state of strengths and equipment holdings of Chinese Army units from mid-1944 to the end of the war.

60th Army (Y-Force), 5 August 1944					
	Army troops	*18th Division*	*182nd Division*	*184th Division*	*Total*
9mm pistols	0	93	70	65	228
.45-cal. submachine guns	0	180	120	180	540
7.92mm rifles	1,127	2,100	2,387	2,433	8,047
Rifle grenade launchers	171	0	0	0	171
Grenade dischargers	0	108	n/a	n/a	340
7.92mm light MGs	58	137	173	179	547
.303-cal. Bren light MGs	0	18	18	18	54
7.92mm medium MGs	2	36	58	60	156
13.2mm heavy MGs	3	0	0	0	3
60mm mortars	19	54	35	27	135
81mm mortars	0	13	12	13	44
82mm mortars	12	10	12	17	51
.55-cal. Boys AT rifles	0	18	18	18	54
37mm AT guns	4	0	0	0	4
20mm guns	9	0	0	0	9

24th Army Group, as of 15 November 1944

	Combat personnel		Non-combat personnel		Totals	Mules
	Officers	Enlisted	Officers	Enlisted		
73rd Army						
HQ Troops	131	1,416	318	8,000	9,865	86
15th Division	228	4,733	201	4,225	9,387	16
77th Division	285	4,429	234	1,796	6,744	18
Temporary 5th Division	167	657	97	555	1,476	4
74th Army						
HQ Troops	437	3,191	293	6,954	10,266	379
51st Division	445	6,107	192	3,557	10,301	146
57th Division	420	4,897	193	3,982	9,492	91
58th Division	414	6,219	200	3,011	9,844	192
100th Army						
HQ Troops	106	818	119	791	1,834	37
19th Division	320	3,377	148	2,500	6,348	50
63rd Division	302	3585	180	3,036	7,103	26
225th Regt/75th Division	81	936	24	550	1,591	8

Note: The source document does not define "non-combat." Presumably many were porters.

Transport, 60th Army (Y-Force), 20 November 1944

	Army HQ	18th Division	182nd Division	184th Division
Porters	0	620	650	720
Pack animals	100	415	450	600
Jeeps	1	0	0	0
2½-ton trucks	5	0	0	0

1st Army Group Weapons, 20 November 1944

	Army group HQ	60th Army		
		Army HQ	182nd Division	184th Division
Pistols	41	70	18	84
Submachine guns .45-cal. Thompson	0	36	165	165
7.92mm rifles				
CKS	171	370	147	621
Belgian	0	0	0	0
Belgian Model 24	0	407	999	1,585
Czech	94	125	222	0
German	10	0	289	0
French	0	0	0	225
Hanyang	200	0	0	0
Standard	0	221	773	0
Rifle grenade launchers	0	3	84	84
Grenade dischargers	0	0	121	120
Light MGs				
Chellali 7.62mm	0	0	0	0
Czech 7.92mm	29	34	154	147
Browning BAR 7.92mm	3	9	14	19
Hotchkiss 7.92mm	0	10	3	6
Madsen 7.92mm	0	0	0	0
Chellali 7.92mm	0	0	0	0
Bren .303-cal.	0	18	0	18
Medium MGs 7.92mm				
Hotchkiss	2	6	8	10
Madsen	4	0	32	35
Czech	0	0	2	0
Maxim	4	2	12	10
Heavy MGs, 13.2mm Hotchkiss	0	0	5	0
Mortars, 60mm	0	27	0	32
Mortars, 81mm	0	0	12	13
Mortars, 82mm	0	12	12	17
Mortars, 150mm	6	0	0	0
Anti-tank rifles, .55-cal. Boys	0	18	0	18
Anti-tank guns, 20mm	0	1	4	0
Anti-tank guns, 37mm	0	4	0	0
Anti-aircraft guns, 20mm	0	0	0	0
Howitzers, 75mm Krupp-type	0	0	0	0
Pack howitzers, 75mm US	0	12	0	0

Note: Chellali LMG unidentified.

| | 1st Route Army | | | 2nd Route Army | |
Army HQ	18th Division	20th Division	Army HQ	21st Division	22nd Division
0	93	93	19	94	103
0	180	0	0	0	0
0	0	0	0	0	0
0	2,100	0	0	0	0
0	0	2,100	100	0	1,669
0	0	0	0	0	0
0	0	0	0	0	0
0	0	0	0	0	0
0	0	0	0	0	431
0	0	0	0	0	0
0	0	0	0	0	0
0	108	108	0	106	107
0	0	0	0	73	73
0	0	0	3	0	0
0	173	173	0	100	100
0	0	0	0	0	0
0	0	0	2	0	0
0	0	0	0	73	73
0	18	0	0	0	0
0	36	36	0	36	36
0	0	0	0	0	0
0	0	0	0	0	0
0	0	0	0	0	0
12	12	0	0	0	0
0	54	18	0	16	16
0	13	13	0	8	10
0	10	0	0	5	5
0	0	0	0	0	0
0	18	0	0	0	0
0	3	4	0	4	4
0	0	0	0	0	0
0	1	0	0	0	0
0	0	0	0	12	0
0	0	0	0	0	0

Weapons of 52nd Army (Y-Force), 25 November 1944

	Army HQ	2nd Division	25th Division	195th Division
Pistols, 9mm	82	138	265	216
Submachine guns, .45-cal.	33	169	169	169
Rifles, 7.92mm	756	2,292	1,785	2,043
Bayonets	762	1,025	1,600	1,270
Grenade launchers	14	164	168	152
Light MGs, 7.92mm	33	227	175	221
Light MGs, .303-cal. Bren	0	18	18	18
Medium MGs, 7.92mm	15	63	55	74
Mortars, 60mm	0	54	54	54
Mortars, 82mm	2	32	27	27
AT rifles, .55-cal. Boys	0	18	18	18
AT guns, 20mm Madsen	0	4	0	0
AT guns, 37mm	0	0	4	3
AT rocket launchers	3	0	0	0
AA guns, 20mm Solothurn	0	4	7	6
Pack howitzers, 75mm	12	0	0	0

24th Army Group, Guerrilla Unit Weapons, December 1944

	Item	Model	Number
73rd Army	Pistols	Automatic	4
	Rifles	Hanyang	140
	Light machine guns	Czech model	16
74th Army	Pistols	Automatic	148
	Submachine guns	Thompson	5
	Rifles	CKS	539
	Grenade dischargers	Type 27	16
	Light machine guns	Czech made	48
	Medium machine guns	Maxim	2
	Anti-tank rifles	Boys	1
	60mm mortars	US	3
100th Army	Pistols	Automatic	3
	Rifles	CKS	200
	Grenade dischargers	Type 27	9
	Light machine guns	Czech made	18

24th Army Group Weapons, 11 December 1944

	73rd Army	74th Army	100th Army
Pistols, 7.63mm	80	148	27
Revolvers, .32-cal.	0	0	2
Submachine guns	7	465	0
Rifles, 7.92mm	5,235	6,089	3,249
Grenade launchers, Type 28	139	446	0
Grenade dischargers, Type 27	0	72	222
Light machine guns, 7.92mm	508	455	348
Light machine guns, .303-cal.	0	54	0
Medium machine guns, 7.92mm	131	112	76
Anti-tank rifles, .55-cal.	0	50	0
Anti-tank rocket launchers	36	36	36
Anti-tank guns, 20mm	2	1	0
Anti-tank guns, 37mm	0	1	4
Mortars, 60mm	0	136	0
Mortars, 81mm	0	29	0
Mortars, 82mm	59	27	44
Anti-aircraft machine guns, .50-cal.	0	12	0
Anti-aircraft auto cannon, 20mm	0	5	0
Howitzers, 75mm	0	2	2
Field guns, 75mm, Krupp type	0	2	0
Field guns, 75mm, French	0	2	0
Field guns, 76.2mm	0	2	0

31st Army Group, December 1944

	Officers		Enlisted		Horses		Mules	
	TO&E	Actual	TO&E	Actual	TO&E	Actual	TO&E	Actual
Army Group HQ	138	134	760	760	83	60	51	40
HQ attached troops	35	19	239	222	0	0	0	0
78th Army								
Army HQ	269	264	4,089	3,689	60	60	12	12
New 42nd Division	457	445	6,857	5,996	87	51	306	15
New 43rd Division	457	446	6,857	6,315	87	67	306	33
New 44th Division	457	447	6,857	6,339	87	56	306	6
85th Army								
Army HQ	515	473	5,334	5,079	553	137	1,218	437
23rd Division	487	450	9,454	7,195	122	36	594	149
110th Division	487	464	9,454	8,040	122	87	594	247
Temp. 55th Division	487	487	9,454	7,438	122	59	594	35
Totals	3,789	3,629	59,355	51,073	1,323	613	3,981	974

31st Army Group Equipment, December 1944

		Army Group HQ	78th Army HQ
7.63mm pistols	TO&E	30	0
	Actual	0	0
7.9mm rifles	TO&E	200	384
	Actual	190	252
Rifle grenade launcher	TO&E	0	0
	Actual	0	0
Grenade dischargers	TO&E	12	0
	Actual	0	0
Light machine guns	TO&E	12	8
	Actual	5	6
Medium machine guns	TO&E	6	0
	Actual	2	0
82mm mortars	TO&E	0	0
	Actual	0	0
45mm anti-tank guns	TO&E	0	0
	Actual	0	0
75mm mountain guns	TO&E	0	0
	Actual	0	0
20-line switchboards	TO&E	?	0
	Actual	?	0
15-line switchboards	TO&E	?	0
	Actual	?	1
10-line switchboards	TO&E	?	2
	Actual	?	0
5-line switchboards	TO&E	?	0
	Actual	?	1
Telephones	TO&E	?	12
	Actual	?	12
15-watt radios	TO&E	?	1
	Actual	?	1
5-watt radios	TO&E	?	2
	Actual	?	1
Heavy insulated wire (rolls)	TO&E	?	32
	Actual	?	10
Medium insulated wire (rolls)	TO&E	?	0
	Actual	?	0

New 42nd Division	New 43rd Division	New 44th Division	85th Army HQ	23rd Division	110th Division	Temp 55th Division
0	0	0	106	356	356	356
0	0	0	33	100	47	9
2,219	2,219	2,219	722	2,392	2,392	2,392
1,715	1,715	1,715	419	1,734	1,811	1,352
0	0	0	56	178	178	178
171	171	171	0	112	46	60
178	178	178	0	0	0	0
81	81	81	0	0	0	0
171	171	171	36	171	171	171
117	117	117	15	153	152	85
36	36	36	2	54	54	54
36	36	36	0	59	38	34
12	12	12	0	30	30	30
9	9	9	0	26	24	11
0	0	0	0	4	4	4
0	4	0	0	0	0	0
0	0	0	12	0	0	0
0	0	0	7	0	0	0
0	0	0	0	0	0	0
0	0	0	0	1	0	1
1	1	1	0	0	0	0
0	0	0	0	0	0	0
3	3	3	2	3	3	3
4	2	1	2	4	2	3
0	0	0	0	0	0	0
0	2	3	1	1	2	0
42	42	42	12	42	42	42
22	22	22	35	38	16	18
1	1	1	1	1	1	1
1	1	0	0	0	1	0
4	4	4	2	4	4	4
1	1	2	4	2	3	3
32	32	32	48	34	34	34
10	10	10	68	8	8	34
57	57	57	0	57	57	57
21	21	21	34	52	18	19

Guizhou–Guangxi–Hunan Border Force Weapons, 31 December 1944

		Pistols	SMG .45-cal.	Rifles	Type 27 grenade dischargers	Type 28 grenade launchers	Light machine guns
9th Army	TO&E	0	0	7,898	0	590	542
	Actual	105	0	5,098	326	0	521
13th Army	TO&E	0	0	7,901	0	590	542
	Actual	526	300	5,342	0	598	680
29th Army	TO&E	0	0	7,898	0	590	542
	Actual	74	0	5,935	15	320	428
74th Army	TO&E	0	0	7,898	0	590	542
	Actual	228	463	8,010	0	462	530
87th Army	TO&E	0	0	5,506	0	412	371
	Actual	248	0	4,309	0	382	367
94th Army	TO&E	0	0	7,898	0	590	542
	Actual	197	0	5,268	367	110	422
97th Army	TO&E	0	0	5,506	0	412	371
	Actual	106	0	2,500	0	107	300
100th Army	TO&E	0	0	7,898	0	590	542
	Actual	86	0	5,242	185	180	519
Artillery command	Actual	0	0	?	0	0	?
Anti-tank regiment	Actual	4	20	472	0	0	24
AT battalion of 48th Division	Actual	0	0	61	0	0	33
18th Engineer Regiment	Actual	4	0	288	0	0	15

Medium machine guns	60mm mortars	82mm mortars	Boys anti-tank rifles	Anti-tank rocket launchers	37mm anti-tank guns	75mm pack howitzers	Field guns	Anti-aircraft machine guns	20mm anti-aircraft guns	150mm howitzers	155mm howitzers
164	0	90	0	0	12	12	0	0	0	0	0
94	0	37	0	0	0	0	0	0	0	0	0
164	0	90	0	0	12	12	0	0	0	0	0
139	30	60	0	0	3	6	0	0	4	0	0
164	0	90	0	0	12	12	0	0	0	0	0
128	0	72	0	0	0	0	0	0	0	0	0
164	0	90	0	0	12	12	0	0	0	0	0
151	140	79	50	36	11	9	10	12	6	0	0
110	0	60	0	0	8	12	0	0	0	0	0
114	0	52	0	0	8	12	0	0	0	0	0
164	0	90	0	0	12	12	0	0	0	0	0
143	0	70	0	0	8	22	0	0	0	0	0
110	0	60	0	0	8	12	0	0	0	0	0
98	3	55	0	0	3	0	0	0	0	0	0
164	0	90	0	0	12	12	0	0	0	0	0
121	0	67	0	24	0	0	0	0	0	0	0
?	0	0	0	0	0	45	3	0	0	9	4
0	0	0	0	26	27	0	0	0	0	0	0
3	0	0	0	0	16	0	0	0	0	0	0
0	0	0	0	0	0	0	0	0	0	0	0

13th Army Weapons, January 1945

		Army HQ	4th Division	89th Division	Temporary 16th Division
Revolvers, Colt .32-cal.	TO&E	0	0	0	0
	Actual	1	4	0	0
Pistols, Browning 7.65mm	TO&E	0	0	0	0
	Actual	1	22	0	0
Revolvers	TO&E	0	0	0	0
	Actual	1	32	0	8
Pistols, Mauser 7.63mm	TO&E	0	0	0	0
	Actual	80	332	41	1
Pistols, 9mm	TO&E	0	0	0	0
	Actual	1	0	0	0
Submachine guns, .45-cal.	TO&E	0	0	0	0
	Actual	54	246	0	0
Rifles, 7.92mm	TO&E	722	2,393	2,393	2,393
	Actual	612	1,536	1,709	1,455
Rifle grenade launchers, Type 28	TO&E	56	178	178	178
	Actual	16	241	221	110
Light machine guns, 7.92mm	TO&E	29	171	171	171
	Actual	74	277	226	103
Medium machine guns, 7.92mm	TO&E	2	54	54	54
	Actual	6	36	52	45
Mortars, 60mm	TO&E	0	0	0	0
	Actual	0	28	2	0
Mortars, 82mm	TO&E	0	30	30	30
	Actual	0	24	24	12
Anti-tank guns, 37mm German	TO&E	0	4	4	4
	Actual	0	3	0	0
Cannon, 20mm Oerlikon	TO&E	0	0	0	0
	Actual	4	0	0	0
Pack artillery, 75mm Bofors	TO&E	12	0	0	0
	Actual	6	0	0	0

17th Army Strength & Weapons, 23 February 1945

	Army HQ	84th Division	New 2nd Division
TO&E			
Officers	267	513	513
Enlisted	2,307	9,902	9,902
Actual			
Officers	242	465	448
Enlisted	1,949	7,708	7,291
TO&E			
Pistols	0	0	0
Rifles	495	2,421	2,421
Grenade launchers	48	178	178
Light machine guns	15	167	167
Medium machine guns	2	54	54
Mortars, 82mm	0	30	30
Actual			
Pistols	38	118	7
Rifles			
Japanese, 6.5mm	6	131	116
Russian, 7.62mm	67	0	30
Czech, 7.92mm	332	796	154
Hanyang Cavalry, 7.92mm	0	4	56
Hanyang, 7.92mm	566	647	1,210
CKS, 7.92mm	2	115	15
Double-barrel, 7.92mm	84	0	0
Other, 7.92mm	70	74	50
Grenade dischargers, Type 27	63	124	138
Light machine guns			
Russian, 7.62mm	3	0	0
Various, 7.92mm	57	119	108
Medium machine guns			
Japanese, 6.5mm	1	0	0
Various, 7.92mm	0	35	37
Mortars, 82mm	6	9	10

Note: Double-barrel 7.92mm rifle unidentified

IV War Zone Strength & Weapons, 29 March 1945

Personnel & Animals

	TO&E	Actual	TO&E requirements
Officers	5,976	7,611	
Enlisted	116,625	83,209	
Horses & mules	16,072	1,118	

Weapons

	TO&E	Actual	TO&E requirements
Pistols	513	2,542	each div 57
Submachine guns, Thompson	0	368	not required in new TO&E
Rifles	26,883	15,294	each div 2,829 & Army HQ 474
Rifle grenade launchers	2,517	1,898	each div 261 & Army HQ 56
Light machine guns, 7.92mm	2,529	1,344	each div 266 & Army HQ 54
Light machine guns, .303cal	0	84	not required in new TO&E
Medium machine guns, 7.92mm	492	398	each div 54 & Army HQ 2
Mortars, 60mm	486	129	each div 54
Mortars, 81mm or 82mm	270	165	each div 30
Anti-tank rifles, .55-cal.	0	39	not required in new TO&E
Anti-tank rocket launchers	0	47	not required in new TO&E
Anti-tank guns, 37mm	36	4	each div 4
Pack howitzers, 75mm	144	11	each div 12 & Army HQ 12

Ammunition

	TO&E	Actual	TO&E requirements
Cartridges, 7.92mm ball for rifle	4,072,450	820,122	2,316,856 req for wpns on hand
Cartridges, 7.92mm ball for LMG	6,069,600	247,404	3,225,600 req for wpns on hand
Cartridges, 7.92mm ball for HMG	2,214,000	281,457	1,791,000 req for wpns on hand
Total, 7.92mm ball	12,356,050	1,348,983	7,333,456 req for wpns on hand
Cartridges, .303-cal. ball	0	32,662	
Cartridges, .45-cal. ball	0	4,219	
Rifle grenades	15,510	3,516	11,696 req for wpns on hand
Shells, HE for 60mm Mortar	58,320	1,281	15,480 req for wpns on hand
Shells, HE for 81/82mm Mortar	32,400	3,415	19,800 req for wpns on hand
Rockets, HEAT	0	645	
Shells, HE & AP for 37mm	10,800	0	1,200 req for wpns on hand
Hand grenades	60,000	23,214	

I War Zone Artillery, May 1945

Weapon	Quantity	Ammo on hand	Ammo in storage	Ammo shortage
Mountain guns, 75mm Shanghai	8	700	1,430	670
Mountain guns, 75mm Japanese model	9	479	4,598	0
Mountain guns, 76mm Russian	10	1,014	0	2,500
Field guns, 75mm French	43	3,851	5,330	5,944
Field guns, 75mm Czech (?) made	15	1,841	3,943	193
Field guns, 76mm Russian	13	1,683	3,761	0
Howitzers, 105mm German leFH18	18	1,734	873	3,693
Howitzers, 114mm Russian	8	1,123	2,700	0
Howitzers, 150mm German	6	1,600	1,598	0
Heavy mortars, 150mm	31	1,390	6,342	1,568
Light anti-aircraft guns, 20mm Swiss	18	6,926	3,300	1,400
Infantry guns, 37mm Manchurian	4	50	50	1,700
Infantry guns, 37mm Russian	23	4,557	11,881	0
Anti-tank guns, 47mm British (45mm Rus?)	14	3,247	3,500	0
Anti-tank guns, 37mm Russian	10	1,974	9,900	0
Anti-tank guns, 37mm German	36	6,801	4,100	4,948
Anti-tank guns, 47mm Bohler	17	2,028	0	5,422
Small guns, 53mm Chinese	8	43	0	2,757

I War Zone Transport Assets, May 1945

	Quantity on hand	Shortage
Field Armies		
Bus & sedan cars	41	92
Trucks	456	432
Special cars	126	701
Animal-drawn carts	1,508	1,138
Pack animals	5,021	3,961
Porters	49,982	17,341
Rear Services		
Trucks	247	15
Rubber-tired animal-drawn carts	527	619
Ox-drawn carts	1,045	836
Animal-drawn carts	4,089	2,559
Hand carts	524	295
Pack mules	1,250	2,740
Pack donkeys	421	155
Porters	4,177	2,805
Army boats	184	?

I War Zone Signal Equipment, May 1945

	Holdings	Shortages
Switchboards, 20-drop	35	0
Switchboards, 15-drop	6	27
Switchboards, 10-drop	236	42
Switchboards, 5-drop	102	0
Radio sets, 15-watt	91	0
Radio sets, 5-watt	193	59

Strength of 2nd Army Group, May 1945

	Officers	Enlisted	Porters
2nd Army Group HQ		612	
Guard Regiment		2,282	
8th Engineer Regiment		1,004	
1st Border Police Battalion		533	
2nd Border Police Battalion		596	
1st Commando Battalion		427	
2nd Commando Battalion		482	
LPA troops		1,082	
46th Army			
HQ Troops	433	2,372	
New 19th Division	644	5,534	
175th Division	667	5,990	
188th Division	584	6,043	
62nd Army			
HQ Troops	378	2,388	230
95th Division	574	8,270	
151st Division	527	7,971	15
157th Division	519	5,234	229
64th Army			
HQ Troops	241	1,864	
131st Division	535	9,634	
156th Division	531	5,513	
159th Division	520	6,777	

13th Army Porter Transport Strength, June 1945

	TO&E				Actual			
	Officers	Enlisted	Poles	Ropes	Officers	Enlisted	Poles	Ropes
13th Army Transport Regiment	167	2,341	1,728	3,456	165	2,093	608	608
4th Division Transport Battalion	40	535	432	864	40	282	60	40
10th Inf Regt Transport Company	8	135	108	216	8	126	40	60
11th Inf Regt Transport Company	8	135	108	216	8	107	20	20
12th Inf Regt Transport Company	8	135	108	216	7	123	36	36
54th Division Transport Battalion	40	535	432	864	40	421	280	280
160th Inf Regt Transport Company	8	135	108	216	8	137	50	50
161st Inf Regt Transport Company	8	135	108	216	8	109	84	84
162nd Inf Regt Transport Company	8	135	108	216	5	101	64	64
89th Division Transport Battalion	40	535	432	864	12	460	120	120
265th Inf Regt Transport Company	8	135	108	216	6	93	0	0
266th Inf Regt Transport Company	8	135	108	216	8	116	86	172
267th Inf Regt Transport Company	8	135	108	216	8	125	60	120

Note: Each porter was to be provided with one shoulder ("yo-yo") pole and a rope for each end. Actual useful porter strength was determined by the number of ropes and poles available.

13th Army Pack Transport Strength, April 1945

| | TO&E | | | | | Actual | | | | |
	Pack animals	Riding animals	Packs	Saddles	Horses	Saddles	Mules	Packs	Saddles
4th Division Transport Battalion	907	90	907	90	16	29	10	13
10th Inf Regt Transport Company	140	23	140	23	16	62	8	6
11th Inf Regt Transport Company	140	23	140	23	16	59	18	5
12th Inf Regt Transport Company	140	23	140	23	10	74	24	0
54th Division Transport Battalion	907	90	907	90	33	41	37	35
160th Inf Regt Transport Company	140	23	140	23	15	11	?	?
161st Inf Regt Transport Company	140	23	140	23	16	50	52	10
162nd Inf Regt Transport Company	140	23	140	23	15	45	45	13

VIII War Zone Weapons, June 1945

	Pistols	Submachine guns	Rifles & carbines	Rifle grenade launchers	Grenade dischargers	
War Zone HQ	116	2	231	12	0	
War Zone troops	219	95	2,186	0	2	
West Bank Garrison HQ	5	0	526	12	54	
3rd Army Group						
HQ troops	10	0	0	12	0	
91st Army						
HQ troops	15	0	411	56	61	
10th Cavalry Division	57	0	1,615	80	0	
New 4th Division	0	0	2,152	37	117	
17th Army Group						
HQ Troops	375	24	265	0	300	
11th Army						
HQ Troops	149	4	2,989	30	0	
168th Division	197	0	3,027	30	0	
Temporary 9th Division	142	36	3,224	90	0	
Temporary 31st Division	83	107	1,420	90	0	
81st Army						
HQ Troops	239	16	2,694	64	10	
35th Division	61	62	2,940	40	0	
Temporary 60th Division	61	62	2,940	40	0	
3rd Artillery Battalion	40	0	585	0	0	

Light machine guns	Medium machine guns	Mortars	Infantry guns	Anti-tank guns	Anti-aircraft machine guns	Mountain artillery	Field artillery	Anti-aircraft guns
21	12	0	0	0	0	0	0	0
29	28	9	0	0	0	0	0	0
39	12	4	0	0	0	0	0	0
12	6	0	0	0	0	0	0	0
26	2	0	0	0	0	0	0	0
119	12	2	0	0	0	0	0	0
148	108	20	0	0	0	0	0	0
29	20	8	0	0	0	0	0	0
52	12	10	0	4	0	0	3	0
27	26	11	0	0	0	12	0	0
33	23	12	0	0	0	12	0	0
69	22	0	0	0	0	0	0	0
75	7	13	0	4	0	26	0	0
82	36	12	0	0	0	0	0	0
82	36	12	0	0	0	0	0	0
6	0	0	0	0	0	0	18	0

VIII War Zone Weapons, June 1945 (*continued*)

	Pistols	Submachine guns	Rifles & carbines	Rifle grenade launchers	Grenade dischargers	
40th Army Group						
HQ Troops	?	?	?	?	?	
82nd Army						
HQ Troops	436	0	757	150	9	
100th Division	199	0	3,286	0	60	
New 8th Cavalry Division	200	0	1,650	0	0	
Temporary 61st Division	181	0	3,224	120	31	
5th Cavalry Army						
HQ Troops	448	42	2,825	0	0	
3rd Cavalry Division	151	0	2,279	0	0	
Temporary 1st Cavalry Division	151	0	2,437	0	0	
Temporary 2nd Cavalry Division	259	27	2,208	0	40	
35th Army						
HQ Troops	52	2	618	1	0	
31st Division	71	0	1,680	130	0	
32nd Division	13	0	1,475	60	0	
Temporary 3rd Army						
HQ Troops	1	0	268	0	0	
Temporary 10th Division	17	0	445	0	0	
Temporary 11th Division	21	0	1,592	105	0	
Temporary 17th Division	21	0	1,593	108	0	
4th Cavalry Army						
HQ Troops	0	3	390	0	0	
New 3rd Cavalry Division	25	0	998	0	0	
New 4th Cavalry Division	5	2	473	18	0	
unknown Infantry Division	36	183	1,217	0	0	

Light machine guns	Medium machine guns	Mortars	Infantry guns	Anti-tank guns	Anti-aircraft machine guns	Mountain artillery	Field artillery	Anti-aircraft guns
?	?	?	?	?	?	?	?	0
161	56	22	0	4	0	6	0	0
88	12	12	4	0	0	0	0	0
52	8	4	0	0	0	0	0	0
84	12	12	0	0	0	0	0	0
70	9	0	0	0	0	9	0	0
24	12	0	0	0	0	0	0	0
23	16	0	0	0	0	0	0	0
41	6	0	0	0	0	0	0	0
24	10	12	0	0	0	0	0	0
143	30	9	0	4	0	0	0	0
138	30	9	0	4	0	0	0	0
0	0	0	0	0	0	0	0	0
0	0	0	0	0	0	0	0	0
92	30	9	0	0	0	0	0	0
124	30	9	0	0	0	0	0	0
0	0	3	0	0	0	0	0	0
21	4	2	0	0	0	0	0	0
56	12	6	0	0	0	0	0	0
163	24	4	0	0	0	0	0	0

VIII War Zone Weapons, June 1945 (*continued*)

	Pistols	Submachine guns	Rifles & carbines	Rifle grenade launchers	Grenade dischargers	
Shanxi–Chahar–Suiyuan Border Army						
HQ Troops	?	?	?	?	?	
22nd Army						
HQ Troops	277	131	2,775	202	0	
86th Division	460	0	3,612	0	0	
6th Cavalry Division	186	35	2,279	0	0	
67th Army						
HQ Troops	16	57	831	0	28	
New 26th Division	36	0	1,827	161	0	
7th Cavalry Division	334	0	2,268	50	25	
New 11th Brigade	88	12	2,013	80	0	
Manchuria Command Unit						
HQ Troops	24	0	612	8	0	
New 5th Cavalry Division	61	15	845	26	0	
New 6th Cavalry Division	8	14	1,258	26	0	
Shanxi–Chahar–Suiyuan Border Command	25	132	1,403	0	0	
12th Division	9	0	1,509	0	77	
4th Bn/52nd Artillery Regiment	16	0	48	0	0	
52nd Artillery Regiment	25	48	169	0	0	
2nd Battalion/46th Artillery Regiment	0	10	52	0	0	
2nd Battalion/44th Artillery Regiment	0	0	0	0	0	
Can-Chou Garrison Regiment	9	0	699	54	18	
22nd Military Police Regiment	68	0	750	0	3	
East Gansu Signal HQ	93	54	877	0	0	

Light machine guns	Medium machine guns	Mortars	Infantry guns	Anti-tank guns	Anti-aircraft machine guns	Mountain artillery	Field artillery	Anti-aircraft guns
?	?	?	?	?	?	?	?	0
66	36	17	0	0	0	12	0	0
90	36	18	0	0	0	8	0	0
57	12	6	0	0	0	0	0	0
81	4	2	0	0	0	0	0	0
156	26	8	0	0	0	0	0	0
149	12	10	0	6	0	0	0	0
88	11	6	0	0	0	0	0	0
21	0	2	0	0	0	0	0	0
23	9	1	0	0	0	0	0	0
19	7	0	0	0	0	0	0	0
16	32	8	0	0	0	0	0	0
134	36	3	0	0	0	0	0	0
5	0	0	0	8	0	0	0	0
1	0	0	0	2	0	13	2	0
0	0	0	0	0	0	0	0	8
0	0	0	0	0	2	0	0	4
0	0	0	0	0	0	0	0	0
0	0	0	0	0	0	0	0	0
0	2	4	0	0	0	0	0	0

3rd Cavalry Army, mid-1945

	Army HQ & troops		9th Cavalry Division		New 7th Cavalry Division	
	TO&E	Actual	TO&E	Actual	TO&E	Actual
Officers	217	207	493	416	288	281
Enlisted	1,911	1,035	6,932	4,151	3,725	2,332
Horses	2,184	517	6,171	2,250	3,952	1,264
Mules	0	51	966	114	0	56
Carts	84	20	279	120	32	0
Pistols	168	0	185	123	205	13
Submachine guns	0	29	0	2	0	9
Rifles	905	297	4,586	1,797	1,400	1,297
Grenade launchers	30	12	52	56	52	50
Light machine guns	72	21	156	91	80	48
Medium machine guns	4	2	18	16	12	4
Mortars	0	0	6	2	4	0
37mm infantry guns	0	0	12	0	0	0
37mm anti-tank guns	0	0	8	0	0	0
AA machine guns	0	0	16	0	0	0
Telephones	32	22	70	42	48	10
Switchboards	5	2	17	5	8	2
Wire reels	32	11	70	15	48	6
15-watt radios	1	2	1	1	1	1
5-watt radios	2	5	4	4	4	4

4th Front Army, 10 July 1945			
	Officers	*Enlisted*	*Horses & Mules*
Alpha Units			
TO&E HQ Troops	438	1,420	50
TO&E Signal Bn	167	901	15
TO&E Army HQ Troops	558	4,799	901
TO&E Division	680	10,329	871
Field Army HQ Troops	438	1,420	50
New 6th Army			
HQ Troops	649	5,891	75
14th Division	669	10,868	967
22nd Division	701	12,014	1,608
18th Army			
HQ Troops	392	3,464	164
11th Division	653	8,124	590
18th Division	654	8,757	265
118th Division	585	7,480	131
73rd Army			
HQ Troops	455	3,682	102
15th Division	638	8,477	227
77th Division	635	8,134	144
193rd Division	571	6,371	70
74th Army			
HQ Troops	472	4,136	378
51st Division	679	9,077	417
57th Division	675	8,764	380
58th Division	608	7,755	145
Non-Alpha Units			
TO&E Army HQ Troops	315	3,078	625
TO&E Division	592	11,926	1,164
92nd Army			
HQ Troops	278	1,247	?
21st Division	532	8,800	?
56th Division	587	10,932	?
142nd Division	571	8,662	?
100th Army			
HQ Troops	311	2,486	299
19th Division	529	6,931	54
63rd Division	541	7,373	52
Total TO&E	13,907	200,982	20,320
Total Actual	12,968	161,568	>6,133

Appendix XII

Artillery Unit Surveys

In late 1942 General Stilwell instructed Brigadier General Jerome Waters to conduct personal surveys of a number of Chinese artillery units that might be incorporated into his planned Y-Force. The inspections, carried out in January 1943, show the disparity among the various artillery formations, which ranged from very good to nearly useless. The spellings of names and places have been retained as shown in the original documents.

Second Army Artillery Regiment – 15 January 1943

3. This regiment consists of two battalions of pack howitzers. They are well trained, a mobile and effective artillery unit.

4. The following is a detailed list of materiel, fire-control, and signal equipment in the possession of the regiment.

   a. *Materiel:* 22 x 3-inch Russian pack howitzers; 3 x 75mm Krupp mountain howitzers. These howitzers are in excellent condition and there is available 1,249 rounds of 3-inch Russian pack howitzer ammunition with the unit.

   b. *Fire control equipment:* 9 x 80cm range finders, 4 x 75cm range finders, 10 BC scopes (German), 6 BC scopes (Russian), 6 aiming circles (Russian), 8 aiming circles (German), 1 pr field glasses (12x), 3 prs field glasses (8x), 71 prs field glasses (6 x), 33 slide rules. The above equipment is in excellent condition.

   c. *Signal equipment:* 73 field telephones, 22 x 800m reels of light wire (not very good wire). The telephones are in good condition but require batteries, which I will try to get for them.

   d. *Transportation:* Each howitzer is drawn by four mules hitched to a limber. All officers, details, and NCOs were mounted. Drivers ride the near animals and handled them well. All animals were in good condition. In addition to the animals there were several hundred men available to carry all weapons where animals could not take them.

   e. *Personnel:* 170 officers, 2,960 enlisted men. All personnel appeared in good condition and well disciplined. Enlisted men wore sandles and should, if available, be equipped with tennis shoes. The headquarters batteries were equipped with 72 Chinese rifles and 229 German rifles, 6 Bren LMG, and 6 Browning LMG.

   f. *Training:* These men are well trained. A demonstration of going into action and gun drill was excellent. In addition to the demonstration, a problem on advance guard action was conducted. The battalion commander and battery performed in a creditable manner. The commanding general is desirous of assistance by US artillery officers.

5. This regiment is considered to be a mobile pack artillery unit and can be expected to perform its mission. One battalion has received orders to join the Sixth Army. Will place field artillery officers with each battalion as soon as they arrive and have issued such signal equipment as necessary when they go through Kunming.

Fifth Army Artillery Regiment – 5 January 1943

3. The following is a detailed list of materiel, fire control equipment and signal equipment which is in the possession of this unit at various localities.

    a. *Materiel:* 20 US 75mm pack howitzers: Nine of these are at Yangling, one at arsenal near Kunming and ten located at Luchow. All are to be sent to Yangling. 7 US 75mm field howitzers: Three of these are enroute to Yangling from Luchow and four at arsenal near Kweiyang [Guiyang] . The nine US 75mm pack howitzers inspected were in very good condition and with some minor repairs will be in serviceable condition. 6 Schneider 75mm pack (light) howitzers: These hows can be placed in serviceable condition and the ordnance department have been requested to send a mobile repair unit to Yangling to repair all materiel and equipment of that unit.

    b. *Fire Control Equipment:* 8 BC telescopes, 12 aiming circles, 5 1-meter base rangefinders, 2 75cm rangefinders, 1 80cm rangefinder, 5 8 x 50 field glasses, 34 6 x 30 field glasses, 12 quadrants. The above is a list of equipment in the possession of artillery at various localities and said to be in good condition. Of the above I inspected the following: 1 1-meter base rangefinder, 2 aiming circles, 1 BC telescope. All were in excellent condition.

    c. *Signal Equipment:* 2 EE8A telephones, 2 Siemens switchboards, 2 Chinese switchboards. Of the above only the two telephones were inspected and found in excellent condition.

    d. *Transportion:* The organization does not have any pack animals. The US howitzers have been transported by truck which is unsatisfactory. Animals should be procured at once. It is further believed that with care in the selection of animals that they can be obtained large enough to carry the heavier loads by pack. In any event they can be transported by the Ramgarh type cart, twenty of which have been ordered sent to Kunming. The six Schneider light pack hows have also been hauled in trucks. The Schneider howitzers break down into light loads and we can have ordnance prepare adapters to fit frames on our Phillips saddles which will give them greater mobility than the carts.

    e. *Personnel:* The organization turned out eleven cannoneers per gun and six officers. Colonel Chu, regimental commander, appeared desirous of assistance. The enlisted men are large men and appeared in good physical condition.

    f. *Training:* One battery put on a standing gun drill, consisting of disassembly and assembly of howitzers and a few fire commands. Their state of training is unsatisfactory.

Fifty-Second Army Artillery Battalion – 24 March 1943

2. The 52nd Army was reported as having a total of twelve 75mm Japanese model howitzers of which six were present for the inspection. Of the absent howitzers four were reported as being at Nin Chao being repaired by the Army's own personnel. Two howitzers were reported as being at Pi Sai enroute to Wenshan after being repaired.

3. The following is a detailed list of equipment and pertinent comments on training and personnel:
    a. Six Japanese model howitzers (includes only those present at the inspection). Four of the six howitzers were made in Japan, and two were Chinese made but copied after the Japanese model. The six absent howitzers were all reported as Chinese made. All six of the howitzers present have excessive play in the traversing mechanism, and one was so bad as to be considered unserviceable (100 mils play). The following additional materiel was on hand: 2 Luger pistols, 84 rifles, 12 automatic pistols, 746 rounds of ammunition on hand.
    b. *Fire control equipment*: 3 BC scopes, 3 aiming circles, 1 range finder. Of the fire control equipment, 1 BC scope, 2 aiming circles and the one range finder were serviceable. Two BC scopes were unserviceable (excessive play, 40 and 50 mils respectively) and one aiming circle was unserviceable (defective needle).
    c. *Signal equipment:* 10 telephones, German type, 1 switchboard. An estimated five miles [8km] of wire, all of which would be unserviceable in wet weather.
    d. *Personnel* (present only): 34 officers, 390 enlisted men. The men appeared healthy and vigorous, but they had very badly worn clothing. It was reported that they were issued one summer uniform and one winter uniform only, which had to do for two years. They were equipped with sandals instead of sneakers for footwear.
    e. *Animals* (present): 48 horses, 70 mules. In general, the animals were in excellent condition. Many of them were fairly large and strong, and are suitable for use as pack animals to transport artillery materiel.
    f. The unit gave a demonstration on gun drill, packing, marching, RSOP, and firing. The gun drill, packing, marching and operation of the gun squads in firing was very satisfactory. The conduct of the RSOP and conduct of fire by the officers was far too slow and unsatisfactory. In the service of the piece the firing was slowed down by excessive checking

4. Conclusion: It is believed that this organization can be developed into a very satisfactory battalion in a short time if brought up to strength in men and animals and given supervision by an experienced American artillery officer.

Fifty-Fourth Army Artillery – 30 January 1943

2. The 54th Army has a total of twelve 75mm Japanese howitzers of which four are considered in fair condition and remainder unserviceable.

3. Herewith a detailed list of materiel, fire control and signal equipment in possession of the artillery:

   a. *Materiel*: 4 75mm Japanese howitzers, 3 light machine guns, 8 Mauser pistols. These weapons are old and worn. Only one howitzer is equipped with a panoramic sight. The unit has 797 rounds of ammunition on hand.
   b. *Fire Control Equipment*: 2 BC scopes, 2 aiming circles, 1 range finder, 4 prs field glasses.
   c. *Signal Equipment*: 4 telephones (no batteries), 1 switchboard, 1 Very pistol. The wire is all in unserviceable condition.
   d. *Personnel:* 13 officers, 435 enlisted men. Officers and men have been consolidated into one battery due to lack of materiel.
   e. *Animals*: 82 mules and horses. These animals are all old and badly underfed.
   f. *Training*: The unit gave a demonstration of packing and gun drill which was satisfactory.

4. This organization cannot perform its mission with present weapons and training.

Seventy-First Army Artillery – 22 February 1943

1. This battalion was inspected while on the march approximately 24km west of Kunming. The battalion had marched from the Pao-Shan Front during the past 20 days including a few days rest for the Chinese New Year.

2.
   a. *Equipment*: The equipment included eleven 75mm French guns, Model 1897, horse and mule drawn. Fire control equipment was mostly Russian. Signal equipment was considered adequate except they had no radios.
   b. *Animals*: The animals totaled about 125 of which 81 were mules. Of these mules about 30% were of excellent size and conformation. All animals were very thin, but casualties enroute had been extremely low. Prior to this inspection, the Battalion had marched approximately 640km in less than 20 days.
   c. *Ammunition*: 140 rounds per battery or a total of 420 rounds had been left at Yung Ping. No ammunition was transported with the battalion.

3. General Condition. I consider that this Battalion has made a very satisfactory march. Their animals need a rest with good veterinary attention and forage. At the end of one month, if given good care, about 30% of the mules would be suitable for pack artillery.

First Battalion, Tenth Artillery Regiment – 15 January 1943

2. The 10th Artillery Regiment consists of three battalions. The 2nd and 3rd Battalions are at present in Hunan, at Yuanling and Lingling, respectively. They are said to be equipped similarly to the 1st Battalion, and in the same state of training.

3. The following is a detailed list of the materiel, fire control equipment, and signal equipment now in the possession of the 1st Battalion.

> a. *Materiel*: 6 Krupp 150mm guns. These guns are in excellent condition. They have not been fired for over a year and a half, and are to be inspected by an ordnance officer. The battalion has in its possession 402 rounds of ammunition.
>
> b. *Fire Control Equipment*: 3 BC scopes, 6 aiming circles, 3 range finders, 26 field glasses. All in excellent condition.
>
> c. *Signal Equipment*: 31 field telephones, 2 switchboards, 1 15-watt radio, 3 Very pistols. All in good condition. The battalion has very little wire.
>
> d. *Transportation*: 10 1941 model GMC 2½ ton trucks, 12 1934 model GMC 2½ ton trucks, 4 1937 model Studebaker trucks, 15 Henschel diesel heavy trucks. The diesel trucks are used as prime movers, and are in need of overhauling. The 1941 GMC trucks are in good condition; the other light trucks are in need of overhauling. Some of the 1934 model trucks probably cannot be repaired and should be discarded.
>
> e. *Personnel*: 39 officers, 587 men. These men are in good condition and morale is excellent. Enlisted men wear rope sandals, which should be replaced by sneakers if available. For close defense there are 6 light machine guns and a considerable number of rifles.
>
> f. *Training:* This battalion has been training for a year and a half. Prior to that it took part in three major engagements. At present its state of training is superior. Both officers and men are thoroughly familiar with their duties.
>
> g. *Necessary equipment:* The battalion lacks the following necessary equipment and supplies: 8 to 10 miles [13–16km] of telephone wire, 6 rounds of dummy ammunition, crocus cloth, medical supplies of all sorts.
>
> h. *Service practice:* It would be desirable to make some ammunition available for service practice. At present the battalion commander has orders not to use any of the ammunition for this purpose.

4. This is the best unit inspected to date and they are anxious for assistance.

Second Battalion, Thirteenth Artillery Regiment – 11 January 1943

3. The 13th Artillery Regiment consists of three battalions. The 1st Battalion lost all its materiel and equipment in Burma. The 3rd Battalion is now in Tungkwan, Shensi [Tongguan, Shaanxi], and is reported to be equipped identically with the 2nd Battalion.

4. The following is a detailed list of materiel, fire control equipment and signal equipment in the possession of the 2nd Battalion 13th Artillery Regiment.

   a. *Materiel*: 6 German Rheinmetall 105mm howitzers. These howitzers are in excellent condition. 465 rounds of ammunition are available with the battalion.
   b. *Fire Control Equipment*: 3 BC scopes, 4 German aiming circles, 17 6 x 30 field glasses. All are in good condition.
   c. *Signal Equipment*: 26 field telephones, 21 ½-mile reels of single strand wire, 1 15-watt radio transmitter. All are apparently in good condition.
   d. *Transportation*: 7 Heavy prime mover trucks, 6 1.5-ton trucks. These are reported in running condition but were not tested due to lack of gas.
   e. *Personnel*: 22 officers, 301 enlisted men. All officers and men were equipped with gas masks. Small arms consisted of 69 rifles and 10 pistols in good condition. In spite of the meager ration of 24 oz rice, ¼ oz salt and meat once a week, the men appeared in good condition.
   f. *Training:* The state of training of this unit, while not entirely satisfactory, is better than others observed. With some help they can be made into an excellent unit. A demonstration of gun drill was given with indirect laying and with gas masks.

5. Were ammunition available for this unit it could with assistance be made into an excellent unit. Since ammunition is not available, it is recommended that, when air transportation becomes available, that this unit be converted into a pack battalion as it would take but a short time to make them an effective unit.

Yunnan Provincial Artillery Regiment – 12 January 1943

3. The provincial regiment consists of three pack battalions and one mule-drawn 120mm mortar battery. The second battalion, now in Chiensueh (200km from Kunming) is reported to be equipped identically with the 3rd Battalion. One battery each from the 1st and 3rd Battalions has been ordered to Paoshan, and one battery each has been assigned to Regimental Headquarters. Therefore, only one battery each from the 1st and 3rd Battalions and the mortar battery were present at the inspection.

4 The following is a detailed list of materiel, fire control and signal equipment in the possession of the 1st and 3rd battalions and the mortar battery.

   a. *Materiel:*
   1st Battalion: 12 Schneider 75mm pack howitzers. The four guns inspected are old but in serviceable condition. The battalion has 600 rounds of ammunition on hand.
   3rd Battalion: 12 Krupp 75mm pack howitzers. The guns are obsolete. They are equipped for direct laying only. 1,500 rounds of ammunition are on hand in the battalion.

Mortar Battery: 4 French Brandt 120mm mortars, 4 ammunition carriers. These mortars are in excellent condition and are reported to have a range of 7,000 meters. 60 rounds of ammunition are available.

b. *Fire Control Equipment:*

1st Battalion: 3 BC scopes, 3 aiming circles, 3 range finders. One of each was inspected and appeared to be in good condition.

3rd Battalion: 1 BC scope, 1 aiming circle, 1 range finder. These instruments appeared to be in good condition. More must be provided if this unit is equipped with modern guns.

Mortar Battery: 1 BC scope, 1 aiming circle, 1 range finder. These instruments appeared to be in good condition.

c. *Signal Equipment*: Each of the 7 batteries has 4 field telephones and four ½-mile reels of single strand wire

d. *Transportation:* The pack batteries had sufficient large mules, pack saddles and attachments to pack out the entire battery. The animals were in fair condition, although insufficient forage is provided. The mortar battery is drawn by four mules to each mortar and ammunition carrier. Since each of these are equipped with high-speed axles they could be drawn by trucks. Riding animals were provided for all officers.

e. *Personnel:* In 1st Battalion there were approximately 150 men in the battery inspected. There were ten cannoneers and nine drivers for each howitzer. In the ammunition section there were twenty drivers and twenty-two ammunition handlers. There were thirty men in the detail, equipped with one Hotchkiss light machine gun and ten rifles.

f. *Training:* The battery from the 1st Battalion gave a demonstration of packing, moving a short distance and going into action. Both men and animals performed well in packing and unpacking, but they are not satisfactory in service of the piece and firing.

5. This unit can be made into an effective and mobile pack regiment with American howitzers in a short time as they have animals and equipment. With their present weapons they are ineffective due to ammunition and other obsolete guns.

Appendix XIII

Field Artillery Center Throughput

Brigadier General Jerome Walters had been instructed in December 1942 to conduct a survey of Chinese artillery units tentatively assigned to Y-Force. In furtherance of that he established a firing range 20km east of Kunming at which units could demonstrate their proficiency. On 19 January 1943 General Walters was informed that the US Army's CBI Theater was planning to open a field artillery training center in Yunnan province in a month's time to train Chinese units on the American 75mm howitzer, and directed him to begin searching for a location and working on buildings and translations of instructional materials.

Officers were hurriedly assigned and the first Chinese unit, the artillery battalion of the 71st Army, arrived on 27 March. This unit was probably chosen because it had already been equipped with, but not trained on, US 75mm howitzers. It departed a little under six months later at full strength and with a full set of equipment. Others followed, with the curriculum being adjusted to reflect battlefield feed-back; in particular the near elimination of training on battalion fire direction in favor of more dispersed battery-level fire.

Other than the German-trained and -equipped howitzer battalions and the CAI units, the FATC graduates were the only artillery in the NRA capable of modern fire control. As such they played an outsize, if somewhat belated, role in army effectiveness and would have been critical to operations had Japan not surrendered.

Units passing through the FATC are detailed in the tables that follow.

Arrival

Unit	Date	Officers	Enlisted	Horses	Mules	Weapons
71st Army Artillery Bn	27 Mar 43	40	343	26	100	11 US 75mm pk how
1st Bty, 1st Bn, 93rd Army Arty Bn	12 Apr 43	0	124	9	63	3 Russian 76mm guns
2nd Bty, 1st Bn, 10th Arty Regt	15 Apr 43	10	141	0	0	3 German 150mm hov
2nd Bn, 2nd Army Arty Regt	18 Apr 43	42	658	100	280	12 Rus. 75mm pk how
1st Bty, 1st Bn, 1st Arty Group[a]	18 May 43	5	131	20	0	4 US 75mm pk how
2nd Bty, 1st Bn, 93rd Army Arty Bn	4 Jul 43	7	108	9	61	3 Russian 76mm guns
6th Army Artillery Bn	8 Jul 43			new		
3rd Bn, 5th Artillery Regt	20 Aug 43	40	550	20	215	none
53rd Army Artillery Bn	6 Oct 43	35	593	14	83	4 Chinese 75mm pk ho
54th Army Artillery Bn	15 Nov 43	28	542	118	33	4 Chinese 75mm pk ho
8th Army Artillery Bn	3 May 44	45	817	11	19	none
1st Bn, 5th Army Artillery Regt	16 May 44	42	600	83	220	none
1st Bn, 30th Artillery Regt	26 May 44	41	616	60	216	none
2nd Bn, 30th Artillery Regt	21 Aug 44	37	641	91	294	none
HQ, 30th Artillery Regt	23 Aug 44	40	205	20	0	none
2nd Bn, 5th Army Artillery Regt	16 Sep 44	34	530	98	226	
2nd Yunnan Artillery Bn	1 Dec 44	37	644	29	257	
2nd Bn, 53rd Army Artillery Regt[b]	17 Jan 45	36	537	17	38	none
11th Division Artillery Bn[b]	17 Jan 45	39	538	17	38	none
103rd Division Artillery Bn[b]	17 Jan 45	31	533	18	39	none
18th Division Artillery Bn[b]	17 Jan 45	35	337	17	37	none
45th Division Artillery Bn[c]	17 Feb 45	42	592	45	167	11 US 75mm pk how
HQ, 5th Artillery Regt	1 Apr 45	21	101	4 vehs		none
1st Bn, 5th Artillery Regt	1 Apr 45	46	350	100 vehs		12 US 105mm how
2nd Bty, 12th Artillery Regt	1 Apr 45	9	100	16 vehs		4 US 155mm how
New 6th Army Howitzer Bn	31 Mar 45	51	373	3 vehs		48 .50cal MG
198th Division Artillery Bn[b]	17 Jan 45	42	532	17	37	none
New 1st Army Howitzer Bn[d]	21 Jun 45	62	583	88 vehs		12 US 105mm how
13th Army Howitzer Bn[e]	19 Apr 45	35	213	no vehs		none
54th Army Howitzer Bn[e]	16 Mar 45	35	204	no vehs	0	none
6th Training Bn[b]	1 Apr 45	44	130	0	0	none
7th Training Bn[b]	1 Apr 45	20	140	0	0	none
8th Training Bn[b]	15 May 45	35	242	5	43	none
9th Training Bn[b]	10 Mar 45	35	435	5	0	none
1st Bty, 26th Artillery Regt	14 Apr 45	9	116	no vehs		none
18th Army Howitzer Bn[e]	21 Jun 45	38	191	82 vehs		12 US 105mm how
71st Army Howitzer Bn[e]	24 May 45	22	197	81 vehs		12 US 105mm how
94th Army Howitzer Bn[e]	8 Jun 45	25	185	81 vehs		12 US 105mm how

a Training unit.   b Date of arrival is date of activation.   c Formerly 1st Bn, 5th Artillery Regt.
d Unit previously trained at Ramgarh.   e Cadre from Ramgarh.   f Still at FATC at war's end.

Departure

Unit	Date	Officers	Enlisted	Horses	Mules	Weapons
st Army Artillery Bn	3 Sep 43	40	645	148	300	12 US 75mm pk how
t Bty, 1st Bn, 93rd Army Arty Bn	9 Sep 43	0	132	9	61	3 Russian 76mm guns
d Bty, 1st Bn, 10th Arty Regt	15 Oct 43	10	145	0	0	3 German 150mm how
d Bn, 2nd Army Arty Regt	19 Nov 43	44	574	121	299	12 US 75mm pk how
t Bty, 1st Bn, 1st Arty Group[a]	18 Oct 44	5	160	20	0	4 US 75mm pk how
d Bty, 1st Bn, 93rd Army Arty Bn	9 Sep 44	8	124	9	61	4 US 75mm pk how
h Army Artillery Bn	21 Nov 44	44	605	122	255	?
d Bn, 5th Artillery Regt	12 May 44	45	610	77	238	12 US 75mm pk how
rd Army Artillery Bn	21 Apr 44	49	775	104	216	12 US 75mm pk how
th Army Artillery Bn	9 Apr 44	46	643	195	225	12 US 75mm pk how
h Army Artillery Bn	22 Jul 44	41	890	117	180	12 US 75mm pk how
t Bn, 5th Army Artillery Regt	7 Sep 44	42	642	99	239	12 US 75mm pk how
t Bn, 30th Artillery Regt	7 Jan 45	40	626	94	227	12 US 75mm pk how
d Bn, 30th Artillery Regt	10 Jan 45	48	695	95	222	12 US 75mm pk how
Q, 30th Artillery Regt	1 Jan 45	40	212	22	3	none
d Bn, 5th Army Artillery Regt	28 Feb 45	34	530	98	226	12 US 75mm pk how
d Yunnan Artillery Bn	15 Jan 45	37	645	29	256	12 US 75mm pk how
d Bn, 53rd Army Artillery Regt[b]	19 May 45	46	690	43	141	12 US 75mm pk how
th Division Artillery Bn[b]	6 Jun 45	47	721	47	133	12 US 75mm pk how
3rd Division Artillery Bn[b]	22 May 45	42	730	45	143	12 US 75mm pk how
th Division Artillery Bn[b]	9 Jun 45	49	721	48	135	12 US 75mm pk how
th Division Artillery Bn[c]	31 Mar 45	42	696	48	181	11 US 75mm pk how
Q, 5th Artillery Regt	6 Jun 45	33	32	3 vehs		none
t Bn, 5th Artillery Regt	7 May 45	63	536	100 vehs		12 US 105mm how
d Bty, 12th Artillery Regt	15 Jun 45	11	119	16 vehs		4 US 155mm how
ew 6th Army Howitzer Bn	f	51	373	n/a		12 US 105mm how
8th Division Artillery Bn[b]	14 Jun 45	49	721	47	127	12 US 75mm pk how
ew 1st Army Howitzer Bn[d]		55	583	90 vehs		12 US 105mm how
th Army Howitzer Bn[e]		60	486	82 vehs		12 US 105mm how
th Army Howitzer Bn[e]		64	534	82 vehs		12 US 105mm how
h Training Bn[b]		47	700	0	6	12 US 75mm pk how
h Training Bn[b]		49	663	0	6	12 US 75mm pk how
h Training Bn[b]	f	41	656	5	35	12 US 75mm pk how
h Training Bn[b]		44	652	4	6	12 US 75mm pk how
t Bty, 26th Artillery Regt		8	115	4 vehs		4 US 75mm fld how
th Army Howitzer Bn[e]		61	569	82 vehs		12 US 105mm how
st Army Howitzer Bn[e]		59	433	82 vehs		12 US 105mm how
th Army Howitzer Bn[e]		65	595	82 vehs		12 US 105mm how

Higher Command Organs

Ultimate command authority in the KMT government rested, of course, with Chiang Kai-shek. He exercised this authority as chairman of the Military Affairs Committee (also known as the National Military Council), where he was assisted by his chief of staff, General He Yingqin, and the vice chief of staff, General Bai Chongxi. Subordinate to Chiang were the Ministry of Military Operations and the Ministry of Military Administration, the former responsible for operational matters and the latter for training, logistics, and political indoctrination.

In theory, orders to the field originated with Chiang and went from him (or his personal office), through the appropriate military ministry and thence to the war zone commander(s) for action. In practice subordinates quickly learned that Chiang sent what he considered important orders directly, bypassing the ministries. Inevitably, directives from Chiang or his personal office were thus treated as orders, while those from the operations or administrative ministries were often regarded more as strong suggestions. Compounding this was Chiang's tendency to bypass not only the ministries but the chain of command in the field as well. Orders would flow directly to army groups or even armies in the field, often without even notifying their superior headquarters. Understandably, coordination often suffered.

Further, the various commanders had varying degrees of loyalty to the Chongqing government. Yan of II War Zone, Li of V War Zone and Long in Yunnan were examples of commanders who owed their positions not to any regular appointment system but to the fact that the forces under them were actually their own private armies.

War Zones

To help manage the war effort over an area as large as China the MAC activated five war zones on 20 August 1937. Each was responsible for both administrative and tactical functions in their area. Further numbered war zones were added and moved as the operational requirements changed. There were also a few named war zones, smaller than the numbered ones, intended to control guerrilla operations.

I War Zone: covered Hebei and northern Henan provinces to defend the Beijing–Hankou railway and the northern portion of the Tianjin–Nanjing railway. Chiang commanded this directly, although General Cheng Qian served as acting commander and assumed actual command in October. In May 1938 the zone assumed responsibility for western Shandong, although the main force was directed to withdraw west of the Beijing–Hankou railway. Once the Yellow River dikes were blown the main force of the war zone was effectively insulated from the remainder of the war.

II War Zone: covered Shanxi, Suiyuan, and Chahar provinces, although the latter two were lost to the Japanese within months of the start of the war and allocated by them to the Mongol puppet regime. It was commanded by Yan Xishan, the Shanxi warlord, and thus was essentially little more than a recognition of his authority in the area. It also nominally included the communist 8th Route Army.

III War Zone: covered southern Jiangsu and Zhejiang, including responsibility for Shanghai. This war zone was also commanded directly by Chiang. After the fall of the city command was handed off to General Gu Zhutong with orders to carry out guerrilla warfare. Much of the zone remained unoccupied through the war, however, and new forces were brought in to maintain the government's authority.

IV War Zone: covered Fujian and Guangdong provinces, essentially the central China coast, including the area behind Hong Kong. Commanded by He Yingqin, who was also minister of war. Following the war zone's poor performance he was replaced in March 1940 by Zhang Fakui. It supervised the battle for Guilin–Liuzhou in August 1944 and was deactivated in December of that year.

V War Zone: covered Shandong and northern Hubei, commanded by Li Zongren until 1943. Li was the foremost member of the Guangxi Clique of warlords and following his appointment three Guangxi armies moved north to serve under their master. The deputy commander was Han Fuju, the Shandong warlord until his execution in January 1938. Pulled out to the west in May 1938 and thereafter centered on Hubei. Li was removed from effective power in 1943.

VI War Zone: carved out of I War Zone on 7 September 1937 to defend the northern portion of the Tianjin–Nanjing railway. Placed under Feng Yuxiang, a Chiang adversary known as the Christian General, in hopes that he could rally former colleagues. It performed poorly and was deactivated the next month.

VI War Zone: A second incarnation of this zone was activated in October 1939 in Hubei and shifted south to occupy southern Hubei and northern Hunan. At war's end it accepted the surrender of the Japanese 6th Army.

VII War Zone: activated in October 1937 in Sichuan under the local warlord Liu Xiang. Liu led his 15th (Sichuan) Army into battle at Shanghai and Nanjing, but died in January 1938. With the arrival of the central government in Chongqing the war zone was disestablished in March 1939.

VII War Zone: the second incarnation of VII War Zone was activated in September 1944 to control forces in Guangdong province, mostly operating in the guerrilla role.

VIII War Zone: created in November 1937 to safeguard the northwest, particularly Gansu with its large airbase used by the Soviets and Ningxia with its overland routes to the USSR. Qinghai and Suiyuan were added in March 1940.

IX War Zone: Created July 1938 using the Wuhan Garrison HQ as a basis with Chen Cheng commanding. He was succeeded in 1939 by Xue Yue, who remained in command as one of the better field generals until the end of the war, fighting four ferocious battles for Changsha.

X War Zone: formed in October 1939 from the Generalissimo's Xian HQ. Occupying Shaanxi Province, it saw little combat, but did dispatch forces in May 1944 to the combat areas to the east.

XI & XII War Zones: these were formed in August 1945, the former to accept the surrender of the Japanese North China Area Army in Beijing, and the latter to accept the surrender of the Mongolian Frontier Army.

Shandong–Jiangsu War Zone: Formed in March 1939 under Yu Xuezhong, who also served as chairman of Shandong province, to conduct guerrilla warfare. It was divided into two subordinate HQs, one for each province.

Hebei War Zone: Formed in 1939 as a small element to conduct guerrilla operations.

Hebei–Chahar War Zone: Formed in 1939 for guerrilla operations, usually controlling a single army, to the end of the war.

Field Headquarters

One field HQ was formed to control mobile operations, the HQ, Chinese Army Forces (also sometimes referred to as the Chinese Army Central HQ). This was activated in December 1944 to carry out offensive operations in the south using largely American-equipped divisions. This was to be accomplished via the subordinate 1st, 2nd, 3rd, and 4th Front Armies activated at the same time, commanding a total of 14 armies and 42 divisions with 199 mountain guns.

There were also a variety of command organs known as Generalissimo's Field Head-quarters. Most of the early HQs, notably those for Chengdu, Chongqing, Guangzhou, Nanchang, Shijiazhuang, and Tianshui were small elements for limited areas and were abolished within the first year or two of the war.

Two others, those for Guilin and Xian, were larger. The former was formed in 1939 with no fewer than five army groups and lasted until late 1944. The Xian Field HQ was formed prewar and had up to ten armies, although all of these had been transferred out by early 1939.

Sources

Bin Shih, *China's Small Arms of the 2nd Sino-Japanese War* (2011)

Collier, Harry H. and Paul Chin-Chih Lai, *Organizational Changes in the Chinese Army 1895–1950* (Office of the [Taiwan] Military Historian, 1969). Summarizes the tables of organization used by the Chinese Army, useful coverage, particularly before about 1930, less detailed after that.

Dorn, Frank, *The Sino-Japanese War 1937–41* (Macmillan, 1974). An early, interesting and highly opinionated history of the first phase of the war by an American military attaché to China at the time.

Howard, Joshua H., *Workers at War: Labor in China's Arsenals 1937–1953* (Stanford University Press, 2004)

Hsu Long-hsuen and Chang Ming-kai, *History of the Sino-Japanese War (1937–1945)* (Chung Wu, 1971). An abridged version of the multi-volume Taiwanese official history.

Kataoka, Tetsuya, *Resistance and Revolution in China: The Communists and the Second United Front* (University of California, 1974)

Liu, F. F., *Military History of Modern China, 1924–49* (Princeton, 1956). An early but still useful overview.

Mitter, Rana; *Forgotten Ally: China's World War II 1937–1945* (Houghton Mifflin Harcourt, 2013). A good general, rather than purely military, history of China's war effort.

Peattie, Mark, Edward Drea, and Hans van de Ven; *The Battle for China: Essays on the Military History of the Sino-Japanese War of 1937–1945* (Stanford University Press, 2011). A large collection of essays examining the war from both the Japanese and Chinese perspectives. Currently the best single source on the war.

Pettibone, Charles D., *The Organization and Order of Battle of Militaries in World War II, Vol VIII – China* (Trafford, 2013). A large book detailing the command structures of the various Chinese units, down to division level, of 1937–45 as drawn from English-language sources.

Romanus, Charles, and Riley Sunderland, *Stilwell's Mission to China*; *Stilwell's Command Problems*;*Time Runs Out in CBI* (US Army CMH, 1952, 1956, 1959). The three-volume US Army official history of the China–Burma–India theater.

Skřivan, Aleš, "Export of Zbrojovka Brno (Czechoslovak Arms Factory of Brno) to China in the Interwar Period," in *Prague Papers on History of International Relations* (Charles University, Prague, 2005).

Stratton, Roy Olin, *SACO – The Rice Paddy Navy* (C. S. Palmer, 1950)

van de Ven, Hans J.; *War and Nationalism in China 1925–45* (Routledge, 2003)

van Slyke, Lyman P. (ed.), *The Chinese Communist Movement, A Report of the United States War Department, July 1945* (Stanford University, 1968). Republication of the wartime US Army report, based in part on the Yenan Mission that visited the communist HQ for a year at that point. Generally sympathetic to the communist faction in China.

[no editor listed], *Soviet Volunteers in China 1925–1945, Articles and Reminiscences* (Progress Publishers, 1980)

The Japanese Monographs provide an invaluable glimpse into the war in China from the other side. They were written by Japanese officers after the war under the auspices of HQ, US Army, Japan. Naturally, they play down the use of chemical weapons and wartime atrocities. Subsequent research has revealed minor inaccuracies, but for the most part they remain a unique resource. A great benefit is that being copyright-free most are available online. These are:

no. 70   China Area Operations Record (Revised) (July 1937–November 1941)
no. 71   Army Operations in China (December 1941–December 1943)
no. 72   Army Operations in China (January 1944–August 1945)
no. 74   Operations in the Kun-Lun-Kuan Area (November 1939–February 1940)
no. 129   China Area Operations Record, Command of the China Expeditionary Army (August 1943–August 1945)
no. 178   North China Area Operations (July 1937–May 1941)
no. 179   Central China Area Operations Record (1937–1941)
no. 180   South China Area Operations Record (1937–1941)

American Archives

The US Army had a substantial advisory element in China from mid-1943 onwards, although it had contact only with a minority of Chinese units. The records of the China–Burma–India Theater and, later, China Theater, are voluminous and are to be found in Record Group 493 of the National Archives at College Park, Maryland. The majority of records of interest are found in the files of China Theater, Y-FOS and its successor China Combat Command, Z-FOS, and the Eastern and Central Commands. Some are filed in correspondence and general files under the decimals 320 to 323.

Consolidated groups of records can also be found in the following entries:

UD-UP 334 – Reports of US inspectors and observers of Chinese units 1944
UD-UP 406 – Tables of Organization & Equipment (US & Chinese) 1944–5
UD-UP 530 – Z Force supply, 1944
UD-UP 537 – Records Related to Chinese Army Units, 1945
UD-UP 538 – CCC Reports 1945
UD-UP 577 – Records of 18th Army Combat Section
UD-UP 578 – Records of 74th Army Combat Section, 1945
UD-UP 581 – Records of 1st War Area Liaison Team 1944–5

French Archives

A mostly complete monthly list of arms sales by France to China for the 1930s can be found in the files of the military attachés to China in Army boxes 7N3311 to 7N3313 in the Service Historique de l'Armée de Terre, now part of the Service historique de la Défense (SHD).

The Archives Diplomatiques Français also include records of licenses for arms sales in Asie 1918–1940: Chine, Vol. 166; Asie 1918–1929: Chine Vol. 164; Asie 1918–1929: Chine Vol. 161; Asie 1930–1940: Chine Vol. 534; Asie 1930–1940: Chine Vol. 541 & 542.

British Archives

The Vickers corporate files, held by Cambridge University Library, detail such sales to China as took place in the 1930s.

The National Archives (formerly the PRO) of Britain documents arms sales to China as discussed by the Foreign Office's Political Department in FO 371/18060; the War Office's plans in 1942–3 for aid to China are discussed in WO 106/3555-3558B. A gold mine of information on arms traffic to China between the fall of Shanghai in 1937 and the fall of Burma in 1942 can be found in CO/129/567/4&5, CO129/575/15 and CO129/583/13 which catalog the import of munitions into China through the customs offices of Hong Kong and Burma, the two remaining ports of entry.

Chinese Language Sources

Unfortunately, neither the Chinese nor the Taiwanese archives have released significant number of documents and those that have been released are almost always in the form of curated collections published as books.

China's Modern Ordnance Industry Historical Records (1–4) [中國近代兵器工業檔案史料 (一~四)]: Modern China Ordnance Industry Historical Records Committee, 1993, Ordnance Industry Press, Beijing. An outstanding collection of documents on Chinese arms production.

China's Modern Ordnance Industries: From Late Qing Period to the Republic [中國近代兵器工業], Modern China Ordnance Industry Committee, 1st edition, 1998, Defense Industry Press, Beijing.

The Chongqing Ordnance Industry During the war [抗戰時期重慶的兵器工業], Lu Dayue [陸大鉞], Tang Runming [唐潤明主編], Chongqing War of Resistance Series Committee, 1st edition, 1995, Chongqing Press, Chongqing.

The China Domestic Produced Small Arms Review [國造槍械列傳], Lin Zuoyi [林佐乙], 1999, Global Defense Magazine, Taipei, Taiwan.

Shandong Guerilla Bases [山東根據地], Xue Xingfu [薛幸福],1990, Ordnance Industry Press, Beijing.

Shanxi, Henan and Hebei Guerilla Bases [晉冀豫根據地], Wu Dongcai [吳東才], 1990, Ordnance Industry Press, Beijing.

Ordnance Records of Shanxi, Chahar and Hebei Guerilla Bases [晉察冀根據地軍工史料], China Ordnance History Records Edit Committee, Fang Min [方敏], 1993, China Ordnance Industry Corp.

Ordnance Records of Shanxi and Suiyuan Gerilla Bases [晉綏根據地軍工史料], China Ordnance History Records Editorial Committee, Xue Xingfu [薛幸福], 1990, China Ordnance Industry Corp.

Shaanxi, Ganxu and Ningxia Frontal Regions [陝甘寧邊區], Xue Xingfu [薛幸福], 1990, Ordnance Industry Press, Beijing.

Jiangxu Modern Ordnance History [江蘇近代兵工史略], Jiangxu Historical Records Editorial Department, Jiang Hong [江洪], Hou Futong [侯福全], 1989, Nanjing, China.

Jiangnan Manufacturing Records [江南製造局記], Qing, Wei Yungong [魏允恭], 1997 reprint by Shanghai Ancient Book Press.

General Shooting and Ordnance Info. [大眾射擊與兵器知識], Qian Shijian [錢石堅], 1939, Shenhua Press.

Infantry Weapons Manual, in English and Chinese, China Expedition Forces Command, India, 1943.

Ordnance Designs and Theories [槍炮構造及理論], Li Daichen [李待琛], Vol. 1 and 2, 1938, Ordnance School.

Guns – Volume 1 of Ordnance References [槍械－兵器參考材料之一], Ordnance Research Office, The third Field Corp. of Eastern China, August, 1952.

China's Ordnance Development History [中國兵器製造業發展史], Wang Guoqiang [王國強], 1987, Liming Culture Inc., Taipei, Taiwan.

The Complete Book of the Type Triple-Tens Machine Gun [三十節式機關槍全書], Zong Mingjie [宗明杰], 1930, Minshen Monthly, Hankou, China.

Type 24 Maxim Machine Gun Instruction Manual [二十四年式馬克沁機關槍說明書], 6th edition, 21st Arsenal, 1948.

Type 28 Grenade Launcher Instruction [二八式槍榴彈教程], 80th Arsenal, 1947.

Type 27 Grenade Discharger Instructions [二七式擲彈筒使用法], 2nd edition, 30th Arsenal, 1940.

The Specification of Chinese Army Small Arms in Service [我國陸軍現用各武器諸元手冊], Ordnance Office of the Combined Services Command, September, 1947.

Munitions Identification [彈藥識別], Ordnance Department, Supply Command, Eastern China Military Zone, 25 February 1949.

A Brief of Eight Years of War of Resistance [八年抗戰經過概要]: General Chen Cheng, Chief of China's General Staff, 1946.

Japanese Language Sources

Shinagun Heiki Yoran (*Guide to the Weapons of the Chinese Army*), WDC164382, Library of Congress, Washington Document Center

Arms & Ammunition of Japan – A Catalog of Taihei Kumiai [日本陸軍兵器資料集 -(泰平組合目錄)], Munkakata Kazuhro, Hyodo Nishohachi, 1999, Namiki Press, Tokyo.